THE KORÂN

THE KORÂN

TRANSLATED INTO ENGLISH
FROM THE ORIGINAL ARABIC

BY

GEORGE SALE

WITH EXPLANATORY NOTES
FROM THE MOST APPROVED COMMENTATORS

WITH AN INTRODUCTION

BY

SIR EDWARD DENISON ROSS
C.I.E., Ph.D., ETC.

FREDERICK WARNE

LONDON

297
Kor

FREDERICK WARNE (Publishers) LTD
LONDON ENGLAND

Gift of Norwich Bahá'í Community
11/81

ISBN 0 7232 0261 3

Printed and bound in Great Britain by
Fakenham Press Limited, Fakenham, Norfolk

D 6035. 979

INTRODUCTION

THERE is surely no need to-day to insist on the importance of a close study of the Korân for all who would comprehend the many vital problems connected with the Islamic World ; and yet few of us, I imagine, among the many who possess translations of this book have been at pains to read it through. It must, however, be borne in mind that the Korân plays a far greater rôle among the Muhammadans than does the Bible in Christianity in that it provides not only the canon of their faith, but also the text-book of their ritual and the principles of their Civil Law.

It was the Great Crusades that first brought the West into close touch with Islam, but between the years 1096 and 1270 we only hear of one attempt to make known to Europe the Sacred Book of the Moslems, namely, the Latin version made in 1143, by Robert of Retina (who, Sale tells us, was an Englishman), and Hermann of Dalmatia, on the initiative of Petrus Venerabilis, the Abbot of Clugny, which version was ultimately printed by T. Bibliander in Basel in 1543, nearly a hundred years after the fall of Constantinople.

During the seventeenth and eighteenth centuries, several translations appeared both in Latin and in French, and one of the latter, by André du Ryer, was translated into English by Alexander Ross in 1649. But by far the most important work on the Korân was that of Luigi Marracci which was published in Padua in 1698.

George Sale's translation first appeared in November, 1734, in a quarto volume ; in 1764 it was first printed in medium octavo, and the reprint of 1825 contained the sketch of Sale's life by Richard Alfred Davenant which has been utilized in the article on Sale in the *Dictionary of National Biography*. The Chandos Classics edition in crown octavo was first issued in 1877.

Soon after the death of the Prophet, early Muhammadan theologians began to discuss, not only the correct reading of the text itself, but also to work out on the basis of first-hand reports the story connected with the revelation of each chapter. As the book at present stands in its original form the chapters are arranged more or less according to their respective length, beginning with the longest ; except in the case of the opening chapter, which holds a place by itself, not only in the sacred book of Islam, corresponding as it does in a manner to our Pater Noster, but also in its important ceremonial usages. The presumed order in which the various chapters were revealed is given in the tabular list of Contents, but it may be mentioned that neither Muhammadan theologians, nor, in more recent times, European scholars, are in entire agreement upon the exact chronological position of all the chapters.

It is well for all who study the Korân to realize that the actual text is never the composition of the Prophet, but is the word of God addressed to the Prophet ; and that in quoting the Korân the formula is " He (may he be exalted) said " or some such phrase. The Prophet himself is of course quoted by Muhammadan theologians, but such quotations refer to his traditional sayings known as " Hadîs," which have been handed down from mouth to mouth with the strictest regard to genealogical continuity.

It would probably be impossible for any Arabic scholar to produce a translation of the Korân which would defy criticism, but this much may be said of Sale's version : just as, when it first appeared, it had no rival in the field, it may be fairly claimed to-day that it has been superseded by no subsequent translations. Equally remarkable with his translation is the famous *Preliminary Discourse* which constitutes a *tour de force* when we consider how little critical work had been done in his day in the field of Islamic research. Practically the only works of first-class importance were Dr. Pocock's *Specimen Historiæ Arabum*, to which, in his original Address to the Reader, Sale acknowledges his great indebtedness, and Marracci's Korân.

In spite of the vast number of eminent scholars who have worked in the same field since the days of George Sale, his *Preliminary Discourse* still remains the best Introduction in any European language to the study of the religion promulgated by the Prophet of Arabia ; but as Wherry says : " Whilst regarding the *Preliminary Discourse* as a most masterly, and on the whole reliable, presentation of the peculiar doctrines, rites, ceremonies, customs, and institutions of Islam, we recognize the fact that modern research has brought to light many things concerning the history of the ancient Arabs which greatly modify the statements made in the early paragraphs."

For many centuries the acquaintance which the majority of Europeans possessed of Muhammadanism was based almost entirely on distorted reports of fanatical Christians which led to the dissemination of a multitude of gross calumnies. What was good in Muhammadanism was entirely ignored, and what was not good, in the eyes of Europe, was exaggerated or misinterpreted.

It must not, however, be forgotten that the central doctrine preached by Muhammad to his contemporaries in Arabia, who worshipped the Stars ; to the Persians, who acknowledged Ormuz and Ahriman ; the Indians, who worshipped idols ; and the Turks, who had no particular worship, was the unity of God, and that the simplicity of his creed was probably a more potent factor in the spread of Islam than the sword of the Ghazis.

Islam, although seriously affecting the Christian world, brought a spiritual religion to one half of Asia, and it is an amazing circumstance that the Turks, who on several occasions let loose their Central Asian hordes over India, and the Middle East, though irresistible in the onslaught of their arms, were all conquered in their turn by the Faith of Islam, and founded Muhammadan dynasties.

The Mongols of the thirteenth century did their best to wipe out all traces of Islam when they sacked Baghdad, but though the Caliphate was relegated to obscurity in Egypt the newly founded Empires quickly became Muhammadan states, until finally it was a Turk who took the title of Caliph which has been held by the house of Othman ever since.

Thus through all the vicissitudes of thirteen hundred years the Korân has remained the sacred book of all the Turks and Persians and of nearly a quarter of the population of India. Surely such a book as this deserves to be widely read in the West, more especially in these days when space and time have been almost annihilated by modern invention, and when public interest embraces the whole world

It is difficult to decide to what extent Sale's citations in the notes represent first-hand use of the Arabic commentators, but I fear that the result of a close inquiry only points to very little original research on his part. He says himself in his Address to the Reader : " As I have had no opportunity of consulting public libraries, the manuscripts of which I have made use throughout the whole work have been such as I had in my own study, except only the Commentary of Al Baidhâwi " . . . which " belongs to the library of the Dutch Church in Austin Friars."

Now with regard to these manuscripts which Sale had in his " own study " we happen to possess first-hand information, for a list of them was printed by the executor of his will under the following title : " A choice collection of most curious and inestimable manuscripts in the Turkish, Arabic and Persian languages from the library of the late learned and ingenious Mr. George Sale. Which books are now in the possession of Mr. William Hammerton Merchant in Lothbury where they may be seen on Wednesdays and Fridays till either they are sold or sent abroad. N.B. These MSS. are to be sold together and not separately." They were purchased in the first instance by the Rev. Thomas Hunt of Oxford for the Radcliffe Library, and they are now permanently housed in the Bodleian Library.

The British Museum possesses a copy of this list which is drawn up in English and French on opposite pages and comprises eighty-six works in all. The list contains very few Arabic works of first-rate importance, but is rich in Turkish and Persian Histories. What is most significant, however, is the fact that it contains hardly any of the Arabic works and *none* of the Commentaries which are referred to on every page of Sale's translation of the Korân.

I have therefore been forced to the conclusion that with the exception of Al-Baidhâwi, Sale's sources were all consulted at second hand ; and an examination of Marracci's great work makes the whole matter perfectly clear. Sale says of Marracci's translation that it is " generally speaking very exact ; but adheres to the Arabic idiom too literally to be easily understood . . . by those who are not versed in the Muhammadan learning. The notes he has added are indeed of great use ; but his refutations, which swell the work to a large volume, are of little or none at all, being often unsatisfactory, and sometimes impertinent. The work, however, with all its faults is very valuable, and I should be guilty of ingratitude, did I not acknowledge myself much obliged thereto ; but still being in Latin it can be of no use to those who understand not that tongue."

Such is Sale's own confession of his obligation to Marracci but it does not go nearly far enough. A comparison of the two versions shows that so much had been achieved by Marracci that Sale's work might almost have been performed with a knowledge of Latin alone, as far as regards the quotations from Arabic authors. I do not wish to imply that Sale did not know Arabic, but I do maintain that his work as it stands gives a misleading estimate of his original researches, and that his tribute to Marracci falls far short of his actual indebtedness.

It must be mentioned that Marracci not only reproduced the whole of the Arabic text of the Korân but furthermore gives the original text and the translation of all his quotations from Arabic writers. It is indeed a profoundly learned work and has never received the recognition it deserves. Marracci had at his disposal rich collections of MSS. belonging to the Libraries of Italy. How he learnt his Arabic we do not know. Voltaire says he was never in the East. He was confessor to Pope Innocent XI, and his work which appeared in Padua in 1698 is dedicated to the Holy Roman Emperor Leopold I. By way of Introduction to his Korân Marracci published a companion folio volume called *Prodromus* which contains practically all that was known in his day regarding Muhammad and the Religion of Islam.

It may in any case be claimed that the present work presents to the Western student all the essentials of a preliminary study of Islam : for Sale's translation and footnotes will give him as clear an idea as can be obtained, without laborious years of study in Arabic, of what is regarded by so many millions of men from Fez to the Far East as the revealed word of God and the unshakable basis of their faith.

George Sale was born about 1697 and died in 1736. Every biography calls attention to the statement made by Voltaire in his *Dictionnaire Philosophique* to the effect that Sale spent over twenty years among the Arabs. I think this must have been a *lapsus calami* on Voltaire's part, because it is unlikely that he would have invented such a story. Sale must also have been well versed in Hebrew, both biblical and post-biblical, as his numerous allusions to Rabbinical writings testify.

Two years after the publication of his great work Sale died in Surrey Street, Strand, his age being then under forty. In 1720 he had been admitted a student of the Inner Temple —son of Samuel Sale, citizen and merchant of London— and the same year the Patriarch of Antioch had sent Solomon Negri (Suleiman Alsadi) to London from Damascus to urge the Society for Promoting Christian Knowledge, then established in the Middle Temple, to issue an Arabic New Testament for the Syrian Christians. It is surmised that Negri was Sale's first instructor in Arabic, though Dadichi, the King's Interpreter, a learned Greek of Aleppo, guided him, we are told, "through the labyrinth of oriental dialects."

Whatever Sale may have known before—and he certainly had the gift of languages—it is on the Society's records that on August 30, 1726, he offered his services as one of the correctors of the Arabic New Testament and soon became the chief worker on it, besides being the Society's solicitor and holding other honorary offices. That translation of the New Testament into Arabic was followed by the translation of the Korân into English.

In this edition the proper names have been left for the most part as in the original, but the reader must understand that in Sale's day there was a freedom in regard to oriental orthography that allowed of many variations. In spite, however, of the want of a scientific system, Sale's transcription is on the whole clear, and far less confusing than those adopted by contemporary Anglo-Indian scholars, who utterly distorted Muhammadan names—including place names in India—by rendering the short *a* by *u* and so forth. As a few examples of names spelled in more than one way, the correct modern way being given first, we have Al-Qor'án, Coran, Korân, etc. ; Muhammad, Mohammed, Mahomet, etc. ; Al-Baidhâwi, Al-Beidâwi ; Muttalib, Motalleb, Motaleb, etc. ; Jalâl ud-Din, Jallâlo'ddîn ; Anas, Ans ; Khalîfa, Caliph, Khalif, etc.

It is only within quite recent times that scholars have troubled to render each letter of the Arabic alphabet by an equivalent and distinct letter of the Roman alphabet—and although no particular system has been universally adopted by European orientalists, every writer has some system by which any reader with a knowledge of Arabic is able to turn back every name into the original script. The chief advantage of any such system is that a distinction is made between the two varieties of *s*, *k*, and *t*, and the presence of the illusive Arabic letter *'ayn* is always indicated.

E. DENISON ROSS.

A TABLE OF THE CHAPTERS OF
THE KORÂN
ACCORDING TO THE ARABIC TEXT
WITH THEIR ORDER OF DATE AND NUMBER OF VERSES

NOTE.—The order of date is according to Nöldeke.

THE KORÂN

I

THE PREFACE, OR INTRODUCTION [1]
Revealed at Mecca.

IN THE NAME OF THE MOST MERCIFUL GOD.

PRAISE be to GOD, the LORD of all creatures ; [2] the most merciful, the king of the day of judgment. Thee do we worship, and of thee do we beg assistance. Direct us in the right way, in the way of those to whom thou hast been gracious ; not of those against whom thou art incensed, nor of those who go astray. [3]

[1] In Arabic *Al Fâtihat*. This chapter is a prayer, and held in great veneration by the Mohammedans, who give it several other honourable titles ; as the chapter of *prayer*, of *praise*, of *thanksgiving*, of *treasure*, etc. They esteem it as the quintessence of the whole Korân, and often repeat it in their devotions both public and private, as the Christians do the Lord's Prayer. (Bobovium de Precib. Mohammed, p. 3, et seq.) The " Bismillah " to all the chapters except the ninth, " In the Name of the most merciful God," is otherwise rendered as " In the Name of the merciful and compassionate God," and " In the Name of God, the Compassionate, the Merciful." The Mohammedans say it whenever they slaughter an animal and at the commencement of their reading, and of all important actions. It is with them what the sign of the cross is with Christians.

[2] The original words are, *Rabbi'l âlamîna,* which literally signify *Lord of the worlds*, but *âlamîna* in this and other places of the Korân properly means the three species of rational creatures, men, genii, and angels.

[3] This last sentence contains a petition, that GOD would lead the supplicants unto the true religion, by which is meant the Mohammedan, in the Korân often called *the right way* ; in this place more particularly defined to be, *the way of those to whom* GOD *hath been gracious*, that is, of the prophets and faithful who preceded Mohammed ; under which appellations are also comprehended the Jews and Christians, such as they were in the times of their primitive purity, before they had deviated from their respective institutions ; *not the way of the modern* Jews, whose signal calamities are marks of the just *anger* of GOD against them for their obstinacy and disobedience ; *nor of the* Christians *of this age,* who have departed from the true doctrine of Jesus, and are bewildered in a labyrinth of *error.* (Jallalo'ddin, Al Beidâwi, &c.)

This is the common exposition of the passage although Al Zamakhshari, and some others, by a different application of the negatives, refer the whole

II

THE CHAPTER OF THE COW [1]

Revealed partly at Mecca, and partly at Medina.

IN THE NAME OF THE MOST MERCIFUL GOD.

A. L. M. [2] There is no doubt in this book ; *it is* a direction to the pious, who believe in the mysteries [3] *of faith,* who observe the appointed times of prayer, and distribute *alms* out of what we have bestowed on them ; and who believe in that *revelation,* which hath been sent down unto thee, and that which hath been sent down *unto the prophets* before thee, [4] and have firm assurance in the life to come : [5] these are directed by their LORD, and they shall prosper. As for the unbelievers, it will be equal to them whether thou admonish them, or do not admonish them ; they will not believe. GOD hath sealed up their hearts and their hearing ;

to the true believers ; and then the sense will run thus : *The way of those to whom thou hast been gracious, against whom thou art not incensed, and who have not erred.* Which translation the original will very well bear.

This chapter has been metrically translated by Sir Richard Burton as follows :—

1. In the Name of Allah, the Merciful, the Compassionate !
2. Praise be to Allah, who the *three* worlds made.
3. The Merciful, the Compassionate.
4. The King of the Day of Fate.
5. Thee *alone* do we worship, and of Thee *alone* do we ask aid.
6. Guide us to the path that is straight.
7. The path of those to whom Thy love is great,
        Not those in whom is hate,
        Nor they that deviate. Amen,—

thus giving an idea of the rhymes of the original.

[1] This title was occasioned by the story of the *red heifer,* mentioned p. 9. It is also called the chapter of the Heifer.

[2] As to the meaning of these letters, see Sale Preliminary Discourse, Sect. III, p. 64.

[3] The Arabic word is *gheib,* which properly signifies a thing that is *absent, at a great distance,* or *invisible,* such as the resurrection, paradise, and hell. And this is agreeable to the language of scripture, which defines faith to be *the evidence of things not seen.* (Heb. xi. 1. See also Rom. xxiv. 25 ; 2 Cor. iv. 18 and v. 7.)

[4] The Mohammedans believe that GOD gave written revelations not only to Moses, Jesus, and Mohammed, but to several other prophets (Reland de Relig. Moham. p. 34, and Dissert. de Samaritanis, p. 34, etc.) ; though they acknowledge none of those which preceded the Korân to be now extant, except the Pentateuch of Moses, the Psalms of David, and the Gospel of Jesus ; which yet they say were even before Mohammed's time altered and corrupted by the Jews and Christians ; and therefore will not allow our present copies to be genuine.

[5] The original word *al-âkherat* properly signifies *the latter part* of anything, and by way of excellence *the next life, the latter* or *future state* after death ; and is opposed to *al-donya, this world* ; and *al-oula,* the *former* or *present life.* The Hebrew word *ahharith,* from the same root, is used by Moses in this sense, and is translated *latter end.* (Numb. xxiv. 20 ; Deut. viii. 16).

a dimness covereth their sight, and they shall suffer a grievous punishment. There are some who say, We believe in
GOD and the last day, but are not *really* believers ; they
seek to deceive GOD, and those who do believe, but they
deceive themselves only, and are not sensible thereof. There
is an infirmity in their hearts, and GOD hath increased that
infirmity ; [1] and they shall suffer a most painful punishment
because they have disbelieved. When one saith unto them,
Act not corruptly [2] in the earth, they reply, Verily, we are
men of integrity.[3] Are not they themselves corrupt doers ?
but they are not sensible thereof. And when one saith unto
them, Believe ye as others [4] believe ; they answer, Shall we
believe as fools believe ? Are not they themselves fools ?
but they know it not. When they meet those who believe,
they say, We do believe : but when they retire privately
to their devils,[5] they say, We really *hold* with you, and only
mock *at those people* : GOD shall mock at them, and continue them in their impiety ; they shall wander in confusion.
These are *the men* who have purchased error at the price of
true direction : but their traffic hath not been gainful, neither
have they been *rightly* directed. They are like unto one who
kindleth a fire,[6] and when it hath enlightened all around him,[7]
GOD taketh away their light [8] and leaveth them in darkness,
they shall not see ; *they are* deaf, dumb, and blind, therefore
will they not repent. Or like a stormy cloud from heaven,

[1] Mohammed here, and elsewhere frequently, imitates the truly inspired
writers, in making GOD by operation on the minds of reprobates to prevent
their conversion. This fatality or predestination, as believed by the Mohammedans, hath been sufficiently treated of in the Preliminary Discourse.

[2] Literally *corrupt not in the earth*, by which some expositors understand
the sowing of false doctrine, and corrupting people's principles.

[3] According to the explication in the preceding note, this word must be
translated *reformers*, who promote true piety by their doctrine and example.

[4] The first companions and followers of Mohammed. (Jallalo'ddin.)

[5] The prophet, making use of the liberty zealots of all religions have, by
prescription, of giving ill language, bestows this name on the Jewish rabbins
and Christian priests ; though he seems chiefly to mean the former, against
whom he had by much the greater spleen.

[7] In this passage, Mohammed compares those who believed not on him,
to a man who wants to kindle a fire, but as soon as it burns up, and the
flames give a light, shuts his eyes, lest he should see. As if he had said :
You, O Arabians, have long desired a prophet of your own nation, and
now I am sent unto you, and have plainly proved my mission by the excellence of my doctrine and revelation, you resist conviction, and refuse to
believe in me ; therefore shall GOD leave you in your ignorance.

[7] The sense seems to be here imperfect, and may be completed by adding
the words, He *turns from it, shuts his eyes*, or the like.

[8] That is of the unbelievers, to whom the word *their*, being in the plural,
seems to refer ; though it is not unusual for Mohammed, in affectation
of the prophetic style, suddenly to change the number against all rules
of grammar.

fraught with darkness, thunder, and lightning,[1] they put their fingers in their ears, because of the noise of the thunder, for fear of death ; GOD encompasseth the infidels : the lightning wanteth but little of taking away their sight ; so often as it enlighteneth them, they walk therein, but when darkness cometh on them, they stand still ; and if GOD so pleased, He would certainly deprive them of their hearing and their sight, for GOD is almighty. O men of *Mecca* ! serve your LORD who hath created you, and those who have been before you : peradventure ye will fear *him* ; who hath spread the earth as a bed for you, and the heaven as a covering, and hath caused water to descend from heaven, and thereby produced fruits for your sustenance. Set not up therefore any equals unto GOD, against your own knowledge. If ye be in doubt concerning that *revelation* which we have sent down unto our servant, produce a chapter like unto it, and call upon your witnesses, besides GOD,[2] if ye say truth. But if ye do *it* not, nor shall *ever be able to* do *it*, justly fear the fire whose fuel is men and stones, prepared for the unbelievers. But bear good tidings unto those who believe, and do good works, that they shall have gardens watered by rivers ; so often as they eat of the fruit thereof for sustenance they *shall* say, This is what we have formerly eaten of ; and they shall be supplied with *several sorts of fruit* having a mutual resemblance to one another.[3] There shall they enjoy wives subject to no impurity, and there shall they continue for ever. Moreover GOD will not be ashamed to propound in a parable a gnat, or even a more despicable thing : [4] for they who believe will know it to be the truth from their LORD ; but the unbelievers will say, What meaneth God by this parable ? he will thereby mislead many, and will direct many thereby : but he will not mislead

[1] Here he compares the unbelieving Arabs to people caught in a violent storm. To perceive the beauty of this comparison, it must be observed, that the Mohammedan doctors say, this tempest is a type or image of the Korân itself : the thunder signifying the threats therein contained ; the lightning, the promises ; and the darkness, the mysteries. The terror of the threats makes them stop their ears, unwilling to hear truths so disagreeable ; when the promises are read to them, they attend with pleasure ; but when anything mysterious or difficult of belief occurs, they stand stock still, and will not submit to be directed.

[2] *i.e.*, Your false gods and idols.

[3] Some commentators (Jallalo'ddin) approve of this sense, supposing the fruits of paradise, though of various tastes, are alike in colour and outward appearance : but others (Al Zamakhshari) think the meaning to be, that the inhabitants of that place will find there fruits of the same or the like kinds as they used to eat while on earth.

[4] This was revealed to take off an objection made to the Korân by the infidels, for condescending to speak of such insignificant insects as the ant, the bee, &c. (Yahya.)

any thereby, except the transgressors, who make void the covenant of GOD after the establishing thereof, and cut in sunder that which GOD hath commanded to be joined, and act corruptly in the earth ; they shall perish.   How *is it that* ye believe not in GOD ? since ye were dead, and he gave you life ; [1] he will hereafter cause you to die, and will again restore you to life ; then shall ye return unto him.   It is he who hath created for you whatsoever is on earth, and then set his mind to *the creation of* heaven, and formed it into seven heavens ; he knoweth all things.   When thy LORD said unto the angels, I am going to place a substitute on earth,[2] they said, Wilt thou place there one who will do evil therein, and shed blood ? but we celebrate thy praise, and sanctify thee. GOD answered, Verily I know that which ye know not ; and he taught Adam the names of all things, and then proposed them to the angels, and said, Declare unto me the names of these things if ye say truth.   They answered, Praise be unto thee, we have no knowledge but what thou teachest us, for thou art knowing and wise.   GOD said, O Adam, tell them their names.   And when he had told them their names, GOD said, Did I not tell you that I know the secrets of heaven and earth, and know that which ye discover, and that which ye conceal ? [3]   And when we said unto the angels, Wor-

[1] *i.e.*, Ye were dead while in the loins of your fathers, and he gave you life in your mothers' wombs ; and after death ye shall be again raised at the resurrection.   (Jallalo'ddin.)

[2] Concerning the creation of Adam, here intimated, the Mohammedans have several peculiar traditions.   They say the angels, Gabriel, Michael, and Israfil, were sent by GOD, one after another, to fetch for that purpose seven handfuls of earth from different depths, and of different colours whence some account for the various complexions of mankind (Al Termedi, from a tradition of Abu Musa al Ashàri) ; but the earth being apprehensive of the consequence, and desiring them to represent her fear to GOD that the creature he designed to form would rebel against him, and draw down his curse upon her, they returned without performing GOD's command ; whereupon he sent Azraël on the same errand, who executed his commission without remorse, for which reason GOD appointed that angel to separate the souls from the bodies, being therefore called *the angel of death.*   The earth he had taken was carried into Arabia, to a place between Mecca and Tayef, where, being first kneaded by the angels, it was afterwards fashioned by GOD himself into a human form, and left to dry (Kor. c. lv) for the space of forty days, or, as others say, as many years, the angels in the meantime often visiting it, and Eblis (then one of the angels who are nearest to GOD's presence, afterwards the devil) among the rest ; but he, not contented with looking on it, kicked it with his foot till it rung, and knowing GOD designed that creature to be his superior, took a secret resolution never to acknowledge him as such.   After this, GOD animated the figure of clay and endued it with an intelligent soul, and when he had placed him in paradise, formed Eve out of his left side.   (Khondamir. Jallalo'ddin. Comment in Korân, &c.   D'Herbelot, Biblioth. Orient. p. 55.)

[3] This story Mohammed borrowed from the Jewish traditions, which say that the angels having spoken of man with some contempt when GOD

ship[1] Adam, they *all* worshipped *him*, except Eblîs, *who* refused, and was puffed up with pride, and became of the *number
of* unbelievers.[2] And we said, O Adam, dwell thou and thy
wife in the garden,[3] and eat *of the fruit* thereof plentifully
wherever ye will ; but approach not this tree,[4] lest ye become of *the number of* the transgressors. But Satan caused
them to forfeit *paradise*,[5] and turned them out of *the state
of happiness* wherein they had been ; whereupon we said,
Get ye down,[6] the one of you an enemy unto the other ; and

consulted them about his creation, GOD made answer that the man was
wiser than they ; and to convince them of it, he brought all kinds of animals
to them, and asked them their names ; which they not being able to tell,
he put the same question to the man, who named them one after another ;
and being asked his own name and GOD's name, he answered very justly,
and gave GOD the name of JEHOVAH. (Rivin. Serpent. seduct. p. 56.)
The angels' adoring of Adam is also mentioned in the Talmud. (R. Moses
Haddarshan, in Bereshit rabbah.)

[1] The original word signifies properly to *prostrate one's self* till the forehead
touches the ground, which is the humblest posture of adoration, and strictly
due to GOD only ; but it is sometimes, as in this place, used to express
that civil worship or homage, which may be paid to creatures. (Jallalo'ddin.)

[2] This occasion of the devil's fall has some affinity with an opinion which
has been pretty much entertained among Christians (Irenæus, Lact. Greg.
Nyssen, &c.), viz., that the angels being informed of GOD's intention to
create man after his own image, and to dignify human nature by CHRIST's
assuming it, some of them, thinking their glory to be eclipsed thereby,
envied man's happiness, and so revolted.

[3] Mohammed, as appears by what presently follows, does not place this
garden or paradise on earth, but in the seventh heaven. (Marracc. in Alc.
p. 24.)

[4] Concerning this tree or the forbidden fruit, the Mohammedans, as well
as the Christians, have various opinions. Some say it was an ear of wheat ;
some will have it to have been a fig-tree, and others a vine. (Marracc. p. 24.)
The story of the Fall is told, with some further circumstances, in the beginning of the seventh chapter.

[5] They have a tradition that the devil offering to get into paradise to tempt
Adam, was not admitted by the guard ; whereupon he begged of the animals,
one after another, to carry him in, that he might speak to Adam and his
wife ; but they all refused him except the serpent, who took him between
two of his teeth, and so introduced him. They add that the serpent was
then of a beautiful form, and not in the shape he now bears. (Marracc, p. 24.)

[6] The Mohammedans say that when they were cast down from paradise,
Adam fell on the isle of Ceylon or Serendib, and Eve near Joddah (the port
of Mecca) in Arabia ; and that after a separation of 200 years, Adam was,
on his repentance, conducted by the angel Gabriel to a mountain near Mecca,
where he found and knew his wife, the mountain being thence named Arafat ;
and that he afterwards retired with her to Ceylon, where they continued
to propagate their species. (D'Herbelot, Bib. Orient. p. 55.) It may not
be improper here to mention another tradition concerning the gigantic
stature of our first parents. Their prophet, they say, affirmed Adam to
have been as tall as a high palm-tree (Yahya); but this would be too much
in proportion, if that were really the print of his foot, which is pretended to
be such, on the top of a mountain in the isle of Ceylon, thence named Pico
de Adam, and by the Arab writers Rahûn, being somewhat above two spans
long. Moncony's Voyage, part i. p. 372, &c. Knox's Account of Ceylon)
--though others say it is 70 cubits long, and that when Adam set one foot
here, he had the other in the sea (Anciennes Relations des Indes, &c., p. 3)—
and too little, if Eve were of so enormous a size, as is said, when her head

there shall be a dwelling-place for you on earth, and a provision for a season. And Adam learned words *of prayer* from his LORD, and GOD turned unto him, for he is easy to be reconciled and merciful. We said, Get ye all down from hence ; hereafter shall there come unto you a direction from me,[1] and whoever shall follow my direction, on them shall no fear come, neither shall they be grieved ; but they who shall be unbelievers, and accuse our signs[2] of falsehood, they shall be the companions of *hell* fire, therein shall they remain for ever. O children of Israel,[3] remember my favour wherewith I have favoured you ; and perform *your* covenant with me, and I will perform *my* covenant with you ; and revere me : and believe in the *revelation* which I have sent down, confirming that which is with you, and be not the first who believe not therein, neither exchange my signs for a small price ; and fear me. Clothe not the truth with vanity, neither conceal the truth against your own knowledge ; observe the stated times of prayer, and pay your legal alms, and bow down yourselves with those who bow down. Will ye command men to do justice, and forget your own souls ? yet ye read the book *of the law* : do ye not therefore understand ? Ask help with perseverance and prayer ; this indeed is grievous, unless to the humble, who *seriously* think they shall meet their LORD, and that to him they shall return. O children of Israel, remember my favour wherewith I have favoured you, and that I have preferred you above all nations : dread the day *wherein one* soul shall not make satisfaction for *another* soul, neither shall any intercession be accepted from them, nor shall any compensation be received, neither shall they be helped. *Remember* when we delivered you from the people

lay on one hill near Mecca, her knees rested on two others in the plain, about two musket-shots asunder. (Moncony's Voyage, ubi sup.)

[1] GOD here promises Adam that his will should be revealed to him and his posterity ; which promise the Mohammedans believe was fulfilled at several times by the ministry of several prophets, from Adam himself, who was the first, to Mohammed, who was the last. The number of books revealed unto Adam they say was ten. (Hottinger Hist. Orient. p. 11. Reland. de Relig. Mohammed. p. 21.)

[2] This word has various significations in the Korân ; sometimes, as in this passage, it signifies *divine revelation*, or *scripture* in general ; sometimes the *verses* of the Korân in particular, and at other times *visible miracles*. But the sense is easily distinguished by the context.

[3] The Jews are here called upon to receive the Korân, as verifying and confirming the Pentateuch, particularly with respect to the unity of God and the mission of Mohammed. (Yahya.) And they are exhorted not to conceal the passages of their law which bear witness to those truths, nor to corrupt them by publishing false copies of the Pentateuch, for which the writers were but poorly paid. (Jallalo'ddin.)

of Pharaoh, who grievously oppressed you, they slew your male children, and let your females live ; therein was a great trial from your LORD. And when we divided the sea for you and delivered you, and drowned Pharaoh's people while ye looked on.[1] And when we treated with Moses forty nights ; then ye took the calf[2] *for your God*, and did evil ; yet afterwards we forgave you, that peradventure ye might give thanks. And we gave Moses the book *of the law*, and the distinction *between good and evil*, that peradventure ye might be directed. And when Moses said unto his people, O my people, verily ye have injured your own souls, by your taking the calf *for your God* ; therefore be turned unto your Creator, and slay those among you *who have been guilty of that crime*,[3] this will be better for you in the sight of your Creator : and *thereupon* he turned unto you, for he is easy to be reconciled, and merciful. And when ye said O Moses, we will not believe thee, until we see GOD manifestly ; therefore a punishment came upon you, while ye looked on ; then we raised you to life after ye had been dead, that peradventure ye might give thanks.[4] And we caused clouds to overshadow you, and

[1] See the story of Moses and Pharaoh more particularly related, Chaps. vii. and xx., &c.

[2] The person who cast this calf, the Mohammedans say, was (not Aaron but) Al Sâmeri, one of the principal men among the children of Israel, some of whose descendants it is pretended still inhabit an island of that name in the Arabian Gulf. (Geogr. Nubiens. p. 45.) It was made of the rings (Kor. c. vii.) and bracelets of gold, silver, and other materials, which the Israelites had borrowed of the Egyptians ; for Aaron, who commanded in his brother's absence, having ordered Al Sâmeri to collect those ornaments from the people, who carried on a wicked commerce with them, and to keep them together till the return of Moses ; Al Sâmeri, understanding the founder's art, put them altogether into a furnace to melt them down into one mass, which came out in the form of a calf. (Exod. xxxii. 24.) The Israelites, accustomed to the Egyptian idolatry, paying a religious worship to this image, Al Sâmeri went farther, and took some dust from the footsteps of the horse of the angel Gabriel, who marched at the head of the people, and threw it into the mouth of the calf, which immediately began to low, and became animated (Kor. c. VII) ; for such was the virtue of that dust. (Jallalo'ddin. D'Herbelot, Bibl. Orient. p. 650.) One writer says that all the Israelites adored this calf, except only 12,000. (Abulfeda.)

[3] In this particular, the narration agrees with that of Moses, who ordered the Levites to slay *every man his brother* (Exod. xxxii. 26, 27), but the scripture says, *there fell of the people that day about* 3,000 (the Vulgate says 23,000) *men* (Ibid. 28) ; whereas the commentators of the Korân make the number of the slain to amount to 70,000 ; and add, that GOD sent a dark cloud which hindered them from seeing one another, lest the sight should move those who executed the sentence to compassion. (Jallalo'ddin, &c.)

[4] The persons here meant are said to have been seventy men, who were made choice of by Moses, and heard the voice of GOD talking with him. But not being satisfied with that, they demanded to see GOD ; whereupon they were all struck dead by lightning, and on Moses's intercession restored to life. (Ismael Ebn Ali.)

manna and quails[1] to descend upon you, *saying,* Eat of the
good things which we have given you for food : and they
injured not us, but injured their own souls. And when we
said, Enter into this city,[2] and eat *of the provisions* thereof
plentifully as ye will ; and enter the gate worshipping, and
say, Forgiveness ![3] we will pardon you your sins, and give
increase unto the well-doers. But the ungodly changed the
expression into another,[4] different from what had been spoken
unto them ; and we sent down upon the ungodly indignation from heaven,[5] because they had transgressed. And
when Moses asked drink for his people, we said, Strike the
rock[6] with thy rod ; and there gushed thereout twelve
fountains [7] *according to the number of the tribes,* and all men

---

[1] The eastern writers say these quails were of a peculiar kind, to be found
nowhere but in Yaman, from whence they were brought by a south wind in
great numbers to the Israelites' camp in the desert. (Psalm lxxviii. 26.)
The Arabs call these birds *Salwâ,* which is plainly the same with the Hebrew
Salwim, and say they have no bones, but are eaten whole. (D'Herbelot,
Bibl. Orient. p. 477.)

[2] Some commentators suppose it to be Jericho, others Jerusalem.

[3] The Arabic word is *Hittaton,* which some take to signify that profession
of the unity of GOD so frequently used by the Mohammedans, *La ilâha illa
'llaho, There is no god but* GOD.

[4] According to Jallalo'ddin, instead of *Hittaton,* they cried *Habbat fi
shaïrat—i.e., a grain in an ear of barley* ; and in ridicule of the divine command to enter the city in an humble posture, they indecently crept in upon
their breech.

[5] A pestilence which carried off near 70,000 of them. (Jallalo'ddin.)

[6] The commentators say this was a stone which Moses brought from
Mount Sinai, and the same that fled away with his garments which he laid
upon it one day while he washed ; they add that Moses ran after the stone
naked, till he found himself, ere he was aware, in the midst of the people,
who, on this accident, were convinced of the falsehood of a report which
had been raised of their prophet, that he was bursten, or, as others write,
an hermaphrodite. (Jallalo'ddin, Yahya.) They describe it to be a square
piece of white marble, shaped like a man's head ; wherein they differ not
much from the accounts of European travellers, who say this rock stands
among several lesser ones, about 100 paces from Mount Horeb, and appears
to have been loosened from the neighbouring mountains, having no coherence
with the others ; that it is a huge mass of red granite, almost round on
one side, and flat on the other, twelve feet high, and as many thick, but
broader than it is high, and about fifty feet in circumference. (Breydenbach,
Itinerar. Chartâ m. p. 1. Sicard, dans les Mémoires des Missions, vol. vii.
p. 14.)

[7] Marracci thinks this circumstance looks like a Rabbinical fiction, or
else that Mohammed confounds the water of the rock at Horeb with the
twelve wells at Elim (Exod. xv. 27; Numb. xxxiii. 9) ; for he says several
who have been on the spot affirm there are but three orifices whence the
water issued. (Marracc. Prodr. part iv. p. 80.) But it is to be presumed
that Mohammed had better means of information in this respect than to
fall into such a mistake ; for the rock stands within the borders of Arabia,
and some of his countrymen must needs have seen it, if he himself did not,
as it is most probable he did. And in effect he seems to be in the right.
For one who went into those parts in the end of the fifteenth century tells
us expressly that the water issued from twelve places of the rock, according
to the number of the tribes of Israel ; *egressæ sunt aquæ largissimæ in*

knew their *respective* drinking-place. Eat and drink of the bounty of GOD, and commit not evil in the earth, acting unjustly. And when ye said, O Moses, we will by no means be satisfied with one *kind of* food ; pray unto thy Lord therefore for us, that he would produce for us of that which the earth bringeth forth, herbs, and cucumbers, and garlic, and lentils, and onions ;[1] Moses answered, Will ye exchange that which is better, for that which is worse ? Get ye down into Egypt, for *there* shall ye find what ye desire : and they were smitten with vileness and misery, and drew on themselves indignation from GOD. This *they suffered*, because they believed not in the signs of GOD, and killed the prophets unjustly ; this, because they rebelled and transgressed. Surely those who believe, and those who Judaize, and Christians, and Sabians,[2] whoever believeth in GOD, and the last day, and doth that which is right, they shall have their reward with their LORD ; *there shall come* no fear on them, neither shall they be grieved. *Call to mind* also when we

---

duodecim locis petræ, juxta numerum duodecim tribuum Israel. (Breydenbach, ubi sup.) A late curious traveller (Sicard, ubi sup.) observes that there are twenty-four holes in the stone, which may be easily counted—that is to say, twelve on the flat side, and as many on the opposite round side, every one being a foot deep, and an inch wide ; and he adds, that the holes on one side do not communicate wth those on the other, which a less accurate spectator not perceiving (for they are placed horizontally, within two feet of the top of the rock), might conclude they pierced quite through the stone, and so reckon them to be but twelve.

[1] See Numb. xi. 5, &c.

[2] From these words, which are repeated in the fifth chapter, several writers (Selden, de Jure Nat. et Gent. sec. Hebr. l. 6, c. 12. Angel, a St. Joseph. Gazophylac. Persic. p. 365. Nic. Cusanus in Cribratione Al-corani, I. 3, c. 2, &c.) have wrongly concluded that the Mohammedans hold it to be the doctrine of their prophet that every man may be saved in his own religion, provided he be sincere and lead a good life. It is true, some of their doctors do agree this to be the purport of the words (Chardin's Voyages, vol. ii. p. 326, 331) ; but then they say the latitude hereby granted was soon revoked, for that this passage is abrogated by several others in the Korân, which expressly declare that none can be saved who is not of the Mohammedan faith, and particularly by those words of the third chapter, *Whoever followeth any other religion than* Islâm (*i e.*, the Moham-medan) *it shall not be accepted of him, and at the last day he shall be of those who perish.* (Abu'lkasem Hebatallah de abrogante et abrogato.) However, others are of opinion that this passage is not abrogated, but interpret it differently, taking the meaning of it to be that no man, whether he be a Jew, a Christian, or a Sabian, shall be excluded from salvation, provided he quit his erroneous religion and become a Moslem, which they say is intended by the following words, *Whoever believeth in* GOD *and the last day, and doth that which is right.* And this interpretation is approved by Mr. Reland, who thinks the words here import no more than those of the apostle, *In every nation he that feareth* GOD, *and worketh righteousness, is accepted with him* (Acts x. 35) ; from which it must not be inferred that the religion of nature, or any other, is sufficient to save, without faith in Christ. (Reland. de Rel. Moham. p. 128 &c.)

accepted your covenant, and lifted up the mountain *of Sinai* over you,[1] *saying*, Receive *the law* which we have given you, with a resolution *to keep it*, and remember that which is contained therein, that ye may beware. After this ye again turned back, so that if it had not been for GOD's indulgence and mercy towards you, ye had certainly been destroyed. Moreover ye know *what befell* those of your nation who transgressed on the sabbath day;[2] We said unto them, Be ye *changed into* apes, driven away *from the society of men*. And we made them an example unto those who were contemporary with them, and unto those who came after them, and a warning to the pious. And when Moses said unto his people, Verily GOD commandeth you to sacrifice a cow;[3]

[1] The Mohammedan tradition is, that the Israelites refusing to receive the law of Moses, GOD tore up the mountain by the roots, and shook it over their heads, to terrify them into a compliance. (Jallalo'ddin.)

[2] The story to which this passage refers, is as follows. In the days of David some Israelites dwelt at Ailah, or Elath, on the Red Sea, where on the night of the sabbath the fish used to come in great numbers to the shore, and stay there all the sabbath, to tempt them; but the night following they returned into the sea again. At length some of the inhabitants, neglecting GOD's command, caught fish on the sabbath, and dressed and ate them; and afterwards cut canals from the sea, for the fish to enter, with sluices, which they shut on the sabbath, to prevent their return to the sea. The other part of the inhabitants, who strictly observed the sabbath, used both persuasion and force to stop this impiety, but to no purpose, the offenders growing only more and more obstinate; whereupon David cursed the sabbath-breakers, and GOD transformed them into apes. It is said that one going to see a friend of his that was among them, found him in the shape of an ape, moving his eyes about wildly; and asking him whether he was not such a one, the ape made a sign with his head that it was he; whereupon the friend said to him, Did not I advise you to desist? at which the ape wept. They add that these unhappy people remained three days in this condition, and were afterwards destroyed by a wind which swept them all into the sea. (Abulfeda.)

[3] The occasion of this sacrifice is thus related. A certain man at his death left his son, then a child, a cow-calf, which wandered in the desert till he came of age; at which time his mother told him the heifer was his, and bid him fetch her, and sell her for three pieces of gold. When the young man came to the market with his heifer, an angel in the shape of a man accosted him, and bid him six pieces of gold for her; but he would not take the money till he had asked his mother's consent; which when he had obtained, he returned to the market-place, and met the angel, who now offered him twice as much for the heifer, provided he would say nothing of it to his mother; but the young man refusing, went and acquainted her with the additional offer. The woman perceiving it was an angel, bid her son go back and ask him what must be done with the heifer; whereupon the angel told the young man that in a little time the children of Israel would buy that heifer of him at any price. And soon after it happened that an Israelite, named Hammiel, was killed by a relation of his, who, to prevent discovery, conveyed the body to a place considerably distant from that where the deed was committed. The friends of the slain man accused some other persons of the murder before Moses; but they denying the fact, and there being no evidence to convict them, GOD commanded a cow, of such and such particular marks, to be killed; but there being no other which answered the description except the orphan's heifer, they were obliged to buy her for as much gold as her

they answered, Dost thou make a jest of us ? Moses said,
GOD forbid that I should be *one* of the foolish. They said,
Pray for us unto thy LORD, that he would show us what *cow*
it is. Moses answered, He saith, She is neither an old cow,
nor a young heifer, but of a middle age between both : do
ye therefore that which ye are commanded. They said,
Pray for us unto thy LORD, that he would show us what colour
she is of. Moses answered, He saith, She is a red cow,[1]
intensely red, her colour rejoiceth the beholders. They
said, Pray for us unto thy LORD, that he would *further* show
us what *cow* it is, for *several* cows with us are like one another,
and we, if GOD please, will be directed. Moses answered, He
saith, She is a cow not broken to plough the earth, or water
the field, a sound one, there is no blemish in her. They said,
Now hast thou brought the truth. Then they sacrificed her ;
yet they wanted little of leaving it undone.[2] And when
ye slew a man, and contended among yourselves concerning
him, GOD brought forth *to light* that which ye concealed.
For we said, Strike *the dead body* with part of *the sacrificed
cow* :[3] so GOD raiseth the dead to life, and showeth you his
signs, that peradventure ye may understand. Then were
your hearts hardened after this, even as stones, or exceeding
them in hardness : for from some stones have rivers bursted
forth, others have been rent in sunder, and water hath issued
from them, and others have fallen down for fear of GOD.
But GOD is not regardless of that which ye do. Do ye therefore desire that *the Jews* should believe you ? yet a part of
them heard the word of GOD, and then perverted it, after
they had understood it, against their own conscience. And
when they meet the true believers, they say, We believe : but
when they are privately assembled together, they say, Will
ye acquaint them with what GOD hath revealed unto you,
that they may dispute with you concerning it in the presence

hide would hold ; according to some, for her full weight in gold, and as
others say, for ten times as much. This heifer they sacrificed, and the
dead body being, by divine direction, struck with a part of it, revived,
and standing up, named the person who had killed him ; after which it
immediately fell down dead again. (Abulfeda.) The whole story seems
to be borrowed from the red heifer which was ordered by the Jewish law
to be burnt, and the ashes kept for purifying those who happened to touch
a dead corpse (Numb. xix.) ; and from the heifer directed to be slain for the
expiation of an uncertain murder. (See Deut. xxi. 1–9.)

[1] The epithet in the original is *yellow* ; but this word we do not use in
speaking of the colour of cattle.

[2] Because of the exorbitant price which they were obliged to pay for the
heifer.

[3] *i.e.*, Her tongue, or the end of her tail. (Jallalo'ddin.)

of your LORD ? Do ye nòt therefore understand ? Do not they know that GOD knoweth that which they conceal as well as that which they publish ? But there are illiterate men among them, who know not the book *of the law*, but only lying stories, although they think otherwise. And woe unto them who transcribe *corruptly* the book *of the law* [1] with their hands, and then say, This is from GOD : that they may sell it for a small price. Therefore woe unto them because of that which their hands have written ; and woe unto them for that which they have gained. They say, The fire *of hell* shall not touch us but for a *certain* number of days. [2] Answer, Have ye received any promise from GOD *to that purpose* ? for GOD will not act contrary to his promise : or do ye speak concerning GOD that which ye know not ? Verily whoso doth evil, [3] and is encompassed by his iniquity, they *shall be* the companions of *hell* fire, they shall remain therein for ever : but they who believe and do good works, they shall be the companions of paradise, they shall continue therein for ever. *Remember* also, when we accepted the covenant of the children of Israel, *saying*, Ye shall not worship *any other* except GOD, and *ye shall show* kindness to *your* parents and kindred, and to orphans, and to the poor, and speak that which is good unto men, and be constant at prayer, and give alms. Afterwards ye turned back, except a few of you, and retired afar off. And when we accepted your covenant, *saying*, Ye shall not shed your *brother's* blood, nor dispossess one another of your habitations. Then ye confirmed *it*, and were witnesses *thereto*. Afterwards ye were they who slew one another, [4] and turned several of your *brethren* out of their

---

[1] Mohammed again accuses the Jews of corrupting their scripture.

[2] That is, says Jallalo'ddin, forty ; being the number of days that their forefathers worshipped the golden calf ; after which they gave out that their punishments should cease. It is a received opinion among the Jews at present, that no person, be he ever so wicked, or of whatever sect, shall remain in hell above eleven months, or at most a year ; except Dathan and Abiram, and atheists, who will be tormented there to all eternity. (Bartoloccii Biblioth. Rabbinic. tom. ii. p. 128, et tom. iii. p. 421.)

[3] By *evil* in this place the commentators generally understand polytheism or idolatry ; which sin the Mohammedans believe, unless repented of in this life, is unpardonable and will be punished by eternal damnation ; but all other sins they hold will at length be forgiven. This therefore is that irremissible impiety, in their opinion, which in the New Testament is called *the sin against the Holy Ghost*.

[4] This passage was revealed on occasion of some quarrels which arose between the Jews of the tribes of Koreidha, and those of Al Aws, Al Nadhir, and Al Khazraj, and came to that height that they took arms and destroyed one another's habitations, and turned one another out of their houses ; but when any were taken captive, they redeemed them. When they were asked the reason of their acting in this manner, they answered, That they

houses, mutually assisting each other against them with injustice and enmity; but if they come captives unto you, ye redeem them : yet it is *equally* unlawful for you to dispossess them. Do ye therefore believe in part of the book *of the law*, and reject other parts thereof ? But whoso among you doth this, shall have no other reward than shame in this life, ánd on the day of resurrection they shall be sent to a most grievous punishment ; for GOD is not regardless of that which ye do. These are they who have purchased this present life, at the price of that which is to come ; wherefore their punishment shall not be mitigated neither shall they be helped. We formerly delivered the book *of the law* unto Moses, and caused apostles to succeed him, and gave evident miracles to Jesus the son of Mary, and strengthened him with the holy spirit.[1] Do ye therefore, whenever an apostle cometh unto you with that which your souls desire not, proudly reject *him*, and accuse some of imposture, and slay others ? *The Jews say*, Our hearts are uncircumcised : but GOD hath cursed them with their infidelity, therefore few shall believe. And when a book came unto them from GOD, confirming *the scriptures* which were with them, although they had before prayed for assistance against those who believed not,[2] *yet* when that came unto them which they knew *to be from God*, they would not believe therein : therefore the curse of GOD shall be on the infidels. For a vile *price* have they sold their souls, that they should not believe in that which GOD hath sent down ;[3] out of envy, because GOD sendeth down his favours to such of his servants as he pleaseth : therefore they brought on themselves indignation on indignation ; and the unbelievers shall suffer an ignominious punishment. When one saith unto them, Believe in that which GOD hath sent down ; they answer, We believe in that which hath been sent down unto us ;[4] and they reject what *hath been revealed* since, although it be the truth, confirming that which is with them. Say, Why therefore have ye slain the prophets of GOD in times past, if ye be true believers ? Moses formerly came unto you with evident signs, but ye

were commanded by their law to redeem the captives, but that they fought out of shame, lest their chiefs should be despised. (Jallalo'ddin.)

[1] We must not imagine Mohammed here means the Holy Ghost in the Christian acceptation. The commentators say this spirit was the angel Gabriel, who sanctified Jesus and constantly attended on him. (Jallalo'ddin.)

[2] The Jews in expectation of the coming of Mohammed (according to the tradition of his followers) used this prayer, *O God, help us against the unbelievers by the prophet who is to be sent in the last times.* (Jallalo'ddin.)

[3] The Korân.   [4] The Pentateuch.

afterwards took the calf *for your god* and did wickedly. And when we accepted your covenant, and lifted the mountain of *Sinai* over you,[1] *saying*, Receive *the law* which we have given you, with a resolution *to perform it*, and hear ; they said, We have heard, and have rebelled : and they were made to drink down the calf into their hearts [2] for their unbelief. Say, A grievous thing hath your faith commanded you,if ye be true believers.[3] Say, If the future mansion with GOD be *prepared* peculiarly for you, exclusive of the rest of mankind, wish for death, if ye say truth : but they will never wish for it, because of that which their hands have sent before them ;[4] GOD knoweth the wicked doers ; and thou shalt surely find them of all men the most covetous of life, even *more* than the idolaters : one of them would desire his life to be prolonged a thousand years, but none shall reprieve himself from punishment, that his life may be prolonged : GOD seeth that which they do. Say, Whoever is an enemy to Gabriel [5] (for he hath caused *the Korân* to descend on thy heart, by the permission of GOD, confirming that which was before *revealed*, a direction, and good tidings to the faithful) ; whosoever is an enemy to GOD, or his angels, or his apostles, or to Gabriel, or Michael, verily GOD is an enemy to the unbelievers. And now we have sent down unto thee evident signs,[6] and none will disbelieve them but the evil-doers. Whenever they make a covenant, will

[1] See before.

[2] Moses *took the calf which they had made, and burnt it in the fire, and ground it to powder, and strewed it upon the water (of the brook that descended from the mount), and made the children of* Israel *drink of it.* (Exod. xxxii. 20 ; Deut. ix. 21.)

[3] Mohammed here infers from their forefathers' disobedience in worshipping the calf, at the same time that they pretended to believe in the law of Moses, that the faith of the Jews in his time was as vain and hypocritical, since they rejected him, who was foretold therein, as an impostor. (Jallalo'ddin, Yahya, Al Beidâwi.)

[4] That is, by reason of the wicked forgeries which they have been guilty of in respect to the scriptures. An expression much like that of St. Paul, where he says, *that some men's sins are open beforehand, going before to judgment* (1 Tim. v. 24.)

[5] The commentators say that the Jews asked what angel it was that brought the divine revelations to Mohammed ; and being told that it was Gabriel, they replied that he was their enemy, and the messenger of wrath and punishment ; but if it had been Michael, they would have believed on him, because that angel was their friend, and the messenger of peace and plenty. And on this occasion, they say, this passage was revealed. (Jallalo'ddin ; Al Zamakh ; Yahya.) That Michael was really the protector or guardian angel of the Jews, we know from scripture (Dan. xii. 1) ; and it seems that Gabriel was, as the Persians call him, *the angel of revelations*, being frequently sent on messages of that kind (Dan. c. viii. 16, and ix. 21 ; Luke i. 19, 26. Hyde de Rel. Vet. Persar. p. 263) ; for which reason it is probable Mohammed pretended he was the angel from whom he received the Korân.

[6] *i.e.*, the revelations of this book.

some of them reject it ? yea, the greater part of them do not believe. And when there came unto them an apostle from GOD, confirming that *scripture* which was with them, some of those to whom the scriptures were given, cast the book of GOD behind their backs, as if they knew it not : and they followed *the device* which the devils devised against the kingdom of Solomon ;[1] and Solomon was not an unbeliever ; but the devils believed not, they taught men sorcery, and that which was sent down to the two angels at *Babel*, Harût and Marût ;[2] yet those two taught no man until they had said, Verily we are a temptation, therefore be not an unbeliever. So men learned from those two a . charm by which they might cause division between a man and his wife ; but they hurt none thereby, unless by GOD's permission ; and they learned that which would hurt them, and not profit them ; and yet they knew that he who bought that *art* should have no part in the life to come, and woeful *is the price* for which they have sold their souls, if they knew it. But if they had believed and feared *God*, verily the reward *they would have had* from GOD would have been better, if they had known it. O true believers, say not *to our apostle*, Raïna ;

[1] The devils having, by GOD's permission, tempted Solomon without success, they made use of a trick to blast his character. For they wrote several books of magic, and hid them under that prince's throne, and after his death, told the chief men that if they wanted to know by what means Solomon had obtained his absolute power over men, genii, and the winds, they should dig under his throne ; which having done, they found the aforesaid books, which contained impious superstitions. The better sort refused to learn the evil arts therein delivered, but the common people did ; and the priests published this scandalous story of Solomon, which obtained credit among the Jews, till GOD, say the Mohammedans, cleared that king by the mouth of their prophet, declaring that Solomon was no idolater. (Yahya. Jallalo'ddin.)

[2] Some say only that these were two magicians, or angels sent by GOD to teach men magic, and to tempt them. (Jallalo'ddin.) But others tell a longer fable ; that the angels expressing their surprise at the wickedness of the sons of Adam, after prophets had been sent to them with divine commissions, GOD bid them choose two out of their own number to be sent down to be judges on earth. Whereupon they pitched upon Harût and Marût, who executed their office with integrity for some time, till Zohara, or the planet Venus, descended and appeared before them in the shape of a beautiful woman, bringing a complaint against her husband (though others say she was a real woman). As soon as they saw her, they fell in love with her, and endeavoured to prevail on her to satisfy their desires ; but she flew up again to heaven, whither the two angels also returned, but were not admitted. However, on the intercession of a certain pious man, they were allowed to choose whether they would be punished in this life, or in the other ; whereupon they chose the former, and now suffer punishment accordingly in Babel, where they are to remain till the day of judgment. They add that if a man has a fancy to learn magic, he may go to them, and hear their voice, but cannot see them. (Yahya, &c.) This story Mohammed took directly from the Persian Magi, who mention two

but say, Ondhorna ;[1] and hearken : the infidels shall suffer a grievous punishment. It is not the desire of the unbelievers, either among those unto whom the scriptures have been given, or among the idolaters, that any good should be sent down unto you from your LORD : but GOD will appropriate his mercy unto whom he pleaseth ; for GOD is exceeding beneficent. Whatever verse we shall abrogate, or cause *thee* to forget, we will bring a better than it, or one like unto it. Dost thou not know that GOD is almighty ? Dost thou not know that unto GOD belongeth the kingdom of heaven and earth ? neither have ye any protector or helper except GOD. Will ye require of your apostle according to that which was formerly required of Moses ? [2] but he that hath exchanged faith for infidelity, hath already erred from the straight way. Many of those unto whom the scriptures have been given, desire to render you again unbelievers, after ye have believed ; out of envy from their souls, even after the truth is become manifest unto them ; but forgive *them*, and avoid *them*, till GOD shall send his command ; for GOD is omnipotent. Be constant in prayer, and give alms ; and what good ye have sent before for your souls, ye shall find it with God ; surely GOD seeth that which ye do. They say, Verily none shall enter paradise, except they who are Jews or Christians :[3] this is their wish. Say, Produce your proof *of this*, if ye speak truth. Nay, but he who resigneth himself[4] to GOD, and doth that which is right,[5] he shall have his reward with his LORD ; there shall *come* no fear on them, neither shall they be grieved. The Jews say, The Christians are *grounded* on nothing ;[6] and the Christians say, The Jews are *grounded*

---

rebellious angels of the same names, now hung up by the feet, with their heads downwards, in the territory of Babel. (Hyde, ubi sup. c. 12.) And the Jews have something like this, of the angel Shamhozai, who, having debauched himself with women, repented, and by way of penance hung himself up between heaven and earth. (Bereshit rabbah, in Gen. vi. 2.)

[1] These two Arabic words have both the same signification, viz., *Look on us* ; and are a kind of salutation. Mohammed had a great aversion to the first, because the Jews frequently used it in derision, it being a word of reproach in their tongue. (Jallalo'ddin.) They alluded, it seems, to the Hebrew verb רוע *ruá*, which signifies to *be bad* or *mischievous*.

[2] Namely, to see GOD manifestly. (See before.)

[3] This passage was revealed on occasion of a dispute which Mohammed had with the Jews of Medina, and the Christians of Najrân, each of them asserting that those of their religion only should be saved. (Jallalo'ddin.)

[4] Literally, *resigneth his face*, &c.

[5] That is, asserteth the unity of GOD. (Jallalo'ddin.)

[6] The Jews and Christians are here accused of denying the truth of each other's religion, notwithstanding they read the scriptures. Whereas the Pentateuch bears testimony to Jesus, and the Gospel bears testimony to Moses. (Jallalo'ddin.)

on nothing : yet they *both* read the scriptures. So likewise say they who know not the *scripture*, according to their saying. But GOD shall judge between them on the day of the resurrection, concerning that about which they *now* disagree. Who is more unjust than he who prohibiteth the temples of GOD,[1] that his name should be remembered therein, and who hasteth to destroy them ? Those men cannot enter therein, but with fear : they shall have shame in this world, and in the next a grievous punishment. To GOD *belongeth* the east and the west ; therefore, whithersoever ye turn yourselves to pray, there is the face of GOD ; for GOD is omnipresent and omniscient. They say, GOD hath begotten children :[2] GOD forbid ! To him *belongeth* whatever is in heaven, and on earth ; all is possessed by him, the Creator of heaven and earth ; and when he decreeth a thing, he only saith unto it, Be, and it is. And they who know not *the scriptures* say, Unless GOD speak unto us, or thou show us a sign, *we will not believe*. So said those before them, according to their saying : their hearts resemble each other. We have already shown manifest signs unto people who firmly believe ; we have sent thee in truth, a bearer of good tidings, and a preacher ; and thou shalt not be questioned concerning the companions of hell. But the Jews will not be pleased with thee, neither the Christians, until thou follow their religion ; say, The direction of GOD is the *true* direction. And verily if thou follow their desires, after the knowledge which hath been given thee, thou shalt find no patron or protector against GOD. They to whom we have given the book *of the Korân*, and who read it with its true reading, they believe therein ; and whoever believeth not therein, they shall perish. O children of Israel, remember my favour wherewith I have favoured you, and that I have preferred you before all nations ; and dread the day wherein *one* soul shall not make satisfaction for *another* soul, neither shall any compensation be accepted from them, nor shall any intercession avail, neither shall they be helped. *Remember* when

---

[1] Or hindereth men from paying their adorations to GOD in those sacred places. This passage, says Jallalo'ddin, was revealed on news being brought that the Romans had spoiled the temple of Jerusalem ; or else when the idolatrous Arabs obstructed Mohammed's visiting the temple of Mecca, in the expedition of Al Hodeibiya, which happened in the sixth year of the Hejra. (Abulfeda, Vit. Moham. p. 84, &c.)

[2] This is spoken not only of the Christians and of the Jews (for they are accused of holding Ozair, or Ezra, to be the Son of GOD), but also the pagan Arabs, who imagined the angels to be the daughters of GOD.

the LORD tried Abraham by *certain* words,[1] which he fulfilled :
God said, Verily I will constitute thee a model of religion[2]
unto mankind ; he answered, And also of my posterity ;
God said, My covenant doth not comprehend the ungodly.
And when we appointed the *holy* house[3] *of Mecca* to be the
place of resort for mankind, and a place of security ; and
said, Take the station of Abraham[4] for a place of prayer ;
and we covenanted with Abraham and Ismael, that they
should cleanse my house for those who should compass *it*,
and those who should be devoutly assiduous *there*, and those
who should bow down and worship. And when Abraham
said, LORD, make this a territory of security, and bounteously
bestow fruits on its inhabitants, such of them as believe in
GOD and the last day ; *God* answered, And whoever believeth
not, I will bestow on him little, afterwards I will drive him
to the punishment of *hell* fire ; an ill journey shall it be !
And when Abraham and Ismael raised the foundations of
the house, *saying*, LORD, accept *it* from us, for thou art he
who heareth and knoweth : LORD, make us also resigned [5]
unto thee, and of our posterity a people resigned unto thee,
and show us our holy ceremonies, and be turned unto us, for
thou art easy to be reconciled and merciful ; LORD, send them
likewise an apostle from among them, who may declare thy
signs unto them, and teach them the book *of the Korân* and
wisdom, and may purify them ; for thou art mighty and
wise. Who will be averse to the religion of Abraham, but he
whose mind is infatuated ? Surely we have chosen him in
this world, and in that which is to come he shall be one
of the righteous. When his LORD said unto him, Resign
thyself *unto me* ; he answered, I have resigned myself unto
the LORD of all creatures. And Abraham bequeathed this

[1] GOD tried Abraham chiefly by commanding him to leave his native
country, and to offer his son. But the commentators suppose the trial
here meant related only to some particular ceremonies, such as circumcision,
pilgrimage to the Caaba, several rites of purification, and the like. (Jallalo'-
ddin.)

[2] I have rather expressed the meaning, than truly translated the Arabic
word Imâm, which answers to the Latin *Antistes*. This title the Mohammedans give to their priests, who begin the prayers in their mosques, and
whom all the congregation follow.

[3] That is, the Caaba, which is usually called, by way of eminence, *the
House*. Of the sanctity of this building, and other particulars relating to it,
see Sale Prel. Disc. Sect. IV. p. 123.

[4] A place so called within the inner enclosure of the Caaba, where they
pretend to show the print of his foot in a stone. (Sale Prel. Disc. Sec. IV.)

[5] The Arabic word is Moslemûna, in the singular Moslem, which the
Mohammedans take as a title peculiar to themselves. The Europeans generally
write and pronounce it Musulman.

religion to his children, and Jacob *did the same, saying*, My children, verily GOD hath chosen this religion for you, therefore die not, unless ye also be resigned. Were ye present when Jacob was at the point of death ? when he said to his sons, Whom will ye worship after me ? They answered, We will worship thy GOD, and the GOD of thy fathers, Abraham, and Ismael, and Isaac, one GOD, and to him will we be resigned. That people are now passed away, they have what they have gained,[1] and ye shall have what ye gain ; and ye shall not be questioned concerning that which they have done. They say, Become Jews or Christians that ye may be directed. Say, Nay, *we follow* the religion of Abraham the orthodox, who was no idolater. Say, We believe in GOD, and that which hath been sent down unto us, and that which hath been sent down unto Abraham, and Ismael, and Isaac, and Jacob, and the tribes, and that which was delivered unto Moses, and Jesus; and that which was delivered unto the prophets from their LORD : We make no distinction between any of them, and to *God* are we resigned. Now if they believe according to what ye believe, they are surely directed, but if they turn back, they are in schism. GOD shall support thee against them, for he is the hearer, the wise.[2] The baptism of GOD[3] *have we received*, and who is better than GOD to baptize ? him do we worship. Say, Will ye dispute with us concerning GOD,[4] who is our LORD, and your LORD ? we have our works, and ye have your works, and unto him are we sincerely devoted. Will ye say, Truly Abraham, and Ismael, and Isaac, and Jacob, and the tribes were Jews or Christians ? Say, Are ye wiser, or GOD ? And who is more unjust than he who hideth the testimony which

[1] Or deserved. The Mohammedan notion, as to the imputation of moral actions to man, which they call *gain*, or *acquisition*, is sufficiently explained in Sale's Preliminary Discourse.

[2] This is the verse which was stained with blood in the copy of the Korân the Khalif Othman held in his hand when he was murdered. Ibn Batutah says he saw the actual copy in the mosque at Basra.

[3] By *baptism* is to be understood the religion which GOD instituted in the beginning ; because the signs of it appear in the person who professes it, as the signs of water appear in the clothes of him that is baptized. (Jallalo'-ddin.) Palmer renders this—" The dye of God ! and who is better than God at dyeing ? " and says that the metaphor is derived from dyeing cloth, and should not be translated baptism.

[4] These words were revealed because the Jews insisted that they first received the scriptures, that their Keblah was more ancient, and that no prophets could arise among the Arabs ; and therefore if Mohammed was a prophet, he must have been of their nation. (Jallalo'ddin.)

[5] The Jews are again accused of corrupting and suppressing the prophecies in the Pentateuch relating to Mohammed.

he hath *received* from GOD ? But GOD is not regardless of that which ye do. That people are passed away, they have what they have gained, and ye shall have what ye gain, nor shall ye be questioned concerning that which they have done. (II.)[1] The foolish men will say, What hath turned them from their Keblah, towards which they formerly *prayed* ?[2] Say, Unto GOD *belongeth* the east and the west : he directeth whom he pleaseth into the right way. Thus have we placed you, *O Arabians*, an intermediate nation,[3] that ye may be witnesses against *the rest of* mankind, and that the apostle may be a witness against you. We appointed the Keblah towards which thou didst formerly *pray*, only that we might know him who followeth the apostle, from him who turneth back on his heels ;[4] though this *change* seem a great matter, unless unto those whom GOD hath directed. But GOD will not render your faith of none effect ; [5] for GOD is gracious and merciful unto man. We have seen thee turn about thy face towards heaven *with uncertainty*, but we will cause thee to turn thyself towards a Keblah that will please thee. Turn therefore thy face towards the holy temple *of Mecca* ; and wherever ye be, turn your faces towards that *place.* They to whom the scripture hath been given, know this to be truth from their LORD. GOD is not regardless of that which ye do. Verily although thou shouldest show unto those to whom the scripture hath been given all kinds of signs, yet they will not follow thy Keblah, neither shalt thou follow their Keblah ; nor will one part of them follow the Keblah of the other. And if thou follow their desires, after the knowledge which hath been given thee, verily thou wilt become *one* of the ungodly. They to whom we have given

---

[1] Section II begins here. See Sale, Prel. Disc. p. 63.

[2] At first, Mohammed and his followers observed no particular rite in turning their faces towards any certain place, or quarter of the world, when they prayed ; it being declared to be perfectly indifferent. (See before.) Afterwards, when the prophet fled to Medina, he directed them to turn towards the temple of Jerusalem (probably to ingratiate himself with the Jews), which continued to be their Keblah for six or seven months ; but either finding the Jews too intractable, or despairing otherwise to gain the pagan Arabs, who could not forget their respect to the temple of Mecca, he ordered that prayers for the future should be towards the last. This change was made in the second year of the Hejra (Abulfeda, Vit. Moham. p. 54), and occasioned many to fall from him, taking offence at his inconstancy. (Jallalo'ddin.)

[3] Some commentators (Jallalo'ddin, Yahya, &c.) take this to mean that the Arabians are here declared to be a most *just* and *good* nation.

[4] *i.e.,* Returneth to Judaism.

[5] Or will not suffer it to go without its reward, while ye prayed towards Jerusalem.

the scripture know *our apostle*, even as they know their own children ; but some of them hide the truth, against their own knowledge. Truth is from thy LORD, therefore thou shalt not doubt. Every sect hath a certain tract *of heaven* to which they turn themselves *in prayer* ; but do ye strive to run after good things : wherever ye be, GOD will bring you all back *at the resurrection*, for GOD is almighty. And from what place soever thou comest forth, turn thy face towards the holy temple ; for this is truth from thy LORD ; neither is GOD regardless of that which ye do. From what place soever thou comest forth, turn thy face towards the holy temple ; and wherever ye be, thitherward turn your faces, lest men have matter of dispute against you ; but as for those among them who are unjust doers, fear them not, but fear me, that I may accomplish my grace upon you, and that ye may be directed. As we have sent unto you an apostle from among you,[1] to rehearse our signs unto you, and to purify you, and to teach you the book *of the Korân* and wisdom, and to teach you that which ye knew not : therefore remember me, and I will remember you, and give thanks unto me, and be not unbelievers. O *true* believers, beg assistance with patience and prayer, for GOD is with the patient. And say not of those who are slain in fight for the religion of GOD,[2] that *they are* dead ; yea, *they are* living :[3] but ye do not understand. We will surely prove you by *afflicting you* in some measure with fear, and hunger, and decrease of wealth, and *loss* of lives, and *scarcity* of fruits : but bear good tidings unto the patient, who when a misfortune befalleth them, say, We are GOD's, and unto him shall we surely return.[4] Upon them shall be blessings from their LORD and mercy, and they are the rightly directed. Moreover Safâ and Merwâ are *two* of the monuments of GOD : whoever therefore goeth on pilgrimage to the temple *of Mecca* or visiteth *it*, it shall be no crime in him if he compass them both.[5] And as for him who voluntarily performeth a good

[1] That is, of your own nation.

[2] The original words are literally, *who are slain in the way of* GOD ; by which expression, frequently occurring in the Korân, is always meant war undertaken against unbelievers for the propagation of the Mohammedan faith.

[3] The souls of martyrs (for such they esteem those who die in battle against infidels), says Jallalo'ddin, are in the crops of green birds, which have liberty to fly wherever they please in paradise, and feed on the fruits thereof.

[4] An expression frequently in the mouths of the Mohammedans, when under any great affliction, or in any imminent danger.

[5] Safâ and Merwâ are two mountains near Mecca, whereon were anciently two idols, to which the pagan Arabs used to pay a superstitious veneration.

work ; verily GOD is grateful and knowing.   They who conceal any of the evident signs, or the direction which we have
sent down, after what we have manifested unto men in the
scripture, GOD shall curse them ; and they who curse shall
curse them.[1]   But as for those who repent and amend, and
make known *what they concealed*, I will be turned unto them,
for I am easy to be reconciled and merciful.   Surely they
who believe not, and die in their unbelief, upon them shall be
the curse of GOD, and of the angels and of all men ; they
shall remain under it for ever, their punishment shall not
be alleviated, neither shall they be regarded.[2]   Your GOD
is one GOD, there is no GOD but He, the most merciful.   Now
in the creation of heaven and earth, and the vicissitude of
night and day, and in the ship which saileth in the sea, *laden*
with what is profitable for mankind, and in the *rain*-water
which GOD sendeth from heaven, quickening thereby the
dead earth, and replenishing the same with all sorts of cattle,
and in the change of winds, and the clouds that are compelled
to do service[3] between heaven and earth, are signs to people
of understanding : yet some men take idols beside GOD, and
love them as with the love *due to* GOD ; but the true believers
are more fervent in love towards GOD.   Oh that they who act
unjustly did perceive,[4] when they behold their punishment,
that all power belongeth unto GOD, and that he is severe in
punishing !   When those who have been followed, shall

(Sale, Prel. Disc. p. 22.)   Jallalo'ddin says this passage was revealed because
the followers of Mohammed made a scruple of going round these mountains,
as the idolaters did.   But the true reason of his allowing this relic of ancient
superstition seems to be the difficulty he found in preventing it.   Abul
Kâsem Hebato'llah thinks these last words are abrogated by those other,
Who will reject the religion of Abraham, *except he who hath infatuated his
soul* ?   (See before, p. 19.)   So that he will have the meaning to be quite
contrary to the letter, as if it had been, *it shall be no crime in him if he do not
compass them*.   However, the expositors are all against him (Marracc. in
Alc. p. 69, &c.), and the ceremony of running between these two hills is still
observed at the pilgrimage.   (Sale, Prel. Disc. Sect. IV p. 128.)
   [1] That is, the angels, the believers, and all things in general.   (Jallalo'ddin.)
But Yahya interprets it of the curses which will be given to the wicked,
when they cry out because of the punishment of the sepulchre (Sale, Prel.
Disc. Sect. IV p. 82), by all who hear them, that is, by all creatures except
men and genii.
   [2] Or, as Jallalo'ddin expounds it, GOD will not wait for their repentance.
   [3] The original word signifies properly *that are pressed or compelled to do
personal service without hire* ; which kind of service is often exacted by the
eastern princes of their subjects, and is called by the Greek and Latin writers,
Angaria.   The Scripture often mentions this sort of compulsion or force.
(Matth. v. 41 ; xxvii. 32, &c.)
   [4] Or it may be translated, *Although the ungodly will perceive*, &c.   But
some copies instead of *yara*, in the third person, read *tara*, in the second ;
and then it must be rendered, *Oh if thou didst see when the ungodly behold
their punishment*, &c.

separate themselves from their followers,[1] and shall see the punishment, and the cords *of relation* between them shall be cut in sunder ; the followers shall say, If we could return *to life*, we would separate ourselves from them, as they have *now* separated themselves from us. So GOD will show them their works ; they shall sigh grievously, and shall not come forth from the fire *of hell.* O men, eat of that which is lawful and good on the earth ; and tread not in the steps of the devil, for he is your open enemy. Verily he commandeth you evil and wickedness, and that ye should say that of GOD which ye know not. And when it is said unto them *who believe not*, Follow that which GOD hath sent down ; they answer, Nay, but we will follow that which we found our fathers practise. What ? though their fathers knew nothing, and were not *rightly* directed ? The unbelievers are like unto one who crieth aloud to that which heareth not so much as *his* calling, or the sound of *his* voice. *They are* deaf, dumb, and blind, therefore they do not understand. O true believers, eat of the good things which we have bestowed on you for food, and return thanks unto GOD, if ye serve him. Verily he hath forbidden you *to eat* that which dieth of itself, and blood, and swine's flesh, and that on which any other name but GOD's hath been invocated.[2] But he who is forced by necessity, not lusting, nor returning *to transgress*, it shall be no crime in him *if he eat of those things*, for GOD is gracious and merciful. Moreover they who conceal *any part* of the scripture which God hath sent down unto them, and sell it for a small price, they shall swallow into their bellies nothing but fire ; GOD shall not speak unto them on the day of resurrection, neither shall he purify them, and they shall suffer a grievous punishment. These are they who have sold direction for error, and pardon for punishment : but how great will their suffering be in the fire ! This *they shall endure*, because GOD sent down the book *of the Korân* with truth, and they who disagree concerning that book, are certainly in a wide mistake. It is not righteousness that ye turn your faces *in prayer* towards the east and the west, but righteousness is of him who believeth in GOD and the last day, and the angels and the scriptures, and the prophets ; who

[1] That is, when the broachers or heads of new sects shall at the last day forsake or wash their hands of their disciples, as if they were not accomplices in their superstitions.

[2] For this reason, whenever the Mohammedans kill any animal for food, they always say, *Bismillah*, or *In the name of* GOD ; which, if it be neglected, they think it not lawful to eat of it.

giveth money for *God's* sake unto his kindred, and unto orphans, and the needy, and the stranger, and those who ask, and for redemption of captives ; who is constant at prayer, and giveth alms ; and of those who perform their covenant, when they have covenanted, and who behave themselves patiently in adversity, and hardships, and in time of violence: these are they who are true, and these are they who fear *God*. O true believers, the law of retaliation is ordained you for the slain : the free *shall die* for the free, and the servant for the servant, and a woman for a woman :[1] but he whom his brother shall forgive, may be prosecuted, *and obliged to make satisfaction* according to what is just, and a fine shall be set on him[2] with humanity. This is indulgence from your LORD, and mercy. And he who shall transgress after this, *by killing the murderer*, shall suffer a grievous punishment. And in this law of retaliation ye have life, O ye of understanding, that peradventure ye may fear. It is ordained you, when any of you is at the point of death, if he leave any goods, *that he bequeath* a legacy to his parents, and kindred, according to what shall be reasonable.[3] This is a duty *incumbent* on those who fear GOD. But he who shall change *the legacy*, after he hath heard it *bequeathed by the dying person*, surely the sin thereof shall be on those who change it, for GOD is he who heareth and knoweth. Howbeit he who apprehendeth from the testator any mistake or injustice, and shall compose *the matter* between them, that shall be no crime in him, for GOD is gracious and merciful. O true believers, a fast is ordained you, as it was ordained unto those before you, that ye may fear *God*. A certain number of days *shall ye fast* : but he among you who shall be sick, or on a journey, *shall fast an equal* number of other days. And those who can[4] *keep it, and do not*, must redeem *their*

[1] This is not to be strictly taken ; for according to the Sonna, a man also is to be put to death for the murder of a woman. Regard is also to be had to difference in religion, so that a Mohammedan, though a slave, is not to be put to death for an infidel, though a freeman. (Jallalo'ddin.) But the civil magistrates do not think themselves always obliged to conform to this last determination of the Sonna.

[2] This is the common practice in Mohammedan countries, particularly in Persia (Chardin, Voyage de Perse, t. ii. p. 299, &c.), where the relations of the deceased may take their choice, either to have the murderer put into their hands to be put to death, or else to accept of a pecuniary satisfaction.

[3] That is, the legacy was not to exceed a third part of the testator's substance, nor to be given where there was no necessity. But this injunction is abrogated by the law concerning inheritances.

[4] The expositors differ much about the meaning of this passage, thinking it very improbable that people should be left entirely at liberty either to fast or not, on compounding for it in this manner. Jallalo'ddin, therefore,

neglect by maintaining of a poor man.[1] And he who voluntarily dealeth better *with the poor man than he is obliged*, this shall be better for him. But if ye fast it will be better for you, if ye knew it. The month of Ramadân *shall ye fast*, in which the Korân was sent down *from heaven*,[2] a direction unto men, and declarations of direction, and the distinction *between good and evil*. Therefore let him among you who shall be present[3] in this month, fast the same *month* ; but he who shall be sick, or on a journey, *shall fast* the *like* number of other days. GOD would *make this* an ease unto you, and would not *make it* a difficulty unto you ; that ye may fulfil the number *of days*, and glorify GOD, for that he hath directed you, and that ye may give thanks. When my servants ask thee concerning me, Verily I am near ; I will hear the prayer of him that prayeth, when he prayeth unto me ; but let them hearken unto me, and believe in me, that they may be rightly directed. It is lawful for you on the night of the fast to go in unto your wives,[4] they are a garment[5] unto you, and ye are a garment unto them. GOD knoweth that ye defraud yourselves *therein*, wherefore he turneth unto you, and forgiveth you. Now therefore go in unto them ; and earnestly desire that which GOD ordaineth you, and eat and drink, until ye can plainly distinguish a white thread from a black thread by the daybreak : then keep the fast until night, and go not in unto them, but be constantly present in the places of worship. These are the prescribed bounds of GOD, therefore draw not near them *to transgress them*. Thus GOD

supposes the negative particle *not* to be understood, and that this is allowed only to those who are *not able* to fast, by reason of age or dangerous sickness ; but afterwards he says, that in the beginning of Mohammedism it was free for them to choose whether they would fast or maintain a poor man, which liberty was soon after taken away, and this passage abrogated by the following, *Therefore let him who shall be present in this month, fast the same month.* Yet this abrogation, he says, does not extend to women with child or that give suck, lest the infant suffer. Al Zamakhshari, having first given an explanation of Ebn Abbâs, who, by a different interpretation of the Arabic word *Yotikûnaho* which signifies *can* or *are able to fast*, renders it, *Those who find great difficulty therein*, &c., adds an exposition of his own, by supposing something to be understood, according to which the sense will be, *Those who can fast* and yet have a legal excuse to break it, *must redeem it*, &c.

[1] According to the usual quantity which a man eats in a day and the custom of the country. (Jallalo'ddin.)

[2] Sale, Prel. Disc. p. 69.

[3] *i.e.*, At home, and not in a strange country, where the fast cannot be performed, or on a journey.

[4] In the beginning of Mohammedism, during the fast, they neither lay with their wives, nor ate nor drank after supper. But both are permitted by this passage. (Jallalo'ddin.)

[5] A metaphorical expression, to signify the mutual comfort a man and his wife find in each other.

declareth his signs unto men, that ye may fear *him*. Consume not your wealth among yourselves in vain ; nor present it unto judges, that ye may devour part of men's substance unjustly, against your own consciences. They will ask thee concerning the phases of the moon. Answer, They are times appointed unto men, and to *show the season of* the pilgrimage to *Mecca*. It is not righteousness that ye enter *your* houses by the back part thereof,[1] but righteousness is of him who feareth *God*. Therefore enter *your* houses by their doors ; and fear GOD, that ye may be happy. And fight for the religion of GOD against those who fight against you, but transgress not *by attacking them first*, for GOD loveth not the transgressors. And kill them wherever ye find them, and turn them out of that whereof they have dispossessed you ; for temptation *to idolatry* is more grievous than slaughter : yet fight not against them in the holy temple, until they attack you therein ; but if they attack you, slay them *there*. This shall be the reward of the infidels. But if they desist, GOD is gracious and merciful. Fight therefore against them, until there be no temptation *to idolatry*, and the religion be GOD's : but if they desist, then let there be no hostility, except against the ungodly. A sacred month for a sacred month,[2] and the holy limits *of Mecca, if they attack you therein, do ye also attack them therein in* retaliation ; and whoever transgresseth against you *by so doing*, do ye transgress against him in like manner as he hath transgressed against you, and fear GOD, and know that GOD is with those who fear *him*. Contribute *out of your substance* towards the defence of the religion of GOD, and throw not *yourselves* with your own hands into perdition ;[3] and do good, for GOD loveth those who do good. Perform the pilgrimage *of Mecca*, and the visitation of GOD ; and if ye be besieged, *send* that offering which shall be the easiest ; and shave not your heads,[4] until your offering reacheth the place of sacrifice. But whoever among you is sick, or is troubled with any distemper of the head,

[1] Some of the Arabs had a superstitious custom after they had been at Mecca (in pilgrimage, as it seems), on their return home, not to enter their house by the old door, but to make a hole through the back part for a passage, which practice is here reprehended.

[2] As to these sacred months, wherein it was unlawful for the ancient Arabs to attack one another. See Sale, Prel. Disc. Sect. VII.

[3] *i.e.*, Be not accessory to your own destruction, by neglecting your contributions towards the wars against infidels, and thereby suffering them to gather strength.

[4] For this was a sign they had completed their vow, and performed all the ceremonies of the pilgrimage. (Jallalo'ddin.)

must redeem *the shaving his head* by fasting, or alms, or some offering.[1] When ye are secure *from enemies*, he who tarrieth in the visitation *of the temple of Mecca*[2] until the pilgrimage, shall *bring* that offering which shall be the easiest. But he who findeth not *anything to offer*, shall fast three days in the pilgrimage, and seven when ye are returned : they shall be ten *days* complete. This *is incumbent* on him whose family shall not be present at the holy temple. And fear GOD, and know that GOD is severe in punishing. The pilgrimage *must be performed in* the known months ; [3] whosoever therefore purposeth to go on pilgrimage therein, let him not know a woman, nor transgress, nor quarrel in the pilgrimage. The good which ye do, GOD knoweth it. Make provision *for your journey* ; but the best provision is piety : and fear me, O ye of understanding. It shall be no crime in you, if ye seek an increase from your LORD, *by trading during the pilgrimage.* And when ye go in procession [4] from Arafat,[5] remember GOD near the holy monument,[6] and remember him for that he hath directed you, although ye were before this of *the number of* those who go astray. Therefore go in procession from whence the people go in procession, and ask pardon of GOD, for GOD is gracious and merciful. And when ye have finished your holy ceremonies, remember GOD, according as ye remember your fathers, or with a more reverent commemoration. There are some men who say, O LORD, give us *our portion* in this world ; but such shall have no portion in the next life : and there are others who say, O

[1] That is, either by fasting three days, or feeding six poor people, or sacrificing a sheep.

[2] This passage is somewhat obscure. Yahya interprets it of him who marries a wife during this visitation, and performs the pilgrimage the year following. But Jallalo'ddin expounds it of him who stays within the sacred enclosures, in order to complete the ceremonies which (as it should seem) he had not been able to do within the prescribed time.

[3] *i.e.*, Shawâl, Dhu'lkaada, and Dhu'lhajja. See Sale, Preliminary Discourse, Sect. IV, p. 127.

[4] The original word signifies *to rush forward impetuously* ; as the pilgrims do when they proceed from Arafat to Mozdalifa.

[5] A mountain near Mecca, so called because Adam there met and *knew* his wife, after a long separation. (See before.) Yet others say that Gabriel, after he had instructed Abraham in all the sacred ceremonies, coming to Arafat, there asked him, if he *knew* the ceremonies which had been shown him ; to which Abraham answering in the affirmative, the mountain had thence its name. (Al Hasan.)

[6] In Arabic, *Al Masher al harâm.* It is a mountain in the farther part of Mozdalifa, where it is said Mohammed stood praying and praising GOD, till his face became extremely shining. (Jallalo'ddin.) Bobovius calls it Farkh (Bohov. de Peregr. Meccana, p. 15), but the true name seems to be Kazah ; the variation being occasioned only by the different pointing of the Arabic letters

LORD, give us good in this world, and also good in the next world, and deliver us from the torment of *hell* fire. They shall have a portion of that which they have gained : GOD is swift in taking an account.[1]   Remember GOD the *appointed* number of days :[2] but if any haste *to depart from the valley of* Mina in two days, it shall be no crime in him.   And if any tarry longer, it shall be no crime in him, in him who feareth GOD.   Therefore fear GOD, and know that unto him ye shall be gathered.   There is a man who causeth thee to marvel[3] by his speech concerning this present life, and calleth GOD to witness that which is in his heart, yet he is most intent in opposing thee ;   and when he turneth away *from thee*, he hasteth to act corruptly in the earth, and to destroy that which is sown, and springeth up :[4] but GOD loveth not corrupt doing.   And if one say unto him, Fear GOD ;   pride seizeth him, together with wickedness ;   but hell shall be his reward, and an unhappy couch shall it be.   There is also a man who selleth his soul for the sake of those things which are pleasing unto GOD ;[5] and GOD is gracious unto *his* servants.   O *true* believers, enter into the true religion wholly, and follow not the steps of Satan, for he is your open enemy.   If ye have slipped after the declarations *of our will* have come unto you, know that GOD is mighty and wise.   Do *the infidels* expect less than that GOD should come down to them overshadowed with clouds, and the angels *also* ?   but the thing is decreed, and to GOD shall *all* things return.   Ask the children of Israel how many evident signs we have showed them ;   and whoever shall change the grace of GOD, after it shall have come unto him, verily GOD will be severe in punishing *him*. The present life was ordained for those who believe not, and they laugh the faithful to scorn ;   but they who fear GOD shall be above them, on the day of the resurrection :   for GOD is bountiful unto whom he pleaseth without measure. Mankind was of one faith, and God sent prophets bearing good tidings, and denouncing threats, and sent down with

---

[1] For he will judge all creatures, says Jallalo'ddin, in the space of half a day.

[2] *i.e.*, Three days after slaying the sacrifices.

[3] This person was Al Akhnas Ebn Shoraik, a fair-spoken dissembler, who swore that he believed in Mohammed, and pretended to be one of his friends, and to contemn this world.   But GOD here reveals to the prophet his hypocrisy and wickedness.   (Jallalo'ddin.)

[4] Setting fire to his neighbour's corn, and killing his asses by night. (Jallalo'ddin.)

[5] The person here meant was one Soheib, who being persecuted by the idolaters of Mecca, forsook all he had, and fled to Medina.   (Jallalo'ddin.)

them the scripture in truth, that it might judge between men of that concerning which they disagreed : and none disagreed concerning it, except those to whom the same *scriptures* were delivered, after the declarations *of* GOD's *will* had come unto them, out of envy among themselves. And GOD directed those who believed, to that truth concerning which they disagreed, by his will : for GOD directeth whom he pleaseth into the right way. Did ye think ye should enter paradise, when as yet no such thing had happened unto you, as *hath happened* unto those who have been before you ? They suffered calamity and tribulation, and were afflicted ; so that the apostle, and they who believed with him, said, When *will* the help of GOD *come* ? Is not the help of GOD nigh ? They will ask thee what they shall bestow *in alms* : Answer, The good which ye bestow, *let it be given* to parents, and kindred, and orphans, and the poor, and the stranger. Whatsoever good ye do, GOD knoweth it. War is enjoined you *against the Infidels* ; but this is hateful unto you : yet perchance ye hate a thing which is better for you, and perchance ye love a thing which is worse for you : but GOD knoweth and ye know not. They will ask thee concerning the sacred month, *whether they may* war therein : Answer, To war therein is grievous ; but to obstruct the way of God, and infidelity towards him, and *to keep men* from the holy temple, and to drive out his people from thence, is more grievous in the sight of GOD, and the temptation *to idolatry* is more grievous than to kill *in the sacred months*. They will not cease to war against you, until they turn you from your religion, if they be able : but whoever among you shall turn back from his religion, and die an infidel, their works shall be vain in this world and the next ; they shall be the companions of *hell* fire, they shall remain therein for ever. But they who believe, and who fly for the sake of religion, and fight in GOD's cause, they shall hope for the mercy of GOD ; for GOD is gracious and merciful. They will ask thee concerning wine [1] and lots : [2] Answer, In both there is great sin, and *also some* things of use unto men ; [3] but their sinfulness is

[1] Under the name of *wine* all sorts of strong and inebriating liquors are comprehended. (Sale, Prel. Disc. Sect. V.)

[2] The original word, *Meiser*, properly signifies a particular game performed with arrows, and much in use with the pagan Arabs. But by *lots* we are here to understand all games whatsoever, which are subject to chance or hazard, as dice, cards, &c. (Sale, Prel. Disc. Sect. V.)

[3] From these words some suppose that only drinking to excess and too frequent gaming are prohibited. (Jallalo'ddin, Al Zamakhshari.) And the moderate use of wine they also think is allowed by these words of the

greater than their use. They will ask thee also what they shall bestow *in alms* : Answer, What ye have to spare. Thus GOD showeth *his* signs unto you, that peradventure ye might seriously think of this present world, and of the next. They will also ask thee concerning orphans : Answer, To deal righteously with them is best ; and if ye intermeddle with *the management of what belongs to* them, *do them no wrong* ; they are your brethren : GOD knoweth the corrupt dealer from the righteous ; and if GOD please, he will surely distress you,[1] for GOD is mighty and wise. Marry not *women who are* idolaters, until they believe : verily a maid-servant who believeth is better than an idolatress, although she please you *more*. And give not *women who believe* in marriage to the idolaters, until they believe ; for verily a servant who is a true believer, is better than an idolater, though he please you *more*. They invite unto *hell* fire, but GOD inviteth unto paradise and pardon through his will, and declareth his signs unto men, that they may remember. They will ask thee also concerning the courses of women : Answer, They are a pollution : therefore separate yourselves from women in their courses, and go not near them until they be cleansed. But when they are cleansed, go in unto them as GOD hath commanded you,[2] for GOD loveth those who repent, and loveth those who are clean. Your wives are your tillage ; go in therefore unto your tillage in what manner soever ye will :[3] and do first some act *that may be profitable* unto your souls ;[4] and fear GOD, and know that ye must meet him ; and bear good tidings unto the faithful. Make not GOD the object of your oaths,[5] that ye will deal justly, and be devout, and make peace among men ;[6] for GOD is he who heareth and

16th chapter, *And of the fruits of palm-trees and grapes ye obtain inebriating drink, and also good nourishment*. But the more received opinion is, that both drinking wine or other strong liquors in any quantity, and playing at any game of chance, are absolutely forbidden. (Sale, Prel. Disc. ubi sup.)

[1] viz., By his curse, which shall certainly bring to nothing what ye shall wrong the orphans of.

[2] But not while they have their courses, nor by using preposterous venery. (Ebn Abbas, Jallalo'ddin.)

[3] It has been imagined that these words allow that preposterous lust, which the commentators say is forbidden by the preceding ; but I question whether this can be proved. (Jallalo'ddin, Yahya, Al Zamakhshari. Lucret. de Rer. Nat. I. 4. v. 1258, &c.)

[4] *i.e.*, Perform some act of devotion or charity.

[5] So as to swear frequently by him. The word translated *object*, properly signifies a butt to shoot at with arrows. (Jallalo'ddin.)

[6] Some commentators (Jallalo'ddin, Yahya) expound this negatively, *That ye will not deal justly, nor be devout*, &c. For such wicked oaths, they say, were customary among the idolatrous inhabitants of Mecca ; which gave occasion to the following saying of Mohammed : *When you swear to*

knoweth. GOD will not punish you for an inconsiderate word[1] in your oaths ; but he will punish you for that which your hearts have assented unto : GOD is merciful and gracious. They who vow *to abstain* from their wives, are *allowed* to wait four months ;[2] but if they go back *from their vow*, verily GOD is gracious and merciful ; [3] and if they resolve on a divorce, GOD is he who heareth and knoweth. The *women who are* divorced shall wait concerning themselves until they have their courses thrice,[4] and it shall not be lawful for them to conceal that which GOD hath created in their wombs,[5] if they believe in GOD and the last day ; and their husbands will act more justly to bring them back at this *time*, if they desire a reconciliation. The women ought also *to behave towards their husbands* in like manner as *their husbands should behave* towards them, according to what is just : but the men ought to have a superiority over them. GOD is mighty and wise. Ye may divorce *your wives* twice ; and then either retain *them* with humanity, or dismiss *them* with kindness. But it is not lawful for you to take away anything of what ye have given them, unless both fear that they cannot observe the ordinances of GOD.[6] And if ye fear that they cannot observe the ordinances of GOD, it shall be no crime in either of them on account of that for which *the wife* shall redeem herself.[7] These are the ordinances of GOD ; therefore trans-

---

do a thing, and afterwards find it better to do otherwise, do that which is better and make void your oath.

[1] When a man swears inadvertently, and without design.

[2] That is, they may take so much time to consider ; and shall not, by a rash oath, be obliged actually to divorce them.

[3] *i.e.*, If they be reconciled to their wives within four months, or after, they may retain them, and GOD will dispense with their oath.

[4] This is to be understood of those only with whom the marriage has been consummated ; for as to the others there is no time limited. Those who are not quite past childbearing (which a woman is reckoned to be after her courses cease, and she is fifty-five lunar years, or about fifty-three solar years old), and those who are too young to have children, are allowed three months only ; but they who are with child must wait till they be delivered. (Jallalo'ddin.)

[5] That is, they shall tell the real truth, whether they have their courses, or be with child, or not ; and shall not, by deceiving their husband, obtain a separation from him before the term be accomplished : lest the first husband's child should, by that means, go to the second ; or the wife in case of the first husband's death, should set up her child as his heir, or demand her maintenance during the time she went with such child, and the expenses of her lying-in, under pretence that she waited not her full prescribed time. (Yahya.)

[6] For if there be a settled aversion on either side, their continuing together may have very ill, and perhaps fatal consequences.

[7] *i.e.*, If she prevail on her husband to dismiss her, by releasing part of her dowry.

gress them not ; for whoever transgresseth the ordinances
of GOD, they are unjust doers. But if *the husband* divorce
her *a third time*, she shall not be lawful for him again, until
she marry another husband. But if he *also* divorce her, it
shall be no crime in them if they return to each other, if they
think they can observe the ordinances of GOD ; and these are
the ordinances of GOD, he declareth them to people of understanding. But when ye divorce women, and they have
fulfilled their prescribed time, either retain them with
humanity, or dismiss them with kindness ; and retain them
not by violence, so that ye transgress ;[1] for he who doth this,
surely injureth his own soul. And make not the signs of
GOD a jest : but remember GOD's favour towards you, and
that he hath sent down unto you the book *of the Korân*, and
wisdom, admonishing you thereby : and fear GOD, and
know that GOD is omniscient. But when ye have divorced
your wives, and they have fulfilled their prescribed time,
hinder them not from marrying their husbands, when they
have agreed among themselves according to what is honourable. This is given in admonition unto him among you who
believeth in GOD, and the last day. This is most righteous
for you, and most pure. GOD knoweth, but ye know not.
Mothers *after they are divorced* shall give suck unto their children two full years, to him who desireth the time of giving suck
to be completed ; and the father shall be obliged to maintain
them and clothe them *in the mean time*, according to that
which shall be reasonable. No person shall be obliged beyond
his ability. A mother shall not be compelled *to what is unreasonable* on account of her child, nor a father on account of his
child. And the heir *of the father* shall be obliged to do in
like manner. But if they choose to wean *the child before
the end of two years*, by common consent and on mutual
consideration, it shall be no crime in them. And if ye have a
mind to provide a nurse for your children, it shall be no crime
in you, in case ye fully pay what ye offer *her*, according to
that which is just. And fear GOD, and know that GOD seeth
whatever ye do. Such of you as die, and leave wives, *their
wives* must wait concerning themselves four months and ten
days,[2] and when they shall have fulfilled their term, it shall
be no crime in you, for that which they shall do with them-

---

[1] viz., By obliging them to purchase their liberty with part of their dowry.
[2] That is to say, before they marry again ; and this, not only for the sake
of decency, but that it may be known whether they be with child by the
deceased or not.

selves,[1] according to what is reasonable. God well knoweth that which ye do. And it shall be no crime in you, whether ye make public overtures of marriage unto *such* women, *within the said four months and ten days*, or whether ye conceal *such your designs* in your minds : GOD knoweth that ye will remember them. But make no promise unto them privately, unless ye speak honourable words ; and resolve not on the knot of marriage, until the prescribed time be accomplished ; and know that GOD knoweth that which is in your minds, therefore beware of him, and know that God is gracious and merciful. It shall be no crime in you, if ye divorce your wives, so long as ye have not touched them, nor settled any dowry on them. And provide for them (he who is at his ease must *provide* according to his circumstances, and he who is straitened according to his circumstances) necessaries, according to what shall be reasonable. *This is* a duty *incumbent* on the righteous. But if ye divorce them before ye have touched them, and have already settled a dowry on them, *ye shall give them* half of what ye have settled, unless they release *any part*, or he release *part* in whose hand the knot of marriage is ;[2] and if ye release *the whole*, it will approach nearer unto piety. And forget not liberality among you, for GOD seeth that which ye do. Carefully observe the *appointed* prayers, and the middle prayer,[3] and be assiduous *therein*, with devotion towards GOD. But if ye fear *any danger*, *pray* on foot or on horseback ; and when ye are safe, remember GOD, how he hath taught you what as yet ye knew not. And such of you as shall die and leave wives, ought to bequeath their wives a year's maintenance, without putting them out *of their houses* : but if they go out *voluntarily*, it shall be no crime in you, for that which they shall do with themselves, according to what shall be reasonable ; GOD is mighty and wise. And unto those who are divorced, a reasonable provision *is also due* ; *this is* a duty *incumbent* on those who fear *God*. Thus GOD declareth his signs unto you, that ye may understand. Hast thou not

[1] That is, if they leave off their mourning weeds, and look out for new husbands.

[2] *i.e.*, Unless the wife agree to take less than half her dowry, or unless the husband be so generous as to give her more than half, or the whole, which is here approved of as most commendable.

[3] Y ahya interprets this from a tradition of Mohammed, who, being asked which was the *middle prayer*, answered,The evening prayer,which was instituted by the prophet Solomon. But Jallalo'ddin allows a greater latitude, and supposes it may be the afternoon prayer, the morning prayer, the noon prayer, or any other.

considered those who left their habitations (and they were thousands) for fear of death ?[1] And GOD said unto them, Die ; then he restored them to life, for GOD is gracious towards mankind ; but the greater part of men do not give thanks. Fight for the religion of GOD, and know that GOD is he who heareth and knoweth. Who is he that will lend unto GOD on good usury ? [2] verily he will double it unto him manifold ; for GOD contracteth and extendeth *his hand* as he pleaseth, and to him shall ye return. Hast thou not considered the assembly of the children of Israel, after *the time of* Moses ; when they said unto their prophet *Samuel,* Set a king over us, that we may fight for the religion of GOD ? *The prophet* answered, If ye are enjoined to go to war, will ye be near refusing to fight ? They answered, And what should ail us that we should not fight for the religion of GOD, seeing we are dispossessed of our habitations, and *deprived* of our children ? But when they were enjoined to go to war, they turned back, except a few of them : and GOD knew the ungodly. And their prophet said unto them, Verily GOD hath set Talût[3] king over you : they answered, How shall he reign over us, seeing we are more worthy of the kingdom than he, neither is he possessed of great riches ? *Samuel* said, Verily GOD hath chosen him before you, and hath caused him to increase in knowledge and stature, for GOD giveth his kingdom unto whom he pleaseth ; GOD is bounteous and wise. And their prophet said unto them, Verily the sign of his kingdom shall be, that the ark shall come unto you :[4]

---

[1] These were some of the children of Israel, who abandoned their dwellings because of a pestilence, or, as others say, to avoid serving in a religious war ; but, as they fled, GOD struck them all dead in a certain valley. About eight days or more after, when their bodies were corrupted, the prophet Ezekiel, the son of Buzi, happening to pass that way, at the sight of their bones wept ; whereupon GOD said to him, *Call to them, O Ezekiel, and I will restore them to life.* And accordingly on the prophet's call they all arose, and lived several years after ; but they retained the colour and stench of dead corpses as long as they lived, and the clothes they wore changed as black as pitch, which qualities they transmitted to their posterity. (Jallalo'ddin, Yahya, Abulfeda, &c.) As to the number of these Israelites the commentators are not agreed : they who reckon least say they were 3,000, and they who reckon most, 70,000. This story seems to have been taken from Ezekiel's vision of the resurrection of dry bones. (Ezek. xxxvii. 1–10.) Some of the Mohammedan writers will have Ezekiel to have been one of the judges of Israel, and to have succeeded Othniel the son of Caleb. They also call this prophet *Ebn al ajûs,* or *the son of the old woman* ; because they say his mother obtained him by her prayers in her old age. (Al Thalabi, Abu Ishak, &c.)

[2] viz., By contributing towards the establishment of his true religion.

[3] So the Mohammedans name Saul.

[4] This ark, says Jallalo'ddin, contained the images of the prophets, and was sent down from heaven to Adam, and at length came to the Israelites, who put great confidence therein, and continually carried it in the front of

therein shall be tranquillity from your Lord,[1] and the relics[2] which have been left by the family of Moses, and the family of Aaron ; the angels shall bring it. Verily this shall be a sign unto you, if ye believe. And when Talût departed with his soldiers, he said, Verily GOD will prove you by the river : for he who drinketh thereof, shall not be on my side (but he who shall not taste thereof he shall be on my side) except he who drinketh a draught out of his hand. And they drank thereof, except a few of them.[3] And when they had passed *the river*, he and those who believed with him, they said, We have no strength to-day against Jalut [4] and his forces. But they who considered that they should meet GOD *at the resurrection*, said, How often hath a small army discomfited a great army, by the will of GOD ? and GOD is with those who patiently persevere. And when they went forth to battle against Jalut and his forces, they said, O LORD, pour on us patience, and confirm our feet, and help us against the unbelieving people. Therefore they discomfited them, by the will of GOD, and David slew Jalut. And GOD gave him the kingdom and wisdom, and taught him his will ;[5] and if GOD had not prevented men, the one by the other, verily the earth had been corrupted : but GOD is beneficent towards *his* creatures. These are the signs of GOD : we rehearse them unto thee with truth, and thou art surely *one* of those who have been sent *by* GOD. (III.) These are the apostles ; we have preferred some of them before others : some of them hath GOD spoken unto, and hath exalted the degree of others of them. And we gave unto Jesus the son of Mary manifest

their army, till it was taken by the Amalekites. But on this occasion the angels brought it back, in the sight of all the people, and placed it at the feet of Talût ; who was thereupon unanimously acknowledged for their king. This relation seems to have arisen from some imperfect tradition of the taking and sending back the ark by the Philistines. (1 Sam. iv. v. and vi.)

[1] That is, because of the great confidence the Israelites placed in it, having won several battles by its miraculous assistance. I imagine, however, that the Arabic word *Sakinat*, which signifies *tranquillity* or *security of mind*, and is so understood by the commentators, may not improbably mean the *divine presence* or *glory*, which used to appear on the ark, and which the Jews express by the same word Shechinah.

[2] These were the shoes and rod of Moses, the mitre of Aaron, a pot of manna, and the broken pieces of the two tables of the law. (Jallalo'ddin.)

[3] The number of those who drank out of their hands was about 313. (Jallalo'ddin, Yahya.) It seems that Mohammed has here confounded Saul with Gideon, who by the divine direction took with him against the Midianites such of his army only as lapped water out of their hands, which were 300 men. (Judges vii.)

[4] Or Goliath.

[5] Or *what he pleased* to teach him. Yahya most rationally understands

signs, and strengthened him with the holy spirit.[1] And if
GOD had pleased, they who came after those *apostles* would
not have contended among themselves, after manifest signs
had been shown unto them. But they fell to variance ;
therefore some of them believed, and some of them believed
not ; and if GOD had so pleased, they would not have contended among themselves, but GOD doth what he will. O
true believers, give *alms* of that which we have bestowed on
you, before the day cometh wherein there shall be no merchandizing, nor friendship, nor intercession. The infidels are
unjust doers. GOD! there is no GOD but he ;[2] the living,
the self-subsisting : neither slumber nor sleep seizeth him ;
to him *belongeth* whatsoever is in heaven, and on earth. Who
is he that can intercede with him, but through his good
pleasure ? He knoweth that which is past, and that which
is to come unto them, and they shall not comprehend anything of his knowledge, but so far as he pleaseth. His throne
is extended over heaven and earth,[3] and the preservation of
both is no burden unto him. He is the high, the mighty.
Let there be no violence in religion.[4] Now is right direction
manifestly distinguished from deceit : whoever therefore
shall deny Tagut,[5] and believe in God, he shall surely take
hold on a strong handle, which shall not be broken ; GOD
is he who heareth and seeth. GOD is the patron of those who
believe ; he shall lead them out of darkness into light ; but
as to those who believe not, their patrons are Tagut ; they
shall lead them from the light into darkness ; they shall be

hereby the divine revelations which David received from GOD ; but Jallalo'-
ddin the art of making coats of mail, which the Mohammedans believe was
that prophet's peculiar trade (Chap. xxi.), and the knowledge of the
language of birds.

[1] With the previous passage Section III begins.

[2] The following seven lines contain a magnificent description of the divine
majesty and providence ; but it must not be supposed the translation comes
up to the dignity of the original. This passage is justly admired by the
Mohammedans, who recite it in their prayers ; and some of them wear it
about them, engraved on an agate or other precious stone. (Bobov. de
Prec. Moham. p. 5, et Reland. Dissert. de Gemmis Arab. p. 235, 239.)

[3] This throne, in Arabic called Corsi, is by the Mohammedans supposed to
be GOD's tribunal, or seat of justice ; being placed under that other called
Al Arsh, which they say is his imperial throne. The Corsi allegorically
signifies the divine providence, which sustains and governs the heaven and
the earth, and is infinitely above human comprehension. (D'Herbelot,
Bibl. Orient. Art. Corsi.)

[4] This passage was particularly directed to some of Mohammed's first
proselytes, who, having sons that had been brought up in idolatry or Judaism,
would oblige them to embrace Mohammedism by force. (Jallalo'ddin.)

[5] This word properly signifies *an idol*, or whatever is worshipped besides
GOD—particularly the two idols of the Meccans, Allât and Al Uzza ; and
also the devil, or any seducer.

the companions of *hell* fire, they shall remain therein for ever.
Hast thou not considered him who disputed with Abraham
concerning his LORD,[1] because GOD had given him the kingdom ? When Abraham said, My LORD is he who giveth life,
and killeth : he answered, I give life, and I kill. Abraham
said, Verily GOD bringeth the sun from the east, now do
thou bring it from the west. Whereupon the infidel was
confounded ; for GOD directeth not the ungodly people.
Or *hast thou not considered* how he *behaved* who passed by a
city which had been destroyed, even to her foundations ?[2]
He said, How shall GOD quicken this *city*, after she hath been
dead ? And GOD caused him to die for an hundred years,
and afterwards raised him to life. *And God* said, How long
hast thou tarried *here* ? He answered, A day, or part of a
day. *God* said, Nay, thou hast tarried *here* an hundred years.
Now look on thy food and the drink, they are not yet corrupted ; and look on thine ass : and this *have we done* that
we might make thee a sign unto men. And look on the bones
of thine ass, how we raise them, and afterwards clothe them
with flesh. And when *this* was shown unto him, he said, I
know that GOD is able to do all things. And when Abraham
said, O LORD, show me how thou wilt raise the dead ;[3] *God*
said, Dost thou not yet believe ? He answered, Yea ; but
I ask this that my heart may rest at ease. *God* said, take
therefore four birds, and divide them ;[4] then lay a part of

[1] This was Nimrod, who, as the commentators say, to prove his power
of life and death by ocular demonstration, caused two men to be brought
before him at the same time, one of whom he slew, and saved the other
alive. As to this tyrant's persecution of Abraham, see Chap. xxi. and the
notes thereon.

[2] The person here meant was Ozair or Ezra, who riding on an ass by the
ruins of Jerusalem, after it had been destroyed by the Chaldeans, doubted
in his mind by what means GOD could raise the city and its inhabitants
again ; whereupon GOD caused him to die, and he remained in that condition
100 years ; at the end of which GOD restored him to life, and he found a
basket of figs and a cruse of wine he had with him not in the least spoiled
or corrupted ; but his ass was dead, the bones only remaining, and these,
while the prophet looked on, were raised and clothed with flesh, becoming
an ass again, which being inspired with life, began immediately to bray.
(Jallalo'ddin, Yahya, &c. D'Herbel. Bibl. Orient. Art. Ozair.) This apocryphal story may perhaps have taken its rise from Nehemiah's viewing the
ruins of Jerusalem. (Nehem. ii. 12, &c.)

[3] The occasion of this request of Abraham is said to have been on a doubt
proposed to him by the devil, in human form, how it was possible for the
several parts of the corpse of a man which lay on the sea-shore, and had been
partly devoured by the wild beasts, the birds and the fish, to be brought
together at the resurrection. (D'Herbelot, p. 13.)

[4] These birds, according to the commentators, were an eagle (a dove,
say others), a peacock, a raven, and a cock, which Abraham cut to pieces
and mingled their flesh and feathers together, or, as some tell us, pounded
all in a mortar, and dividing the mass into four parts, laid them on so many

them on every mountain ; then call them, and they shall come swiftly unto thee ; and know that GOD is mighty and wise. The similitude of those who lay out their substance for advancing the religion of GOD, is as a grain *of corn* which produceth seven ears, and in every ear an hundred grains ; for GOD giveth twofold unto whom he pleaseth : GOD is bounteous and wise. They who lay out their substance for the religion of GOD, and afterwards follow not what they have *so* laid out by reproaches or mischief,[1] they shall have their reward with their LORD ; upon them shall no fear come, neither shall they be grieved. A fair speech, and to forgive, is better than alms followed by mischief. GOD is rich and merciful. O true believers, make not your alms of none effect by reproaching, or mischief, as he who layeth out what he hath to appear unto men *to give alms*, and believeth not in GOD and the last day. The likeness of such a one is as a flint covered with earth, on which a violent rain falleth, and leaveth it hard. They cannot prosper in anything which they have gained, for GOD directeth not the unbelieving people. And the likeness of those who lay out their substance from a desire to please GOD, and for an establishment for their souls, is as a garden on a hill, on which a violent rain falleth, and it bringeth forth its fruits twofold ; and if a violent rain falleth not on it, yet the dew *falleth thereon* : and GOD seeth that which ye do. Doth any of you desire to have a garden of palm-trees and vines,[2] through which rivers flow, wherein he may have all *kinds of* fruits, and that he may attain to old age, and have a weak offspring ? then a violent fiery wind shall strike it, so that it shall be burned. Thus GOD declareth his signs unto you, that ye may consider. O true believers, bestow *alms* of the good things which ye have gained, and of that which we have produced for you out of the earth, and choose not the bad thereof, to give it *in alms*, such as ye would not accept yourselves,

mountains, but kept the heads, which he had preserved whole, in his hand. Then he called them each by their name, and immediately one part flew to the other, till they all recovered their first shape, and then came to be joined to their respective heads. (Jallalo'ddin. D'Herbelot, ubi supra.) This seems to be taken from Abraham's sacrifice of birds mentioned by Moses (Gen. xv.) with some additional circumstances.

[1] *i.e.*, Either by reproaching the person whom they have relieved with what they have done for him, or by exposing his poverty to his prejudice (Jallalo'ddin.)

[2] This garden is an emblem of alms given out of hypocrisy, or attended with reproaches, which perish, and will be of no service hereafter to the giver. (Jallalo'ddin.)

otherwise than by connivance ;[1] and know that GOD is rich and worthy to be praised. The devil threateneth you with poverty, and commandeth you filthy covetousness ; but GOD promiseth you pardon from himself and abundance : GOD is bounteous and wise. He giveth wisdom unto whom he pleaseth ; and he unto whom wisdom is given, hath received much good : but none will consider, except the *wise* of heart. And whatever alms ye shall give, or *whatever* vow ye shall vow, verily GOD knoweth it ; but the ungodly shall have none to help *them*. If ye make your alms to appear, it is well ; but if ye conceal them, and give them unto the poor, this *will be* better for you, and will atone for your sins : and GOD is well informed of that which ye do. The direction of them belongeth not unto thee ; but GOD directeth whom he pleaseth. The good that ye shall give *in alms shall redound* unto yourselves ; and ye shall not give unless out of desire of *seeing* the face of GOD.[2] And what good thing ye shall give *in alms*, it shall be repaid you, and ye shall not be treated unjustly . unto the poor who are wholly employed in fighting for the religion of GOD, and cannot go to and fro in the earth ; whom the ignorant man thinketh rich, because of their modesty : thou shalt know them by this mark, they ask not men with importunity ; and what good ye shall give *in alms*, verily GOD knoweth it. They who distribute *alms* of their substance night and day, in private and in public, shall have their reward with the LORD ; on them shall no fear come, neither shall they be grieved. They who devour usury shall not arise *from the dead*, but as he ariseth whom Satan hath infected by a touch :[3] this *shall happen to them* because they say, Truly selling is but as usury : and yet GOD hath permitted selling and forbidden usury. He therefore who when there cometh unto him an admonition from his Lord, abstaineth *from usury for the future*, shall have what is past *forgiven him*, and his affair belongeth unto GOD. But whoever returneth *to usury*, they shall be the companions of *hell* fire, they shall continue therein for ever. GOD shall take his blessing from usury, and shall increase alms : for GOD loveth no infidel, or ungodly person. But they who believe and do that which

---

[1] That is, on having some amends made by the seller of such goods, either by abatement of the price, or giving something else to the buyer to make up the value.

[2] *i.e.*, For the sake of a reward hereafter, and not for any worldly consideration. (Jallalo'ddin.)

[3] viz., Like *dæmoniacs* or possessed persons, that is, in great horror and distraction of mind and convulsive agitation of body.

is right, and observe the stated times of prayer, and pay their legal alms, they shall have their reward with their LORD : there shall come no fear on them, neither shall they be grieved. O true believers, fear GOD, and remit that which remaineth of usury,[1] if ye *really* believe ; but if ye do it not, hearken unto war, *which is declared against you* from GOD and his apostle : yet if ye repent, ye shall have the capital of your money. Deal not unjustly *with others*, and ye shall not be dealt with unjustly. If there be any *debtor* under a difficulty *of paying his debt, let his creditor* wait till it be easy *for him to do it* ; but if ye remit it as alms, it will be better for you, if ye knew it. And fear the day wherein ye shall return unto GOD ; then shall every soul be paid what it hath gained and they shall not be treated unjustly. O true believers, when ye bind yourselves one to the other in a debt for a certain time, write it down ; and let a writer write between you according to justice, and let not the writer refuse writing according to what GOD hath taught him ; but let him write, and let him who oweth the debt dictate, and let him fear GOD his LORD, and not diminish ought thereof. But if he who oweth the debt be foolish, or weak, or be not able to dictate himself, let his agent[2] dictate according to equity ; and call to witness two witnesses of your *neighbouring* men ; but if there be not two men, *let there be* a man and two women of those whom ye shall choose for witnesses ; if one of those *women* should mistake, the other of them will cause her to recollect. And the witnesses shall not refuse, whensoever they shall be called. And disdain not to write it down, be it a large *debt*, or be it a small one, until its time *of payment* : this will be more just in the sight of GOD, and more right for bearing witness, and more easy, that ye may not doubt. But if it be a present bargain which ye transact between yourselves, it shall be no crime in you, if ye write it not down. And take witnesses when ye sell one to the other, and let no harm be done to the writer, nor to the witness ; *which* if ye do, it will surely be injustice in you : and fear GOD, and GOD will instruct you, for GOD knoweth all things. And if ye be on a journey, and find no writer, *let* pledges *be* taken : but if one of you trust the other, let him who is trusted return

---

[1] Or the interest due before usury was prohibited. For this some of Mohammed's followers exacted of their debtors, supposing they lawfully might. (Jallalo'ddin.)

[2] Whoever manages his affairs, whether his father, heir, guardian, or interpreter. (Jallalo'ddin.)

what he is trusted with, and fear GOD his LORD. And conceal not the testimony, for he who concealeth it hath surely a wicked heart : GOD knoweth that which ye do. Whatever is in heaven and on earth is GOD'S ; and whether ye manifest that which is in your minds, or conceal it, GOD will call you to account for it, and will forgive whom he pleaseth, and will punish whom he pleaseth ; for GOD is almighty. The apostle believeth in that which hath been sent down unto him from his LORD, and the faithful *also*. Every one *of them* believeth in GOD, and his angels, and his scriptures, and his apostles : we make no distinction at all between his apostles.[1] And they say, We have heard, and do obey : *we implore* thy mercy, O LORD, for unto thee must we return. GOD will not force any soul beyond its capacity : it shall have *the good* which it gaineth, and it shall suffer *the evil* which it gaineth. O LORD, punish us not, if we forget, or act sinfully : O LORD, lay not on us a burden like that which thou hast laid on those who have been before us ;[2] neither make us, O LORD, to bear what we have not strength to *bear*, but be favourable unto us, and spare us, and be merciful unto us. Thou art our patron, help us therefore against the unbelieving nations.

III

THE CHAPTER OF THE FAMILY OF IMRÂN [3]

Revealed at Medina.

IN THE NAME OF THE MOST MERCIFUL GOD.

A L. M.[4] There is no GOD but GOD, the living, the self-subsisting : He hath sent down unto thee the book *of the Korân* with truth, confirming that which was *revealed* before it ; for he had formerly sent down the law and the gospel, a direction unto men ; and he had also sent down

---

[1] But this, say the Mohammedans, the Jews do, who receive Moses but reject Jesus ; and the Christians, who receive both those prophets, but reject Mohammed. (Jallalo'ddin.)

[2] That is, on the Jews, who, as the commentators tell us, were ordered to kill a man by way of atonement, to give one-fourth of their substance in alms, and to cut off an unclean ulcerous part (Jallalo'ddin), and were forbidden to eat fat, or animals that divided the hoof, and were obliged to observe the sabbath, and other particulars wherein the Mohammedans are at liberty. (Yahya.)

[3] This name is given in the Korân to the father of the Virgin Mary. See below, p. 35.

[4] For the meaning of these letters the reader is referred to Sale, Prel. Disc. Sect. III, p. 64.

the distinction *between good and evil.* Verily those who believe not the signs of GOD, shall suffer a grievous punishment ; for GOD is mighty, able to revenge.   Surely nothing is hidden from GOD, *of that which is* on earth, or in heaven : it is he who formeth you in the wombs, as he pleaseth ; there is no GOD but he, the mighty, the wise.   It is he who hath sent down unto thee the book, wherein are some verses clear to be understood, they are the foundation of the book ; and others are parabolical.[1]   But they whose hearts are perverse will follow that which is parabolical therein, out of love of schism, and a desire of the interpretation thereof ; yet none knoweth the interpretation thereof, except GOD.   But they who are well grounded in knowledge say, We believe therein, the whole is from our LORD ; and none will consider except the prudent. O LORD, cause not our hearts to swerve *from truth,* after thou hast directed us : and give us from thee mercy, for thou art he who giveth.   O LORD, thou shalt surely gather mankind together, unto a day *of resurrection* : there is no doubt of it, for GOD will not be contrary to the promise.   As for the infidels, their wealth shall not profit them anything, nor their children, against GOD : they shall be the fuel of *hell* fire. According to the wont of the people of Pharaoh, and of those who went before them, they charged our signs with a lie ; but GOD caught them in their wickedness, and GOD is severe in punishing.   Say unto those who believe not, Ye shall be overcome, and thrown together into hell ; an unhappy couch *shall it be.*   Ye have already had a miracle *shown you* in two armies, which attacked each other :[2] one army fought for

[1] This passage is translated according to the exposition of Al Zamakhshari and Al Beidâwi, which seems to be the truest.   The contents of the Korân are here distinguished into such passages as are to be taken in the literal sense, and such as require a figurative acceptation.   The former being plain and obvious to be understood, compose the fundamental part, or, as the original expresses it, *the mother* of the book, and contain the principal doctrines and precepts ; agreeably to and consistently with which, those passages which are wrapt up in metaphors, and delivered in an enigmatical, allegorical style, are always to be interpreted.   (Sale, Prel. Disc. p. 73.)

[2] The sign or miracle here meant, was the victory gained by Mohammed in the second year of the Hejra, over the idolatrous Meccans, headed by Abu Sofiân, in the valley of Bedr, which is situated near the sea, between Mecca and Medina.   Mohammed's forces consisted of no more than three hundred and nineteen men, but the enemy's army of near a thousand, notwithstanding which odds he put them to flight, having killed seventy of the principal Koreish, and taken as many prisoners, with the loss of only fourteen of his own men.   (Elmacin. p. 5.   Hottinger, Hist. Orient. I. 2, c. 4.   Abulfed. Vit. Moham. p. 56, &c.   Prideaux's Life of Mahom. p. 71, &c.)   This was the first victory obtained by the prophet, and though it may seem no very considerable action, yet it was of great advantage to him, and the foundation of all his future power and success.   For which reason it is famous in the Arabian history, and more than once vaunted in the Korân (see this chapter

GOD's true religion, but the other were infidels ; they saw *the faithful* twice as many as themselves in *their* eyesight, for GOD strengtheneth with his help whom he pleaseth. Surely herein was an example unto men of understanding. The love and eager desire of wives, and children, and sums heaped up of gold and silver, and excellent horses, and cattle, and land, is prepared for men : this is the provision of the present life ; but unto GOD shall be the most excellent return. Say, Shall I declare unto you better *things* than this ? For those who are devout *are prepared* with their LORD, gardens through which rivers flow ; therein shall they continue for ever : and *they shall enjoy* wives free from impurity, and the favour of GOD ; for GOD regardeth *his* servants ; who say, O LORD, we do sincerely believe ; forgive us therefore our sins, and deliver us from the pain of *hell* fire : the patient, and the lovers of truth, and the devout, and the almsgivers, and those who ask pardon *early* in the morning. GOD hath borne witness that there is no GOD but he ; and the angels, and *those who are* endowed with wisdom, *profess the same* ; who executeth righteousness ; there is no GOD but he ; the mighty, the wise. Verily the *true* religion in the sight of GOD, is Islâm ;[1] and they who had received the scriptures dissented not *therefrom*, until after the knowledge *of God's unity* had come unto them, out of envy among themselves ; but whosoever believeth not in the signs of GOD, verily GOD will be swift in *bringing him to* account. If they dispute with thee, say, I have resigned myself unto GOD, and he who followeth me *doth the same* : and say unto them who have received the scriptures and to the ignorant,[2] Do ye profess *the religion of*

---

below, and Chaps. VIII. and XXXII,) as an effect of the divine assistance. The miracle, it is said, consisted in three things—1. Mohammed, by the direction of the angel Gabriel, took a handful of gravel and threw it towards the enemy in the attack, saying, *May their faces be confounded* ; whereupon they immediately threw the gravel himself, yet it is told in the Korân (Chap. VIII., not far from the beginning) that it was not he, but GOD, who threw it, that is to say, by the ministry of his angel. 2. The Mohammedan troops seemed to the infidels to be twice as many in number as themselves, which greatly discouraged them. And 3. GOD sent down to their assistance first a thousand and afterwards three thousand angels, led by Gabriel, mounted on his horse Haizûm ; and, according to the Korân (Chap. VIII.), these celestial auxiliaries really did all the execution, though Mohammed's men imagined themselves did it, and fought stoutly at the same time.

[1] The proper name of the Mohammedan religion, which signifies the *resigning* or *devoting one's self* entirely to GOD and his service. This they say is the religion which all the prophets were sent to teach, being founded on the unity of GOD. (Jallalo'ddin, Al Beidâwi.)

[2] *i.e.*, The pagan Arabs, who had no knowledge of the Scriptures. (Jallalo'-ddin, Al Beidâwi.)

Islâm? Now if they embrace Islâm, they are surely directed; but if they turn their backs, verily unto thee *belongeth* preaching *only*; for GOD regardeth his servants. And unto those who believe not in the signs of GOD, and slay the prophets without a cause, and put those men to death who teach justice; denounce unto them a painful punishment. These are they whose works perish in this world, and in that which is to come; and they shall have none to help them. Hast thou not observed those unto whom part of the scripture was given?[1] They were called unto the book of GOD, that it might judge between them;[2] then some of them turned their backs, and retired afar off. This *they did* because they said, The fire *of hell* shall by no means touch us, but for a *certain* number of days:[3] and that which they had falsely devised, hath deceived them in their religion. How then *will it be with them*, when we shall gather them together at the day *of judgment*,[4] of which there is no doubt; and every

[1] That is, the Jews.

[2] This passage was revealed on occasion of a dispute Mohammed had with some Jews, which is differently related by the commentators. Al Beidâwi says that Mohammed going one day into a Jewish synagogue, Naïm Ebn Amru and Al Hareth Ebn Zeid asked him what religion he was of? To which he answering, " Of the religion of Abraham ; " they replied "Abraham was a Jew." But on Mohammed's proposing that the Pentateuch might decide the question, they would by no means agree to it. But Jallalo'ddin tells us that two persons of the Jewish religion having committed adultery, their punishment was referred to Mohammed, who gave sentence that they should be stoned, according to the law of Moses. This the Jews refused to submit to, alleging there was no such command in the Pentateuch ; but on Mohammed's appealing to the book, the said law was found therein. Whereupon the criminals were stoned, to the great mortification of the Jews. It is very remarkable that this law of Moses concerning the stoning of adulterers is mentioned in the New Testament— John viii. 5—(though I know some dispute the authenticity of that whole passage), but is not now to be found, either in the Hebrew or Samaritan Pentateuch, or in the Septuagint ; it being only said that such *shall be put to death*. (Levit. xx. 10. Whiston's Essay towards restoring the true text of the Old Test. p. 99, 100.) This omission is insisted on by the Mohammedans as one instance of the corruption of the law of Moses by the Jews. It is also observable that there was a verse once extant in the Korân, commanding adulterers to be stoned ; and the commentators say the words only are abrogated, the sense or law still remaining in force. (Sale, Prel. Disc. Sect. III, p. 71.)

[3] *i.e.*, Forty ; the time their forefathers worshipped the calf. (See before, p. 2, note 13.) Al Beidâwi adds, that some of them pretended their punishment was to last but seven days, that is, a day for every thousand years which they supposed the world was to endure ; and that they imagined they were to be so mildly dealt with, either by reason of the intercession of their fathers the prophets, or because GOD had promised Jacob that his offspring should be punished but slightly.

[4] The Mohammedans have a tradition that the first banner of the infidels that shall be set up, on the day of judgment, will be that of the Jews ; and that GOD will first reproach them with their wickedness, over the heads of those who are present, and then order them to hell. (Al Beidâwi.)

soul shall be paid that which it hath gained, neither shall they be treated unjustly ? Say, O GOD, who possessest the kingdom ; thou givest the kingdom unto whom thou wilt, and thou takest away the kingdom from whom thou wilt : thou exaltest whom thou wilt, and thou humblest whom thou wilt : in thy hand is good, for thou art almighty. Thou makest the night to succeed the day : thou bringest forth the living out of the dead, and thou bringest forth the dead out of the living ;[1] and providest food for whom thou wilt without measure. Let not the faithful take the infidels for their protectors, rather than the faithful : he who doth this shall not be *protected* of GOD at all ; unless ye fear any danger from them : but GOD warneth you to beware of himself ; for unto GOD must ye return. Say, Whether ye conceal that which is in your breasts, or whether ye declare it, GOD knoweth it : for he knoweth whatever is in heaven, and whatever is on earth : GOD is almighty. On the *last* day every soul shall find the good which it hath wrought, present ; and the evil which it hath wrought, it shall wish that between itself and that were a wide distance : but GOD warneth you to beware of himself ; for GOD is gracious unto his servants. Say, If ye love GOD, follow me : *then* GOD shall love you, and forgive you your sins ; for GOD is gracious and merciful. Say, Obey GOD, and *his* apostle : but if ye go back, verily GOD loveth not the unbelievers, GOD hath surely chosen Adam, and Noah, and the family of Abraham, and the family of Imrân[2] above the *rest of the* world ; a race *descending* the

---

[1] As a man from seed, and a bird from an egg; and *vice versâ*. (Jallalo'-ddin.)

[2] Or Amrân. This is the name of two several persons, according to the Mohammedan tradition. One was the father of Moses and Aaron ; and the other was the father of the Virgin Mary (Al Zamakhshari. Al Beidâwi) ; but he is called by some Christian writers Joachim. The commentators suppose the first, or rather both of them, to be meant in this place ; however, the person intended in the next passage, it is agreed, was the latter ; who besides Mary the mother of Jesus, had also a son named Aaron (Chap. XIX), and another sister, named Ishâ (or Elizabeth), who married Zacharias, and was the mother of John the Baptist ; whence that prophet and Jesus are usually called by the Mohammedans, *The two sons of the aunt*, or the cousins german. From the identity of names it has been generally imagined by Christian writers (Reland. de Rel. Moh. p. 211. Marracc. in Alc. p. 115, &c. Prideaux, Letter to the Deists, p. 185) that the Korân here confounds Mary the mother of Jesus, with Mary or Miriam the sister of Moses and Aaron ; which intolerable anachronism, if it were certain, is sufficient of itself to destroy the pretended authority of this book. But though Mohammed may be supposed to have been ignorant enough in ancient history and chronology to have committed so gross a blunder, yet I do not see how it can be made out from the words of the Korân. For it does not follow, because two persons have the same name, and have each a father and brother who bear the same names, that they must therefore necessarily be the same person :

one from the other : GOD is he who heareth and knoweth. *Remember* when the wife of Imrân[1] said, LORD, verily I have vowed unto thee that which is in my womb, to be dedicated *to thy service* :[2] accept *it* therefore of me ; for thou art he who heareth and knoweth. And when she was delivered of it, she said, LORD, verily I have brought forth a female (and GOD well knew what she had brought forth), and a male is not as a female :[3] I have called her Mary ; and I commend her to thy protection, and *also* her issue, against Satan driven away with stones.[4] Therefore the Lord accepted her with a gracious acceptance,[5] and caused her to bear an excellent

besides, such a mistake is inconsistent with a number of other places in the Korân, whereby it manifestly appears that Mohammed well knew and asserted that Moses preceded Jesus several ages. And the commentators accordingly fail not to tell us that there had passed about one thousand eight hundred years between Amrân the father of Moses, and Amrân the father of the Virgin Mary : they also make them the sons of different persons ; the first, they say, was the son of Yeshar, or Izhar—though he was really his brother—(Exod. vi. 18), the son of Kâhath, the son of Levi ; and the other was the son of Mathân (Al Zamakh. Al Beidâwi), whose genealogy they trace, but in a very corrupt and imperfect manner, up to David, and thence to Adam. (Reland. ubi sup. D'Herbelot, Bibl. Orient. p. 383.) It must be observed that though the Virgin Mary is called in the Korân (Chap. XIX.) the sister of Aaron, yet she is nowhere called the sister of Moses ; however, some Mohammedan writers have imagined that the same individual Mary, the sister of Moses, was miraculously preserved alive from his time till that of Jesus Christ, purposely to become the mother of the latter. (Guadagnol. Apolog. pro Rel. Christ. contra Ahmed Ebn Zein al Abedin. p. 279.)

[1] The Imrân here mentioned was the father of the Virgin Mary, and his wife's name was Hannah, or Ann, the daughter of Fakudh. This woman, say the commentators, being aged and barren, on seeing a bird feed her young ones, became very desirous of issue, and begged a child of GOD, promising to consecrate it to his service in the temple ; whereupon she had a child, but it proved a daughter. (Al Beidâwi. Al Thalabi.)

[2] The Arabic word is *free*, but here signifies particularly one that is *free* or detached from all worldly desires and occupations, and wholly devoted to GOD's service. (Jallalo'ddin. Al Zamakhshari.)

[3] Because a female could not minister in the temple as a male could. (Jallalo'ddin.)

[4] This expression alludes to a tradition, that Abraham, when the devil tempted him to disobey GOD in not sacrificing his son, drove the fiend away by throwing stones at him ; in memory of which, the Mohammedans, at the pilgrimage of Mecca, throw a certain number of stones at the devil, with certain ceremonies, in the valley of Mina. (Prelim. Disc. Sect. IV.) It is not improbable that the pretended immaculate conception of the Virgin Mary is intimated in this passage ; for according to a tradition of Mohammed, every person that comes into the world is touched at his birth by the devil, and therefore cries out : Mary and her son only excepted, between whom and the evil spirit GOD placed a veil, so that his touch did not reach them. (Jallalo'ddin. Al Beidâwi.) And for this reason, they say, neither of them were guilty of any sin, like the rest of the children of Adam (Kitada) : which peculiar grace they obtained by virtue of this recommendation of them by Hannah to GOD's protection.

[5] Though the child happened not to be a male, yet her mother presented her to the priests who had the care of the temple, as one dedicated to GOD ; and they having received her, she was committed to the care of Zacharias, as will be observed by-and-bye, and he built her an apartment in the temple,

offspring. And Zacharias took care of *the child* ; whenever Zacharias went into the chamber to her, he found provisions with her : [1] *and* he said, O Mary, whence hadst thou this ? she answered, This is from God ; for GOD provideth for whom he pleaseth without measure. [2] There Zacharias called on his LORD, *and* said, LORD, give me from thee a good offspring, for thou art the hearer of prayer. And the angels [3] called to him, while he stood praying in the chamber, *saying*, Verily GOD promiseth thee *a son named* John, who shall bear witness to the Word [4] *which cometh* from God ; an honourable person, chaste, [5] and one of the righteous prophets. He answered, LORD, how shall I have a son, when old age hath overtaken me, [6] and my wife is barren ? *The angel* said, So GOD doth that which he pleaseth. *Zacharias* answered, LORD, give me a sign. *The angel* said, Thy sign shall be, that thou shalt speak unto no man [7] for three days, otherwise than by gesture : remember thy LORD often, and praise *him* evening and morning. And when the angels said, O Mary, verily GOD hath chosen thee, and hath purified thee, and hath chosen thee above *all* the women of the world : O Mary, be devout towards thy LORD, and worship, and bow down with those who bow down. This is a secret history : we reveal it unto thee, although thou wast not present with them when they threw in their rods *to cast lots* which of them should have

and supplied her with necessaries. (Jallalo'ddin. Al Beidâwi. Lud de Dieu, in not. ad Hist. Christi Xaveril, p. 542.)

[1] The commentators say that none went into Mary's apartment but Zacharias himself, and that he locked seven doors upon her, yet he found she had always winter fruits in summer, and summer fruits in winter. (Al Beidâwi. Vide de Dieu, ubi sup. p. 548.)

[2] There is a story of Fâtema, Mohammed's daughter, that she once brought two loaves and a piece of flesh to her father, who returned them to her, and having called for her again, when she uncovered the dish, it was full of bread and meat ; and on Mohammed's asking her whence she had it, she answered in the words of this passage : *This is from* GOD ; *for* GOD *provideth for whom he pleaseth without measure.* Whereupon he blessed GOD, who thus favoured her, as he had the most excellent of the daughters of Israel. (Al Beidâwi.)

[3] Though the word be in the plural, yet the commentators say it was the angel Gabriel only. The same is to be understood where it occurs in the following passages.

[4] That is, Jesus, who, Al Beidâwi says, is so called because he was conceived by the word or command of GOD without a father.

[5] The original word signifies one who refrains not only from women, but from all other worldly delights and desires. Al Beidâwi mentions a tradition, that during his childhood some boys invited him to play, but he refused, declaring that he was not created to play.

[6] Zacharias was then ninety-nine years old, and his wife eighty-nine. (Al Beidâwi.)

[7] Though he could not speak to anybody else, yet his tongue was at liberty to praise GOD, as he is directed to do by the following words.

the education of Mary :[1] neither wast thou with them, when they strove among themselves.   When the angels said, O Mary, verily GOD sendeth thee good tidings, *that thou shalt bear* the Word, *proceeding* from himself ; his name shall be CHRIST JESUS the son of Mary, honourable in this world and in the world to come, and *one* of those who approach near *to the presence of God* ; and he shall speak unto men in the cradle,[2] and when he is grown up ;[3] and he shall be *one* of the righteous : she answered, LORD, how shall I have a son, since a man hath not touched me ?   *The angel* said, So GOD createth that which he pleaseth : when he decreeth a thing, he only saith unto it, Be, and it is : *God* shall teach him the scripture, and wisdom, and the law, and the gospel ; and *shall appoint him his* apostle to the children of Israel ; *and he shall say,* Verily I come unto you with a sign from your LORD ; for I will make before you, of clay, as it were the figure of a bird ; [4]

[1] When Mary was first brought to the temple, the priests, because she was the daughter of one of their chiefs, disputed among themselves who should have the education of her. Zacharias insisted that he ought to be preferred, because he had married her aunt ; but the others not consenting that it should be so, they agreed to decide the matter by casting of lots ; whereupon twenty-seven of them went to the river Jordan and threw in their rods (or arrows without heads or feathers, such as the Arabs used for the same purpose), on which they had written some passages of the law ; but they all sank except that of Zacharias, which floated on the water ; and he had thereupon the care of the child committed to him. (Al Beidâwi. Jallalo'-ddin, etc.)

[2] Besides an instance of this given in the Korân itself (Chap. XIX), which I shall not here anticipate, a Mohammedan writer (of no very great credit, indeed) tells two stories, one of Jesus's speaking while in his mother's womb, to reprove her cousin Joseph for his unjust suspicions of her (Sikii notas in Evang. Infant. p. 5) ; and another of his giving an answer to the same person soon after he was born. For Joseph being sent by Zacharias to seek Mary (who had gone out of the city by night to conceal her delivery) and having found her, began to expostulate with her, but she made no reply ; whereupon the child spoke these words : *Rejoice, O Joseph, and be of good cheer ; for God hath brought me forth from the darkness of the womb, to the light of the world ; and I shall go to the children of Israel, and invite them to the obedience of God.* (Al Kessai, apud eundem.) These seem all to have been taken from some fabulous traditions of the Eastern Christians, one of which is preserved to us in the spurious gospel of the Infancy of Christ ; where we read that Jesus spoke while yet in the cradle, and said to his mother, *Verily I am Jesus the son of God, the word which thou hast brought forth, as the angel Gabriel did declare unto thee; and my father hath sent me to save the world.* (Evang. Infant. p. 5.)

[3] The Arabic word properly signifies a man in full age, that is, between thirty or thirty-four, and fifty-one ; and the passage may relate to Christ's preaching here on earth.   But as he had scarce attained this age when he was taken up into heaven, the commentators choose to understand it of his second coming. (Jallalo'ddin. Al Beidâwi.)

[4] Some say it was a bat (Jallalo'ddin), though others suppose Jesus made several birds of different sorts. (Al Thala' i.) This circumstance is also taken from the following fabulous tradition, which may be found in the spurious gospel above mentioned. Jesus being seven years old, and at play with several children of his age, they made several figures of birds and beasts, for

then I will breathe thereon, and it shall become a bird, by the permission of GOD ;[1] and I will heal him that hath been blind from his birth, and the leper ; and I will raise the dead[2] by the permission of GOD : and I will prophesy unto you what ye eat, and what ye lay up for store in your houses. Verily herein will be a sign unto you, if ye believe. And *I come* to confirm the Law which was *revealed* before me, and to allow unto you as lawful, part of that which hath been forbidden you :[3] and I come unto you with a sign from your LORD ; therefore fear GOD, and obey me. Verily GOD is my LORD, and your LORD : therefore serve him. This is the right way. But when Jesus perceived their unbelief, he said, Who *will be* my helpers towards GOD ? The apostles[4] answered, We *will be* the helpers of GOD ; we believe in GOD, and do thou bear witness that we are true believers. O LORD, we believe in that which thou hast sent down, and we have followed thy apostle ; write us down therefore with those who bear witness *of him.* And *the Jews* devised a stratagem *against him ;*[5] but GOD devised a stratagem *against them ;*[6]

their diversion, c clay ; and each preferring his own workmanship, Jesus told them, that he would make his walk and leap ; which accordingly, at his command, they did. He made also several figures of sparrows and other birds, which flew about or stood on his hands as he ordered them, and also ate and drank when he offered them meat and drink. The children telling this to their parents, were forbidden to play any more with Jesus, whom they held to be a sorcerer. (Evang. Infant. p. iii, &c.)

[1] The commentators observe that these words are added here, and in the next sentence, lest it should be thought Jesus did these miracles by his own power, or was GOD. (Al Beidâwi, &c.)

[2] Jallalo'ddin mentions three persons whom Christ restored to life, and who lived several years after, and had children ; viz., Lazarus, the widow's son, and the publican's (I suppose he means the ruler of the synagogue's) daughter. He adds that he also raised Shem the son of Noah, who, as another writes (Al Thalabi), thinking he had been called to judgment, came out of his grave with his head half grey, whereas men did not grow grey in his days ; after which he immediately died again.

[3] Such as the eating of fish that have neither fins nor scales, the caul and fat of animals, and camel's flesh, and to work on the sabbath. These things, say the commentators, being arbitrary institutions in the law of Moses, were abrogated by Jesus ; as several of the same kind, instituted by the latter have been since abrogated by Mohammed. (Al Beidâwi. Jallalo'ddin.)

[4] In Arabic, *Hawâriyûn* ; which word they derive from *Hâra, to be white,* and suppose the apostles were so called either from the *candour* and *sincerity* of their minds, or because they were princes and wore white garments, or else because they were by trade *fullers.* (Al Beidâwi). According to which last opinion, their vocation is thus related ; that as Jesus passed by the seaside, he saw some fullers at work, and accosting them, said, *Ye cleanse these clothes, but cleanse not your hearts* ; upon which they believed on him. But the true etymology seems to be from the Ethiopic verb *Hawyra, to go* ; whence *Hawârya* signifies *one that is sent,* a *messenger* or *apostle.* (Ludolfi Lexic. Æthiop. col. 40, et Golii notas ad cap. 61 Korâni, p. 205.)

[5] *i e.,* They laid a design to take away his life.

[6] This stratagem of GOD's was the taking of Jesus up into heaven, and

and GOD is the best deviser of stratagems. When GOD said, O Jesus, verily I will cause thee to die,[1] and I will take thee

stamping his likeness on another person, who was apprehended and crucified in his stead. For it is the constant doctrine of the Mohammedans that it was not Jesus himself who underwent that ignominious death, but somebody else in his shape and resemblance. (Chap. IV.) The person crucified some will have to be a spy that was sent to entrap him; others that it was one Titian, who by the direction of Judas entered in at a window of the house where Jesus was, to kill him; and others that it was Judas himself, who agreed with the rulers of the Jews to betray him for thirty pieces of silver, and led those who were sent to take him. They add, that Jesus after his crucifixion in *effigy*, was sent down again to the earth, to comfort his mother and disciples, and acquaint them how the Jews were deceived; and was then taken up a second time into heaven. (Marracc. in Alc. p. 113, &c.; et in Prodr. part iii. p. 63, &c.) It is supposed by several that this story was an original invention of Mohammed's; but they are certainly mistaken; for several sectaries held the same opinion, long before his time. The Basilidians (Irenæus, l. 1, c. 23, &c. Epiphan. Hæres. 24, num. iii.), in the very beginning of Christianity, denied that Christ himself suffered, but that Simon the Cyrenean was crucified in his place. The Cerinthians before them, and the Carpocratians next (to name no more of those who affirmed Jesus to have been a mere man), did believe the same thing; that it was not himself, but one of his followers very like him that was crucified. Photius tells us, that he read a book entitled, The Journeys of the Apostles, relating the acts of Peter, John, Andrew, Thomas and Paul; and among other things contained therein, this was one, *that Christ was not crucified, but another in his stead*, and that therefore *he laughed at his crucifiers* (Photius, Bibl. Cod. 114, col. 291), or those who thought they had crucified him. (Toland's Nazarenus, p. 17, &c.) I have in another place (Sale, Prel. Disc. Sect. IV) mentioned an apocryphal gospel of Barnabas, a forgery originally of some nominal Christians, but interpolated since by Mohammedans; which gives this part of the history of Jesus with circumstances too curious to be omitted. It is therein related, that the moment the Jews were going to apprehend Jesus in the garden, he was snatched up into the third heaven, by the ministry of four angels, Gabriel, Michael, Raphael, and Uriel; that he will not die till the end of the world, and that it was Judas who was crucified in his stead; GOD having permitted that traitor to appear so like his master, in the eyes of the Jews, that they took and delivered him to Pilate. That this resemblance was so great, that it deceived the Virgin Mary and the apostles themselves; but that Jesus Christ afterwards obtained leave of GOD to go and comfort them. That Barnabas having then asked him, why the divine goodness had suffered the mother and disciples of so holy a prophet to believe even for one moment that he had died in so ignominious a manner? Jesus returned the following answer. "O Barnabas, believe me that every sin, how small soever, is punished by GOD with great torment, because GOD is offended with sin. My mother therefore and faithful disciples, having loved me with a mixture of earthly love, the just GOD has been pleased to punish this love with their present grief, that they might not be punished for it hereafter in the flames of hell. And as for me, though I have myself been blameless in the world, yet other men having called me GOD, and the son of GOD; therefore GOD, that I might not be mocked by the devils at the day of judgment, has been pleased that in this world I should be mocked by men with the death of Judas, making everybody believe that I died upon the cross. And hence it is that this mocking is still to continue till the coming of Mohammed, the messenger of GOD; who coming into the world, will undeceive every one who shall believe in the law of GOD from this mistake. (See the Menagians, tom. iv. p. 326, &c.)

[1] It is the opinion of a great many Mohammedans that Jesus was taken up into heaven without dying; which opinion is consonant to what is delivered in the spurious gospel above mentioned. Wherefore several of

up unto me,[1] and I will deliver thee from the unbelievers ;
and I will place those who follow thee above the unbelievers,
until the day of resurrection : [2] then unto me shall ye return,
and I will judge between you of that concerning which ye
disagree. Moreover, as for the infidels, I will punish them
with a grievous punishment in this world, and in that which is
to come ; and there shall be none to help them. But they
who believe, and do that which is right, he shall give them
their reward ; for GOD loveth not the wicked doers. These
signs and this prudent admonition do we rehearse unto thee.
Verily the likeness of Jesus in the sight of GOD is as the likeness of Adam : he created him out of the dust, and then said
unto him, Be ; and he was.[3] *This is* the truth from thy
LORD ; be not therefore *one* of those who doubt : and whoever shall dispute with thee concerning him,[4] after the knowledge which hath been given thee, say *unto them,* Come, let
us call together our sons, and your sons, and our wives, and
your wives, and our selves, and your selves ; then let us make
imprecations, and lay the curse of GOD on those who lie.[5]

the commentators say that there is a *hysteron proteron* in these words, *I will
cause thee to die, and I will take thee up unto me* ; and that the copulative
does not import order, or that he died before his assumption ; the meaning
being this, viz., that GOD would first take Jesus up to heaven, and deliver
him from the infidels, and afterwards cause him to die ; which they suppose
is to happen when he shall return into the world again, before the last day.
(Sale, Prel. Disc. Sect. IV.) Some, thinking the order of the words is not
to be changed, interpret them figuratively, and suppose their signification
to be that Jesus was lifted up while he was asleep, or that GOD caused him
to die a spiritual death to all worldly desires. But others acknowledge that
he actually died a natural death, and continued in that state three hours, or,
according to another tradition, seven hours ; after which he was restored
to life, and then taken up to heaven. (Al Beidâwi.)
    [1] Some Mohammedans say this was done by the ministry of Gabriel ;
but others that a strong whirlwind took him up from Mount Olivet. (Al
Thalabi. See 2 Kings ii. 1, 11.)
    [2] That is, they who believe in Jesus (among whom the Mohammedans
reckon themselves) shall be for ever superior to the Jews, both in arguments
and in arms. And accordingly, says Al Beidâwi, to this very day the Jews
have never prevailed either against the Christians or Moslems, nor have
they any kingdom or established government of their own.
    [3] He was like to Adam in respect of his miraculous production by the
immediate power of GOD (Jallalo'ddin, &c.)
    [4] Namely, Jesus.
    [5] To explain this passage their commentators tell the following story.
That some Christians, with their bishop named Abu Hareth, coming to
Mohammed as ambassadors from the inhabitants of Najrân, and entering
into some disputes with him touching religion and the history of Jesus Christ,
they agreed the next morning to abide the trial here mentioned, as a quick
way of deciding which of them were in the wrong. Mohammed met them
accordingly, accompanied by his daughter Fâtema, his son-in-law Ali, and
his two grandsons, Hasan and Hosein, and desired them to wait till he had
said his prayers. But when they saw him kneel down, their resolution
failed them, and they durst not venture to curse him, but submitted to pay
him tribute. (Jallalo'ddin. Al Beidâwi.)

Verily this is a true history : and there is no GOD but GOD ; and GOD is most mighty, and wise. If they turn back, GOD well knoweth the evil-doers. Say, O ye who have received the scripture, come to a just determination between us and you ;[1] that we worship not *any* except GOD and associate no creature with him ; and that the one of us take not the other for lords,[2] beside GOD. But if they turn back, say, Bear witness that we are true believers. O ye to whom the scriptures have been given, why do ye dispute concerning Abraham,[3] since the Law and the Gospel were not sent down until after him ? Do ye not therefore understand ? Behold ye are they who dispute concerning that which ye have some knowledge of ; why therefore do ye dispute concerning that which ye have no knowledge of ?[4] GOD knoweth, but ye know not. Abraham was neither a Jew, nor a Christian ; but he was of the true religion, one resigned *unto God*, and was not of the *number of the* idolaters. Verily the men who are the nearest *of kin* unto Abraham, are they who follow him ; and this prophet, and they who believe *on him* : GOD is the patron of the faithful. Some of those who have received the scriptures desire to seduce you ;[5] but they seduce themselves only, and they perceive *it* not. O ye who have received the scriptures, why do ye not believe in the signs of GOD, since ye are witnesses *of them* ? O ye who have received the scriptures, why do ye clothe truth with vanity, and knowingly hide the truth ?[6] And some of those to whom the scriptures were given, say, Believe in that which hath been sent down unto those who believe, in the beginning of the day, and deny *it* in the end thereof ; that they may go back *from their faith* :[7]

[1] That is, to such terms of agreement as are indisputably consonant to the doctrine of all the prophets and scriptures, and therefore cannot be reasonably rejected. (Al Beidâwi.)

[2] Besides other charges of idolatry on the Jews and Christians, Mohammed accused them of paying too implicit an obedience to their priests and monks, who took upon them to pronounce what things were lawful, and what unlawful, and to dispense with the laws of GOD. (Al Beidâwi.)

[3] viz., By pretending him to have been of your religion.

[4] *i.e.*, Ye perversely dispute even concerning those things which ye find in the law and the gospel, whereby it appears they were both sent down long after Abraham's time ; why then will ye offer to dispute concerning such points of Abraham's religion of which your scriptures say nothing, and of which ye consequently can have no knowledge ? (Al Beidâwi.)

[5] This passage was revealed when the Jews endeavoured to pervert Hodheifa, Ammâr, and Moâdh to their religion. (Al Beidâwi.)

[6] The Jews and Christians are again accused of corrupting the scriptures and stifling the prophecies concerning Mohammed.

[7] The commentators, to explain this passage, say that Caab Ebn al Ashraf and Malec Ebn al Seif (two Jews of Medina) advised their companions, when the Keblah was changed (See Chapter II), to make as if they believed it was

and believe him only who followeth your religion. Say, Verily the *true* direction is the direction of GOD, that there may be given unto some other *a revelation* like unto what hath been given unto you. Will they dispute with you before your LORD? Say, Surely excellence is in the hand of GOD, he giveth it unto whom he pleaseth; GOD is bounteous and wise: he will confer peculiar mercy on whom he pleaseth; for GOD is endued with great beneficence. There is of those who have received the scriptures, unto whom if thou trust a talent, he will restore it unto thee;[1] and *there is also* of them, unto whom if thou trust a dinâr, he will not restore it unto thee, unless thou stand over him continually *with great urgency*.[2] This *they do* because they say, We are not obliged to observe justice with the heathen: but they utter a lie against GOD, knowingly. Yea; whoso keepeth his covenant,

done by the divine direction, and to pray towards the Caaba in the morning, but that in the evening they should pray, as formerly, towards the temple of Jerusalem; that Mohammed's followers, imagining the Jews were better judges of this matter than themselves, might imitate their example. But others say these were certain Jewish priests of Khaibar, who directed some of their people to pretend in the morning that they had embraced Mohammedism, but in the close of the day to say that they had looked into their books of scripture, and consulted their Rabbins, and could not find that Mohammed was the person described and intended in the law, by which trick they hoped to raise doubts in the minds of the Mohammedans. (Al Beidâwi.)

[1] As an instance of this, the commentators bring Abd'allah Ebn Salâm, a Jew, very intimate with Mohammed (Prideaux's Life of Mahom. p. 33), to whom one of the Koreish lent 1,200 ounces of gold, which he very punctually repaid at the time appointed. (Al Beidâwi. Jallalo'ddin.)

[2] Al Beidâwi produces an example of such a piece of injustice in one Phineas Ebn Azûra, a Jew, who borrowed a *dinâr*, which is a gold coin worth about ten shillings, of a Koreishite, and afterwards had the conscience to deny it. But the person more directly struck at in this passage was the above-mentioned Caab Ebn al Ashraf, a most inveterate enemy of Mohammed and his religion, of whom Jallalo'ddin relates the same story as Al Beidâwi does of Phineas. This Caab, after the battle of Bedr, went to Mecca, and there, to excite the Koreish to revenge themselves, made and recited verses lamenting the death of those who were slain in that battle, and reflecting very severely on Mohammed; and he afterwards returned to Medina, and had the boldness to repeat them publicly there also, at which Mohammed was so exceedingly provoked that he proscribed him, and sent a party of men to kill him, and he was circumvented and slain by Mohammed Ebn Moslema, in the third year of the Hejra. (Al Jannâbi, Elmacin.) Dr. Prideaux (Life of Mahom. p. 78, etc.) has confounded the Caab we are now speaking of with another very different person of the same name, and a famous poet, but who was the son of Zohair, and no Jew, as a learned gentleman has already observed. (Gagnier, in not. ad Abufed. Vit. Moh. p. 64 and 122.) In consequence of which mistake, the doctor attributes what the Arabian historians write of the latter to the former, and wrongly affirms that he was not put to death by Mohammed. Some of the commentators, however, suppose that in the former part of this passage the Christians are intended, who, they say, are generally people of some honour and justice; and in the latter part the Jews, who, they think, are more given to cheating and dishonesty. (Al Beidâwi.)

and feareth *God*, GOD, surely loveth those who fear *him*. But they who make merchandise of GOD's covenant, and of their oaths, for a small price, shall have no portion in the next life, neither shall GOD speak to them or regard them on the day of resurrection, nor shall he cleanse them ; but they shall suffer a grievous punishment. And there are certainly some of them, who read the scriptures perversely, that ye may think *what they read* to be really in the scriptures, yet it is not in the scripture ; and they say, This is from GOD ; but it is not from GOD : and they speak that which is false concerning GOD, against their own knowledge. It is not *fit* for a man, that GOD should give him a book *of revelations*, and wisdom, and prophecy ; and then he should say unto men, Be ye worshippers of me, besides GOD ; but *he ought to say*, Be ye perfect in knowledge and in works, since ye know the scriptures, and exercise yourselves therein.[1] *God* hath not commanded *you* to take the angels and the prophets for *your* Lords : Will he command *you* to become infidels, after ye have been true believers ? And *remember* when GOD accepted the covenant of the prophets,[2] *saying, This* verily *is* the scripture and the wisdom which I have given you : hereafter shall an apostle come unto you, confirming the truth of that *scripture* which is with you ; ye shall surely believe on him, and ye shall assist him. *God* said, Are ye firmly resolved, and do ye accept my covenant on this *condition* ? They answered, We are firmly resolved : *God* said, Be ye therefore witnesses ; and I also bear witness with you : and whosoever turneth back after this, they are surely the transgressors. Do they therefore seek any other religion but GOD's ? since to him is resigned whosoever is in heaven or on earth, voluntarily, or of force : and to him shall they return. Say, We believe in GOD, and that which hath been sent down unto us, and that which was sent down unto Abraham, and Ismael, and Isaac, and Jacob, and the tribes, and that which was delivered to Moses, and Jesus, and the

---

[1] This passage was revealed, say the commentators, in answer to the Christians, who insisted that Jesus had commanded them to worship him as GOD. Al Beidâwi adds that two Christians named Abu Râfé al Koradhi and Al Seyid al Najrâni, offered to acknowledge Mohammed for their Lord, and to worship him : to which he answered, GOD *forbid that we should worship any besides* GOD.

[2] Some commentators interpret this of the children of Israel themselves, of whose race the prophets were. But others say the souls of all the prophets, even of those who were not then born, were present on Mount Sinai when GOD gave the law to Moses, and that they entered into the covenant here mentioned with him. A story borrowed by Mohammed from the Talmudists, and therefore most probably his true meaning in this place.

prophets from their LORD ; we make no distinction between any of them ; and to him are we resigned. Whoever followeth any other religion than Islâm, it shall not be accepted of him ; and in the next life he shall be of those who perish. How shall GOD direct men who have become infidels after they had believed, and borne witness that the apostle was true, and manifest declarations *of the divine will* had come unto them ? for GOD directeth not the ungodly people. Their reward shall be, that on them *shall fall* the curse of GOD, and of angels, and of all mankind : they shall remain under the same for ever ; their torment shall not be mitigated, neither shall they be regarded ; except those who repent after this, and amend ; for GOD is gracious and merciful. Moreover they who become infidels after they have believed, and yet increase in infidelity, their repentance shall in no wise be accepted, and they are those who go astray. Verily they who believe not, and die in their unbelief, the world full of gold shall in no wise be accepted from any of them, even though he should give it for his ransom ; they shall suffer a grievous punishment, and they shall have none to help them. (IV.) [1] Ye will never attain unto righteousness, until ye give in alms of that which ye love : and whatever ye give, GOD knoweth it. All food was permitted unto the children of Israel, except what Israel forbade unto himself[2] before the Pentateuch was sent down.[3] Say *unto the Jews*, Bring hither the Pentateuch and read it, if ye speak truth. Whoever therefore contriveth a lie against GOD after this, they will be evil-doers. Say, GOD is true : follow ye therefore the religion of Abraham the orthodox ; for he was no idolater. Verily the first house appointed unto men *to worship in*

[1] Section IV begins here. See Sale, Prel. Disc. p. 63.

[2] This passage was revealed on the Jews reproaching Mohammed and his followers with their eating of the flesh and milk of camels (Levit. xi. 4 ; Deut. xiv. 7), which they said was forbidden Abraham, whose religion Mohammed pretended to follow. In answer to which he tells them that GOD ordained no distinction of meats before he gave the law to Moses, though Jacob voluntarily abstained from the flesh and milk of camels ; which some commentators say was the consequence of a vow made by that patriarch, when afflicted with the sciatica, that if he were cured he would eat no more of that meat which he liked best ; and that was camel's flesh : but others suppose he abstained from it by the advice of physicians only. (Al Beidâwi. Jallalo'ddin.) This exposition seems to be taken from the children of Israel's not eating of the sinew on the hollow of the thigh, because the angel, with whom Jacob wrestled at Peniel, touched *the hollow of his thigh in the sinew that shrank*. (Gen. xxxii. 32.)

[3] Wherein the Israelites, because of their wickedness and perverseness, were forbidden to eat certain animals which had been allowed their predecessors. (Chap. IV. See the notes there.)

was that which is in Becca ;[1] blessed, and a direction to all creatures.[2]   Therein are manifest signs : [3] the place where Abraham stood ; and whoever entereth therein, shall be safe. And *it is a duty* towards GOD, *incumbent* on those who are able to go thither,[4] to visit this house : but whosoever disbelieveth, verily GOD needeth not *the service of* any creature. Say, O ye who have received the scriptures, why do ye not believe in the signs of GOD ?   Say, O ye who have received the scriptures, why do ye keep back from the way of GOD him who believeth ?   Ye seek to make it crooked, and yet are witnesses *that it is the right* : but GOD will not be unmindful of what ye do.   O true believers, if ye obey some of those who have received the scriptures, they will render you infidels, after ye have believed : [5] and how can ye be infidels, when the signs of GOD are read unto you, and his apostle is among

[1] Mohammed received this passage when the Jews said that their Keblah, or the temple of Jerusalem, was more ancient than that of the Mohammedans, or the Caaba.   (Al Beidâwi. Jallalo'ddin.)   Becca is another name of Mecca. (Sale, Prel. Disc. page 3.)   Al Beidâwi observes that the Arabs used the " M " and " B " promiscuously in several words.

[2] *i.e.*, The Keblah, towards which they are to turn their faces in prayer.

[3] Such is the stone wherein they show the print of Abraham's feet, and the inviolable security of the place immediately mentioned ; that the birds light not on the roof of the Caaba, and wild beasts put off their fierceness there; that none who came against it in a hostile manner ever prospered (Jallalo'ddin.   Al Beidâwi), as appeared particularly in the unfortunate expedition of Abraha al Ashram (Chap. CV.); and other fables of the same stamp which the Mohammedans are taught to believe.

[4] According to an exposition of this passage attributed to Mohammed, he is supposed to be able to perform the pilgrimage, who can supply himself with provisions for the journey, and a beast to ride upon.   Al Shâfeï has decided that those who have money enough, if they cannot go themselves, must hire some other to go in their room.   Mâlec Ebn Ans thinks he is to be reckoned *able* who is strong and healthy, and can bear the fatigue of the journey on foot, if he has no beast to ride, and can also earn his living by the way.   But Abu Hanifa is of opinion that both money sufficient and health of body are requisite to make the pilgrimage a duty.   (Al Beidâwi.)

[5] This passage was revealed on occasion of a quarrel excited between the tribes of Al Aws and Al Khazraj, by one Shâs Ebn Kais, a Jew ; who—passing by some of both tribes as they were sitting and discoursing familiarly together and being inwardly vexed at the friendship and harmony which reigned among them on their embracing Mohammedism, whereas they had been, for 120 years before, most inveterate and mortal enemies, though descendants of two brothers—in order to set them at variance, sent a young man to sit down by them, directing him to relate the story of the battle of Boâth (a place near Medina), wherein, after a bloody fight, Al Aws had the better of Al Khazraj, and to repeat some verses on that subject.   The young man executed his orders ; whereupon those of each tribe began to magnify themselves, and to reflect on and irritate the other, till at length they called to arms, and great numbers getting together on each side, a dangerous battle had ensued, if Mohammed had not stepped in and reconciled them ; by representing to them how much they would be to blame if they returned to paganism, and revived those animosities which Islâm had composed ; and telling them that what had happened was a trick of the devil to disturb their present tranquillity   (Al Beidâwi.)

you? But he who cleaveth firmly unto GOD, is already directed into the right way. O believers, fear GOD with his true fear; and die not unless ye also be true believers. And cleave all *of you* unto the covenant[1] of GOD, and depart not *from it*, and remember the favour of GOD towards you : since ye were enemies, and he reconciled your hearts, and ye became companions and brethren by his favour : and ye were on the brink of a pit of fire, and he delivered you thence. Thus GOD declareth unto you his signs, that ye may be directed. Let there be people among you, who invite to the best *religion* ; and command that which is just, and forbid that which is evil ; and they shall be happy. And be not as they who are divided, and disagree *in matters of religion*,[2] after manifest proofs have been brought unto them : they shall suffer a great torment. On the day *of resurrection some* faces shall become white, and *other* faces shall become black.[3] And unto them whose faces shall become black, *God will say*, Have ye returned unto *your* unbelief, after ye had believed ? therefore taste the punishment, for that ye have been unbelievers : but they whose faces shall become white *shall be* in the mercy of GOD, therein shall they remain for ever. These are the signs of GOD : we recite them unto thee with truth. GOD will not deal unjustly with *his* creatures. And to GOD *belongeth* whatever is in heaven and on earth ; and to GOD shall *all* things return. Ye are the best nation that hath been raised up unto mankind : ye command that which is just, and ye forbid that which is unjust, and ye believe in GOD. And if they who have received the scriptures had believed, it had surely been the better for them : there are believers among them,[4] but the greater part of them are transgressors. They shall not hurt you, unless with a *slight* hurt ; and if they fight against you, they shall turn their backs to you, and they shall not be helped.[5] They are smitten with vile-

---

[1] Literally, *Hold fast by the cord of* GOD. That is, *Secure yourselves by adhering to* Islâm, which is here metaphorically expressed by a *cord*, because it is as sure a means of saving those who profess it from perishing hereafter, as holding by a rope is to prevent one's falling into a well, or other like place. It is said that Mohammed used for the same reason to call the Korân, Habl Allah al matin, *i.e.*, *the sure cord of* GOD. (Al Beidâwi.)

[2] *i.e.*, As the Jews and Christians, who dispute concerning the unity of GOD, the future state, &c. (Al Beidâwi.)

[3] Sale, Prel. Disc. Sect. IV.

[4] As Abd'allah Ebn Salâm and his companions (Al Beidâwi), and those of the tribes of Al Aws and Al Khazraj who had embraced Mohammedism.

[5] This verse, Al Beidâwi says, is one of those whose meaning is mysterious, and relates to something future : intimating the low condition to which the Jewish tribes of Koreidha, Nadir, Banu Kainokâ, and those who dwelt at Khaibar, were afterwards reduced by Mohammed.

ness wheresoever they are found ; unless *they obtain security* by *entering into* a treaty with GOD, and a treaty with men ;[1] and they draw on themselves indignation from GOD, and they are afflicted with poverty. This *they suffer*, because they disbelieved the signs of GOD, and slew the prophets unjustly ; this, because they were rebellious, and transgressed. *Yet* they are not *all* alike : there are of those who have received the scriptures, upright people ;[2] they meditate on the signs of GOD[3] in the night season, and worship ; they believe in GOD and the last day ; and command that which is just, and forbid that which is unjust, and zealously strive *to excel* in good works ; these are of the righteous. And ye shall not be denied *the reward of* the good which ye do ;[4] for GOD knoweth the pious. As for the unbelievers, their wealth shall not profit them at all, neither their children, against GOD : they *shall be* the companions of *hell* fire ; they shall continue therein for ever. The likeness of that which they lay out in this present life, is as a wind wherein there is a scorching cold : it falleth on the standing corn of those men who have injured their own souls, and destroyeth it. And GOD dealeth not unjustly with them ; but they injure their own souls. O true believers, contract not an intimate friendship *with any* besides yourselves :[5] they will not fail to corrupt you. They wish for that which may cause you to perish : their hatred hath already appeared from out of their mouths ; but what their breasts conceal is yet more inveterate. We have already shown you signs *of their ill will towards you*, if ye understand. Behold, ye love them, and they do not love you : ye believe in all the scriptures, and when they meet you, they say, We believe ; but when they assemble privately together, they bite their fingers' ends out of wrath against you. Say *unto them*, Die in your wrath : verily GOD knoweth the innermost part of *your* breasts. If good happen unto you, it grieveth them ; and if evil befall you, they rejoice at it. But if ye be patient, and fear *God*, their subtlety shall not hurt you at all ; for GOD comprehendeth whatever they do. *Call to mind* when thou wentest forth early from thy family, that thou mightest prepare the faithful a camp

---

[1] *i.e.*, Unless they either profess the Mohammedan religion, or submit to pay tribute.

[2] Those namely who have embraced Islâm.

[3] That is, the Korân.

[4] Some copies have a different reading in this passage, which they express in the third person : *They shall not be denied*, &c.

[5] *i.e.*, Of a different religion.

for war ; [1] and GOD heard and knew *it* ; when two companies
of you were anxiously thoughtful, so that ye became faint-
hearted ; [2] but GOD was the supporter of them both ; and in
GOD let the faithful trust. And GOD had already given you
the victory at Bedr,[3] when ye were inferior *in number* ;
therefore fear GOD, that ye may be thankful. When thou
saidst unto the faithful, Is it not enough for you, that your
LORD should assist you with three thousand angels, sent
down *from heaven* ? Verily if ye persevere, and fear *God*,
and *your enemies* come upon you suddenly, your LORD will
assist you with five thousand angels, distinguished *by their
horses and attire*.[4] And this GOD designed only as good
tidings for you[5] that your hearts might rest secure : for
victory is from GOD alone, the mighty, the wise. That he
should cut off the uttermost part of the unbelievers, or cast
them down, or that they should be overthrown and unsuc-

---

[1] This was at the battle of Ohod, a mountain about four miles to the north
of Medina. The Koreish, to revenge their loss at Bedr (see before), the
next year being the third of the Hejra, got together an army of 3,000 men,
among whom there were 200 horse, and 700 armed with coats of mail. These
forces marched under the conduct of Abu Sofiân and sat down at Dhu'lholeifa,
a village about six miles from Medina. Mohammed, being much inferior
to his enemies in numbers, at first determined to keep himself within the
town, and receive them there ; but afterwards, the advice of some of his
companions prevailing, he marched out against them at the head of 1,000
men (some say he had 1,050 men, others but 900), of whom 100 were armed
with coats of mail, but he had no more than one horse, besides his own, in
his whole army. With these forces he formed a camp in a village near Ohod,
which mountain he contrived to have on his back ; and the better to secure
his men from being surrounded, he placed fifty archers in the rear, with
strict orders not to quit their post. When they came to engage, Mohammed
had the better at first, but afterwards by the fault of his archers, who left
their ranks for the sake of the plunder, and suffered the enemies' horse
to encompass the Mohammedans and attack them in the rear, he lost the
day, and was very near losing his life, being struck down by a shower of
stones, and wounded in the face with two arrows, on pulling out of which
his two foreteeth dropped out. Of the Moslems seventy men were slain,
and among them Hamza the uncle of Mohammed, and of the infidels twenty-
two. (Abulfeda, in Vita Moham. p. 64, &c. Elmacin. l. x. Prideaux's
Life of Mahomet, p. 80.) To excuse the ill success of this battle, and to
raise the drooping courage of his followers, is Mohammed's drift in the
remaining part of this chapter.
[2] These were some of the families of Banu Salma of the tribe of Al Khazraj,
and Banu'l Hareth of the tribe of Al Aws, who composed the two wings of
Mohammed's army. Some ill impression had been made on them by Abo-
a'llah Ebn Obba Solûl, then an infidel, who having drawn off 300 men, told
them that they were going to certain death, and advised them to return
back with him ; but he could prevail on but a few, the others being kept
firm by the divine influence, as the following words intimate. (Al Beidâwi.
[3] See before.
[4] The angels who assisted the Mohammedans at Bedr, rode, say the
commentators, on black and white horses, and had on their heads white
and yellow sashes, the ends of which hung down between their shoulders.
[5] *i.e.*, As an earnest of future success.

cessful, *is nothing to thee.* It is no business of thine ; whether *God* be turned unto them, or whether he punish them ; they are surely unjust doers.[1] To GOD belongeth whatsoever is in heaven and on earth : he spareth whom he pleaseth, and he punisheth whom he pleaseth ; for GOD is merciful. O true believers, devour not usury, doubling it twofold ; but fear GOD, that ye may prosper : and fear the fire which is prepared for the unbelievers ; and obey GOD, and *his* apostle, that ye may obtain mercy. And run with emulation to *obtain* remission from your LORD, and paradise, whose breath *equalleth* the heavens and the earth, which is prepared for the godly ; who give alms in prosperity and adversity ; who bridle their anger and forgive men : for GOD loveth the beneficent.[2] And who, after they have committed a crime, or dealt unjustly with their own souls, remember GOD, and ask pardon for their sins (for who forgiveth sins except God ?) and persevere not in what they have done knowingly : their reward shall be pardon from their LORD, and gardens wherein rivers flow, they shall remain therein for ever : and how excellent is the reward of those who labour ! There have already been before you examples of punishment *of infidels,* therefore go through the earth, and behold what hath been the end of those who accuse *God's apostles* of imposture. This *book* is a declaration unto men, and a direction, and an admonition to the pious. And be not dismayed, neither be ye grieved ; for ye shall be superior *to the unbelievers* if ye believe. If a wound hath happened unto you *in war,*[3] a like wound hath already happened unto the *unbelieving* people :[4] and we cause these days *of different success* interchangeably to succeed each other among men ; that GOD

[1] This passage was revealed when Mohammed received the wounds above mentioned at the battle of Ohod, and cried out, *How shall that people prosper who have stained their prophet's face with blood, while he called them to their Lord ?* The person who wounded him was Otha the son of Abu Wakkâs. (Al Beidâwi. Abulfeda, ubi supra.)

[2] It is related of Hasan the son of Ali, that a slave having once thrown a dish on him boiling hot, as he sat at table, and fearing his master's resentment, fell immediately on his knees, and repeated these words, *Paradise is for those who bridle their anger* ; Hasan answered, *I am not angry.* The slave proceeded, *and for those who forgive men. I forgive you,* said Hasan. The slave, however, finished the verse, adding, *for GOD loveth the beneficent. Since it is so,* replied Hasan, *I give you your liberty, and four hundred pieces of silver.* (D'Herbelot, Bibl. Orient.) A noble instance of moderation and generosity.

[3] That is, by your being worsted at Ohod.

[4] When they were defeated at Bedr. It is observable that the number of Mohammedans slain at Ohod, was equal to that of the idolaters slain at Bedr ; which was so ordered by GOD for a reason to be given elsewhere. (Chap. VIII.)

may know those who believe, and may have martyrs from among you (GOD loveth not the workers of iniquity) ; and that GOD might prove those who believe, and destroy the infidels. Did ye imagine that ye should enter paradise, when as yet GOD knew not those among you who fought strenuously *in his cause* ; nor knew those who persevered with patience ? Moreover ye did sometime wish for death before that ye met it ;[1] but ye have now seen it, and ye looked on, *but retreated from it.* Mohammed is no more than an apostle ; the *other* apostles have already deceased before him : if he die therefore, or be slain, will ye turn back on your heels ?[2] but he who turneth back on his heels, will not hurt GOD at all ; and GOD will surely reward the thankful. No soul can die unless by the permission of GOD, according to *what is written in* the book containing the determinations of things.[3] And whoso chooseth the reward of this world, we will give him thereof : but whoso chooseth the reward of the world to come, we will give him thereof and we will surely reward the thankful. How many prophets have encountered those who had many myriads *of troops* : and yet they desponded not in their mind for what had befallen them in fighting for the religion of GOD, and were not weakened, neither behaved themselves in an abject manner ? GOD loveth those who persevere patiently. And their speech was no other than that they said, Our LORD forgive us our offences, and our transgressions in our business ; and confirm our feet, and help us against the unbelieving people. And

[1] Several of Mohammed's followers who were not present at Bedr, wished for an opportunity of obtaining, in another action, the like honour as those had gained who fell martyrs in that battle ; yet were discouraged on seeing the superior numbers of the idolaters in the expedition of Ohod. On which occasion this passage was revealed. (Al Beidâwi.)

[2] These words were revealed when it was reported in the battle of Ohod that Mohammed was slain ; whereupon the idolaters cried out to his followers, *Since your prophet is slain, return to your ancient religion, and to your friends : if Mohammed had been a prophet he had not been slain.* It is related that a Moslem named Ans Ebn al Nadar, uncle to Mâlec Ebn Ans, hearing these words, said aloud to his companions, *My friends, though Mohammed be slain, certainly Mohammed's Lord liveth and dieth not ; therefore value not your lives since the prophet is dead, but fight for the cause for which he fought ;* then he cried out, *O God, I am excused before thee, and acquitted in thy sight of what they say* ; and drawing his sword, fought valiantly till he was killed. (Al Beidâwi.)

[3] Mohammed, the more effectually to still the murmurs of his party on their defeat, represents to them that the time of every man's death is decreed and predetermined by GOD, and that those who fell in the battle could not have avoided their fate had they stayed at home ; whereas they had now obtained the glorious advantage of dying martyrs for the faith. Of the Mohammedan doctrine of absolute predestination I have spoken in another place. (Sale, Prel. Disc. Sect. IV, p. 111.)

GOD gave them the reward of this world, and a glorious reward in the life to come ; for GOD loveth the well-doers. O ye who believe, if ye obey the infidels, they will cause you to turn back on your heels, and ye will be turned back and perish :[1] but GOD is your LORD ; and he is the best helper. We will surely cast a dread into the hearts of the unbelievers,[2] because they have associated with GOD that concerning which he sent them down no power : their dwelling shall be the fire *of hell* ; and the receptacle of the wicked shall be miserable. GOD had already made good unto you his promise, when ye destroyed them by his permission,[3] until ye became faint-hearted, and disputed concerning the command *of the apostle*, and were rebellious ;[4] after *God* had shown you what ye desired. Some of you chose this present world, and others of you chose the world to come.[5] Then he turned you *to flight* from before them, that he might make trial of you (but he hath now pardoned you ; for GOD is endued with beneficence toward the faithful) ; when ye went up *as ye fled*, and looked not back on any ; while the apostle called you, in the uttermost part of you.[6] Therefore *God* rewarded you with affliction on affliction, that ye be not grieved *hereafter* for the *spoils* which ye fail of, nor for that which befalleth you ;[7] for GOD is well acquainted with whatever ye do.   Then

[1] This passage was also occasioned by the endeavours of the Koreish to seduce the Mohammedans to their old idolatry, as they fled in the battle of Ohod.

[2] To this Mohammed attributed the sudden retreat of Abu Sofiân and his troops, without making any farther advantage of their success ; only giving Mohammed a challenge to meet them next year at Bedr, which he accepted.   Others say that as they were on their march home, they repented they had not utterly extirpated the Mohammedans, and began to think of going back to Medina for that purpose, but were prevented by a sudden consternation or panic fear, which fell on them from GOD.   (Al Beidâwi.)

[3] *i.e.*, In the beginning of the battle, when the Moslems had the advantage, putting the idolaters to flight, and killing several of them.

[4] That is, till the bowmen, who were placed behind to prevent their being surrounded, seeing the enemy fly, quitted their post, contrary to Mohammed's express orders, and dispersed themselves to seize the plunder ; whereupon Khâled Ebn al Walid perceiving their disorder, fell on their rear with the horse which he commanded, and turned the fortune of the day.   It is related that though Abda'llah Ebn Johair, their captain, did all he could to make them keep their ranks, he had not ten that stayed with him out of the whole fifty.   (Al Beidâwi. Abulfeda, Vit. Moh. p. 65, 66, and note.)

[5] The former were they who, tempted by the spoil, quitted their post ; and the latter they who stood firm by their leader.

[6] Crying aloud, *Come hither to me, O servants of* GOD !   *I am the apostle of* GOD ; *he who returneth back shall enter paradise.*   But notwithstanding all his endeavours to rally his men, he could not get above thirty of them about him.

[7] *i.e.*, GOD punished your avarice and disobedience by suffering you to be beaten by your enemies, and to be discouraged by the report of your prophet's

he sent down upon you after affliction security ; a soft sleep which fell on some part of you ; but *other* part were troubled by their own souls ;[1] falsely thinking of GOD a foolish imagination, saying, Will anything of the matter *happen* unto us ?[2] Say, Verily the matter *belongeth* wholly unto GOD. They concealed in their minds what they declared not unto thee : saying,[3] If anything of the matter had happened unto us,[4] we had not been slain here. Answer, If ye had been in your houses, verily they would have gone forth to fight, whose slaughter was decreed, to the places where they died, and *this came to pass* that GOD might try what was in your breasts, and might discern what was in your hearts ; for GOD knoweth the innermost parts of the breasts *of men.* Verily they among you who turned their backs on the day whereon the two armies met each other *at Ohod*, Satan caused them to slip, for some *crime* which they had committed :[5] but now hath GOD forgiven them ; for GOD is gracious and ·nerciful. O true believers, be not as they who believe not, and said of their brethren, when they had journeyed in the land or had been at war, If they had been with us, those had not died, nor had these been slain : *whereas what befell them was so ordained* that GOD might make it *matter of* sighing in their hearts. GOD giveth life, and causeth to die : and GOD seeth that which ye do. Moreover if ye be slain, or die in defence of the religion of GOD ; verily pardon from GOD, and mercy, are better than what they heap together *of worldly riches.* And if ye die, or be slain, verily unto GOD shall ye be gathered. And as to the mercy *granted unto the disobedient* from GOD, thou, *O Mohammed*, hast been mild towards them ; but if thou hadst been severe and hard-hearted, they had surely separated themselves from about thee. Therefore forgive them, and ask pardon for them : and consult them in the

death ; that ye might be inured to patience under adverse fortune, and not repine at any loss or disappointment for the future.

[1] After the action, those who had stood firm in the battle were refreshed as they lay in the field by falling into an agreeable sleep, so that the swords fell out of their hands ; but those who had behaved themselves ill were troubled in their minds, imagining they were now given over to destruction. (Al Beidâwi. Jallalo'ddin,)

[2] That is, is there any appearance of success, or of the divine favour and assistance which we have been promised ? (Al Beidâwi.)

[3] *i.e.*, To themselves, or to one another in private.

[4] If GOD had assisted us according to his promise ; or, as others interpret the words, if we had taken the advice of Abda'llah Ebn Obba Solûl, and had kept within the town of Medina, our companions had not lost their lives, (Al Beidâwi.)

[5] viz., For their covetousness in quitting their post to seize the plunder.

affair *of war* ; and after thou hast deliberated, trust in GOD ; for GOD loveth those who trust *in him.* If GOD help you, none shall conquer you ; but if he desert you, who is it that will help you after him ?   Therefore in GOD let the faithful trust.   It is not *the part* of a prophet to defraud,[1] for he who defraudeth, shall bring with him what he hath defrauded *any one of,* on the day of the resurrection.[2]   Then shall every soul be paid what he hath gained ; and they shall not be treated unjustly.   Shall he therefore who followeth that which is well pleasing unto GOD, be as he who bringeth on himself wrath from GOD, and whose receptacle is hell ?   an evil journey shall it be *thither.*   There shall be degrees *of rewards and punishments* with GOD, for GOD seeth what they do.   Now hath GOD been gracious unto the believers when he raised up among them an apostle of their own nation,[3] who should recite his signs unto them, and purify them, and teach them the book *of the Korân* and wisdom :[4] whereas they were before in manifest error.   After a misfortune hath befallen you *at Ohod* (ye had already obtained two equal advantages),[5] do ye say, Whence *cometh* this ?   Answer, This is from yourselves :[6] for GOD is almighty.   And what happened unto you, on the day whereon the two armies met, was certainly by the permission of GOD ; and that he might know the faithful, and that he might know the ungodly. It was said unto them, Come, fight for the religion of GOD, or drive back *the enemy* : they answered, If we had known *ye went out* to fight, we had certainly followed you.[7]   They were

---

[1] This passage was revealed, as some say, on the division of the spoil at Bedr ; when some of the soldiers suspected Mohammed of having privately taken a scarlet carpet made all of silk and very rich, which was missing. (Al Beidâwi. Jallalo'ddin.) Others suppose the archers, who occasioned the loss of the battle of Ohod, left their station because they imagined Mohammed would not give them their share of the plunder ; because, as it is related, he once sent out a party as an advanced guard, and in the meantime attacking the enemy, took some spoils which he divided among those who were with him in the action, and gave nothing to the party that was absent on duty.   (Al Beidâwi)

[2] According to a tradition of Mohammed, whoever cheateth another will on the day of judgment carry his fraudulent purchase publicly on his neck.

[3] Some copies, instead of *min anfosihim, i.e., of themselves,* read *min-anfasihim, i.e., of the noblest among them ;* for such was the tribe of Koreish, of which Mohammed was descended.   (Al Beidâwi.)

[4] *i.e.,* The Sonna.   (Al Beidâwi.)

[5] viz., In the battle of Bedr, where ye slew seventy of the enemy, equalling the number of those who lost their lives at Ohod, and also took as many prisoners.

[6] It was the consequence of your disobeying the orders of the prophet, and abandoning your post for the sake of plunder.

[7] That is, if we had conceived the least hope of success when ye marched out of Medina to encounter the infidels, and had not known that ye went

on that day nearer unto unbelief than they were to faith : they spake with their mouths what was not in their hearts : but GOD perfectly knew what they concealed ; who said of their brethren, *while themselves* stayed *at home,* if they had obeyed us, they had not been slain. Say, Then keep back death from yourselves, if ye say truth. Thou shalt in no wise reckon those who have been slain *at Ohod* in the cause of GOD, dead ; nay, they are sustained alive with their LORD,[1] rejoicing for what GOD of his favour hath granted them ; and being glad for those who, coming after them, have not as yet overtaken them ;[2] because there shall no fear come on them, neither shall they be grieved. They are filled with joy for the favour *which they have received* from GOD, and *his* bounty ; and for that GOD suffereth not the reward of the faithful to perish. They who hearkened unto GOD and *his* apostle, after a wound had befallen them *at Ohod,*[3] such of them as do good works, and fear GOD, shall have a great reward ; unto whom *certain* men said, Verily the men *of Mecca* have already gathered *forces* against you, be ye therefore afraid of them :[4] but *this* increaseth their faith, and they said,

---

rather to certain destruction than to battle, we had gone with you. But this Mohammed here tells them was only a feigned excuse ; the true reason of their staying behind being their want of faith and firmness in their religion. (Al Beidâwi.)

[1] See before, p. 22.

[2] *i.e.,* Rejoicing also for their sakes, who are destined to suffer martyrdom but have not as yet attained it. (Rev. vi. 11.)

[3] The commentators differ a little as to the occasion of this passage. When news was brought to Mohammed, after the battle of Ohod, that the enemy, repenting of their retreat, were returning towards Medina, he called about him those who had stood by him in the battle, and marched out to meet the enemy as far as Homarâ al Asad, about eight miles from that town, notwithstanding several of his men were so ill of their wounds that they were forced to be carried ; but a panic fear having seized the army of the Koreish, they changed their resolution and continued their march home ; of which Mohammed having received intelligence, he also went back to Medina ; and, according to some commentators, the Korân here approves the faith and courage of those who attended the prophet on this occasion. Others say the persons intended in this passage were those who went with Mohammed the next year, to meet Abu Sofiân and the Koreish, according to their challenge, at Bedr, where they waited some time for the enemy, and then returned home ; for the Koreish, though they set out from Mecca, yet never came so far as the place of appointment, their hearts failing them on their march ; which Mohammed attributed to their being struck with a terror from GOD. (Al Beidâwi.) This expedition the Arabian histories call the *second,* or *lesser expedition of* Bedr.

[4] The persons who thus endeavoured to discourage the Mohammedans were, according to one tradition, some of the tribe of Abd Kais, who, going to Medina, were bribed by Abu Sofiân with a camel's load of dried raisins ; and, according to another tradition, it was Noaim Ebn Masúd al Ashjaï who was also bribed with a she-camel ten months gone with young (a valuable present in Arabia). This Noaim, they say, finding Mohammed and his men

God is our support, and the most excellent patron. Wherefore they returned with favour from God, and advantage, no evil befell them : and they followed what was well pleasing unto God ; for God is endowed with great liberality. Verily that devil [2] would cause you to fear his friends : but be ye not afraid of them ; but fear me, if ye be true believers. They shall not grieve thee, who emulously hasten unto infidelity ; for they shall never hurt God at all. God will not give them a part in the next life, and they shall suffer a great punishment. Surely those who purchase infidelity with faith, shall by no means hurt God at all, but they shall suffer a grievous punishment. And let not the unbelievers think, because we grant them lives long and prosperous, that it is better for their souls : we grant them long and prosperous lives only that their iniquity may be increased ; and they shall suffer an ignominious punishment. God is not *disposed* to leave the faithful in the condition which ye are now in,[3] until he sever the wicked from the good ; nor is God *disposed* to make you acquainted with what is a hidden secret, but God chooseth such of his apostles as he pleaseth, *to reveal his mind unto* :[4] believe therefore in God, and his apostles ; and if ye believe, and fear *God*, ye shall receive a great reward. And let not those who are covetous of what God of his bounty hath granted them, imagine that *their avarice* is better for them : nay, rather it is worse for them. That which they have covetously reserved shall be bound as a collar about their neck,[5] on the day of the resurrection : unto God *belongeth* the inheritance of heaven and earth ; and God is well acquainted with what ye do. God hath already heard the saying of those who said, Verily God is

preparing for the expedition, told them that Abu Sofiân, to spare them the pains of coming so far as Bedr, would seek them in their own houses, and that none of them could possibly escape otherwise than by timely flight. Upon which Mohammed, seeing his followers a little dispirited, swore that he would go himself though not one of them went with him. And accordingly he set out with seventy horsemen, every one of them crying out, *Hashna Allah, i.e.*, God *is our support*. (Al Beidâwi. Jallalo'ddin.)

[1] While they stayed at Bedr expecting the enemy, they opened a kind of fair there, and traded to very considerable profit. (Al Beidâwi.)

[2] Meaning either Noaim, or Abu Sofiân himself.

[3] That is, he will not suffer the good and sincere among you to continue indiscriminately mixed with the wicked and hypocritical.

[4] This passage was revealed on the rebellious and disobedient Mohammedans telling Mohammed that if he was a true prophet he could easily distinguish those who sincerely believed from the dissemblers. (Al Beidâwi.)

[5] Mohammed is said to have declared, that whoever pays not his legal contribution of alms duly shall have a serpent twisted about his neck at the resurrection. (Al Beidâwi. Jallalo'ddin.)

poor, and we are rich :[1] we will surely write down what they have said, and the slaughter which they have made of the prophets without a cause ; and we say *unto them,* Taste ye the pain of burning.   This *shall they suffer* for the *evil* which their hands have sent before them, and because GOD is not unjust towards mankind ; who *also* say, Surely GOD hath commanded us, that we should not give credit to *any* apostle, until *one* should come unto us with a sacrifice, which should be consumed by fire.[2]   Say, Apostles have already come unto you before me,[3] with plain proofs, and with the *miracle* which ye mention :   why therefore have ye slain them, if ye speak truth ?   If they accuse thee of imposture, the apostles before thee have also been accounted impostors, who brought evident demonstrations, and the scriptures, and the book which enlightened *the understanding.*   Every soul shall taste of death, and ye shall have your rewards on the day of resurrection ;   and he who shall be far removed from *hell* fire, and shall be admitted into paradise, shall be happy ;   but the present life is only a deceitful provision.   Ye shall surely be

---

[1] It is related that Mohammed, writing to the Jews of the tribe of Kainokâ to invite them to Islâm, and exhorting them, among other things, in the words of the Korân (Chap. II.), *to lend unto* GOD *on good usury,* Phineas Ebn Azûra, on hearing that expression, said, *Surely* GOD *is poor, since they ask to borrow for him.*   Whereupon Abu Becr, who was the bearer of that letter, struck him on the face, and told him that if it had not been for the truce between them, he would have struck off his head ; and on Phineas's complaining to Mohammed of Abu Becr's ill usage, this passage was revealed.   (Al Beidâwi.)

[2] The Jews, say the commentators, insisted that it was a peculiar proof of the mission of all the prophets sent to them, that they could, by their prayers, bring down fire from heaven to consume the sacrifice, and therefore they expected Mohammed should do the like.   And some Mohammedan doctors agree that GOD appointed this miracle as the test of all their prophets, except only Jesus and Mohammed (Jallalo'ddin) ; though others say any other miracle was a proof full as sufficient as the bringing down fire from heaven.   (Al Beidâwi.)   The Arabian Jews seem to have drawn a general consequence from some particular instances of this miracle in the Old Testament.   (Levit. ix. 24 ; 1 Chron. xxi. 26 ; 2 Chron. vii. 1 ; 1 Kings xviii. 38.)   And the Jews at this day say, that first the fire which fell from heaven on the altar of the tabernacle (Levit. ix. 24), after the consecration of Aaron and his sons, and afterwards that which descended on the altar of Solomon's temple, at the dedication of that structure (2 Chron. vii. 1), was fed and constantly maintained there by the priests, both day and night, without being suffered once to go out, till it was extinguished, as some think, in the reign of Manasses (Talmud, Zebachim, c. 6), but, according to the more received opinion, when the temple was destroyed by the Chaldeans.   Several Christians (Prideaux's Connect. part i. bk. iii. p. 158) have given credit to this assertion of the Jews, with what reason I shall not here inquire ; and the Jews, in consequence of this notion, might probably expect that a prophet who came to restore GOD's true religion, should rekindle for them this heavenly fire, which they have not been favoured with since the Babylonish captivity.

[3] Among these the commentators reckon Zacharias and John the Baptist.

proved in your possessions, and *in* your persons ; and ye shall bear from those unto whom the scripture was delivered before you, and from the idolaters, much hurt : but if ye be patient, and fear *God*, this is a matter that is absolutely determined. And when GOD accepted the covenant of those to whom the book *of the law* was given, *saying*, Ye shall surely publish it unto mankind, ye shall not hide it ; yet they threw it behind their backs, and sold it for a small price ; but woeful *is the price* for which they have sold *it*.[1]   Think not that they who rejoice at what they have done, and expect to be praised for what they have not done ; [2] think not, *O prophet*, that they shall escape from punishment, for they shall suffer a painful punishment ; and unto GOD *belongeth* the kingdom of heaven and earth ; GOD is almighty.   Now in the creation of heaven and earth, and the vicissitude of night and day, are signs unto those who are endued with understanding ; who remember GOD standing, and sitting, and *lying* on their sides ;[3] and meditate on the creation of heaven and earth, *saying*, O LORD, thou hast not created this in vain ; far be it from thee : therefore deliver us from the torment of *hell* fire : O LORD, surely whom thou shalt throw into the fire, thou wilt also cover with shame ; nor shall the ungodly have any to help them.   O LORD, we have heard of a preacher[4] inviting *us* to the faith, *and saying*, Believe in your LORD : and we believed.   O LORD, forgive us therefore our sins, and expiate our evil deeds from us, and make us to die with the righteous.   O LORD, give us also *the reward* which thou hast promised by thy apostles ; and cover us not with shame on the day of resurrection ; for thou art not contrary to the promise.   Their LORD therefore answereth them, *saying*, I will not suffer the work of him among you who worketh

---

[1] *i.e.*, Dearly shall they pay hereafter for taking bribes to stifle the truth. *Whoever concealeth the knowledge which* GOD *has given him*, says Mohammed, GOD *shall put on him a bridle of fire on the day of resurrection.*

[2] *i.e.*, Who think they have done a commendable deed in concealing and dissembling the testimonies in the Pentateuch concerning Mohammed, and in disobeying GOD'S commands to the contrary.   It is said that, Mohammed, once asking some Jews concerning a passage in their law, they gave him an answer very different from the truth, and were mightily pleased that they had, as they thought, deceived him.   Others, however, think this passage relates to some pretended Mohammedans who rejoiced in their hypocrisy, and expected to be commended for their wickedness.   (Al Beidâwi.)

[3] viz., At all times and in all postures.   Al Beidâwi mentions a saying of Mohammed to one Imrân Ebn Hosein, to this purpose : *Pray standing, if thou art able; if not, sitting; and if thou canst not sit up, then as thou liest along.*   Al Shâfeï directs that the sick should pray lying on their right side.

[4] Namely, Mohammed, with the Korân.

to be lost, whether he be male or female :[1] the one of you is from the other. They therefore who have left their country, and have been turned out of their houses, and have suffered for my sake, and have been slain in battle ; verily I will expiate their evil deeds from them, and I will surely bring them into gardens watered by rivers ; a reward from GOD : and with GOD is the most excellent reward. Let not the prosperous dealing of the unbelievers in the land deceive thee :[2] *it is but* a slender provision ;[3] *and* then their receptacle shall be hell ; an unhappy couch *shall it be*. But they who fear their LORD shall have gardens through which rivers flow, they shall continue therein for ever : this is the gift of GOD ; for what is with GOD shall be better for the righteous *than short-lived worldly prosperity*. There are some of those who have received the scriptures, who believe in GOD, and that which hath been sent down unto you, and that which hath been sent down to them, submitting themselves unto GOD ;[4] they tell not the signs of GOD for a small price : these shall have their reward with their LORD ; for GOD is swift in taking an account.[5] O true believers, be patient, and strive to excel in patience, and be constant-minded, and fear GOD, that ye may be happy.

[1] These words were added, as some relate, on Omm Salma, one of the prophet's wives, telling him that she had observed GOD often made mention of the men who fled their country for the sake of their faith, but took no notice of the women. (Al Beidâwi.)

[2] The original word properly signifies success in the affairs of life, and particularly in trade. It is said that some of Mohammed's followers observing the prosperity the idolaters enjoyed, expressed their regret that those enemies of GOD should live in such ease and plenty, while they themselves were perishing for hunger and fatigue ; whereupon this passage was revealed. (Al Beidâwi.)

[3] Because of its short continuance.

[4] The persons here meant, some will have to be Abda'llah Ebn Salâm (see before, p. 58) and his companions ; others suppose they were forty Arabs of Najrân, or thirty-two Ethiopians, or else eight Greeks, who were converted from Christianity to Mohammedism ; and others say this passage was revealed in the ninth year of the Hejra, when Mohammed, on Gabriel's bringing him the news of the death of Ashama king of Ethiopia, who had embraced the Mohammedan religion some years before (Sale, Prel. Disc. Sect. II, 48), prayed for the soul of the departed ; at which some of his hypo-critical followers were displeased, and wondered that he should pray for a Christian proselyte whom he had never seen. (Al Beidâwi.)

[5] See Sale, Prel. Disc. Sect. IV.

IV

THE CHAPTER OF WOMEN [1]

Revealed at Medina.

ıN THE NAME OF THE MOST MERCIFUL GOD.

O MEN, fear your LORD, who hath created you out of one man, and out of him created his wife, and from the two hath multiplied many men and women : and fear GOD by whom ye beseech one another ; [2] and *respect* women, [3] *who have borne you,* for GOD is watching over you. And give the orphans *when they come to age* their substance ; and render *them* not in exchange bad for good : [4] and devour not their substance, *by adding it* to your substance ; for this is a great sin. And if ye fear that ye shall not act with equity towards orphans *of the female sex,* take in marriage of such *other* women as please you, two, or three, or four, *and not more.* [5] But if ye fear that ye cannot act equitably *towards so many, marry* one *only,* or the slaves which ye shall have acquired. [6] This will be easier, that ye swerve not *from righteousness.* And give women their dowry freely ; but if they voluntarily remit unto you any part of it, enjoy it with satisfaction and advantage. And give not unto those who are weak of understanding, the substance which GOD hath appointed you to preserve *for them* ; but maintain them thereout, and clothe

[1] This title was given to this chapter, because it chiefly treats of matters relating to women ; as, marriages, divorces, dower, prohibited degrees, &c.

[2] Saying, I beseech thee for GOD's sake. (Al Beidâwi.)

[3] Literally, *the wombs.*

[4] That is, take not what ye find of value among their effects to your own use, and give them worse in its stead.

[5] The commentators understand this passage differently. The true meaning seems to be as it is here translated ; Mohammed advising his followers that if they found they should wrong the female orphans under their care, either by marrying them against their inclinations, for the sake of their riches or beauty, or by not using or maintaining them so well as they ought, by reason of their having already several wives, they should rather choose to marry other women, to avoid all occasion of sin. (Al Beidâwi.) Others say that when this passage was revealed, many of the Arabians, fearing trouble and temptation, refused to take upon them the charge of orphans, and yet multiplied wives to a great excess, and used them ill ; or, as others write, gave themselves up to fornication ; which occasioned the passage. And according to these, its meaning must be either that if they feared they could not act justly towards orphans, they had as great reason to apprehend they could not deal equitably with so many wives, and therefore are commanded to marry but a certain number ; or else, that since fornication was a crime as well as wronging of orphans, they ought to avoid that also, by marrying according to their abilities. (Al Beidâwi. Jallalo'ddin.)

[6] For slaves requiring not so large a dower, nor so good and plentiful a maintenance as free women, a man might keep several of the former, as easily as one of the latter.

them, and speak kindly unto them. And examine the orphans[1] until they attain *the age of* marriage :[2] but if ye perceive they are able to manage their affairs well, deliver their substance unto them ; and waste it not extravagantly, or hastily, because they grow up.[3] Let him who is rich abstain *entirely from the orphan's estates* ; and let him who is poor take *thereof* according to what shall be reasonable.[4] And when ye deliver their substance unto them, call witnesses *thereof* in their presence : GOD taketh sufficient account *of your actions*. Men ought to have a part of what *their* parents and kindred leave *behind them when they die* : and women *also* ought to have a part of what *their* parents and kindred leave,[5] whether it be little, or whether it be much ; a determinate part *is due to them*. And when they who are of kin are present at the dividing *of what is left*, and also the orphans, and the poor ; distribute unto them *some part* thereof ; and *if the estate be too small, at least* speak comfortably unto them. And let those fear *to abuse orphans*, who if they leave behind them a weak offspring, are solicitous for them : let them therefore fear GOD, and speak that which is convenient.[6] Surely they who devour the possessions of orphans unjustly, shall swallow down nothing but fire into their bellies, and shall broil in raging flames. GOD hath *thus* commanded you concerning your children. A male shall have as much as the share of two females :[7] but if they be females *only, and* above two *in number*, they shall have two third parts of what *the deceased* shall leave ;[8] and if there be *but* one, she shall have the half.[9] And the parents of *the*

---

[1] *i.e.*, Try whether they be well grounded in the principles of religion and have sufficient prudence for the management of their affairs. Under this expression is also comprehended the duty of a curator's instructing his pupils in those respects.

[2] Or age of maturity, which is generally reckoned to be fifteen ; a decision supported by a tradition of their prophet, though Abu Hanifah thinks eighteen the proper age. (Al Beidâwi.)

[3] *i.e.*, Because they will shortly be of age to receive what belongs to them.

[4] That is, no more than what shall make sufficient recompence for the trouble of their education.

[5] This law was given to abolish a custom of the pagan Arabs, who suffered not women or children to have any part of their husband's or father's inheritance, on pretence that they only should inherit who were able to go to war. (Al Beidâwi.)

[6] viz., Either to comfort the children, or to assure the dying father they shall be justly dealt by. (Al Beidâwi.)

[7] This is the general rule to be followed in the distribution of the estate of the deceased, as may be observed in the following cases. (Sale, Prel. Disc. Sect. VI.)

[8] Or if there be two and no more, they will have the same share.

[9] And the remaining third part, or the remaining moiety of the estate,

deceased shall have each of them a sixth part of what he shall leave, if he have a child : but if he have no child, and his parents be his heirs, then his mother shall have the third part.[1]   And if he have brethren, his mother shall have a sixth part, after the legacies [2] which he shall bequeath, and his debts *be paid*. Ye know not whether your parents or your children be of greater use unto you.   *This is* an ordinance from GOD, and GOD is knowing and wise.   Moreover ye may claim half of what your wives shall leave, if they have no issue ; but if they have issue, then ye shall have the fourth part of what they shall leave, after the legacies which they shall bequeath, and the debts *be paid*.   They also shall have the fourth part of what ye shall leave, in case ye have no issue ; but if ye have issue, then they shall have the eighth part of what ye shall leave, after the legacies which ye shall bequeath and your debts *be paid*.   And if a man or woman's *substance* be inherited by a distant relation,[3] and he *or she* have a brother or sister ;   each of the two shall have a sixth part *of the estate* [4]   But if there be more than this *number*, they shall be *equal* sharers in a third part, after *payment of* the legacies which shall be bequeathed, and the debts, without prejudice *to the heirs*.   *This is* an ordinance from GOD : and GOD is knowing and gracious.   These are the statutes of GOD.   And whoso obeyeth GOD and his apostle, GOD shall lead him into gardens wherein rivers flow, he shall continue therein for ever ; and this shall be great happiness.   But whoso disobeyeth GOD, and his apostle, and transgresseth his statutes, GOD shall cast him into *hell* fire ; he shall remain therein for ever, and he shall suffer a shameful punishment.   If any of your women be guilty of whore-

---

which is not here expressly disposed of, if the deceased leaves behind him no son, nor a father, goes to the public treasury.   It must be observed that Mr. Selden is certainly mistaken when, in explaining this passage of the Korân, he says that where there is a son and an only daughter, each of them will have a moiety (Selden, de Success. ad Leges Ebræor. l. 1, c. 1.), for the daughter can have a moiety but in one case only, that is, where there is no son ; for if there be a son, she can have but a third, according to the above-mentioned rule.

[1] And his father consequently the other two-thirds.   (Al Beidâwi.)

[2] By *legacies*, in this and the following passages, are chiefly meant those bequeathed to pious uses ; for the Mohammedans approve not of a person's giving away his substance from his family and near relations on any other account.

[3] For this may happen by contract, or on some other special occasion.

[4] Here and in the next case, the brother and sister are made equal sharers, which is an exception to the general rule of giving a male twice as much as a female ; and the reason is said to be because of the smallness of the portions, which deserve not such exactness of distribution ; for in other

dom,[1] produce four witnesses from among you against them,
and if they bear witness *against them*, imprison them in
separate apartments until death release them, or GOD afford-
eth them a way *to escape*.[2]   And if two of you commit the
like *wickedness*,[3] punish them both :[4] but if they repent
and amend, let them both alone ; for GOD is easy to be
reconciled and merciful.   Verily repentance *will be accepted*
with GOD, from those who do evil ignorantly, and then repent
speedily ; unto them will GOD be turned : for GOD is knowing
and wise.   But no repentance *shall be accepted* from those who
do evil until *the time* when death presenteth itself unto one of
them, *and he* saith, Verily I repent now ; nor unto those who
die unbelievers : for them have we prepared a grievous
punishment.   O true believers, it is not lawful for you to be
heirs of women against their will,[5] nor to hinder them *from
marrying others*,[6] that ye may take away part of what ye
have given them *in dowry* ; unless they have been guilty of a

---

cases the rule holds between brother and sister, as well as other relations.
(See this chapter, near the end.)

[1] Either adultery or fornication.

[2] Their punishment, in the beginning of Mohammedism, was to be
immured till they died, but afterwards this cruel doom was mitigated, and
they might avoid it by undergoing the punishment ordained in its stead by
the Sonna, according to which the maidens are to be scourge i with a hundred stripes, and to be banished for a full year ; and the married women to
be stoned. (Jallalo'ddin.)

[3] The commentators are not agreed whether the text speaks of fornication
or sodomy. Al Zamakhshari, and from him, Al Beidâwi, supposes the former
is here meant ; but Jallalo'ddin is of opinion that the crime intended in this
passage must be committed between two men, and not between a man and
a woman ; not only because the pronouns are in the masculine gender, but
because both are ordered to suffer the same slight punishment, and are
both allowed the same repentance and indulgence ; and especially tor that a
different and much severer punishment is appointed for the women in the
preceding words. Abu'l Kâsem Hebatallah takes simple fornication to be
the crime intended, and that this passage is abrogated by that of the 24th
chapter, where the man and the woman who shall be guilty of fornication
are ordered to be scourged with a hundred stripes each.

[4] The original is, *Do them some hurt* or *damage* : by which some understand
that they are only to reproach them in public (Jallalo'ddin, Yahya, Abul
Kâsem Hebatallah, Al Beidâwi). or strike them on the head with their
slippers (Jallalo'ddin, Al Beidâwi)—a great indignity in the East,—though
some imagine they may be scourged. (Al Beidâwi.)

[5] It was customary among the pagan Arabs, when a man died, for one
of his relations to claim a right to his widow, which he asserted by throwing
his garment over her ; and then he either married her himself, if he thought
fit, on assigning her the same dower that her former husband had done,
or kept her dower and married her to another, or else refused to let her marry
unless she redeemed herself by quitting what she might claim of her husband's
goods. (Al Beidâwi.) This unjust custom is abolished by this passage.

[6] Some say these words are directed to husbands who used to imprison
their wives without any just cause, and out of covetousness, merely to make
them relinquish their dower or their inheritance. (Al Beidâwi.)

manifest crime :[1] but converse kindly with them. And if ye hate them, it may happen that ye may hate a thing wherein GOD hath placed much good. If ye be desirous to exchange a wife for *another* wife,[2] and ye have already given one of them a talent ;[3] take not away anything therefrom :[4] will ye take it by slandering *her*, and *doing her* manifest injustice ? And how can ye take it, since the one of you hath gone in unto the other, and they have received from you a firm covenant ? Marry not women whom your fathers have had to wife (except what is already past) : for this is uncleanness, and an abomination, and an evil way. Ye are forbidden *to marry* your mothers, and your daughters, and your sisters, and your aunts both on the father's and on the mother's side, and your brother's daughters, and your sister's daughters, and your mothers who have given you suck, and your foster-sisters, and your wives' mothers, and your daughters-in-law which are under your tuition, *born* of your wives unto whom ye have gone in (but if ye have not gone in unto them, it shall be no sin in you *to marry them*), and the wives of your sons who *proceed* out of your loins ; and *ye are also forbidden* to take to wife two sisters ;[5] except what is already past : for GOD is gracious and merciful. (V.) *Ye are* also *forbidden to take to wife* free women *who are married*, except those *women* whom your right hands shall possess *as slaves.*[6] *This is* ordained you from GOD. Whatever is beside this, is allowed you ; that ye may with your substance provide *wives* for yourselves, acting that which is right, and avoiding whoredom. And for the advantage which ye receive from them, give them their reward,[7] according to what is ordained : but it shall be no crime in you to make any other agreement among yourselves, [8] after the ordinance *shall be complied with* ; for GOD is knowing and wise. Whoso among you hath

---

[1] Such as disobedience, ill behaviour, immodesty, and the like. (A Beidâwi.)
[2] That is, by divorcing one, and marrying another.
[3] *i.e.*, Ever so large a dower.
[4] See Chap. II.
[5] The same was also prohibited by the Levitical law. (Levit. xviii. 18.)
[6] According to this passage—with which Section V begins—it is not lawful to marry a free woman that is already married, be she Mohammedan or not, unless she be legally parted from her husband by divorce ; but it is lawful to marry those who are slaves, or taken in war, after they shall have gone through the proper purifications, though their husbands be living. According to Abu Hanifah, it is not lawful to marry such whose husbands shall be taken, or in actual slavery with them. (Al Beidâwi.)
[7] That is, assign them their dower.
[8] That is, either to increase the dower, or to abate some part or even the whole of it.

not means sufficient that he may marry free women, who are believers, *let him marry* with such of your maid-servants whom your right hands possess, as are true believers ; for GOD well knoweth your faith. Ye are the one from the other :[1] therefore marry them with the consent of their masters ; and give them their dower according to justice ; *such as are* modest, not guilty of whoredom, nor entertaining lovers. And when they are married, if they be guilty of adultery, they shall suffer half the punishment which *is appointed* for the free women.[2] This *is allowed* unto him among you, who feareth to sin *by marrying free women* ; but if ye abstain *from marrying slaves, it will be* better for you ; GOD is gracious and merciful. GOD is willing to declare *these things* unto you, and to direct you according to the ordinances of those who *have gone* before you,[3] and to be merciful unto you. GOD is knowing and wise. GOD desireth to be gracious unto you ; but they who follow *their* lusts,[4] desire that ye should turn aside *from the truth* with great deviation. GOD is minded to make *his religion* light unto you : for man was created weak.[5] O true believers, consume not your wealth among yourselves in vanity ;[6] unless there be merchandising among you by mutual consent : neither slay yourselves ;[7] for GOD is merciful towards you : and whoever doth this maliciously[8] and wickedly, he will surely cast him to be broiled in *hell* fire ; and this is easy with GOD. If ye turn aside from the grievous sins,[9] of those which ye are forbidden *to commit,* we will

[1] Being alike descended from Adam, and of the same faith. (Al Beidâwi.)

[2] The reason of this is because they are not presumed to have had so good an education. A slave, therefore, in such a case, is to have fifty stripes, and to be banished for half a year ; but she shall not be stoned, because it is a punishment which cannot be inflicted by halves. (Al Beidâwi.)

[3] viz., Of the prophets, and other holy and prudent men of former ages. (Jallalo'ddin Al Beidâwi.)

[4] Some commentators suppose that these words have a particular regard to the Magians, who formerly were frequently guilty of incestuous marriages, their prophet Zerdusht having allowed them to take their mothers and sisters to wife ; and also to the Jews, who likewise might marry within some of the degrees here prohibited. (Al Beidâwi.)

[5] Being unable to refrain from women, and too subject to be led away by carnal appetites. (Al Beidâwi. Jallalo'ddin)

[6] That is, employ it not in things prohibited by GOD ; such as usury, extortion, rapine, gaming, and the like. (Al Beidâwi.)

[7] Literally, *slay not your souls* ; *i.e.,* says Jallalo'ddin, by committing mortal sins, or such crimes as will destroy them. Others, however, are of opinion that self-murder, which the gentile Indians did, and still do, often practise in honour of their idols, or else the taking away the life of any true believer, is hereby forbidden. (Al Beidâwi.)

[8] See Wisdom xvi. 14, in the Vulgate.

[9] These sins Al Beidâwi, from a tradition of Mohammed, reckons to be seven (equalling in number the sins called deadly by Christians), that is to

cleanse you from your *smaller* faults ; and will introduce you
into paradise with an honourable entry. Covet not that
which GOD hath bestowed on some of you preferably to
others.[1]   Unto the men *shall be given* a portion of what they
shall have gained, and unto the women *shall be given* a portion
of what they shall have gained ; [2] therefore ask GOD of his
bounty ; for GOD is omniscient. We have appointed unto
every one kindred, *to inherit part* of what their parents and
relations shall leave *at their deaths*. And unto those with
whom your right hands have made an alliance, give their
part *of the inheritance* ;[3] for GOD is witness of all things.   Men
shall have the pre-eminence above women, because of those
advantages wherein GOD hath caused the one of them to excel
the other,[4] and for that which they expend of their substance
in maintaining their wives. The honest women *are* obedient,
careful in the absence *of their husbands*,[5] for that GOD preserveth *them, by committing them to the care and protection of
the men*. But those, whose perverseness ye shall be apprehensive of, rebuke ; and remove them into separate apartments,[6] and chastise them.[7]   But if they shall be obedient

say, idolatry, murder, falsely accusing modest women of adultery, wasting
the substance of orphans, taking of usury, desertion in a religious expedition,
and disobedience to parents. But Ebn Abbâs says they amount to near
seven hundred ; and others suppose that idolatry only, of different kinds,
in worshipping idols or any creature, either in opposition to or jointly with
the true GOD, is here intended ; that sin being generally esteemed by
Mohammedans, and in a few lines after declared by the Korân itself, to be the
only one which GOD will not pardon. (Al Beidâwi.)

[1] Such as honour, power, riches, and other worldly advantages.   Some,
however, understand this of the distribution of inheritances according to
the preceding determinations, whereby some have a larger share than others.
(Al Beidâwi.)

[2] That is, they shall be blessed according to their deserts ; and ought,
therefore, instead of displeasing GOD by envying others, to endeavour to
merit his favour by good works, and to apply to him by prayer.

[3] A precept conformable to an old custom of the Arabs, that where persons
mutually entered into a strict friendship or confederacy, the surviving friend
should have a sixth part of the deceased's estate. But this was afterwards
abrogated, according to Jallalo'ddin and Al Zamakhshari, at least as to
infidels. The passage may likewise be understood of a private contract,
whereby the survivor is to inherit a certain part of the substance of him
that dies first. (Al Beidâwi.)

[4] Such as superior understanding and strength, and the other privileges
of the male sex, which enjoys the dignities in church and state, goes to war
in defence of GOD's true religion, and claims a double share of their deceased
ancestors' estates. (Al Beidâwi.)

[5] Both to preserve their husband's substance from loss or waste, and
themselves from all degrees of immodesty. (Al Beidâwi, Jallalo'ddin.)

[6] That is, banish them from your bed.

[7] By this passage the Mohammedans are in plain terms allowed to beat
their wives, in case of stubborn disobedience ; but not in a violent or dangerous manner. (Al Beidâwi.)

unto you, seek not an occasion *of quarrel* against them ; for God is high and great. And if ye fear a breach between the *husband and wife*, send a judge[1] out of his family, and a judge out of her family : if they shall desire a reconciliation, God will cause them to agree ; for God is knowing and wise. Serve God, and associate no creature with him ; and *show* kindness unto parents, and relations, and orphans, and the poor, and *your* neighbour who is of kin to you,[2] and also *your* neighbour who is a stranger, and to *your* familiar companion, and the traveller, and *the captives* whom your right hands shall possess ; for God loveth not the proud *or* vainglorious, who are covetous, and recommend covetousness unto men, and conceal that which God of his bounty hath given them[3] (we have prepared a shameful punishment for the unbelievers) ; and who bestow their wealth *in charity* to be observed of men, and believe not in God, nor in the last day ; and whoever hath Satan for a companion, an evil companion *hath he* ! And what *harm would befall* them if they should believe in God and the last day, and give alms out of that which God hath bestowed on them ? since God knoweth them *who do this*. Verily God will not wrong *any one even* the weight of an ant :[4] and if it be a good action, he will double it, and will recompense *it* in his sight with a great reward. How *will it be with the unbelievers* when we shall bring a witness out of each nation *against itself*,[5] and shall bring thee, *O Mohammed*, a witness against these *people* ?[6] In that day they who have not believed, and have rebelled against the apostle *of God*, shall wish the earth was levelled with them ; and they shall not *be able to* hide any matter from God. O true believers, come not to prayers when ye are drunk,[7] until ye

---

[1] *i.e.*, Let the magistrate first send two arbitrators or mediators, one on each side, to compose the difference, and prevent, if possible, the ill consequences of an open rupture.

[2] Either of your own nation or religion.

[3] Whether it be wealth, knowledge, or any other talent whereby they may help their neighbour.

[4] Either by diminishing the recompence due to his good actions, or too severely punishing his sins. On the contrary, he will reward the former in the next life far above their deserts. The Arabic word *dharra*, which is translated *an ant*, signifies a very small sort of that insect, and is used to denote a thing that is exceeding small, as a *mite*.

[5] When the prophet who was sent to each nation in particular, shall on the last day be produced to give evidence against such of them as refused to believe on him, or observed not the laws which he brought.

[6] That is, the Arabians, to whom Mohammed was, as he pretended, more peculiarly sent.

[7] It is related, that before the prohibition of wine, Abd'alrahmân Ebn Awf made an entertainment, to which he invited several of the apostle's

understand what ye say ; nor when ye are polluted by emission of seed, unless ye be travelling on the road, until ye wash yourselves. But if ye be sick, or on a journey, or any of you come from easing nature, or have touched women, and find no water ; take fine clean sand and rub your faces and your hands *therewith* ;[1] for GOD is merciful and inclined to forgive. Hast thou not observed those unto whom part of the scripture[2] was delivered ? they sell error, and desire that ye may wander from the *right* way ; but GOD well knoweth your enemies. GOD is a sufficient patron, and GOD is a sufficient helper. Of the Jews there are some who pervert words from their places ;[3] and say, We have heard, and have disobeyed ; and do thou hear without understanding *our meaning*,[4] and look upon us :[5] perplexing with their tongues, and reviling the *true* religion. But if they had said, We have heard, and do obey ; and do thou hear, and regard us :[6] certainly it were better for them, and more right. But GOD hath cursed them by reason of their infidelity ; therefore a few *of them* only shall believe. O *ye* to whom the scriptures have been given, believe in the *revelation* which we have sent down, confirming that which is with you ; before we deface *your* countenances, and render them as the back parts thereof ;[7] or curse them, as we cursed those who transgressed on the sabbath day ;[8] and the command of GOD was fulfilled. Surely GOD will not pardon the giving him an equal ;[9] but will pardon any other *sin*, except that, to whom he pleaseth :[10] and whoso giveth a

companions ; and after they had ate and drunk plentifully, the hour of evening prayer being come, one of the company rose up to pray, but being overcome with liquor, made a shameful blunder in reciting a passage of the Korân ; whereupon to prevent the danger of any such indecency for the future, this passage was revealed. (Al Beidâwi.)

[1] Sale, Prel. Disc. Sect. IV, p. 113.

[2] Meaning the Jews, and particularly their Rabbins.

[3] That is (according to the commentators), who change the true sense of the Pentateuch by dislocating passages, or by wresting the words according to their own fancies and lusts. (Al Beidâwi, Jallalo'ddin.) But Mohammed seems chiefly to intend here the Jews bantering of him in their addresses, by making use of equivocal words, seeming to bear a good sense in Arabic, but spoken by them in derision according to their acceptation in Hebrew ; an instance of which he gives in the following words.

[4] Literally, *without being made to hear* or apprehend what we say.

[5] The original word is *Raina*, which being a term of reproach in Hebrew, Mohammed forbade their using to him.

[6] In Arabic, *Ondhorna* ; which having no ill equivocal meaning, the prophet ordered them to use instead of the former.

[7] That is, perfectly plain, without eyes, nose, or mouth. The original, however, may also be translated, *and turn them behind*, by wringing their necks backward.

[8] And were therefore changed into apes.

[9] That is, idolatry of all kinds.

[10] viz., To those who repent. (Al Beidâwi.)

companion unto GOD, hath devised a great wickedness. Hast thou not observed those who justify themselves ?[1] But GOD justifieth whomsoever he pleaseth, nor shall *they* be wronged a hair.[2] Behold, how they imagine a lie against GOD ; and therein is iniquity sufficiently manifest. Hast thou not considered those to whom part of the scripture hath been given ? They believe in false gods and idols,[3] and say of those who believe not, These are more rightly directed in the way *of truth* than they who believe *on Mohammed*. Those are *the men* whom *God* hath cursed ; and unto him whom God shall curse, thou shalt surely find no helper. Shall they have a part of the kingdom,[4] since even then they would not bestow the smallest matter[5] on men ? Do they envy *other* men that which GOD of his bounty hath given them ?[6] We formerly gave unto the family of Abraham a book of *revelations* and wisdom ; and we gave them a great kingdom.[7] There is of them who believeth on him ;[8] and there is of them who turneth aside from him ; but the raging fire of hell is *a* sufficient *punishment*. Verily, those who disbelieve our signs, we will surely cast to be broiled in *hell* fire ; so often as their skins shall be well burned, we will give them other skins in exchange, that they may taste the *sharper* torment ; for GOD is mighty

---

[1] *i.e.*, The Christians and Jews, who called themselves *the children of* GOD *and his beloved people.* (Al Beidâwi, Jallalo'ddin. See Chap. V, not far from the beginning.)

[2] The original word signifies a little skin in the cleft of a date-stone, and is used to express a thing of no value.

[3] The Arabic is, "in Jibt and Taghût ". The former is supposed to have been the proper name of some idol ; but it seems rather to signify any false deity in general. The latter we have explained already. It is said that this passage was revealed on the following occasion. Hoyai Ebn Akhtab and Caab Ebn al Ashraf, two chief men among the Jews, with several others of that religion, went to Mecca, and offered to enter into a confederacy with the Koreish, and to join their forces against Mohammed. But the Koreish, entertaining some jealousy of them, told them, that the Jews pretended to have a written revelation from heaven, as well as Mohammed, and the doctrines and worship approached much nearer to what he taught, than the religion of their tribe ; wherefore, said they, if you would satisfy us that you are sincere in the matter, do as we do, and worship our gods. Which proposal, if the story be true, these Jews complied with, out of their inveterate hatred to Mohammed. (Al Beidâwi.)

[4] For the Jews gave out that they should be restored to their ancient power and grandeur (Al Beidâwi) ; depending, it is to be presumed, on the victorious Messiah whom they expected.

[5] The original word properly signifies a small dent on the back of a date-stone, and is commonly used to express a thing of little or no value.

[6] viz., The spiritual gifts of prophecy, and divine revelations ; and the temporal blessings of victory and success, bestowed on Mohammed and his followers.

[7] Wherefore GOD will doubtless show equal favour to this prophet (a descendant also of Abraham), and those who believe on him. (Al Beidâwi.)

[8] Namely, on Mohammed.

and wise. But those who believe and do that which is right, we will bring into gardens watered by rivers, therein shall they remain for ever, *and* there shall they enjoy wives free from all impurity ; and we will lead them into perpetual shades. Moreover GOD commandeth you to restore what ye are trusted with, to the owners ;[1] and when ye judge between men, that ye judge according to equity : and surely an excellent *virtue it is* to which GOD exhorteth you ; for GOD *both* heareth and seeth. O true believers, obey GOD, and obey the apostle, and those who are in authority among you : and if ye differ in anything, refer it unto GOD[2] and the apostle, if ye believe in GOD and the last day : this is better, and a fairer *method of* determination. Hast thou not observed those who pretend they believe in what hath been revealed unto thee, and what hath been revealed before thee ? They desire to go to judgment before Taghût,[3] although they have been commanded not to believe in him ; and Satan desireth to seduce them into a wide error. And when it is said unto them, Come unto *the book* which GOD hath sent down, and to the apostle ; thou seest the ungodly turn aside from thee, with *great* aversion. But how *will they behave* when a misfortune shall befall them, for that which their hands have sent before them ?

---

[1] This passage, it is said, was revealed on the day of the taking of Mecca, the primary design of it being to direct Mohammed to return the keys of the Caaba to Othmân Ebn Telha Ebn Abdaldâr, who had then the honour to be keeper of that holy place (Prideaux's Life of Mahomet, p. 2) and not to deliver them to his uncle Al Abbâs, who having already the custody of the well Zemzem, would fain have had also that of the Caaba. The prophet obeying the divine order, Othmân was so affected with the justice of the action, notwithstanding he had at first refused him entrance, that he immediately embraced Mohammedism ; whereupon the guardianship of the Caaba was confirmed to this Othmân and his heirs for ever. (Al Beidâwi. D'Herbel. Bibl. Orient. p. 220, 221.)

[2] *i.e.*, To the decision of the Korân.

[3] That is, before the tribunals of infidels. This passage was occasioned by the following remarkable accident. A certain Jew having a dispute with a wicked Mohammedan, the latter appealed to the judgment of Caab Ebn al Ashraf, a principal Jew, and the former to Mohammed. But at length they agreed to refer the matter to the prophet singly, who, giving it in favour of the Jew, the Mohammedan refused to acquiesce in his sentence, but would needs have it re-heard by Omar, afterwards Khalif. When they came to him the Jew told him that Mohammed had already decided the affair in his favour, but that the other would not submit to his determination ; and the Mohammedan confessing this to be true, Omar bid them stay a little, and fetching his sword, struck off the obstinate Moslem's head, saying aloud, *This is the reward of him who refuseth to submit to the judgment of* GOD *and his apostle.* And from this action Omar had the surname of Al Farûk, which alludes both to his *separating* that knave's head from his body, and to his *distinguishing* between truth and falsehood. (Jallalo'ddin, Al Beidâwi, D'Herbel, Bibl. Orient. p. 688, and Ockley's Hist. of the Sarac. v. 1, p. 365.) The name of Taghût, therefore, in this place, seems to be given to Caab Ebn al Ashraf.

Then will they come unto thee, and swear by GOD, *saying*. If we intended any other than to do good, and to reconcile *the parties*.[1] GOD knoweth what is in the hearts of these *men* ; therefore let them alone, and admonish them, and speak unto them a word which may affect their souls. We have not sent any apostle, but that he might be obeyed by the permission of GOD : but if they, after they have injured their own souls,[2] come unto thee, and ask pardon of GOD, and the apostle ask pardon for them, they shall surely find GOD easy to be reconciled and merciful. And by thy LORD they will not *perfectly* believe, until they make thee judge of their controversies ; and shall not afterwards find in their own minds any hardship in what thou shalt determine, but shall acquiesce *therein* with *entire* submission. And if we had commanded them, *saying*, Slay yourselves, or depart from your houses ;[3] they would not have done it, except a few of them. And if they had done what they were admonished, it would certainly have been better for them, and more efficacious for confirming *their faith* ; and we should then have surely given them in our sight an *exceeding* great reward, and we should have directed them in the right way. Whoever obeyeth GOD and the apostle, they *shall be* with those unto whom GOD hath been gracious, of the prophets, and the sincere, and the martyrs, and the righteous ; and these are the most excellent company. This is bounty from GOD ; and GOD is sufficiently knowing. O true believers, take your *necessary* precaution[4] *against your enemies*, and *either* go forth *to war* in separate parties, or go forth all together *in a body*. There is of you who tarrieth behind ;[5] and if a misfortune befall you, he saith, Verily GOD hath been gracious unto me, that I was not present with them : but if success attend you from GOD, he will say (as if there was no friendship between you and him),[6] Would to

---

[1] For this was the excuse of the friends of the Mohammedan whom Omar slew, when they came to demand satisfaction for his blood. (Al Beidâwi.)

[2] viz., By acting wickedly, and appealing to the judgment of infidels.

[3] Some understand these words of their venturing their lives in a religious expedition ; and others, of their undergoing the same punishments which the Israelites did for their idolatry in worshipping the golden calf. (Al Beidâwi.)

[4] *i.e.*, Be vigilant, and provide yourselves with arms and necessaries.

[5] Mohammed here upbraids the hypocritical Moslems, who, for want of faith and constancy in their religion, were backward in going to war for its defence.

[6] *i.e.*, As one who attendeth not to the public, but his own private interest. Or else these may be the words of the hypocritical Mohammedan himself, insinuating that he stayed not behind the rest of the army by his own fault, but was left by Mohammed, who chose to let the others share in his good fortune, preferably to him. (Al Beidâwi.)

GOD I had been with them, for I should have acquired great merit. Let them therefore fight for the religion of GOD, who part with the present life in exchange for that which is to come ;[1] for whosoever fighteth for the religion of GOD, whether he be slain, or be victorious,[2] we will surely give him a great reward. And what ails you, that ye fight not for GOD's true religion, and *in defence of* the weak among men, women, and children,[3] who say, O LORD, bring us forth from this city, whose inhabitants are wicked ; grant us from before thee a protector, and grant us from thee a defender.[4] They who believe fight for the religion of GOD ; but they who believe not fight for the religion of Taghût. Fight therefore against the friends of Satan, for the stratagem of Satan is weak. Hast thou not observed those unto whom it was said, Withhold your hands *from war*, and be constant at prayers, and pay the legal alms ?[5] But when war is commanded them, behold, a part of them fear men as they should fear GOD, or with a greater fear, and say, O LORD, wherefore hast thou commanded us to go to war, and hast not suffered us to wait *our* approaching end ?[6] Say *unto them*, The provision of this life is *but* small ; but the future *shall be* better for him who feareth *God* ; and ye shall not be in the least injured *at the day of judgment*. Wheresoever ye be, death will overtake you, although ye be in lofty towers. If good befall them, they say, This is from GOD ; but if evil befall them, they say, This is from thee, O Mohammed :[7] say, All is from GOD ; and what aileth these people, that they are so far from understanding what is said *unto them* ? Whatever good befalleth thee, *O man*, it is from GOD ; and whatever

[1] By venturing their lives and fortunes in defence of the faith.

[2] For no man ought to quit the field till he either fall a martyr or gain some advantage for the cause. (Al Beidâwi.)

[3] viz., Those believers who stayed behind at Mecca, being detained there either forcibly by the idolaters, or for want of means to fly for refuge to Medina. Al Beidâwi observes that *children* are mentioned here to show the inhumanity of the Koreish, who persecuted even that tender age.

[4] This petition, the commentators say, was heard. For GOD afforded several of them an opportunity and means of escaping, and delivered the rest at the taking of Mecca by Mohammed, who left Otâb Ebn Osaid governor of the city : and under his care and protection, those who had suffered for their religion became the most considerable men in the place.

[5] These were some of Mohammed's followers, who readily performed the duties of their religion so long as they were commanded nothing that might endanger their lives.

[6] That is, a natural death.

[7] As the Jews, in particular, who pretended that their land was grown barren, and provisions scarce, since Mohammed came to Medina. (Al Beidâwi.)

evil befalleth thee, it is from thyself.[1] We have sent thee an
apostle unto men, and GOD is a sufficient witness *thereof*.
Whoever obeyeth the apostle, obeyeth GOD ; and whoever
turneth back, we have not sent thee *to be* a keeper over them.[2]
They say, Obedience : yet when they go forth from thee, part
of them meditate by night *a matter* different from what thou
speakest ; but GOD shall write down what they meditate by
night ; therefore let them alone, and trust in GOD, for GOD
is a sufficient protector. Do they not attentively consider
the Korân ? If it had been from any besides GOD, they
would certainly have found therein many contradictions.
When any news cometh unto them, either of security or fear,
they *immediately* divulge it ; but if they told it to the apostle
and to those who are in authority among them, such of them
would understand *the truth of* the matter, as inform themselves thereof *from the apostle and his chiefs*. And if the
favour of GOD and his mercy *had* not *been* upon you, ye had
followed the devil, except a few *of you*.[3] Fight therefore for
the religion of GOD, and oblige not any to what is difficult,[4]
except thyself ; however, excite the faithful *to war*, perhaps
GOD will restrain the courage of the unbelievers ; for GOD is
stronger *than they*, and more able to punish. He who intercedeth *between men* with a good intercession[5] shall have a
portion thereof ; and he who intercedeth with an evil intercession shall have a portion thereof ; for GOD overlooketh all
things. When ye are saluted with a salutation, salute *the
person* with a better salutation,[6] or *at least* return the same ;

[1] These words are not to be understood as contradictory to the preceding,
That all proceeds from GOD ; since the evil which befalls mankind, though
ordered by GOD, is yet the consequence of their own wicked actions.

[2] Or, to take an account of their actions, for this is GOD's part.

[3] That is, if GOD had not sent his apostle with the Korân to instruct you
in your duty, ye had continued in idolatry and been doomed to destruction ;
except only those who, by GOD's favour and their superior understanding,
should have true notions of the divinity ; such, for example, as Zeid Ebn
Amru Ebn Nofail (Millium, de Mohammedismo ante Moh. p. 311) and Waraka
Ebn Nawfal (Sale, Prel. Disc. Sect II), who left idols, and acknowledged but
one GOD, before the mission of Mohammed. (Al Beidâwi.)

[4] It is said this passage was revealed when the Mohammedans refused
to follow their prophet to the lesser expedition of Bedr, so that he was obliged
to set out with no more than seventy. Some copies vary in this place, and
instead of *la tokallafo*, in the second person singular, read *la nokallafo*, in
the first person plural, *We do not oblige*, &c. The meaning being, that the
prophet only was under an indispensable necessity of obeying GOD's commands, however difficult, but others might choose, though at their peril.

[5] *i.e.*, To maintain the right of a believer, or to prevent his being wronged.

[6] By adding something farther. As when one salutes another by this
form, *Peace be unto thee*, he ought not only to return the salutation, but to
add, *and the mercy of* GOD *and his blessing*.

for GOD taketh an account of all things. GOD! there is no
GOD but he; he will surely gather you together on the day of
resurrection; there is no doubt of it: and who is more true
than GOD in what he saith? Why are ye *divided* concerning
the ungodly into two parties;[1] since GOD hath overturned
them for what they have committed? Will ye direct him
whom GOD hath led astray; since for him whom GOD shall
lead astray, thou shalt find no *true* path? They desire that
ye should become infidels, as they are infidels, and that ye
should be equally *wicked with themselves*. Therefore take not
friends from among them, until they fly *their country* for the
religion of GOD; and if they turn back *from the faith*, take
them, and kill them wherever ye find them; and take no
friend from among them, nor any helper, except those who go
unto a people who are in alliance with you,[2] or those who
come unto you, their hearts forbidding them either to fight
against you, or to fight against their own people.[3] And if
GOD pleased he would have permitted them to have prevailed
against you, and they would have fought against you. But
if they depart from you, and fight not against you, and
offer you peace, GOD doth not allow you *to take or kill* them.
Ye shall find others who are desirous to enter into a confidence with you, and *at the same time* to preserve a confidence
with their own people:[4] so often as they return to sedition,
they shall be subverted therein; and if they depart not
from you, and offer you peace, and restrain their hands *from
warring against you*, take them and kill them wheresoever
ye find them; over these have we granted you a manifest
power. It is not *lawful* for a believer to kill a believer, unless *it
happen* by mistake;[5] and whoso killeth a believer by mistake,

[1] This passage was revealed, according to some, when certain of Mohammed's followers, pretending not to like Medina, desired leave to go elsewhere,
and, having obtained it, went farther and farther, till they joined the
idolaters or, as others say, on occasion of some deserters at the battle of
Ohod; concerning whom the Moslems were divided in opinion whether they
should be slain as infidels or not.

[2] The people here meant, say some, were the tribe of Khozâah, or, according to others, the Aslamians, whose chief, named Helâl Ebn Owaimar, agreed
with Mohammed, when he set out against Mecca, to stand neuter; or, as
others rather think, Banu Becr Ebn Zeid. (Al Beidâwi, Jallalo'ddin.)

[3] These, it is said, were the tribe of Modlaj, who came in to Mohammed,
but would not be obliged to assist him in war. (Al Beidâwi.)

[4] The persons hinted at here were the tribes of Asad and Ghatfân, or as
some say, Banu Abdaldâr, who came to Medina and pretended to embrace
Mohammedism, that they might be trusted by the Moslems, but when they
returned, fell back to their old idolatry. (Al Beidâwi.)

[5] That is, by accident and without design. This passage was revealed
to decide the case of Ayâsh Ebn Abi Rabia, the brother, by the mother's

the penalty shall be the freeing of a believer from slavery, and a fine to be paid to the family of *the deceased,*[1] unless they remit *it* as alms ; and if *the slain person* be of a people at enmity with you, and be a true believer, *the penalty shall be* the freeing of a believer ;[2] but if he be of a people in confederacy with you, a fine to be paid to his family, and the freeing of a believer. And he who findeth not *wherewith to do this,* shall fast two months consecutively, *as* a penance *enjoined* from GOD ; and GOD is knowing and wise. But whoso killeth a believer designedly, his reward shall be hell ; he shall remain therein *for ever ;*[3] and GOD shall be angry with him, and shall curse him, and shall prepare for him a great punishment. O true believers, when ye are on a march in defence of the true religion, justly discern *such as ye shall happen to meet,* and say not unto him who saluteth you, Thou art not a true believer ;[4] seeking the accidental goods of the present life ;[5] for with GOD is much spoil. Such have ye formerly been ; but GOD hath been gracious unto you ;[6] therefore make a just discernment, for GOD is well acquainted with that which ye do. Those believers who sit still *at home,* not having any hurt,[7] and those who employ their fortunes and their persons for the religion of GOD, shall not be held equal. GOD hath preferred those who employ their fortunes and their persons *in that cause,* to a degree *of honour* above those who sit at home :

side, of Abu Jahl, who meeting Hareth Ebn Zeid on the road, and not knowing that he had embraced Mohammedism, slew him. (Al Beidâwi.)

[1] Which fine is to be distributed according to the laws of inheritances given in the beginning of this chapter. (Al Beidâwi.)

[2] And no fine shall be paid, because in such case his relations, being infidels and at open war with the Moslems, have no right to inherit what he leaves.

[3] That is, unless he repent. Others, however, understand not here an eternity of damnation (for it is the general doctrine of the Mohammedans that none who profess that faith shall continue in hell for ever), but only a long space of time. (Al Beidâwi.)

[4] On pretence that he only feigns to be a Moslem that he might escape from you. The commentators mention more instances than one of persons slain and plundered by Mohammed's men under this pretext, notwithstanding they declared themselves Moslems by repeating the usual form of words, and saluting them ; for which reason this passage was revealed, to prevent such rash judgments for the future.

[5] That is, being willing to judge him an infidel, only that ye may kill and plunder him.

[6] viz., At your first profession of Islâmism, before ye had given any demonstrations of your sincerity and zeal therein.

[7] *i.e.,* Not being disabled from going to war by sickness, or other just impediment. It is said that when the passage was first revealed there was no such exception therein, which occasioned Ebn Omm Mactûm, on his hearing it repeated, to object, *And what though I be blind* ? Whereupon Mohammed, falling into a kind of trance, which was succeeded by strong agitations, pretended he had received the divine direction to add these words to the text. (Al Beidâwi.)

GOD hath indeed promised every one paradise, but GOD hath preferred those who fight *for the faith* before those who sit still, *by adding unto them* a great reward, *by* degrees *of honour conferred on them* from him, and *by granting them* forgiveness and mercy ; for GOD is indulgent *and* merciful.   Moreover unto those whom the angels put to death, having injured their own souls,[1] *the angels* said, Of what *religion* were ye ? they answered, We were weak in the earth.[2]   *The angels* replied, Was not GOD's earth wide *enough*, that ye might fly therein *to a place of refuge* ?[3]   Therefore their habitation shall be hell ; and an evil journey *shall it be thither* : except the weak among men, and women, and children, who were not able to find means, and were not directed in the way ; these peradventure GOD will pardon, for GOD is ready to forgive *and* gracious.   Whosoever flieth *from his country* for the sake of GOD's true religion, shall find in the earth many forced *to do the same*, and plenty *of provisions*.   And whoever departeth from his house, and flieth unto GOD and his apostle, if death overtake him *in the way*,[4] GOD will be obliged to reward him, for GOD is gracious *and* merciful.   When ye march *to war* in the earth, it shall be no crime in you if ye shorten your prayers, in case ye fear the infidels may attack you ; for the infidels are your open enemy.   But when thou, *O prophet*, shalt be among them, and shalt pray with them, let a party of them arise to prayer with thee, and let them take their arms ; and when they shall have worshipped, let them stand behind you,[5] and let another party come that hath not prayed, and let them pray with thee, and let them be cautious and take their arms.   The unbelievers would that ye should neglect your arms and your baggage *while ye pray*, that they might turn upon you at once.   It shall be no crime in you, if ye be incommoded by rain, or be sick, that ye lay down your arms ; but take your *necessary* precaution :[6] GOD hath

---

[1] These were certain inhabitants of Mecca, who held with the hare and ran with the hounds, for though they embraced Mohammedism, yet they would not leave that city to join the prophet, as the rest of the Moslems did, but on the contrary went out with the idolaters, and were therefore slain with them at the battle of Bedr.   (Al Beidâwi, Jallalo'ddin.)

[2] Being unable to fly, and compelled to follow the infidels to war.

[3] As they did who fled to Ethiopia and to Medina.

[4] This passage was revealed, says Al Beidâwi, on account of Jondob Ebn Damra.   This person being sick, was, in his flight, carried by his sons on a couch, and before he arrived at Medina, perceiving his end approached, he clapped his right hand on his left, and solemnly plighting his faith to GOD and his apostle, died.

[5] To defend those who are at prayers, and to face the enemy.

[6] By keeping strict guard.

prepared for the unbelievers an ignominious punishment. And when ye shall have ended *your* prayer, remember GOD, standing, and sitting, and *lying* on your sides.[1] But when ye are secure *from danger*, complete *your* prayers ; for prayer is commanded the faithful, *and* appointed *to be said* at the stated times. Be not negligent in seeking out the *unbelieving* people, though ye suffer *some inconvenience* ; for they *also* shall suffer, as ye suffer, and ye hope for *a reward* from GOD which they cannot hope for ; and GOD is knowing *and* wise.[2] We have sent down unto thee the book *of the Korân* with truth, that thou mayest judge between men through that *wisdom* which GOD showeth thee *therein* ; and be not an advocate for the fraudulent ;[3] but ask pardon of GOD *for thy wrong intention*, since GOD is indulgent *and* merciful. Dispute not for those who deceive one another, for GOD loveth not him who is a deceiver *or* unjust.[4] *Such* conceal themselves from men, but they conceal not themselves from GOD ; for he is with them when they imagine by night a saying which pleaseth *him* not,[5] and GOD comprehendeth what they do. Behold, ye are they who have disputed for them in this present life ; but who shall dispute with GOD for them on the day of resurrection, or who will become their patron ? yet he who doth evil, or injureth his own soul, and afterwards asketh pardon of GOD, shall find GOD gracious *and* merciful. Whoso committeth wickedness, committeth it against his own soul : GOD is knowing *and* wise. And whoso committeth a sin or iniquity, and afterwards layeth it on the innocent, he shall surely bear *the guilt of* calumny and manifest injustice. If the

[1] That is, in such posture as ye shall be able.

[2] This verse was revealed on occasion of the unwillingness of Mohammed's men to accompany him in the lesser expedition of Bedr. (Al Beidâwi.)

[3] Tíma Ebn Obeirak, of the sons of Dhafar, one of Mohammed's companions, stole a coat of mail from his neighbour, Kitâda Ebn al Nomân, in a bag of meal, and hid it at a Jew's named Zeid Ebn al Samîn ; Tíma, being suspected, the coat of mail was demanded of him, but he, denying he knew anything of it, they followed the track of the meal, which had run out through a hole in the bag, to the Jew's house, and there seized it, accusing him of the theft ; but he producing witnesses of his own religion that he had it of Tíma, the sons of Dhafar came to Mohammed and desired him to defend his companion's reputation and condemn the Jew ; which he having some thoughts of doing, this passage was revealed, reprehending him for his rash intention, and commanding him to judge not according to his own prejudice and opinion, but according to the merit of the case. (Al Beidâwi, Jallalo'ddin, Yahya.)

[4] Al Beìdâwi, as an instance of the divine justice, adds, that Tíma, after the fact above mentioned, fled to Mecca, and returned to idolatry ; and there undermining the wall of a house, in order to commit a robbery, the wall fell in upon him and crushed him to death.

[5] That is, when they secretly contrive means, by false evidence or otherwise, to lay their crimes on innocent persons.

indulgence and mercy of GOD had not been upon thee, surely a part of them had studied to seduce thee ;[1] but they shall seduce themselves only, and shall not hurt thee at all. GOD hath sent down unto thee the book *of the Korân* and wisdom, and hath taught thee that which thou knewest not ;[2] for the favour of GOD hath been great towards thee. There is no good in the multitude of their private discourses, unless *in the discourse* of him who recommendeth alms, or that which is right, or agreement amongst men ; whoever doth this out of a desire to please GOD we will surely give him a great reward. But whoso separateth himself from the apostle, after *true* direction hath been manifested unto him, and followeth any other way than that of the true believers, we will cause him to obtain that to which he is inclined,[3] and will cast him to be burned in hell ; and an unhappy journey shall it be *thither*. Verily GOD will not pardon the giving him a companion, but he will pardon *any crime* besides that, unto whom he pleaseth : and he who giveth a companion unto GOD, is surely led aside into a wide mistake : the *infidels* invoke beside him only female *deities*,[4] and only invoke rebellious Satan. GOD cursed him ; and he said, Verily I will take of thy servants a part cut off *from the rest*,[5] and I will seduce them, and will insinuate *vain* desires into them, and I will command them, and they shall cut off the ears of cattle ;[6] and I will command them, and they shall change GOD's creature.[7] But whoever taketh Satan for his patron, besides GOD,[8] shall surely perish with a manifest destruction, He maketh them promises, and insinuateth into them vain desires ; yet Satan maketh them only deceitful promises. The receptacle of these shall be hell, they

[1] Meaning the sons of Dhafar.

[2] By instructing thee in the knowledge of right and wrong, and the rules of justice.

[3] viz., Error, and false notions of religion.

[4] Namely, Allât, Al Uzza, and Menât, the idols of the Meccans ; or the angels, whom they called the *daughters of* GOD. (Sale, Prel. Disc. p. 19.)

[5] Or, as the original may be translated, a part *destined* or *predetermined* to be seduced by me.

[6] Which was done out of superstition by the old pagan Arabs. See more of this custom in the notes to the fifth chapter.

[7] Either by maiming it, or putting it to uses not designed by the Creator. Al Beidâwi supposes the text to intend not only the superstitious amputations of the ears and other parts of cattle, but the castration of slaves, the marking their bodies with figures, by pricking and dyeing them with wood or indigo (as the Arabs did and still do), the sharpening their teeth by filing ; and also sodomy, and the unnatural amours between those of the female sex, the worship of the sun, moon, and other parts of nature, and the like.

[8] *i.e.*, By leaving the service of GOD, and doing the works of the devil.

shall find no refuge from it. But they who believe, and do good works, we will surely lead them into gardens, through which rivers flow ; they shall continue therein for ever, *according to* the true promise of GOD ; and who is more true than GOD in what he saith ? It shall not be according to your desires, nor *according to* the desires of those who have received the scriptures.[1] Whoso doth evil, shall be rewarded for it ; and shall not find any patron or helper, beside GOD ; but whoso doth good works, whether he be male or female, and is a true believer, he shall be admitted into paradise, and shall not in the least be unjustly dealt with. Who is better in point of religion than he who resigneth himself unto GOD, and is a worker of righteousness, and followeth the law of Abraham the orthodox ? since GOD took Abraham for his friend :[2] and to GOD *belongeth* whatsoever is in heaven and on earth ; GOD comprehendeth all things. They will consult thee concerning women ;[3] Answer, GOD instructeth you concerning them,[4] and that which is read unto you in the book *of the Korân* concerning female orphans, to whom ye give not that which is ordained them, neither will ye marry them,[5]

---

[1] That is, the promises of GOD are not to be gained by acting after your own fancies, nor yet after the fancies of the Jews or Christians, but by obeying the commands of GOD. This passage, they say, was revealed on a dispute which arose between those of the three religions, each preferring his own, and condemning the others. Some, however, suppose the persons here spoken to in the second person were not the Mohammedans, but the idolaters. (Al Beidâwi, Jallalo'ddin, Yahya.)

[2] Therefore the Mohammedans usually call that patriarch, as the scripture also does, Khalil Allah, the *Friend of* GOD, and simply Al Khalil ; and they tell the following story. That Abraham in a time of dearth sent to a friend of his in Egypt for a supply of corn ; but the friend denied him, saying in his excuse, that though there was a famine in their country also, yet had it been for Abraham's own family, he would have sent what he desired, but he knew he wanted it only to entertain his guests and give away to the poor, according to his usual hospitality. The servants whom Abraham had sent on this message, being ashamed to return empty, to conceal the matter from their neighbours, filled their sacks with fine white sand, which in the East pretty much resembles meal. Abraham being informed by his servants, on their return, of their ill success, the concern he was under threw him into a sleep ; and in the meantime Sarah, knowing nothing of what had happened, opening one of the sacks, found good flour in it, and immediately set out about making of bread. Abraham awaking and smelling the new bread, asked her whence she had the flour ? *Why*, says she, *from your friend in Egypt. Nay*, replied the Patriarch, *it must have come from no other than my friend* GOD *Almighty*. (Al Beidâwi. D'Herbel. Bibl. Orient. p. 14, and Morgan's Mahometism Explained, vol. I. p. 132.)

[3] *i.e.*, As to the share they are to have in the distribution of the inheritances of their deceased relations ; for it seems that the Arabs were not satisfied with Mohammed's decision on this point, against the old customs.

[4] *i.e.*, He hath already made his will known unto you, by revealing the passages concerning inheritances in the beginning of this chapter.

[5] Or the words may be rendered in the affirmative, *and whom ye desire to marry*. For the pagan Arabs used to wrong their female orphans in both

and concerning weak infants,[1] and that ye observe justice towards orphans : whatever good ye do, GOD knoweth it. If a woman fear ill usage, or aversion, from her husband, it shall be no crime in them if they agree the matter amicably between themselves ;[2] for a reconciliation is better *than a separation.* *Men's* souls are naturally inclined to covetousness :[3] but if ye be kind *towards women,* and fear *to wrong them,* GOD is well acquainted with what ye do. Ye can by no means carry yourselves equally between women *in all respects,* although ye study *to do it* ; therefore turn not *from a wife* with all *manner of* aversion,[4] nor leave her like one in suspense :[5] if ye agree, and fear *to abuse your wives,* GOD is gracious *and* merciful ; but if they separate, GOD will satisfy *them* both of his abundance ;[6] for GOD is extensive *and* wise, and unto GOD *belongeth* whatsoever is in heaven and on earth. We have already commanded those unto whom the scriptures were given before you, and *we command* you also, *saying,* Fear GOD ; but if ye disbelieve, unto GOD *belongeth* whatsoever is in heaven and on earth ; and GOD is self-sufficient,[7] *and* to be praised ; for unto GOD *belongeth* whatsoever is in heaven and on earth, and GOD is a sufficient protector. If he pleaseth he will take you away, O men, and will produce others[8] *in your stead* ; for GOD is able to do this. Whoso desireth the reward of this world, verily with GOD is the reward of this world, and *also* of that which is to come ; GOD *both* heareth *and* seeth. O true believers, observe justice when ye bear witness before GOD, although *it be* against yourselves, or *your* parents, or relations ; whether *the party*

instances ; obliging them to marry against their inclinations, if they were beautiful or rich ; or else not suffering them to marry at all, that they might keep what belonged to them. (Al Beidâwi.)

[1] That is, male children of tender years, to whom the Arabs, in the time of paganism, used to allow no share in the distribution of their parents' estate. (See before, p. 72, note 9.)

[2] By the wife's remitting part of her dower or other dues.

[3] So that the woman, on the one side, is unwilling to part with any of her right ; and the husband, on the other, cares not to retain one he has no affection for ; or, if he should retain her, she can scarce expect he will use her in all respects as he ought. (Al Beidâwi.)

[4] *i.e.,* Though you cannot use her equally well with a beloved wife, yet observe some measures of justice towards her ; for if a man is not able perfectly to perform his duty, he ought not, for that reason, entirely to neglect it. (Al Beidâwi.)

[5] Or like one that neither has a husband, nor is divorced, and at liberty to marry elsewhere.

[6] That is, either will bless them with a better and more advantageous match, or with peace and tranquillity of mind. (Al Beidâwi.)

[7] Wanting the service of no creature.

[8] *i.e.,* Either another race of men or a different species of creatures.

be rich, or *whether he be* poor ; for GOD is more worthy than
them both : therefore follow not *your own* lust *in bearing
testimony*, so that ye swerve *from justice*. And whether ye
wrest *your evidence*, or decline *giving it*, GOD is well acquainted
with that which ye do. O true believers, believe in GOD and
his apostle, and the book which he hath caused to descend
unto his apostle, and the book which he hath formerly sent
down.[1] And whosoever believeth not in GOD, and his
angels, and his scriptures, and his apostles, and the last day,
he surely erreth in a wide mistake. Moreover they who
believed, and afterwards became infidels, and then believed
again, and after that disbelieved, and increased in infidelity,[2]
GOD will by no means forgive them, nor direct them into
the *right* way. Declare unto the ungodly,[3] that they shall
suffer a painful punishment. They who take the unbelievers
for their protectors, besides the faithful, do they seek for
power with them ? since all power belongeth unto GOD.
And he hath already revealed unto you, in the book *of the
Korân*,[4] *the following passage* : When ye shall hear the signs
of GOD, they shall not be believed, but they shall be laughed
to scorn. Therefore sit not with them *who believe not*, until
they engage in different discourse ; for *if ye do*, ye will certainly *become* like unto them. GOD will surely gather the
ungodly and the unbelievers together in hell. They who
wait *to observe what befalleth* you, if victory be *granted* you
from GOD, say, Were we not with you ?[5] But if any advantage happen to the infidels, they say *unto them*, Were we not
superior to you,[6] and have we not defended you against the
believers ? GOD shall judge between you on the day of

[1] It is said that Abda'llah Ebn Salâm and his companions told Mohammed
that they believed in him, and his Korân, and in Moses, and the Pentateuch,
and in Ezra, but no farther ; whereupon this passage was revealed, declaring
that a partial faith is little better than none at all, and that a true believer
must believe in all GOD's prophets and revelations without exception.
(Al Beidâwi.)

[2] These were the Jews, who first believed in Moses and afterwards fell
into idolatry by worshipping the golden calf ; and though they repented
of that, yet in after ages rejected the prophets who were sent to
them, and particularly Jesus, the son of Mary, and now filled up the
measure of their unbelief by rejecting Mohammed. (Al Beidâwi.)

[3] Mohammed here means those who hypocritically pretended to believe
in him but really did not, and by their treachery did great mischief to his
party. (Al Beidâwi.)

[4] Chap. VI.

[5] *i.e.*, Did we not assist you ? Therefore give us part of the spoil. (Al
Beidâwi.)

[6] Would not our army have cut you off if it had not been for our faint
assistance, or rather desertion, of the Moslems, and our disheartening them ?
(Al Beidâwi.)

resurrection ; and GOD will not grant the unbelievers means *to prevail* over the faithful. The hypocrites act deceitfully with GOD, but he will deceive them ; and when they stand up to pray, they stand carelessly, affecting to be seen of men, and remember not GOD, unless a little,[1] wavering between *faith and infidelity, and adhering* neither unto these nor unto those :[2] and for him whom GOD shall lead astray, thou shalt find no true path. O true believers, take not the unbelievers for *your* protectors, besides the faithful. Will ye furnish GOD with an evident argument *of impiety* against you ? Moreover the hypocrites shall be in the lowest bottom of *hell* fire,[3] and thou shalt not find any to help them *thence*. But they who repent and amend, and adhere firmly unto GOD, and approve the sincerity of their religion to GOD, they shall be *numbered* with the faithful ; and GOD will surely give the faithful a great reward. And how should GOD go about to punish you, if ye be thankful and believe ? for GOD is grateful *and* wise. (VI.)[4] GOD loveth not the speaking ill *of anyone* in public, unless he who is injured *call for assistance* ; and GOD heareth *and* knoweth : whether ye publish a good *action*, or conceal it, or forgive evil, verily GOD is gracious *and* powerful. They who believe not in GOD and his apostles, and would make a distinction between GOD and his apostles, and say, We believe in some *of the prophets*, and reject others *of them*, and seek to take a *middle* way in this *matter* ; these are really unbelievers, and we have prepared for the unbelievers an ignominious punishment. But they who believe in GOD and his apostles, and make no distinction between any of them, unto those will we surely give their reward ; and GOD is gracious *and* merciful. They who have received the scriptures[5] will demand of thee, that thou cause a book to descend unto them from heaven : they formerly asked of Moses a greater *thing* than this ; for they said, Show us GOD visibly.[6] Wherefore a storm of fire from heaven destroyed them, because of their iniquity. Then they took the calf *for their God*, after that evident proofs *of the divine unity* had come unto them :

---

[1] That is, with the tongue, and not with the heart.
[2] Neither to the Moslems nor the infidels.   [3] Sale, Prel. Disc. Sect. IV, p. 98.
[4] The sixth section begins here. See Sale, Prel. Disc. p. 63
[5] That is, the Jews ; who demanded of Mohammed, as a proof of his mission, that they might see a book of revelations descend to him from heaven, or that he would produce one written in a celestial character, like the two tables of Moses.
[6] This story seems to be an addition to what Moses says of the seventy elders, who went up to the mountain with him, and with Aaron, Nadab, and Abihu, and saw the GOD of Israel. (Exod. xxiv. 9, 10, 11.)

but we forgave *them* that, and gave Moses a manifest power *to punish them.* And we lifted the mountain *of Sinai* over them, *when we exacted from them* their covenant ; and said unto them, Enter the gate *of the city* worshipping. We also said unto them, Transgress not on the sabbath day. And we received from them a firm covenant, *that they would observe these things.* Therefore for that[1] they have made void their covenant, and have not believed in the signs of GOD, and have slain the prophets unjustly, and have said, Our hearts are uncircumcised (but GOD hath sealed them up, because of their unbelief ; therefore they shall not believe, except a few *of them*) : and for that they have not believed *on Jesus,* and have spoken against Mary a grievous calumny ;[2] and have said, Verily we have slain Christ Jesus the son of Mary, the apostle of GOD ; yet they slew him not, neither crucified him, but he was represented *by one* in his likeness ; and verily they who disagreed concerning him,[3] were in a doubt as to this *matter,* and had no *sure* knowledge thereof, but followed only an *uncertain* opinion. They did not really kill him ; but GOD took him up into himself : and GOD is mighty *and* wise. And *there shall not be one* of those who have received the scriptures, who shall not believe in him, before his death,[4] and on the day of resurrection he shall be a witness against

[1] There being nothing in the following words of this sentence, to answer to the casual *for that,* Jallalo'ddin supposes something to be understood to complete the sense, as *therefore we have cursed them,* or the like.

[2] By accusing her of fornication. (Chap. XIX, and that virulent book entitled Toldoth Jesu.)

[3] For some maintained that he was justly and really crucified ; some insisted that it was not Jesus who suffered, but another who resembled him in the face, pretending that the other parts of his body, by their unlikeness, plainly revealed the imposition ; some said he was taken up into heaven ; and others, that his manhood only suffered, and that his godhead ascended into heaven. (Al Beidâwi.)

[4] This passage is expounded two ways. Some, referring the relative *his* to the first antecedent, take the meaning to be, that no Jew or Christian shall die before he believes in Jesus : for they say, that when one of either of those religions is ready to breathe his last, and sees the angel of death before him, he shall then believe in that prophet as he ought, though his faith will not then be of any avail. According to a tradition of Hejâj, when a Jew is expiring, the angels will strike him on the back and face, and say to him, *O thou enemy of* GOD, *Jesus was sent as a prophet unto thee, and thou didst not believe on him* ; to which he will answer, *I now believe him to be the servant of* GOD ; and to a dying Christian they will say, *Jesus was sent as a prophet unto thee, and thou hast imagined him to be* GOD, *or the son of* GOD ; whereupon he will believe him to be the servant of GOD only, and his apostle. Others, taking the above-mentioned relative to refer to Jesus, suppose the intent of the passage to be, that all Jews and Christians in general shall have a right faith in that prophet before his death, that is, when he descends from heaven and returns into the world, where he is to kill Antichrist, and to establish the Mohammedan religion, and a most perfect tranquillity and

them.[1] Because of the iniquity of those who Judaize, we have forbidden them good things, which had been *formerly* allowed them ; and because they shut out many from the way of GOD, and have given usury, which was forbidden them *by the law*, and devoured men's substance vainly : we have prepared for such of them as are unbelievers a painful punishment. But those among them who are well grounded in knowledge,[2] and the faithful, who believe in that which hath been sent down unto thee, and that which hath been sent down *unto the prophets* before thee, and who observe the stated times of prayer, and give alms, and believe in GOD and the last day ; unto these will we give a great reward. Verily we have revealed *our will* unto thee, as we have revealed *it* unto Noah and the prophets who succeeded him ; and *as* we revealed *it* unto Abraham, and Ismael, and Isaac, and Jacob, and the tribes, and unto Jesus, and Job, and Jonas, and Aaron, and Solomon ; and *we have given thee the Korân, as* we gave the Psalms unto David : *some* apostles *have we sent*, whom we have formerly mentioned unto thee ; and *other* apostles *have we sent*, whom we have not mentioned unto thee ; and GOD spake unto Moses, discoursing *with him* ; apostles declaring good tidings, and denouncing threats, lest men should have an argument *of excuse* against GOD, after the apostles *had been sent unto them* ; GOD is mighty *and* wise. GOD is witness of that *revelation* which he hath sent down unto thee ; he sent it down with his s*pecial* knowledge ; the angels also are witnesses *thereof* ; but GOD is a sufficient witness. They who believe not, and turn aside *others* from the way of GOD, have erred in a wide mistake. Verily those who believe not, and act unjustly, GOD will by no means forgive, neither will he direct them into *any other* way than the way of hell ; they shall remain therein for ever : and this is easy with GOD. O men, now is the apostle come unto you, with truth from your LORD ; believe therefore, *it will be* better for you. But if ye disbelieve, verily unto GOD *belongeth* whatsoever *is* in heaven and on earth ; and GOD is knowing *and* wise. O ye who have received the scriptures, exceed not the just bounds in your religion,[3] neither say of GOD

security on earth. (Jallalo'ddin, Yahya, Al Zamakhshari, and Al Beidâwi. Prelim. Disc. Sect. IV.)

[1] *i e.*, Against the Jews, for rejecting him ; and against the Christians for calling him GOD, and the son of GOD. (Al Beidâwi.)

[2] As Abda'llah Ebn Salâm, and his companions. (Al Beidâwi.)

[3] Either by rejecting and contemning Jesus as the Jews do ; or raising him to an equality with GOD, as do the Christians. (Al Beidâwi.)

her than the truth. Verily Christ Jesus the son of Mary apostle of GOD, and his Word, which he conveyed into and a spirit *proceeding* from him. Believe therefore in GOD, and his apostles, and say not, *There are* three *Gods* ;[1] forbear *this* ; it will be better for you. GOD is but one GOD. Far be it from him that he should have a son ! unto him *belongeth* whatsoever *is* in heaven and on earth ; and GOD is a sufficient protector. Christ doth not proudly disdain to be a servant unto GOD ; neither the angels who approach near *to his presence* ; and whoso disdaineth his service, and is puffed up with pride, *God* will gather them all to himself, *on the last day.* Unto those who believe, and do that which is right, he shall give their rewards, and shall *superabundantly* add unto them of his liberality : but those who are disdainful and proud, he will punish with a grievous punishment ; and they shall not find any to protect or to help them, besides GOD. O men, now is an evident proof come unto you from your LORD, and we have sent down unto you manifest light. [2] They who believe in GOD and firmly adhere to him, he will lead them into mercy from him, and abundance ; and he will direct them in the right way to himself.[3] They will consult thee *for thy decision in certain cases* ; say *unto them,* GOD giveth you *these* determinations, concerning the more remote degrees of kindred.[4] If a man die without issue, and have a sister, she shall have the half of what he shall leave :[5] and he shall be heir to her,[6] in case she have no issue. But if there be two *sisters,* they shall have *between them* two third parts of what he shall leave ; and if there be *several, both* brothers and sisters, a male shall have as much as the portion of two females. GOD declareth unto you *these precepts,* lest ye err : and GOD knoweth all things.

---

[1] Namely, God, Jesus, and Mary. (Al Beidâwi, Jallalo'ddin, Yahya.) For the eastern writers mention a sect of Christians which held the Trinity to be composed of those three (Elmacin. p. 227. Eutych. p. 120. Prelim. Disc. Sect. II); but it is allowed that this heresy has been long since extinct. (Ahmed Ebn Abd'al Halim.) The passage, however, is equally levelled against the Holy Trinity, according to the doctrine of the orthodox Christians, who, as Al Beidâwi acknowledges, believe the divine nature to consist of three persons, the Father, the Son, and the Holy Ghost ; by the Father understanding GOD's essence ; by the Son his knowledge ; and by the Holy Ghost his life.

[2] That is, Mohammed and his Korân.

[3] viz., Into the religion of Islâm, in this world, and the way to paradise in the next. (Al Beidâwi.)

[4] See the beginning of this chapter, p. 71.

[5] And the other half will go to the public treasury.

[6] That is, he shall inherit her whole substance.

V

THE CHAPTER OF THE TABLE [1]

Revealed at Medina.

IN THE NAME OF THE MOST MERCIFUL GOD.

O TRUE believers, perform your contracts. Ye are allowed *to eat* the brute cattle,[2] other than what ye are commanded *to abstain from*; except the game which ye are allowed *at other times, but not* while ye are on pilgrimage *to Mecca*; GOD ordaineth that which he pleaseth. O true believers, violate not the holy rites of GOD,[3] nor the sacred month,[4] nor the offering, nor the ornaments hung *thereon*,[5] nor those who are travelling to the holy house, seeking favour from their LORD, and to please *him*. But when ye shall have finished *your pilgrimage*, then hunt. And let not the malice of some, in that they hindered you *from entering* the sacred temple,[6] provoke you to transgress, *by taking revenge on them in the sacred months*. Assist one another according to justice and piety, but assist not one another in injustice and malice: therefore fear GOD; for GOD is severe in punishing. Ye are forbidden *to eat* that which dieth of itself, and blood, and swine's flesh, and that on which the name of any besides GOD hath been invocated;[7] and that which hath been strangled, or killed by a blow, or by a fall, or by the horns *of another beast*, and that which hath been eaten by a wild beast,[8] except what ye shall kill *yourselves*;[9] and that which hath been sacrificed unto idols.[10] *It is likewise unlawful for you* to

---

[1] This title is taken from the Table, which, towards the end of the chapter, is fabled to have been let down from heaven to Jesus. It is sometimes also called the chapter of *Contracts*, which word occurs in the first verse.

[2] As camels, oxen, and sheep; and also wild cows, antelopes, &c. (Jallalo'-ddin, Al Beidâwi); but not swine, nor what is taken in hunting during the pilgrimage.

[3] i.e., The ceremonies used in the pilgrimage of Mecca.

[4] Sale, Prel. Disc. Sect. VII.

[5] The offering here meant is the sheep led to Mecca, to be there sacrificed, about the neck of which they used to hang garlands, green boughs, or some other ornament, that it might be distinguished as a thing sacred (Sale, Prel. Disc. Sect. IV.)

[6] In the expedition of Al Hodeibiya. (Sale, Prel. Disc. Sect. II. p. 56.)

[7] For the idolatrous Arabs used, in killing any animal for food, to consecrate it, as it were, to their idols, by saying, In the name of Allât, or Al Uzza. (See Chap. II.)

[8] Or by a creature trained up to hunting. (Al Beidâwi.)

[9] That is, unless ye come up time enough to find life in the animal, and to cut its throat.

[10] The word also signifies certain stones, which the pagan Arabs used to set up near their houses, and on which they superstitiously slew animals, in honour of their gods. (Al Beidâwi.)

make division by casting lots with arrows.[1] This is an impiety. On this day,[2] woe be unto those who have apostatized from their religion ; therefore fear not them, but fear me. This day have I perfected your religion for you,[3] and have completed my mercy upon you ;[4] and I have chosen for you Islâm, *to be your* religion. But whosoever shall be driven by necessity through hunger *to eat of what we have forbidden*, not designing to sin, surely GOD *will be* indulgent *and* merciful *unto him*. They will ask thee what is allowed them *as lawful to eat* ? Answer, Such things as are good[5] are allowed you ; and what ye shall teach animals of prey *to catch*,[6] training them up for hunting after the manner of dogs, *and* teaching them according to the *skill* which GOD hath taught you. Eat therefore of that which they shall catch for you ; and commemorate the name of GOD thereon ;[7] and fear GOD, for GOD is swift in taking an account. This day are ye allowed to eat such things as are good, and the food of those to whom the scriptures were given [8] is *also* allowed as lawful unto you ; and your food is allowed as lawful unto them. And *ye are also allowed to marry* free women that are believers, and also free women of those who have received the scriptures before you, when ye shall have assigned them their dower ; living chastely *with them*, neither committing fornication, nor taking *them for* concubines. Whoever shall renounce the faith, his work shall be vain, and in the next life he shall be of those who perish. O true believers, when ye prepare yourselves to pray, wash your faces, and your hands unto the elbows ; and rub your heads, and your feet unto the ankles ; and if ye be polluted by having lain with a woman, wash yourselves *all over*. But if ye be sick, or on a journey, or any of you cometh from the privy, or *if* ye have touched women, and ye find no water, take fine clean sand, and rub your faces and your hands therewith ; GOD would

---

[1] Sale, Prel. Disc. Sect. V.

[2] This passage, it is said, was revealed on Friday evening, being the day of the pilgrims' visiting Mount Arafat, the last time Mohammed visited the temple of Mecca, therefore called the *pilgrimage of valediction*. (Al Beidâwi. Prid. Life of Mahom. p. 99.)

[3] And therefore the commentators say, that after this time, no positive or negative precept was given. (Vide Abulfed. Vit. Moh. p. 131.)

[4] By having given you a true and perfect religion ; or, by the taking of Mecca, and the destruction of idolatry.

[5] Not such as are filthy, or unwholesome.

[6] Whether beasts or birds.

[7] Either when ye let go the hound, hawk, or other animal, after the game ; or when ye kill it.

[8] viz., Slain or dressed by Jews or Christians

not put a difficulty upon you ; but he desireth to purify you, and to complete his favour upon you, that ye may give thanks. Remember the favour of GOD towards you, and his covenant which he hath made with you, when ye said, We have heard, and will obey.[1] Therefore fear GOD, for God knoweth the innermost parts of the breasts *of men*. O true believers, observe justice when ye appear as witnesses before GOD, and let not hatred towards any induce you to do wrong : *but* act justly ; this will approach nearer unto piety ; and fear GOD, for GOD is fully acquainted with what ye do. GOD hath promised unto those who believe, and do that which is right, that they shall receive pardon and a great reward. But they who believe not, and accuse our signs of falsehood, they shall be the companions of hell. O true believers, remember GOD's favour towards you, when certain men designed to stretch forth their hands against you, but he restrained their hands from *hurting* you ;[2] therefore fear GOD, and in GOD let the faithful trust. GOD formerly accepted the covenant of the children of Israel, and we appointed out of them twelve leaders : and GOD said, Verily, I am with you :[3] if ye observe prayer, and give alms, and believe in my apostles, and assist

[1] These words are the form used at the inauguration of a prince ; and Mohammed here intends the oath of fidelity which his followers had taken to him at Al Akaba. (Vide Abulfed. ibid. p. 43, and Sale, Prel. Disc. p. 51.)

[2] The commentators tell several stories as the occasion of this passage. One says, that Mohammed and some of his followers being at Osfân (a place not far from Mecca, in the way to Medina), and performing their noon devotions, a company of idolaters, who were in view, repented they had not taken that opportunity of attacking them, and therefore waited till the hour of evening prayer, intending to fall upon them then : but GOD defeated their design, by revealing the verse of *fear*. Another relates, that the prophet going to the tribe of Koreidha (who were Jews) to levy a fine for the blood of two Moslems, who had been killed by mistake by Amru Ebn Ommeya al Dimri, they desired him to sit down and eat with them, and they would pay the fine ; Mohammed complying with their request, while he was sitting, they laid a design against his life, one Amru Ebn Jahâsh undertaking to throw a millstone upon him ; but GOD withheld his hand, and Gabriel immediately descended to acquaint the prophet with their treachery, upon which he rose up and went his way. A third story is, that Mohammed having hung up his arms on a tree, under which he was resting himself, and his companions being dispersed some distance from him, an Arab of the desert came up to him and drew his sword, saying, *Who hindereth me from killing thee* ? To which Mohammed answered, GOD ; and Gabriel beating the sword out of the Arab's hand, Mohammed took it up, and asked him the same question, *Who hinders me from killing thee* ? the Arab replied, *nobody*, and immediately professed Mohammedism. (Al Beidâwi.) Abûlfeda (Vit. Moh. p. 73) tells the same story, with some variation of circumstances.

[3] After the Israelites had escaped from Pharaoh, GOD ordered them to go against Jericho, which was then inhabited by giants, of the race of the Canaanites, promising to give it into their hands ; and Moses, by the divine direction, appointed a prince or captain over each tribe, to lead them in that expedition, (Numb. i. 4, 5), and when they came to the borders of the land

them, and lend unto GOD on good usury,[1] I will surely expiate your evil *deeds* from you, and I will lead you into gardens, wherein rivers flow : but he among you who disbelieveth after this, erreth from the straight path.   Wherefore because they have broken their covenant, we have cursed them, and hardened their hearts ; they dislocate the words *of the Pentateuch* from their places, and have forgotten part of what they were admonished ; and thou wilt not cease to discover deceitful practices among them, except a few of them.   But forgive them,[2] and pardon them, for GOD loveth the beneficent.   And from those who say, We are Christians, we have received their covenant ; but they have forgotten part of what they were admonished ; wherefore we have raised up enmity and hatred among them, till the day of resurrection ; and GOD will *then* surely declare unto them what they have been doing.   O ye who have received the scriptures, now is our apostle come unto you, to make manifest unto you many *things* which ye concealed in the scriptures ;[3] and to pass over[4] many *things*.   Now is light and a perspicuous book *of revelations* come unto you from GOD. Thereby will GOD direct him who shall follow his good pleasure, into the paths of peace ; and shall lead them out of darkness into light, by his will, and shall direct them in the right way.   They are infidels, who say, Verily GOD is Christ the son of Mary.   Say unto them, And who could obtain any thing from GOD *to the contrary*, if he pleased to destroy Christ the son of Mary, and his mother, and all those who are on the earth ?   For unto GOD *belongeth* the kingdom of heaven and earth, and whatsoever *is contained* between them ; he createth what he pleaseth, and GOD is almighty.   The Jews and the Christians say, We are the children of GOD, and his beloved.   Answer, Why therefore doth he punish you for your sins ?   Nay, but ye are men, of those whom he hath created.   He forgiveth whom he pleaseth, and punisheth

of Canaan, sent the captains as spies to get information of the state of the country, enjoining them secrecy ; but they being terrified at the prodigious size and strength of the inhabitants, disheartened the people by publicly telling what they had seen, except only Caleb the son of Yufanna (Jephunneh) and Joshua the son of Nun.   (Al Beidâwi.   Numb. xiii. and xiv.)

[1] By contributing towards this holy war.

[2] That is, if they repent and believe, or submit to pay tribute.   Some, however, think these words are abrogated by the verse of the *sword*.   (Al Beidâwi.)

[3] Such as the verse of stoning adulterers (see Chap. III.), the description of Mohammed, and Christ's prophecy of him by the name of Ahmed.   (Al Beidâwi.)

[4] *i.e.*, Those which it was not necessary to restore.

whom he pleaseth ; and unto GOD *belongeth* the kingdom of
heaven and earth, and of what *is contained* between them
both ; and unto him shall *all things* return.　O ye who have
received the scriptures, now is our apostle come unto you,
declaring unto you *the true religion*, during the cessation of
apostles,[1] lest ye should say, There came unto us no bearer
of good tidings, nor any warner : but now is a bearer of good
tidings and a warner come unto you ; and GOD is almighty.
Call to mind when Moses said unto his people, O my people,
remember the favour of GOD towards you, since he hath
appointed prophets among you, and constituted you kings,[2]
and bestowed on you what he hath given to no *other nation*
in the world.[3]　O my people, enter the holy land, which GOD
hath decreed you, and turn not your backs, lest ye be subverted and perish.　They answered, O Moses, verily there
are a gigantic people in the *land*,[4] and we will by no means
enter it, until they depart thence ; but if they depart thence,
then will we enter *therein*.　*And* two men[5] of those who
feared *God*, unto whom GOD had been gracious, said, Enter
ye upon them *suddenly by* the gate *of the city* ; and when ye
shall have entered the same, ye shall surely be victorious :
therefore trust in GOD, if ye are true believers.　They replied,
O Moses, we will never enter *the land*, while they remain
therein : go therefore thou, and thy LORD, and fight ; for
we will sit here.　Moses said, O LORD, surely I am not master
of any except myself, and my brother ; therefore make
a distinction between us and the ungodly people.　*God*
answered, Verily the *land* shall be forbidden them forty
years ; *during which time* they shall wander *like men astonished*
in the earth ;[6] therefore be not thou solicitous for the un-

---

[1] The Arabic *Fatra* signifies the intermediate space of time between two
prophets, during which no new revelation or dispensation was given ; as
the interval between Moses and Jesus, and between Jesus and Mohammed.

[2] This was fulfilled either by GOD's giving them a kingdom, and a long
series of princes ; or by his having made them *kings* or *masters* of themselves,
by delivering them from the Egyptian bondage.

[3] Having divided the Red Sea for you, and guided you by a cloud, and
fed you with quails and manna, &c.　(Al Beidâwi.)

[4] The largest of these giants, the commentators say, was Og, the son of
Anak ; concerning whose enormous stature, his escaping the Flood, and
the manner of his being slain by Moses, the Mohammedans relate several
absurd fables.　(Marracc. in Alcor. p. 231, &c.　D'Herbel. Bibl. Orient.
p. 336.)

[5] Namely, Caleb and Joshua.

[6] The commentators pretend that the Israelites, while they thus wandered
in the desert, were kept within the compass of about eighteen (or, as some
say, twenty-seven miles ; and that though they travelled from morning to
night, yet they constantly found themselves the next day at the place from
whence they set out.　(Al Beidâwi, Jallalo'ddin.)

godly people. Relate also unto them the history of the two sons of Adam,[1] with truth. When they offered[2] *their* offering and it was accepted from one of them,[3] and was not accepted from the other, *Cain* said *to his brother*, I will certainly kill thee. *Abel* answered, GOD only accepteth *the offering* of the pious ; if thou stretchest forth thy hand against me, to slay me, I will not stretch forth my hand against thee, to slay thee ; for I fear GOD the LORD of all creatures.[4] I choose that thou shouldest bear my iniquity and thine own iniquity ; and that thou become a companion of *hell* fire ; for that is the reward of the unjust.[5] But his soul suffered him to slay his brother, and he slew him ;[6] wherefore he became *of the number* of those who perish. And GOD sent a raven, which scratched the earth, to show him how he should hide the shame of his brother,[7] *and* he said, Woe is me ! am I unable to be like this raven, that I may hide my brother's shame ? and he became *one* of those who repent. Wherefore we commanded the children of Israel, that he who slay-

---

[1] viz., Cain and Abel, whom the Mohammedans call Kâbîl and Hâbîl.

[2] The occasion of their making this offering is thus related, according to the common tradition in the East. (Abulfarag, p. 6, 7 ; Eutych. Annal. p. 15, 16 ; and D'Herbelot, Bibl. Orient. Art. Cabil.) Each of them being born with a twin sister, when they were grown up, Adam, by GOD's direction, ordered Cain to marry Abel's twin sister, and that Abel should marry Cain's (for it being the common opinion that marriages ought not to be had in the nearest degrees of consanguinity, since they must necessarily marry their sisters, it seemed reasonable to suppose they ought to take those of the remoter degree), but this Cain refusing to agree to, because his own sister was the handsomer, Adam ordered them to make their offerings to GOD, thereby referring the dispute to his determination. (Al Beidâwi.) The commentators say Cain's offering was a sheaf of the very worst of his corn, but Abel's a fat lamb, of the best of his flock.

[3] Namely, from Abel, whose sacrifice GOD declared his acceptance of in a visible manner, by causing fire to descend from heaven and consume it, without touching that of Cain. (Al Beidâwi, Jallalo'ddin.)

[4] To enhance Abel's patience, Al Beidâwi tells us, that he was the stronger of the two, and could easily have prevailed against his brother.

[5] The conversation between the two brothers is related somewhat to the same purpose in the Jerusalem Targum and that of Jonathan ben Uzziel.

[6] Some say he knocked out his brains with a stone (Eutych. ubi supra) ; and pretend that as Cain was considering which way he should effect the murder, the devil appeared to him in a human shape, and showed him how to do it, by crushing the head of a bird between two stones. (D'Herbelot, ubi sup.)

[7] *i.e.*, His dead corpse. For Cain, having committed this fratricide, became exceedingly troubled in his mind, and carried the dead body about on his shoulders for a considerable time, not knowing where to conceal it, till it stank horribly ; and then GOD taught him to bury it by the example of a raven, who having killed another raven in his presence, dug a pit with his claws and beak, and buried him therein. (Al Beidâwi, Jallalo'ddin.) For this circumstance of the raven Mohammed was beholden to the Jews, who tell the same story, except only that they make the raven to appear to Adam, and that he thereupon buried his son. (R. Eliezer, Pirke, c. 20.)

eth a soul, without having slain a soul, or committed wickedness in the earth,[1] *shall be* as if he had slain all mankind :[2]
but he who saveth *a soul* alive, *shall be* as if he had saved the
lives of all mankind.   Our apostles formerly came unto them,
with evident *miracles* ; then were many of them, after this,
transgressors on the earth.   But the recompence of those who
fight against GOD and his apostles, and study to act corruptly
in the earth, *shall be*, that they shall be slain, or crucified, or
have their hands and their feet cut off on the opposite *sides*,
or be banished the land.[3]   This shall be their disgrace in this
world, and in the next world they shall suffer a grievous
punishment ; except those who shall repent, before ye prevail
against them ; for know that GOD *is* inclined to forgive,
and merciful.   O true believers, fear GOD, and earnestly
desire a near conjunction with him, and fight for his religion,
that ye may be happy.   Moreover they who believe not,
although they had whatever *is* in the earth, and as much
more withal, that they might therewith redeem themselves
from punishment on the day of resurrection ; it shall not be
accepted from them, but they shall suffer a painful punishment.   They shall desire to go forth from the fire, but they
shall not go forth from it, and their punishment shall be
permanent.   If a man or a woman steal, cut off their hands,[4]
in retribution for that which they have committed ; *this
is* an exemplary punishment *appointed* by GOD ; and GOD
is mighty *and* wise.   But whoever shall repent after his
iniquity, and amend, verily GOD will be turned unto him,[5]

---

[1] Such as idolatry, or robbing on the highway. (Al Beidâwi.)

[2] Having broken the commandment which forbids the shedding of blood.

[3] The lawyers are not agreed as to the applying of these punishments.
But the commentators suppose that they who commit murder only are to
be put to death in the ordinary way ; those who murder and rob too, to be
crucified ; those who rob without committing murder, to have their right
hand and their left foot cut off ; and they who assault persons and put them
in fear, to be banished. (Al Beidâwi, Jallalo'ddin.)   It is also a doubt whether
they who are to be crucified shall be crucified alive, or be first put to death,
or whether they shall hang on the cross till they die. (Al Beidâwi.)

[4] But this punishment, according to the Sonna, is not to be inflicted, unless
the value of the thing stolen amount to four *dinârs*, or about forty shillings.
For the first offence, the criminal is to lose his right hand, which is to be
cut off at the wrist ; for the second offence, his left foot, at the ankle ; for
the third, his left hand ; for the fourth, his right foot ; and if he continue
to offend, he shall be scourged at the discretion of the judge. (Al Beidâwi,
Jallalo'ddin.)

[5] That is, GOD will not punish him for it hereafter ; but his repentance
does not supersede the execution of the law here, nor excuse him from making
restitution.   Yet, according to Al Shâfeï, he shall not be punished if the
party wronged forgive him before he be carried before a magistrate. (Jallalo'-
ddin, Al Beidâwi.)

for GOD *is* inclined to forgive *and* merciful. Dost thou not know that the kingdom of heaven and earth is GOD's. He punisheth whom he pleaseth, and he pardoneth whom he pleaseth ; for GOD is almighty. O apostle, let not them grieve thee, who hasten to infidelity,[1] *either* of those who say, We believe, with their mouths, but whose hearts believe not ;[2] or of the Jews, who hearken to a lie, *and* hearken to other people ;[3] *who* come not unto thee : they pervert the words *of the law* from their *true* places,[4] *and* say, If this be brought unto you, receive it ; but if it be not brought unto you, beware *of receiving ought else* ;[5] and in behalf of him whom GOD shall resolve to reduce, thou shalt not prevail with GOD at all. They whose hearts GOD shall not please to cleanse, shall suffer shame in this world, and a grievous punishment in the next : who hearken to a lie, *and* eat that which is forbidden.[6] But if they come unto thee *for judgment,* either judge between them, or leave them ;[7] and if thou leave them, they shall not hurt thee at all. But if thou *undertake to* judge, judge between them with equity ; for GOD loveth those who observe justice. And how will they submit to thy decision, since they have the law, containing the judg-

---

[1] *i.e.*, Who take the first opportunity to throw off the mask, and join the unbelievers.

[2] viz., The hypocritical Mohammedans.

[3] These words are capable of two senses ; and may either mean that they attended to the lies and forgeries of their rabbins, neglecting the remonstrances of Mohammed ; or else, that they came to hear Mohammed as spies only, that they might report what he said to their companions, and represent him as a liar. (Al Beidâwi.)

[4] See Chapter IV. p. 79.

[5] That is, if what Mohammed tells you agrees with scripture, as corrupted and dislocated by us, then you may accept it as the word of GOD ; but if not, reject it. These words, it is said, relate to the sentence pronounced by that prophet on an adulterer and an adulteress (Chap. III), both persons of some figure among the Jews. For they, it seems, though they referred the matter to Mohammed, yet directed the persons who carried the criminals before him, that if he ordered them to be scourged and to have their faces blackened (by way of ignominy), they should acquiesce in his determination ; but in case he condemned them to be stoned, they should not. And Mohammed pronouncing the latter sentence against them, they refused to execute it, till Ebn Sûriya (a Jew), who was called upon to decide the matter, acknowledged the law to be so—whereupon they were stoned at the door of the mosque. (Al Beidâwi.)

[6] Some understand this of unlawful meats ; but others of taking or *devouring* as it is expressed, of usury and bribes. (Al Beidâwi.)

[7] *i.e.*, Take thy choice, whether thou wilt determine their differences or not. Hence Al Shâfeï was of opinion that a judge was not obliged to decide causes between Jews or Christians ; though if one or both of them be tributaries, or under the protection of the Mohammedans, then he is obliged : this verse not regarding them. Abu Hanífa, however, thought that the magistrates were obliged to judge all cases which were submitted to them. (Al Beidâwi.)

ment of GOD ?[1] Then will they turn their backs, after this ;[2] but those are not true believers.[3] We have surely sent down the law, containing direction, and light : thereby did the prophets, who professed the true religion, judge these who Judaized ; and the doctors and priests *also judged* by the book of GOD, which had been committed to their custody ; and they were witnesses thereof.[4] Therefore fear not men, but fear me ; neither sell my signs for a small price.   And whoso judgeth not according to what GOD hath revealed, they are infidels.   We have therein commanded them, that *they should give* life for life,[5] and eye for eye, and nose for nose, and ear for ear, and tooth for tooth ; and *that* wounds *should also be punished by* retaliation :[6] but whoever should remit it as alms, it *should be accepted as* an atonement for him.   And whoso judgeth not according to what GOD hath revealed, they are unjust.   We also caused Jesus the son of Mary to follow the footsteps of *the prophets*, confirming the law which *was sent down* before him ; and we gave him the gospel, containing direction and light ; confirming also the law which *was given* before it, and a direction and admonition unto those who fear *God* : that they who have received the gospel might judge according to what GOD hath revealed therein : and whoso judgeth not according to what GOD hath revealed, they are transgressors.   We have also sent down unto thee the book *of the Korân* with truth, confirming that scripture which *was revealed* before it ; and preserving the same safe *from corruption*.   Judge therefore between them according to that which GOD hath revealed ; and follow not their desires, *by swerving* from the truth which hath come unto thee.   Unto every of you have we given a law, and an open path ; and if GOD had pleased, he had surely made you one people ;[7] but *he hath thought fit to give you different laws*, that

---

[1] In the following passage Mohammed endeavours to answer the objections of the Jews and Christians, who insisted that they ought to be judged, the former by the law of Moses, and the latter by the gospel. He allows that the law was the proper rule of judging till the coming of Jesus Christ, after which the gospel was the rule ; but pretends that both are set aside by the revelation of the Korân, which is so far from being contradictory to either of the former, that it is more full and explicit ; declaring several points which had been stifled or corrupted therein, and requiring a rigorous execution of the precepts in both, which had been too remissly observed, or rather neglected, by the later professors of those religions.

[2] That is, notwithstanding their outward submission, they will not abide by thy sentence, though conformable to the law, if it contradict their own false and loose decisions.

[3] As gainsaying the doctrine of the books which they acknowledge for scripture.   [4] That is, vigilant, to prevent any corruptions therein.

[5] The original word is *soul*.   [6] See Exod. xxi, 24, &c.

[7] *i.e.*, He had given you the same laws, which should have continued

he might try you in that which he hath given you *respectively*. Therefore strive to excel each other in good works : unto GOD shall ye all return, and *then* will he declare unto you that concerning which ye have disagreed. Wherefore *do thou, O prophet,* judge between them according to that which GOD hath revealed, and follow not their desires ; but beware of them, lest they cause thee to err[1] from part of those *precepts* which GOD hath sent down unto thee ; and if they turn back [2] know that GOD is pleased to punish them for some of their crimes ; for a great number of men are transgressors. Do they therefore desire the judgment of *the time of* ignorance ?[3] but who is better than GOD, to judge between people who reason aright ? O true believers, take not the Jews or Christians for *your* friends ; they are friends the one to the other ; but whoso among you taketh them for *his* friends, he *is* surely *one* of them : verily GOD directeth not unjust people. Thou shalt see those in whose hearts there is an infirmity, to hasten unto them, saying, We fear lest some adversity befall us ;[4] but it is easy for GOD to give victory, or a command from him,[5] that they may repent of that which they concealed in their minds. And they who believe will say, Are these *the men* who have sworn by GOD, with a most firm oath, that they surely *held* with you ?[6] their works are become vain, and they are of those who perish. O true believers, whoever of you apostatizeth from his religion, GOD will certainly bring other people to *supply his place,*[7] whom he will love, and who

in force through all ages, without being abolished or changed by new dispensations ; or he could have forced you all to embrace the Mohammedan religion. (Al Beidâwi.)

[1] It is related that certain of the Jewish priests came to Mohammed with a design to entrap him ; and having first represented to him that if they acknowledged him for a prophet, the rest of the Jews would certainly follow their example, made this proposal—that if he would give judgment for them in a controversy of moment which they pretended to have with their own people, and which was agreed to be referred to his decision, they would believe him—but this Mohammed absolutely refused to comply with. (Al Beidâwi.)   [2] Or refused to be judged by the Korân.

[3] That is, to be judged according to the customs of paganism, which indulge the passions and vicious appetites of mankind : for this, it seems, was demanded by the Jewish tribes of Koreidha and Al Nadir. (Al Beidâwi.)

[4] These were the words of Ebn Obba, who, when Obâdah Ebn al Sâmat publicly renounced the friendship of the infidels, and professed that he took GOD and his apostle for his patrons, said that he was a man apprehensive of the fickleness of fortune, and therefore would not throw off his old friends, who might be of service to him hereafter. (Al Beidâwi.)

[5] To extirpate and banish the Jews ; or to detect and punish the hypocrites.

[6] These words may be spoken by the Mohammedans either to one another or to the Jews, since these hypocrites had given their oaths to both. (Al Beidâwi.)

[7] This is one of those accidents which, it is pretended, were foretold by

will love him ; *who shall be* humble towards the believers, *but* severe to the unbelievers ; they shall fight for the religion of GOD, and shall not fear the obloquy of the detractor. This *is* the bounty of GOD, he bestoweth it on whom he pleaseth : GOD *is* extensive *and* wise. Verily your protector is GOD, and his apostle, and those who believe, who observe the stated times of prayer, and give alms, and who bow down *to worship*. And whoso taketh GOD, and his apostle, and the believers for his friends, *they are* the party of GOD, *and* they *shall be* victorious. O true believers, take not such of those to whom the scriptures were delivered before you, or of the infidels, for your friends, who make a laughing-stock and a jest of your religion ;[1] but fear GOD if ye be true believers ; *nor those who*, when ye call to prayer, make a laughing-stock and a jest of it ;[2] this *they do* because they are people who do

the Korân long before they came to pass. For in the latter days of Mohammed, and after his death, considerable numbers of the Arabs quitted his religion, and returned to Paganism, Judaism, or Christianity. Al Beidâwi reckons them up in the following order. 1. Three companies of Banu Modlaj, seduced by Dhu'lhamâr al Aswad al Ansi, who set up for a prophet in Yaman, and grew very powerful there. (Sale, Prel. Disc. Sect. VIII.) 2. Banu Honeifa, who followed the famous false prophet Moseilama. (Sale, Prel. Disc. Sect. VIII.) 3. Banu Asad, who acknowledged Toleiha Ebn Khowailed, another pretender to divine revelation (Sale, Prel. Disc. Sect. VIII.) for their prophet. All these fell off in Mohammed's lifetime. The following, except only the last, apostatized in the reign of Abu Becr. 4. Certain of the tribe of Fezârah, headed by Oyeyma Ebn Hosein. 5. Some of the tribe of Ghatfân whose leader was Korrah Ebn Salma. 6. Banu Soleim, who followed Al Fajâah Ebn Abd Yal l. 7. Banu Yarbu, whose captain was Malec Ebn Noweirah Ebn Kais. 8. Part of the tribe of Tamîm, the proselytes of Sajâj the daughter of Al Mondhar, who gave herself out for a prophetess. (Prelim. Disc. Sect. VIII.) 9. The tribe of Kendah, led by Al Ashâth Ebn Kais. 10. Banu Becr Ebn al Wayel, in the province of Bahrein, headed by Al Hotam Ebn Zeid. And, 11. Some of the tribe of Ghassán, who, with their prince Jabalah Ebn al Ayham, renounced Mohammedism in the time of Omar, and returned to their former profession of Christianity. (Sale, Prel. Disc. Sect. I.) But as to the persons who fulfilled the other part of this prophecy, by supplying the loss of so many renegades, the commentators are not agreed. Some will have them to be the inhabitants of Yaman, and others the Persians ; the authority of Mohammed himself being vouched for both opinions. Others, however, suppose them to be 2,000 of the tribe of Al Nakhâ (who dwelt in Yaman), 5,000 of those of Kendah and Bajilah, and 3,000 of unknown descent (D'Herbel. Bibl. Orient. p. 226), who were present at the famous battle of Kadesia, fought in the Khalîfat of Omar, and which put an end to the Persian empire. (Al Beidâwi.)

[1] This passage was primarily intended to forbid the Moslems entering into a friendship with two hypocrites named Refâa Ebn Zeid, and Soweid Ebn al Hareth, who, though they had embraced Mohammedism, yet ridiculed it on all occasions, and were notwithstanding greatly beloved among the prophet's followers.

[2] These words were added on occasion of a certain Christian, who hearing the Muedhdhin, or crier, in calling to prayers, repeat this part of the usual form, *I profess that* Mohammed *is the apostle of* GOD, said aloud, *May* GOD *burn the liar* : but a few nights after his own house was accidentally set

not understand. Say, O ye who have received the scriptures, do ye reject us *for any other reason* than because we believe in GOD, and that *revelation* which hath been sent down unto us, and that which was formerly sent down, and for that the greater part of you are transgressors? Say, Shall I denounce unto you a worse *thing* than this, *as to* the reward *which ye are to expect* with GOD? He whom GOD hath cursed, and with whom he hath been angry, having changed *some* of them into apes and swine,[1] and *who* worship Taghût,[2] they *are* in the worse condition, and err more *widely* from the straightness of the path. When they came unto you, they said, We believe: yet they entered *into your company* with infidelity, and went forth *from you* with the same; but GOD well knew what they concealed. Thou shalt see many of them hastening unto iniquity and malice, and to eat things forbidden;[3] and woe *unto them for* what they have done. Unless *their* doctors and priests forbid them uttering wickedness, and eating things forbidden; woe *unto them for* what they shall have committed. The Jews say, the hand of GOD is tied up.[4] Their hands shall be tied up,[5] and they shall be cursed for that which they have said. Nay, his hands are both stretched forth; he bestoweth as he pleaseth: that which hath been sent down unto thee from thy LORD,[6] shall increase the transgression and infidelity of many of them; and we have put enmity and hatred between them, until the day of resurrection. So often as they shall kindle a fire for war, GOD shall extinguish it;[7] and they

on fire by a servant, and himself and his family perished in the flames (Al Beidâwi.)

[1] The former were the Jews of Ailah, who broke the sabbath (See Chap. II); and the latter those who believed not in the miracle of the table which was let down from heaven to Jesus. (See towards the end of this chapter.) Some, however, imagine that the Jews of Ailah only are meant in this place, pretending that the young men among them were metamorphosed into apes, and the old men into swine. (Al Beidâwi.)

[2] See Chap. II. p. 37.

[3] See before.

[4] That is, he is become niggardly and close-fisted. These were the words of Phineas Ebn Azrûa (another indecent expression of whom, almost to the same purpose, is mentioned in Chap. III.), when the Jews were much impoverished by a dearth, which the commentators will have to be a judgment on them for their rejecting of Mohammed; and the other Jews who heard him, instead of reproving him, expressed their approbation of what he had said. (Al Beidâwi.)

[5] *i.e.*, They shall be punished with want and avarice. The words may also allude to the manner wherein the reprobates shall appear at the last day, having their right hands tied up to their necks (Sale, Prel. Disc. Sect. IV.); which is the proper signification of the Arabic word.

[6] viz., The Korân.

[7] Either by raising feuds and quarrels among themselves, or by granting the victory to the Moslems. Al Beidâwi adds, that on the Jews neglecting

shall set their minds to act corruptly in the earth, but GOD loveth not the corrupt doers. Moreover, if they who have received the scriptures believe, and fear *God*, we will surely expiate their sins from them, and we will lead them into gardens of pleasure ; and if they observe the law, and the gospel, and *the other scriptures* which have been sent down unto them from their LORD, they shall surely eat *of good things* both from above them and from under their feet.[1] Among them there are people who act uprightly ; but how evil is that which many of them do work ! O apostle, publish *the whole of* that which hath been sent down unto thee from thy LORD : for if thou do not, thou dost not *in effect* publish any part thereof ;[2] and GOD will defend thee against *wicked* men ;[3] for GOD directeth not the unbelieving people. Say, O ye who have received the scriptures, ye are not *grounded* on anything, until ye observe the law and the gospel, and that which hath been sent down unto you from your LORD. That which hath been sent down unto thee from thy LORD shall surely increase the transgression and infidelity of many of them : but be not thou solicitous for the unbelieving people. Verily they who believe, and those who Judaize, and the Sabians, and the Christians, whoever *of them* believeth in GOD and the last day, and doth that which is right, *there shall come* no fear on them, neither shall they be grieved.[4] We formerly accepted the covenant of the children of Israel, and sent apostles unto them. So often as an apostle came unto them with that which their souls desired not, they accused some of them of imposture, and some of them they killed : and they imagined that there should be no punishment *for those crimes*, and they became blind and deaf.[5] Then was GOD turned unto them ;[6] afterwards many of them *again*

the true observance of their law, and corrupting their religion, GOD has successively delivered them into the hands, first of Bakht Nasr or Nebuchadnezzar, then of Titus the Roman, and afterwards of the Persians, and has now at last subjected them to the Mohammedans.

[1] That is, they shall enjoy the blessings both of heaven and earth.

[2] That is, if thou do not complete the publication of all thy revelations, without exception, thou dost not answer the end for which they were revealed ; because the concealing of any part renders the system of religion which GOD has thought fit to publish to mankind by thy ministry lame and imperfect. (Al Beidâwi, Jallalo'ddin.)

[3] Until this verse was revealed, Mohammed entertained a guard of armed men for his security, but on his receiving this assurance of GOD's protection, he immediately dismissed them. (Al Beidâwi, Jallalo'ddin.)

[4] See Chap II. p. 10.

[5] Shutting their eyes and ears against conviction and the remonstrance of the law ; as when they worshipped the calf.

[6] *i.e.*, Upon their repentance.

became blind and deaf; but GOD saw what they did. They are surely infidels, who say, Verily GOD is Christ the son of Mary; since Christ said, O children of Israel, serve GOD, my LORD and your LORD; whoever shall give a companion unto GOD, GOD shall exclude him from paradise, and his habitation shall be *hell* fire; and the ungodly shall have none to help them. They are certainly infidels, who say, GOD is the third of three :[1] for there is no GOD besides one GOD; and if they refrain not from what they say, a painful torment shall surely be inflicted on such of them as are unbelievers. Will they not therefore be turned unto GOD, and ask pardon of him? since GOD is gracious *and* merciful. Christ the son of Mary is no more than an apostle; *other* apostles have preceded him; and his mother was a woman of veracity :[2] they *both* ate food.[3] Behold, how we declare unto them the signs *of God's unity*; and then behold, how they turn aside *from the truth*. Say *unto them*, Will ye worship, besides GOD, that which can cause you neither harm nor profit? GOD *is* he who heareth *and* seeth. Say, O ye who have received the scriptures, exceed not *the just bounds* in your religion,[4] *by speaking* beside the truth; neither follow the desires of people who have heretofore erred, and who have seduced many, and have gone astray from the strait path.[5] Those among the children of Israel who believed not, were cursed by the tongue of David, and of Jesus the son of Mary.[6] This *befell them* because they were rebellious and transgressed : they forbade not one another the wickedness which they committed; and woe *unto them for* what they committed. Thou shalt see many of them take for their friends those who believe not. Woe *unto them* for what their souls have sent before them,[7] for that GOD is incensed against them, and they shall remain in torment *for ever*. But, if they had believed in GOD, and the prophet, and that which hath been revealed unto him, they had not taken them for *their* friends; but many of them are evil-doers. Thou shalt surely find the most violent of *all* men in enmity against the true believers, *to be* the Jews and

---

[1] See Chap IV. p. 96.

[2] Never pretending to partake of the divine nature, or to be the mother of GOD. (Jallalo'ddin.)

[3] Being obliged to support their lives by the same means, and being subject to the same necessities and infirmities as the rest of mankind, and therefore no Gods. (Al Beidâwi, Jallalo'ddin.)

[4] See Chap IV. p. 96. But here the words are principally directed to the Christians.

[5] That is, of their prelates and predecessors, who erred in ascribing divinity to Christ, before the mission of Mohammed. (Al Beidâwi Jallalo'ddin.)

[6] See p. 108.   [7] See Chap. II.

the idolaters ; and thou shalt surely find those among them *to be* the most inclinable to *entertain* friendship for the true believers, who say, We are Christians. This *cometh to pass,* because there are priests and monks among them ; and because they are not elated with pride.[1] (VII.) And when they hear that which hath been sent down to the apostle *read unto them,* thou shalt see their eyes overflow with tears, because of the truth which they perceive *therein,*[2] saying, O LORD, we believe ; write us down therefore with those who bear witness *to the truth* : and what *should hinder* us from believing in GOD, and the truth which hath come unto us, and from earnestly desiring that our LORD would introduce us *into paradise* with the righteous people ? Therefore hath GOD rewarded them, for what they have said, with gardens through which rivers flow ; they shall continue therein *for ever* ; and this is the reward of the righteous. But they who believe not, and accuse our signs of falsehood, they *shall be* the companions of hell. O true believers, forbid not the good things which GOD hath allowed you ;[3] but transgress not, for GOD loveth not the transgressors. And eat of what GOD hath given you for food *that which is* lawful *and* good : and fear GOD, in whom ye believe. GOD will not punish you for an inconsiderate word in your oaths ;[4] but he will punish you for what ye solemnly swear *with deliberation.* And the expiation of such *an oath shall be* the feeding of ten poor men with such moderate *food* as ye feed your own families withal ; or to

---

[1] Being humble and well disposed to receive the truth ; qualities which are to be commended even in infidels. (Al Beidâwi.) The sixth section ends with this passage.

[2] The persons directly intended in this passage were, either Ashama, king of Ethiopia, and several bishops and priests, who, being assembled for that purpose, heard Jaafar Ebn Abi Taleb, who fled to that country in the first flight (Sale, Prel. Disc. Sect. II.), read the 29th and 30th, and afterwards the 18th and 19th chapters of the Korân ; on hearing of which the king and the rest of the company burst into tears, and confessed what was delivered therein to be conformable to truth ; that prince himself, in particular, becoming a proselyte to Mohammedism. (Al Beidâwi, Al Thalabi. Abulfed. Vit. Moham. p. 25, &c. Marracc. Prodr. ad Refut. Alcor. part i. p. 45) ; or else, thirty, or as others say, seventy persons, sent ambassadors to Mohammed by the same king of Ethiopia, to whom the prophet himself read the 36th chapter, entitled Y.S. Whereupon they began to weep, saying, *How like is this to that which was revealed unto Jesus !* and immediately professed themselves Moslem. (Al Beidâwi, Jallalo'ddin. Vide Marracc. ubi sup.)

[3] These words were revealed when certain of Mohammed's companions agreed to oblige themselves to continual fasting and watching, and to abstain from women, eating flesh, sleeping on beds, and other lawful enjoyments of life, in imitation of some self-denying Christians ; but this the prophet disapproved, declaring that he would have no *monks* in his religion. (Al Beidâwi, Jallalo'ddin.)   [4] See Chap. II. p. 32.

clothe them ;[1] or to free the neck *of a true believer from captivity* ; but he who shall not find *wherewith to perform one of these three things*, shall fast three days.[2]   This is the expiation, of your oaths, when ye swear *inadvertently*.   Therefore keep your oaths.   Thus GOD declareth unto you his signs, that ye may give thanks.   O true believers, surely wine, and lots,[3] and images,[4] and divining arrows,[5] *are* an abomination of the work of Satan ; therefore avoid them, that ye may prosper. Satan seeketh to sow dissension and hatred among you, by means of wine and lots, and to divert you from remembering GOD, and from prayer ; will ye not therefore abstain *from them* ?   Obey GOD, and obey the apostle, and take heed *to yourselves* : but if ye turn back, know that the duty of our apostle is only to preach publicly.[6]   In those who believe and do good works, it is no sin that they have tasted *wine or gaming before they were forbidden* ; if they fear *God*, and believe, and do good works, and *shall for the future* fear *God*, and believe, and *shall persevere to* fear *him*, and *to* do good ;[7] for GOD loveth those who do good.   O true believers, GOD will surely prove you in *offering you plenty of* game, which ye may take with your hands or your lances,[8] that GOD may know who feareth him in secret ; but whoever transgresseth after this, shall suffer a grievous punishment.   O true be-

---

[1] The commentators give us the different opinions of the doctors, as to the quantity of food and clothes to be given in this case ; which I think scarce worth transcribing.

[2] That is, three days together, says Abu Hanifa.   But this is not observed in practice, being neither explicitly commanded in the Korân, nor ordered in the Sonna.   (Al Beidâwi.)

[3] That is, all inebriating liquors, and games of chance.   (Sale, Prel. Disc. Sect. V., and Chap. II. p. 30.)

[4] Al Beidâwi and some other commentators expound this of idols ; but others, with more probability, of the carved pieces or men with which the pagan Arabs played at chess, being little figures of men, elephants, horses, and dromedaries ; and this is supposed to be the only thing Mohammed disliked in that game : for which reason the Sonnites play wth plain pieces of wood or ivory ; but the Persians and Indians, who are not so scrupulous, still make use of the carved ones.   (Sale, Prel. Disc. Sect. V.)

[5] Sale, Prel. Disc. Sect V.

[6] Sale, Prel. Disc. Sect. II. p. 52.

[7] The commentators endeavour to excuse the tautology of this passage by supposing the threefold repetition of *fearing* and *believing* refers either to the three parts of time, past, present, and future, or to the threefold duty of man, towards GOD, himself, and his neighbour, &c. (Al Beidâwi.)

[8] This temptation or trial was at Al Hodeibiya, where Mohammed's men, who had attended him thither with an intent to perform a pilgrimage to the Caaba, and had initiated themselves with the usual rites, were surrounded by so great a number of birds and beasts that they impeded their march ; from which unusual accident, some of them concluded that GOD had allowed them to be taken ; but this passage was to convince them of the contrary. (Al Beidâwi, Jallalo'ddin.)

lievers, kill no game while ye are on pilgrimage ;[1] whosoever among you shall kill any designedly, shall restore the like of what ye shall have killed, in domestic animals,[2] according to the determination of two just persons among you, to be brought as an offering to the Caaba ; or in atonement thereof shall feed the poor ; or instead thereof shall fast, that he may taste the heinousness of his deed. GOD hath forgiven what is past, but whoever returneth *to transgress*, GOD will take vengeance on him ; for GOD is mighty *and* able to avenge. It is lawful for you to fish in the sea,[3] and to eat *what ye shall catch*, as a provision for you and for those who travel ; but it is unlawful for you to hunt by land, while ye are performing the rites of pilgrimage ;[4] therefore fear GOD, before whom ye shall be assembled *at the last day*. GOD hath appointed the Caaba, the holy house, an establishment[5] for mankind ; and *hath ordained* the sacred month,[6] and the offering, and the ornaments hung *thereon*.[7] This *hath he done* that ye might know that GOD knoweth whatsoever *is* in heaven and on earth, and that GOD is omniscient. Know that GOD is severe in punishing, and that GOD *is also* ready to forgive *and* merciful. The duty of our apostle is to preach only ;[8] and GOD knoweth that which ye discover, and that which ye conceal. Say, Evil and good shall not be equally esteemed of, though the abundance of evil pleaseth thee ; [9]

[1] Literally, *while ye are* Mohrims, or have actually initiated yourselves as pilgrims, by putting on the garment worn at that solemnity. Hunting and fowling are hereby absolutely forbidden to persons in this state, though they are allowed to kill certain kinds of noxious animals. (Sale, Prel. Disc. Sect. V.)

[2] That is, he shall bring an offering to the temple of Mecca, to be slain there and distributed among the poor, of some domestic or tame animal, equal in value to what he shall have killed ; as a sheep, for example, in lieu of an antelope, a pigeon for a partridge, &c. And of this value two prudent persons were to be judges. If the offender was not able to do this, he was to give a certain quantity of food to one or more poor men ; or, if he could not afford that, to fast a proportionable number of days. (Al Beidâwi, Jallalo'ddin.)

[3] This, says Jallalo'ddin, is to be understood of fish that live altogether in the sea, and not of those that live in the sea and on land both, as crabs, &c. The Turks, who are Hanifites, never eat this sort of fish; but the sect of Mâlec Ebn Ans, and perhaps some others, make no scruple of it.

[4] See above, note[1].

[5] That is, the place where the practice of their religious ceremonies is chiefly established ; where those who are under any apprehension of danger may find a sure *asylum*, and the merchant certain gain, &c. (Al Beidâwi, Jallalo'ddin.)

[6] Al Beidâwi understands this of the month of Dhu'lhajja, wherein the ceremonies of the pilgrimage are performed ; but Jallalo'ddin supposes all the four sacred months are here intended. (Sale, Prel. Disc. Sect. VII.)

[7] See before.   [8] Sale, Prel. Disc. Sect. II. p. 52.

[9] For judgment is to be made of things not from their plenty or scarcity, but from their intrinsic good or bad qualities. (Al Beidâwi.)

therefore fear GOD, O ye of understanding, that ye may be happy. O true believers, inquire not concerning things which, if they be declared unto you, may give you pain ; [1] but if ye ask concerning them when the Korân is sent down, they will be declared unto you : GOD pardoneth *you as to* these matters ; for GOD is ready to forgive *and* gracious. People who have been before you formerly inquired concerning them ; and afterwards disbelieved therein. GOD hath not ordained *anything* concerning Bahîra, nor Sâïba, nor Wasîla, nor Hâmi ; [2] but the unbelievers have invented a lie against GOD : and the greater part of them do not understand. And when it was said unto them, Come unto that which GOD hath revealed, and to the apostle ; they answered, That *religion* which we found our fathers *to follow* is sufficient for us. What though their fathers knew nothing, and were not *rightly* directed ? O true believers, take care of your souls. He who erreth shall not hurt you, while ye are *rightly* directed : [3] unto GOD shall ye all return, and he will tell you that which ye have done. O true believers, let witnesses be taken between you, when death approaches any of you, at the time of *making* the testament ; *let there be* two *witnesses*, just men, from among you ; [4] or two others of *a* different *tribe or faith* from yourselves, [5] if ye be journeying in the earth, and the accident of death befall you. Ye shall shut them both up, after the *afternoon* prayer, [6] and they shall swear by GOD, if ye

[1] The Arabs continually teasing their prophet with questions, which probably he was not always prepared to answer, they are here ordered to wait, till GOD should think fit to declare his pleasure by some further revelation ; and, to abate their curiosity, they are told, at the same time, that very likely the answers would not be agreeable to their inclinations. Al Beidâwi says, that when the pilgrimage was first commanded, Sorâka Ebn Malec asked Mohammed whether they were obliged to perform it every year ? To this question the prophet at first turned a deaf ear, but being asked it a second and a third time, he at last said, *No ; but if I had said yes it would have become a duty, and, if it were a duty, ye would not be able to perform it ; therefore give me no trouble as to things wherein I give you none :* whereupon this passage was revealed.

[2] These were the names given by the pagan Arabs to certain camels or sheep which were turned loose to feed, and exempted from common services, in some particular cases ; having their ears slit, or some other mark, that they might be known ; and this they did in honour of their gods. (Sale, Prel. Disc. Sect. V.) Which superstitions are here declared to be no ordinances of GOD, but the inventions of foolish men.

[3] This was revealed when the infidels reproached those who embraced Mohammedism and renounced their old idolatry, that by so doing they arraigned the wisdom of their forefathers. (Al Beidâwi.)

[4] That is, of your kindred or religion.

[5] They who interpret these words of persons of another religion, say they are abrogated, and that the testimony of such ought not to be received against a Moslem. (Al Beidâwi.)

[6] In case there was any doubt, the witnesses were to be kept apart from

if ye be true believers. They said, We desire to eat thereof,
and that our heart may rest at ease, and that we may know
that thou hast told us the truth, and that we may be witnesses
thereof. Jesus, the son of Mary, said, O GOD our LORD, cause
a table to descend unto us from heaven, that *the day of its
descent* may become a festival day[1] unto us, unto the first of
us, and unto the last of us, and a sign from thee ; and do
thou provide food for us, for thou art the best provider. GOD
said, Verily I will cause it to descend unto you ; but whoever
among you shall disbelieve hereafter, I will surely punish
him with a punishment wherewith I will not punish any
other creature. And when GOD shall say *unto Jesus, at the
last day*, O Jesus, son of Mary, hast thou said unto men, Take
me and my mother for two gods, beside GOD ? He shall
answer, Praise be unto thee ! it is not for me to say that which
I ought not ; if I had said so, thou wouldst surely have known
it : thou knowest what is in me, but I know not what is in
thee ; for thou art the knower of secrets. I have not spoken
to them *any other* than what thou didst command me ;
namely, Worship GOD, my LORD and your LORD : and I was
a witness *of their actions* while I stayed among them ; but
since thou hast taken me to thyself,[2] thou hast been the
watcher over them ; for thou art witness of all things. If
thou punish them, they are surely thy servants ; and if thou
forgive them, thou art mighty *and* wise. GOD will say, This
day shall their veracity be of advantage unto those who
speak truth ; they shall have gardens wherein rivers flow,
they shall remain therein for ever : GOD hath been well
pleased in them, and they have been well pleased in him.
This *shall* be great felicity. Unto GOD *belongeth* the kingdom
of heaven and of earth, and of whatever therein is ; and he is
almighty.

are also told, which are scarce worth transcribing. (Marracc. in Alc. p.
238, &c.)

[1] Some say the table descended on a Sunday, which was the reason of
the Christians observing that day as sacred. Others pretend this day is
still kept among them as a very great festival ; and it seems as if the story
had its rise from an imperfect notion of Christ's last supper, and the
institution of the Eucharist.

[2] Or, *since thou hast caused me to die* : but as it is a dispute among the
Mohammedans whether Christ actually died or not, before his assumption
(See Chap. III. p. 50), and the original may be translated either way, I have
chosen the former expression, which leaves the matter undecided.

VI

THE CHAPTER OF CATTLE [1]

Revealed at Mecca. [2]

IN THE NAME OF THE MOST MERCIFUL GOD.

PRAISE be unto GOD, who hath created the heavens and the earth, and hath ordained the darkness and the light ; nevertheless they who believe not in the LORD, equalize *other gods with him*. It is he who hath created you of clay ; and then decreed the term *of your lives* ; and the prefixed term is with him :[3] yet do we doubt *thereof*. He is GOD in heaven and in earth ; he knoweth what ye keep secret, and what ye publish, and knoweth what ye deserve. There came not unto them any sign, of the signs of their LORD, but they retired from the same ; and they have gainsaid the truth, after that it hath come unto them ; but a message shall come unto them, concerning that which they have mocked at.[4] Do they not consider how many generations we have destroyed before them ? We had established them in the earth in a manner wherein we have not established you ;[5] we sent the heaven to rain abundantly upon them, and we gave *them* rivers which flowed under *their feet* : yet we destroyed them in their sins, and raised up other generations after them. Although we had caused to descend unto thee a book *written* on paper, and they had handled it with their hands, the unbelievers had surely said, This *is* no other than manifest sorcery. They said, Unless an angel be sent down unto him *we will not believe*. But if we had sent down an angel, verily the matter had been decreed,[6] and they should not have been

[1] This chapter is so entitled, because some superstitious customs of the Meccans, as to certain cattle, are therein incidentally mentioned.

[2] Except only six verses, or, say others, three verses, which are taken notice of in the notes.

[3] By the last term some understand the time of the resurrection. Others think that by the first term is intended the space between creation and death, and by the latter, that between death and the resurrection.

[4] That is, they shall be convinced of the truth which they have made a jest of, when they see the punishment which they shall suffer for so doing, both in this world and the next ; or when they shall see the glorious success of Mohammedism.

[5] *i.e.*, We had blessed them with greater power and length of prosperity than we have granted you, O men of Mecca. (Al Beidâwi). Mohammed seems here to mean the ancient and potent tribes of Ad and Thamûd, &c. (Sale, Prelim. Disc. Sect. I. p. 6.)

[6] That is to say, As they would not have believed, even if an angel had descended to them from heaven, GOD has shown his mercy in not complying with their demands ; for if he had, they would have suffered immediate condemnation, and would have been allowed no time for repentance.

borne with, *by having time granted them to repent.* And if we had appointed an angel *for our messenger,* we should have sent him *in the form of a man,*[1] and have clothed *him* before them, as they are clothed. *Other* apostles have been laughed to scorn before thee ; but *the judgment* which they made a jest of, encompassed those who laughed them to scorn. Say, Go through the earth, and behold what hath been the end of those who accused *our prophets* of imposture. Say, Unto whom *belongeth* whatsoever is in heaven and earth ? Say, Unto GOD. He hath prescribed unto himself mercy. He will surely gather you together on the day of resurrection ; there is no doubt of it. They who destroy their own souls *are those who* will not believe. Unto him *is owing* whatsoever happeneth by night or by day ; *it is* he who heareth and knoweth. Say, Shall I take any other protector than GOD, the creator of heaven and earth, who feedeth *all* and is not fed *by any* ? Say, Verily I am commanded to be the first who professeth Islâm,[2] and *it was said unto me,* Thou shalt by no means be *one* of the idolaters. Say, Verily I fear, if I should rebel against my LORD, the punishment of the great day ; from whomsoever it shall be averted on that day, *God* will have been merciful unto him ; this *will be* manifest salvation. If GOD afflict thee with any hurt, there is none who can take it off *from thee,* except himself ; but if he cause good to befall thee, he is almighty ; he is the supreme *Lord* over his servants ; and he *is* wise *and* knowing. Say, What thing is the strongest in bearing testimony ?[3] Say, GOD ; *he is* witness between me and you. And this Korân was revealed unto me, that I should admonish you thereby, and *also* those unto whom it shall reach. Do ye really profess that there are other gods together with GOD ? Say, I do not profess *this.* Say, Verily he is one GOD ; and I am guiltless of what ye associate *with him.* They unto whom we have given the scripture know *our apostle,* even as they know their own children ;[4] *but* they who destroy their own souls, will not believe. Who is more unjust than he who inventeth a lie against GOD,[5] or

---

[1] As Gabriel generally appeared to Mohammed ; who, though a prophet, was not able to bear the sight of him when he appeared in his proper form, much less would others be able to support it.

[2] That is, the first of my nation. (Al Beidâwi.)

[3] This passage was revealed when the Koreish told Mohammed that they had asked the Jews and Christians concerning him, who assured them they found no mention or description of him in their books of scripture, *Therefore,* said they, *who bears witness to thee, that thou art the Apostle of God* ? (Al Beidâwi. Jallalo'ddin,)   [4] See Chap. II. p. 22.

[5] Saying the angels are the daughters of God, and intercessors for us with him, &c. (Al Beidâwi.)

chargeth his signs with imposture ? Surely the unjust shall not prosper. And on the day *of resurrection* we will assemble them all ; then will we say unto those who associated *others with God*, Where are your companions,[1] whom ye imagined *to be those of God* ? But they shall have no other excuse, than that they shall say, By GOD our LORD, we have not been idolaters. Behold, how they lie against themselves, and what they have *blasphemously* imagined *to be the companion of God* flieth from them.[2] There is of them who hearkeneth unto thee *when thou readest the Korân* ;[3] but we have cast veils over their hearts, that they should not understand it, and a deafness in their ears : and though they should see all *kinds of* signs, they will not believe therein ; *and their infidelity will arrive to that height* that they will even come unto thee, to dispute with thee. The unbelievers will say, This is nothing but silly fables of ancient *times*. And they will forbid *others* from *believing therein*, and will retire afar off from it ; but they will destroy their own souls only, and they are not sensible *thereof*. If thou didst see, when they shall be set over the fire *of hell* ! and they shall say, Would to GOD we might be sent back *into the world* ; we would not charge the signs of our LORD with imposture, and we would become true believers : nay, but that is become manifest unto them, which they formerly concealed ;[4] and though they should be sent back *into the world*, they would surely return to that which was forbidden them ; and they are surely liars. And they said, There is no *other life* than our present life ; neither shall we be raised again. But if thou couldst see, when they shall be set before their LORD ![5] He shall say *unto them*, Is not this in truth *come to pass* ? They shall answer, Yea, by our LORD. *God* shall say, Taste therefore the punishment *due unto you*, for that ye have disbelieved. They are lost who reject as falsehood the meeting of GOD *in the next life*, until the hour [6] cometh suddenly upon them. *Then will* they say,

---

[1] *i.e.*, Your idols and false gods.

[2] That is, their imaginary deities prove to be nothing, and disappear like vain phantoms and chimeras.

[3] The persons here meant were Abu Sofiân, Al Walʿd, Al Nodar, Otba, Abu Jahl, and their comrades, who went to hear Mohammed repeat some of the Korân ; and Nodar being asked what he said, answered, with an oath, that he knew not, only that he moved his tongue, and told a parcel of foolish stories, as he had done to them. (Al Beidâwi.)

[4] Their hypocrisy and vile actions ; nor does their promise proceed from any sincere intention of amendment, but from the anguish and misery of their condition. (Al Beidâwi.)

[5] Viz., In order for judgment.

[6] The last day is here called *the hour*, as it is in Scripture (1 John v. 25, &c.);

Alas ! for that we have behaved ourselves negligently in *our lifetime* ; and they shall carry their burdens on their backs ;[1] will it not be evil which they shall be laden with ? This present life is no other than a play and a vain amusement ; but surely the future mansion *shall be* better for those who fear *God* : will they not therefore understand ? Now we know that what they speak grieveth thee : yet they do not accuse thee of falsehood ; but the ungodly contradict the signs of GOD.[2] And apostles before thee have been accounted liars : but they patiently bore their being accounted liars, and their being vexed, until our help came unto them ; for there is none who can change the words of GOD : and thou hast received some information concerning those who have been *formerly* sent *from him*.[3] If their aversion *to thy admonitions* be grievous unto thee, if thou canst seek out a den *whereby thou mayest penetrate* into *the inward parts of* the earth, or a ladder *by which thou mayest ascend* into heaven, that thou mayest show them a sign, *do so, but thy search will be fruitless* ; for if GOD pleased he would bring them all to the *true* direction : be not therefore *one* of the ignorant.[4] He will give a favourable answer unto those only who shall hearken *with attention* : and GOD will raise the dead ; then unto him shall they return. The *infidels* say, Unless some sign be sent down unto him from his LORD, *we will not believe* : answer, Verily GOD is able to send down a sign : but the

and the preceding expression of *meeting* GOD on that day is also agreeable to the same (1 Thess. iv. 17).

[1] When an infidel comes forth from his grave, says Jallalo'ddin, his works shall be represented to him under the ugliest form that ever he beheld, having a most deformed countenance, a filthy smell, and a disagreeable voice ; so that he shall cry out, GOD *defend me from thee, what art thou ? I never saw anything more detestable !* To which the figure will answer, *Why dost thou wonder at my ugliness ? I am thy evil works* (Milton's Paradise Lost, bk. ii. v. 737, &c.) ; *thou didst ride upon me while thou wast in the world ; but now will I ride upon thee, and thou shalt carry me.* And immediately it shall get upon him ; and whatever he shall meet shall terrify him, and say, *Hail, thou enemy of God, thou art he who was meant by* (these words of the Korân), *and they shall carry their burdens*, &c.

[2] That is, it is not thou but GOD whom they injure by their impious gainsaying of what has been revealed to thee. It is said that Abu Jahl once told Mohammed that they did not accuse him of falsehood, because he was known to be a man of veracity, but only they did not believe the revelations which he brought them ; which occasioned this passage. (Al Beidâwi.)

[3] *i.e.*, Thou hast been acquainted with the stories of several of the preceding prophets ; what persecutions they suffered from those to whom they were sent, and in what manner GOD supported them and punished their enemies, according to his unalterable promise. (Al Beidâwi.)

[4] In this passage Mohammed is reproved for his impatience in not bearing with the obstinacy of his countrymen, and for his indiscreet desire of effecting what GOD hath not decreed, namely, the conversion and salvation of all men. (Al Beidâwi.)

greater part of them know *it* not.¹ There is no *kind of* beast
on earth, nor fowl which flieth with its wings, but *the same is*
a people like unto you ;² we have not omitted anything in
the book³ *of our decrees* : then unto their LORD shall they
return.⁴ They who accuse our signs of falsehood, *are* deaf
and dumb, *walking* in darkness : GOD will lead into error
whom he pleaseth, and whom he pleaseth he will put in the
right way. Say, What think ye ? if the punishment of GOD
come upon you, or the hour *of the resurrection* come upon you,
will ye call upon' any other than GOD, if ye speak truth ?
yea, him shall ye call upon, and he shall free *you* from that
which ye shall ask him *to deliver you from*, if he pleaseth ; and
ye shall forget that which ye associated *with him*.⁵ We have
already sent *messengers* unto *sundry* nations before thee, and
we afflicted them with trouble and adversity that they might
humble themselves : yet when the affliction *which we sent*
came upon them, they did not humble themselves : but their
hearts became hardened, and Satan prepared for them that
which they committed. And when they had forgotten that
concerning which they had been admonished, we opened unto
them the gates of all things ;⁶ until, while they were rejoicing
for that which had been given them, we suddenly laid hold
on them, and behold, they *were* seized with despair ; and the
utmost part of the people which had acted wickedly, was cut
off ; praise be unto GOD, the LORD of all creatures ! Say,
what think ye ? if GOD should take away your hearing and
your sight, and should seal up your hearts ; what god besides
GOD will restore them unto you ? See how variously we
show forth the signs *of God's unity* ;⁷ yet do they turn aside

---

¹ Being both ignorant of GOD's almighty power, and of the consequence
of what they ask, which might prove their utter destruction.

² Being created and preserved by the same omnipotence and providence
as ye are.

³ That is, in the *preserved table*, wherein GOD's decrees are written, and
all things which come to pass in this world, as well the most minute as the
more momentous, are exactly registered. (Sale, Prelim. Disc. Sect. IV.)

⁴ For, according to the Mohammedan belief, the irrational animals will
also be restored to life at the resurrection, that they may be brought to
judgment, and have vengeance taken on them for the injuries they did one
another while in this world. (Sale, Prelim. Disc. Sect. IV. p. 88.)

⁵ That is, ye shall then forsake your false gods, when ye shall be effectually
convinced that GOD alone is able to deliver you from eternal punishment.
But others rather think that this forgetting will be the effect of the distress
and terror which they will then be in. (Al Beidâwi.)

⁶ That is, we gave them all manner of plenty ; that since they took no
warning by their afflictions, their prosperity might become a snare to them,
and they might bring down upon themselves swifter destruction.

⁷ Laying them before you in different views, and making use of arguments
and motives drawn from various considerations.

from them. Say *unto them,* What think ye ? if the punishment of GOD come upon you suddenly, or in open view ;[1] will *any* perish, except the ungodly people ?   We send not *our* messengers otherwise than bearing good tidings and denouncing threats.   Whoso therefore shall believe and amend, on them shall no fear come, neither shall they be grieved :   but whoso shall accuse our signs of falsehood, a punishment shall fall on them, because they have done wickedly.   Say, I say not unto you, The treasures of GOD are in my power : neither *do I say,* I know the secrets *of God* : neither do I say unto you, Verily I am an angel : I follow only that which is revealed unto me.   Say, shall the blind and the seeing be held equal ? do ye not therefore consider ?   Preach it unto those who fear that they shall be assembled before their LORD : they shall have no patron nor intercessor, except him ; that peradventure they may take heed to themselves.   Drive not away those who call upon their LORD morning and evening, desiring *to see* his face ;[2] it belongeth not unto thee to pass any judgment on them,[3] nor doth it belong unto them to pass any judgment on thee : therefore *if* thou drive them away, thou wilt become *one* of the unjust.   Thus have we proved some part of them by other part, that they may say, Are these *the people* among us unto whom GOD hath been gracious ?[4] Doth not GOD most truly know *those who are* thankful ? And when they who believe in our signs shall come unto thee, say, Peace *be* upon you.   Your Lord hath prescribed unto himself mercy ; so that whoever among you worketh evil through ignorance, and afterwards repenteth and amendeth, *unto him will* he surely *be* gracious *and* merciful.   Thus have we distinctly propounded *our* signs, that the path of the

[1] That is, says Al Beidâwi, either without any previous notice, or after some warning given.

[2] These words were occasioned when the Koreish desired Mohammed not to admit the poor or more inferior people, such as Ammâr, Soheib, Khobbâb, and Salmân, into his company pretending that then they would come and discourse with him ; but he refusing to turn away any believers, they insisted at least that he should order them to rise up and withdraw when they came, which he agreed to do.   Others say that the chief men of Mecca expelled all the poor out of their city, bidding them go to Mohammed ; which they did, and offered to embrace his religion ; but he made some difficulty to receive them, suspecting their motive to be necessity, and not real conviction (Al Beidâwi, Jallalo'ddin) ; whereupon this passage was revealed.

[3] *i.e.*, Rashly to decide whether their intentions be sincere or not ; since thou canst not know their heart, and their faith may possibly be firmer than that of those who would persuade thee to discard them.

[4] That is to say, the noble by those of mean extraction, and the rich by the poor ; in that God chose to call the latter to the faith before the former.   (Al Beidâwi.)

wicked might be made known. Say, Verily I am forbidden
to worship *the false deities* which ye invoke, besides God. Say,
I will not follow your desires ; for then should I err, neither
should I be *one* of *those who are rightly* directed. Say, I
behave according to the plain declaration *which I have received*
from my LORD ; but ye have forged lies concerning him.
That which ye desire should be hastened, is not in my power :[1]
judgment *belongeth* only unto GOD ; he will determine the
truth ; and he is the best discerner. Say, if what ye desire
should be hastened were in my power, the matter had been
determined between me and you :[2] but GOD well knoweth
the unjust.   With him are the keys of the secret *things* ; none
knoweth them besides himself : he knoweth that which is
on the dry land and in the sea ; there falleth no leaf, but he
knoweth it ; neither *is there* a single grain in the dark parts
of the earth, neither a green thing, nor a dry thing, but it is
written in the perspicuous book.[3]   It is he who causeth you to
sleep by night, and knoweth what ye merit by day ; he also
awaketh you thereon, that the prefixed term *of your lives*
may be fulfilled ; then unto him shall ye return, and he shall
declare unto you that which ye have wrought.   He is
supreme over his servants, and sendeth the guardian *angel
to watch* over you,[4] until, when death overtaketh one of you,
our messengers[5] cause him to die ; and they will not neglect
our commands.   Afterwards shall they return unto GOD,
their true LORD : doth not judgment *belong* unto him ? he
is the most quick in taking an account.[6]   Say, who delivereth
you from the darkness[7] of the land, and of the sea, *when* ye
call upon him humbly and in private, *saying*, Verily if thou
deliver us[8] from these *dangers*, we will surely be thankful ?
Say, GOD delivereth you from them, and from every grief of
mind ; *yet* afterwards ye give *him* companions.[9]   Say, He is
able to send on you a punishment from above you,[10] or from

[1] This passage is an answer to the audacious defiances of the infidels,
who bade Mohammed, if he were a true prophet, to call for a shower of stones
from heaven, or some other sudden and miraculous punishment, to destroy
them. (Al Beidâwi.)

[2] For I should ere now have destroyed you, out of zeal for God's honour,
had it been in my power. (Al Beidâwi.)

[3] *i.e.*, The preserved table, or register of GOD's decrees.

[4] Sale, Prel. Disc. Sect. IV.

[5] That is, the angel of death and his assistants. (Sale, Prelim. Disc.
Sect. IV.)   [6] Sale, Prel. Disc. Sect IV.

[7] That is, the dangers and distresses.

[8] The Cufic copies read it in the third person, *if he deliver us*, &c.

[9] Returning to your old idolatry.

[10] That is, by storms from heaven, as he destroyed the unbelieving people

under your feet,[1] or to engage you in dissension, and to make some of you taste the violence of others. Observe how variously we show forth *our* signs, that peradventure they may understand. This people hath accused the *revelation which thou hast brought* of falsehood, although it be the truth. Say, I am not a guardian over you : every prophecy hath its fixed time *of accomplishment* ; and ye will hereafter know *it*. When thou seest those who are engaged in *cavilling at or ridiculing* our signs ; depart from them, until they be engaged in some other discourse : and if Satan cause thee to forget *this precept*, do not sit with the ungodly people, after recollection. They who fear *God* are not at all accountable for them, but *their duty is* to remember, that they may take heed to themselves.[2] Abandon those who make their religion a sport and a jest ; and whom the present life hath deceived : and admonish *them* by *the Korân*, that a soul becometh liable to destruction for that which it committeth : it shall have no patron nor intercessor besides GOD ; and if it could pay the utmost price of redemption, it would not be accepted from it. They who are delivered over to perdition for that which they have committed, shall have boiling water to drink, and shall suffer a grievous punishment, because they have disbelieved. Say, Shall we call upon that, besides GOD, which can neither profit us nor hurt us ? and shall we turn back on our heels, after that GOD hath directed us ; like him whom the devils have infatuated, wandering amazedly in the earth, *and yet* having companions who call him to the *true* direction, *saying*, Come unto us ? Say, The direction of GOD is the *true* direction : we are commanded to resign ourselves unto the LORD of all creatures ; and *it is also commanded us*, *saying*, Observe the stated times of prayer, and fear him ; for it is he before whom ye shall be assembled. It is he who hath created the heavens and the earth in truth ; and whenever he saith *unto a thing*, Be, it is. His word is the truth ; and his will be the kingdom on the day whereon

of Noah, and of Lot, and the army of Abraha, the lord of the elephant. (Al Beidâwi).

[1] Either by drowning you, as he did Pharaoh and his host, or causing the earth to open and swallow you up, as happened to Korah, or (as the Mohammedans name him) Karun. (Al Beidâwi.)

[2] And therefore need not be troubled at the indecent and impious talk of the infidels, provided they take care not to be infected by them. When the preceding passage was revealed, the Moslems told their prophet that if they were obliged to rise up whenever the idolaters spoke irreverently of the Korân, they could never sit quietly in the temple, nor perform their devotions there ; whereupon these words were added. (Al Beidâwi, Jallalo'ddin.)

the trumpet shall be sounded :[1] he knoweth whatever is
secret, and whatever is public : he is the wise, the knowing.
Call to mind when Abraham said unto his father Azer,[2] Dost
thou take images for gods ?[3] Verily I perceive that thou
and thy people *are* in a manifest error. And thus did we
show unto Abraham the kingdom of heaven and earth, that
he might become *one* of those who firmly believe.[4] And
when the night overshadowed him, he saw a star, *and* he said,
This is my LORD ;[5] but when it set, he said, I like not *gods*

[1] Sale, Prel. Disc. Sect. IV.

[2] This is the name which the Mohammedans give to Abraham's father,
named in scripture Terah. However, some of their writers pretend that Azer
was the son of Terah, (Tarikh Montakhab, apud D'Herbel. Bibl. Orient. p.
12.) an l D'Herbelot says that the Arai s always distinguish them in their
genealogies as different persons; but that because Abraha n was the son of
Terah according to Moses, it is therefore supposed (l y European writers)
that Terah is the same with the Azer of the Arabs. (D'Herbel. Bibl. Orient.
p. 12.) How true this observation may be in relation to some authors, I cannot
say, but I am sure it cannot be true of all ; for several Arab and Turkish
writers expressiy make Azer and Terah the same person. (Al Beidâwi,
Jallalo'ddin, Yahya, Ebn Shohnah, Mirat Kainat, &c. Vide etiam
Pharhang Jehanghiri, apud Hyde, De Rel. Vet. Persar. p. 68.) Azer, in
ancient times, was the name of the planet Mars, and the month of
March was so called by the most ancient Persians ; for the word originaIly
signifying *fire* (as it still does), it was therefore given by them and the
Chaldeans to that planet (Hyde, De Rel. Vet. Persar. p. 63). which partaking,
as was supposed, of a fiery nature, was acknowledged by the Chaldeans
and Assyrians as a god or planetary deity, whom in old times they worshipped
under the form of a pillar : whence Azer became a name among the nobility,
who esteemed it honourable to be denominated from their gods (Hyde, De
Rel. Vet. Persar. p. 64), and is found in the composition of several Babylonish
names. For these reasons a learned author supposes Azer to have been the
heathen name of Terah, and that the other was given him on his conversion.
(Hyde, De Rel. Vet. Persar. p. 62). Al Beidâwi confirms this conjecture,
saying that Azer was the name of the idol which he worshipped. It may be
observed that Abraham's father is also called Zarah in the Talmud, and
Athar by Eusebius.

[3] That Azer, or Terah, was an idolater is allowed on all hands ; nor can it
be denied, since he is expressly said in scripture to have served strange gods.
(Josh. xxiv. 2, 14.) The eastern authors unanimously agree that he was a
statuary or carver of idols ; and he is represented as the first who made
images of clay, pictures only having been in use before (Epiphan. adv. Hær.
l. 1, p. 7, 8), and taught that they were to be adored as gods (Suidas in
Lexico, voce Σερύχ). However, we are told his employment was a very
honourable one (Hyde, De Rel. Vet. Persar. p. 63), and that he was a great lord,
and in high favour with Nimrod, whose son-in-law he was (D'Herbel. Bibl.
Orient.), because he made his idols for him, and was excellent in his art.
Some of the rabbins say Terah was a priest, and chief of the order (Shalshel.
hakkab. p. 94.)

[4] That is, we gave him a right apprehension of the government of the
world and of the heavenly bodies, that he might know them all to be ruled
by GOD, by putting him on making the following reflections.

[5] Since Abraham's parents were idolaters, it seems to be a necessary consequence that he was one also in his younger years ; the scripture not
obscurely intimates as much (Josh. xxiv. 2, 14, and Hyde, De Rel. Vet.
Persar. p. 59), and the Jews themselves acknowledge it. (Joseph. Ant. l.
l. c. 7. Maimon. More Nev. part iii. c. 29, et Yad Hazzak. de Id. c. 1, &c.)

which set. And when he saw the moon rising, he said, This
is my LORD ; but when he saw it set, he said, Verily if my
LORD direct me not, I shall become *one* of the people who go
astray. And when he saw the sun rising, he said, This is my
LORD, this is the greatest ; but when it set, he said, O my
people, verily I am clear of that which ye associate *with God* :
I direct my face unto him who hath created the heavens and
the earth ; *I am* orthodox, and am not *one* of the idolaters.
And his people disputed with him : *and he* said, Will ye
dispute with me concerning GOD ? since he hath now directed
me, and I fear not that which ye associate *with him*, unless
that my LORD willeth a thing ; *for* my LORD comprehendeth
all things by *his* knowledge ;[1] will ye not therefore consider ?
And how should I fear that which ye associate *with* GOD, since
ye fear not to have associated with GOD that concerning
which he hath sent down unto you no authority ? which
therefore of the two parties is the more safe, if ye understand *aright* ? They who believe, and clothe not their faith
with injustice,[2] they shall enjoy security, and they *are rightly*
directed. And this is our argument wherewith we furnished

At what age he came to the knowledge of the true GOD and left idolatry,
opinions are various. Some Jewish writers tell us he was then but three
years old (Tanchuma, Talmud, Nedarim, 32, 1, et apud Maimon. Yad
Hazzak.), and the Mohammedans likewise suppose him very young, and
that he asked his father and mother several shrewd questions when a child.
(D'Herbel. Bibl. Orient. Art. Abraham.) Others, however, allow him to
have been a middle-aged man at that time. (Maimon. More Nev. part III. c.
29. R. Abr. Zacuth in Sefer Juchasin, Shalshel. hakkab, &c.) Maimonides,
in particular, and R. Abraham Zacuth think him to have been forty years
old, which age is also mentioned in the Korân. But the general opinion of the
Mohammedans is that he was about fifteen or sixteen. (Hyde, De Rel. Vet.
Persar. p. 60, 61, et. Hotting. Smegma Orient. p. 290, &c. Genebr. in
Chron.) As the religion wherein Abraham was educated was the Sabian,
which consisted chiefly in the worship of the heavenly bodies (Sale, Prel. Disc.
p. 33.), he is introduced examining their nature and properties, to see
whether they had a right to the worship which was paid them or not ; and
the first which he observed was the planet Venus, or, as others will have it,
Jupiter. (Al Beidâwi.) This method of Abraham's attaining to the knowledge of the supreme Creator of all things, is conformable with what Josephus
writes, viz. : That he drew his notions from the changes which he had
observed in the earth and the sea, and in the sun and the moon, and the
rest of the celestial bodies ; concluding that they were subject to the command
of a superior power, to whom alone all honour and thanks are due. (Joseph.
Ant. l. 1, c. 7.) The story itself is certainly taken from the Talmud. (R.
Bechai in Midrash. Bartolocc. Bibl. Rabb. part i. p. 640). Some of the
commentators, however, suppose this reasoning of Abraham with himself
was not the first means of his conversion, but that he used it only by way of
argument to convince the idolaters among whom he then lived.

[1] That is, I am not afraid of your false gods, which cannot hurt me, except
GOD permitteth it, or is pleased to afflict me himself.

[2] By injustice, in this place, the commentators understand idolatry, or
open rebellion against GOD.

Abraham *that he might make use of it* against his people : we exalt unto degrees *of wisdom and knowledge* whom we please ; for thy LORD is wise *and* knowing.   And we gave unto him Isaac and Jacob ; we directed *them* both : and Noah had we before directed, and of his posterity[1] David and Solomon ; and Job,[2] and Joseph, and Moses, and Aaron : thus do we reward the righteous : and Zacharias, and John, and Jesus, and Elias ;[3] all *of them were* upright men : and Ismael, and Elisha,[4] and Jonas,[5] and Lot ;[6] all *these* have we favoured above *the rest of* the world ; and *also divers* of their fathers, and their issue, and their brethren ; and we chose them, and directed them into the right way.   This is the direction of GOD, he directeth thereby such of his servants as he pleaseth ; but if they had been guilty of idolatry, that which they wrought would have become utterly fruitless unto them. Those *were the persons* unto whom we gave the scripture, and wisdom, and prophecy ; but if these[7] believe not therein, we will commit the care of them to a people who shall not disbelieve the same.   Those *were the persons* whom GOD hath directed, therefore follow their direction.   Say *unto the inhabitants of Mecca,* I ask of you no recompence for *preaching the Korân* ; it is no other than an admonition unto *all* creatures.   They make not a due estimation of GOD,[8] when they say, GOD hath not sent down unto man anything at all :[9] Say, Who sent down the book which Moses brought, a

[1] Some refer the relative *his* to Abraham, the person chiefly spoken of in this passage ; some to Noah, the next antecedent, because Jonas and Lot were not (say they) of Abraham's seed ; and others suppose the persons named in this and the next verse are to be understood as the descendants of Abraham, and those in the following verse as those of Noah.   (Al Beidâwi.)

[2] The Mohammedans say he was of the race of Esau.   (See Chaps. XXI. and XXXVIII.

[3] See Chap. XXXVII.

[4] This prophet was the successor of Elias, and, as the commentators will have it, the son of Okhtûb, though the Scripture makes him the son of Shaphat.

[5] See Chaps. X., XXI., and XXXVII.

[6] See Chaps. VII., &c.

[7] That is, the Koreish.   (Al Beidâwi.)

[8] That is, they know him not truly, nor have just notions of his goodness, and mercy towards man.   The persons here meant, according to some commentators, are the Jews, and according to others, the idolaters.   (Al Beidâwi.)   This verse and the two next, as Jallalo'ddin thinks, were revealed at Medina.

[9] By these words the Jews (if they were the persons meant) chiefly intended to deny the Korân to be of divine revelation, though they might in strictness insist that GOD never revealed, or *sent down,* as the Korân expresses it, any real composition or material writing from heaven in the manner that Mohammed pretended his revelations were delivered (Sale, Prel. Disc. Sect. III.), if we except only the Decalogue, GOD having left to the inspired penmen not only

light and a direction unto men; which ye transcribe on papers, whereof ye publish *some part*, and great part *whereof* ye conceal? and ye have been taught *by Mohammed* what ye knew not, neither your fathers. Say, GOD *sent it down*: then leave them to amuse themselves with their vain discourse. This book which we have sent down *is* blessed; confirming that which was *revealed* before it; and *is delivered unto thee* that thou mayest preach *it* unto the metropolis *of Mecca* and to those who are round about it. And they who believe in the next life will believe therein, and they will diligently observe their *times of* prayer. Who is more wicked than he who forgeth a lie concerning GOD?[1] or saith, *This* was revealed unto me, when nothing hath been revealed unto him?[2] and who saith, I will produce a revelation like unto that which GOD hath sent down?[3] If thou didst see when the ungodly *are* in the pangs of death, and the angels[4] reach out their hands, *saying*, Cast forth your souls; this day shall ye receive an ignominious punishment for that which ye have falsely spoken concerning GOD; and because ye have proudly rejected his signs. And now are ye come unto us alone,[5] as we created you at first,[6] and ye have left that which we had bestowed on you, behind your backs; neither do we see with you your intercessors,[7] whom ye thought to have been partners *with* GOD among you: now is *the relation* between you cut off, and what ye imagined hath deceived you.[8] GOD causeth the grain and the date-stone to put forth: he

---

the labour of writing, but the liberty, in a great measure at least, of putting the truths into their own words and manner of expression.

[1] Falsely pretending to have received revelations from him, as did Moseilama, Al Aswad al Ansi, and others.

[2] As did Abda'llah Ebn Saad Ebn Abi Sarah, who for some time was the prophet's amanuensis, and when these words were dictated to him as revealed, viz., *We created man of a purer kind of clay*, &c. (Chap. XXIII.), cried out, by way of admiration, *Blessed be* GOD *the best Creator !* and being ordered by Mohammed to write these words down also, as part of the inspired passage, began to think himself as great a prophet as his master. (Al Beidâwi.) Whereupon he took upon himself to corrupt and alter the Korân according to his own fancy, and at length apostatizing, was one of the ten who were proscribed at the taking of Mecca (Sale, Prelim. Disc. p. 59), and narrowly escaped with life on his recantation, by the interposition of Othmân Ebn Affân, whose foster-brother he was. (Abulfeda, Vit. Moh. p. 109.)

[3] For some Arabs, it seems, had the vanity to imagine, and gave out, that if they pleased, they could write a book nothing inferior to the Korân.

[4] See before, p. 124, note.

[5] That is, without your wealth, your children, or your friends, which ye so much depended on in your lifetime.

[6] *i.e.*, Naked and helpless.

[7] Or false gods.

[8] Concerning the intercession of your idols, or the disbelief of future rewards and punishments.

bringeth forth the living from the dead, and he bringeth forth the dead from the living.[1] This *is* GOD. Why therefore are ye turned away *from him* ? He causeth the morning to appear ; and hath ordained the night for rest, and the sun and the moon for the computing *of time*. This is the disposition of the mighty, the wise *God*. It is he who hath ordained the stars for you, that ye may be directed thereby in the darkness of the land and of the sea. We have clearly shown forth *our* signs, unto people who understand. It is he who hath produced you from one soul ; and *hath provided for you* a sure receptacle and a repository.[2] We have clearly shown forth *our* signs, unto people who are wise. It is he who sendeth down water from heaven, and we have thereby produced the springing buds of all things, and have thereout produced the green thing, from which we produce the grain growing in rows, and palm-trees from whose branches proceed clusters of dates *hanging* close together ; and gardens of grapes, and olives, and pomegranates, *both* like and unlike to one another. Look on their fruits, when they bear fruit, and their growing to maturity. Verily herein are signs, unto people who believe. *Yet* they have set up the genii[3] as partners with GOD, although he created them : and they have falsely attributed unto him sons and daughters,[4] without knowledge. Praise be unto him ; and far be that from him which they attribute *unto him* ! *He is* the maker of heaven and earth : how should he have issue, since he hath no consort ? he hath created all things, and he is omniscient. This is GOD your LORD ; there is no GOD but he, the creator of all things ; therefore serve him ; for he taketh care of all things. The sight comprehendeth him not, but he comprehendeth the sight ; he *is* the gracious,[5] the wise. Now have evident demonstrations come unto you from your LORD ; whoso seeth *them, the advantage thereof will redound* to his own soul ; and whoso is *wilfully* blind, *the consequence will be* to

---

[1] See Chap. III. p. 46.

[2] Namely, in the loins of your fathers, and the wombs of your mothers. (Al Beidâwi.)

[3] This word signifies properly the *genus* of rational, *invisible* beings, whether angels, devils, or that intermediate species usually called *genii*. Some of the commentators therefore, in this place, understand the angels whom the pagan Arabs worshipped ; and others the devils, either because they became their servants by adoring idols at their instigation, or else because, according to the Magian system, they looked on the devil as a sort of creator, making him the author and principle of all evil, and GOD the author of good only. (Al Beidâwi.)

[4] Sale, Prel. Disc. p. 19.

[5] Or, as the word may be translated, *the incomprehensible*. (Al Beidâwi.)

himself. I am not a keeper over you. Thus do we variously explain *our* signs ; that they may say, Thou hast studied diligently ;[1] and that we may declare them unto people of understanding. Follow that which hath been revealed unto thee from thy LORD ; there is no GOD but he : retire therefore from the idolaters. If GOD had *so* pleased, they had not been guilty of idolatry. We have not appointed thee a keeper over them ; neither art thou a guardian over them. Revile not the *idols* which they invoke besides GOD, lest they maliciously revile GOD, without knowledge. Thus have we prepared for every nation their works : hereafter unto GOD shall they return, and he shall declare unto them that which they have done. They have sworn by GOD, by the most solemn oath, that if a sign came unto them, they would certainly believe therein : Say, Verily signs are in the power of GOD alone ; and he permitteth you not to understand that when they come, they will not believe.[2] And we will turn aside their hearts and their sight *from the truth*, as they believed not therein[3] the first time ; and we will leave them to wander in their error. (VIII.)[4] And though we had sent down angels unto them, and the dead had spoken unto them, and we had gathered together before them all things in one view ;[5] they would not have believed, unless GOD had so pleased : but the greater part of them know *it* not. Thus have we appointed unto every prophet an enemy ; the devils of men, and of genii : who privately suggest the one to the other specious discourses to deceive : but if thy LORD pleased, they would not have done it. Therefore leave them, and that which they have falsely imagined ; and let the hearts of those be inclined thereto, who believe not in the life to come ; and let them please themselves therein, and let them gain that which they are gaining. Shall I seek

[1] That is, Thou hast been instructed by the Jews and Christians in these matters, and only retailest to us what thou hast learned of them. For this the infidels objected to Mohammed, thinking it impossible for him to discourse on subjects of so high a nature in so pertinent a manner, without being well versed in the doctrines and sacred writings of those people.

[2] In this passage Mohammed endeavours to excuse his inability of working a miracle, as had been demanded of him ; declaring that GOD did not think fit to comply with their desires ; and that if he had so thought fit, yet it had been in vain, because if they were not convinced by the Korân, they would not be convinced by the greatest miracle. (Luke xvi. 31.)

[3] *i.e.*, in the Korân.

[4] Section VIII. begins. (See Sale, Prel. Disc. p. 63.)

[5] For the Meccans required that Mohammed should either show them an angel descending from heaven in their sight, or raise their dead fathers, that they might discourse with them, or prevail on GOD and his angels to appear to them in a body.

after any *other* judge besides GOD *to judge between us* ? It
is he who hath sent down unto you the book *of the Korân,*
distinguishing *between good and evil* ; and they to whom we
gave the scripture know that it is sent down from thy LORD,
with truth. Be not therefore *one* of those who doubt *thereof.*
The words of thy LORD are perfect in truth and justice ;
there is none who can change his words :[1] he *both* heareth
and knoweth. But if thou obey the greater part of them
who are in the earth, they will lead thee aside from the path
of GOD : they follow an *uncertain* opinion only,[2] and speak
nothing but lies ; verily thy LORD well knoweth those who
go astray from his path, and well knoweth those who are
rightly directed. Eat of that whereon the name of GOD
hath been commemorated,[3] if ye believe in his signs : and
why do ye not eat of that whereon the name of GOD hath
been commemorated ? since he hath plainly declared unto
you what he hath forbidden you ; except that which ye be
compelled to *eat of* by necessity ; many lead *others* into error,
because of their appetites, being void of knowledge ; but thy
LORD well knoweth *who are* the transgressors. Leave both
the outside of iniquity, and the inside thereof ;[4] for they who
commit iniquity shall receive the reward of that which they
shall have gained. Eat not therefore of that whereon the
name of GOD hath not been commemorated ; for this is
certainly wickedness : but the devils will suggest unto their
friends, that they dispute with you *concerning this precept*;
but if ye obey them, ye *are* surely idolaters. Shall he who
hath been dead, and whom we have restored unto life, and
unto whom we have ordained a light, whereby he may walk
among men, *be* as he whose similitude is in darkness, from
whence he shall not come forth ?[5] Thus was that which the
infidels are doing, prepared for them. And thus have we
placed in every city chief leaders of the wicked *men* thereof,[6]

[1] Some interpret this of the immutability of GOD's decree, and the certainty of his threats and promises ; others, of his particular promise to
preserve the Korân from any such alterations or corruptions as they imagine
to have happened to the Pentateuch and the Gospel (Sale, Prel. Disc., and
Chap. XV.) ; and others of the unalterable duration of the Mohammedan
law, which they hold is to last till the end of the world, there being no other
prophet, law, or dispensation to be expected after it.

[2] Imagining that the true religion was that which their idolatrous ancestors
professed.

[3] See Chap. II., p. 24, and Chap. V., p. 97.

[4] That is, both open and secret sins.

[5] The persons primarily intended in this passage, were Hamza, Mohammed's uncle, and Abu Jahl ; others, instead of Hamza, name Omar, or
Ammâr.

[6] In the same manner as we have done in Mecca.

that they may act deceitfully therein ; but they shall act deceitfully against their own souls only ; and they know *it* not. And when a sign[1] cometh unto them, they say, We will by no means believe until *a revelation* be brought unto us, like unto that which hath been delivered unto the messengers of GOD.[2] GOD best knoweth whom he will appoint for his messenger.[3] Vileness in the sight of GOD shall fall upon those who deal wickedly, and a grievous punishment, for that they have dealt deceitfully. And whomsoever GOD shall please to direct, he will open his breast to *receive the faith of* Islâm : but whomsoever he shall please to lead into error, he will render his breast straight *and* narrow, as though he were climbing up to heaven.[4] Thus doth GOD inflict a terrible punishment on those who believe not. This is the right way of thy LORD. Now have we plainly declared *our* signs unto those people who will consider. They shall have a dwelling of peace with their LORD, and he shall be their patron, because of that which they have wrought. *Think on* the day *whereon* GOD shall gather them all together, *and shall say*, O company of genii,[5] ye have been much concerned with mankind ;[6] and their friends from among mankind *shall* say, O LORD, the one of us hath received advantage from the other,[7] and we are arrived at our limited term[8] which thou hast appointed us. GOD will say, *Hell* fire *shall be* your habitation, therein shall ye remain *for ever* ; unless as GOD shall please *to mitigate your pains*,[9] for thy LORD *is* wise *and*

---

[1] *i.e.*, Any verse or passage of the Korân.

[2] These were the words of the Koreish, who thought that there were persons among themselves more worthy of the honour of being GOD's messenger than Mohammed.

[3] Literally, *Where he will place his commission.* GOD, says Al Beidâwi, bestows not the gift of prophecy on any one on account of his nobility or riches, but for their spiritual qualifications ; making choice of such of his servants as he pleases, and who he knows will execute their commissions faithfully.

[4] Or had undertaken the most impossible thing in the world. In like manner shall the heart of such a man be incapable of receiving the truth.

[5] That is, of devils. (Al Beidâwi.)

[6] In tempting and seducing them to sin.

[7] The advantage which men received from the evil spirits, was their raising and satisfying their lusts and appetites ; and that which the latter received in return, was the obedience paid them by the former, &c. (Al Beidâwi, Jallalo'ddin.)

[8] viz., The day of resurrection, which we believed not in the other world.

[9] The commentators tell us that this alleviation of the pains of the damned will be when they shall be taken out of the fire to drink the boiling water (Jallalo'ddin), or to suffer the extreme cold, called Al Zamharîr, which is to be one part of their punishment ; but others think the respite which GOD will grant to some before they are thrown into hell, is here intended. (Al Beidâwi.) According to the exposition of Ebn Abbas, these words may be

knowing. Thus do we set some of the unjust over others of them, because of that which they have deserved. O company of genii and men, did not messengers from among yourselves come unto you,[1] rehearsing my signs unto you, and forewarning you of the meeting of this your day ? They shall answer, We bear witness against ourselves : the present life deceived them : and they shall bear witness against themselves that they were unbelievers. This *hath been the method of* GOD's *dealing with his creatures*, because thy LORD would not destroy the cities in *their* iniquity, while their inhabitants were careless.[2] Every one shall *have* degrees *of recompence* of that which they shall do ; for thy LORD is not regardless of that which they do, and thy LORD is self-sufficient *and* endued with mercy. If he pleaseth he can destroy you, and cause such as he pleaseth to succeed you, in like manner as he produced you from the posterity of other people. Verily that which is threatened you shall surely come to pass ; neither shall ye cause *it* to fail. Say *unto those of Mecca*, O my people, act according to your power ; verily I will act *according to my duty* : [3] and hereafter shall ye know whose will be the reward of paradise. The ungodly shall not prosper. *Those of Mecca* set apart unto GOD a portion of that which he hath produced of the fruits of the earth, and of cattle ; and say, This *belongeth* unto GOD (according to their imagination), and this unto our companions.[4] And that which is *destined* for their companions cometh not unto GOD ; yet that which *is set apart* unto GOD cometh unto their companions.[5] How ill do they judge ! In like manner have their companions induced many of the

rendered, *Unless him whom* GOD *shall please* to deliver thence. (Sale, Prelim. Disc. Sect. IV.)

[1] It is the Mohammedan belief that apostles were sent by GOD for the conversion both of *genii* and of men ; being generally of the human race (as Mohammed, in particular, who pretended to have a commission to preach to both kinds) ; according to this passage, it seems there must have been prophets of the race of *genii* also, though their mission be a secret to us.

[2] Or considered not their danger ; but GOD first sent some prophet to them to warn them of it, and to invite them to repentance.

[3] That is, ye may proceed in your rebellion against GOD and your malice towards me, and be confirmed in your infidelity ; but I will persevere to bear your insults with patience, and to publish those revelations which GOD has commanded me. (Al Beidâwi.)

[4] *i.e.*, Our idols. In which sense this word is to be taken through the whole passage.

[5] As to this custom of the pagan Arabs, see Sale, Prel. Disc. p. 17. To what is there said we may add, that the share set apart for GOD was employed chiefly in relieving the poor and strangers, and the share of the idols, for paying their priests and providing sacrifices for them. (Al Beidâwi, Jallalo'ddin.)

idolaters to slay their children,[1] that they might bring them
to perdition, and that they might render their religion obscure
and confused unto them.[2] But if GOD had pleased, they
had not done this : therefore leave them, and that which
they falsely imagine. They also say, These cattle and fruits
of the earth are sacred ; none shall eat thereof but who we
please [3] (according to their imagination) ; and *there are*
cattle whose backs are forbidden *to be ridden on, or laden with
burdens* ;[4] and *there are* cattle on which they commemorate
not the name of GOD *when they slay them,*[5] devising a lie
against him : GOD shall reward them for that which they
falsely devise. And they say, That which is in the bellies
of these cattle,[6] *is* allowed our males *tc eat,* and *is* forbidden
to our wives : but if it prove abortive, then they are *both*
partakers thereof.[7] GOD shall give them the reward of
their attributing *these things to him* : he *is* knowing *and* wise.
They are utterly lost who have slain their children foolishly,[8]
without knowledge ; [9] and have forbidden that which
GOD hath given them for food, devising a lie against GOD.
They have erred, and were not *rightly* directed. He it is who
produceth gardens of *vines, both those which are* supported
on trails *of wood,* and *those which are* not supported, and[10]
palm-trees, and the corn affording various food, and olives,
and pomegranates, alike and unlike unto one another. Eat
of their fruit, when they bear fruit, and pay the due thereof
on the day whereon ye shall gather it ;[11] but be not pro-

[1] Either by that inhuman custom, which prevailed among those of Kendah
and some other tribes of burying their daughters alive, so soon as they were
born, if they apprehended they could not maintain them (Chap. LXXXI.);
or else by offering them to their idols, at the instigation of those who had the
custody of their temples. (Al Beidâwi.)

[2] By corrupting with horrid superstitions that religion which Ismael had
left to his posterity. (Al Beidâwi.)

[3] That is, those who serve our idols, and are of the male sex ; for the
women were not allowed to eat of them. (Al Beidâwi.)

[4] Which they superstitiously exempted from such services, in some
particular cases, as they did the Bahîra, the Sâïba, and the Hâmi. (See
Chap. V., p. 97, and Sale, Prel. Disc. Sect. V., p. 138.)

[5] See Chap. V., p. 97.

[6] That is, the *fœtus* or embryos of the Bahîra and the Sâïba, which shall
be brought forth alive.

[7] For if those cattle cast their young, the women might eat thereof as
well as the men.

[8] See above, note.[1]

[9] Not having a due sense of GOD's providence.

[10] Or, as some choose to interpret the words, *Trees or plants which are
planted by the labour of man, and those which grow naturally in the deserts and
on mountains.*

[11] That is, give alms thereof to the poor. And these alms, as Al Beidâwi
observes, were what they used to give before the Zacât, or legal alms, was

fuse,[1] for GOD loveth not those who are too profuse. And GOD *hath given you* some cattle fit for bearing of burdens, and *some* fit for slaughter only. Eat of what GOD hath given you for food ; and follow not the steps of Satan, for he is your declared enemy. Four pairs [2] *of cattle hath* GOD *given you* ; of sheep one pair, and of goats one pair. Say *unto them*, Hath GOD forbidden the two males, *of sheep and of goats*, or the two females ; or that which the wombs of the two females contain ? Tell me with certainty, if ye speak truth. And of camels *hath* GOD *given you* one pair, and of oxen one pair. Say, Hath he forbidden the two males *of these*, or the two females ; or that which the wombs of the two females contain ? [3] Were ye present when GOD commanded you this ? And who is more unjust than he who deviseth a lie against GOD,[4] that he may seduce men without understanding ? Verily GOD directeth not unjust people. Say, I find not in that which hath been revealed unto me, anything forbidden unto the eater, that he eat it not, except it be that which dieth of itself, or blood poured forth,[5] or swine's flesh : for this is an abomination : or *that which is* profane, having been slain in the name of some other than of GOD. But whoso shall be compelled by necessity *to eat of these things*, not lusting, nor *wilfully* transgressing, verily thy LORD *will be* gracious *unto him* and merciful. Unto the Jews did we forbid every *beast* having an *undivided* hoof ; and of bullocks and sheep, we forbade them the fat of both ; except that which should be on their backs, or their inwards,[6] or which should be intermixed with the bone.[7] This have we rewarded them with, because of their iniquity ; and we

---

instituted, which was done after Mohammed had retired from Mecca, where this verse was revealed. Yet some are of another opinion, and for this very reason will have the verse to have been revealed at Medina.

[1] *i.e.*, Give not so much thereof in alms as to leave your own families in want, for charity begins at home.

[2] Or, literally, eight males and females paired together ; that is, four of each sex, and two of every distinct kind.

[3] In this passage Mohammed endeavours to convince the Arabs of their superstitious folly in making it unlawful, one while, to eat the males of these four kinds of cattle ; another while, the females ; and at another time, their young. (Al Beidâwi.)

[4] The person particularly intended here, some say, was Amru Ebn Lohai, king of Hejâz, a great introducer of idolatry and superstition among the Arabs. (Al Beidâwi; Sale, Prel. Disc., and Pocock Spec. p. 80.)

[5] That is, fluid blood ; in opposition to what the Arabs suppose to be also blood, but not fluid, as the liver and the spleen. (Al Beidâwi, Jallalo'ddin.)

[6] See Levit. vii. 23, and iii. 16.

[7] viz., The fat of the rumps or tails of sheep, which are very large in the East, a small one weighing ten or twelve pounds, and some, it is reported, no less than threescore.

are surely speakers of truth. If they accuse thee of imposture, say, Your LORD is endued with extensive mercy; but his severity shall not be averted from wicked people. The idolaters will say, If GOD had pleased, we had not been guilty of idolatry, neither our fathers; and *pretend that* we have not forbidden *them* anything. Thus did they who were before them accuse *the prophets* of imposture, until they tasted our severe punishment. Say, Is there with you any *certain* knowledge *of what ye allege*, that ye may produce it unto us? Ye follow only a *false* imagination; and ye only utter lies. Say, Therefore unto GOD *belongeth* the most evident demonstration; for if he had pleased, he had directed you all. Say, Produce your witnesses, who can bear testimony that GOD hath forbidden this. But if they bear testimony *of this*, do not thou bear testimony with them, nor do thou follow the desires of those who accuse our signs of falsehood, and who believe not in the life to come, and equalize *idols* with their LORD. Say, Come,[1] I will rehearse that which your LORD hath forbidden you; *that is to say*, that ye be not guilty of idolatry, and *that ye show* kindness to *your* parents, and that ye murder not your children *for fear* lest ye be reduced to poverty: we will provide for you and them; and draw not near unto heinous crimes,[2] neither openly nor in secret; and slay not the soul which GOD hath forbidden *you to slay*, unless for a just cause.[3] This hath he enjoined you that ye may understand. And meddle not with the substance of the orphan, otherwise than for the improving *thereof*, until he attain his age of strength; and use a full measure and a just balance. We will not impose *a task* on *any* soul, beyond its ability. And when ye pronounce *judgment* observe justice, although it be *for or against* one who is near of kin, and fulfil the covenant of GOD. This hath *God* commanded you, that ye may be admonished; and *that ye may know* that this is my right way: therefore follow it, and follow not the paths *of others*, lest ye be scattered from the path *of God*. This hath he commanded you, that ye may take heed. We gave also unto Moses the book *of the Law*; a perfect rule unto him who should do right, and a determination concerning all things *needful*, and a direction, and mercy; that *the children of Israel* might believe the

[1] This and the two following verses Jallalo'ddin supposes to have been revealed at Medina.
[2] The original word signifies peculiarly fornication and avarice.
[3] As for murder, apostasy, or adultery (Al Beidâwi.)

meeting of their LORD. And this book which we have *now* sent down, is blessed ; therefore follow it and fear *God*, that ye may obtain mercy : lest ye should say, The scriptures were only sent down unto two people[1] before us ; and we neglected to peruse them with attention : [2] or lest ye should say, If a book *of divine revelations* had been sent down unto us, we would surely have been better directed than they.[3] And now hath a manifest declaration come unto you from your LORD, and a direction and mercy : and who is more unjust than he who deviseth lies against the signs of GOD, and turneth aside from them ? We will reward those who turn aside from our signs with a grievous punishment, because they have turned aside. Do they wait for *any other* than that the angels should come unto them, *to part their souls from their bodies* ; or that thy LORD should come *to punish them* ; or that some of the signs of thy LORD should come to pass, *showing the day of judgment to be at hand*.[4] On the day whereon some of thy LORD'S signs shall come to pass, its faith shall not profit a soul which believed not before, or wrought not good in its faith.[5] Say, Wait ye *for this day* ; we surely do wait *for it*. They who make a division in their religion,[6] and become sectaries, have thou nothing to do with them ; their affair *belongeth* only unto GOD. Hereafter shall he declare unto them that which they have done. He who shall appear with good works, shall receive a tenfold recompence for the same ; but he who shall appear with evil works, shall receive only an equal *punishment* for the same ; and they shall not be treated unjustly. Say, Verily my LORD hath directed me into a

[1] That is, the Jews and the Christians.

[2] Either because we knew nothing of them, or did not understand the language wherein they were written.

[3] Because of the acuteness of our wit, the clearness of our understanding, and our facility of learning sciences—as appears from our excelling in history, poetry, and oratory, notwithstanding we are illiterate people. (Al Beidâwi.)

[4] Al Beidâwi, from a tradition of Mohammed, says that ten signs will precede the last day, viz., the smoke, the beast of the earth, an eclipse in the east, another in the west, and a third in the peninsula of Arabia, the appearance of Antichrist, the sun's rising in the west, the irruption of Gog and Magog, the descent of Jesus on earth, and fire which shall break forth from Aden. (Sale, Prel. Disc. Sect. IV., p. 85.)

[5] For faith in the next life will be of no advantage to those who have not believed in this ; nor yet faith in this life without good works.

[6] That is, who believe in part of it, and disbelieve other parts of it, or who form schisms therein. Mohammed is reported to have declared that the Jews were divided into seventy-one sects, and the Christians into seventy-two ; and that his own followers would be split into seventy-three sects; and that all of them would be damned. except only one of each. (Al Beidâwi.)

right way, a true religion, the sect of Abraham the orthodox ;
and he was no idolater. Say, Verily my prayers, and my
worship, and my life, and my death *are dedicated* unto GOD,
the LORD of all creatures : he hath no companion. This
have I been commanded : I am the first Moslem.[1] Say,
shall I desire any other LORD besides GOD ? since he is the
LORD of all things ; and no soul shall acquire *any merits
or demerits* but for itself ; and no burdened *soul* shall bear
the burden of another.[2] Moreover unto your LORD shall
ye return ; and he shall declare unto you that concerning
which ye *now* dispute. It is he who hath appointed you to
succeed *your predecessors* in the earth, and hath raised some
of you above others by *various* degrees *of worldly advantages,*
that he might prove you by that which he hath bestowed
on you. Thy LORD is swift in punishing ; and he *is also*
gracious *and* merciful.

VII

THE CHAPTER OF AL ARÂF [3]

Revealed at Mecca.[4]

IN THE NAME OF THE MOST MERCIFUL GOD.

A L. M. S.[5] A book hath been sent down unto thee :
and therefore let there be no doubt in thy breast
concerning it ; that thou mayest preach the same, and *that
it may be* an admonition unto the faithful. Follow that
which hath been sent down unto you from your LORD ;
and follow no guides besides him : how little will ye be
warned ! How many cities have we destroyed ; which our
vengeance overtook by night,[6] or while they were reposing
themselves at noonday ![7]   And their supplication, when our

[1] See before, p. 119.
[2] This was revealed in answer to the pressing instances of the idolaters,
who offered to take the crime upon themselves, if Mohammed would conform
to their worship. (Al Beidâwi.)
[3] Al Arâf signifies the partition between paradise and hell, which is
mentioned in this chapter. (Sale, Prel. Disc. Sect. IV., p. 101.)
[4] Some, however, except five or eight verses, begin at these words, *And
ask them concerning the city,* &c.
[5] The signification of those letters the more sober Mohammedans confess
GOD alone knows. Some, however, imagine they stand for Allah, Gabriel,
Mohammed, *on whom be peace.* (See Sale, Prel. Disc. p. 64.)
[6] As it did the inhabitants of Sodom and Gomorrah, to whom Lot was
sent.
[7] As happened to the Midianites, to whom Shoaib preached.

punishment came upon them, was no other than that they said, Verily we have been unjust. We will surely call those to an account, unto whom *a prophet* hath been sent; and we will *also* call those to account who have been sent *unto them*. And we will declare *their actions* unto them with knowledge; for we are not absent *from them*. The weighing *of men's actions* on that day *shall be* just;[1] and they whose balances *laden with their good works* shall be heavy, are those who *shall be* happy; but they whose balances shall be light, are those who have lost their souls, because they injured our signs. And now have we placed you on the earth, and have provided you food therein: *but* how little are ye thankful! We created you, and afterwards formed you; and then said unto the angels, Worship Adam; and they *all* worshipped *him*, except Eblîs, *who* was not one of those who worshipped.[2] *God* said *unto him*, What hindered thee from worshipping *Adam*, since I had commanded thee? He answered, I am more excellent than he: thou hast created me of fire, and hast created him of clay. *God* said, Get thee down therefore from *paradise*; for it is not *fit* that thou behave thyself proudly therein: get thee *hence*; thou shalt *be* one of the contemptible. He answered, Give me respite until the day of resurrection. *God* said, Verily thou shalt be *one* of those *who are* respited.[3] *The devil* said, Because thou hast depraved me, I will lay wait for *men* in thy strait way; then will I come upon them from before, and from behind, and from their right hands, and from their left;[4] and thou shalt not find the greater part of them thankful. *God* said *unto him*, Get thee hence, despised, and driven *far away*: verily whoever of them shall follow thee, I will surely fill hell with you all: but *as for thee*, O Adam, dwell thou and thy wife in paradise; and eat *of the fruits thereof* wherever ye will; but approach not this tree, lest ye become *of the number* of the unjust. And Satan suggested to them both, that he would discover unto them their nakedness, which was hidden from them; and he said, Your LORD hath not for-

---

[1] Sale, Prel. Disc. Sect. IV., p. 96.

[2] Chap. II., p. 5, &c.

[3] As the time till which the devil is reprieved is not particularly expressed, the commentators suppose his request was not wholly granted; but agree that he shall die, as well as other creatures, at the second sound of the trumpet. (Al Beidâwi. Sale, Prel. Disc. Sect. IV., and D'Herbelot, Bibl. Orient. Art. Eblis.)

[4] *i.e.*, I will attack them on every side that I shall be able. The other two ways, viz., from above and from under their feet, are omitted, say the commentators, to show that the devil's power is limited. (Al Beidâwi.)

bidden you this tree, *for any other reason* but lest ye should become angels, or lest ye become immortal. And he sware unto them, *saying*, Verily I am *one* of those who counsel you aright. And he caused them to fall through deceit.[1] And when they had tasted of the tree, their nakedness appeared unto them ;[2] and they began to join together the leaves of paradise,[3] to cover themselves. And their LORD called to them, *saying*, Did I not forbid you this tree ; and *did I not* say unto you, Verily Satan is your declared enemy ? They answered, O LORD, we have dealt unjustly with our own souls ; and if thou forgive us not, and be not merciful unto us, we shall *surely* be of those who perish. *God* said, Get ye down, the one of you an enemy unto the other ; and ye shall have a dwelling-place upon earth, and a provision for a season. He said, Therein shall ye live, and therein shall ye die, and from thence shall ye be taken forth *at the resurrection*. O children of Adam, we have sent down unto you apparel,[4] to conceal your nakedness, and fair garments ; but the clothing of piety is better. This *is one* of the signs of GOD ; that peradventure ye may consider. O children of Adam, let not Satan seduce you, as he expelled your parents out of paradise, by stripping them of their clothing, that he might show them their nakedness : verily he seeth you, *both* he and his companions, whereas ye see not them.[5] We have appointed the devils *to be* the patrons of those who believe not : and when they commit a filthy action, they say, We found our fathers *practising* the same ; and GOD hath com-

[1] The Mohammedan gospel of Barnabas tells us, that the sentence which GOD pronounced on the serpent for introducing the devil into paradise (see the notes to Chap. II. p. 5). was, that he should not only be turned out of paradise, but that he should have his legs cut off by the angel Michael, with the sword of GOD ; and that the devil himself, since he had rendered our first parents unclean, was condemned to eat the excrements of them and all their posterity ; which two last circumstances I do not remember to have read elsewhere. The words of the manuscript are these : *Y llamó [Dios] a la serpiente, y a Michael, aquel que tiene la espada de Dios, y le dixo ; Aquesta sierpe es acelerada, echala la primera del parayso, y cortale las piernas, y si quisiere caminar, arrastrara la vida por tierra. Y llamó à Satanas, el qual vino riendo, y dixole ; Porque tu reprobo has engañado a aquestos, y los has hecho immundos ? Yo quiero que toda immundicia suya, y de todos sus hijos, en saliendo de sus cuerpos entre por tu boca, porque en verdad ellos haran penitencia, y tu quedaras harto de immundicia.*

[2] Which they had not perceived before ; being clothed, as some say, with light, or garments of paradise, which fell from them on their disobedience. Yahya imagines their nakedness was hidden by their hair. (Chap. II. 5.)

[3] Which it is said were fig leaves. (Chap. II. 5.)

[4] Not only proper materials, but also ingenuity of mind and dexterity of hand to make use of them. (Chap. II. 5.)

[5] Because of the subtlety of their bodies, and their being void of all colour. (Jallalo'ddin.)

manded us *to do* it.   Say, Verily GOD commandeth not filthy
actions.   Do ye speak concerning GOD that which ye know
not ?   Say, My LORD hath commanded me *to observe* justice ;
therefore set your faces *to pray* at every place of worship,
and call upon him, approving unto him the sincerity of *your*
religion.   As he produced you at first, *so unto him* shall ye
return.   A part *of mankind* hath he directed ; and a part
hath been justly led into error, because they have taken the
devils for *their* patrons besides GOD, and imagine that they
are *rightly* directed.   O children of Adam, take your decent
apparel at every place of worship,[1] and eat and drink,[2]
but be not guilty of excess ; for he loveth not those who are
guilty of excess.   Say, Who hath forbidden the decent
apparel of GOD, which he hath produced for his servants,
and the good things *which he hath provided* for food ?   Say,
These things *are* for those who believe, in this present life,
but peculiarly on the day of resurrection.[3]   Thus do we
distinctly explain *our* signs unto people who understand.
Say, Verily my LORD hath forbidden filthy actions, both
that which is discovered thereof, and that which is concealed,
and also iniquity, and unjust violence ;   and *hath forbidden*
you to associate with GOD that concerning which he hath
sent you down no authority, or to speak of GOD that which
ye know not.   Unto every nation *there is* a prefixed term ;
therefore when their term is expired, they shall not have
respite for an hour, neither shall they be anticipated.   O
children of Adam, verily apostles from among you shall come
unto you, who shall expound my signs unto you : whosoever
therefore shall fear *God* and amend, there shall come no fear
on them, neither shall they be grieved.   But they who shall
accuse our signs of falsehood, and shall proudly reject them,
they shall be the companions of *hell* fire ;   they shall remain

[1] This passage was revealed to reprove an immodest custom of the pagan
Arabs, who used to encompass the Caaba naked, because clothes, they said,
were the signs of their disobedience to GOD. (Al Beidâwi, Jallalo'ddin.)
The Sonna orders that, when a man goes to prayers, he should put on his
better apparel, out of respect to the divine majesty before whom he is to
appear.   But as the Mohammedans think it indecent, on the one hand, to
come into God's presence in a slovenly manner, so they imagine, on the other,
that they ought not to appear before him in habits too rich or sumptuous,
and particularly in clothes adorned with gold or silver, lest they should seem
proud.

[2] The sons of Amer, it is said, when they performed the pilgrimage to
Mecca, used to eat no more than was absolutely necessary, and that not of
the more delicious sort of food, which abstinence they looked upon as a piece
of merit, but they are here told the contrary. (Al Beidâwi, Jallalo'ddin.)

[3] Because then the wicked, who also partook of the blessings of this life,
will have no share in the enjoyments of the next.

therein for ever. And who is more unjust than he who deviseth a lie concerning GOD, or accuseth his signs of imposture ? Unto these shall be given their portion *of worldly happiness*, according to *what is written in* the book *of God's decrees*, until our messengers [1] come unto them, *and* shall cause them to die ; saying, Where *are the idols* which ye called upon, besides GOD ? They shall answer, They have disappeared from us. And they shall bear witness against themselves, that they were unbelievers. *God* shall say *unto them at the resurrection*, Enter ye with the nations which have preceded you, of genii and of men, into *hell* fire ; so often as one nation shall enter, it shall curse its sister,[2] until they shall all have successively entered therein. The latter of them shall say of the former of them, O LORD, these have seduced us ; therefore inflict on them a double punishment of the fire *of hell*. *God* shall answer, *It shall be* doubled unto all ; [3] but ye know *it* not. And the former of them shall say unto the latter of them, Ye have not therefore any favour above us ; taste the punishment for that which ye have gained. Verily they who shall charge our signs with falsehood, and shall proudly reject them, the gates of heaven shall not be opened unto them,[4] neither shall they enter into paradise, until a camel pass through the eye of a needle ; [5] and thus will we reward the wicked doers. Their couch shall be in hell, and over them shall be coverings *of fire* ; and thus will we reward the unjust. But they who believe and do that which is right (we will not load any soul but according to its ability), they shall be the companions of paradise ; they shall remain therein for ever. And we will remove all grudges from their minds ; [6] rivers shall run at their feet, and they shall say, Praised be GOD, who hath directed us unto this *felicity* ! for we should not have been

---

[1] viz., The angel of death and his assistants.

[2] That is, the nation whose example betrayed them into their idolatry and other wickedness.

[3] Unto those who set the example, because they not only transgressed themselves, but were also the occasion of the others' transgression ; and unto those who followed them, because of their own infidelity and their imitating an ill example. (Al Beidâwi, Jallalo'ddin.)

[4] That is, when their souls shall, after death, ascend to heaven, they shall not be admitted, but shall be thrown down into the dungeon under the seventh earth. (Jallalo'ddin. Sale, Prel. Disc. Sect. IV.)

[5] This expression was probably taken from our Saviour's words in the gospel (Matt. xix. 24), though it be proverbial in the East.

[6] So that, whatever differences or animosities there had been between them in their lifetime, they shall now be forgotten, and give place to sincere love and amity. This Ali is said to have hoped would prove true to himself and his inveterate enemies, Othmân, Telha and Al Zobeir. (Al Beidâwi.)

rightly directed, if GOD had not directed us : now *are we convinced by demonstration that* the apostles of our LORD came *unto us* with truth. And it shall be proclaimed unto them, This is paradise, whereof ye are made heirs, *as a reward* for that which ye have wrought. And the inhabitants [1] of paradise shall call out to the inhabitants of *hell* fire, *saying*, Now have we found that which our LORD promised us *to be* true ; have ye *also* found that which your LORD promised you *to be* true ? They shall answer, Yea. And a crier [2] shall proclaim between them, The curse of GOD *shall be* on the wicked ; who turn *men* aside from the way of GOD, and seek *to render* it crooked, and who deny the life to come. And between the *blessed and the damned* there shall be a veil ; and men *shall stand* on Al Arâf,[3] who shall know every one *of them* by their marks ; [4] and shall call unto the inhabitants of paradise, *saying*, Peace be upon you : *yet* they shall not enter therein, although they earnestly desire *it*.[5] And when they shall turn their eyes towards the companions of *hell* fire, they shall say, O LORD, place us not with the ungodly people ! And those who stand on Al Arâf shall call unto *certain* men,[6] whom they shall know by their marks, *and* shall say, What hath your gathering *of riches* availed you, and that ye were puffed up with pride ? Are these the men on whom ye sware that GOD would not bestow mercy ? [7] Enter ye into paradise ; *there shall come* no fear on you, neither shall ye be grieved.[8] And the inhabitants of *hell* fire shall call unto the inhabitants of paradise, *saying*, Pour upon us some water, or of those *refreshments* which GOD

---

[1] Literally, *the companions*.

[2] This crier, some say, will be the angel Israfil.

[3] Al Arâf is the name of the wall or partition which, as Mohammed taught, will separate paradise from hell. But as to the persons who are to be placed thereon the commentators differ, as has been elsewhere observed. (Sale, Prel. Disc. Sect. IV. p. 101.)

[4] *i.e.*, Who shall distinguish the blessed from the damned by their proper characteristics ; such as the whiteness and splendour of the faces of the former, and the blackness of those of the latter. (Al Beidâwi.)

[5] From this circumstance, it seems that their opinion is the most probable who make this intermediate partition a sort of purgatory for those who, though they deserve not to be sent to hell, yet have not merits sufficient to gain them immediate admittance into paradise, and will be tantalized here for a certain time with a bare view of the felicity of that place.

[6] That is, the chiefs and ringleaders of the infidels. (Al Beidâwi.)

[7] These were the inferior and poorer among the believers, whom they despised in their lifetimes as unworthy of God's favour.

[8] These words are directed by an apostrophe, to the poor and despised believers above mentioned. Some commentators, however, imagine these and the next preceding words are to be understood of those who will be confined in Al Arâf ; and that the damned will, in return for their reproachful

hath bestowed on you.[1] They shall answer, Verily GOD hath forbidden them unto the unbelievers; who made a laughing-stock and a sport of their religion, and whom the life of the world hath deceived : therefore this day will we forget them, as they did forget the meeting of this day, and for that they denied our signs *to be from God*. And now we have brought unto those *of Mecca* a book *of divine revelations* : we have explained it with knowledge ; a direction and mercy unto people who shall believe. Do they wait *for any other* than the interpretation thereof ? [2] On the day whereon the interpretation thereof shall come, they who had forgotten the same before, shall say, Now *are we convinced by demonstration that* the messengers of our LORD came *unto us* with truth : shall we therefore have any intercessors, who will intercede for us ? or shall we be sent back *into the world*, that we may do other *works* than what we did *in our lifetime* ? But now have they lost their souls ; and that which they impiously imagined, hath fled from them.[3] Verily your LORD is GOD, who created the heavens and the earth in six days ; and then ascended *his* throne : he causeth the night to cover the day ; it succeedeth the same swiftly : *he* also *created* the sun and the moon, and the stars, *which are* absolutely subject unto his command. Is not the whole creation, and the empire *thereof*, his ? Blessed be GOD, the LORD of all creatures ! Call upon your LORD humbly and in secret ; for he loveth not those who transgress.[4] And act not corruptly in the earth, after its reformation ; [5] and call upon him with fear and desire : for the mercy of GOD is near unto the righteous. It is he who sendeth the winds, spread abroad [6] before his mercy,[7] until they

speech, swear that they shall never enter paradise themselves ; whereupon GOD of his mercy shall order them to be admitted by these words. (Al Beidâwi.)

[1] *i.e.*, Of the other liquors or fruits of paradise. Compare this passage with the parable of Dives and Lazarus.

[2] That is, the event of the promises and menaces therein.

[3] See Chap. VI. p. 120.

[4] Behaving themselves arrogantly while they pray ; or praying with an obstreperous voice, or a multitude of words and vain repetitions. (Al Beidâwi.)

[5] *i.e.*. After that GOD hath sent his prophets, and revealed his laws, for the reformation and amendment of mankind.

[6] Or ranging over a large extent of land. Some copies, instead of *noshran*, which is the reading I have here followed, have *boshran*, which signifies *good tidings* ; the rising of the wind in such a manner being the forerunner of rain.

[7] That is, rain. For the east wind, says Al Beidâwi, raises the clouds, the north wind drives them together, the south wind agitates them, so as to make the rain fall, and the west wind disperses them again. (Al Beidâwi.)

bring a cloud heavy *with rain*, which we drive unto a dead country ;[1] and we cause water to descend thereon by which we cause all *sorts of* fruits to spring forth. Thus will we bring forth the dead *from their graves* ;[2] that peradventure ye may consider. From a good country shall its fruit spring forth *abundantly*, by the permission of its LORD ; but from the *land* which is bad, it shall not spring forth otherwise than scarcely. Thus do we explain the *signs of divine providence* unto people who are thankful. We formerly sent Noah[3] unto his people : and he said, O my people, worship GOD : ye have no other GOD than him.[4] Verily I fear for you the punishment of the great day.[5] The chiefs of his people answered *him*, We surely perceive thee *to be* in a manifest error. He replied, O my people, there is no error in me ; but I am a messenger from the LORD of all creatures. I bring unto you the messages of my LORD ; and I counsel you aright : for I know from GOD that which ye know not. Do ye wonder that an admonition hath come unto you from your LORD by a man[6] from among you, to warn you, that ye may take heed to yourselves, and that

[1] Or a dry and parched land.

[2] Sale, Prel. Disc. Sect. IV. p. 89.

[3] Noah the son of Lamech, according to the Mohammedan writers, was one of the six principal prophets (Sale, Prel. Disc.), though he had no written revelations delivered to him (Reland. de Relig. Moh., p. 34), and the first who appeared after his great-grandfather Edris or Enoch. They also say he was by trade a carpenter, which they infer from his building the ark, and that the year of his mission was the fiftieth, or, as others say, the fortieth of his age. (Al Zamakhshari.)

That Noah was a preacher of righteousness unto the wicked antediluvians is testified by Scripture (2 Pet. ii. 5). The Eastern Christians say that when GOD ordered Noah to build the ark, he also directed him to make an instrument of wood, such as they make use of at this day in the East, instead of bells, to call the people to church, and named in Arabic Nâkûs, and in modern Greek Semandra ; on which he was to strike three times every day, not only to call together the workmen that were building the ark, but to give him an opportunity of daily admonishing his people of the impending danger of the Deluge, which would certainly destroy them if they did not repent. (Eutych. Annal., p. 37.)

Some Mohammedan authors pretend Noah was sent to convert Zohâk, one of the Persian kings of the first race, who refused to hearken to him ; and that he afterwards preached GOD's unity publicly. (D'Herbel. Bibl. Orient. p. 675.)

[4] From these words, and other passages of the Korân where Noah's preaching is mentioned, it appears that, according to Mohammed's opinion, a principal crime of the antediluvians was idolatry. (Chap. LXXI., and Sale, Prel. Disc. Sect. I.)

[5] viz., Either the day of resurrection, or that whereon the Flood was to begin.

[6] For, said they, if GOD had pleased, He would have sent an angel, and not a man ; since we never heard of such an instance in the times of our fathers. (Al Beidâwi.)

peraдventure ye may obtain mercy? And they accused him of imposture: but we delivered him and those who *were* with him in the ark,[1] and we drowned those who charged our signs with falsehood; for they were a blind people. And unto *the tribe of* Ad [2] *we sent* their brother Hûd.[3] He said, O my people, worship GOD: ye have no other GOD than him; will ye not fear *him*? The chiefs of those among his people who believed not,[4] answered, Verily we perceive that thou *art guided* by folly; and we certainly esteem thee *to be one* of the liars. He replied, O my people, *I am* not *guided by* folly; but I am a messenger unto you from the LORD of all creatures: I bring unto you the messages of my LORD; and I am a faithful counsellor unto you. Do ye wonder that an admonition hath come unto you from your LORD, by a man from among you, that he may warn you? Call to mind how he hath appointed you successors unto the people of Noah,[5] and hath added unto you in stature largely.[6] Remember the benefits of GOD, that ye may prosper. They said, Art thou come unto us, that we should worship GOD alone, and leave *the deities* which our fathers worshipped? Now bring down that *judgment* upon us, with which thou threatenest us, if thou speakest truth. *Hûd* answered, Now shall there suddenly fall upon you from

[1] That is, those who believed on him, and entered into that vessel with him. Though there be a tradition among the Mohammedans, said to have been received from the prophet himself, and conformable to the Scripture, that eight persons, and no more, were saved in the ark, yet some of them report the number variously. One says they were but six, another ten, another twelve, and another seventy-eight, and another fourscore, half men and half women (Al Zamakhshari, Jallalo'ddin, Ebn Shohnah), and that one of them was the elder Jorham (Sale, Prel. Disc. Sect. I.), the preserver, as some pretend, of the Arabian language. (Pocock, Orat. Præfix. Carm. Tograi.)

[2] Ad was an ancient and potent tribe of Arabs (Sale, Prel. Disc. Sect. I.) and zealous idolaters (Abulfeda). They chiefly worshipped four deities, Sâkia, Hâfedha, Râzeka, and Sâlema; the first, as they imagined, supplying them with rain, the second preserving them from all dangers abroad, the third providing food for their sustenance, and the fourth restoring them to health when afflicted with sickness (D'Herbel. Bibl. Orient. Art. Houd), according to the signification of the several names.

[3] Generally supposed to be the same person with Heber (Sale, Prel. Disc.); but others say he was the son of Abda'llah, the son of Ribâh, the son of Kholûd, the son of Ad, the son of Aws or Uz, the son of Aram, the son of Sem. (Al Beidâwi.)

[4] These words were added because some of the principal men among them believed on Hûd, one of whom was Morthed Ebn Saad. (Al Beidâwi.)

[5] Dwelling in the habitations of the antediluvians, who preceded them not many centuries, or having the chief sway in the earth after them. For the kingdom of Shedâd, the son of Ad, is said to have extended from the sands of Alaj to the trees of Omân. (Al Beidâwi.)

[6] Sale, Prel. Disc. p. 7.

your LORD vengeance and indignation. Will ye dispute
with me concerning the names which ye have named,[1]
and your fathers ; as to which GOD hath not revealed unto
you any authority ? Do ye wait therefore, and I will be
one of those who wait with you. And we delivered him,
and them who *believed* with him, by our mercy ; and we
cut off the uttermost part of those who charged our signs
with falsehood, and were not believers.[2] And unto *the
tribe of* Thamûd *we sent* [3] their brother Sâleh.[4] He said, O
my people, worship GOD : ye have no GOD besides him.
Now hath a manifest proof come unto you from your LORD.
This she-camel of GOD *is* a sign unto you :[5] therefore dismiss

[1] That is, concerning the idols and imaginary objects of your worship,
to which ye wickedly gave the names, attributes, and honour due to the
only true GOD.

[2] The dreadful destruction of the Adites we have mentioned in another
place (Sale, Prel. Disc. Sect. I.), and shall only add here some further circumstances of that calamity, and which differ a little from what is there
said ; for the Arab writers acknowledge many inconsistencies in the histories of these ancient tribes. (Al Beidâwi. D'Herbelot, Bibl. Orient. Art.
Houd.)

The tribe of Ad having been for their incredulity previously chastised
with a three years' drought, sent Kail Ebn Ithar and Morthed Ebn Saad,
with seventy other principal men, to the temple of Mecca to obtain rain.
Mecca was then in the hands of the tribe of Amalek, whose prince was
Moâwiyah Ebn Becr ; and he, being without the city when the ambassadors
arrived, entertained them there for a month in so hospitable a manner that
they had forgotten the business they came about had not the king reminded
them of it, not as from himself, lest they should think he wanted to be rid
of them, but by some verses which he put into the mouth of a singing woman.
At which, being roused from their lethargy, Morthed told them the only
way they had to obtain what they wanted would be to repent and obey
their prophet ; but this displeasing the rest, they desired Moâwiyah to
imprison him, lest he should go with them ; which being done, Kail with
the rest entering Mecca, begged of GOD that he would send rain to the people
of Ad. Whereupon three clouds appeared, a white one, a red one, and
a black one ; and a voice from heaven ordered Kail to choose which he
would. Kail failed not to make choice of the last, thinking it to be laden
with the most rain ; but when this cloud came over them, it proved to be
fraught with the divine vengeance, and a tempest broke forth from it which
destroyed them all. (Sale, Prel. Disc. Sect. I.)

[3] Thamûd was another tribe of the ancient Arabs who fell into idolatry.
(Sale, Prel. Disc. Sect. I.)

[4] Al Beidâwi deduces his genealogy thus : Sâleh, the son of Obeid, the
son of Asaf, the son of Masekh, the son of Obeid, the son of Hâdher, the
son of Thamûd. (Abulfeda, Al Zamakhshari, D'Herbel. Bibl. Orient. Art.
Sâleh.)

[5] The Thamûdites, insisting on a miracle, proposed to Sâleh that he
should go with them to their festival, and that they should call on their
gods, and he on his, promising to follow that deity which should answer.
But after they had called on their idols a long time to no purpose, Jonda
Ebn Amru, their prince, pointed to a rock standing by itself, and bade
Sâleh cause a she-camel big with young to come forth from it, solemnly
engaging that, if he did, he would believe, and his people promised the same.
Whereupon Sâleh asked it of GOD, and presently the rock, after several
throes as if in labour, was delivered of a she-camel answering the description

her freely, that she may feed in GOD's earth ; and do her
no hurt, lest a painful punishment seize you. And call to
mind how he hath appointed you successors unto *the tribe
of* Ad, and hath given you a habitation on earth ; ye built
yourselves castles on the plains thereof, and cut out the
mountains into houses.[1] Remember therefore the benefits
of GOD, and commit not violence in the earth, acting corruptly. The chiefs among his people who were puffed
up with pride, said unto those who were esteemed weak,
namely, unto those who believed among them, Do ye know
that Sâleh hath been sent from his LORD ? They answered,
We do surely believe in that wherewith he hath been sent.
Those who were elated with pride replied, Verily we believe
not in that wherein ye believe. And they cut off the feet
of the camel,[2] and insolently transgressed the command of
their LORD,[3] and said, O Sâleh, cause that to come upon us
with which thou hast threatened us, if thou art *one* of those
who have been sent *by* GOD. Whereupon a terrible noise
from heaven [4] assailed them ; and in the morning they were

of Jonda, which immediately brought forth a young one, ready weaned, and,
as some say, as big as herself. Jonda, seeing this miracle, believed on the
prophet, and some few with him ; but the greater part of the Thamûdites
remained, notwithstanding, incredulous. Of this camel the commentators
tell several very absurd stories : as that, when she went to drink, she never
raised her head from the well or river till she had drunk up all the water in
it, and then she offered herself to be milked, the people drawing from her
as much milk as they pleased ; and some say that she went about the town
crying aloud, *If any wants milk let him come forth.* (Sale, Prel. Disc. p. 8.)

[1] The tribe of Thamûd dwelt first in the country of the Adites, but their
numbers increasing, they removed to the territory of Hejr for the sake of
the mountains, where they cut themselves habitations in the rocks, to be
seen at this day.

[2] This extraordinary camel frightening the other cattle from their pasture,
a certain rich woman named Oneiza Omm Ganem, having four daughters,
dressed them out and offered one Kedâr his choice of them if he would
kill the camel. Whereupon he chose one, and with the assistance of eight
other men, hamstrung and killed the dam, and pursuing the young one,
which fled to the mountain, killed that also and divided his flesh among
them. (Abulfeda.) Others tell the story somewhat differently, adding Sadaka
Bint al Mokhtâr as a joint conspiratress with Oneiza, and pretending that
the young one was not killed ; for they say that having fled to a certain
mountain named Kâra, he there cried three times, and Sâleh bade them
catch him if they could, for then there might be hopes of their avoiding the
divine vengeance ; but this they were not able to do, the rock opening
after he had cried, and receiving him within it. (Al Beidâwi, D'Herbel.
ubi supra.)

[3] Defying the vengeance with which they were threatened ; because
they trusted in their strong dwellings hewn in the rocks, saying that the
tribe of Ad perished only because their houses were not built with sufficient
strength. (Al Kessai.)

[4] Like violent and repeated claps of thunder, which some say was no
other than the voice of the angel Gabriel (Sale, Prel. Disc.), and which
rent their hearts (Abulfeda, Al Beidâwi). It is said that after they had

found in their dwellings prostrate on their breasts and *dead*.[1] And Sâleh departed from them, and said,[2] O my people, now have I delivered unto you the message of my LORD ; and I advised you well, but ye love not those who advise *you* well. And *remember* Lot,[3] when he said unto his people, Do ye commit a wickedness, wherein no creature hath set you an example ? Do ye approach lustfully unto men, leaving the women ? Certainly ye are people who transgress *all modesty*. But the answer of his people was no other than that they said *the one to the other*, Expel them [4] your city ; for they are men who preserve themselves pure *from the crimes which ye commit*. Therefore we delivered him and his family, except his wife ; she was *one* of those who stayed *behind* :[5] and we rained a shower *of stones* upon them.[6] Behold therefore what was the end of the wicked. And unto Madian,[7]

killed the camel, Sâleh told them that on the morrow their faces should become yellow, the next day red, and the third day black, and that on the fourth GOD's vengeance should light on them ; and that the first three signs happening accordingly, they sought to put him to death, but GOD delivered him by sending him into Palestine. (Al Beidâwi.)

[1] Mohammed, in the expedition of Tabûc, which he undertook against the Greeks in the ninth year of the Hejra, passing by Hejr, where this ancient tribe had dwelt, forbade his army, though much distressed with heat and thirst, to draw any water there, but ordered them if they had drunk of that water to bring it up again, or if they had kneaded any meal with it to give it to their camels (Abulfed. Vit. Moh. p. 124) ; and wrapping up his face in his garment, he set spurs to his mule, crying out, *Enter not the houses of those wicked men, but rather weep, lest that happen unto you which befell them* ; and having so said, he continued galloping full speed with his face muffled up, till he had passed the valley (Al Bokhari).

[2] Whether this speech was made by Sâleh to them at parting, as seems most probable, or after the judgment had fallen on them, the commentators are not agreed.

[3] The commentators say, conformably to the Scripture, that Lot was the son of Haran, the son of Azer or Terah, and consequently Abraham's nephew, who brought him with him from Chaldea into Palestine, where they say he was sent by GOD to reclaim the inhabitants of Sodom and the other neighbouring cities which were overthrown with it, from the unnatural vice to which they were addicted. (D'Herbelot, Bibl. Orient. Art. Loth.) And this Mohammedan tradition seems to be countenanced by the words of the apostle, that this *righteous man dwelling among them, in seeing and hearing vexed his righteous soul from day to day with their unlawful deeds* (2 Pet. ii. 8) ; whence it is probable that he omitted no opportunity of endeavouring their reformation. The story of Lot is told with further circumstances in the eleventh chapter.

[4] viz., Lot, and those who believe on him.

[5] See Chap. XI.

[6] See Chap. XI.

[7] Or Midian, a city of Hejâz, and the habitation of a tribe of the same name, the descendants of Midian, the son of Abraham by Keturah (Gen. xxv. 2), who afterwards coalesced with the Ismaelites, as it seems ; Moses naming the same merchants who sold Joseph to Potiphar, in one place Ismaelites (Gen. xxxix. 1), and in another Midianites (Gen. xxxvii. 36).

This city was situated on the Red Sea, south-east of Mount Sinai, and is doubtless the same with the Modiana of Ptolemy ; what was remaining

we sent their brother Shoaib.[1] He said *unto them*, O my people, worship GOD ; ye have no GOD besides him. Now hath an evident demonstration [2] come unto you from your LORD. Therefore give full measure and just weight, and diminish not unto men *aught of* their matters ; [3] neither act corruptly in the earth, after its reformation. This will be better for you, if ye believe. And beset not every way, threatening *the passenger*,[4] and turning aside from the path of GOD him who believeth in him, and seeking to make it crooked. And remember, when ye were few, and GOD multiplied you : and behold, what hath been the end of those who acted corruptly. And if part of you believe in that wherewith I am sent, and part believe not, wait patiently until GOD judge between us ; for he is the best judge. (IX.)[5] The chiefs of his people, who were elated with pride, answered, We will surely cast thee, O Shoaib, and those who believe with thee, out of our city ; or else thou shalt certainly return unto our religion. He said, What, though we be averse *thereto* ? We shall surely imagine a lie against GOD, if we return unto your religion, after that GOD hath delivered us from the same : and we have no *reason* to return unto it, unless GOD our LORD shall please *to abandon*

---

of it in Mohammed's time was soon after demolished in the succeeding wars (Golit. not. in Alfrag. p. 143), and it remains desolate to this day. The people of the country pretend to show the well whence Moses watered Jethro's flocks. (Abulfed. Desc. Arab. p. 42. Geogr. Nub. p. 10).

[1] Some Mohammedan writers make him the son of Mikaïl, the son of Yashjar, the son of Madian (Al Beidâwi, Tarikh Montakhab) ; and they generally suppose him to be the same person with the father-in-law of Moses, who is named in Scripture Reuel or Raguel, and Jethro (Exod. ii. 18 ; iii. 1). But Ahmed Ebn Abd'alhalim charges those who entertain this opinion with ignorance. Al Kessâi says that his father's name was Sanûn, and that he was first called Boyûn, and afterwards Shoaib : and adds that he was a comely person, but spare and lean, very thoughtful and of few words. Doctor Prideaux writes this name, after the French translation, Chaib. (Life of Mah. p. 24.)

[2] This demonstration the commentators suppose to have been a power of working miracles, though the Korân mentions none in particular. However, they say (after the Jews) that he gave his son-in-law that wonder-working rod (Al Beidâwi, Shalshel hakkab. p. 12), with which he performed all those miracles in Egypt and the desert, and also excellent advice and instructions (Exod. xviii. 13, &c.), whence he had the surname of Khatîb al anbiyâ, or the *preacher to the prophets* (D'Herbelot, Bibl. Orient.)

[3] For one of the great crimes which the Midianites were guilty of was the using of diverse measures and weights, a great and a small, buying by one and selling by another (Al Beidâwi. Deut. xxv. 13, 14).

[4] Robbing on the highway, it seems, was another crying sin frequent among these people. But some of the commentators interpret this passage figuratively, of their besetting the way of truth, and threatening those who gave ear to the remonstrances of Shoaib. (Al Beidâwi.)

[5] Here Section IX. begins.

us. Our LORD comprehendeth everything by *his* knowledge. In GOD do we put our trust. O LORD, do thou judge between us and our nation with truth ; for thou art the best judge. And the chiefs of his people, who believed not, said, If ye follow Shoaib, ye shall surely perish. Therefore a storm from heaven [1] assailed them, and in the morning they were found in their dwellings *dead and* prostrate. They who accused Shoaib of imposture *became* as though they had never dwelt therein ; they who accused Shoaib of imposture perished themselves. And he departed from them, and said, O my people, now have I performed unto you the messages of my LORD ; and I advised you aright : but why should I be grieved for an unbelieving people ? We have never sent any prophet unto a city, but we afflicted the inhabitants thereof with calamity and adversity, that they might humble themselves. Then we gave *them* in exchange good in lieu of evil, until they abounded, and said, Adversity and prosperity formerly happened unto our fathers, *as unto us.* Therefore we took vengeance on them suddenly, and they perceived it not *beforehand.* But if the inhabitants of *those* cities had believed and feared *God,* we would surely have opened to them blessings both from heaven and earth. But they charged *our apostles* with falsehood ; wherefore we took vengeance on them, for that which they had been guilty of. Were the inhabitants therefore of *those* cities secure that our punishment should not fall on them by night, while they slept ? Or were the inhabitants of *those* cities secure that our punishment should not fall on them by day, while they sported ? Were they therefore secure from the stratagem of GOD ? [2] But none will think himself secure from the stratagem of GOD, except the people who perish. And hath it not manifestly appeared unto those who have inherited the earth after the *former* inhabitants thereof, that, if we please, we can afflict them for their sins ? But we will seal up their hearts ; and they shall not hearken. We will relate unto thee some stories of these cities. Their apostles had come unto them with evident miracles, but they were not *disposed*

---

[1] Like that which destroyed the Thamûdites. Some suppose it to have been an earthquake, for the original word signifies either or both ; and both these dreadful calamities may well be supposed to have jointly executed the divine vengeance.

[2] Hereby is figuratively expressed the manner of GOD's dealing with proud and ungrateful men, by suffering them to fill up the measure of their iniquity, without vouchsafing to bring them to a sense of their condition by chastisements and afflictions till they find themselves utterly lost, when they least expect it. (Al Beidâwi.)

to believe in that which they had before gainsaid. Thus
will GOD seal up the hearts of the unbelievers. And we
found not in the greater part of them any *observance of their*
covenant ; but we found the greater part of them wicked
doers. Then we sent, after the *above-named apostles*, Moses
with our signs unto Pharaoh[1] and his princes ; who treated
them unjustly : [2] but behold what was the end of the corrupt
doers. And Moses said, O Pharaoh, verily I am an apostle
sent from the LORD of all creatures. It is just that I should
not speak of GOD other than the truth. Now am I come unto
you with an *evident* sign from your LORD : send therefore the
children of Israel away with me. Pharaoh answered, If
thou comest with a sign, produce it, if thou speakest truth.
Wherefore he cast down his rod ; and behold, it *became*
a visible serpent.[3] And he drew forth his hand *out of his*
bosom ; and behold, it *appeared* white unto the spectators. [4]

---

[1] This was the common title or name of the kings of Egypt (signifying
king in the Coptic tongue), as Ptolemy was in after times ; and as Cæsar
was that of the Roman emperors, and Khosrû that of the kings of Persia.
But which of the kings of Egypt this Pharaoh of Moses was, is uncertain.
Not to mention the opinions of the European writers, those of the East
generally suppose him to have been Al Walîd, who, according to some, was
an Arab of the t ibe of Ad, or, according to others, the son of Masâb, the
son of Riyán, the son of Wal d (Sale, Prel. Disc.) the Amalekite (Abulfeda,
&c.). There are historians, however, who suppose Kabûs, the brother
and predecessor Al Walîd, was the prince we are speaking of ; and pretend
he lived six hundred and twenty years, and reigned four hundred. Which
is more reasonable, at least, than the opinion of those who imagine it was
his father Masâb, or grandfather Riyân (Kitâb Tafsir Lebâb, and Al Keshâf).
Abulfeda says that Masâb being one hundred and seventy years old, and
having no child, while he kept the herds saw a cow calve, and heard her
say, at the same time, O Masáb, *be not grieved, for thou shalt have a wicked*
son, who will be at length cast into hell. And he accordingly had this Walîd,
who afterwards coming to be king of Egypt, proved an impious tyrant.

[2] By not believing therein.

[3] The Arab writers tell enormous fables of this serpent or dragon. For
they say that he was hairy, and of so prodigious a size, that when he opened
his mouth, his jaws were fourscore cubits asunder, and when he laid his
lower jaw on the ground, his upper reached to the top of the palace ; that
Pharaoh seeing this monster make towards him, fled from it, and was so
terribly frightened that he befouled himself ; and that the whole assembly
also betaking themselves to their heels, no less than twenty-five thousand
of them lost their lives in the press. They add that Pharaoh upon this
adjured Moses by GOD who had sent him, to take away the serpent, and
promised he would believe on him, and let the Israelites go ; but when
Moses had done what he requested, he relapsed, and grew as hardened as
before. (Al Beidâwi.)

[4] There is a tradition that Moses was a very swarthy man ; and that
when he put his hand into his bosom, and drew it out again, it became extremely white and splendid, surpassing the brightness of the sun. (Al Beidâwi.)
Marracci (in Alc. p. 284) says we do not read in Scripture that Moses showed
this sign before Pharaoh. It is true, the Scripture does not expressly say
so, but it seems to be no more than a necessary inference from that passage
where GOD tells Moses that if they will not hearken to the first sign, they

The chiefs of the people of Pharaoh said, This *man* is certainly an expert magician : he seeketh to dispossess you of your land ; what therefore do ye direct ? They answered, Put off him and his brother *by fair promises for some time,* and *in the meanwhile* send unto the cities persons who may assemble and bring unto thee every expert magician. So the magicians [1] came unto Pharaoh ; *and* they said, Shall we surely receive a reward, if we do overcome ? He answered Yea ; and ye shall certainly be of those who approach near *unto my throne.* They said, O Moses, either do thou cast down *thy rod first,* or we will cast down *ours. Moses* answered, Do ye cast down *your rods first.* And when they had cast *them* down, they enchanted the eyes of the men *who were present,* and terrified them ; and they performed a great enchantment. [2] And we spake by revelation unto Moses, *saying,* Throw down thy rod. And behold, it swallowed up *the rods* which they had *caused falsely to appear* changed *into serpents.* [3] Wherefore the truth was confirmed, and that which they had wrought vanished. And *Pharaoh and his magicians* were overcome there, and were rendered contemptible. And the magicians prostrated themselves, worshipping ; *and* they said, We believe in the LORD of all creatures, the LORD of Moses and Aaron. [4] Pharaoh said, Have ye believed on him, before I have given you permission ? Verily this is a plot which ye have contrived in the city, that ye might cast forth from thence the inhabitants

will believe the latter sign, and if they will not believe these two signs then directs him to turn the water into blood (Exod. iv. 8, 9).

[1] The Arabian writers name several of these magicians, besides their chief priest Simeon, viz., Sadûr and Ghadûr, Jaath and Mosfa, Warân and Zamân, each of whom came attended with their disciples, amounting in all to several thousands. (D'Herbelot, Bibl. Orient. Art. Mousa, p. 643, &c. Al Kessâi.)

[2] They provided themselves with a great number of thick ropes and long pieces of wood, which they contrived, by some means, to move, and make them twist themselves one over the other, and so imposed on the beholders, who at a distance took them to be true serpents. (Al Beidâwi. D'Herbelot, ubi. sup. and Chap. XX.)

[3] The expositors add, that when this serpent had swallowed up all the rods and cords, he made directly towards the assembly, and put them into so great a terror that they fled, and a considerable number were killed in the crowd ; then Moses took it up, and it became a rod in his hand as before. Whereupon the magicians declared that it could be no enchantment, because in such case their rods and cords would not have disappeared. (Al Beidâwi).

[4] It seems probable that all the magicians were not converted by this miracle, for some writers introduce Sadûr and Ghadûr only, acknowledging Moses' miracle to be wrought by the power of GOD. These two, they say, were brothers, and the sons of a famous magician, then dead ; but on their being sent for to court on this occasion, their mother persuaded them to go to their father's tomb to ask his advice. Being come to the tomb, the

thereof.[1] But ye shall surely know *that I am your master*;
for I will cause your hands and your feet to be cut off on the
opposite sides,[2] then will I cause you all to be crucified.[3]
The *magicians* answered, We shall certainly return unto our
LORD, *in the next life*; for thou takest vengeance on us only
because we have believed in the signs of our LORD, when
they have come unto us. O LORD, pour on us patience, and
cause us to die Moslems.[4] And the chiefs of Pharaoh's
people said, Wilt thou let Moses and his people go, that they
may act corruptly in the earth, and leave thee and thy gods?[5]
Pharaoh answered, We will cause their male children to be
slain and we will suffer their females to live;[6] and *by that
means* we shall prevail over them. Moses said unto his
people, Ask assistance of GOD, and suffer patiently; for
the earth is GOD'S, he giveth it for an inheritance unto such
of his servants as he pleaseth: and the *prosperous* end *shall
be* unto those who fear *him*. They answered, We have been
afflicted *by having our male children slain*, before thou camest
unto us, and also since thou hast come unto us. *Moses*
said, Peradventure it may happen that your LORD will
destroy your enemy, and will cause you to succeed *him* in
the earth, that he may see how ye will act *therein*. And

father answered their call; and when they had acquainted him with the
affair, he told them that they should inform themselves whether the rod
of which they spoke became a serpent while its masters slept, or only when
they were awake; for, said he, enchantments have no effect while the
enchanter is asleep, and therefore if it be otherwise in this case, you may
be assured that they act by a divine power. These two magicians then,
arriving at the capital of Egypt, on inquiry found, to their great astonishment,
that when Moses and Aaron went to rest, their rod became a serpent, and
guarded them while they slept. (D'Herbel. ubi sup.) And this was the
first step towards their conversion.

[1] *i.e.*, This is a confederacy between you and Moses, entered into before
ye left the city to go to the place of appointment, to turn out the Copts,
or native Egyptians, and establish the Israelites in their stead. (Al Beidâwi.)

[2] That is, your right hands and your left feet.

[3] Some say Pharaoh was the first inventor of this ignominious and painful
punishment.

[4] Some think these converted magicians were executed accordingly;
but others deny it, and say that the king was not able to put them to death,
insisting on these words of the Korân (Chap. XXVIII.), *You two, and they
who follow you, shall overcome.*

[5] Which were the stars, or other idols. But some of the commentators,
from certain expressions of this prince, recorded in the Korân (Chaps.
XXVI., XXVIII., &c.), whereby he sets up himself as the only god of his
subjects, suppose that he was the object of their worship, and therefore
instead of *alihataca, thy gods*, read *ilahataca, they worship* (Al Beidâwi).

[6] That is, we will continue to make use of the same cruel policy to keep
the Israelites in subjection, as we have hitherto done. The commentators
say that Pharaoh came to this resolution because he had either been admonished in a dream, or by the astrologers or diviners, that one of that nation
should subvert his kingdom. (Al Beidâwi, Jallalo'ddin.)

we formerly punished the people of Pharaoh with dearth and scarcity of fruits, that they might be warned. Yet when good happened unto them, they said, This *is owing* unto us : but if evil befell them, they attributed *the same* to the ill luck of Moses, and those who *were* with him.[1] Was not their ill luck with GOD ? [2] but most of them knew *it* not. And they said *unto Moses*, Whatever sign thou show unto us, to enchant us therewith, we will not believe on thee. Wherefore we sent upon them a flood,[3] and locusts, and l ice,[4] and frogs, and blood ; distinct miracles : but they behaved proudly, and became a wicked people. And when the plague[5] fell on them, they said, O Moses, entreat thy LORD for us, according to that which he hath covenanted with thee, verily if thou take the plague from off us, we will surely believe thee, and we will let the children of Israel go with thee. But when we had taken the plague from off them, until the term *which God had granted them* was expired, behold, they broke their promise. Wherefore we took vengeance on them, and drowned them in the *Red* Sea ; [6] because they charged our signs with falsehood, and neglected them. And we caused the people who had been rendered weak, to inherit the eastern parts of the earth and the western parts thereof,[7] which we blessed *with fertility* ; and the gracious word of thy LORD was fulfilled on the children of Israel, for that they had endured with patience : and we destroyed the *structures* which Pharaoh and his people had

---

[1] Looking on him and his followers as the occasion of those calamities. The original word properly signifies to *take an ominous and sinister presage* of any future event, from the flight of birds, or the like.

[2] By whose will and decree they were so afflicted, as a punishment for their wickedness.

[3] This inundation, they say, was occasioned by unusual rains, which continued eight days together, and the overflowing of the Nile ; and not only covered their lands, but came into their houses, and rose as high as their backs and necks ; but the children of Israel had no rain in their quarters (Jallalo'ddin, Abulfed.) As there is no mention of any such miraculous inundation in the Mosaic writings, some have imagined this plague to have been either a pestilence, or the small-pox, or some other epidemical distemper. (A! Beidâwi.) For the word *tufân*, which is used in this place, and is generally rendered a *deluge*, may also signify any other universal destruction or mortality.

[4] Some will have these insects to have been a larger sort of tick; others, the young locusts before they have wings. (Al Beidâwi.)

[5] viz., Any of the calamities already mentioned, or the pestilence which GOD sent upon them afterwards.

[6] See this wonderful event more particularly described in the tenth and twentieth chapters.

[7] That is, the land of Syria, of which the eastern geographers reckon Palestine a part, and wherein the commentators say the children of Israel succeeded the kings of Egypt and the Amalekites. (Al Beidâwi.)

made, and that which they had erected.[1] And we caused
the children of Israel to pass through the sea, and they came
unto a people who gave themselves up to *the worship of
their idols* ;[2] and they said, O Moses, make us a god in like
manner as these *people* have gods. *Moses* answered, Verily
ye are an ignorant people : for *the religion* which these follow
will be destroyed, and that which they do is vain. He said,
Shall I seek for you any other god than GOD ; since he hath
preferred you to the *rest of the* world ? And *remember*
when we delivered you from the people of Pharaoh, who
grievously oppressed you ; they slew your male children,
and let your females live : therein was a great trial from your
LORD. And we appointed unto Moses *a fast of* thirty nights
before we gave him the law,[3] and we completed them by
adding of ten *more* ; and the stated time of his LORD was
fulfilled in forty nights. And Moses said unto his brother
Aaron, Be thou my deputy among my people *during my
absence* ; and behave uprightly, and follow not the way of
the corrupt doers. And when Moses came at our appointed
time, and his LORD spake unto him,[4] he said, O LORD,
Show me *thy glory*, that I may behold thee. *God* answered,
Thou shalt in no wise behold me ; but look towards the
mountain,[5] and if it stand firm in its place, then shalt thou
see me. But when his LORD appeared with glory in the
mount,[6] he reduced it to dust. And Moses fell down in a
swoon. And when he came to himself, he said, Praise be
unto thee ! I turn unto thee with repentance, and I *am*

[1] Particularly the lofty tower which Pharaoh caused to be built, that
he might attack the GOD of Moses. (Chaps. XXVIII. and XL.)

[2] These people some will have to be of the tribe of Amalek, whom Moses
was commanded to destroy, and others of the tribe of Lakhm. Their
idols, it is said, were images of oxen, which gave the first hint to the making
of the golden calf. (Al Beidâwi.)

[3] The commentators say that GOD, having promised Moses to give him
the law, directed him to prepare himself for the high favour of speaking
with GOD in person by a fast of thirty days ; and that Moses accordingly
fasted the whole month of Dhu'lkaada ; but not liking the savour of his
breath, he rubbed his teeth with a dentifrice, upon which the angels told
him that his breath before had the odour of musk (Sale, Prel. Disc. Sect.
IV.), but that his rubbing his teeth had taken it away. Whereupon GOD
ordered him to fast ten days more, which he did ; and these were the first
ten days of the succeeding month Dhu'lhajja. Others, however, suppose
that Moses was commanded to fast and pray thirty days only, and that
during the other ten GOD discoursed with him. (Al Beidâwi, Jallalo'ddin.)

[4] Without the mediation of any other, and face to face, as he speaks unto
the angels. (Al Beidâwi. D'Herbel. Bibl. Orient. p. 650.)

[5] This mountain the Mohammedans name Al Zabir.

[6] Or, as it is literally, *unto the mount.* For some of the expositors pretend
that GOD endued the mountain with life and the sense of seeing.

the first of true believers.[1] *God* said *unto him*, O Moses, I
have chosen thee above *all men*, *by honouring thee* with my
commissions, and by my speaking *unto thee* : receive therefore that which I have brought thee, and be *one* of those who
give thanks.[2] And we wrote for him on the tables [3] an
admonition concerning every matter, and a decision in every
case,[4] *and said*, Receive this with reverence ; and command
thy people that they live according to the most excellent
precepts thereof. I will show you the dwelling of the wicked.[5]
I will turn aside from my signs those who behave themselves
proudly in the earth, without justice : and although they
see every sign, yet they shall not believe therein ; and
although they see the way of righteousness, yet they shall not
take that way ; but if they see the way of error, they shall
take that way. This *shall come to pass* because they accuse
our signs of imposture, and neglect the same. But as for
them who deny the truth of our signs and the meeting of the
life to come, their works shall be vain, shall they be rewarded
otherwise than *according to* what they shall have wrought ?
And the people of Moses, after his *departure*, took a corporeal
calf,[6] *made* of their ornaments,[7] which lowed.[8] Did they
not see that it spake not unto them, neither directed them
in the way ? *yet* they took it *for their god*, and acted wickedly.
But when they repented with sorrow,[9] and saw that they

---

[1] This is not to be taken strictly. See the like expression in Chap. VI.

[2] The Mohammedans have a tradition that Moses asked to see GOD on
the day of Arafat, and that he received the law on the day they slay the
victims at the pilgrimage of Mecca, which days are the ninth and tenth
of Dhu'lhajja.

[3] These tables, according to some, were seven in number, and according
to others ten. Nor are the commentators agreed whether they were cut
out of a kind of lote-tree in paradise called the Sedra, or whether they were
chrysolites, emeralds, rubies, or common stone. (Al Beidâwi.) But they
say that they were each ten or twelve cubits long ; for they suppose that
not only the ten commandments but the whole law was written thereon :
and some add that the letters were cut quite through the tables, so that
they might be read on both sides (D'Herbel. ubi sup.)—which is a fable
of the Jews.

[4] That is, a perfect law, comprehending all necessary instructions, as
well in regard to religious and moral duties, as the administration of justice.

[5] viz., The desolate habitations of the Egyptians, or those of the impious
tribes of Ad and Thamûd, or perhaps hell, the dwelling of the ungodly in
the other world.

[6] That is, as some understand it, consisting of flesh and blood ; or, as
others, being a mere body or mass of metal, without a soul. (Al Beidâwi.
See Chap. XX. and the notes to Chap. II.)

[7] Such as their rings and bracelets of gold and silver. (Chaps. II. and XX.)

[8] See Chap. XX., and the notes to Chap. II.

[9] Father Marracci seems not to have understood the meaning of this
phrase, having literally translated the Arabic words, *wa lamma sokita fi
eidihim*, without any manner of sense, *Et cum cadere factus fuisset in manibus
eorum.*

had gone astray, they said, Verily if our LORD have not mercy upon us, and forgive us not, we shall certainly become *of the number* of those who perish. And when Moses returned unto his people, full of wrath and indignation, he said, An evil thing is it that ye have committed after my *departure* ; have ye hastened the command of your LORD ? [1] And he threw down the tables,[2] and took his brother by the *hair of the* head, and dragged him unto him. *And Aaron* said unto him, Son of my mother, Verily the people prevailed against me,[3] and it wanted little but they had slain me : make not *my* enemies therefore to rejoice over me, neither place me with the wicked people. *Moses* said, O LORD, forgive me and my brother, and receive us into thy mercy ; for thou art the most merciful of those who exercise mercy. Verily as for them who took the calf *for their god*, indignation shall overtake them from their LORD,[4] and ignominy in this life : thus will we reward those who imagine falsehood. But unto them who do evil, and afterwards repent and believe *in God*, verily thy LORD *will* thereafter *be* clement *and* merciful. And when the anger of Moses was appeased, he took the tables ; [5] and in what was written thereon was a direction and mercy unto those who feared their LORD. And Moses chose out of his people seventy men, *to go up with him to the mountain* at the time appointed by us : and when a storm of thunder and lightning had taken them away,[6] he said, O LORD, if thou hadst pleased, thou hadst destroyed them before, and me *also* ; wilt thou destroy us for that which the foolish *men* among us have committed ? This is only thy trial ; thou wilt thereby lead into error whom thou pleasest, and thou wilt direct whom thou pleasest. Thou art our protector, therefore forgive us, and be merciful unto us ; for thou art the best of those who forgive. And write down for us good in this world, and in the life to come ; for unto thee are we directed. *God* answered, I will inflict my punishment on whom I please ; and my mercy extendeth over all things ; and I will write down *good* unto those who shall fear *me*. and give alms, and who shall believe in our

---

[1] By neglecting his precepts, and bringing down his swift vengeance on you.

[2] Which were all broken and taken up to heaven, except one only ; and this, they say, contained the threats and judicial ordinances, and was afterwards put into the ark. (Al Beidâwi. D'Herbel. ubi sup. p. 649.)

[3] Literally, *rendered me weak*.

[4] See Chap. II.

[5] Or the fragments of that which was left.

[6] See Chap. II. and Chap. IV.

signs ; who shall follow the apostle, the illiterate prophet,[1] whom they shall find written down [2] with them in the law and the gospel : he will command them that which is just, and will forbid them that which is evil ; and will allow unto them as lawful the good things *which were before forbidden,*[3] and will prohibit those which are bad ; [4] and he will ease them of their heavy burden, and of the yokes which were upon them.[5]   And those who believe on him, and honour him, and assist him, and follow the light which hath been sent down with him, *shall be* happy.   Say, O men, Verily I am the messenger of GOD unto you all : [6] unto him *belongeth* the kingdom of heaven and earth ; there is no GOD but he ; he giveth life, and he causeth to die.   Believe therefore in GOD and his apostle, the illiterate prophet, who believeth in GOD and his word ; and follow him, that ye may be *rightly* directed.   Of the people of Moses *there is* a party [7] who direct *others* with truth, and act justly according to the same. And we divided them into twelve tribes, *as into so many* nations.   And we spake by revelation unto Moses, when his people asked drink of him, *and we said*, Strike the rock with thy rod ; and there gushed thereout twelve fountains,[8] and men knew their *respective* drinking-places.   And we caused clouds to overshadow them, and manna and quails [9] to descend upon them, *saying*, Eat of the good things which we have given you for food : and they injured not us, but they injured their own souls.   And *call to mind* when it was said unto them, Dwell in this city,[10] and eat *of the provisions* thereof wherever ye will, and say, Forgiveness!

---

[1] That is, Mohammed. See, Sale, Prel. Disc. Sect. II. p. 45.

[2] *i.e.,* Both foretold by name and certain description.

[3] See Chap. III.

[4] As the eating of blood and swine's flesh, and the taking of usury, &c.

[5] See Chap. II.

[6] That is, to all mankind in general, and not to one particular nation, as the former prophets were sent.

[7] viz., Those Jews who seemed better disposed than the rest of their brethren to receive Mohammed's law ; or perhaps such of them as had actually received it. Some imagine they were a Jewish nation dwelling somewhere beyond China, which Mohammed saw the night he made his journey to heaven, and who believed on him. (Al Beidâwi.)

[8] See Chap. II. To what is said in the notes there, we may add that, according to a certain tradition, the stone on which this miracle was wrought was thrown down from paradise by Adam, and came into the possession of Shoaib, who gave it with the rod to Moses ; and that, according to another, the water issued thence by three orifices on each of the four sides of the stone, making twelve in all, and that it ran in so many rivulets to the quarter of each tribe in the camp. (Al Beidâwi.)

[9] See Chap. II. p. 9.

[10] See this passage explained, ibid.

and enter the gate worshipping : we will pardon you your sins, *and* will give increase unto the well-doers. But they who were ungodly among them changed the expression into another,[1] which had not been spoken unto them. Wherefore we sent down upon them indignation from heaven, because they had transgressed. And ask them concerning the city,[2] which was situate on the sea, when they transgressed on the sabbath day : when their fish came unto them on their sabbath day, *appearing* openly *on the water* ; but on the day whereon they celebrated no sabbath, they came not unto them. Thus did we prove them, because they were wicked doers. And when a party of them [3] said *unto the others*, Why do ye warn a people whom GOD will destroy, or will punish with a grievous punishment ? They answered, *This is* an excuse *for us* unto your LORD ; [4] and peradventure they will beware. But when they had forgotten the admonitions which had been given them, we delivered those who forbade *them* to do evil ; and we inflicted on those who had transgressed, a severe punishment, because they had acted wickedly. And when they proudly refused *to desist* from what had been forbidden them, we said unto them, Be ye *transformed into* apes, driven away *from the society* of men. And *remember* when thy LORD declared that he would surely send against *the Jews*, until the day of resurrection, *some nation* who should afflict them with a grievous oppression : [5] for thy LORD is swift in punishing, and he *is* also ready to forgive *and* merciful : and we dispersed them among the nations in the earth. *Some* of them are upright persons, and *some* of them are otherwise. And we proved them with prosperity and with adversity, that they might return *from their disobedience* ; and a succession *of*

[1] Professor Sike says, that being prone to leave spiritual for worldly matters, instead of Hittaton they said Hintaton, which signifies wheat (Sike, in not. ad Evang. Infant. p. 71), and comes much nearer the true word than the expression I have in the last place quoted, set down from Jallalo'ddin. Whether he took this from the same commentator or not does not certainly appear, though he mentions him just before ; but if he did, his copy must differ from that which I have followed.

[2] This city was Ailah or Elath, on the Red Sea ; though some pretend it was Midian, and others Tiberias. The whole story is already given in the notes to Chap. II. Some suppose the following five or eight verses to have been ·evealed at Medina.

[3] viz., The religious persons among them, who strictly observed the Sabbath, and endeavoured to reclaim the others, till they despaired of success. But some think these words were spoken by the offenders in answer to the admonitions of the others.

[4] That we have done our duty in dissuading them from their wickedness.

[5] See Chap. V.

their posterity hath succeeded after them, who have inherited the book *of the law*, who receive the temporal *goods* of this world,[1] and say, It will surely be forgiven us : and if a temporal *advantage* like the former be offered them, they accept it *also*. Is not the covenant of the book *of the law* established with them, that they should not speak of GOD *aught* but the truth ? [2] Yet they diligently read that which is therein. But the enjoyment of the next life *will be* better for those who fear *God than the wicked gains of these people* (Do ye not therefore understand ?) and for those who hold fast the book *of the law*, and are constant at prayer : for we will by no means suffer the reward of the righteous to perish. And when we shook the mountain *of Sinai* over them,[3] as though it had been a covering, and they imagined that it was falling upon them ; *and we said*, Rece... the *law* which we have brought you, with reverence ; and remember that which is *contained* therein, that ye may take heed. And when thy LORD drew forth their posterity from the loins of the sons of Adam,[4] and took them to witness against themselves, *saying*, Am not I your LORD ? They answered, Yea : we do bear witness. *This was done* lest ye should say, at the day of resurrection, Verily we were negligent as to this *matter, because we were not apprised thereof*: or lest ye should say, Verily our fathers were formerly guilty of idolatry, and we are *their* posterity who have succeeded them ; wilt thou therefore destroy us for that which vain men have committed ? Thus do we explain *our* signs, that they may return *from their vanities*. And relate unto *the Jews* the history of him unto whom we brought our signs,[5] and he

[1] By accepting of bribes for wresting judgment, and for corrupting the copies of the Pentateuch, and by extorting of usury, &c. (Al Beidâwi.)

[2] Particularly by giving out that GOD will forgive their corruption without sincere repentance and amendment.

[3] See Chap. II.

[4] This was done in the plain of Dahia in India, or, as others imagine, in a valley near Mecca. The commentators tell us that GOD stroked Adam's back, and extracted from his loins his whole posterity, which should come into the world until the resurrection, one generation after another ; that these men were actually assembled all together in the shape of small ants, which were endued with understanding ; and that after they had, in the presence of the angels, confessed their dependence on GOD, they were again caused to return into the loins of their great ancestor. (Al Beidâwi, Jallalo'ddin, Yahya. D'Herbelot, Bibl. Orient. p. 54.) From this fiction it appears that the doctrine of pre-existence is not unknown to the Mohammedans ; and there is some little conformity between it and the modern theory of generation *ex animalculis in semine marium*.

[5] Some suppose the person here intended to be a Jewish rabbi, or one Ommeya Ebn Abi'lsalt, who read the Scriptures, and found thereby that GOD would send a prophet about that time, and was in hopes that he might be the man ; but when Mohammed declared his mission, believed not on

departed from them ; wherefore Satan followed him, and
he became *one* of those who were seduced.   And if we had
pleased, we had surely raised him thereby *unto wisdom* ; but
he inclined unto the earth, and followed his own desire.[1]
Wherefore his likeness is as the likeness of a dog, which if
thou drive him away, putteth forth his tongue, or, if thou
let him alone, putteth forth his tongue *also*.   This is the
likeness of the people who accuse our signs of falsehood.
Rehearse therefore *this* history *unto them*, that they may
consider.   Evil is the similitude of those people who accuse
our signs of falsehood and injure their own souls.   Whomsoever GOD shall direct, he *will be rightly* directed ; and
whomsoever he shall lead astray, they shall perish.   Moreover we have created for hell many of the genii and of men ;
they have hearts by which they understand not, and they
have eyes by which they see not, and they have ears by
which they hear not.   These are like the brute beasts ;
yea, they go more astray : these are the negligent.   GOD
hath most excellent names : [2] therefore call on him by the
same ; and withdraw from those who use his names perversely : [3] they shall be rewarded for that which they shall
have wrought.   And of those whom we have created there
are a people who direct *others* with truth, and act justly
according thereto.[4]   But those who devise lies against our
signs, we will suffer them to fall gradually into ruin, by a
method which they know not : [5] and I will grant them to

him through envy.   But according to the more general opinion, it was Balaam,
the son of Beor, of the Canaanitish race, well acquainted with part at least
of the Scripture, having even been favoured with some revelations from GOD;
who being requested by his nation to curse Moses and the children of Israel,
refused it at first, saying, *How can I curse those who are protected by the angels ?*
But afterwards he was prevailed on by gifts ; and he had no sooner done it,
than he began to put out his tongue like a dog, and it hung down upon his
breast.   (Al Beidâwi, Jallalo'ddin, Al Zamakhshari.   D'Herbel. Bibl. Orient.
Art. Balaam.)

[1] Loving the wages of unrighteousness, and running greedily after error
for reward.   (2 Peter ii. v. ; Jude 11.)

[2] Expressing his glorious attributes.   Of these the Mohammedan Arabs
have no less than ninety-nine, which are reckoned up by Marracci.   (In Alc.
p. 414.)

[3] As did Walîd Ebn al Mogheira, who hearing Mohammed give GOD
the title of Al Rahmân, or *the merciful*, laughed aloud, saying he knew none
of that name, except a certain man who dwelt in Yamama (Marrac. Vit. Moh.
p. 19) ; or as the idolatrous Meccans did, who deduced the names of their
idols from those of the true GOD ; deriving, for example, Allât from Allah,
Al Uzza from Al Azîz, *the mighty*, and Manât from Al Mannân, *the bountiful.*
(Al Beidâwi, Jallalo'ddin.   Sale, Prel. Disc. Sect. I.)

[4] As it is said a little above that GOD hath created many to eternal misery,
so here he is said to have created others to eternal happiness.   (Al Beidâwi.)

[5] By flattering them with prosperity in this life, and permitting them to

enjoy a long and prosperous life; for my stratagem is
effectual. Do they not consider that there is no devil in
their companion?[1] He is no other than a public preacher.
Or do they not contemplate the kingdom of heaven and
earth, and the things which GOD hath created; and *consider*
that peradventure it may be that their end draweth nigh?
And in what new declaration will they believe, after this?[2]
He whom GOD shall cause to err, shall have no director;
and he shall leave them in their impiety, wandering in
confusion. They will ask thee concerning the *last* hour;
at what time its coming is fixed? Answer, Verily the
knowledge thereof is with my LORD, none shall declare the
fixed time thereof, except he. *The expectation thereof* is
grievous in heaven and on earth:[3] it shall come upon you no
otherwise than suddenly. They will ask thee, as though
thou wast well acquainted therewith. Answer, Verily the
knowledge thereof is with GOD alone: but the greater part
of men know it not. Say, I am able neither to procure
advantage unto myself, nor to avert mischief *from me*, but as
GOD pleaseth. If I knew the secrets *of* GOD, I should surely
enjoy abundance of good, neither should evil befall me.
Verily, I am no other than a denouncer of threats, and a
messenger of good tidings unto people who believe. It is he
who hath created you from one person, and out of him produced his wife, that he might dwell with her; and when he
had known her, she carried a light burden *for a time*, wherefore she walked *easily* therewith. But when it became more
heavy,[4] they called upon GOD, their LORD, *saying*, If thou
give us *a child* rightly shaped, we will surely be thankful.
Yet when he had given them *a child* rightly shaped, they attributed companions unto him, for that which he had given
them.[5] But far be that from GOD, which they associated

sin in an uninterrupted security, till they find themselves unexpectedly
ruined. (Al Beidâwi.)
    [1] viz., In Mohammed, whom they gave out to be possessed when he went
up to Mount Safâ, and from thence called to the several families of each
respective tribe in order, to warn them of GOD's vengeance if they continued
in their idolatry. (Al Beidâwi.)
    [2] *i.e.*, After they have rejected the Korân. For what more evident revela-
tion can they hereafter expect? (Al Beidâwi.)
    [3] Not only to men and genii, but to the angels also.
    [4] That is, when the child grew bigger in her womb.
    [5] For the explaining of this whole passage, the commentators tell the
following story:—
    They say, that when Eve was big with her first child, the devil came to
her and asked her whether she knew what she carried within her, and which
way she should be delivered of it, suggesting that possibly it might be a
beast. She, being unable to give an answer to this question, went in a fright

with him ! Will they associate *with him false gods* which create nothing, but are themselves created ; and can neither give them assistance nor help themselves ? And if ye invite them to the *true* direction, they will not follow you : it will be equal unto you, whether ye invite them, or whether ye hold your peace. Verily the *false deities* whom ye invoke besides GOD, are servants like unto you.[1] Call therefore upon them, and let them give you an answer if ye speak truth. Have they feet, to walk with ? Or have they hands, to lay hold with ? Or have they eyes, to see with ? Or have they ears, to hear with ? Say, Call upon your companions, and then lay a snare for me, and defer *it* not ; for GOD *is* my protector, who sent down the book *of the Korân* ; and he protecteth the righteous. But they whom ye invoke besides him, cannot assist you, neither do they help themselves ; and if ye call on them to direct you, they will not hear. Thou seest them look towards thee, but they see not. Use indulgence,[2] and command that which is just, and withdraw far from the ignorant. And if an evil suggestion from Satan be suggested unto thee, *to divert thee from thy duty*, have recourse unto GOD ; for he heareth *and* knoweth. Verily they who fear GOD, when a temptation from Satan assaileth them, remember *the divine commands*, and behold, they clearly see *the danger of sin and the wiles of the devil.* But as for the

to Adam, and acquainted him with the matter, who, not knowing what to think of it, grew sad and pensive. Whereupon the devil appeared to her again (or, as others say, to Adam), and pretended that he by his prayers would obtain of GOD that she might be safely delivered of a son in Adam's likeness, provided they would promise to name him Abda'lhareth, or the *servant of Al Hareth* (which was the devil's name among the angels), instead of Abd'allah, or *the servant of* GOD, as Adam had designed. This proposal was agreed to, and accordingly, when the child was born, they gave it that name, upon which it immediately died. (Al Beidâwi, Yahya, D'Herbelot, Bibl. Orient. p. 438, et Selden. de Jure Nat. Sec. Hebr. l. 5, c. 8.) And with this Adam and Eve are here taxed, as an act of idolatry. The story looks like a rabbinical fiction, and seems to have no other foundation than Cain's being called by Moses Obed Adâmah, that is, *a tiller of the ground*, which might be translated into Arabic by Abd'alhareth.

Al Beidâwi, thinking it unlikely that a prophet (as Adam is, by the Mohammedans, supposed to have been) should be guilty of such an action, imagines the Korân in this place means Kosai, one of Mohammed's ancestors, and his wife, who begged issue of GOD, and, having four sons granted them, called them Abd Menâf, Abd Shams, Abd'al Uzza, and Abd'al Dâr, after the names of four principal idols of the Koreish. And the following words also he supposes to relate to their idolatrous posterity.

[1] Being subject to the absolute command of GOD. For the chief idols of the Arabs were the sun, moon, and stars. (Sale, Prel. Disc. Sect. I.)

[2] Or, as the words may also be translated, *Take the superabundant overplus*—meaning that Mohammed should accept such voluntary alms from the people as they could spare. But the passage, if taken in this sense, was abrogated by the precept of legal alms, which was given at Medina.

brethren *of the devils*, they shall continue them in error ; and afterwards they shall not preserve themselves *therefrom*. And when thou bringest not a verse *of the Korân* unto them, they say, Hast thou not put it together ?[1]   Answer, I follow that only which is revealed unto me from my LORD.   This *book containeth* evident proofs from your LORD, and *is* a direction and mercy unto people who believe.   And when the Korân is read, attend thereto, and keep silence ; that ye may obtain mercy.   And meditate on thy LORD in thine own mind, with humility and fear, and without loud speaking, evening and morning ;   and be not *one* of the negligent. Moreover *the angels* who are with my LORD, do not proudly disdain his service, but they celebrate his praise and worship him.

VIII

THE CHAPTER OF THE SPOILS [2]

Revealed at Medina.[3]

IN THE NAME OF THE MOST MERCIFUL GOD.

THEY will ask thee concerning the spoils : Answer, The *division of the* spoils *belongeth* unto God and the apostle.[4] Therefore fear GOD, and compose the matter amicably among you ; and obey GOD and his apostle, if ye are true believers.   Verily the true believers *are those* whose hearts fear when GOD is mentioned, and whose faith increaseth when his signs are rehearsed unto them, and *who* trust in their LORD ; who observe the stated times of prayer, and give alms out of that which we have bestowed on them.   These are really believers : they shall have *superior* degrees of

---

[1] *i.e.*, Hast thou not yet contrived what to say ; or canst thou obtain no revelation from GOD ?

[2] This chapter was occasioned by the disputes which happened about the division of the spoils taken at the battle of Bedr (see Chap. III.), between the young men who had fought, and the old men who had stayed under the ensigns ; the former insisting they ought to have the whole, and the latter that they deserved a share (Al Beidâwi, Jallalo'ddin). To end the contention, Mohammed pretended to have received orders from heaven to divide the booty among them equally, having first taken thereout a fifth part for the purposes which will be mentioned hereafter.

[3] Except seven verses, beginning at these words, *And call to mind when the unbelievers plotted against the*, &c. Which some think were revealed at Mecca.

[4] It is related that Saad Ebn Abi Wakkâs, one of the companions, whose brother Omair was slain in this battle, having killed Saîd Ebn al As, took

felicity with their LORD, and forgiveness, and an honourable provision. As thy LORD brought thee forth from thy house[1] with truth ; and part of the believers were averse *to thy directions* :[2] they disputed with thee concerning the truth, after it had been made known unto them ;[3] no otherwise than as if they had been led forth to death, and had seen *it with their eyes.*[4] And *call to mind* when GOD promised you one

his sword, and carrying it to Mohammed, desired that he might be permitted to keep it ; but the prophet told him that it was not his to give away, and ordered him to lay it with the other spoils. At this repulse, and the loss of his brother, Saad was greatly disturbed ; but in a very little while this chapter was revealed, and thereupon Mohammed gave him the sword, saying, You asked the sword of me when I had no power to dispose of it, but now I have received authority from GOD to distribute the spoils, you may take it. (Al Beidâwi.)

[1] *i.e.*, From Medina. The particle *as* having nothing in the following words to answer it, Al Beidâwi supposes the connection to be that the division of the spoils belonged to the prophet, notwithstanding his followers were averse to it, as they had been averse to the expedition itself.

[2] For the better understanding of this passage, it will be necessary to mention some further particulars relating to the expedition of Bedr. Mohammed having received private information (for which he pretended he was obliged to the angel Gabriel) of the approach of a caravan belonging to the Koreish, which was on its return from Syria with a large quantity of valuable merchandise, and was guarded by no more than thirty, or, as others say, forty men, set out with a party to intercept it. Abu Sofiân, who commanded the little convoy, having notice of Mohammed's motions, sent to Mecca for succours ; upon which Abu Jahl, and all the principal men of the city, except only Abu Laheb, marched to his assistance, with a body of nine hundred and fifty men. Mohammed had no sooner received advice of this, than Gabriel descended with a promise that he should either take the caravan or beat the succours ; whereupon he consulted with his companions which of the two he should attack. Some of them were for setting upon the caravan, saying that they were not prepared to fight such a body of troops as were coming with Abu Jahl : but this proposal Mohammed rejected, telling them that the caravan was at a considerable distance by the seaside, whereas Abu Jahl was just upon them. The others, however, insisted so obstinately on pursuing the first design of falling on the caravan, that the prophet grew angry, but by the interposition of Abu Becr, Omar, Saad Ebn Obadah, and Mokdâd Ebn Amru, they at length acquiesced in his opinion. Mokdâd in particular assured him they were all ready to obey his orders, and would not say to him, as the children of Israel did to Moses, *Go thou and thy LORD to fight, for we will sit here* (Kor. Chap. V.) ; but, *Go thou and thy LORD to fight, and we will fight with you.* At this Mohammed smiled, and again sat down to consult with them, applying himself chiefly to the Ansârs or *helpers*, because they were the greater part of his forces, and he had some apprehension lest they should not think themselves obliged by the oath they had taken to him at the Akaba (Sale, Prel. Disc. Sect. I.) to assist him against any other than such as should attack him in Medina. But Saad Ebn Moâdh, in the name of the rest, told him that they had received him as the apostle of GOD, and had promised him obedience, and were therefore all to a man ready to follow him where he pleased, though it were into the sea. Upon which the prophet ordered them in GOD's name to attack the succours, assuring them of the victory. (Al Beidâwi.)

[3] That is, concerning their success against Abu Jahl and the Koreish ; notwithstanding they had GOD's promise to encourage them.

[4] The reason of this great backwardness was the smallness of their number, in comparison to the enemy, and their being unprepared ; for they were

of the two parties, that it should be *delivered* unto you ;[1] and ye desired that the *party* which was not furnished with arms[2] should be *delivered* unto you ; but GOD purposed to make known the truth in his words, and to cut off the uttermost part of the unbelievers ; [3] that he might verify the truth, and destroy falsehood, although the wicked were averse *thereto*. When ye asked assistance of your LORD,[4] and he answered you, Verily I will assist you with a thousand[5] angels, following one another *in order*. And this GOD designed only as good tidings[6] for you, and that your hearts might thereby rest secure : for victory *is* from GOD alone ; and GOD is mighty *and* wise. When a sleep fell on you as a security from him, and he sent down upon you water from heaven, that he might thereby purify you, and take from you the abomination of Satan,[7] and that he might confirm your hearts, and establish *your* feet thereby. *Also* when thy LORD spake unto the angels, *saying*, Verily I am with you ; wherefore confirm those who believe. I will cast a dread into the hearts of the unbelievers. Therefore strike off *their* heads,

all foot. having but two horses among them, whereas the Koreish had no less than a hundred horse. (Al Beidâwi, Abulfed. Vit. Moh. p. 56.)

[1] That is, either the caravan or the succours from Mecca. Father Marracci mistaking *al ir* and *al nafir*, which are appellatives and signify *the caravan* and *the troop* or body of succours, for proper names, has thence coined two families of the Koreish never heard of before, which he calls Airenses and Naphirenses. (Marracc. in Alc. p. 297.)

[2] viz., The caravan, which was guarded by no more than forty horse ; whereas the other party was strong and well appointed.

[3] As if he had said, Your view was only to gain the spoils of the caravan. and to avoid danger ; but God designed to exalt his true religion by extirpating its adversaries. (Al Beidâwi.)

[4] When Mohammed's men saw they could not avoid fighting, they recommended themselves to GOD's protection ; and their prophet prayed with great earnestness, crying out, O GOD, *fulfil that which thou hast promised me : O GOD, if this party be cut off, thou wilt no more be worshipped on earth.* And he continued to repeat these words till his cloak fell from off his back. (Al Beidâwi. Abulfed. Vit. Moh. p. 58.)

[5] Which were afterwards reinforced with three thousand more (see Chap. III.). Wherefore some copies instead of a *thousand*, read *thousands* in the plural.

[6] See Chap. III.

[7] It is related, that the spot where Mohammed's little army lay was a dry and deep sand, into which their feet sank as they walked, the enemy having the command of the water ; and that having fallen asleep, the greater part of them were disturbed with dreams, wherein the devil suggested to them that they could never expect GOD's assistance in the battle, since they were cut off from the water, and besides suffering the inconvenience of thirst, must be obliged to pray without washing, though they imagined themselves to be the favourites of God, and that they had his apostle among them. But in the night rain fell so plentifully that it formed a little brook, and not only supplied them with water for all their uses, but made the sand between them and the infidel army firm enough to bear them ; whereupon the diabolical suggestions ceased. (Al Beidâwi.)

and strike off all the ends of their *fingers*.[1] This *shall they suffer*, because they have resisted GOD and his apostle : and whosoever shall oppose GOD and his apostle, verily GOD *will be severe* in punishing *him*. This *shall be your punishment ;* taste it therefore : and the infidels shall *also* suffer the torment of *hell* fire. O true believers, when ye meet the unbelievers marching *in great numbers against you*, turn not *your* backs unto them : for whoso shall turn his back unto them on that day, unless he turneth aside to fight, or retreateth to *another* party *of the faithful*,[2] shall draw on himself the indignation of GOD, and his abode shall be hell ; an ill journey *shall it be thither* ! And ye slew not those *who were slain at Bedr yourselves*, but GOD slew them.[3] Neither didst thou, O *Mohammed*, cast *the gravel into their eyes*, when thou didst *seem to cast it* ; but GOD cast *it*,[4] that he might prove the true believers by a gracious trial from himself ; for GOD heareth *and* knoweth. This *was done* that GOD might also weaken the crafty devices of the unbelievers. If ye desire a decision *of the matter between us*, now hath a decision come unto you :[5] and if ye desist *from opposing the apostle*, it *will be* better for you. But if ye return *to attack him*, we will also return *to his assistance* ; and your forces shall not be of advantage unto you at all, although they be numerous ; for GOD is with the faithful. O true believers, obey GOD and his apostle, and turn not back from him, since ye hear *the admonitions of the Korân*. And be not as those who say, We hear, when they do not hear. Verily the worst *sort of* beasts in the sight of GOD, are the deaf *and* the dumb, who understand not. If GOD had known any good in them, he would certainly have caused them to hear :[6] and if he had caused them to hear, they would surely have

[1] This is the punishment expressly assigned the enemies of the Mohammedan religion ; though the Moslems did not inflict it on the prisoners they took at Bedr, for which they are reprehended in this chapter.

[2] That is, if it be not downright running away, but done either with design to rally and attack the enemy again, or by way of feint or stratagem, or to succour a party which is hard pressed, &c.   (Al Beidâwi.)

[3] See Chap. III.

[4] See ibid.

[5] These words are directed to the people of Mecca, whom Mohammed derides, because the Koreish, when they were ready to set out from Mecca, took hold of the curtains of the Caaba, saying, *O* GOD, *grant the victory to the superior army, the party that is most rightly directed, and the most honourable*. (Al Beidâwi.)

[6] That is, to hearken to the remonstrances of the Korân. Some say that the infidels demanded of Mohammed that he should raise Kosai, one of his ancestors, to life, to bear witness to the truth of his mission, saying he was a man of honour and veracity, and they would believe his testimony : but they are here told that it would have been in vain. (Al Beidâwi. See Chap. VI.)

turned back, and have retired afar off. O true believers, answer GOD and *his* apostle, when he inviteth you unto that which giveth you life ; and know that GOD goeth between a man and his heart,[1] and that before him ye shall be assembled. Beware of sedition ;[2] it will not affect those who are ungodly among you particularly, *but all of you in general* ; and know that GOD is severe in punishing. And remember when ye were few, *and* reputed weak in the land ;[3] ye feared lest men should snatch you away ; but *God* provided you a place of refuge, and he strengthened you with his assistance, and bestowed on you good things, that ye might give thanks. O true believers, deceive not GOD and *his* apostle ;[4] neither violate your faith, against your own knowledge. And know that your wealth, and your children *are* a temptation *unto you* ;[5] and that with GOD is a great reward. O true believers, if ye fear GOD, he will grant you a distinction,[6] and will expiate your sins from you, and will forgive you ; for GOD is endued with great liberality. And *call to mind* when the unbelievers plotted against thee, that they might either detain thee *in bonds*, or put thee to death, or expel thee *the city* ;[7] and they plotted *against thee* : but GOD laid a plot

---

[1] Not only knowing the innermost secrets of his heart, but overruling a man's designs, and disposing him either to belief or infidelity.

[2] The original word signifies any epidemical crime, which involves a number of people in its guilt ; and the commentators are divided as to its particular meaning in this place.

[3] viz., At Mecca. The persons here spoken to are the Mohâjerin, or refugees who fled from thence to Medina.

[4] Al Beidâwi mentions an instance of such treacherous dealing in Abu Lobâba, who was sent by Mohammed to the tribe of Koreidha, then besieged by that prophet for having broken their league with him and perfidiously gone over to the enemies at the war of the ditch (Prid. Life of Mah. p. 85. Abulf. Vit. Moh. p. 76, and the notes to Kor. Chap. XXXIII.), to persuade them to surrender at the discretion of Saad Ebn Moadh, prince of the tribe of Aws, their confederates, which proposal they had refused. But Abu Lobâba's family and effects being in the hands of those of Koreidha, he acted directly contrary to his commission, and instead of persuading them to accept Saad as their judge, when they asked his advice about it, drew his hand across his throat, signifying that he would put them all to death. However, he had no sooner done this than he was sensible of his crime, and going into a mosque, tied himself to a pillar, and remained there seven days without meat or drink, till Mohammed forgave him.

[5] As they were to Abu Lobâba.

[6] *i.e.*, A direction that you may distinguish between truth and falsehood ; or success in battle to distinguish the believers from the infidels ; or the like.

[7] When the Meccans heard of the league entered into by Mohammed with those of Medina, being apprehensive of the consequences, they held a council, whereat they say the devil assisted in the likeness of an old man of Najd. The point under consideration being what they should do with Mohammed, Abu'lbakhtari was of opinion that he should be imprisoned, and the room walled up, except a little hole, through which he should have necessaries given him, till he died. This the devil opposed, saying that he might prob-

against them ;[1] and GOD is the best layer of plots. And when our signs are repeated unto them, they say, We have heard ; if we pleased we could certainly pronounce *a composition* like unto this : this is nothing but fables of the ancients.[2] And when they said, O GOD, if this be the truth from thee, rain down stones upon us from heaven, or inflict on us some *other* grievous punishment.[3] But GOD was not *disposed* to punish them, while thou wast with them ; nor was GOD *disposed* to punish them when they asked pardon.[4] But they have nothing to *offer in excuse* why GOD should not punish them, since they hindered *the believers* from *visiting* the holy temple,[5] although they are not the guardians thereof.[6] The guardians thereof are those only who fear *God* ; but the greater part of them know it not. And their prayer at the house *of God* is no other than whistling and clapping of the hands.[7] Taste therefore the punishment, for that ye have been unbelievers. They who believe not, expend their wealth to obstruct the way of GOD :[8] they shall expend it, but after-

ably be released by some of his own party. Heshâm Ebn Amru was for banishing him, but his advice also the devil rejected, insisting that Mohammed might engage some other tribes in his interest, and make war on them. At length Abu Jahl gave his opinion for putting him to death, and proposed the manner, which was unanimously approved. (Al Beidâwi. Sale, Prel. Disc. Sect. I.)

[1] Revealing their conspiracy to Mohammed, and miraculously assisting him to deceive them and make his escape (Sale, Prel. Disc. p. 54) ; and afterwards drawing them to the battle of Bedr.

[2] See Chap. VI.

[3] This was the speech of Al Nodar Ebn al Hareth. (Al Beidâwi.)

[4] Saying, GOD *forgive us !* Some of the commentators, however, suppose the persons who asked pardon were certain believers who stayed among the infidels ; and others think the meaning to be, that GOD would not punish them, *provided they asked pardon.*

[5] Obliging them to fly from Mecca, and not permitting them so much as to approach the temple, in the expedition of Al Hodeibiya. (Sale, Prel. Disc. p. 41.)

[6] Because of their idolatry and indecent deportment there. For otherwise the Koreish had a right to the guardianship of the Caaba, and it was continued in their tribe and in the same family even after the taking of Mecca. (See Chap. IV.)

[7] It is said that they used to go round the Caaba naked (see Chap. VII.), both men and women, whistling at the same time through their fingers, and clapping their hands. Or, as others say, they made this noise on purpose to disturb Mohammed when at his prayers, pretending to be at prayers also themselves. (Al Beidâwi.)

[8] The persons particularly meant in this passage were twelve of the Koreish, who gave each of them ten camels every day to be killed for provisions for their army in the expedition of Bedr ; or according to others, the owners of the effects brought by the caravan, who gave great part of them to the support of the succours from Mecca. It is also said that Abu Sofiân, in the expedition of Ohod, hired two thousand Arabs, who cost him a considerable sum, besides the auxiliaries which he had obtained *gratis.* (Al Beidâwi.)

wards it shall become *matter of* sighing *and regret* unto them, and at length they shall be overcome ; and the unbelievers shall be gathered together into hell ; that GOD may distinguish the wicked from the good, and may throw the wicked one upon the other, and may gather them all in a heap, and cast them into hell. These are they who shall perish. Say unto the· unbelievers, that if they desist *from opposing thee,* what is already past shall be forgiven them ; but if they return *to attack thee,* the exemplary punishment of the former *opposers of the prophets* is already past, *and the like shall be inflicted on them.* Therefore fight against them until there be no opposition *in favour of idolatry,* and the religion be wholly GOD'S. If they desist, verily GOD seeth that which they do : but if they turn back, know that GOD is your patron ; *he is* the best patron and the best helper. (X).[1] And know that whenever ye gain any *spoils* a fifth part thereof belongeth unto GOD, and to the apostle, and *his* kindred, and the orphans, and the poor, and the traveller ;[2] if ye believe in GOD, and that which we have sent down unto our servant on the day of distinction,[3] on the day whereon the two armies met ; and GOD is almighty. When ye were *encamped* on the hithermost side of the valley,[4] and they were *encamped* on the further side, and the caravan *was* below you ;[5] and if ye had mutually appointed *to come to a battle,* ye would certainly have declined the appointment ;[6] but *ye were brought to an engagement without any previous appointment,* that GOD might accomplish the thing which was *decreed to be* done,[7] that he who perisheth *hereafter* may perish after demonstrative evidence, and that he who liveth may live by *the same* evidence ; GOD *both* heareth *and* knoweth. When

[1] Section X. begins here.

[2] According to this law, a fifth part of the spoils is appropriated to the particular uses here mentioned, and the other four-fifths are to be equally divided among those who were present at the action : but in what manner or to whom the first fifth is to be distributed, the Mohammedan doctors differ, as we have elsewhere observed. (Sale, Prel. Disc. Sect. VI.) Though it be the general opinion that this verse was revealed at Bedr, yet there are some who suppose it was revealed in the expedition against the Jewish tribe of Kainokâ, which happened a little above a month after. (Al Beidâwi.)

[3] *i.e.,* Of the battle of Bedr ; which is so called because it *distinguished* the true believers from the infidels.

[4] Which was much more inconvenient than the other, because of the deep sand and want of water.

[5] By the seaside, making the best of their way to Mecca.

[6] Because of the great superiority of the enemy, and the disadvantages ye lay under.

[7] By granting a miraculous victory to the faithful, and overthrowing their enemies ; for the conviction of the latter, and the confirmation of the former.

thy LORD caused *the enemy* to appear unto thee in thy sleep, *few in number* ;[1] and if he had caused them to appear numerous unto thee, ye would have been disheartened and would have disputed concerning the matter ;[2] but GOD preserved *you from this* ; for he knoweth the innermost parts of the breasts *of men.* And when he caused them to appear unto you, when ye met, *to be* few in your eyes ;[3] and diminished your *numbers* in their eyes ; [4] that GOD might accomplish the thing which *was decreed to be* done : and unto GOD shall *all* things return. O true believers, when ye meet a party *of the infidels,* stand firm and remember GOD frequently, that ye may prosper : and obey GOD and his apostle, and be not refractory, lest ye be discouraged, and your success depart from you ; but persevere with patience, for GOD *is* with those who persevere. And be not as those who went out of their houses in an insolent manner, and to appear with ostentation unto men, [5] and turned aside from the way of GOD ; for GOD comprehendeth that which they do. And *remember* when Satan prepared their works for them,[6] and said, No man shall prevail against you to-day ; and I will surely be near *to assist* you. But when the two armies appeared in sight of each other, he turned back on his heels and said, Verily, I am clear of you : I certainly see that which ye see not ; I fear GOD, for GOD is severe in punishing.[7] When the hypocrites,

[1] With which vision Mohammed acquainted his companions for their encouragement.

[2] Whether ye should attack the enemy or fly.

[3] It is said that Ebn Masúd asked the man who was next him whether he did not see them to be about seventy, to which he replied that he took them to be a hundred. (Al Beidâwi.)

[4] This seeming contradictory to a passage in the third chapter (page 44), where it is said that the Moslems appeared to the infidels to be twice their own number, the commentators reconcile the matter by telling us that, just before the battle began, the prophet's party seemed fewer than they really were, to draw the enemy to an engagement; but that so soon as the armies were fully engaged, they appeared superior, to terrify and dismay their adversaries. It is related that Abu Jahl at first thought them so inconsiderable a handful, that he said one camel would be as much as they could all eat. (Al Beidâwi, Jallalo'ddin, Yahya.)

[5] These were the Meccans, who, marching to the assistance of the caravan, and being come as far as Johfa, were there met by a messenger from Abu Sofiân, to acquaint them that he thought himself out of danger, and there·fore they might return home ; upon which, Abu Jahl, to give the greater opinion of the courage of himself and his comrades, and of their readiness to assist their friends, swore that they would not return till they had been at Bedr, and had there drunk wine and entertained those who should be present, and diverted themselves with singing women. (Al Beidâwi.) The event of which bravado was very fatal, several of the principal Koreish, and Abu Jahl in particular, losing their lives in the expedition.

[6] By inciting them to oppose the prophet.

[7] Some understand this passage figuratively, of the private instigation

and those in whose hearts *there was* an infirmity, said, Their religion hath deceived these *men* :[1] but whosoever confideth in GOD *cannot be deceived* ; for GOD *is* mighty *and* wise. And if thou didst behold when the angels cause the unbelievers to die ; they strike their faces and their backs,[2] and *say unto them*, Taste ye the pain of burning : this *shall ye suffer* for that which your hands have sent before you ;[3] and because GOD is not unjust towards *his* servants. *These have acted* according to the wont of the people of Pharaoh, and of those before them, who disbelieved in the signs of GOD ; therefore GOD took them away in their iniquity ; for GOD *is* mighty *and* severe in punishing. This *hath come to pass* because GOD changeth not *his* grace, wherewith he hath favoured any people, until they change that which is in their souls ; and for that GOD *both* heareth *and* seeth. According to the wont of the people of Pharaoh, and of those before them, who charged the signs of their LORD with imposture, *have they acted* : wherefore we destroyed them in their sins, and we drowned the people of Pharaoh ; for they were all unjust persons. Verily the worst cattle in the sight of GOD are those who are *obstinate* infidels, and will not believe. As to those who enter into a league with thee, and afterwards violate their league at every *convenient* opportunity,[4] and fear not GOD ; if thou

of the devil, and of the defeating of his designs and the hopes with which he had inspired the idolaters. But others take the whole literally, and tell us that when the Koreish, on their march, bethought themselves of the enmity between them and the tribe of Kenâna, who were masters of the country about Bedr, that consideration would have prevailed on them to return, had not the devil appeared in the likeness of Sorâka Ebn Malec, a principal person of that tribe, and promised them that they should not be molested, and that himself would go with them. But when they came to join battle, and the devil saw the angels descending to the assistance of the Moslems, he retired ; and Al Hareth Ebn Heshâm, who had him then by the hand, asking him whither he was going, and if he intended to betray them at such a juncture, he answered, in the words of this passage : *I am clear of you, for I see that which ye see not* ; meaning the celestial succours. They say further, that when the Koreish, on their return, laid the blame of their overthrow on Sorâka, he swore that he did not so much as know of their march till he heard they were routed : and afterwards, when they embraced Mohammedism, they were satisfied it was the devil. (Al Beidâwi, Jallalo'ddin.)

[1] In tempting them to so great a piece of folly, as to attack so large a body of men with such a handful.

[2] This passage is generally understood of the angels who slew the infidels at Bedr, and who fought (as the commentators pretend) with iron maces, which shot forth flames of fire at every stroke. (Al Beidâwi, Jallalo'ddin.) Some, however, imagine that the words hint, at least, at the examination of the sepulchre, which the Mohammedans believe every man must undergo after death, and will be very terrible to the unbelievers. (Sale, Prel. Disc. Sect. IV. p. 82.)

[3] See Chap. II.

[4] As did the tribe of Koreidha.

take them in war, disperse, by *making* them *an example*, those *who shall come* after them, that they may be warned ; or if thou apprehend treachery from any people, throw back *their league* unto them, with like treatment ; for GOD loveth not the treacherous. And think not[1] that the unbelievers have escaped GOD's *vengeance*,[2] for they shall not weaken *the power of* GOD. Therefore prepare against them what force ye are able, and troops of horse, whereby ye may strike a terror into the enemy of GOD, and your enemy, and into other *infidels* besides them, whom ye know not, *but* GOD knoweth them. And whatsoever ye shall expend in the defence of the religion of GOD, it shall be repaid unto you, and ye shall not be treated unjustly. And if they incline unto peace, do thou *also* incline thereto ; and put thy confidence in GOD, for it is he who heareth *and* knoweth. But if they seek to deceive thee, verily GOD *will be* thy support. It is he who hath strengthened thee with his help, and with *that of* the faithful ; and hath united their hearts. If thou hadst expended whatever *riches are* in the earth, thou couldst not have united their hearts,[3] but GOD united them ; for he *is* mighty *and* wise. O prophet, GOD is thy support, and such of the true believers who followeth thee.[4] O prophet, stir up the faithful to war : if twenty of you persevere *with constancy*, they shall overcome two hundred, and if there be one hundred of you, they shall overcome a thousand of those who believe not ; because they are a people which do not understand. Now hath GOD eased you, for he knew that ye were weak. If there be a hundred of you who persevere *with constancy*, they shall overcome two hundred ; and if there be a thousand of you, they shall overcome two thousand,[5] by the permission of GOD ; for GOD is with those who persevere. It hath not been *granted* unto any prophet, that he should possess captives, until he had made a great slaughter *of the infidels* in the earth.[6] Ye seek the accidental *goods* of this world, but

[1] Some copies read it in the third person, *Let not the unbelievers think*, &c.
[2] viz., Those who made their escape from Bedr.
[3] Because of the inveterate enmity which reigned among many of the Arab tribes ; and therefore this reconciliation is reckoned by the commentators as no inconsiderable miracle, and a strong proof of their prophet's mission.
[4] This passage, as some say, was revealed in a plain called Al Beidâ, between Mecca and Medina, during the expedition of Bedr ; and, as others, in the sixth year of the prophet's mission, on the occasion of Omar's embracing Mohammedism.
[5] See Levit. xxvi. 8 ; Josh. xxiii. 10.
[6] Because severity ought to be used where circumstances require it, though clemency be more preferable where it may be exercised with safety.

GOD regardeth the life to come ; and GOD *is* mighty *and* wise. Unless a revelation had been previously delivered from GOD, verily a severe punishment had been inflicted on you, for *the ransom* which ye took *from the captives at Bedr.*[1] Eat therefore of what ye have acquired,[2] *that which is* lawful *and* good ; for GOD *is* gracious *and* merciful. O prophet, say unto the captives who are in your hands, If GOD shall know any good *to be* in your hearts, he will give you better than what hath been taken from you ;[3] and he will forgive you, for

While the Mohammedans, therefore were weak, and their religion in its infancy, GOD's pleasure was that the opposers of it should be cut off, as is particularly directed in this chapter. For which reason, they are here upbraided with their preferring the lucre of the ransom to their duty.

[1] That is, had not the ransom been, in strictness, lawful for you to accept by GOD's having in general terms allowed you the spoil and the captives, ye had been severely punished. Among the seventy prisoners which the Moslems took in this battle were Al Abbâs, one of Mohammed's uncles, ; nd Okail, the son of Abu Tâleb and brother of Ali. When they were brought before Mohammed, he asking the advice of his companions what should be done with them, Abu Becr was for releasing them on their paying ransom, saying that they were near relations to the prophet, and GOD might possibly forgive them on their repentance ; but Omar was for striking off their heads, as professed patrons of infidelity. Mohammed did not approve of the latter advice, but observed that Abu Becr resembled Abraham, who interceded for offenders and that Omar was like Noah, who prayed for the utter extirpation of the wicked antediluvians ; and thereupon it was agreed to accept a ransom from them, and their fellow captives. Soon after which, Omar, going into the prophet's tent, found him and Abu Becr weeping, and, asking them the reason of their tears, Mohammed acquainted him that this verse had been revealed, condemning their ill-timed lenity towards their prisoners, and that they had narrowly escaped the divine vengeance for it, adding that, if GOD had not passed the matter over, they had certainly been destroyed to a man, excepting only Omar and Saad Ebn Moadh, a person of as great severity, and who was also for putting the prisoners to death. Yet did not this crime go absolutely unpunished ; for in the battle of Ohod the Moslems lost seventy men, equal to the number of prisoners taken at Bedr (see Chap. III.), which was so ordered by GOD, as a retaliation or atonement for the same.

[2] *i.e.*, Of the ransom which ye have received of your prisoners. For it seems, on this rebuke, they had some scruple of conscience whether they might convert it to their own use or not. (Al Beidâwi.)

[3] That is, if ye repent and believe, GOD will make you abundant retribution for the ransom ye have now paid. It is said that this passage was revealed on the particular account of Al Abbâs, who, being obliged by Moham-med, though his uncle, to ransom both himself and his two nephews, Okail and Nawfal Ebn al Hareth, complained that he should be reduced to beg alms of the Koreish as long as he lived. Whereupon Mohammed asked him what was become of the gold which he delivered to Omm al Fadl when he left Mecca, telling her that he knew not what might befall him in the expedition, and therefore, if he lost his life, she might keep it herself for the use of her and her children ? Al Abbâs demanded who told him this, to which Mohammed replied that GOD had revealed it to him. And upon this Al Abbâs immediately professed Islâmism, declaring that none could know of that affair except GOD, because he gave her the money at midnight. Some years after, Al Abbâs reflecting on this passage, confessed it to be fulfilled ; for he was then not only possessed of a large substance, but had the custody of the well Zemzem, which, he said, he preferred to all the riches of Mecca. (Al Beidâwi. D'Herbel. Bibl. Orient. Art. Abbâs.)

GOD *is* gracious *and* merciful. But if they seek to deceive thee,[1] verily they have deceived GOD before ; wherefore he hath given *thee* power over them ; and GOD *is* knowing *and* wise. Moreover they who have believed, and have fled their country, and employed their substance and their persons in fighting for the religion of GOD, and they who have given *the prophet* a refuge *among them*, and have assisted *him*, these *shall be deemed* the one nearest of kin to the other.[2] But they who have believed, but have not fled their country, shall have no *right of* kindred at all with you, until they *also* fly. Yet if they ask assistance of you on account of religion, *it belongeth* unto you *to give them* assistance ; except against a people between whom and yourselves *there shall be* a league *subsisting* : and GOD seeth that which ye do. And as to the infidels, let them be *deemed* of kin the one to the other. Unless ye do this, there will be a sedition in the earth, and grievous corruption. But as for them who have believed, and left their country, and have fought for GOD's true religion, and who have allowed *the prophet* a retreat *among* them, and have assisted *him*, these are really believers, they shall receive mercy, and an honourable provision. And they who have believed since, and have fled their country, and have fought with you, these *also* are of you. And those who are related by consanguinity *shall be deemed* the nearest of kin to each other, *preferably to strangers*, according to the book of GOD ; GOD knoweth all things.

IX

THE CHAPTER OF THE DECLARATION OF IMMUNITY [3]

Revealed at Medina.

A DECLARATION of immunity from GOD and his apostle, unto the idolaters with whom ye have entered

[1] By not paying the ransom agreed on.

[2] And shall consequently inherit one another's substance, preferably to their relations by blood. And this, they say, was practised for some time, the Mohâjerin and Ansârs being judged heirs to one another, exclusive of the deceased's other kindred, till this passage was abrogated by the following : *Those who are related by blood shall be deemed the nearest of kin to each other.*

[3] The reason why the chapter had this title appears from the first verse. Some, however, give it other titles, and particularly that of *Repentance*, which is mentioned immediately after.

It is observable that this chapter alone has not the auspiciatory form, *In the name of the most merciful* GOD, prefixed to it ; the reason of which

into league.¹ Go to and fro in the earth *securely* four months;²
and know that ye shall not weaken GOD, and that GOD will
disgrace the unbelievers.   And a declaration from GOD and
his apostle unto the people, on the day of the greater pilgrimage,³ that GOD is clear of the idolaters, and his apostle *also*.
Wherefore if ye repent, this will be better for you ; but if
ye turn back, know that ye shall not weaken GOD : and
denounce unto those who believe not, a painful punishment.

omission, as some think, was, because these words imply a concession of
security, which is utterly taken away by this chapter, after a fixed time ;
wherefore some have called it the chapter of *Punishment* ; others say that
Mohammed (who died soon after he had received this chapter), had
given no direction where it should be placed, nor for the prefixing the Bismillah to it, as had been done to the other chapters ; and the argument
of this chapter bearing a near resemblance to that of the preceding, his
companions differed about it, some saying that both chapters were but
one, and together made the seventh of the seven long ones, and others that
they were two distinct chapters ; whereupon, to accommodate the dispute,
they left a space between them, but did not interpose the distinction of
the Bismillah. (Al Beidâwi, Jallalo'ddin, Yahya, &c.) It is agreed that
this chapter was the last which was revealed ; and the only one, as Mohammed declared, which was revealed entire and at once, except the hundred
and tenth. Some will have the two last verses to have been revealed at
Mecca.
¹ Some understand this sentence of the *immunity* or *security* therein
granted to the infidels for the space of four months ; but others think that
the words properly signify that Mohammed is here declared by GOD to be
absolutely *free* and *discharged* from all truce or league with them, after
the expiration of that time (Al Beidâwi) ; and this last seems to be the
truest interpretation. Mohammed's thus renouncing all league with those
who would not receive him as the apostle of GOD, or submit to become
tributary, was the consequence of the great power to which he was now
arrived. But the pretext he made use of was the treachery he had met
with among the Jewish and idolatrous Arabs—scarce any keeping faith
with him, except Banu Damra, Banu Kenâna, and a few others. (Al Beidâwi.)
² These months were Shawâl, Dhu'lkaada, Dhu'lhajja, and Moharram ;
the chapter being revealed in Shawâl. Yet others compute them from
the tenth of Dhu'lhajja, when the chapter was published at Mecca, and
consequently make them expire on the tenth of the former Rabî (Al
Beidâwi, Al Zamaksh., Jallalo'ddin.)
³ viz., The tenth of Dhu'lhajja, when they slay the victims at Mina ;
which day is their great feast, and completes the ceremonies of the pilgrimage. Some suppose the adjective *greater* is added here to distinguish the
pilgrimage made at the appointed time from *lesser pilgrimages*, as they
may be called, or *visitations* of the Caaba, which may be performed at any
time of the year ; or else because the concourse at the pilgrimage this year
was greater than ordinary, both Moslems and idolaters being present at it.
The promulgation of this chapter was committed by Mohammed to Ali,
who rode for that purpose on the prophet's slit-eared camel from Medina
to Mecca ; and on the day above mentioned, standing up before the whole
assembly at Al Akaba, told them that he was the messenger of the apostle
of GOD unto them. Whereupon they asking him what was his errand,
he read twenty or thirty verses of the chapter to them, and then said, *I
am commanded to acquaint you with four things* : 1. *That no idolater is to
come near the temple of Mecca after this year* ; 2. *That no man presume to
compass the Caaba naked for the future* (see before, Chap. VII.) ; 3. *That none
but true believers shall enter paradise* ; *and* 4. *That public faith is to be kept.*
(Al Beidâwi. Abulfed Vit. Moh. p. 127, &c.)

Except such of the idolaters with whom ye shall have entered into a league, and who afterwards shall not fail you in any instance, nor assist any *other* against you.[1] Wherefore perform the covenant *which ye shall have made* with them, until their time *shall be elapsed* ; for GOD loveth those who fear *him*. And when the months *wherein ye are* not allowed *to attack them* shall be past, kill the idolaters wheresoever ye shall find them,[2] and take them *prisoners*, and besiege them, and lay wait for them in every convenient place. But if they shall repent, and observe the appointed times of prayer, and pay the legal alms, dismiss them freely ; for GOD *is* gracious *and* merciful. And if any of the idolaters shall demand protection of thee, grant him protection, that he may hear the word of GOD ; and afterwards let him reach the place of his security.[3] This *shalt thou do*, because they are people which know not *the excellency of the religion thou preachest.* How shall the idolaters be admitted into a league with GOD and with his apostle ; except those with whom ye entered into a league at the holy temple ?[4] So long as they behave with fidelity towards you, do ye *also* behave with fidelity towards them ; for GOD loveth those who fear *him*. How *can they be admitted into a league with you*, since, if they prevail against you, they will not regard in you *either* consanguinity or faith ? They will please you with their mouths, but their hearts will be averse *from you* ; for the greater part of them are wicked doers. They sell the signs of GOD for a small price, and obstruct his way ; it is certainly evil which they do. They regard not in a believer *either* consanguinity or faith ; and these are the transgressors. Yet if they repent, and observe the appointed times of prayer, and give alms, *they shall be deemed* your brethren in religion. We distinctly propound *our* signs unto people who understand. But if they violate their oaths, after their league, and revile your religion, oppose the leaders of infidelity (for there is no trust in them), that they may desist *from their treachery.* Will ye not fight against people who have violated their oaths, and conspired to expel the apostle *of God* ; and who of their own

[1] So that notwithstanding Mohammed renounces all leagues with those who had deceived him, he declares himself ready to perform his engagements to such as had been true to him.

[2] Either within or without the sacred territory.

[3] That is, you shall give him a safe-conduct, that he may return home again securely, in case he shall not think fit to embrace Mohammedism.

[4] These are the persons before excepted.

accord assaulted you the first time?[1] Will ye fear them?
But it is more just that ye should fear GOD, if ye are true
believers. Attack them *therefore*; GOD shall punish them
by your hands, and will cover them with shame, and will
give you the victory over them; and he will heal the breasts
of the people who believe,[2] and will take away the indignation of their hearts: for GOD will be turned unto whom he
pleaseth; and GOD *is* knowing *and* wise. Did ye imagine
that ye should be abandoned, whereas GOD did not yet know
those among you who sought *for his religion*, and took not
any besides GOD, and his apostle, and the faithful *for their*
friends? God is well acquainted with that which ye do.
It is not *fitting* that the idolaters should visit the temples of
GOD, being witnesses against their own souls of *their* infidelity.
The works of these *men* are vain; and they shall remain in
hell fire for ever. But he only shall visit the temples of GOD,
who believeth in GOD and the last day, and is constant at
prayer, and payeth the legal alms, and feareth GOD alone.
These perhaps may become of *the number of* those who are
rightly directed.[3] Do ye reckon the giving drink to the
pilgrims, and the visiting of the holy temple, *to be actions as
meritorious* as *those performed by* him who believeth in GOD
and the last day, and fighteth for the religion of GOD?[4] They
shall not be held equal with GOD; for GOD directeth not the
unrighteous people. They who have believed, and fled their
country, and employed their substance and their persons in
the defence of GOD's true religion, shall be in the highest
degree *of honour* with GOD; and these are they who shall be
happy. Their LORD sendeth them good tidings of mercy

---

[1] As did the Koreish in assisting the tribe of Becr against those of Khozâah (Sale, Prel. Disc.), and laying a design to ruin Mohammed, without
any just provocation; and as several of the Jewish tribes did, by aiding
the enemy, and endeavouring to oblige the prophet to leave Medina, as
he had been obliged to leave Mecca (Al Beidâwi).

[2] viz., Those of Khozâah; or, as others say, certain families of Yaman
and Saba, who went to Mecca, and there professed Mohammedism, but
were very injuriously treated by the inhabitants; whereupon they complained to Mohammed, who bade them take comfort, for that joy was
approaching. (Al Beidâwi.)

[3] These words are to warn the believers from having too great a confidence
in their own merits, and likewise to deter the unbelievers; for if the faithful
will but *perhaps* be saved, what can the others hope for? (Al Beidâwi.)

[4] This passage was revealed on occasion of some words of Al Abbâs,
Mohammed's uncle, who, when he was taken prisoner, being bitterly
reproached by the Moslems, and particularly by his nephew Ali, answered:
*You rip up our ill actions, but take no notice of our good ones; we visit the
temple of Mecca, and adorn the Caaba with hangings, and give drink to the
pilgrims* (of Zemzem water, I suppose) *and free captives.* (Al Beidâwi.)

from him, and goodwill, and of gardens wherein they shall enjoy lasting pleasure ; they shall continue therein for ever : for GOD is a great reward. O true believers, take not your fathers or your brethren for friends, if they love infidelity above faith ; and whosoever among you shall take them for *his* friends, they will be unjust doers. Say, If your fathers, and your sons, and your brethren, and your wives, and your relations, and *your* substance which ye have acquired, and *your* merchandise which ye apprehend may not be sold off, and *your* dwellings wherein ye delight, be more dear unto you than GOD, and his apostle, and the advancement of his religion ; wait, until GOD shall send his command :[1] for GOD directeth not the ungodly people. Now hath GOD assisted you in many engagements, and *particularly* at the battle of Honein ;[2] when ye pleased yourselves in your multitude, but it was no manner of advantage unto you, and the earth became too strait for you,[3] notwithstanding it was spacious ; then did ye retreat and turn your backs. Afterwards GOD sent down his security[4] upon his apostle and upon the faithful, and sent down troops *of angels*[5] which ye saw not ; and he

[1] Or shall punish you. Some suppose the taking of Mecca to be here intended. (Al Beidâwi.)

[2] This battle was fought in the eighth year of the Hejra, in the valley of Honein, which lies about three miles from Mecca towards Tâyef, between Mohammed, who had an army of twelve thousand men, and the tribes of Hawâzen and Thakif, whose forces did not exceed four thousand. The Mohammedans, seeing themselves so greatly superior to their enemies, made sure of the victory ; a certain person, whom some suppose to have been the prophet himself, crying out, *These can never be overcome by so few.* But GOD was so highly displeased with this confidence, that in the first encounter the Moslems were put to flight (Prid. Life of Mahomet, p. 96, &c. Hotting. Hist. Orient. p. 271, &c. D'Herbel. Bibl. Orient. p. 601), some of them running away quite to Mecca, so that none stood their ground except Mohammed himself, and some few of his family ; and they say the prophet's courage was so great, that his uncle Al Abbâs, and his cousin Abu Sofiân Ebn al Hareth, had much ado to prevent his spurring his mule into the midst of the enemy, by laying hold of the bridle and stirrup. Then he ordered Al Abbâs, who had the voice of a Stentor, to recall his flying troops ; upon which they rallied, and the prophet throwing a handful of dust against the enemy, they attacked them a second time, and by the divine assistance gained the victory. (Al Beidâwi, Jallalo'ddin, Abulfeda, Vit. Moh. p. 112, &c.)

[3] For the valley being very deep, and encompassed by craggy mountains, the enemy placed themselves in ambush on every side, attacking them in the straits and narrow passages, and from behind the rocks, with great advantage. (Ebn. Ishak.)

[4] The original word is Sak'nat, which the commentators interpret in this sense ; but it seems rather to signify the *divine presence*, or Shechinah, appearing to aid the Moslems. (See Chap. II.)

[5] As to the number of these celestial auxiliaries, the commentators differ ; some say they were five thousand, some eight thousand, and others sixteen thousand. (Al Beidâwi.)

punished those who disbelieved : and this was the reward of the unbelievers.   Nevertheless GOD will hereafter be turned unto whom he pleaseth ;[1] for GOD *is* gracious *and* merciful. O true believers, verily the idolaters are unclean ; let them not therefore come near unto the holy temple after this year.[2]   And if ye fear want, *by the cutting off trade and communication with them,* GOD will enrich you of his abundance,[3] if he pleaseth ; for GOD *is* knowing *and* wise.   Fight against them who believe not in GOD, nor in the last day,[4] and forbid not that which GOD and his apostle have forbidden, and profess not the true religion, of those unto whom the scriptures have been delivered, until they pay tribute by right of subjection,[5] and they be reduced low.   The Jews say, Ezra

[1] Besides a great number of proselytes who were gained by this battle, Mohammed, on their request, was so generous as to restore the captives (which were no less than six thousand) to their friends, and offered to make amends himself to any of his men who should not be willing to part with his prisoners ; but they all consented to it. (Al Beidâwi.)

[2] Which was the ninth year of the Hejra.   In consequence of this prohibition, neither Jews nor Christians, nor those of any other religion, are suffered to come near Mecca to this day.

[3] This promise, says Al Beidâwi, was fulfilled by GOD's sending plenty of rain, and disposing the inhabitants of Tebâla and Jorash, two towns in Yaman, to embrace Islâm, who thereupon brought sufficient provisions to Mohammed's men ; and also by the subsequent coming in of the Arabs from all quarters to him.

[4] That is, who have not a just and true faith in these matters ; but either believe a plurality of gods, or deny the eternity of hell torments (see Chaps. II. and III.), or the delights of paradise as described in the Korân.   For as it appears by the following words, the Jews and Christians are the persons here chiefly meant.

[5] This I think the true meaning of the words *an yadin,* which literally signify *by* or *out of hand,* and are variously interpreted : some supposing they mean that the tribute is to be paid *readily,* or by their *own hands* and not by another ; or that tribute is to be exacted of the *rich* only, or those who are able to pay it, and not of the poor ; or else that it is to be taken as a *favour* that the Mohammedans are satisfied with so small an imposition, &c. (Al Beidâwi.)   That the Jews and Christians are, according to this law, to be admitted to protection on payment of tribute, there is no doubt : though the Mohammedan doctors differ as to those of other religions.   It is said that Omar at first refused to accept tribute from a Magian, till Abd'alrahmân Ebn Awf assured him that Mohammed himself had granted protection to a Magian, and ordered that the professors of that religion should be included among *the people of the book,* or those who found their religion on some book which they suppose to be of divine original.   And it is the more received opinion that these three religions only ought to be tolerated on the condition of paying tribute : others, however, admit the Sabians also.   Abu Hanîfa supposed people of any religion might be suffered, except the idolatrous Arabs ; and Malec excepted only apostates from Mohammedism.   The least tribute that can be taken from every such person, is generally agreed to be a *dinâr,* or about ten shillings, a year ; nor can he be obliged to pay more unless he consent to it ; and this, they say, ought to be laid as well on the poor as on the rich. (Reland. de Jure Militari Mohammedanor. p. 17 and 50.)   But Abu Hanîfa decided that the rich should pay forty-eight *dirhems* (twenty, and sometimes twenty-five, of which made a *dinâr*) a year ; one in middling circumstances half that sum ; and

is the son of GOD :[1] and the Christians say, Christ is the son of GOD. This is their saying in their mouths : they imitate the saying of those who were unbelievers in former times. May GOD resist them. How are they infatuated ! They take their priests and their monks for *their* lords, besides GOD,[2] and Christ the son of Mary ; although they are commanded to worship one GOD only : there is no GOD but he ; far be that from him, which they associate *with him* ! They seek to extinguish the light of GOD with their mouths ; but GOD willeth no other than to perfect his light, although the infidels be averse *thereto*. It is he who hath sent his apostle with the direction, and true religion : that he may cause it to appear superior to every *other* religion ; although the idolaters be averse *thereto*. O true believers, verily many of the priests and monks devour the substance of men in vanity,[3] and obstruct the way of GOD. But unto those who treasure

a poor man, who was able to get his living, a quarter of it : but that he who was not able to support himself should pay nothing. (Al Beidâwi.)

[1] This grievous charge against the Jews the commentators endeavour to support by telling us that it is meant of some ancient heterodox Jews, or else of some Jews of Medina ; who said so for no other reason than for that the law being utterly lost and forgotten during the Babylonish captivity, Ezra, having been raised to life after he had been dead one hundred years (see Chap. II.), dictated the whole anew to the scribes, out of his own memory ; at which they greatly marvelled, and declared that he could not have done it unless he were the son of GOD. (Al Beidâwi, Al Zamakhshari, &c.) Al Beidâwi adds that the imputation must be true, because this verse was read to the Jews, and they did not contradict it ; which they were ready enough to do in other instances.

That Ezra did thus restore not only the Pentateuch, but also the other books of the Old Testament, by divine revelation, was the opinion of several of the Christian fathers, who are quoted by Dr. Prideaux (Connect. part i. l. 5, p. 329), and of some other writers (Athanasius junior, in Synopsi S. Script. tom. ii. p. 86. Leontius Byzantin. de Sectis, p. 428) ; which they seem to have first borrowed from a passage in that very ancient apocryphal book, called (in our English Bible) the *second book* of Esdras (Cap. xiv. 20, &c.). Dr. Prideaux (loco citat.) tells us that herein the |fathers attributed more to Ezra than the Jews themselves, who suppose that he only collected and set forth a correct edition of the Scriptures, which he laboured much in, and went a great way in the perfecting of it. It is not improbable, however, that the fiction came originally from the Jews, though they be now of another opinion, and I cannot fix it upon them by any direct proof. For, not to insist on the testimony of the Mohammedans (which yet I cannot but think of some little weight in a point of this nature), it is allowed by the most sagacious critics that the second book of Ezra was written by a Christian indeed (see 2 Esdras ii. 43–47 ; and vii. 28, &c.), but yet one who had been bred a Jew, and was intimately acquainted with the fables of the Rabbins (Dodwelli Dissert. Cyprian. Dissert, 4, & 2. Whiston's Essay on the Apostolical Constit. p. 34, 76, and 304, &c. ; Fabricii Codic. Apocryph. Novi Test. part ii. p. 936, &c.) ; and the story itself is perfectly in the taste and way of thinking of those men.

[2] See Chap. III.

[3] By taking of bribes, meaning, probably, the money they took for dispensing with the commands of GOD, and by way of commutation. (Al Beidâwi.)

up gold and silver, and employ it not for the advancement of GOD's true religion, denounce a grievous punishment. On the day *of judgment their treasures* shall be intensely heated in the fire of hell, and their foreheads, and their sides and their backs shall be stigmatized therewith; *and their tormentors shall say*, This is what ye have treasured up for your souls; taste therefore that which ye have treasured up. Moreover, the *complete* number of months with GOD, is twelve months,[1] *which were ordained* in the book of GOD,[2] on the day whereon he created the heavens and the earth: of these, four are sacred.[3] This is the right religion: therefore deal not unjustly with yourselves therein. But attack the idolaters in all *the months*, as they attack you in all;[4] and know that GOD is with those who fear *him*. Verily the transferring *of a sacred month to another month* is an additional infidelity.[5] The unbelievers are led into an error thereby: they allow *a month* to be violated one year, and declare it sacred *another* year,[6] that they may agree in the number of *months* which GOD hath commanded to be kept sacred; and they allow that which GOD hath forbidden. The evil of their actions hath been prepared for them: for GOD directeth not the unbelieving people. O true believers, what ailed you, that, when it was said unto you, Go forth *to fight* for the religion of GOD, ye inclined heavily towards the earth?[7] Do ye prefer

[1] According to this passage, the intercalation of a month every third or second year, which the Arabs had learned of the Jews, in order to reduce their lunar years to solar years, is absolutely unlawful. For by this means they fixed the time of the pilgrimage and of the fast of Ramadân to certain seasons of the year which ought to be ambulatory. (Prid. Life of Mahomet, p. 65, &c., and Sale, Prel. Disc. Sect. IV. and VII.)

[2] viz., The preserved table.

[3] See Sale, Prel. Disc. Sect. VII. p. 159.

[4] For it is not reasonable that you should observe the sacred months with regard to those who do not acknowledge them to be sacred, but make war against you therein (Chap. II).

[5] This was an invention or innovation of the idolatrous Arabs, whereby they avoided keeping a sacred month, when it suited not their conveniency, by keeping a profane month in its stead; transferring, for example, the observance of Moharram to the succeeding month Safar. The first man who put this in practice, they say, was Jonâda Ebn Awf, of the tribe of Kenâna. (Al Beidâwi, Jallalo'ddin. Poc. Spec. p. 323, and Sale, Prel. Disc. Sect. VII.) These ordinances relating to the months were promulgated by Mohammed himself at the pilgrimage of *valediction*. (Abulfeda, Vit. Moh., p. 132.)

[6] As did Jonâda, who made public proclamation at the assembly of pilgrims, that their gods had allowed Moharram to be profane, whereupon they observed it not; but the next year he told them that the gods had ordered it to be kept sacred. (Al Beidâwi.)

[7] viz., In the expedition of Tabûc, a town situate about half-way between Medina and Damascus, which Mohammed undertook against the Greeks, with an army of thirty thousand men, in the ninth year of the Hejra. On

the present life to that which is to come ? But the provision of this life, in *respect of* that which is to come, is but slender. Unless ye go forth *when ye are summoned to war, God* will punish you with a grievous punishment ; and he will place another people in your stead,[1] and ye shall not hurt him at all ; for GOD is almighty. If ye assist not *the prophet*, verily GOD *will assist him, as he* assisted him formerly, when the unbelievers drove him out *of Mecca*, the second of two :[2] when they *were* both in the cave : when he said unto his companion, Be not grieved, for GOD is with us.[3] And GOD sent down his security[4] upon him, and strengthened him with armies *of angels*, whom ye saw not.[5] And he made the word of those who believed not to be abased, and the word of GOD was exalted ; for GOD *is* mighty *and* wise. Go forth *to battle*, both light and heavy,[6] and employ your substance and your persons for the advancement of GOD'S religion. This will be better for you, if ye know it. If it had been a near advantage and a moderate journey, they had surely followed thee ;[7] but the way seemed tedious unto them : and yet they will swear by GOD, *saying*, If we had been able, we had surely gone forth with you. They destroy their own souls ; for GOD knoweth that they are liars. GOD forgive thee ! why didst thou give them leave *to stay at home*,[8] until they who speak the truth, *when they excuse themselves*, had become manifested unto thee, and thou hadst known the liars ? They who believe in GOD and the last day, will not ask leave of

this expedition the Moslems set out with great unwillingness, because it was undertaken in the midst of the summer heats, and at a time of great drought and scarcity ; whereby the soldiers suffered so much, that this army was called the *distressed army* : besides, their fruits were just ripe, and they had much rather have stayed to have gathered them. (Al Beidâwi, Jallalo'ddin. Abulfeda, Vit. Moh. p. 123.)

[1] See Chap. V.

[2] That is, having only Abu Becr with him.

[3] Sale, Prel. Disc. Sect. II.

[4] See before, p. 181.

[5] Who, as some imagine, guarded him in the cave. Or the words may relate to the succours from heaven which Mohammed pretended to have received in several encounters ; as at Bedr, the war of the ditch, and the battle of Honein.

[6] *i.e.*, Whether the expedition be agreeable or not ; or whether ye have sufficient arms and provisions or not ; or whether ye be on horseback or on foot, &c.

[7] That is, had there been no difficulties to surmount in the expedition of Tabûc, and the march thither had been short and easy, so that the plunder might have cost them little or no trouble, they would not have been so backward.

[8] For Mohammed excused several of his men, at their request, from going on this expedition ; as Abda'llah Ebn Obba and his hypocritical adherents, and also three of the Ansàrs, for which he is here reprehended.

thee to be excused from employing their substance and their persons for the advancement of GOD's true religion ; and GOD knoweth those who fear *him*. Verily they only will ask leave of thee *to stay behind*, who believe not in GOD and the last day, and whose hearts doubt *concerning the faith* : wherefore they are tossed to and fro in their doubting. If they had been willing to go forth *with thee*, they had certainly prepared for that *purpose* a provision *of arms and necessaries* : but GOD was averse to their going forth ; wherefore he rendered them slothful, and it was said *unto them*, Sit ye still with those who sit still.[1] If they had gone forth with you, they had only been a burden unto you, and had run to and fro between you, stirring you up to sedition ; and *there would have been some* among you who would have given ear unto them : and GOD knoweth the wicked. They formerly sought to raise a sedition,[2] and they disturbed thy affairs, until the truth came, and the decree of GOD was made manifest ; although they were averse thereto. There is of them who saith *unto thee*, Give me leave *to stay behind*, and expose me not to temptation.[3] Have they not fallen into temptation *at home* ?[4] But hell will surely encompass the unbelievers. If good happen unto thee, it grieveth them : but if a misfortune befall thee, they say, We ordered our business before ;[5] and they turn their backs, and rejoice *at thy mishap*. Say, Nothing shall befall us, but what GOD hath decreed for us : he is our patron : and on GOD let the faithful trust. Say, Do ye expect *any other should befall* us than one of the two most excellent things ; *either victory or martyrdom* ? But we expect concerning you, that GOD inflict a punishment on you, *either* from himself, or by our hands.[6] Wait therefore *to see what will be the end of both* ; for we will wait with you. Say, Expend *your money in pious uses, either* voluntarily or by constraint ; it shall not be accepted of you, because ye are wicked people. And nothing hindereth their contributions from being accepted of them, but that they believe not in

[1] *i.e.*, With the women and children, and other impotent people.

[2] As they did at the battle of Ohod (Chap. III.).

[3] By obliging me to go, against my will, on an expedition, the hardships of which may tempt me to rebel or to desert. It is related that one Jadd Ebn Kais said that the Ansârs well knew he was much given to women, and he dared not trust himself with the Greek girls ; wherefore he desired he might be left behind, and he would assist them with his purse. Al (Beidâwi.)

[4] Discovering their hypocrisy by their backwardness to go to war for the promotion of the true religion.

[5] That is, we took care to keep out of harm's way by staying at home.

[6] *i.e.*, Either by some signal judgment from heaven, or by remitting their punishment to the true believers.

GOD and his apostle, and perform not the *duty of* prayer, otherwise than sluggishly ; and expend not *their money for God's service*, otherwise than unwillingly. Let not therefore their riches or their children cause thee to marvel. Verily GOD intendeth only to punish them by these things in this world ; and that their souls may depart while they are unbelievers. They swear by GOD that they are of you ;[1] yet they are not of you, but are people who stand in fear.[2] If they find a place of refuge, or caves, or a retreating hole, they surely turn towards the same, and in a headstrong manner haste *thereto.* There is of them also who spreadeth ill reports of thee, in relation to *thy distribution of* the alms ; yet if they receive *part* thereof, they are well pleased ; but if they receive not *a part* thereof, behold, they are angry.[3] But if they had been pleased with that which GOD and his apostle had given them, and had said, GOD is our support ; GOD will give unto us of his abundance and his prophet *also* ; verily unto GOD do we make our supplications : *it would have been more decent.* Alms *are to be distributed* [4] only unto the poor and the needy,[5] and those who are employed in *collecting and distributing* the same, and unto those whose hearts *are* reconciled,[6] and for *the redemption of* captives, and unto those who are in debt *and insolvent,* and for the advancement of GOD's religion, and unto the traveller. *This is* an ordinance from GOD ; and GOD is knowing *and* wise. There are some of them who injure the prophet, and

[1] viz., Staunch Moslems.

[2] Hypocritically concealing their infidelity, lest ye should chastise them, as ye have done the professed infidels and apostates ; and yet ready to avow their infidelity, when they think they may do it with safety.

[3] This person was Abu'l Jowâdh the hypocrite, who said Mohammed gave them away among the keepers of sheep only ; or, as others suppose, Ebn Dhi'lkhowaisara, who found fault with the prophet's distribution of the spoils taken at Honein, because he gave them all among the Meccans, to reconcile and gain them over to his religion and interest. (Al Beidâwi, Abulfeda, Vit. Moh. p. 118, 119.)

[4] See what is said as to this point in Sale, Prel. Disc. Sect. IV.

[5] The commentators make a distinction between these two words in the original, *fakir* and *meskin* ; one, they say, signifies him who is utterly destitute both of money and means of livelihood ; the other, one who is in want indeed, but is able to get something towards his own support. But to which of the two words either of these different significations properly belongs, the critics differ.

[6] That is, who were lately enemies to the faithful, but have now embraced Mohammedism, and entered into amity with them. For Mohammed, to gain their hearts and confirm them in his religion, made large presents to the chief of the Koreish out of the spoils at Honein, as has been just now mentioned. (Abulfeda, ibid.) But this law they say became of no obligation when the Mohammedan faith was established, and stood not in need of such methods for its support.

say, He is an ear :[1] Answer, He is an ear of good unto you :[2] he believeth in GOD, and giveth credit to the faithful, and *is* a mercy unto such of you who believe. But they who injure the apostle of GOD, shall suffer a painful punishment. They swear unto you by GOD, that they may please you ; but it is more just that they should please GOD and his apostle, if they are true believers. Do they not know that he who opposeth GOD and his apostle, shall without doubt *be punished with* the fire of hell ; *and* shall remain therein for ever ? This will be great ignominy. The hypocrites are apprehensive lest a Sura[3] should be revealed concerning them, to declare unto them that which *is* in their hearts. Say *unto them,* Scoff ye ; *but* GOD will surely bring to light that which ye fear *should be discovered.* And if thou ask them *the reason of this scoffing,* they say, Verily we were only engaged in discourse, and jesting *among ourselves.*[4] Say, Do ye scoff at GOD and his signs, and at his apostle ? offer not an excuse : now are ye become infidels, after your faith. If we forgive a part of you, we will punish a part, for that they have been wicked doers. Hypocritical men and women are the one of them or the other : they command that which is evil, and forbid that which is just, and shut their hands *from giving alms.* They have forgotten GOD ; wherefore he hath forgotten them : verily the hypocrites are those who act wickedly. GOD denounceth unto the hypocrites, both men and women, and to the unbelievers the fire of hell ; they shall remain therein *for ever* : this will be their sufficient *reward* ; GOD hath cursed them, and they shall endure a lasting torment. As they who have been before you, *so are ye.* They were superior to you in strength, and had more abundance of wealth and of children ; and they enjoyed their portion *in this world* ; *and ye* also enjoy your portion *here,* as they who have preceded you enjoyed their portion. And ye engage yourselves in vain discourses, like unto those wherein they engaged themselves. The works of these

---

[1] *i.e.,* He hears everything that we say ; and gives credit to all the stories that are carried to him.

[2] Giving credit to nothing that may do you hurt.

[3] So the Mohammedans call a chapter of the Korân. (Sale, Prel. Disc. Sect. III.)

[4] It is related that in the expedition of Tabûc, a company of hypocrites passing near Mohammed, said to one another, *Behold that man ! he would take the strongholds of Syria. Away ! away !*—which being told the prophet, he called them to him, and asked them why they had said so ? Whereto they replied with an oath that they were not talking of what related to him or his companions, but were only diverting themselves with indifferent discourse to beguile the tediousness of the way. (Al. Beidâwi.)

are vain *both* in this world and that which is to come; and these are they who perish. Have they not been acquainted with the history of those who have been before them? of the people of Noah, and of Ad, and of Thamûd, and of the people of Abraham, and of the inhabitants of Madian, and of the *cities which were* overthrown?[1] Their apostles came unto them with evident demonstrations: and GOD was not disposed to treat them unjustly; but they dealt unjustly with their own souls. And the faithful men and the faithful women are friends one to another: they command that which is just, and they forbid that which is evil; and they are constant at prayer, and pay their appointed alms; and they obey GOD and his apostle: unto these will GOD be merciful: for he *is* mighty *and* wise. GOD promiseth unto the true believers, both men and women, gardens through which rivers flow, wherein they shall remain for ever; and delicious dwellings in gardens of perpetual abode:[2] but goodwill from GOD *shall be their* most excellent *reward*. This *will be* great felicity. O prophet, wage war against the unbelievers and the hypocrites, and be severe unto them, for their dwelling shall be hell; an unhappy journey *shall it be thither*! They swear by GOD that they said not *what they are charged with*: yet they spake the word of infidelity, and became unbelievers, after they had embraced Islâm.[3] And they designed that which they could not effect;[4] and they did not disapprove *the design for any other reason*, than because GOD and his apostle had enriched them, of his bounty.[5] If

---

[1] Namely, Sodom and Gomorrah, and the other cities which shared their fate, and are thence called Al Motakifât, or *the subverted*. (Cap. XI.)

[2] Literally, *gardens* of Eden; but the commentators do not take the word Eden in the sense which it bears in Hebrew, as has been elsewhere observed. (Sale, Prel. Disc. p. 103.)

[3] It is related that Al Jallâs Ebn Soweid hearing some passages of this chapter, which sharply reprehend those who refused to go on the above-mentioned expedition of Tabûc, declared that if what Mohammed said of his brethren was true, they were worse than asses; which coming to the prophet's ear, he sent for him; and he denied the words upon oath. But on the immediate revelation of this passage, he confessed his fault, and his repentance was accepted. (Al Beidâwi.)

[4] The commentators tell us that fifteen men conspired to kill Mohammed in his return from Tabûc by pushing him from his camel into a precipice, as he rode by night over the highest part of Al Akaba. But when they were going to execute their design, Hodheifa, who followed and drove the prophet's camel, which was led by Ammâr Ebn Yâser, hearing the tread of camels and the clashing of arms, gave the alarm, upon which they fled. Some, however, suppose the design here meant was a plot to expel Mohammed from Medina. (Al Beidâwi.)

[5] For Mohammed's residing at Medina was of great advantage to the place, the inhabitants being generally poor, and in want of most conveniences of life; but on the prophet's coming among them, they became

they repent, it will be better for them ; but if they relapse, GOD will punish them with a grievous torment, in this world and in the next ; and they shall have no patron on earth, nor any protector. There are some of them who made a covenant with GOD, *saying*, Verily if he give us of his abundance, we will give alms, and become righteous people.[1] Yet when he had given unto them of his abundance, they became covetous thereof, and turned back, and retired afar off. Wherefore he hath caused hypocrisy to succeed in their hearts, until the day whereon they shall meet him ; for that they failed to perform unto GOD that which they had promised him, and for that they prevaricated. Do they not know that GOD knoweth whatever they conceal and their private discourses ; and that GOD is the knower of secrets ? They who traduce such of the believers as are liberal in *giving* alms *beyond what they are obliged*, and those who find nothing *to give* but *what they gain by* their industry ;[2] and therefore scoff at them : GOD shall scoff at them, and they shall suffer a grievous punishment. Ask forgiveness for them, or do not ask forgiveness for them ; *it will be equal.* If thou ask forgiveness for

possessed of large herds of cattle and money also. Al Beidâwi says that the above-named Al Jallâs in particular, having a servant killed, received by Mohammed's order no less than ten thousand *dirhems*, or about three hundred pounds, as a fine for the redemption of his blood.

[1] An instance of this is given in Thalaba Ebn Hateb, who came to Mohammed and desired him to beg of GOD that he would bestow riches on him. The prophet at first advised him rather to be thankful for the little he had than to covet more, which might become a temptation to him ; but on Thalaba's repeated request and solemn promise that he would make a good use of his riches, he was at length prevailed on, and preferred the petition to GOD. Thalaba in a short time grew vastly rich, which, Mohammed being acquainted with, sent two collectors to gather the alms. Other people readily paid them ; but, when they came to Thalaba, and read the injunction to him out of the Korân, he told them that it was not alms, but tribute, or next kin to tribute, and bid them go back till he had better considered of it. Upon which this passage was revealed ; and when Thalaba came afterwards and brought his alms, Mohammed told him that GOD had commanded him not to accept it, and threw dust upon his head, saying, *This is what thou hast deserved.* He then offered his alms to Abu Becr, who refused to accept them, as did Omar some years after, when he was Khalîf. (Al Beidâwi.)

[2] Al Beidâwi relates that Mohammed, exhorting his followers to voluntary alms, among others, Abda'lrahmân Ebn Awf gave four thousand *dirhems*, which was one-half of what he had ; Asem Ebn Adda gave a hundred beasts' loads of dates ; and Abu Okail a saá, which is no more than a sixtieth part of a load, of the same fruit, but was the half of what he had earned by a night's hard work. This Mohammed accepted : whereupon the hypocrites said that Abda'lrahmân and Asem gave what they did out of ostentation, and that GOD and his apostle might well have excused Abu Okail's mite ; which occasioned this passage. I suppose this collection was made to defray the charge of the expedition of Tabûc, towards which, as another writer tells us, Abu Becr contributed all that he had, and Othmân very largely, viz., as it is said, three hundred camels for slaughter, and a thousand *dinârs* of gold. (Abulfed. Vit. Moh. p. 123.)

them seventy times, GOD will by no means forgive them.[1]
This *is the divine pleasure*, for that they believe not in GOD
and his apostle ; and GOD directeth not the ungodly people.
They who were left at home *in the expedition of Tabûc*, were
glad of their staying behind the apostle of GOD, and were
unwilling to employ their substance and their persons for the
advancement of GOD's true religion ; and they said, Go not
forth in the heat.[2] Say, The fire of hell will be hotter ; if
they understood *this*. Wherefore let them laugh little, and
weep much, as a reward for that which they have done. If
GOD bring thee back unto some of them,[3] and they ask thee
leave to go forth *to war with thee*, say, Ye shall not go forth
with me for the future, neither shall ye fight an enemy with
me ; ye were pleased with sitting *at home* the first time ;
sit ye *at home* therefore with those who stay behind. Neither
do thou ever pray over any of them who shall die,[4] neither
stand at his grave ;[5] for that they believed not in GOD or his
apostle, and die in their wickedness. Let not their riches or
their children cause thee to marvel : for GOD intendeth only to
punish them therewith in this world ; and that their souls
may depart while they are infidels. When a Sura[6] is sent
down, *wherein it is said*, Believe in GOD, and go forth to war
with his apostle ; those who are in plentiful circumstances
among them ask leave of thee *to stay behind*, and say, Suffer

[1] In the last sicknesss of Abda'llah Ebn Obba, the hypocrite (who died
in the ninth year of the Hejra), his son, named also Abda'llah, came and
asked Mohammed to beg pardon of GOD for him, which he did, and thereupon
the former part of this verse was revealed. But the prophet, not taking
that for a repulse, said he would *pray seventy times* for him ; upon which the
latter part of the verse was revealed, declaring it would be absolutely in
vain. It may be observed that the numbers *seven*, and *seventy*, and *seven
hundred*, are frequently used by the eastern writers, to signify not so many
precisely, but only an indefinite number, either greater or lesser (Al Beidâwi),
several examples of which are to be met with in Scripture. (Matth. xviii. 22.)
[2] This they spoke in a scoffing manner to one another, because, as has
been observed, the expedition of Tabûc was undertaken in a very hot and
dry season.
[3] That is, if thou return in safety to Medina to the hypocrites, who are
here called some of them who stayed behind, because they were not all
hypocrites. The whole number is said to have been twelve. (Al Beidâwi.)
[4] This passage was also revealed on account of Abda'llah Ebn Obba. In
his last illness he desired to see Mohammed, and, when he was come, asked
him to beg forgiveness of GOD for him, and requested that his corpse might
be wrapped up in the garment that was next his body (which might have
the same efficacy with the habit of a Franciscan), and that he would pray
over him when dead. Accordingly, when he was dead, the prophet sent
his shirt, or inner vestment, to shroud the corpse, and was going to pray
over it, but was forbidden by these words. Some say they were not revealed
till he had actually prayed for him. (Al Beidâwi.)
[5] Either by assisting at his funeral, or visiting his sepulchre.
[6] That is a chapter of the Korân.

us to be *of the number* of those who sit *at home*. They are well pleased to be with those who stay behind, and their hearts are sealed up; wherefore they do not understand. But the apostle, and those who have believed with him, expose their fortunes and their lives *for God's service*; they shall enjoy the good things *of either life*, and they shall be happy. GOD hath prepared for them gardens through which rivers flow; they shall remain therein *for ever*. This will be great felicity. And certain Arabs of the desert came to excuse themselves,[1] *praying* that they might be permitted *to stay behind*; and they sat *at home* who had renounced GOD and his apostle. But a painful punishment shall be inflicted on such of them as believe not. In those who are weak, or are afflicted with sickness, or in those who find not wherewith to contribute *to the war*,[2] it shall be no crime *if they stay at home*; provided they behave themselves faithfully towards GOD and his apostle. There is no room *to lay blame* on the righteous; for GOD *is* gracious *and* merciful: nor on those unto whom, when they came unto thee, *requesting* that thou wouldest supply them with necessaries for travelling, thou didst answer, I find not wherewith to supply you, returned, their eyes shedding tears for grief, that they found not wherewith to contribute *to the expedition*.[3] But there is reason *to blame* those who ask leave of thee *to sit at home*, when they are rich. They are pleased to be with those who stay behind, and GOD hath sealed up their hearts; wherefore they do not understand. (XI.)[4] They will excuse themselves unto you, when ye are returned unto them. Say, Excuse not yourselves; we will by no means believe you: GOD hath acquainted us with your behaviour; and GOD will observe your actions, and his apostle *also*: and hereafter shall ye be brought before him who knoweth that which is hidden and that which is manifest; and he will declare unto you that which ye have done. They will swear unto you by GOD,

---

[1] These were the tribes of Asad and Ghatfân, who excused themselves on account of the necessities of their families, which their industry only maintained. But some write they were the family of Amer Ebn al Tofail, who said that if they went with the army, the tribe of Tay would fall upon their wives and children, and their cattle. (Al Beidâwi.)

[2] By reason of their extreme poverty; as those of Joheina, Mozeina, and Banu Odhra. (Al Beidâwi.)

[3] The persons here intended were seven men of the Ansârs, who came to Mohammed and begged he would give them some patched boots and soled shoes, it being impossible for them to march so far barefoot in such a season; but he told them he could not supply them; whereupon they went away weeping. Some, however, say these were the Banu Mokren; and others Abu Musa and his companions. (Al Beidâwi.)

[4] The eleventh section begins here.

when ye are returned unto them, that ye may let them alone.[1] Let them alone therefore, for they are an abomination, and their dwelling *shall be* hell, a reward for that which they have deserved. They will swear unto you, that ye may be well pleased with them ; but if ye be well pleased with them, verily GOD will not be well pleased with people who prevaricate. The Arabs of the desert are more obstinate in *their* unbelief and hypocrisy; and it is easier for them to be ignorant of the ordinances of that which GOD hath sent down unto his apostle :[2] and GOD *is* knowing *and* wise. Of the Arabs of the desert there is who reckoneth that which he expendeth *for the service of God, to be as* tribute ;[3] and waiteth that some change *of fortune*[4] *may befall* you. A change for evil *shall happen* unto them ; for GOD *both* heareth *and* knoweth. And of the Arabs of the desert there is who believeth in GOD and in the last day ; and esteemeth that which he layeth out *for the service of God* to be the *means of* bringing him near unto GOD and the prayers of the apostle. Is it not unto them *the means of* a near approach ? GOD shall lead them into his mercy ; for GOD *is* gracious *and* merciful.[5] *As for* the leaders *and* the first of the Mohâjerîn, and the Ansârs,[6] and those who have followed them in well doing ; GOD is well pleased with them, and they are well pleased in him : and he hath prepared for them gardens watered by rivers ; they shall remain therein for ever. This shall be great felicity. And of the Arabs of the desert who *dwell* round about you, *there are* hypocritical persons :[7] and of

[1] And not chastise them.

[2] Because of their wild way of life, the hardness of their hearts, their not frequenting people of knowledge, and the few opportunities they have of being instructed. (Al Beidâwi. Sale, Prel. Disc. Sect. I.)

[3] Or a contribution exacted by force, the payment of which he can in no wise avoid.

[4] Hoping that some reverse may afford a convenient opportunity of throwing off the burden.

[5] The Arabs meant in the former of these two passages, are said to have been the tribes of Asad, Ghatfân, and Banu Tamim ; and those intended in the latter, Abdallah, surnamed Dhû'lbajâd n, and his people. (Al Beidâwi.)

[6] The Mohâjerîn, or *refugees*, were those of Mecca, who fled thence on account of their religion ; and the Ansârs, or *helpers*, were those of Medina, who received Mohammed and his followers into their protection, and assisted them against their enemies. By the leaders of the Mohâjerîn are meant those who believed on Mohammed before the Hejra, or early enough to pray towards Jerusalem, from whi h the Keblah was changed to the temple of Mecca in the second year of the Hejra, or else such of them as were present at the battle of Bedr. The leaders of the Ansârs were those who took the oath of fidelity to him at Al Akaba, either the first or the second time. (Al Beidâwi.)

[7] *i.e.*, In the neighbourhood of Medina. These were the tribes of Joheina, Mozeina, Aslam, Ashjâ, and Ghifâr. (Al Beidâwi.)

the inhabitants of Medina *there are some* who are obstinate in hypocrisy. Thou knowest them not, *O prophet, but* we know them : we will surely punish them twice ;[1] afterwards shall they be sent to a grievous torment. And others have acknowledged their crimes.[2] They have mixed a good action with another *which is* bad :[3] peradventure GOD will be turned unto them ; for GOD *is* gracious *and* merciful. Take alms of their substance, that thou mayest cleanse them and purify them thereby ;[4] and pray for them : for thy prayers shall be a security *of mind* unto them ; and GOD *both* heareth *and* knoweth. Do they not know that GOD accepteth repentance from his servants, and accepteth alms ; and that GOD is easy to be reconciled *and* merciful ? Say *unto them*, Work *as ye will* ; but GOD will behold your work, and his apostle *also*, and the true believers : and ye shall be brought before him who knoweth that which is kept secret, and that which is made public ; and he will declare unto you whatever ye have done. And *there are* others *who* wait with suspense the decree of GOD ; whether he will punish them, or whether he will be turned unto them :[5] but GOD *is* knowing *and* wise. *There are some* who have built a temple to hurt *the faithful* and to *propagate* infidelity, and to *foment* division among the true believers,[6] and for a lurking-place for him who hath

[1] Either by exposing them to public shame, and putting them to death ; or by either of those punishments and the torment of the sepulchre : or else by exacting alms of them by way of fine, and giving them corporal punishment. (Al Beidâwi.)

[2] Making no hypocritical excuses for them. These were certain men, who, having stayed at home instead of accompanying Mohammed to Tabûc, as soon as they heard the severe reprehensions and threats of this chapter against those who had stayed behind, bound themselves to the pillars of the mosque, and swore that they would not loose themselves till they were loosed by the prophet. But when he entered the mosque to pray, and was informed of the matter, he also swore that he would not loose them without a particular command from GOD ; whereupon this passage was revealed, and they were accordingly dismissed. (Al Beidâwi.)

[3] Though they were backward in going to war, and held with the hypocrites, yet then confessed their crime and repented.

[4] When these persons were loosed, they prayed Mohammed to take their substance, for the sake of which they had stayed at home, as alms, to cleanse them from their transgression ; but he told them he had no orders to accept anything from them ; upon which this verse was sent down, allowing him to take their alms. (Al Beidâwi.)

[5] The persons here intended were the three Ansârs whose pardon is granted a little below.

[6] When the Banu Amru Ebn Awf had built the temple or mosque of Kobâ, which will be mentioned by-and-bye, they asked Mohammed to come and pray in it, and he complied with their request. This exciting the envy of their brethren, the Banu Ganem Ebn Awf, they also built a mosque, intending that the Imâm or priest who should officiate there should be Abu Amer, a Christian monk ; but he dying in Syria, they came to Mohammed and desired he would consecrate, as it were, their mosque by praying in it.

fought against GOD and his apostle in time past ;[1] and they swear, *saying,* Verily we intended no other than *to do* for the best : but GOD is witness that they do certainly lie. Stand not *up to pray* therein for ever. *There is* a temple founded on piety,[2] from the first day *of its building. It is* more just that thou stand *up to pray* therein : therein *are* men who love to be purified ;[3] for GOD loveth the clean. Whether therefore is he better, who hath founded his building on the fear of GOD, and *his* goodwill ; or he who hath founded his building on the brink of a bank of earth which is washed away by waters, so that it falleth with him into the fire of hell ? GOD directeth not the ungodly people. Their building which they have built will not cease *to be an occasion of* doubting in their hearts, until their hearts be cut in pieces ;[4]

The prophet accordingly prepared himself to go with them, but was forbidden by the immediate revelation of this passage, discovering their hypocrisy and ill design ; whereupon he sent Malec Ebn al Dokhshom, Maan Ebn Addi, Amer Ebn al Sacan, and Al Wahsha, the Ethiopian, to demolish and burn it, which they performed, and made it a dunghill. According to another account, this mosque was built a little before the expedition of Tabûc, with a design to hinder Mohammed's men from engaging therein ; and when he was asked to pray there, he answered that he was just setting out on a journey, but that when he came back, with GOD's leave, he would do what they desired ; but when they applied to him again, on his return, this passage was revealed. (Al Beidâwi, Jallalo'ddin.)

[1] That is, Abu Amer, the monk, who was a declared enemy to Mohammed, having threatened him at Ohod, that no party should appear in the field against him, but he would make one of them ; and, to be as good as his word, he continued to oppose him till the battle of Honein, at which he was present, and being put to flight with those of Hawâzen, he retreated into Syria, designing to obtain a supply of troops from the Greek emperor to renew the war, but he died at Kinnisrîn. Others say that this monk was a confederate at the war of the ditch, and that he fled thence into Syria. (Al Beidâwi.)

[2] viz., That of Kobâ, a place about two miles from Medina, where Mohammed rested four days before he entered that city, in his flight from Mecca, and where he laid the foundation of a mosque (Al Beidâwi, Ebn Shohnah. Abulfed. Vit. Moh. p. 52. Where the translator, taking this passage of the Korân, which is there cited, for the words of his author, has missed the true sense), which was afterwards built by the Banu Amru Ebn Awf. But according to a different tradition, the mosque here meant was that which Mohammed built at Medina.

[3] Al Beidâwi says, that Mohammed walking once with the Mohâjerîn to Kobâ, found the Ansârs sitting at the mosque door, and asked them whether they were believers ; and, on their being silent, repeated the question : whereupon Omar answered, that they were believers ; and Mohammed demanding whether they acquiesced in the judgment Omar had made of them, they said yes. He then asked them whether they would be patient in adversity and thankful in prosperity ; to which they answering in the affirmative, he swore by the LORD of the Caaba that they were true believers. Afterwards he examined them as to their manner of performing the legal washings, and, particularly, what they did after easing themselves ; they told him that in such a case they used three stones, and after that washed with water : upon which he repeated these words of the Korân to them.

[4] Some interpret these words of their being deprived of their judgment and understanding ; and others of the punishment they are to expect, either of death in this world, or of the rack of the sepulchre, or the pains of hell.

and GOD *is* knowing *and* wise. Verily GOD hath purchased of the true believers their souls and their substance, *promising* them the enjoyment of paradise ; *on condition that* they fight for the cause of GOD : whether they slay or be slain, the promise for the same is assuredly due by the law, and the gospel, and the Korân. And who performeth his contract more faithfully than GOD ? Rejoice therefore in the contract which ye have made. This shall be great happiness. The penitent, *and* those who serve GOD, and praise *him, and* who fast, and bow down, and worship ; *and* who command that which is just, and forbid that which is evil, and keep the ordinances of GOD, *shall likewise be rewarded with paradise* : wherefore bear good tidings unto the faithful. It is not *allowed* unto the prophet, nor those who are true believers, that they pray for idolaters,[1] although they be of kin, after it is become known unto them, that they are inhabitants of hell.[2] Neither did Abraham ask forgiveness for his father, otherwise than in pursuance of a promise which he had promised unto him :[3] but when it became known unto him, that he was an enemy unto GOD, he declared himself clear of him.[4] Verily Abraham was pitiful and compassionate. Nor is GOD *disposed* to lead people into error,[5] after that he hath directed them, until that which they ought to avoid is become known unto them ; for GOD knoweth all things. Verily unto GOD *belongeth* the kingdom of heaven and of earth ; he giveth life, and he causeth to die ; and ye have no patron or helper besides GOD. GOD is reconciled unto the prophet,

---

[1] This passage was revealed, as some think, on account of Abu Taleb, Mohammed's uncle and great benefactor ; who, on his death-bed, being pressed by his nephew to speak a word which might enable him to plead his cause before GOD, that is, to profess Islâm, absolutely refused. Mohammed, however, told him that he would not cease to pray for him, till he should be forbidden by GOD ; which he was by these words. Others suppose the occasion to have been Mohammed's visiting his mother Amena's sepulchre at Al Abwâ, soon after the taking of Mecca ; for they say that while he stood at the tomb he burst into tears, and said, *I asked leave of GOD to visit my mother's tomb, and he granted it me* ; *but when I asked leave to pray for her, it was denied me.* (Al Beidâwi.)

[2] By their dying infidels. For otherwise it is not only lawful, but commendable, to pray for unbelievers, while there are hopes of their conversion.

[3] viz., To pray that GOD would dispose his heart to repentance. Some suppose this was a promise made to Abraham by his father, that he would believe in GOD. For the words may be taken either way.

[4] Desisting to pray for him, when he was assured by inspiration that he was not to be converted ; or after he actually died an infidel.

[5] *i.e.*, To consider or punish them as transgressors. This passage was revealed to excuse those who had prayed for such of their friends as had died idolaters, before it was forbidden; or else to excuse certain people who had ignorantly prayed towards the first Keblah, and drunk wine, &c.

and unto the Mohâjerîn, and the Ansârs,[1] who followed him in the hour of distress,[2] after that it had wanted little but that the hearts of a part of them had swerved *from their duty* : afterwards was he turned unto them : for he *was* compassionate *and* merciful towards them. And *he is* also *reconciled* unto the three who were left behind,[3] so that the earth became too strait for them, notwithstanding its spaciousness, and their souls became straitened within them, and they considered that there was no refuge from GOD, otherwise than *by having recourse* unto him. Then was he turned unto them, that they might repent ; for GOD *is* easy to be reconciled *and* merciful. O true believers, fear GOD, and be with the sincere. There was no *reason* why the inhabitants of Medina, and the Arabs of the desert who dwell around them, should stay behind the apostle of GOD, or should prefer themselves before him.[4] This *is unreasonable* : because they are not distressed either by thirst, or labour, or hunger, for the defence of GOD's true religion ; neither do they stir a step, which may irritate the unbelievers ; neither do they receive from the enemy any damage, but a good work is written down unto them for the same ; for GOD suffereth not the reward of the righteous to perish. And they contribute not any sum either small or great, nor do they pass a valley, but it is written down unto them that GOD may reward them

---

[1] Having forgiven the crime they committed, in giving the hypocrites leave to be absent from the expedition to Tabûc ; or for the other sins which they might, through inadvertence, have been guilty of. For the best men have need of repentance. (Al Beidâwi.)

[2] viz., In the expedition of Tabûc ; wherein Mohammed's men were driven to such extremities that (besides what they endured by reason of the excessive heat) ten men were obliged to ride by turns on one camel, and provisions and water were so scarce that two men divided a date between them, and they were obliged to drink the water out of the camels' stomachs. (Al Beidâwi.)

[3] Or, as it may be translated, *who were left in suspense*, whether they should be pardoned or not. These were three Ansârs, named Caab Ebn Malec. Helâl Ebn Omeyya, and Merâra Ebn Rabî, who went not with Mohammed to Tabûc, and were therefore, on his return, secluded from the fellowship of the other Moslems ; the prophet forbidding any to salute them, or to hold discourse with them. Under which interdiction they continued fifty days, till, on their sincere repentance, they were at length discharged from it, by the revelation of this passage. (Al Beidâwi, Jallalo'ddin, Abulf. Vit. Moh. p. 133, 126.)

[4] By not caring to share with him the dangers and fatigues of war. Al Beidâwi tells us, that after Mohammed had set out for Tabûc, one Abu Khaithama, sitting in his garden, where his wife, a very beautiful woman, had spread a mat for him in the shade, and had set new dates and fresh water before him, after a little reflection, cried out : *This is not well that I should thus take my ease and pleasure, while the apostle of GOD is exposed to the scorching of the sunbeams and the inclemencies of the air* ; and immediately mounting his camel, took his sword and lance, and went to join the army.

with a recompence exceeding that which they have wrought.
The believers are not *obliged* to go forth *to war* all together :
if a part of every band of them go not forth, *it is* that they
may diligently instruct themselves in *their* religion ;[1] and
may admonish their people, when they return unto them,
that they may take heed to themselves. O true believers,
wage war against such of the infidels as are near you ;[2] and let
them find severity[3] in you : and know that GOD is with those
who fear *him*. Whenever a Sura is sent down, there are
some of them who say, Which of you hath this caused to
increase in faith ? It will increase the faith of those who
believe, and they shall rejoice : but unto those in whose
hearts there is an infirmity, it will add *farther* doubt unto
their *present* doubt ; and they shall die in their infidelity.
Do they not see that they are tried every year once or twice ?[4]
yet they repent not, neither are they warned. And whenever a Sura is sent down, they look at one another, *saying*,
Doth anyone see you ?[5] then do they turn aside. GOD
shall turn aside their hearts *from the truth* ; because they are
a people who do not understand. Now hath an apostle come
unto you of our own nation,[6] an excellent *person* : it is
grievous unto him that ye commit wickedness ; *he is* careful
over you, *and* compassionate and merciful towards the
believers. If they turn back, say, GOD is my support :
there is no GOD but he. On him do I trust ; and he is the
LORD of the magnificent throne.

[1] That is, if some of every tribe or town be left behind, the end of their
being so left is that they may apply themselves to study and attain a more
exact knowledge of the several points of their religion, so as to be able to
instruct such as, by reason of their continual employment in the wars,
have no other means of information. They say, that after the preceding
passages were revealed, reprehending those who had stayed at home during
the expedition of Tabûc, every man went to war, so that the study of religion,
which is rather more necessary for the defence and propagation of the faith
than even arms themselves, became wholly laid aside and neglected ; to
prevent which, for the future, a convenient number are hereby directed to be
left behind, that they may have leisure to prosecute their studies.

[2] Either of your kindred or neighbours ; for these claim your pity and care
in the first place, and their conversion ought first to be endeavoured. The
persons particularly meant in this passage are supposed to have been the
Jews of the tribes of Koreidha and Nadhîr, and those of Khaibar ; or else
the Greeks of Syria. (Al Beidâwi.)

[3] Or fierceness in war.

[4] *i.e.*, By various kinds of trials, or by being called forth to war, and by
being made witnesses of GOD's miraculous protection of the faithful.

[5] They wink at one another to rise and leave the prophet's presence,
if they think they can do it without being observed, to avoid hearing
the severe and deserving reproofs which they apprehended in every new
revelation. The persons intended are the hypocritical Moslems.

[6] See Chap. III.

X

THE CHAPTER OF JONAS

Revealed at Mecca.

IN THE NAME OF THE MOST MERCIFUL GOD.

A L. R.[2] These are the signs of the wise book. Is it a strange thing unto the men *of Mecca*, that we have revealed *our will* unto a man from among them,[3] *saying*, Denounce threats unto men *if they believe not*; and bear good tidings unto those who believe, that on the merit of their sincerity they have an interest with their LORD ? The unbelievers say, this is manifest sorcery.[4] Verily your LORD is GOD, who hath created the heavens and the earth in six days ; and then ascended *his* throne, to take on himself the government of *all* things. There is no intercessor, but by his permission.[5] This is GOD, your LORD; therefore serve him. Will ye not consider ? Unto him shall ye all return, *according to* the certain promise of GOD ; for he produceth a creature, and then causeth it to return again ; that he may reward those who believe and do that which is right, with equity. But as for the unbelievers, they shall drink boiling water, and *they shall suffer* a grievous punishment, for that they have disbelieved. It is he who hath ordained the sun to shine *by day*, and the moon for a light *by night* ; and hath appointed her stations, that ye might know the number of years, and the computation *of time*. GOD hath not created this, but with truth. He explaineth *his* signs unto people who understand. Moreover in the vicissitude of night and day, and whatever GOD hath created in heaven and earth, are surely signs unto men who fear *him*. Verily they who hope not to meet us *at the last day*, and delight in this present life, and rest securely in the same, and who are negligent of our signs ; their dwelling shall be *hell* fire, for that which they have deserved. But as to those who

---

[1] This prophet, the Jonah of the Bible, is mentioned towards the end of the chapter.

[2] Sale, Prel., Disc. p. 64.

[3] And not one of the most powerful among them ; so that the Koreish said it was a wonder GOD could find out no other messenger than the orphan pupil of Abu Taleb. (Al Beidâwi.)

[4] Meaning the Korân. According to the reading of some copies, the words may be rendered, *This man (i.e.* Mohammed) *is no other than a manifest sorcerer.*

[5] These words were revealed to refute the foolish opinion of the idolatrous Meccans, who imagined their idols were intercessors with GOD for them.

believe, and work righteousness, their LORD will direct them because of their faith ; they shall have rivers flowing through gardens of pleasure. Their prayer therein *shall be*, Praise be unto thee, O GOD ! and their salutation[1] therein *shall be*, Peace ! and the end of their prayer *shall be*, Praise be unto GOD, the LORD of all creatures ! If GOD should cause evil to hasten unto men, according to their desire of hastening good, verily their end had been decreed. Wherefore we suffer those who hope not to meet us *at the resurrection*, to wander amazedly in their error. When evil befalleth a man ; he prayeth unto us *lying* on his side, or sitting, or standing :[2] but when we deliver him from his affliction, he continueth *his former course of life*, as though he had not called upon us *to defend him* against the evil which had befallen him. Thus was that which the transgressors committed prepared for them. We have formerly destroyed the generations *who were* before you, *O men of Mecca*, when they had acted unjustly, and our apostles had come unto them with evident *miracles*, and they would not believe. Thus do we reward the wicked people. Afterwards did we cause you to succeed them in the earth ; that we might see how ye would act. When our evident signs are recited unto them, they who hope not to meet us *at the resurrection*, say, Bring a different Korân from this ; or make some change therein. Answer, It is not *fit* for me, that I should change it at my pleasure : I follow that only which is revealed unto me. Verily I fear, if I should be disobedient unto my LORD, the punishment of the great day. Say, If GOD had so pleased, I had not read it unto you, neither had I taught you the same. I have already dwelt among you to the age *of forty years*,[3] before *I received* it. Do ye not therefore understand ? And who is more unjust than he who deviseth a lie against GOD, or accuseth his signs of falsehood ? Surely the wicked shall not prosper. They worship besides GOD, that which can neither hurt them nor profit them, and they say, These are

---

[1] Either the mutual salutation of the blessed to one another, or that of the angels to the blessed.

[2] *i.e.*, In all postures, and at all times.

[3] For so old was Mohammed before he took upon him to be a prophet (Sale, Prel. Disc. Sect. II. Abulfeda, Vit. Moh. c. 7); during which time his fellow-citizens well knew that he had not applied himself to learning of any sort, nor frequented learned men, nor had ever exercised himself in composing verses or orations whereby he might acquire the art of rhetoric, or elegance of speech. (Sale, Prel. Disc. Sect. I.) A flagrant proof, says Al Beidâwi, that this book could be taught him by none but GOD.

our intercessors with GOD.[1]   Answer, Will ye tell GOD that
which he knoweth not, neither in heaven nor in earth?[2]
Praise be unto him! and far be that from him, which they
associate *with him*! Men were professors of one religion
only,[3] but they dissented *therefrom*; and if a decree had not
previously issued from thy LORD, *deferring their punishment*,
verily the *matter* had been decided between them, concerning which they disagreed. They say, Unless a sign be sent
down unto him from his LORD, *we will not believe.* Answer,
Verily that which is hidden *is known* only unto GOD: wait
therefore *the pleasure of God*; and I also will wait with you.
And when we caused the men *of Mecca* to taste mercy, after
an affliction which had befallen them, behold, they *devised*
a stratagem against our signs.[4] Say *unto them*, GOD is more
swift in *executing* a stratagem *than ye.* Verily our messengers[5] write down that which ye deceitfully devise. It is he
who hath given you conveniences for travelling by land and
by sea; so that ye be in ships, which sail with them with a
favourable wind, and they rejoice therein. *And when* a tempestuous wind overtaketh them, and waves come upon them
from every side, and they think themselves to be encompassed *with inevitable dangers*; they call upon GOD, exhibiting the pure religion unto him,[6] *and saying*, Verily, if thou
deliver us from this *peril*, we will be of those who give thanks.
But when he hath delivered them, behold, they behave
themselves insolently in the earth, without justice. O men,
Verily the violence which ye commit against your own souls,
is for the enjoyment of this present life only; afterwards unto
us shall ye return, and we will declare unto you that which ye
have done. Verily the likeness of this present life is no other
than as water, which we send down from heaven, and wherewith the productions of the earth are mixed, of which men

---

[1] Sale, Prel. Disc. Sect. I.

[2] viz., That he hath equals or companions either in heaven or on earth;
since he acknowledgeth none.

[3] That is to say, the true religion, or Islâm, which was generally professed,
as some say, till Abel was murdered, or, as others, till the days of Noah.
Some suppose the first ages after the Flood are here intended: others,
the state of religion in Arabia, from the time of Abraham to that of Amru Ebn
Lohai, the great introducer of idolatry into that country.

[4] For it is said that they were afflicted with a dearth for seven years, so
that they were very near perishing; but no sooner relieved by GOD's sending
them plenty, than they began again to charge Mohammed with imposture,
and to ridicule his revelations. (Al Beidâwi.)

[5] *i.e.*, The guardian angels.

[6] That is, applying themselves to GOD only, and neglecting their idols;
their fears directing them in such an extremity to ask help of him only who
could give it.

eat, and cattle *also*, until the earth receive its vesture, and be adorned *with various plants* : the inhabitants thereof imagine that they have power over the same ; *but* our command cometh unto it by night or by day, and we render it *as though it had been* mown, as though it had not yesterday abounded *with fruits*. Thus do we explain *our* signs unto people who consider. GOD inviteth unto the dwelling of peace,[1] and directeth whom he pleaseth into the right way. They who do right shall *receive* a most excellent *reward*, and a super-abundant addition ;[2] neither blackness[3] nor shame shall cover their faces. These *shall be* the inhabitants of paradise ; they shall continue therein *for ever*. But they who commit evil *shall* receive the reward of evil, equal thereunto,[4] and they shall be covered with shame (for they shall have no protector against GOD) ; as though their faces were covered with the profound darkness of the night. These shall be the inhabitants of *hell* fire ; they shall remain therein *for ever*. On the day *of the resurrection* we will gather them all together ; then will we say unto the idolaters, *Get ye* to your place, ye and your companions : [5]and we will separate them from one another ; and their companions shall say *unto them*, Ye did not worship us ;[6] and GOD is a sufficient witness between us and you ; neither did we mind your worshipping *of us*. There shall every soul experience[7] that which it shall have sent before it ;[8] and they shall be brought before GOD, their true LORD ; and the *false deities* which they vainly imagined, shall disappear from before them. Say, Who provideth you food from heaven and earth ; or who hath the absolute power over the hearing and the sight ? and who bringeth forth the living from the dead, and bringeth

---

[1] viz., Paradise.

[2] For their reward will vastly exceed he merit of their good works. Al Ghazâli supposes this *additional recompence* will be the beatific vision. (Sale, Prel. Disc. Sect. IV. p. 107.)

[3] Sale, Prel. Disc. Sect. IV. p. 93.

[4] *i.e.*, Though the blessed will be rewarded beyond their deserts, yet GOD will not punish any beyond their demerits, but treat them with the exactest justice.

[5] That is, your idols, or the companions which ye attributed unto GOD.

[6] But ye really worshipped your own lusts, and were seduced to idolatry, not by us, but by your own superstitious fancies. It is pretended that GOD will, at the last day, enable the idols to speak, and that they will thus reproach their worshippers, instead of interceding for them, as they hoped. Some suppose the angels, who were also objects of the worship of the pagan Arabs, are particularly intended in this place.

[7] Some copies instead of *tablu*, read *tatiu*, *i.e.*, *shall follow*, or *meditate upon*.

[8] See Chap. II. p. 15.

forth the dead from the living ? and who governeth *all* things? They will surely answer, GOD. Say, Will ye not therefore fear *him* ? This is therefore GOD, your true LORD : and what *remaineth there* after truth, except error ? How therefore are ye turned aside *from the truth* ? Thus is the word of thy LORD verified upon them who do wickedly ; that they believe not. Say, Is there any of your companions who produceth a creature, and then causeth it to return *unto himself* ? Say, GOD produceth a creature, and then causeth it to return *unto himself*. How therefore are ye turned aside *from his worship* ? Say, Are there any of your companions who directeth unto the truth ? Say, GOD directeth unto the truth. Whether is he therefore, who directeth unto the truth, more worthy to be followed ; or he who directeth not, unless he be directed ? What aileth you, therefore, that ye judge as ye do ? And the greater part of them follow an *uncertain* opinion only ; but a *mere* opinion attaineth not unto any truth. Verily GOD knoweth that which they do. This Korân could not have been composed by *any* except GOD ; but *it is* a confirmation of that which was *revealed* before it, and an explanation of the scripture ; there is no doubt thereof ; *sent down* from the LORD of all creatures. Will they say, *Mohammed* hath forged it ? Answer, Bring therefore a chapter like unto it ; and call whom ye may *to your assistance*, besides GOD, if ye speak truth. But they have charged that with falsehood, the knowledge whereof they do not comprehend, neither hath the interpretation thereof come unto them. In the same manner did those who were before them, accuse *their prophets* of imposture ; but behold what was the end of the unjust. There are some of them who believe therein ; and there are some of them who believe not therein :[1] and thy LORD well knoweth the corrupt doers. If they accuse thee of imposture, say, I have my work, and ye have your work ; ye shall be clear of that which I do, and I will be clear of that which ye do. There are some of them who hearken unto thee ; but wilt thou make the deaf to hear, although they do not understand ? And there are some of them who look at thee ; but

---

[1] *i.e.*, There are some of them who are inwardly well satisfied of the truth of thy doctrine, though they are so wicked as to oppose it ; and there are others of them who believe it not, through prejudice and want of consideration. Or the passage may be understood in the future tense, of some who should afterwards believe, and repent, and of others who should die infidels. (Al Beidâwi.)

wilt thou direct the blind, although they see not ?[1]   Verily
GOD will not deal unjustly with men in any respect : but
men deal unjustly with their own souls.[2]   On a certain day
he will gather them together, as though they had not
tarried[3] above an hour of a day : they shall know one
another.[4]   Then shall they perish who have denied the
meeting of GOD, and were not *rightly* directed.   Whether
we cause thee to see a part of *the punishment* wherewith we
have threatened them, or whether we cause thee to die *before
thou seest it* ; unto us shall they return : then *shall* GOD *be*
witness of that which they do.   Unto every nation *hath*
an apostle *been sent* : and when their apostle came, *the matter*
was decided between them with equity ;[5] and they were not
treated unjustly.   The *unbelievers* say, When *will* this
threatening *be made good*, if ye speak truth ?   Answer, I am
able neither to procure advantage unto myself, nor to avert
mischief *from me*, but as GOD pleaseth.   Unto every nation is
a fixed term *decreed* ; when their term therefore is expired,
they shall not have respite for an hour, neither shall *their
punishment* be anticipated.   Say, Tell me ; if the punishment of GOD overtake you by night, or by day, what *part*
thereof will the ungodly wish to be hastened ?   When it
falleth *on you*, do ye then believe it ?   Now *do ye believe, and
wish it far from you*, when as ye formerly desired it should be
hastened ?   Then shall it be said unto the wicked, Taste ye
the punishment of eternity : would ye receive *other* than the
reward of that which ye have wrought ?   They will desire
to know of thee whether this be true.   Answer, Yea, by my
LORD, it is certainly true ; neither shall ye weaken *God's
power, so as to escape it*.   Verily, if every soul which hath
acted wickedly had whatever is on the earth, it would *willingly*
redeem itself therewith *at the last day*.   Yet they will conceal
their repentance,[6] after they shall have seen the punish-

---

[1] These words were revealed on account of certain Meccans, who seemed
to attend while Mohammed read the Korân to them, or instructed them in any
point of religion, but yet were as far from being convinced or edified, as
if they had not heard him at all. (Al Beidâwi. See Chap. VI.)

[2] For GOD deprives them not of their senses or understanding ; but
they corrupt and make an ill use of them.

[3] Either in the world or in the grave.

[4] As if it were but a little while since they parted.   But this will happen
during the first moments only of the resurrection ; for afterwards the
terror of the day will disturb and take from them all knowledge of one
another. (Al Beidâwi.)

[5] By delivering the prophet and those who believed on him, and destroying the obstinate infidels.

[6] To hide their shame and regret (Jallalo'ddin), or because their sur-

ment : and *the matter* shall be decided between them with
equity ; and they shall not be unjustly treated. Doth not
whatsoever is in heaven and on earth *belong* unto GOD ? Is
not the promise of GOD true ? But the greater part of them
know *it* not. He giveth life, and he causeth to die ; and
unto him shall ye *all* return. O men, now hath an admonition come unto you from your LORD, and a remedy for the
doubts which are in *your* breasts ; and a direction, and mercy
unto the true believers. Say, Through the grace of GOD, and
his mercy : therein therefore let them rejoice ; this will be
better than what they heap together *of worldly riches*. Say,
Tell me ; of that which GOD hath sent down unto you for
food, have ye declared *part to be* lawful, and *other part to be*
unlawful ? Say, Hath GOD permitted you *to make this
distinction* ? or do ye devise *a lie* concerning GOD ? But
what will be the opinion of those who devise a lie concerning
GOD, on the day of the resurrection ? Verily GOD is endued
with beneficence towards mankind ; but the greater part of
them do not give thanks. Thou shalt be *engaged* in no business, neither shalt thou be *employed* in meditating on *any
passage* of the Korân ; nor shall ye do any action, but we
will be witnesses over you, when ye are employed therein.
Nor is so much as the weight of an ant hidden from thy LORD,
in earth or in heaven : neither *is there anything* lesser than
that, or greater, but it is *written* in the perspicuous book.[1] Are
not the friends of GOD *the persons*, on whom no fear shall come,
and who shall not be grieved ? They who believe and fear
GOD, shall receive good tidings in this life and in that which
is to come. There is no change in the words of GOD. This
shall be great felicity. Let not their discourse[2] grieve thee ;
for all might *belongeth* unto GOD : he *both* heareth *and* knoweth. Is not whoever *dwelleth* in heaven and on earth, *subject*
unto GOD ? What therefore do they follow, who invoke
idols, besides GOD ? They follow nothing but a *vain* opinion ; and they only utter lies. It is he who hath ordained the
night for you, that ye may take your rest therein, and the
clear day *for labour* : verily herein are signs unto people who
hearken. They say, GOD hath begotten children : GOD
forbid ! He is self-sufficient. Unto him *belongeth* whatsoever

---

prise and astonishment will deprive them of the use of speech. (Al Beidâwi.)
Some, however, understand the verb which is here rendered *will conceal*,
in the contrary signification, which it sometimes bears ; and then it must
be translated—*They will openly declare their repentance*, &c.

[1] The preserved table, wherein GOD's decrees are recorded.
[2] The impious and rebellious talk of the infidels.

is in heaven and on earth : ye have no demonstrative proof of this. Do ye speak of GOD that which ye know not ? Say, Verily they who imagine a lie concerning GOD, shall not prosper. *They may enjoy* a provision in this world ; *but* afterwards unto us shall they return, and we will then cause them to taste a grievous punishment for that they were unbelievers. Rehearse unto them the history of Noah : when he said unto his people, O my people, if my standing forth *among you*, and my warning *you* of the signs of GOD, be grievous unto you ; in GOD do I put my trust. Therefore lay your design *against me*, and assemble your false gods ; but let not your design be *carried on* by you *in* the dark : then come forth against me, and delay not. And if ye turn aside *from my admonitions*, I ask not any reward of you *for the same ;*[1] I expect my reward from GOD alone, and I am commanded to be *one* of those who are resigned *unto him*. But they accused him of imposture ; wherefore we delivered him, and those who *were* with him in the ark, and we caused them to survive *the flood*, but we drowned those who charged our signs with falsehood. Behold, therefore, what was the end of those who were warned *by Noah*. Then did we send, after him, apostles unto their *respective* people,[2] and they came unto them with evident demonstrations : yet they were not *disposed* to believe in that which they had before rejected as false. Thus do we seal up the hearts of the transgressors. Then did we send, after them, Moses and Aaron unto Pharaoh and his princes with our signs :[3] but they behaved proudly, and were a wicked people. And when the truth from us had come unto them, they said, Verily this is manifest sorcery. Moses said *unto them*, Do ye speak *this* of the truth, after it hath come unto you ? Is this sorcery ? but sorcerers shall not prosper. They said, Art thou come unto us to turn us aside from that *religion* which we found our fathers practised ; and that ye two may have the command in the land ? But we do not believe you. And Pharaoh said, Bring unto me every expert magician. And when the magicians were come, Moses said unto them, Cast down that which ye are about to cast down. And when they had cast down *their rods and cords*, Moses said *unto them*, The enchantment which ye have performed, shall GOD surely render vain ;

[1] Therefore ye cannot excuse yourselves by saying that I am burdensome to you.

[2] As Hûd, Sâleh, Abraham, Lot, and Shoaib, to those of Ad, Thamûd, Babel, Sodom, and Midian.

[3] See Chap. VII.

for GOD prospereth not the work of the wicked doers. And
GOD will verify the truth of his words, although the wicked
be averse *thereto*. And there believed not *any* on Moses, except
a generation of his people,[1] for fear of Pharaoh and of his
princes, lest he should afflict them. And Pharaoh was lifted
up with pride in the earth, and was surely *one* of the transgressors. And Moses said, O my people, if ye believe in
GOD, put your trust in him, if ye be resigned *to his will*. They
answered, We put our trust in GOD : O LORD, suffer us not
to be afflicted by unjust people ; but deliver us, through thy
mercy, from the unbelieving people. And we spake by inspiration unto Moses and his brother, *saying*, Provide habitations for your people in Egypt, and make your houses a place
of worship,[2] and be constant at prayer ; and bear good news
unto the true believers. And Moses said, O LORD, verily
thou hast given unto Pharaoh and his people *pompous* ornaments,[3] and riches in this present life, O LORD, that they
may be seduced from thy way ; O LORD, bring their riches
to nought, and harden their hearts ; that they may not
believe, until they see *their* grievous punishment. *God* said,
Your petition is heard :[4] be ye upright therefore,[5] and follow
not in the way of those who are ignorant. And we caused
the children of Israel to pass through the sea ; and Pharaoh
and his army followed them in a violent and hostile manner ;
until, when he was drowning, he said, I believe that there is no
GOD but he on whom the children of Israel believe ; and I
am *one* of the resigned.[6] Now *dost thou believe* ; when thou

[1] For when he first began to preach, a few of the younger Israelites only
believed on him ; the others not giving ear to him, for fear of the king.
But some suppose the pronoun *his* refers to Pharaoh, and that these were
certain Egyptians, who, together with his wife Asia, believed on Moses.
(Al Beidâwi.)

[2] So Jallalo'ddin expounds the original word Keblah, which properly
signifies that place or quarter towards which one prays. Wherefore Al
Zamakhshari supposes that the Israelites are here ordered to dispose their
oratories in such a manner that, when they prayed, their faces mighܱ be turned
towards Mecca ; which he imagines was the Keblah of Moses, as it is that of
the Mohammedans. The former commentator adds that Pharaoh had
forbidden the Israelites to pray to GOD ; for which reason they were obliged
to perform that duty privately in their houses.

[3] As magnificent apparel, chariots, and the like.

[4] The pronoun is in the dual number ; the antecedent being Moses and
Aaron. The commentators say that, in consequence of this prayer, all the
treasures of Egypt were turned into stones. (Jallalo'ddin.)

[5] Or, as Al Beidâwi interprets it, Be ye constant and steady in preaching to the people. The Mohammedans pretend that Moses continued in
Egypt no less than forty years after he had first published his mission :
which cannot be reconciled to Scripture.

[6] These words, it is said, Pharaoh repeated often in his extremity, that
he might be heard. But his repentance came too late ; for Gabriel soon

hast been hitherto rebellious, and one of the wicked doers ?
This day will we raise thy body[1] *from the bottom of the sea*,
that thou mayest be a sign unto those who shall be after
thee ; and verily a great number of men are negligent of our
signs. And we prepared for the children of Israel an established dwelling *in the land of Canaan*, and we provided good
things for their sustenance : and they differed not *in point
of religion*, until knowledge had come unto them ;[2] verily
thy LORD will judge between them on the day of resurrection, concerning that wherein they disagreed. If thou art
in a doubt concerning *any part of* that which we have sent
down unto thee,[3] ask them who have read the book *of the
law* before thee. Now hath the truth come unto thee from
thy LORD ; be not, therefore *one* of those who doubt : neither
be thou *one* of those who charge the signs of GOD with falsehood, lest thou become *one* of those who perish. Verily
those against whom the word of thy LORD is decreed, shall
not believe, although there come unto them every *kind of*
miracle ; until they see the grievous punishment *prepared
for them*. And if *it were* not *so*, some city, *among the many
which have been destroyed*, would have believed ; and the faith
of its *inhabitants* would have been of advantage unto them :
but none of them believed before the execution of their sentence,
except the people of Jonas.[4] When they believed, we

stopped his mouth with mud, lest he should obtain mercy ; reproaching him
at the same time in the words which follow.

[1] Some of the children of Israel doubting whether Pharaoh was really
drowned, Gabriel, by GOD's command, caused his naked corpse to swim to
shore, that they might see it (Exod. xiv. 30). The word here translated
body, signifying also a *coat of mail*, some imagine the meaning to be, that his
corpse floated armed with his coat of mail, which they tell us was of gold,
by which they knew that it was he.

[2] *i.e.*, After the law had been revealed, and published by Moses.

[3] That is, concerning the truth of the histories which are here related.
The commentators doubt whether the person here spoken to be Mohammed
himself or his auditor.

[4] viz., The inhabitants of Ninive, which stood on or near the place where Al
Mawsel now stands. This people having corrupted themselves with idolatry,
Jonas the son of Mattai (or Amittai, which the Mohammedans suppose to be
the name of his mother), an Israelite of the tribe of Benjamin, was sent by
GOD to preach to and reclaim them. When the first began to exhort them
to repentance, instead of hearkening to him, they uśed him very ill, so that he
was obliged to leave the city ; threatening them, at his departure, that they
should be destroyed within three days, or, as others say, within forty (Jonah
iii. 4). But when the time drew near, and they saw the heavens overcast
with a black cloud, which shot forth fire, and filled the air with smoke, and
hung directly over their city, they were in a terrible consternation, and
getting into the fields with their families and cattle, they put on sackcloth,
and humbled themselves before GOD, calling aloud for pardon, and sincerely
repenting of their past wickedness. Whereupon GOD was pleased to forgive
them, and the storm blew over. (Al Beidâwi, Jallalo'ddin, Abulfeda.
Chap. XXI. and XXXVII.)

delivered them from the punishment of shame in this world, and suffered them to enjoy *their lives and possessions* for a time.[1] But if thy LORD had pleased, verily all who are in the earth would have believed in general. Wilt thou therefore forcibly compel men to be true believers ? No soul can believe but by the permission of GOD : and he shall pour out *his* indignation on those who will not understand. Say, Consider whatever is in heaven and on earth : but signs are of no avail, neither preachers, unto people who will not believe. Do they therefore expect any other than *some terrible judgment*, like unto the judgments *which have fallen* on those who have gone before them ? Say, Wait ye *the issue* ; and I also will wait with you : then will we deliver our apostles and those who believe. Thus is it a justice due from us, that we should deliver the true believers. Say, O men *of Mecca*, if ye be in doubt concerning my religion, verily I worship not the *idols* which ye worship, besides GOD ; but I worship GOD, who will cause you to die : and I am commanded to be *one* of the true believers. And *it was said unto me*, Set thy face towards the *true* religion, *and be* orthodox ; and by no means be *one* of those who attribute companions *unto* GOD ; neither invoke, besides GOD, that which can neither profit thee nor hurt thee : for if thou do, thou *wilt* then certainly *become one* of the unjust. If GOD afflict thee with hurt, there is none who can relieve thee from it, except he ; and if he willeth thee any good, there is none who can keep back his bounty : he will confer it on such of his servants as he pleaseth ; and he *is* gracious *and* merciful. Say, O men, now hath the truth come unto you from your LORD. He therefore who shall be directed, will be directed to *the advantage of* his own soul : but he who shall err, will err only against the same. I am no guardian over you. Do thou, *O prophet*, follow that which is revealed unto thee : and persevere with patience until GOD shall judge ; for he is the best judge.

[1] *i.e.*, Until they died according to the ordinary course of nature.

XI

THE CHAPTER OF HÛD
Revealed at Mecca.

IN THE NAME OF THE MOST MERCIFUL GOD.

A L. R.[2] *This* book, the verses whereof are guarded against corruption,[3] and are also distinctly explained,[4] *is a revelation* from the wise, the knowing *God* : that ye serve not *any other* than GOD (verily I am a denouncer *of threats*, and a bearer of good tidings unto you from him) ; and that ye ask pardon of your LORD, and then be turned unto him. He will cause you to enjoy a plentiful provision, until a prefixed time : and unto every one that hath merit *by good works*, will he give his abundant *reward*. But if ye turn back, verily I fear for you the punishment of the great day : unto GOD shall ye return ; and he is almighty. Do they not double *the folds of* their breasts,[5] that they may conceal *their designs* from him ? When they cover themselves with their garments, doth not he know that which they conceal, and that which they discover ? For he knoweth the innermost parts of the breasts *of men*.[6] (XII.)[7] There is no *creature* which creepeth on the earth, but GOD *provideth* its food ; and he knoweth the place of its retreat, and where it is laid

---

[1] The story of which prophet is repeated in this chapter.

[2] Sale, Prel. Disc. p. 64, and note to Chap II.

[3] According to the various senses which the verb *ohkimat*, in the original, may bear, the commentators suggest as many different interpretations. Some suppose the meaning to be, according to our version, that the Korân is not liable to be corrupted (Sale, Prel. Disc. Sect. IV.), as the law and the gospel have been, in the opinion of the Mohammedans ; others, that every verse in this particular chapter is in full force, and not one of them abrogated ; others, that the verses of the Korân are disposed in a clear and perspicuous method, or contain evident and demonstrative arguments ; and others that they comprise judicial declarations, to regulate both faith and practice.

[4] The signification of the verb *fossilat*, which is here used, being also ambiguous, the meaning of this passage is supposed to be, either that the verses are distinctly proposed or expressed in a clear manner ; or that the subject matter of the whole may be distinguished or divided into laws, monitions, and examples ; or else that the verses were revealed by parcels.

[5] Or, as it may be translated, *Do they not turn away their breasts*, &c.

[6] This passage was occasioned by the words of certain of the idolaters, who said to one another, *When we let down our curtains* (such as the women use in the east to screen themselves from the sight of the men when they happen to be in the room), *and wrap ourselves up in our garments, and fold up our breasts to conceal our malice against Mohammed, how should he come to the knowledge of it* ? Some suppose the passage relates to certain hypocritical Moslems ; but this opinion is generally rejected, because the verse was revealed at Mecca, and the birth of hypocrisy among the Mohammedans happened not till after the Hejra.

[7] Section XII. begins here.

up.[1] The whole *is written* in the perspicuous book *of his decrees*. It is he who hath created the heavens and the earth in six days (but his throne was above the waters *before the creation thereof*),[2] that he might prove you, *and see* which of you would excel in works. If thou say, Ye shall surely be raised again, after death ; the unbelievers will say, This is nothing but manifest sorcery. And verily if we defer their punishment unto a determined season, they will say, What hindereth it *from falling on us* ? Will it not come upon them on a day wherein there shall be none to avert *it* from them ; and that which they scoffed at shall encompass them ? Verily, if we cause man to taste mercy from us, and afterwards take it away from him, he *will* surely *become* desperate,[3] and ungrateful. And if we cause him to taste favour, after an affliction hath befallen him, he will surely say, The evils *which I suffered* are passed from me ; and he *will become* joyful and insolent : except those who persevere with patience, and do that which is right : they shall *receive* pardon and a great reward. Peradventure thou wilt omit *to publish* part of that which hath been revealed unto thee, and thy breast will become straitened, lest they say, Unless a treasure be sent down unto him, or an angel come with him, *to bear witness unto him, we will not believe*. Verily thou art a preacher *only* ; and God is the governor of all things. Will they say, He hath forged *the Korân* ? Answer, Bring therefore ten chapters[4] like unto it, forged *by yourselves* ; and call on whomsoever ye may *to assist you*, except God, if ye speak truth. But if they *whom ye call to your assistance* hear you not, know that *this book* hath been revealed by the knowledge of God only,[5] and that there is no God but he. *Will* ye therefore *become* Moslems ? Whoso chooseth the

---

[1] *i.e.*, Both during its life and after its death ; or the repository of every animal, before its birth, in the loins and wombs of the parents.

[2] For the Mohammedans suppose this throne, and the waters whereon it stands, which waters they imagine are supported by a spirit or wind, were, with some other things, created before the heavens and earth. This fancy they borrowed from the Jews, who also say that the throne of glory then stood in the air, and was borne on the face of the waters, by the breath of God's mouth. (Rashi ad Gen. i. 2. Reland. de Relig. Moh. p. 50, &c.)

[3] Casting aside all hopes of the divine favour, for want of patience and trust in God.

[4] This was the number which he first challenged them to compose ; but they not being able to do it, he made the matter still easier, challenging them to produce a single chapter only (see Chaps. II. and X.), comparable to the Korân in doctrine and eloquence.

[5] Or containing several passages wrapped up in dark and mysterious expressions, which can proceed from and are perfectly comprehended by none but God. (Chap. III.)

present life, and the pomp thereof, unto them will we give *the recompence of* their works therein, and the same shall not be diminished unto them. These are they for whom no *other reward* is *prepared* in the next life, except the fire *of hell* : that which they have done in *this life* shall perish ; and that which they have wrought *shall be* vain. Shall he therefore *be compared with them*, who followeth the evident declaration of his LORD, and whom a witness from him[1] attendeth, preceded by the book of Moses,[2] *which was revealed for a* guide, and *out of* mercy *to mankind* ? These believe in the *Korân* : but whosoever of the confederate *infidels* believeth not therein, is threatened with the fire *of hell, which threat shall certainly be executed* : be not therefore in a doubt concerning it ; for it is the truth from thy LORD : but the greater part of men will not believe. Who is more unjust than he who imagineth a lie concerning GOD ? They shall be set before their LORD, *at the day of judgment*, and the witnesses[3] shall say, These are they who devised lies against their LORD. Shall not the curse of GOD *fall* on the unjust ; who turn *men* aside from the way of GOD, and seek to render it crooked, and who believe not in the life to come ? These were not able to prevail *against God* on earth, *so as to escape punishment* ; neither had they any protectors besides GOD : their punishment shall be doubled unto them.[4] They could not hear, neither did they see. These are they who have lost their souls ; and the *idols* which they falsely imagined have abandoned them. There is no doubt but they shall be most miserable in the world to come. But as for those who believe, and do good works, and humble themselves before their LORD, they shall be the inhabitants of paradise ; they shall remain therein *for ever*. The similitude of the two parties[5] is as the blind and the deaf, and *as* he who seeth *and* heareth : shall they be compared as equal ? Will ye not therefore consider ? We formerly sent Noah[6] unto his people ; *and he said*, Verily I am a public preacher unto you ; that ye worship GOD alone : verily I fear for you the punishment of the terrible day. But the chiefs of his people, who believed not, answered, We see thee *to be* no other than a man, like unto us ; and we do not see that any follow thee, except those who are the most abject among us, *who have believed on thee*

---

[1] The Korân ; or, as others suppose, the angel Gabriel.
[2] Which bears testimony thereto.
[3] That is, the angels, and prophets, and their own members.
[4] For they shall be punished both in this life and in the next.
[5] *i.e.*, The believers and the infidels.   [6] See Chap. VII.

by a rash judgment ;[1] neither do we perceive any excellence in you above us : but we esteem you to be liars. *Noah* said, O my people, tell me ; if I have *received* an evident declaration from my LORD, and he hath bestowed on me mercy from himself, which is hidden from you, do we compel you to *receive* the same, in case ye be averse thereto ? O my people, I ask not of you any riches, for *my preaching unto you* : my reward is with GOD alone. I will not drive away those who have believed :[2] verily they shall meet their LORD, *at the resurrection* ; but I perceive that ye are ignorant men. O my people, who shall assist me against GOD, if I drive them away ? Will ye not therefore consider ? I say not unto you, The treasures of GOD are in my power ; neither *do I say*, I know the secrets *of God* ; neither do I say, Verily I am an angel ;[3] neither do I say of those whom your eyes do contemn, GOD will by no means bestow good on them (GOD best knoweth that which is in their souls) ; for then should I certainly be *one* of the unjust. They answered, O Noah, thou hast already disputed with us, and hast multiplied disputes with us ; now therefore do thou bring that *punishment* upon us wherewith thou hast threatened us, if thou speakest truth. *Noah* said, Verily GOD alone shall bring it upon you, if he pleaseth ; and ye shall not prevail against him, *so as to escape the same*. Neither shall my counsel profit you, although I endeavour to counsel you aright, if GOD shall please to lead you into error. He is your LORD, and unto him shall ye return. Will the *Meccans* say, *Mohammed* hath forged *the Korân* ? Answer, if I have forged it, on me *be* my guilt ; and let me be clear of that which ye are guilty of. And it was revealed unto Noah, *saying*, Verily none of thy people shall believe, except he who hath already believed : be not therefore grieved for that which they are doing. But make an ark in our presence, *according to the form and dimensions* which we have revealed *unto thee* : and speak not unto me in behalf of those who have acted unjustly ; for they *are doomed to be* drowned. And he built the ark ; and so often as a company of his people passed by him, they derided him :[4]

---

[1] For want of mature consideration, and moved by the first impulse of their fancy.

[2] For this they asked him to do, because they were poor mean people. The same thing the Koreish demanded of Mohammed, but he was forbidden to comply with their request.

[3] See Chap. VI.

[4] For building a vessel in an inland country, and so far from the sea ; and for that he was turned carpenter after he had set up for a prophet. (Al Beidâwi.)

but he said, Though ye scoff at us *now*, we will scoff at you *hereafter*, as ye scoff *at us* ; and ye shall surely know on whom a punishment shall be inflicted, which shall cover him with shame, and on whom a lasting punishment shall fall. *Thus were they employed* until our sentence was put in execution, and the oven poured forth *water*.[1] *And* we said *unto Noah*, Carry into *the ark* of every *species of animals* one pair ;[2] and thy family[3] (except him on whom a previous sentence *of destruction* hath passed),[4] and those who believe.[5] But there believed not with him, except a few.[6] And *Noah* said, Embark thereon, in the name of GOD ; while it moveth for-

[1] Or, as the original literally signifies, *boiled over* ; which is consonant to what the Rabbins say, that the waters of the Deluge were boiling hot.

This oven was, as some say, at Cûfa, in a spot whereon a mosque now stands ; or, as others rather think, in a certain place in India, or else at Ain Warda in Mesopotamia (Al Beidâwi) ; and its exudation was the sign by which Noah knew the flood was coming (Jallalo'ddin, &c.). Some pretend that it was the same oven which Eve made use of to bake her bread in, being of a form different from those we use, having the mouth in the upper part, and that it descended from patriarch to patriarch, till it came to Noah. (D'Herbelot, Bibl. Orient. Art. Noah.) It is remarkable that Mohammed, in all probability, borrowed this circumstance from the Persian Magi, who also fancied that the first waters of the Deluge gushed out of the oven of a certain old woman named Zala Cûfa. (Hyde, de Rel. Vet. Persar., and Lord's Account of the Relig. of the Persees, p. 9.)

But the word *tannûr*, which is here translated *oven*, also signifying the *superficies of the earth*, or *a place whence waters spring forth*, or *where they are collected*, some suppose it means no more in this passage than the spot or fissure whence the first eruption of waters broke forth.

[2] Or, as the words may also be rendered, and some commentators think they ought, two pairs, that is, two males and two females of each species ; wherein they partly agree with divers Jewish and Christian writers (Aben Ezra, Justin Martyr, Origen, &c.), who from the Hebrew expression, *seven and seven*, and *two and two, the male and his female* (Gen. vii. 2), suppose there went into the ark fourteen pair of every clean, and two pair of every unclean species. There is a tradition that GOD gathered together unto Noah all sorts of beasts, birds, and other animals (it being indeed difficult to conceive how he should come by them all without some supernatural assistance), and that as he laid hold on them, his right hand constantly fell on the male, and his left on the female. (Jallalo'ddin.)

[3] Namely, thy wife, and thy sons and their wives. (Al Beidâwi.)

[4] This was an unbelieving son of Noah (Yahya), named Canaan (Jallalo'-ddin, Al Beidâwi), or Yam (Ebn Shohnah) ; though others say he was not the son of Noah, but his grandson by his son Ham, or his wife's son by another husband ; nay, some pretend he was related to him no nearer than by having been educated and brought up in his house (Al Zamakhshari. D'Herbel. Bibl. Orient. p. 676). The best commentators add, that Noah's wife, named Wâila, who was an infidel, was also comprehended in this exception, and perished with her son. (Jallalo'ddin, Al Zamakhshari, Al Beidâwi.)

[5] Noah's family being mentioned before, it is supposed that by these words are intended the other believers. who were his proselytes, but not of his family : whence the common opinion among the Mohammedans, of a greater number than eight being saved in the ark, seems to have taken its rise. (Chap VII.)

[6] viz., His other wife, who was a true believer, his three sons, Shem, Ham, and Japhet, and their wives, and seventy-two persons more. (Chap. VII.)

ward, and while it standeth still ;[1] for my LORD *is* gracious *and* merciful. And *the ark* swam with them between waves like mountains :[2] and Noah called unto his son,[3] who was separated *from him, saying,* Embark with us, my son, and stay not with the unbelievers. He answered, I will get on a mountain, which will secure me from the water. *Noah* replied, There is no security this day from the decree of GOD, except for him on whom he shall have mercy. And a wave passed between them, and he became *one* of those who were drowned. And it was said, O earth, swallow up thy waters, and thou O heaven, withhold *thy rain.* And *immediately* the water abated, and the decree was fulfilled, and *the ark* rested on *the mountain* Al Judi ;[4] and it was said, Away with the

[1] That is, omit no opportunity of getting on board. According to a different reading, the latter words may be rendered, *Who shall cause it to move forward, and to stop,* as there shall be occasion. The commentators tell us that the ark moved forwards, or stood still, as Noah would have it, on his pronouncing only the words, *In the name of* GOD. (Al Beidâwi, &c.) It is to be observed that the more judicious commentators make the dimensions of the ark to be the same with those assigned by Moses (Al Beidâwi, &c.): notwithstanding, others have enlarged them most extravagantly (Yahya, Marracc. in Alcor. p. 340), as some Christian writers (Origen, Contr. Cels. l. 4 ; Kircher. de Arca Noe, c. 8) have also done. They likewise tell us that Noah was two years in building the ark, which was framed of Indian plane-tree (Al Beidâwi ; Vide D'Herbel. p. 675, and Eutych. p. 34), that it was divided into three stories, of which the lower was designed for the beasts, the middle one for the men and women, and the upper for the birds (Al Beidâwi ; Vide Eutych. Annal. p. 34) ; and that the men were separated from the women by the body of Adam, which Noah had taken into the ark (Yahya). This last is a tradition of the Eastern Christians (Jacob. Edessenus, apud Barcepham de Parad, part. i. c. 14 ; Eutych, ubi sup. Vide etiam Eliezer. pirke c. 23), some of whom pretend that the matrimonial duty was superseded and suspended during the time Noah and his family were in the ark (Ambros. de Noa et Arca, c. 21) ; though Ham has been accused of not observing continency on that occasion, his wife, it seems, bringing forth Canaan in the very ark (Heidegger. Hist. Patriarchar. vol. i. p. 409).

[2] The waters prevailing fifteen cubits above the mountains. (Al Beidâwi.)
[3] See p. 214, note 4.
[4] This mountain is one of those which divide Armenia, on the south, from Mesopotamia, and that part of Assyria which is inhabited by the Curds, from whom the mountains took the name of Cardu, or Gardu, by the Greeks turned into Gordyæi, and other names. (See Bochart. Phaleg. l. 1, c. 3.) Mount Al Judi (which name seems to be a corruption, though it be constantly so written by the Arabs, for Jordi, or Giordi) is also called Thamanin (Geogr. Nub. p. 202), probably from a town at the foot of it (D'Herbel. Bibl. Orient. p. 404 and 676, and Agathiam, l. 14, p. 135), so named from the number of persons saved in the ark, the word *thamanin* signifying *eighty,* and overlooks the country of Diyâr Rab ah, near the cities of Mawsel, Forda, and Jaz'rat Ebn Omar, which last place one affirms to be but four miles from the place of the ark, and says that a Mohammedan temple was built there with the remains of that vessel, by the Khalîf Omar Ebn Abd'alaziz, whom he by mistake calls Omar Ebn al Khattâb (Benjamin. Itiner. p. 61). The tradition which affirms the ark to have rested on these mountains, must have been very ancient, since it is the tradition of the Chaldeans themselves (Berosus, apud Joseph. Antiq. l. 1, c. 4) : the Chaldee paraphrasts consent to their opinion (Onkelos et Jonathan, in Gen. viii. 4), which obtained very much formerly, especially among the Eastern Christians (Eutych. Annal. p.

ungodly people! And *Noah* called upon his LORD, and said, O LORD, verily my son is of my family; and thy promise is true :[1] for thou art the most just of those who exercise judgment. *God* answered, O Noah, verily he is not of thy family :[2] this *intercession of thine for him,* is not a righteous work.[3] Ask not of me therefore that wherein thou hast no knowledge : I admonish thee that thou become not *one* of the ignorant. *Noah* said, O LORD, I have recourse unto thee *for the assistance of thy grace,* that I ask not of thee that wherein I have no knowledge : and unless thou forgive me, and be merciful unto me, I shall be *one* of those who perish. It was said *unto him,* O Noah, come down from the *ark,*[4] with peace from us, and blessings upon thee and upon a part of those who are with thee :[5] but as for a part *of them,*[6] we will suffer them to enjoy *the provision of this world* ; and afterwards shall a grievous punishment from us be inflicted on them, *in the life to come.* This is a secret history, which we reveal unto thee : thou didst not know it, neither did thy people, before this. Wherefore persevere with patience : for the *prosperous* issue shall attend the pious. And unto *the tribe of* Ad *we sent* their brother Hûd.[7] He said, O my

41). To confirm it, we are told that the remains of the ark were to be seen on the Gordyæan mountains : Berosus and Abydenus both declare there was such a report in their time (Berosus, apud Joseph. ubi sup. Abydenus, apud Euseb. Præp. Ev. l. 9, c. 4) ; the first observing that several of the inhabitants thereabouts scraped the pitch off the planks as a rarity, and carried it about them for an amulet : and the latter saying that they used the wood of the vessel against many diseases with wonderful success. The relics of the ark were also to be seen here in the time of Epiphanius, if we may believe him (Epiph. Hæres. 18) ; and we are told the emperor Heraclius went from the town of Thamanin up to the mountain Al Jûdi, and saw the place of the ark (Elmacin. l. 1. c. 1). There was also formerly a famous monastery, called *the monastery of the ark,* upon some of these mountains, where the Nestorians used to celebrate a feast day on the spot where they supposed the ark rested ; but in the year of Christ 776, that monastery was destroyed by lightning, with the church, and a numerous congregation in it (Chronic. Dionysii Patriarch. Jacobitar, apud Asseman. Bibl. Orient. t. 2, p. 113). Since which time it seems the credit of this tradition hath declined, and given place to another, which obtains at present, and according to which the ark rested on Mount Masis, in Armenia, called by the Turks Aghir dagh, or *the heavy* or *great mountain,* and situate about twelve leagues south-east of Erivan (Al Beidâwi).

[1] Noah here challenges GOD's promise that he would save his family.
[2] Being cut off from it on account of his infidelity.
[3] According to a different reading, this passage may be rendered, *For he hath acted unrighteously.*
[4] The Mohammedans say that Noah went into the ark on the tenth of Rajeb, and came out of it the tenth of Al Moharram, which therefore became a fast. So that the whole time of Noah's being in the ark, according to them, was six months. (Al Beidâwi. D'Herbel. ubi sup.)
[5] viz., Such of them as continued in their belief.
[6] That is, such of his prosperity as should depart from the true faith and fall into idolatry. [7] See Chap. VII.

people, worship GOD ; ye have no GOD besides him : ye only imagine falsehood, *in setting up idols and intercessors of your own making.* O my people, I ask not of you for this *my preaching,* any recompence : my recompence *do I expect* from him only who hath created me. Will ye not therefore understand ? O my people, ask pardon of your LORD ; and be turned unto him : he will send the heaven to pour forth rain plentifully upon you,[1] and he will increase your strength by *giving* unto you *further* strength :[2] therefore turn not aside to commit evil. They answered, O Hûd, thou hast brought us no proof *of what thou sayest* ; therefore we will not leave our gods for thy saying, neither do we believe thee. We say no other than that some of our gods have afflicted thee with evil.[3] He replied, Verily I call GOD to witness, and do ye also bear witness, that I am clear of that which ye associate *with God,* besides him. Do ye all therefore *join to* devise a plot against me, and tarry not ; for I put my confidence in GOD, my LORD and your LORD. There is no beast, but he holdeth *it* by its forelock :[4] verily my LORD *proceedeth* in the right way. But if ye turn back, I have already declared unto you that with which I was sent unto you ; and my LORD shall substitute another nation in your stead ; and ye shall not hurt him at all : for my LORD *is* guardian over all things. And when our sentence came *to be put in execution,* we delivered Hûd, and those who had believed with him,[5] through our mercy ; and we delivered them from a grievous punishment. And this *tribe of* Ad wittingly rejected the signs of their LORD, and were disobedient unto his messengers, and they followed the command of every rebellious perverse person. Wherefore they were followed in this world by a curse, and *they shall be followed by the same* on the day of resurrection. Did not Ad disbelieve in their LORD ? Was it not *said,* Away with Ad, the people of Hûd ? And unto *the tribe of* Thamûd *we sent* their brother Sâleh.[6] He said *unto them,* O my people, worship GOD ; ye have no GOD besides him. It is he who hath produced you out of the

---

[1] For the Adites were grievously distressed by a drought for three years. (See the notes to Chap. VII, p. 148.)

[2] By giving you children ; the wombs of their wives being also rendered barren during the time of the drought, as well as their lands. (Al Beidâwi.)

[3] Or madness ; having deprived thee of thy reason for the indignities thou hast offered them.

[4] That is, he exerciseth an absolute power over it. A creature held in this manner being supposed to be reduced to the lowest subjection.

[5] Who were in number four thousand. (Al Beidâwi.)

[6] See Chap. VII.

earth, and hath given you an habitation therein. Ask pardon of him, therefore, and be turned unto him ; for my LORD is near, *and* ready to answer. They answered, O Sâleh, thou wast *a person* on whom we placed our hopes before this.[1] Dost thou forbid us to worship that which our fathers worshipped ? But we are certainly in doubt concerning *the religion* to which thou dost invite us, *as* justly to be expected. *Sâleh* said, O my people, tell me ; if I have received an evident declaration from my LORD, and he hath bestowed on me mercy from himself ; who will protect me from *the vengeance of* GOD, if I be disobedient unto him ? For ye shall not add unto me, other than loss. And *he said*, O my people, this she-camel of GOD *is* a sign unto you, therefore dismiss her freely that she may feed in GOD's earth, and do her no harm, lest a swift punishment seize you. Yet they killed her ; and *Sâleh* said, Enjoy *yourselves* in your dwellings for three days ;[2] *after which ye shall be destroyed*. This is an infallible prediction. And when our decree came *to be executed*, we delivered Sâleh and those who believed with him, through our mercy, from the disgrace of that day ; for thy LORD is the strong, the mighty *God*. But a terrible noise *from heaven* assailed those who had acted unjustly ; and in the morning they were found in their houses, lying *dead and* prostrate ; as though they had never dwelt therein. Did not Thamûd disbelieve in their LORD ? Was not Thamûd *cast* far away ? Our messengers[3] also came formerly unto Abraham, with good tidings : they said, Peace *be upon thee*. And he answered, *And on you be* peace ! and he tarried not, but brought a roasted calf. And when he saw that their hands did not touch *the meat*, he misliked them, and entertained a fear of them.[4] *But* they said, Fear not : for we are sent unto the people of Lot.[5] And his wife *Sarah was* standing by,[6] and

[1] Designing to have made thee our prince, because of the singular prudence and other good qualities which we observed in thee ; but thy dissenting from us in point of religious worship has frustrated those hopes. (Al Beidâwi.)

[2] viz., Wednesday, Thursday, and Friday. (Al Beidâwi.) See Chap. VII.

[3] These were the angels who were sent to acquaint Abraham with the promise of Issac, and to destroy Sodom and Gomorrah. Some of the commentators pretend they were twelve, or nine, or ten in number ; but others, agreeably to Scripture, say they were but three, viz., Gabriel, Michael, and Israfîl. (Al Beidâwi, Jallalo'ddin. Gen xviii.)

[4] Apprehending they had some ill design against him, because they would not eat with him.

[5] Being angels, whose nature needs not the support of food. (Al Beidâwi.)

[6] Either behind the curtain, or door of the tent ; or else waiting upon them.

she laughed;[1] and we promised her Isaac, and after Isaac, Jacob. She said, Alas! shall I bear a son, who am old; this my husband also being advanced in years?[2] Verily this *would be* a wonderful thing. *The angels answered*, Dost thou wonder at the *effect of the* command of GOD? The mercy of GOD and his blessings be upon you, the family of the house:[3] for he *is* praiseworthy, *and* to be glorified. And when *his* apprehension had departed from Abraham, and the good tidings *of Isaac's birth* had come unto him, he disputed with us concerning the people of Lot:[4] for Abraham was a pitiful, compassionate, and devout *person. The angels said unto him*, O Abraham, abstain from this; for now is the command of thy LORD come, *to put their sentence in execution*, and an inevitable punishment is ready to fall upon them. And when our messengers came unto Lot, he was troubled for them,[5] and his arm was straitened concerning them,[6] and he said, This is a grievous day. And his people came unto him, rushing upon him: and they had formerly been guilty of wickedness. *Lot* said *unto them*, O my people, these my daughters are more lawful for you: therefore fear GOD, and put me not to shame by *wronging* my guests. Is there not a man of prudence among you? They answered, Thou knowest that we have no need of thy daughters; and thou well knowest what we would have. He said, If I had strength sufficient to *oppose* you, or I could have recourse unto a

---

[1] The commentators are so little acquainted with Scripture, that, not knowing the true occasion of Sarah's laughter, they strain their invention to give some reason for it. One says that she laughed at the angels discovering themselves, and ridding Abraham and herself of their apprehensions; and another, that it was at the approaching destruction of the Sodomites (a very probable motive in one of her sex). Some, however, interpret the original word differently, and will have it that she did not *laugh*, but that *her courses*, which had stopped for several years, *came upon her* at this time, as a previous sign of her future conception. (Al Beidâwi, Jallalo'ddin, Al Zamakhshari.)

[2] Al Beidâwi writes that Sarah was then ninety or ninety-nine years old, and Abraham a hundred and twenty.

[3] Or the stock whence all the prophets were to proceed for the future. Or the expression may perhaps refer to Abraham and Ismael's building the Caaba, which is often called, by way of excellence, *the house*.

[4] That is, he interceded with us for them. (Gen. xviii. 23, &c.) Jallalo'-ddin, instead of the numbers mentioned by Moses, says that Abraham first asked whether GOD would destroy those cities if three hundred righteous persons were found therein, and so fell successively to two hundred, forty, fourteen, and at last came to one: but there was not one righteous person to be found among them, except only Lot and his family.

[5] Because they appeared in the shape of beautiful young men, which must needs tempt those of Sodom to abuse them. (Jallalo'ddin, Al Beidâwi. Joseph. Ant. l. 1, c. 11.)

[6] *i.e.*, He knew himself unable to protect them against the insults of his townsmen.

powerful support, *I would certainly do it. The angels* said,
O Lot, verily we are the messengers of thy LORD ; they shall
by no means come in unto thee.[1] Go forth therefore with thy
family, in some part of the night, and let not any of you turn
back ; but as for thy wife,[2] that shall happen unto her, which
shall happen unto them. Verily the prediction *of their punishment* shall be *fulfilled in* the morning : is not the morning
near ? And when our command came, we turned those *cities*
upside down,[3] and we rained upon them stones of baked clay,[4]
one following another, and being marked,[5] from thy LORD ;
and they *are* not far distant from those who act unjustly.[6]
And unto Madian *we sent* their brother Shoaib :[7] he said,
O my people, worship GOD ; ye have no GOD but him : and
diminish not measure and weight. Verily I see you *to be* in a
happy condition : [8] but I fear for you the punishment of the
day which will encompass *the ungodly*. O my people, give
full measure and just weight ; and diminish not unto men
aught of their matters ; neither commit injustice in the earth,
acting corruptly. The residue *which shall remain unto you
as the gift* of GOD, *after ye shall have done justice to others*, will

[1] Al Beidâwi says that Lot shut his door, and argued the matter with the
riotous assembly from behind it ; but at length they endeavoured to get
over the wall : whereupon Gabriel, seeing his distress, struck them on the
face with one of his wings, and blinded them ; so that they moved oft, crying
out for help, and saying that Lot had magicians in his house.

[2] This seems to be the true sense of the passage ; but according to a different reading of the vowel, some interpret it, *Except thy wife* ; the meaning
being that Lot is here commanded to take his family with him *except his
wife*. Wherefore the commentators cannot agree whether Lot's wife went
forth with him or not ; some denying it, and pretending that she was left
behind and perished in the common destruction ; and others affirming it,
and saying that when she heard the noise of the storm and overthrow of
the cities, she turned back lamenting their fate, and was immediately struck
down and killed by one of the stones mentioned a little lower. A punishment she justly merited for her infidelity and disobedience to her husband.
(Chap. LXVI.)

[3] For they tell us that Gabriel thrust his wing under them, and lifted them
up so high, that the inhabitants of the lower heaven heard the barking of the
dogs and the crowing of the cocks ; and then, inverting them, threw them
down to the earth. (Jallalo'ddin, Al Beidâwi.)

[4] The kiln wherein they were burned some imagine to have been hell.

[5] That is, as some suppose, streaked with white and red, or having some
other peculiar mark to distinguish them from ordinary stones. But the
common opinion is that each stone had the name of the person who was to
be killed by it written thereon. (Al Beidâwi.) The army of Abraha al
Ashram was also destroyed by the same kind of stones.

[6] This is a kind of threat to other wicked persons, and particularly to the
infidels of Mecca, who deserved and might justly apprehend the same punishment.

[7] See Chap. VII.

[8] That is, enjoying plenty of all things, and therefore having the less
occasion to defraud one another, and being the more strongly bound to be
thankful and obedient unto GOD.

be better for you *than wealth gotten by fraud* ; if ye be true believers. I am no guardian over you. They answered, O Shoaib, do thy prayers enjoin thee, that we should leave the *gods* which our fathers worshipped ; or that we should not do what we please with our substance ?[1] Thou *only*, it seems, art the wise *person*, and fit to direct. He said, O my people, tell me ; if I have received an evident declaration from my LORD, and he hath bestowed on me an excellent provision, and I will not consent unto you in that which I forbid you ; do I seek *any other* than *your* reformation, to the utmost of my power ? My support is from GOD alone ; on him do I trust, and unto him do I turn me. O my people, let not *your* opposing of me draw on you *a vengeance* like unto that which fell on the people of Noah, or the people of Hûd, or the people of Sâleh ; neither *were* the people of Lot far distant from you.[2] Ask pardon therefore of your LORD ; and be turned unto him : for my LORD is merciful *and* loving. They answered, O Shoaib, we understand not much of what thou sayest ; and we see thee to be a *man* of no power[3] among us : if it had not been *for the sake of* thy family,[4] we had surely stoned thee, neither couldst thou have prevailed against us. *Shoaib* said, O my people, is my family more worthy in your opinion than GOD ? and do ye cast him behind you with neglect ? Verily my LORD comprehendeth that which ye do. O my people, do ye work according to your condition ; I will surely work *according to my duty*.[5] *And* ye shall certainly know on whom will be inflicted a punishment which shall cover him with shame, and who is a liar. Wait therefore *the event* ; for I also will await *it* with you. Wherefore when our decree came *to be executed*, we delivered Shoaib and those who believed with him, through our mercy : and a terrible noise *from heaven* assailed those who had acted unjustly ; and in the morning they were found in their houses lying *dead and*

[1] For this liberty they imagined was taken from them, by his prohibition of false weights and measures, or to diminish or adulterate their coin. (Al Beidâwi.)

[2] For Sodom and Gomorrah were situate not a great way from you, and their destruction happened not many ages ago ; neither did they deserve it, on account of their obstinacy and wickedness, much more than yourselves.

[3] The Arabic word *daif*, *weak*, signifying also, in the Hamyaritic dialect, *blind*, some suppose that Shoaib was so, and that the Midianites objected that to him as a defect which disqualified him for the prophetic office.

[4] *i.e.*, For the respect we bear to thy family and relations, whom we honour as being of our religion, and not for any apprehension we have of their power to assist you against us. The original word, here translated *family*, signifies any number from three to seven or ten, but not more. (Al Beidâwi.)

[5] See Chap. VI. p. 134.

prostrate, as though they had never dwelt therein. Was not Madian removed *from off the earth*, as Thamûd had been removed? And we formerly sent Moses with our signs, and manifest power, unto Pharaoh and his princes:[1] but they followed the command of Pharaoh; although the command of Pharaoh did not direct *them* aright. *Pharaoh shall precede his people on the day of resurrection, and he shall lead them into hell fire*; an unhappy way *shall it be* which *they* shall be led. They were followed in this *life* by a curse, and on the day of resurrection miserable *shall be* the gift which shall be given *them*. This is *a part* of the histories of the cities, which we rehearse unto thee. Of them there are *some* standing; and *others which are* utterly demolished.[2] And we treated them not unjustly, but they dealt unjustly with their own souls: and their gods which they invoked, besides GOD, were of no advantage unto them at all, when the decree of thy LORD came *to be executed on them*, neither were they any other than a detriment unto them. And thus *was* the punishment of thy LORD *inflicted*, when he punished the cities which were unjust; for his punishment is grievous and severe. Verily herein is a sign unto him who feareth the punishment of the last *day*; that *shall be a* day whereon *all* men shall be assembled, and that *shall be* a day whereon witness shall be borne; we defer it not, but to a determined time. When *that day* shall come, no soul shall speak *to excuse itself, or to intercede for another*, but by the permission of *God*. Of them *one shall be* miserable, and *another shall be* happy. And they who shall be miserable, shall be *thrown* into *hell* fire; there shall they wail and bemoan *themselves*:[3] they shall remain therein so long as the heavens and the earth shall endure;[4] except what thy LORD shall please *to remit of their sentence*;[5] for thy LORD effecteth that which he pleaseth. But they who shall be happy, *shall be admitted* into paradise; they shall remain

[1] See Chap. VII.

[2] Literally, *mown down*; the sentence presenting the different images of corn standing, and cut down, which is also often used by the sacred writers.

[3] The two words in the original signify properly the vehement drawing in and expiration of one's breath, which is usual to persons in great pain and anguish; and particularly the reciprocation of the voice of an ass when he brays.

[4] This is not to be strictly understood as if either the punishment of the damned should have an end, or the heavens and the earth should endure for ever; the expression being only used by way of image or comparison, which need not agree in every point with the thing signified. Some, however, think the future heavens and earth, into which the present shall be changed, are here meant. (Al Beidâwi.)

[5] Sale, Prel. Disc. Sect. IV.

therein so long as the heavens and the earth endure ; besides what thy LORD shall please *to add unto their bliss* ; a bounty which shall not be interrupted. Be not therefore in doubt concerning that which these men worship ; they worship no other than what their fathers worshipped before *them* ; and we will surely give them their full portion, not in the least diminished. We formerly gave unto Moses the book *of the law* ; and disputes arose *among his people* concerning it : and unless a previous decree had proceeded from thy LORD, *to bear with them during this life, the matter* had been surely decided between them. And *thy people are also* jealous *and* in doubt concerning the *Korân*. But unto every one of them will thy LORD render *the reward of* their works ; for he well knoweth that which they do. Be thou steadfast, therefore, as thou hast been commanded ; and *let him also be steadfast* who shall be converted with thee ; and transgress not : for he seeth that which ye do. And incline not unto those who act unjustly, lest the fire *of hell* touch you : for ye have no protectors except GOD ; neither shall ye be assisted *against him*. Pray regularly morning and evening ;[1] and in the former part of the night,[2] for good *works* drive away evils. This is an admonition unto those who consider : wherefore persevere with patience ; for GOD suffereth not the reward of the righteous to perish. Were such of the generations before you, endued with understanding and virtue, who forbade the acting corruptly in the earth, any more than a few only of those whom we delivered ? But they who were unjust followed *the delights* which they enjoyed *in this world*,[3] and were wicked doers :[4] and thy LORD was not *of such a disposition* as to destroy the cities unjustly,[5] while their inhabitants behaved themselves uprightly. And if thy LORD pleased, he would have made *all* men of one religion : but they shall not cease to differ among themselves, unless those on whom thy LORD shall have mercy : and unto this hath he created them ; for the word of thy LORD shall be fulfilled,

[1] Literally, *in the two extremities of the day.*

[2] That is, after sunset and before supper, when the Mohammedans say their fourth prayer, called by them *Salât al moghreb*, or the evening prayer. (Al Beidâwi.)

[3] Making it their sole business to please their luxurious desires and appetites, and placing their whole felicity therein.

[4] Al Beidâwi says that this passage gives the reason why the nations were destroyed of old ; viz., for their violence and injustice, their following their own lusts, and for their idolatry and unbelief.

[5] Or, as the commentator just named explains it, *for their idolatry* only, when they observed justice in other respects.

when he said, Verily, I will fill hell altogether with genii and men.   The whole *which we have related* of the histories of *our* apostles do we relate unto thee, that we may confirm thy heart thereby ; and herein is the truth come unto thee, and an admonition, and a warning unto the true believers.   Say unto those who believe not, Act ye according to your condition ; we surely will act *according to our duty :*[1] and await *the issue*; *for* we certainly await *it also.*   Unto GOD *is known* that which is secret in heaven and earth ; and unto him shall the whole matter be referred.   Therefore worship him, and put thy trust in him ; for thy LORD is not regardless of that which ye do.

XII

THE CHAPTER OF JOSEPH [2]

Revealed at Mecca.

IN THE NAME OF THE MOST MERCIFUL GOD.

A L. R.[3]   These are the signs of the perspicuous book ; which we have sent down in the Arabic tongue, that peradventure ye might understand.   We relate unto thee a most excellent history, by revealing unto thee this Korân,[4] whereas thou wast before *one* of the negligent.[5]   When Joseph said unto his father,[6] O my father, verily I saw *in my dream* eleven stars,[7] and the sun and the moon : I saw them

---

[1] See Chap. VI, p. 145, note[7].

[2] The Koreish, thinking to puzzle Mohammed, at the instigation and by the direction of certain Jewish Rabbins, demanded of him how Jacob's family happened to go down into Egypt, and that he would relate to them the history of Joseph, with all its circumstances : whereupon he pretended to have received this chapter from heaven, containing the story of that patriarch (Al Beidâwi).   It is said, however, to have been rejected by two Mohammedan sects, branches of the Khârejites, called the Ajâredites and the Maimûnians, as apocryphal and spurious.

[3] Sale, Prel. Disc. p. 64.

[4] Or this particular chapter.   For the word *Korân,* as has been elsewhere observed (Sale, Prel. Disc. Sect. III.), properly signifying no more than a *reading* or *lecture,* is often used to denote, not only the whole volume, but any distinct chapter or section of it.

[5] *i e.,* So far from being acquainted with the story, that it never so much as entered into thy thoughts ; a certain argument, says Al Beidâwi, that it must have been revealed to him from heaven.

[6] Who was Jacob, the son of Isaac, the son of Abraham.   (Al Beidâwi, &c.)

[7] The commentators give us the names of these stars (which I think it

make obeisance unto me.   Jacob said, O my child, tell not
thy vision to thy brethren, lest they devise some plot against
thee ;[1] for the devil is a professed enemy unto man ; and
thus, *according to thy dream*, shall thy LORD choose thee,
and teach thee the interpretation of *dark* sayings,[2] and he
shall accomplish his favour upon thee and upon the family of
Jacob, as he hath formerly accomplished it upon thy fathers
Abraham and Isaac ; for thy LORD *is* knowing *and* wise.
Surely in *the history of* Joseph and his brethren there are
signs *of God's providence* to the inquisitive ; when they said
to one another, Joseph and his brother[3] are dearer to our
father than we, who are the greater number : our father
certainly maketh a wrong judgment.   *Wherefore* slay Joseph,
or drive him into some *distant or desert part of the* earth, and
the face of your father shall be cleared towards you ;[4] and ye
shall afterwards be people of integrity.   One of them[5] spoke
and said, Slay not Joseph, but throw him to the bottom of
the well : and some travellers will take him up, if ye do *this*.
They said *unto Jacob*, O father, why dost thou not entrust
Joseph with us, since we are sincere *well-wishers* unto him ?
Send him with us to-morrow, *into the field*, that he may divert
himself, and sport,[6] and we will be his guardians.   *Jacob*
answered, it grieveth me that ye take him away ; and I fear
lest the wolf devour him,[7] while ye are negligent of him.
They said, Surely if the wolf devour him when there are so

needless to trouble the reader with), as Mohammed repeated them, at the
request of a Jew, who thought to entrap him by the question.   (Al Beidâwi,
Al Zamakhshari.)

[1] For they say, Jacob, judging that Joseph's dream portended his
advancement above the rest of the family, justly apprehended his brethren's
envy might tempt them to do him some mischief.

[2] That is, of dreams ; or, as others suppose, of the profound passages of
Scripture, and all difficulties respecting either religion or justice.

[3] viz., Benjamin, his brother by the same mother.

[4] Or, he will settle his love wholly upon you, and ye will have no rival in
his favour.

[5] This person, as some say, was Judah, the most prudent and noble-
minded of them all ; or, according to others, Reuben, whom the Mohammedan
writers call Rubil.   (Al Beidâwi.)   And both these opinions are supported
by the account of Moses, who tells us that Reuben advised them not to kill
Joseph, but to throw him into a pit privately, intending to release him
(Gen. xxvii. 21, 22); and that afterwards Judah, in Reuben's absence, persuaded them not to let him die in the pit, but to sell him to the Ishmaelites.
(Gen. v. 26, 27.)

[6] Some copies read, in the first person plural, *that we may divert ourselves*,
&c.

[7] The reason why Jacob feared this beast in particular, as the com-
mentators say, was, either because the land was full of wolves, or else because
Jacob had dreamed he saw Joseph devoured by one of those creatures.
(Al Beidâwi, Jallalo'ddin, Al Zamakhshari.)

many of us, we shall be weak indeed.[1]   And when they had
carried him with them, and agreed to set him at the bottom
of the well,[2] *they executed their design* : and we sent a revelation unto him,[3] *saying,* Thou shalt *hereafter* declare this their
action unto them ; and they shall not perceive *thee to be
Joseph.*   And they came to their father at even, weeping,
and said, Father, we went and ran races with one another,[4]
and we left Joseph with our baggage, and the wolf hath
devoured him ; but thou wilt not believe us, although we
speak the truth.   And they produced his inner garment
stained with false blood.   *Jacob* answered, Nay, but ye yourselves have contrived the thing for your own sakes :[5] however,
patience is most becoming, and GOD'S assistance is to be
implored *to enable me to support the misfortune* which ye
relate.   And certain travellers[6] came and sent one[7] to draw
water for them : and he let down his bucket,[8] and said, Good

---

[1] *i.e.,* It will be an instance of extreme weakness and folly in us, and we
shall be justly blamed for his loss.

[2] This well, say some, was a certain well near Jerusalem, or not far
from the river Jordan ; but others call it the well of Egypt or Midian.
The commentators tell us that, when the sons of Jacob had gotten Joseph
with them in the field, they began to abuse and to beat him so unmercifully,
that they had killed him, had not Judah, on his crying out for help, insisted
on the promise they had made not to kill him, but to cast him into the well.
Whereupon they let him down a little way ; but, as he held by the sides of
the well, they bound him, and took off his inner garment, designing to
stain it with blood, to deceive their father.   Joseph begged hard to have his
garment returned him, but to no purpose, his brothers telling him, with a
sneer, that the eleven stars and the sun and the moon might clothe him and
keep him company.   When they had let him down half-way, they let him
fall thence to the bottom, and, there being water in the well (though the
Scripture says the contrary), he was obliged to get upon a stone, on which, as
he stood weeping, the angel Gabriel came to him with the revelation mentioned immediately.   (Al Beidâwi.)

[3] Joseph being then but seventeen years old, Al Beidâwi observes that herein
he resembled John the Baptist and Jesus, who were also favoured with the
divine communication very early.   The commentators pretend that Gabriel
also clothed him in the well with a garment of silk of paradise.   For they
say that when Abraham was thrown into the fire by Nimrod (Chap. XXI.),
he was stripped ; and that Gabriel brought this garment and put it on him ;
and that from Abraham it descended to Jacob, who folded it up and put it
into an amulet, which he hung about Joseph's neck, whence Gabriel drew
it out.   (Al Beidâwi, Al Zamakhshari.)

[4] These races they used by way of exercise ; and the commentators
generally understand here that kind of race wherein they also showed
their dexterity in throwing darts, which is still used in the East.

[5] This Jacob had reason to suspect, because, when the garment was
brought to him, he observed that, though it was bloody, yet it was not
torn.   (Al Beidâwi.)

[6] viz., A caravan or company travelling from Midian to Egypt who
rested near the well three days after Joseph had been thrown into it.

[7] The commentators are so exact as to give us the name of this man, who,
as they pretend, was Malec Ebn Dhór, of the tribe of Khozâah.   (Al Beidâwi.)

[8] And Joseph, making use of the opportunity, took hold of the cord, and
was drawn up by the man.

news !¹ this is a youth. And they concealed him,² *that they might sell him* as a piece of merchandise : but GOD knew that which they did. And they sold him for a mean price, for a few pence,³ and valued him lightly. And the Egyptian who bought him ⁴ said to his wife,⁵ Use him honourably ; peradventure he may be serviceable to us, or we may adopt him for our son.⁶ Thus did we prepare an establishment for Joseph in the earth, and we taught him the interpretation of *dark* sayings : for GOD is well able to effect his purpose ; but the greater part of men do not understand. And when he had attained his age of strength, we bestowed on him wisdom and knowledge ; for thus do we recompense the righteous. And she, in whose house he was, desired him to lie with her ; and she shut the doors and said, Come hither. He answered, GOD forbid ! verily my lord⁷ hath made my dwelling *with him* easy ; and the ungrateful shall not prosper. But she resolved within herself *to enjoy* him, and he would have resolved *to enjoy* her, had he not seen the evident demonstration of his LORD.⁸ So we turned away evil and filthi-

¹ The original words are *Ya boshra* : the latter of which some take for the proper name of the water-drawer's companion, whom he called to his assistance ; and then they must be translated, *O Boshra*.

² The expositors are not agreed whether the pronoun *they* relates to Malec and his companions or to Joseph's brethren. They who espouse the former opinion say that those who came to draw water concealed the manner of their coming to him from the rest of the caravan, that they might keep him to themselves, pretending that some people of the place had given him to them to sell for them in Egypt. And they who prefer the latter opinion tell us that Judah carried victuals to Joseph every day while he was in the well, but not finding him there on the fourth day, he acquainted his brothers with it ; whereupon they all went to the caravan and claimed Joseph as their slave, he not daring to discover that he was their brother, lest something worse should befall him ; and at length they agreed to sell him to them. (Al Beidâwi.)

³ Namely, twenty or twenty-two *dirhems*, and those not of full weight; for having weighed one ounce of silver only, the remainder was paid by tale, which is the most unfair way of payment. (Al Beidâwi.)

⁴ His name was Kitfir, or Itfir (a corruption of Potiphar) ; and he was a man of great consideration, being superintendent of the royal treasury. (Al Beidâwi.) The commentators say that Joseph came into his service at seventeen, and lived with him thirteen years ; and that he was made prime minister in the thirty-third year of his age, and died at a hundred and twenty. They who suppose Joseph was twice sold differ as to the price the Egyptian paid for him ; some saying it was twenty *dinârs* of gold, a pair of shoes, and two white garments ; and others, that it was a large quantity of silver or of gold.

⁵ Some call her Raïl ; but the name she is best known by is that of Zoleikha.

⁶ Kitfir having no children. It is said that Joseph gained his master's good opinion so suddenly by his countenance, which Kitfir, who, they pretend, had great skill in physiognomy, judged to indicate his prudence and other good qualities.

⁷ viz., Kitfir. But others understand it to be spoken of GOD.

⁸ That is, had he not seriously considered the filthiness of whoredom, and

ness from him, because he was one of our sincere servants.
And they ran *to get one before the other* to the door ;[1] and she
rent his inner garment behind. And they met her lord at the
door. She said, What *shall be* the reward of him who seeketh
to commit evil in thy family, but imprisonment, and a painful
punishment ? And Joseph said, She asked me to lie with
her. And a witness of her family[2] bore witness, *saying*, If
his garment be rent before, she speaketh truth, and he is a
liar ; but if his garment be rent behind, she lieth, and he is a
speaker of truth. And when *her husband* saw that his garment was torn behind, he said, This is a cunning contrivance
of your *sex* ; for surely your cunning is great. O Joseph,
take no farther notice of this *affair* : and thou, *O woman*, ask
pardon for thy crime, for thou art a guilty person. And
certain women said *publicly*[3] in the city, The nobleman's wife
asked her servant to lie with her : he hath inflamed her
breast with his love ; and we perceive her *to be* in a manifest
error. And when she heard of their subtle behaviour, she sent
unto them,[4] and prepared a banquet for them, and she gave
to each of them a knife ; and she said *unto Joseph*, Come forth
unto them. And when they saw him they praised him greatly[5]

the great guilt thereof. Some, however, suppose that the words mean some
miraculous voice or apparition, sent by GOD to divert Joseph from executing
the criminal thoughts which began to possess him. For they say that he
was so far tempted with his mistress's beauty and enticing behaviour that
he sat in her lap, and even began to undress himself, when a voice called to
him, and bade him beware of her ; but he taking no notice of this admonition, though it was repeated three times, at length the angel Gabriel, or, as
others will have it, the figure of his master, appeared to him : but the more
general opinion is that it was the apparition of his father Jacob, who bit his
fingers' ends, or, as some write, struck him on the breast, whereupon his
lubricity passed out at the ends of his fingers. (Al Beidâwi, Al Zamakhshari, Jallalo'ddin, Yahya.)

For this fable, so injurious to the character of Joseph, the Mohammedans
are obliged to their old friends the Jews (Talm. Babyl. Sed. Nashim, p. 36.
Bartolocc. Bibl. Rabb. part iii. p. 509), who imagine that he had a design to
lie with his mistress, from these words of Moses (Gen. xxxix. xx.): *And
it came to pass—that Joseph went into the house to do his business*, &c.

[1] He flying from her, and she running after to detain him.

[2] viz., A cousin of hers, who was then a child in the cradle.

[3] These women, whose tongues were so free with Zoleikha's character on
this occasion, were five in number, and the wives of so many of the king's
chief officers—viz., his chamberlain, his butler, his baker, his jailer, and his
herdsman. (Al Beidâwi.)

[4] The number of all the women invited was forty, and among them were
the five ladies above mentioned. (Al Beidâwi.)

[5] The old Latin translators have strangely mistaken the sense of the
original word *acbarnaho*, which they render *menstruatœ sunt* ; and then
rebuke Mohammed for the indecency, crying out demurely in the margin,
O fœdum et obscœnum prophetam ! Erpenius (In not. ad Hist. Josephi)
thinks that there is not the least trace of such a meaning in the word ;
but he is mistaken ; for the verb *cabara* in the fourth conjugation, which is

and they cut their own hands,[1] and said, O GOD! this is not a mortal; he is no other than an angel, deserving the highest respect. And *his mistress* said, This is he for whose sake ye blamed me: I asked him to lie with me, but he hath constantly refused. But if he do not perform that which I command him, he shall surely be cast into prison, and he shall be made *one* of the contemptible. *Joseph* said, O LORD, a prison is more eligible unto me than *the crime* to which they invite me; but unless thou turn aside their snares from me, I shall youthfully incline unto them, and I shall become *one* of the foolish. Wherefore his LORD heard him, and turned aside their snare from him; for he *both* heareth *and* knoweth. And it seemed good unto them,[2] *even* after they had seen the signs *of his innocency*, to imprison him for a time. And there entered into the prison with him two *of the king's* servants.[3] One of them[4] said, it seemed to me *in my dream* that I pressed wine *out of grapes*. And the other said, It seemed unto me *in my dream* that I carried bread on my head, whereof the birds did eat. Declare unto us the interpretation of *our dreams*, for we perceive that thou art a beneficent person. *Joseph* answered, No food, wherewith ye may be nourished, shall come unto you, but I will declare unto you the interpretation thereof before it come unto you.[5] This *knowledge is a part* of that which my LORD hath taught me: for I have left the religion

here used, has that import, though the subjoining of the pronoun to it here (which possibly the Latin translators did not observe) absolutely overthrows that interpretation.

[1] Through extreme surprise at the wonderful beauty of Joseph; which surprise Zoleikha foreseeing, put knives into their hands, on purpose that this accident might happen. Some writers have observed, on occasion of this passage, that it is customary in the East for lovers to testify the violence of their passion by cutting themselves, as a sign that they would spend their blood in the service of the person beloved; which is true enough, but I do not find that any of the commentators suppose these Egyptian ladies had any such design.

[2] That is, to Kitfir and his friends. The occasion of Joseph's imprisonment is said to be, either that they suspected him to be guilty, notwithstanding the proofs which had been given of his innocence, or else that Zoleikha desired it, feigning, to deceive her husband, that she wanted to have Joseph removed from her sight, till she could conquer her passion by time; though her real design was to force him to compliance.

[3] viz., His chief butler and baker, who were accused of a design to poison him.

[4] Namely, the butler.

[5] The meaning of this passage seems to be, either that Joseph, to show he used no arts of divination or astrology, promises to interpret their dreams to them immediately, even before they should eat a single meal; or else, he here offers to prophesy to them beforehand, the quantity and quality of the victuals which should be brought them, as a taste of his skill.

of people who believe not in GOD, and who deny the life to come ; and I follow the religion of my fathers, Abraham, and Isaac, and Jacob. It is not *lawful* for us to associate anything with GOD. This *knowledge of the divine unity hath been given us* of the bounty of GOD towards us, and towards mankind ; but the greater part of men are not thankful. O my fellow-prisoners, are sundry lords better, or the only *true* and mighty GOD ? Ye worship not, besides him, other than the names which ye have named,[1] ye and your fathers, concerning which GOD hath sent down no authoritative proof : yet judgment *belongeth* unto GOD alone ; *who* hath commanded that ye worship none besides him. This is the right religion ; but the greater part of men know *it* not. O my fellow-prisoners, verily the one of you shall serve wine unto his lord, *as formerly* ; but the other shall be crucified, and the birds shall eat from off his head. The matter is decreed concerning which ye seek to be informed. And *Joseph* said unto him whom he judged to be the person who should escape of the two, Remember me in the presence of thy lord. But the devil caused him to forget to make mention of *Joseph* unto his lord ;[2] wherefore he remained in the prison some years.[3] And the king *of Egypt*[4] said, Verily, I saw *in my dream* seven fat kine, which seven lean kine devoured, and seven green ears *of corn*, and other *seven* withered *ears*. O nobles, expound my vision unto me, if ye be *able to* interpret a vision. They answered, *They are* confused dreams ; neither are we skilled in the intrepretation of *such kind of* dreams. And *Joseph's fellow-prisoner*, who had been delivered, said (for he remembered *Joseph* after a certain space of time), I will declare unto you the interpretation thereof ; wherefore let me go *unto the person who will interpret it unto me*. *And he went to the prison, and said*, O Joseph, thou man

---

[1] See Chap. VII. p. 148.

[2] According to the explanation of some, who take the pronoun *him* to relate to Joseph, this passage may be rendered, *But the devil caused him* (*i.e.* Joseph) *to forget to make his application unto his Lord* ; and to beg the good offices of his fellow-prisoner for his deliverance, instead of relying on GOD alone, as it became a prophet, especially, to have done. (Al Beidâwi.)

[3] The original word signifying any number from three to nine or ten, the common opinion is that Joseph remained in prison seven years, though some say he was confined no less than twelve years. (Al Beidâwi, Jallalo'ddin.)

[4] This prince, as the oriental writers generally agree, was Riyân, the son of Al Walîd, the Amalekite (Sale, Prel. Disc. Sect. I.), who was converted by Joseph to the worship of the true GOD, and died in the lifetime of that prophet. But some pretend that the Pharaoh of Joseph and of Moses were one and the same person, and that he lived (or rather reigned) four hundred years. (Al Beidâwi. See Chap. VII. p. 153.)

of veracity, teach us *the interpretation* of seven fat kine, which seven lean kine devoured, and of seven green ears *of corn* ; and other *seven* withered *ears, which the king saw in his dream* ; that I may return unto the men *who have sent me*, that peradventure they may understand *the same.* *Joseph* answered, Ye shall sow seven years as usual : and *the corn* which ye shall reap, do ye leave in its ear,[1] except a little whereof ye may eat. Then shall there come, after this, seven grievous *years of famine*, which shall consume what ye shall have laid up as a provision for the same, except a little which ye shall have kept. Then shall there come, after this, a year wherein men shall have plenty of rain,[2] and wherein they shall press *wine and oil.* And *when the chief butler had reported this*, the king said, Bring him unto me. And when the messenger came unto *Joseph*, he said, Return unto thy lord, and ask of him, what was the intent of the women who cut their hands ;[3] for my LORD well knoweth the snare which they laid *for me.*[4] *And when the women were assembled before the king*, he said *unto them*, What was your design when ye solicited Joseph to unlawful love ? They answered, GOD be praised ! we know not any ill of him. The nobleman's wife said, Now is the truth become manifest : I solicited him to lie with me ; and he is *one* of those who speak truth. *And when Joseph was acquainted therewith, he said*, This *discovery hath been made*, that *my lord* might know that I was not unfaithful unto him in *his* absence, and that GOD directeth not the plot of the deceivers. (XIII.)[5] Neither do I *absolutely* justify myself :[6] since *every* soul is prone unto evil, except those on

---

[1] To preserve it from the weevil. (Chap. VII.)

[2] Notwithstanding what some ancient authors write to the contrary (Plato, in Timæo, Pomp. Mela.), it often rains in winter in Lower Egypt, and even snow has been observed to fall at Alexandria, contrary to the express assertion of Seneca. (Nat. Quæst. l. 4.) In Upper Egypt indeed, towards the Nile cataracts, it rains very seldom. (See Greaves' Descr. of the Pyramids, p. 74, &c. Ray's Collection of Travels, tom. ii. p. 92.) Some, however, suppose that the rains here mentioned are intended of those which should fall in Ethiopia, and occasion the swelling of the Nile, or else of those which should fall in the neighbouring countries, which were also afflicted with famine during the same time.

[3] Joseph, it seems, cared not to get out of prison till his innocence was publicly known and declared. It is observed by the commentators that Joseph does not bid the messenger move the king to inform himself of the truth of the affair, but bids him directly to ask the king, to incite him to make the proper inquiry with the greater earnestness. They also observe that Joseph takes care not to mention his mistress, out of respect and gratitude for the favours he had received while in her house. (Al Beidâwi, &c.)

[4] Endeavouring both by threats and persuasions to entice me to commit folly with my mistress.

[5] Section XIII. begins here.

[6] According to a tradition of Ebn Abbâs, Joseph had no sooner spoken

whom my LORD shall show mercy ; for my LORD *is* gracious *and* merciful. And the king said, Bring him unto me : I will take him into my own peculiar service. And when *Joseph was brought unto the king, and* he had discoursed with him, he said, Thou art this day firmly established with us, *and shalt be* entrusted *with our affairs.*[1] *Joseph* answered, Set me over the store-houses of the land ; for I *will be* a skilful keeper *thereof.* Thus did we establish Joseph in the land, that he might provide himself a dwelling therein, where he pleased. We bestow our mercy on whom we please, and we suffer not the reward of the righteous to perish : and certainly the reward of the next life is better, for those who believe and fear GOD. Moreover Joseph's brethren came,[2] and went in unto him ; and he knew them, but they knew not him. And when he had furnished them with their provisions, he said, Bring unto me your brother, *the son* of your father : do ye not see that I give full measure, and that I am the most hospitable receiver of guests ? But if ye bring him not unto me, there shall be no *corn* measured unto you from me, neither shall ye approach *my presence.* They answered, We will endeavour to obtain him of his father, and we will certainly perform *what thou requirest.* And *Joseph* said to his

the foregoing words, asserting his innocency, than Gabriel said to him, *What, not when thou wast deliberating to lie with her* ? Upon which Joseph confessed his frailty. (Al Beidâwi, &c.)

[1] The commentators say that Joseph being taken out of prison, after he had washed and changed his clothes, was introduced to the king, whom he saluted in the Hebrew tongue, and on the king's asking what language that was, he answered that it was the language of his fathers. This prince, they say, understood no less than seventy languages, in every one of which he discoursed with Joseph, who answered him in the same ; at which the king greatly marvelling, desired him to relate his dream, which he did, describing the most minute circumstances : whereupon the king placed Joseph by him on his throne, and made him his Wazîr, or chief minister. Some say that his master Kitfîr dying about this time, he not only succeeded him in his place, but, by the king's command, married the widow, his late mistress, whom he found to be a virgin, and who bare him Ephraim and Manasses. (Al Beidâwi, Kitab Tafasir, &c.) So that according to this tradition, she was the same woman who is called Asenath by Moses. This supposed marriage, which authorized their amours, probably encouraged the Mohammedan divines to make use of the loves of Joseph and Zoleikha, as an allegorical emblem of the spiritual love between the Creator and the creature, GOD and the soul ; just as the Christians apply the Song of Solomon to the same mystical purpose. (D'Herbelot, Bibl. Orient. Art. Jousouf.)

[2] Joseph, being made Wazîr, governed with great wisdom ; for he not only caused justice to be impartially administered, and encouraged the people to industry and the improvement of agriculture during the seven years of plenty, but began and perfected several works of great benefit ; the natives at this day ascribing to the patriarch Joseph almost all the ancient works of public utility throughout the kingdom ; as particularly the rendering the province of the Feyyûm, from a standing pool or marsh, the most fertile and best cultivated land in all Egypt. (Golii not. in Alfragan, p.

servants, Put their money[1] *which they have paid for their corn,*
into their sacks, that they may perceive it, when they shall
be returned to their family : peradventure they will come
back *unto us.* And when they were returned unto their
father, they said, O father, it is forbidden to measure out *corn*
unto us *any more, unless we carry our brother Benjamin with
us* : wherefore send our brother with us, and we shall have
corn measured unto us ; and we will certainly guard him
from any mischance. Jacob answered, Shall I trust him with
you *with any better success* than I trusted your brother *Joseph*
with you heretofore ? But GOD is the best guardian ; and he is
the most merciful of those who show mercy. And when they
opened their provisions, they found their money had been
returned unto them ; *and* they said, O father, what do we
desire *further* ? this our money hath been returned unto us :
we will therefore *return,* and provide corn for our family : we
will take care of our brother ; and we shall receive a camel's
burden more *than we did the last time.* This is a small quantity.[2] *Jacob* said, I will by no means send him with you,

175, &c. Kircher. Oedip. Ægypt. vol. i. p. 8. Lucas, Voy. tom. ii. p. 205,
and tom. iii. p. 53.) When the years of famine came, the effects of which were
felt not only in Egypt, but in Syria and the neighbouring countries, the
inhabitants were obliged to apply to Joseph for corn, which he sold to them,
first for their money, jewels, and ornaments, then for their cattle and lands,
and at length for their persons ; so that all the Egyptians in general became
slaves to the king, though Joseph, by his consent, soon released them, and
returned them their substance. The dearth being felt in the land of Canaan,
Jacob sent all his sons, except only Benjamin, into Egypt for corn. On their
arrival, Joseph (who well knew them) asked them who they were, saying he
suspected them to be spies ; but they told him they came only to buy
provisions, and that they were all the sons of an ancient man, named Jacob,
who was also a prophet. Joseph then asked how many brothers there were
of them ; they answered, Twelve ; but that one of them had been lost in a
desert. Upon which he inquired for the eleventh brother, there being no
more than ten of them present. They said he was a lad, and with their
father, whose fondness for him would not suffer him to accompany them in
their journey. At length Joseph asked them who they had to vouch for
their veracity ; but they told him they knew no man who could vouch for
them in Egypt. Then, replied he, one of you shall stay behind with me as a
pledge, and the others may return home with their provisions ; and when ye
come again, ye shall bring your younger brother with you, that I may know
ye have told me the truth. Whereupon, it being in vain to dispute the
matter, they cast lots who should stay behind, and the lot fell upon Simeon.
When they departed, Joseph gave each of them a camel, and another for
their brother. (Al Beidâwi.)

    [1] The original word signifying not only money, but also goods bartered
or given in exchange for other merchandise, some commentators tell us,
that they paid for their corn, not in money, but in shoes and dressed skins.
(Al Beidâwi.)

    [1] The meaning may be, either that the corn they now brought was not
sufficient for the support of their families, so that it was necessary for them
to take another journey, or else, that a camel's load, more or less, was but a
trifle to the king of Egypt. Some suppose these to be the words of Jacob,
declaring it was too mean a consideration to induce him to part with his son.

    H*

until ye give me a solemn promise, *and swear* by GOD that ye will certainly bring him back unto me, unless ye be encompassed *by some inevitable impediment*. And when they had given him their solemn promise, he said, GOD is witness of what we say. And he said, My sons, enter not *into the city* by one *and the same* gate ; but enter by different gates. But *this precaution* will be of no advantage unto you against *the decree of* GOD ; for judgment belongeth unto GOD alone : in him do I put my trust, and in him let those confide who *seek in whom to* put their trust. And when they entered *the city*, as their father had commanded them, it was of no advantage unto them against *the decree of* GOD ; *and the same served* only *to satisfy* the desire of Jacob's soul, which he had charged *them to perform* : for he was endued with knowledge of that which we had taught him ; but the greater part of men do not understand. And when they entered into the presence of Joseph, he received his brother Benjamin as his guest, *and* said, Verily I am thy brother,[1] be not therefore afflicted for that which they have committed *against us*. And when he had furnished them with their provisions, he put *his* cup[2] in his brother Benjamin's sack. Then a crier cried *after them, saying*, O company of travellers, ye are surely thieves. They said (and turned back unto them), What *is it* that ye miss ? They answered, We miss the prince's cup : and unto him who shall produce it *shall be given* a camel's load *of corn* ; and I *will be* surety for the same. *Joseph's brethren* replied, By GOD, ye do well know that we come not to act corruptly in the land,[3] neither are we thieves. *The Egyptians* said, What shall be the reward of him *who shall appear to have stolen the cup*, if ye be *found* liars ? *Joseph's brethren*: answered, As to the reward of him in whose sack it shall be

---

[1] It is related that Joseph, having invited his brethren to an entertainment, ordered them to be placed two and two together, by which means Benjamin, the eleventh, was obliged to sit alone, and bursting into tears, said, If my brother Joseph were alive, he would have sat with me. Whereupon Joseph ordered him to be seated at the same table with himself, and when the entertainment was over, dismissed the rest, ordering that they should be lodged two and two in a house, but kept Benjamin in his own apartment, where he passed the night. The next day Joseph asked him whether he would accept of himself for his brother, in the room of him whom he had lost, to which Benjamin replied, *Who can find a brother comparable unto thee ? yet thou art not the son of Jacob and Rachel.* And upon this Joseph discovered himself to him. (Al Beidâwi.)

[2] Some imagine this to be a measure holding a saá (or about a gallon), wherein they used to measure corn or give water to the beasts. But others take it to be a drinking-cup of silver or gold.

[3] Both by our behaviour among you, and our bringing again our money which was returned to us without our knowledge.

found, let him become *a bondman in* satisfaction for the same :
thus do we reward the unjust, *who are guilty of theft.*[1]   Then
he began by their sacks, before *he searched* the sack of his
brother ;[2] and he drew out *the cup* from his brother's sack.
Thus did we furnish Joseph with a stratagem.   It was not
lawful for him to take his brother *for a bondman,* by the law
of the king *of Egypt,*[3] had not GOD pleased *to allow it, according to the offer of his brethren.*   We exalt to degrees *of knowledge and honour* whom we please : and *there is one who is*
knowing above all those who are endued with knowledge.
His brethren said, If *Benjamin* be guilty of theft, his brother
Joseph hath been also guilty of theft heretofore.[4]   But
Joseph concealed these things in his mind, and did not discover them unto them ; *and* he said *within himself,* Ye are
in a worse condition *than us two* ; and GOD best knoweth what
ye discourse about.   They said *unto Joseph,* Noble *lord,* Verily
this *lad* hath an aged father ; wherefore take one of us in his
stead ; for we perceive that thou art a beneficent person.
Joseph answered, GOD forbid that we should take *any other*
than him with whom we found our goods ; for then *should*
we certainly *be* unjust.   And when they despaired of *obtaining Benjamin,* they retired to confer privately together.   *And*
the elder of them[5] said, Do ye not know that your father hath
received a solemn promise from you, in the name of GOD ;
and how perfidiously ye behaved heretofore towards Joseph ?
Wherefore I will by no means depart the land *of Egypt,* until
my father give me leave *to return unto him,* or GOD maketh
known his will to me ; for he is the best judge.   Return ye

[1] This was the method of punishing theft used by Jacob and his family ;
for among the Egyptians it was punished in another manner.

[2] Some suppose this search was made by the person whom Joseph sent
after them ; others by Joseph himself, when they were brought back to the
city.

[3] For there the thief was not reduced to servitude, but was scourged, and
obliged to restore the double of what he had stolen.   (Al Beidâwi, Jallalo'-
ddin.)

[4] The occasion of this suspicion, it is said, was, that Joseph having been
brought up by his father's sister, she became so fond of him that, when he
grew up, and Jacob designed to take him from her, she contrived the following stratagem to keep him :—Having a girdle which had once belonged to
Abraham, she girt it about the child, and then, pretending she had lost it,
caused strict search to be made for it ; and it being at length found on Joseph,
he was adjudged, according to the above-mentioned law of the family, to be
delivered to her as her property.   Some, however, say that Joseph actually
stole an idol of gold, which belonged to his mother's father, and destroyed
it ; a story probably taken from Rachel's stealing the images of Laban :
and others tell us that he once stole a goat, or a hen, to give to a poor man.
(Jallalo'ddin.)

[5] viz., Reuben.   But some think Simeon or Judah to be here meant ;
and instead of *the elder,* interpret it *the most prudent of them.*

to your father, and say, O father, verily thy son hath committed theft; we bear witness of no more than what we know, and we could not guard against what we did not foresee: and do thou inquire in the city where we have been, and of the company of merchants with whom we are arrived, and *thou wilt find* that we speak the truth. *And when they were returned, and had spoken thus to their father,* he said, Nay, but rather ye yourselves have contrived the thing for your own sakes: but patience *is* most proper *for me*; peradventure GOD will restore them all[1] unto me; for he *is* knowing *and* wise. And he turned from them and said, Oh, how am I grieved for Joseph! And his eyes became white with mourning,[2] he being oppressed with deep sorrow. *His sons* said, By GOD, thou wilt not cease to remember Joseph, until thou be brought to death's door, or thou be actually destroyed *by excessive affliction.* He answered, I only represent my grief, which I am not able to contain, and my sorrow unto GOD; but I know *by revelation* from GOD that which ye know not.[3] O my sons, go and make inquiry after Joseph and his brother; and despair not of the mercy of GOD; for none despaireth of GOD's mercy, except the unbelieving people. *Wherefore Joseph's brethren returned into Egypt:* and when they came into his presence they said, Noble *lord*, the famine is felt by us and our family, and we are come with a small sum of money:[4] yet give unto us full measure, and bestow *corn* upon us *as* alms; for GOD rewardeth the almsgivers. *Joseph* said *unto them,* Do ye know what ye did unto Joseph and his brother, when ye were ignorant *of the consequences thereof*?[5] They answered, Art thou really Joseph?[6] He

---

[1] *i.e.,* Joseph, Benjamin, and Simeon.

[2] That is, the pupils lost their deep blackness and became of a pearl colour (as happens in suffusions), by his continual weeping: which very much weakened his sight, or, as some pretend, made him quite blind. (Al Beidâwi.)

[3] viz., That Joseph is yet alive, of which some tell us he was assured by the angel of death in a dream; though others suppose he depended on the completion of Joseph's dream, which must have been frustrated had he died before his brethren had bowed down before him. (Al Beidâwi.)

[4] Their money being clipped and adulterated. Some, however, imagine they did not bring money, but goods to barter, such as wool and butter, or other commodities of small value. (Al Beidâwi.)

[5] The injury they did Benjamin was the separating him from his brother; after which they kept him in so great subjection, that he durst not speak to them but with the utmost submission. Some say that these words were occasioned by a letter which Joseph's brethren delivered to him from their father, requesting the releasement of Benjamin, and by their representing his extreme affliction at the loss of him and his brother. The commentators observe that Joseph, to excuse his brethren's behaviour towards him, attributes it to their ignorance, and the heat of youth. (Al Beidâwi.)

[6] They say this question was not the effect of a bare suspicion that he **was**

replied, I am Joseph ; and this is my brother. Now hath
GOD been gracious unto us. For whoso feareth GOD, and
persevereth with patience, *shall at length find relief* ; since
GOD will not suffer the reward of the righteous to perish.
They said, By GOD, now hath GOD chosen thee above us ;
and we have surely been sinners. *Joseph* answered, Let
there be no reproach *cast* on you this day. GOD forgiveth
you ; for he is the most merciful of those who show mercy.
Depart ye with this my inner garment,[1] and throw it on my
father's face ; and he shall recover his sight : and *then* come
unto me with all your family. And when the company of
travellers was departed *from Egypt on their journey towards
Canaan,* their father said *unto those who were about him,*
Verily I perceive the smell of Joseph :[2] although ye think
that I dote. They answered, By GOD, thou art in thy old
mistake.[3] But when the messenger of good tidings[4] was
come *with Joseph's inner garment,* he threw it over his face ;
and he recovered his eyesight. *And Jacob* said, Did I not
tell you that I knew from GOD that which ye knew not ?
They answered, O father, ask pardon of our sins for us, for we
have surely been sinners. He replied, I will surely ask pardon for you of my LORD ;[5] for he *is* gracious *and* merciful.
And when *Jacob and his family arrived in Egypt,* and were
introduced unto Joseph, he received his parents unto him,[6]
and said, Enter ye into Egypt, by GOD's favour, in full

Joseph, but that they actually knew him, either by his face and behaviour,
or by his fore teeth, which he showed in smiling, or else by putting off his
tiara, and discovering a whitish mole on his forehead. (Al Beidâwi.)

[1] Which the commentators generally suppose to be the same garment
with which Gabriel invested him in the well ; which having originally come
from paradise, had preserved the odour of that place, and was of so great
virtue as to cure any distemper in the person who was touched with it.
(Al Beidâwi, Jallalo'ddin.)

[2] This was the odour of the garment above mentioned, brought by the
wind to Jacob, who smelt it, as is pretended, at the distance of eighty parasangs (Al Beidâwi) ; or, as others will have, three, or eight days' journey
off. (Jallalo'ddin.)

[3] Being led into this imagination by thy excessive love of Joseph.

[4] viz., Judah, who, as he had formerly grieved his father by bringing him
Joseph's coat stained with blood, now rejoiced him as much by being the
bearer of this vest, and the news of Joseph's prosperity. (Al Beidâwi.)

[5] Deferring it, as some fancy, till he should see Joseph, and have his
consent.

[6] viz., His father, and Leah, his mother's sister, whom he looked on as
his mother after Rachel's death. (Al Beidâwi. Gen. xxxvii. 10.) Al
Beidâwi tells us that Joseph sent carriages and provisions for his father and
his family ; and that he and the king of Egypt went forth to meet them. He
adds that the number of the children of Israel who entered Egypt with him
was seventy-two ; and that when they were led out thence by Moses, they
were increased to six hundred thousand five hundred and seventy men and
upwards, besides the old people and children.

security. And he raised his parents to the seat of state, and they, *together with his brethren*, fell down and did obeisance unto him.[1] And he said, O my father, this is the interpretation of my vision, *which I saw* heretofore : now hath my LORD rendered it true. And he hath surely been gracious unto me, since he took me forth from the prison, and hath brought me hither from the desert ; after that the devil had sown discord between me and my brethren : for my LORD is gracious unto whom he pleaseth ; and he *is* the knowing, the wise *God*. O LORD, thou hast given me *a part* of the kingdom, and hast taught me the interpretation of *dark* sayings. The Creator of heaven and earth ! thou art my protector in this world, and in that which is to come : make me to die a Moslem, and join me with the righteous.[2] This is a secret history, which we reveal unto thee, *O Mohammed*, although thou wast not present with the *brethren of Joseph*, when they concerted their design, and contrived a plot *against him*. But the greater part of men, although thou earnestly desire it, will not believe. Thou shalt not demand of them any reward for *thy publishing the Korân* ; it is no other than an admonition unto all creatures. And how many signs soever *there be of the being, unity, and providence of God*, in the heavens and the earth ; they will pass by them, and will retire afar off from them. And the greater part of them believe not in GOD, without being also guilty of idolatry.[3] Do they not believe that some overwhelming *affliction* shall fall on them, as a punishment from GOD ; or that the hour *of judgment* shall overtake them suddenly, while they consider not *its approach* ? Say *unto those of Mecca*, This is my way : I invite *you* unto GOD, by an evident demonstration ; *both* I and he who followeth me ; and, praise be unto GOD ! I am

[1] A transposition is supposed to be in these words, and that he seated his father and mother after they had bowed down to him, and not before. (Al Beidâwi.)

[2] The Mohammedan authors write that Jacob dwelt in Egypt twenty-four years, and at his death ordered his body to be buried in Palestine by his father, which Joseph took care to perform ; and then returning into Egypt, died twenty-three years after. They add that such high disputes arose among the Egyptians concerning his burial, that they had like to have come to blows ; but at length they agreed to put his body into a marble coffin, and to sink it in the Nile—out of a superstitious imagination, that it might help the regular increase of the river, and deliver them from famine for the future ; but when Moses led the Israelites out of Egypt, he took up the coffin, and carried Joseph's bones with him into Canaan, where he buried them by his ancestors. (Al Beidâwi.)

[3] With this crime Mohammed charges not only the idolatrous Meccans, but also the Jews and Christians, as has been already observed more than once.

not an idolater. We sent not *any apostles* before thee, except men *unto* whom we revealed *our will, and whom we chose* out of those who dwelt in cities.[1] Will they not go through the earth, and see what hath been the end of those who have preceded them ? But the dwelling of the next life shall surely be better for those who fear *God*. Will they not therefore understand ? *Their predecessors were borne with for a time,* until, when *our* apostles despaired *of their conversion,* and they thought that they were liars, our help came unto them, and we delivered whom we pleased ; but our ven·geance was not turned away from the wicked people. Verily in the histories of *the prophets and their people* there is an instructive example unto those who are endued with understanding. *The Korân* is not a new invented fiction ; but a confirmation of *those scriptures* which *have been revealed* before it, and a distinct explication of everything *necessary, in respect either to faith or practice,* and a direction and mercy unto people who believe.

XIII

THE CHAPTER OF THUNDER [2]

Revealed at Mecca.[3]

IN THE NAME OF THE MOST MERCIFUL GOD.

A L. M. R.[4] These are the signs of the book *of the Korân :* and that which hath been sent down unto thee from thy LORD is the truth ; but the greater part of men will not believe. *It is* GOD who hath raised the heavens without visible pillars ; *and* then ascended his throne, and compelled the sun and the moon to perform their services : each *of the heavenly bodies* runneth an appointed course. He ordereth *all* things. He showeth *his* signs distinctly, that ye may be assured ye must meet your LORD *at the last day. It is* he who hath stretched forth the earth, and placed therein steadfast *mountains,* and rivers ; and hath ordained therein of every

---

[1] And not of the inhabitants of the deserts ; because the former are more knowing and compassionate, and the latter more ignorant and hard-hearted. (Al Beidâwi. Sale, Prel. Disc. Sect. I.)

[2] This word occurs on the next page.

[3] Or, according to some copies, at Medina.

[4] The meaning of these letters is unknown. Of several conjectural explanations which are given of them, the following is one : *I am the most wise and knowing* GOD. See Sale, Prel. Disc. p. 64.

fruit two *different* kinds.[1] He causeth the night to cover the day. Herein are certain signs unto people who consider. And in the earth are tracts *of land of different natures,*[2] *though* bordering on each other ; and also vineyards, and seeds, and palm-trees springing several from the same root, and singly from distinct roots. They are watered with the same water, yet we render some of them more excellent than others to eat. Herein are surely signs unto people who understand. If thou dost wonder *at the infidels denying the resurrection,* surely wonderful is their saying, After we shall have been *reduced to* dust, shall we *be restored* in a new creature ? These are they who believe not in their LORD ; these *shall have* collars on their necks,[3] and these *shall be* the inhabitants of *hell* fire ; therein shall they abide for ever. They will ask of thee to hasten evil rather than good ;[4] although there have already been examples *of the divine vengeance* before them. Thy LORD is surely endued with indulgence towards men, notwithstanding their iniquity ; but thy LORD is also severe in punishing. The infidels say, Unless a sign be sent down unto him from his LORD, *we will not believe.* Thou art *commissioned to be* a preacher only, *and not a worker of miracles* : and unto every people *hath* a director *been appointed.* GOD knoweth what every female beareth *in her womb* ; and what the wombs want or exceed *of their due time, or number of young.* With him is everything *regulated* according to a *determined* measure. *He* knoweth that which is hidden, and that which is revealed. *He is* the great, the most high. He among you who concealeth *his* words, and he who proclaimeth them in public ; he also who seeketh to hide himself in the night, and he who goeth forth openly in the day, is equal *in respect to the knowledge of God.* Each of them hath *angels* mutually succeeding each other, before him, and behind him ; they watch him by the command of GOD.[5] Verily GOD

---

[1] As sweet and sour, black and white, small and large, &c. (Al Beidâwi, Jallalo'ddin.)

[2] Some tracts being fruitful and others barren, some plain and others mountainous, some proper for corn and others for trees, &c. (Al Beidâwi.)

[3] The *collar* here mentioned is an engine something like a pillory, but light enough for the criminal to walk about with. Besides the hole to fix it on the neck, there is another for one of the hands, which is thereby fastened to the neck (Chardin, Voy. de Perse, tom. ii. p. 229). And in this manner the Mohammedans suppose the reprobates will appear at the day of judgment (Chap. V, p. 81). Some understand this passage figuratively, of the infidels being bound in the chains of error and obstinacy (Al Beidâwi).

[4] Provoking and daring thee to call down the divine vengeance on them for their impenitency.

[5] Sale, Prel. Disc. Sect. IV. p. 77.

will not change *his grace* which is in men, until they change the *disposition* in their souls *by sin*. When GOD willeth evil on a people, there shall be none to avert it ; neither shall they have any protector beside him. *It is* he who causeth the lightning to appear unto you, to *strike* fear, and *to raise* hope,[1] and who formeth the pregnant clouds. The thunder celebrateth his praise,[2] and the angels *also*, for fear of him. He sendeth his thunderbolts, and striketh therewith whom he pleaseth, while they dispute concerning GOD ;[3] for he is mighty in power. *It is* he *who* ought of right to be invoked ; and the *idols* which they invoke besides him, shall not hear them at all ; otherwise than as he *is heard*, who stretcheth forth his hand to the water that it may ascend to his mouth, when it cannot ascend *thither* : the supplication of the unbelievers is utterly erroneous. Whatsoever is in heaven and on earth worshippeth GOD, voluntarily or of force ;[4] and their shadows *also*, morning and evening.[5] Say, Who is the LORD of heaven and earth ? Answer, GOD. Say, Have ye therefore taken *unto yourselves* protectors beside him, who are unable either to help, or to *defend* themselves from hurt ? Say, Shall the blind and the seeing be esteemed equal ? or shall darkness and light be accounted the same ? or have they attributed companions unto GOD, who have created as he hath created, so that their creation bear any resemblance

[1] Thunder and lightning being the sign of approaching rain ; a great blessing, in the eastern countries more especially.

[2] Or causeth those who hear it to praise him. Some commentators tell us that by the word *thunder*, in this place, is meant the angel who presides over the clouds, and drives them forwards with twisted sheets of fire. (Al Beidâwi, Jallalo'ddin.)

[3] This passage was revealed on the following occasion :—Amer Ebn al Tofail and Arbad Ebn Rabîah, the brother of Labîd, went to Mohammed with an intent to kill him ; and Amer began to dispute with him concerning the chief points of his doctrine, while Arbad, taking a compass, went behind him to dispatch him with his sword ; but the prophet, perceiving his design, implored GOD's protection ; whereupon Arbad was immediately struck dead by thunder, and Amer was struck with a pestilential boil, of which he died in a short time, in a miserable condition. (Al Beidâwi. Golii not. in Adagia Arab. adject. ad Gram. Erpenii, p. 99.) Jallalo'ddin, however, tells another story, saying that Mohammed, having sent one to invite a certain man to embrace his religion, the person put this question to the missionary, *Who is this apostle, and what is* GOD ? *Is he of gold, or of silver, or of brass ?* Upon which a thunderbolt struck off his head, and killed him.

[4] The infidels and devils themselves being constrained to humble themselves before him, though against their will, when they are delivered up to punishment.

[5] This is an allusion to the increasing and diminishing of the shadows, according to the height of the sun ; so that, when they are the longest, which is in the morning and the evening, they appear prostrate on the ground, in the posture of adoration.

unto his ? Say, GOD is the creator of all things ; he is the one, the victorious *God*. He causeth water to descend from heaven, and the brooks flow according to their *respective* measure, and the floods bear the floating froth : and from *the metals* which they melt in the fire, seeking *to cast* ornaments or vessels *for use, there ariseth* a scum like unto it. Thus GOD setteth forth truth and vanity. But the scum is thrown off, and that which is useful to mankind remaineth on the earth. Thus doth GOD put forth parables. Unto those who obey their LORD *shall be given* the most excellent *reward :* but those who obey him not, although they were possessed of whatever is in the whole earth and as much more, they would give it *all* for their ransom. These will be brought to a terrible account : their abode *shall be* hell ; an unhappy couch *shall it be* ! Shall he, therefore, who knoweth that what hath been sent down unto thee from thy LORD, is truth, be *rewarded* as he who is blind ? The prudent only will consider ; who fulfil the covenant of GOD, and break not *their* contract ; and who join that which GOD hath commanded to be joined,[1] and *who* fear their LORD, and dread an ill account ; and who persevere out of a *sincere* desire to please their LORD, and observe the stated times of prayer, and give alms out of what we have bestowed on them, in secret and openly, and who turn away evil with good : the reward of these *shall be* paradise, gardens of eternal abode,[2] which they shall enter, and *also* whoever shall have acted uprightly, of their fathers, and their wives, and their posterity ; and the angels shall go in unto them by every gate, *saying*, Peace be upon you, because ye have endured with patience ; how excellent a reward is paradise ! But as for those who violate the covenant of GOD, after the establishment thereof, and *who* cut in sunder that which GOD hath commanded to be joined, and act corruptly in the earth, on them shall a curse *fall*, and they shall have a miserable dwelling *in hell*. GOD giveth provision in abundance unto whom he pleaseth, and is sparing *unto whom he pleaseth. Those of Mecca* rejoice in the present life ; although the present life, in respect of the future, is but a *precarious* provision. The infidels say, Unless a sign be sent down unto him from his LORD, *we will not believe.* Answer, Verily GOD will lead into

---

[1] By believing in all the prophets, without exception, and joining thereto the continual practice of their duty, both towards GOD and man. (Al Beidâwi, Jallalo'ddin, Yahya.)

[2] Literally *gardens* of Eden. Chap. IX.

error whom he pleaseth, and will direct unto himself him who repenteth, *and* those who believe, and whose hearts rest securely in the meditation of GOD ; shall not *men's* hearts rest securely in the meditation of GOD ? They who believe and do that which is right *shall enjoy* blessedness, and *partake of* a happy resurrection. Thus have we sent thee to a nation which *other* nations have preceded, *unto whom prophets have likewise been sent*, that thou mayest rehearse unto them that which we have revealed unto thee, even while they believe not in the merciful *God*. Say *unto them*, He is my LORD ; there is no GOD but he : in him do I trust, and unto him must I return. Though a Korân *were revealed* by which mountains should be removed, or the earth cleaved in sunder, or the dead be caused to speak,[1] *it would be in vain*. But the matter *belongeth* wholly unto GOD. Do not therefore the believers know, that if GOD pleased, he would certainly direct all men ? Adversity shall not cease to afflict the unbelievers for that which they have committed, or to sit down near their habitations,[2] until GOD's promise come :[3] for GOD is not contrary to the promise. Apostles before thee have been laughed to scorn ; and I permitted the infidels to enjoy a long and happy life : but afterwards I punished them ; and how *severe* was the punishment which I *inflicted on them* ! Who is it therefore that standeth over every soul, *to observe* that which it committeth ? They attribute companions unto GOD. Say, Name them : will ye declare unto him that which he knoweth not in the earth ? or *will ye name them* in outward speech only ?[4] But the deceitful procedure of the infidels

---

[1] These are miracles which the Koreish required of Mohammed ; demanding that he would, by the power of his Korân, either remove the mountains from about Mecca, that they might have delicious gardens in their room ; or that he would oblige the wind to transport them, with their merchandise, to Syria (according to which tradition, the words here translated *or the earth cleaved in sunder*, should be rendered, *or the earth be travelled over* in an instant) ; or else raise to life Kosai Ebn Kelâb (Chap. VIII:), and others of their ancestors, to bear witness to him ; whereupon this passage was revealed.

[2] It is supposed by some that these words are spoken to Mohammed, and then they must be translated in the second person, *Nor shalt thou cease to sit down*, &c. For they say this verse relates to the idolaters of Mecca, who were afflicted with a series of misfortunes for their ill-usage of their prophet, and were also continually annoyed and harassed by his parties, which frequently plundered their caravans and drove off their cattle, himself sitting down with his whole army near the city in the expedition of Al Hodeib'ya. (Al Beidâwi.)

[3] *i.e.*, Till death and the day of judgment overtake them ; or, according to the exposition in the preceding note, until the taking of Mecca. (Al Beidâwi.)

[4] That is, calling them the companions of GOD, without being able to assign any reason, or give any proof why they deserve to be sharers in the honour and worship due from mankind to him. (Al Beidâwi.)

was prepared for them ; and they are turned aside from the *right* path : for he whom GOD shall cause to err, shall have no director. They shall suffer a punishment in this life ; but the punishment of the next shall be more grievous : and there shall be none to protect them against GOD. *This is* the description of paradise, which is promised to the pious. It is watered by rivers ; its food is perpetual, and its shade *also* : this shall be the reward of those who fear *God*. But the reward of the infidels shall be *hell* fire. Those to whom we have given the scriptures, rejoice at what hath been revealed unto thee.[1] Yet *there are* some of the confederates who deny part thereof.[2] Say *unto them*, Verily I am commanded to worship GOD alone ; and to give him no companion : upon him do I call, and unto him shall I return. To this purpose have we sent down *the Korân*, a *rule of* judgment, in the Arabic language. And verily if thou follow their desires, after the knowledge which hath been given thee, there shall be none to defend or protect thee against GOD. We have formerly sent apostles before thee, and bestowed on them wives and children ;[3] and no apostle had *the power* to come with a sign, unless by the permission of GOD. Every age hath its book *of revelation* : GOD shall abolish and shall confirm *what he pleaseth*. With him is the original of the book.[4] Moreover, whether we cause thee to see any part of that *punishment* wherewith we have threatened them, or whether we cause thee to die *before it be inflicted on them*, verily unto thee *belongeth* preaching *only*, but unto us inquisition. Do they not see that we come into *their* land, and straiten the borders thereof, *by the conquests of the true believers* ? When GOD judgeth, there is none to reverse his judgment ; and he *will be* swift in taking an account. Their

[1] viz.,The first proselytes to Mohammedism from Judaism and Christianity or the Jews and Christians in general, who were pleased to find the Korân so consonant to their own Scriptures (Chap. III :).

[2] That is, such of them as had entered into a confederacy to oppose Mohammed ; as did Caab Ebn al Ashraf, and the Jews who followed him, and Al Seyid al Najrâni, Al Akib, and several other Christians ; who denied such parts of the Korân as contradicted their corrupt doctrines and traditions.

[3] As we have on thee. This passage was revealed in answer to the reproaches which were cast on Mohammed, on account of the great number of his wives. For the Jews said that if he was a true prophet, his care and attention would be employed about something else than women and the getting of children. (Jallalo'ddin, Yahya.) It may be observed that it is a maxim of the Jews that nothing is more repugnant to prophecy than carnality. (Maimon, More Nev. part ii., c. 36, &c.)

[4] Literally, *the mother of the book* ; by which is meant *the preserved table*, from which all the written revelations which have been from time to time published to mankind, according to the several dispensations, are transcripts.

predecessors formerly devised subtle plots *against their prophets* ; but GOD is master of every subtle device. He knoweth that which every soul deserveth : and the infidels shall surely know, whose will be the reward of paradise. The unbelievers[1] will say, Thou art not sent *of God.* Answer, GOD is a sufficient witness between me and you, and he who understandeth the scriptures.

XIV

THE CHAPTER OF ABRAHAM [2]

Revealed at Mecca.

IN THE NAME OF THE MOST MERCIFUL GOD.

A L. R.[3] *This* book have we sent down unto thee, that thou mayest lead men forth from darkness into light, by the permission of their LORD, into the glorious and laudable way. GOD *is he* unto whom *belongeth* whatsoever is in heaven and on earth : and woe be to the infidels, because a grievous punishment *awaiteth them* ; who love the present life above that which is to come, and turn *men* aside from the way of GOD, and seek to render it crooked : these are in an error far distant *from the truth.* We have sent no apostle but with the language of his people, that he might declare *their duty* plainly unto them :[4] for GOD causeth to err whom he pleaseth, and directeth whom he pleaseth ; and he is the mighty, the wise. We formerly sent Moses with our signs, *and commanded him saying,* Lead forth thy people from darkness into light, and remind them of the favours of GOD :[5] verily therein *are* signs unto every patient *and* grateful person. And *call to mind* when Moses said unto his people, Remember the favour of GOD towards you, when he delivered you from the people of Pharaoh : they grievously oppressed you ; and they slew your male children, but let your females live :[6]

---

[1] The persons intended in this passage, it is said, were the Jewish doctors. (Al Beidâwi.)

[2] Mention is made of this patriarch towards the end of the chapter.

[3] Sale, Prel. Disc. p. 64.

[4] That so they might not only perfectly and readily understand those revelations themselves, but might also be able to translate and interpret them unto others. (Al Beidâwi.)

[5] Literally, *the days of* GOD ; which may also be translated, *the battles of* GOD (the Arabs using the word *day* to signify a remarkable engagement, as the Italians do *giornata,* and the French, *journée*), or his wonderful acts manifested in the various success of former nations in their wars. (Al Beidâwi.)

[6] Chap. VII.

therein was a great trial from your LORD. And when your LORD declared *by the mouth of Moses, saying,* If ye be thankful, I will surely increase *my favours towards you;* but if ye be ungrateful, verily my punishment *shall be* severe. And Moses said, if ye be ungrateful, and all who are in the earth *likewise;* verily GOD needeth not *your thanks, though* he deserveth the highest praise. Hath not the history of *the nations* your predecessors reached you; *namely,* of the people of Noah, and of Ad, and of Thamûd,[1] and of those who succeeded them; whose *number* none knoweth except GOD? Their apostles came unto them with evident *miracles;* but they clapped their hands to their mouths *out of indignation,* and said, We do not believe *the message* with which ye *pretend to* be sent; and we are in a doubt concerning the *religion* to which ye invite us, *as justly to be* suspected. Their apostles answered, Is there any doubt concerning GOD, the creator of heaven and earth? He inviteth you *to the true faith* that he may forgive you *part* of your sins,[2] and may respite *your punishment, by granting you space to repent,* until an appointed time. They answered, Ye are but men, like unto us: ye seek to turn us aside from *the gods* which our fathers worshipped: wherefore bring us an evident demonstration *by some miracle, that ye speak truth.* Their apostles replied unto them, We are no other than men like unto you; but GOD is bountiful unto such of his servants as he pleaseth: and it is not in our *power* to give you a miraculous demonstration *of our mission,* unless by the permission of GOD; in GOD therefore let the faithful trust. And what *excuse* have we *to allege,* that we should not put our trust in GOD; since he hath directed us our paths? Wherefore we will certainly suffer with patience the *persecution* wherewith ye shall afflict us: in GOD therefore let those put their confidence who *seek in whom to* put their trust. And those who believed not, said unto their apostles, We will surely expel you out of our land; or ye shall return unto our religion. And their LORD spake unto them by revelation, *saying,* We will surely destroy the wicked doers; and we will cause you to dwell in the earth, after them. This *shall be granted* unto him who shall dread *the appearance at* my tribunal, and shall fear my threatening.

---

[1] Chap. VII.

[2] That is, such of them as were committed directly against GOD, which are immediately cancelled by faith, or embracing Islâm; but not the crimes of injustice, and oppression, which were committed against man (Al Beidâwi): for to obtain remission of these last, besides faith, repentance and restitution, according to a man's ability, are also necessary.

And they asked assistance *of God*,[1] and every rebellious perverse person failed of success. Hell *lieth unseen* before him, and he shall have filthy water[2] given him to drink : he shall sup it up by little and little, and he shall not easily let it pass his throat, *because of its nauseousness* ; death also shall come upon him from every quarter, yet he shall not die ; and before him *shall there stand prepared* a grievous torment. *This is* the likeness of those who believe not in their LORD. Their works are as ashes, which the wind violently scattereth in a stormy day : they shall not be able to *obtain* any *solid advantage* from that which they have wrought. This is an error most distant *from truth*. Dost thou not see that GOD hath created the heavens and the earth in wisdom. If he please, he can destroy you, and produce a new creature *in your stead* : neither will this be difficult with GOD. And they shall all come forth into *the presence of God at the last day* : and the weak among them shall say unto those who behaved themselves arrogantly,[3] Verily we were your followers *on earth* ; will ye not therefore avert from us *some part* of the divine vengeance ? They *shall answer*, If GOD had directed us *aright, we had certainly directed you*.[4] It is equal unto us whether we bear *our torments* impatiently, or whether we endure *them* with patience : *for* we have no way to escape. And Satan shall say, after judgment shall have been given, Verily GOD promised you a promise of truth : and I *also* made you a promise ; but I deceived you. Yet I had not any power over you *to compel you* ; but I called you only, and ye answered me : wherefore accuse not me, but accuse yourselves.[5] I cannot assist you ; neither can ye assist me. Verily I do *now* renounce your having associated me *with* God heretofore.[6] A grievous punishment is *prepared* for

---

[1] The commentators are uncertain whether these were the prophets, who begged assistance against their enemies ; or the infidels, who called for GOD's decision between themselves and them ; or both. And some suppose this verse has no connection with the preceding, but is spoken of the people of Mecca, who begged rain in a great drought with which they were afflicted at the prayer of their prophet, but could not obtain it. (Al Beidâwi.)

[2] Which will issue from the bodies of the damned, mixed with purulent matter and blood.

[3] *i.e.*, The more simple and inferior people shall say to their teachers and princes who seduced them to idolatry, and confirmed them in their obstinate infidelity.

[4] That is, We made the same choice for you, as we did for ourselves : and had not GOD permitted us to fall into error, we had not seduced you.

[5] Lay not the blame on my temptations, but blame your own folly in obeying and trusting to me, who had openly professed myself your irreconcilable enemy.

[6] Or I do now declare myself clear of your having obeyed me, preferably

the unjust.   But they who shall have believed, and wrought righteousness, shall be introduced into gardens, wherein rivers flow ;   they shall remain therein *for ever*, by the permission of their LORD ;   and their salutation therein *shall be*, Peace !¹ Dost thou not see how GOD putteth forth a parable ;   *representing* a good word, as a good tree, whose root is firmly fixed *in the earth*, and whose branches *reach* unto heaven ;   which bringeth forth its fruit in all seasons, by the will of its LORD ? GOD propoundeth parables unto men, that they may be instructed.   And the likeness of an evil word is as an evil tree ; which is torn up from the face of the earth, and hath no stability.²   GOD shall confirm them who believe, by the steadfast word *of faith, both* in this life and in that which is to come :³ but GOD shall lead the wicked into error, for GOD doth that which he pleaseth.   Hast thou not considered those who have changed the grace of GOD to infidelity,⁴ and cause their people to descend into the house of perdition, *namely, into* hell ?   They shall be thrown to burn therein ; and an unhappy dwelling *shall it be*.   They also set up idols as copartners with GOD, that they might cause *men* to stray from his path.   Say *unto them*, Enjoy *the pleasures of this life for a time* ;   but your departure *hence* shall be into *hell* fire.   Speak unto my servants who have believed, that they

to GOD, and worshipped idols at my instigation.   Or the words may be translated, *I believed not heretofore in that Being with whom ye did associate me* ;   intimating his first disobedience in refusing to worship Adam at GOD's command. (Al Beidâwi.)

¹ See Chap. X.

² What is particularly intended in this passage by the *good word*, and the *evil word*, the expositors differ.   But the first seems to mean the profession of GOD's unity, the inviting others to the true religion, or the Korân itself ; and the latter, the acknowledging a plurality of gods, the seducing of others to idolatry, or the obstinate opposition to GOD's prophets. (Al Beidâwi, Jallalo'ddin.)

³ Jallalo'ddin supposes the sepulchre to be here understood ;   in which place when the true believers come to be examined by the two angels concerning their faith, they will answer properly and without hesitation ;   which the infidels will not be able to do. (Sale, Prel. Disc. Sect. IV.)

⁴ That is, who requite his favours with disobedience and incredulity. Or, whose ingratitude obliged GOD to deprive them of the blessings he had bestowed on them ;   as he did the Meccans, who though GOD had placed them in the sacred territory, and given them the custody of the Caaba, and abundant provision of all necessaries and conveniences of life, and had also honoured them by the mission of Mohammed, yet in return for all this became obstinate unbelievers, and persecuted his apostle ;   for which they were not only punished by a famine of seven years, but also by the loss and disgrace they sustained at Bedr ;   so that they who had before been celebrated for their prosperity, were now stripped of that, and become conspicuous only for their infidelity. (Al Beidâwi.)   If this be the drift of the passage, it could not have been revealed at Mecca, as the rest of the chapter is agreed to be ;   wherefore some suppose this verse and the next to have been revealed at Medina.

be assiduous at prayer, and give alms out of that which we
have bestowed on them, *both* privately and in public ; before
the day cometh, wherein there shall be no buying nor selling,
neither any friendship. It is GOD who hath created the
heavens and the earth ; and causeth water to descend from
heaven, and by means thereof produceth fruits for your
sustenance : and by his command he obligeth[1] the ships to
sail in the sea for your service ; and he also forceth the rivers
to supply your uses : he likewise compelleth the sun and the
moon, which diligently perform their courses, to serve you ;
and hath subjected the day and the night to your service. He
giveth you of everything which ye ask him ; and if ye *attempt
to* reckon up the favours of GOD, ye shall not be able to
compute the same. Surely man is unjust *and* ungrateful.
Remember when Abraham said, O LORD, make this land[2]
a place of security ; and grant that I and my children[3] may
avoid the worship of idols ; for they, O LORD, have seduced
a great number of men. Whoever therefore shall follow
me, he *shall be* of me : and whosoever shall disobey me ;
verily thou *wilt be* gracious *and* merciful.[4] O LORD, I have
caused *some* of my offspring[5] to settle in an unfruitful valley,
near thy holy house, O LORD, that they may be constant at
prayer. Grant, therefore, that the hearts of some men[6] may
be affected with kindness toward them ; and do thou bestow
on them *all sorts* of fruits ;[7] that they may give thanks. O

[1] The word used here, and in the following sentences, is *sakhkhara*, which
signifies *forcibly to press into any service.* (Chap. II.)

[2] viz., The territory of Mecca. See the Prelim. Disc. Sect. IV.

[3] This prayer, it seems, was not heard as to all his posterity, particularly as
to the descendants of Ismael ; though some pretend that these latter did not
worship images, but only paid a superstitious veneration to certain stones,
which they set up and compassed, as representations of the Caaba. (Al
Beidâwi. Prelim. Disc. Sect. I.)

[4] That is, by disposing him to repentance. But Jallalo'ddin supposes
these words were spoken by Abraham before he knew that GOD would not
pardon idolatry.

[5] *i.e.*, Ismael and his posterity. The Mohammedans say, that Hagar,
his mother, belonged to Sarah, who gave her to Abraham ; and that, on
her bearing him this son, Sarah became so jealous of her, that she prevailed
on her husband to turn them both out of doors ; whereupon he sent them
to the territory of Mecca, where GOD caused the fountain of Zemzem to
spring forth for their relief, in consideration of which the Jorhamites, who
were the masters of the country, permitted them to settle among them.
(Al Beidâwi.)

[6] Had he said the hearts of men, absolutely, the Persians and the Romans
would also have treated them as friends ; and both the Jews and Christians
would have made their pilgrimages to Mecca. (Al Beidâwi. Jallalo'ddin.)

[7] This part of the prayer was granted ; Mecca being so plentifully supplied,
that the fruits of spring, summer, and autumn, are to be found there at one
and the same time. (Al Beidâwi.)

LORD, thou knowest whatsoever we conceal, and whatsoever we publish ; for nothing is hidden from GOD, either on earth, or in heaven. Praise be unto GOD, who hath given me, in *my* old age, Ismael and Isaac : for my LORD is the hearer of supplication. O LORD, grant that I may be an observer of prayer, and *a part* of my posterity *also*,[1] O LORD ; and receive my supplication. O LORD, forgive me, and my parents,[2] and the faithful, on the day whereon an account shall be taken. Think not, *O prophet,* that GOD *is* regardless of what the ungodly do. He only deferreth their *punishment* unto the day whereon *men's* eyes shall be fixed : they shall hasten forward, *at the voice of the angel calling to judgment,* and shall lift up their heads ; they shall not be able to turn their sight *from the object whereon it shall be fixed,* and their hearts shall be void *of sense, through excessive terror.* Wherefore do thou threaten men with the day, *whereon their* punishment shall be inflicted on them, and *whereon* those who have acted unjustly shall say, O LORD, give us respite unto a term near at hand ; *and* we will obey thy call, and we will follow *thy* apostles. *But it shall be answered unto them,* Did ye not swear heretofore, that no reverse should befall you ?[3] yet ye dwelt in the dwellings of those who had treated their own souls unjustly ;[4] and it appeared plainly unto you how we had dwelt with them ;[5] and we propounded *their destruction as* examples unto you. They employ their utmost subtlety *to oppose the truth* ; but their subtlety *is apparent* unto GOD, *who is able to frustrate their designs* ; although their subtlety were *so great,* that the mountains might be moved thereby. Think not therefore, *O prophet,* that GOD will be contrary to his promise *of assistance, made* unto his apostles ; for GOD *is* mighty, able to avenge. The day *will come, when* the earth shall be changed into another earth, and the heavens *into other heavens* ;[6] and men shall come forth *from their graves*

---

[1] For he knew by revelation that some of them would be infidels.

[2] Abraham put up this petition to GOD before he knew that his parents were the enemies of GOD. (Chap. IX.) Some suppose his mother was a true believer, and therefore read it in the singular, *and my father.* Others fancy that by his *parents* the patriarch here means Adam and Eve. (Jallalo'ddin, Al Beidâwi.)

[3] That is, That ye should not taste of death, but continue in this world for ever ; or that ye should not after death be raised to judgment. (Al Beidâwi, Al Zamakhshari, Yahya.)   [4] viz., Of the Adites and Thamûdites.

[5] Not only by the histories of those people revealed in the Korân, but also by the monuments remaining of them (as the houses of the Thamûdites), and the traditions preserved among you of the terrible judgments which befell them.

[6] This the Mohammedans suppose will come to pass at the last day ; the

to appear before the only, the mighty GOD.   And thou shalt see the wicked on that day bound together in fetters : their inner garments shall be of pitch, and fire shall cover their faces ; that GOD may reward every soul, according to what it shall have deserved ; for GOD is swift in taking an account.   This is a sufficient admonition unto men, that they may be warned thereby, and that they may know that there is but one GOD ; and that those who are endued with under-standing may consider.

XV

THE CHAPTER OF AL HEJR [1]

Revealed at Mecca.

IN THE NAME OF THE MOST MERCIFUL GOD.

A L. R. [2]   These are the signs of the book, and of the (XIV.) [3] perspicuous Korân.   The time may come when the unbelievers shall wish that they had been Moslems. [4] Suffer them to eat, and to enjoy themselves *in this world* ; and let hope entertain them ; but they shall hereafter know *their folly*.   We have not destroyed any city, but a fixed term *of repentance was* appointed them.   No nation shall be *pun-ished* before their time *shall be come* ; neither shall they be respited *after*.   *The Meccans* say, O thou to whom the admonition [5] hath been sent down,   thou art certainly possessed with a devil : wouldest thou not have come unto us with *an attendance of* angels, if thou hadst spoken truth ? *Answer*, We send not down the angels, unless on a just occa-sion ; [6] nor should they be then respited any longer.   We have surely sent down the Korân ; and we will certainly preserve

---

earth becoming white and even, or, as some will have it, of silver ; and the heavens of gold. (Sale, Prel. Disc. Sect. IV.)

[1] Al Hejr—literally the rock—is a territory in the province of Hejaz, between Medina and Syria, where the tribe of Thamûd dwelt.

[2] Sale, Prel. Disc. Sect. III. p. 64.

[3] Section XIV. begins here.

[4] viz., When they shall see the success and prosperity of the true believers ; or when they shall come to die ; or at the resurrection.

[5] *i.e.*, The revelations which compose the Korân.

[6] When the divine wisdom shall judge it proper to use their ministry, as in bearing his revelations to the prophets, and the executing his sentence on wicked people ; but not to humour you with their appearance in visible shapes, which, should your demand be complied with, would only increase your confusion, and bring GOD's vengeance on you the sooner.

the same *from corruption*.[1] We have heretofore sent
apostles before thee, among the ancient sects : and there came
no apostle unto them, but they laughed him to scorn. In
the same manner will we put it into the hearts of the wicked
Meccans to scoff at their prophet : they shall not believe on
him ; and the sentence of the nations of old hath been executed heretofore. If we should open a gate in the heaven
above them, and they should ascend thereto[2] all the day long,
they would surely say, Our eyes are only dazzled ; or rather we
are a people deluded by enchantments. We have placed *the
twelve* signs in the heaven, and have set them out *in various
figures*, for *the observation of* spectators : and we guard
them from every devil[3] driven away with stones ;[4] except
him who listeneth by stealth, at whom a visible flame is
darted.[5] We have also spread forth the earth, and thrown
thereon stable *mountains* ; and we have caused every kind of
vegetables to spring forth in the same, according to a determinate weight : and we have provided therein necessaries
of life for you, and for him whom ye do not sustain.[6] There
is no one thing but the storehouses thereof are in our hands ;
and we distribute not the same *otherwise* than in a determinate measure. We also send the winds driving the pregnant
clouds, and we send down from heaven water, whereof we
give you to drink, and which ye keep not in store. Verily,
we give life, and we put to death ; and we are the heirs *of all
things*.[7] We know those among you who go before ; and
we know those who stay behind.[8] And thy LORD shall gather

[1] Sale, Pre lim. Disc. Sect. IV.

[2] *i.e.*, The incredulous Meccans themselves ; or, as others rather think,
the angels in visible forms.

[3] For the Mohammedans imagine that the devils endeavour to ascend
to the constellations, to pry into the actions and overhear the discourse of
the inhabitants of heaven, and to tempt them. They also pretend that
these evil sprits had the liberty of entering any of the heavens till the
birth of JESUS, when they were excluded from three of them ; but that on
the birth of Mohammed they were forbidden the other four. (Al Beidâwi.)

[4] See Chap. III.

[5] For when a star seems to fall or shoot, the Mohammedans suppose the
angels, who keep guard in the constellations, dart them at the devils who
approach too near.

[6] viz., Your family, servants, and slaves, whom ye wrongly imagine that
ye feed yourselves ; though it is GOD who provides for them as well as you
(Al Beidâwi) : or, as some rather think, the animals, of whom men take no
care (Jallalo'ddin.)

[7] *i.e.*, Alone surviving, when all creatures shall be dead and annihilated.

[8] What these words particularly drive at is uncertain. Some think
them spoken of the different times of men's several entrance into this world,
and their departure out of it ; others of the respective forwardness and
backwardness of Mohammed's men in battle ; and a third says, the passage
was occasioned by the different behaviour of Mohammed's followers, or

them together *at the last day* ; for he *is* knowing *and* wise. We created man of dried clay, of black mud, formed into shape :[1] and we had before created the devil of subtle fire. And *remember* when thy LORD said before the angels, Verily I am about to create man of dried clay, of black mud, wrought into shape ; when therefore I shall have completely formed him, and shall have breathed of my spirit into him ; do ye fall down and worship him.　And all the angels worshipped *Adam* together, except Eblîs, *who* refused to be with those who worshipped *him*.　*And God* said *unto him*, O Eblîs, what *hindered* thee from being with those who worshipped *Adam* ?　He answered, It is not fit that I should worship man, whom thou hast created of dried clay, of black mud, wrought into shape.　*God* said, Get thee therefore hence ; for thou shalt be driven away with stones : and a curse *shall be* on thee, until the day of judgment.　*The devil* said, O LORD, give me respite until the day of resurrection.　*God* answered, Verily thou shalt be *one* of those who are respited until the day of the appointed time.[2]　*The devil* replied, O LORD, because thou hast seduced me, I will surely tempt them *to disobedience* in the earth ; and I will seduce them all, except *such* of them *as shall be* thy chosen servants.　*God* said, This is the right way with me.[3]　Verily *as to* my servants, thou shalt have no power over them ; but *over* those only who shall be seduced, and who shall follow thee.　And hell is surely denounced unto them all : it hath seven gates ; unto every gate a distinct company of them *shall be assigned*.[4] But those who fear *God shall dwell* in gardens, amidst fountains.　*The angels shall say unto them*, Enter ye therein in peace and security.　And we will remove all grudges from their breasts ;[5] *they shall be as* brethren, sitting over against one another[6] on couches : weariness shall not affect them therein, neither shall they be cast out thence *for ever*.　Declare

seeing a very beautiful woman at prayers behind the prophet ; some of them going out of the mosque before her, to avoid looking on her more nearly, and others staying behind, on purpose to view her.　(Al Beidâwi.)

[1] See Chap. II.

[2] See Chaps. II. and VII.

[3] viz., The saving of the elect, and the utter reprobation of the wicked, according to my eternal decree.

[4] Sale, Prel. Disc. Sect. IV.

[5] That is, all hatred and ill-will which they bore each other in their lifetime ; or, as some choose to expound it, all envy or heart-burning on account of the different degrees of honour and happiness to which the blessed will be promoted according to their respective merits. (Chap. VII. p. 143, note [6].)

[6] Never turning their backs to one another (Jallalo'ddin) ; which might be construed a sign of contempt.

unto my servants that I am the gracious, the merciful *God ;* and that my punishment is a grievous punishment. And relate unto them *the history* of Abraham's guests.[1] When they went in unto him, and said, Peace *be unto thee,* he answered, Verily we are afraid of you :[2] *and* they replied, Fear not ; we bring thee the promise of a wise son. He said, Do ye bring me the promise *of a son* now old age hath overtaken me ? what is it therefore that ye tell me ? They said, We have told thee the truth ; be not therefore one of those who despair. He answered, And who despaireth of the mercy of GOD, except those who err ? And he said, What is your errand therefore, O messengers *of God* ? They answered, Verily we are sent to *destroy* a wicked people : but *as for* the family of Lot, we will save them all, except his wife ; we have decreed that she shall be *one* of those who remain behind *to be destroyed with the infidels.* And when the messengers came to the family of Lot, he said *unto them,* Verily ye are people *who are* unknown *to me.* They answered, But we are come unto thee to *execute* that *sentence,* concerning which *your fellow-citizens* doubted : we tell thee *a certain* truth ; and we are *messengers of* veracity. Therefore lead forth thy family, in some time of the night ; and do thou follow behind them, and let none of you turn back ; but go whither ye are commanded.[3] And we gave him this command ; because the utmost remnant of those *people* was to be cut off in the morning. And the inhabitants of the city came *unto Lot* rejoicing at the news *of the arrival of some strangers. And* he said *unto them,* Verily these are my guests : wherefore do not disgrace me *by abusing them* ; but fear GOD, and put me not to shame. They answered, Have we not forbidden thee from *entertaining or protecting* any man ?[4] *Lot* replied, These *are* my daughters ; *therefore rather make use of them,* if ye *be resolved to* do *what ye purpose.* As thou livest they wander in their folly.[5] Wherefore a terrible storm from heaven assailed them at sunrise : and we turned *the city* upside down ; and we rained on them stones of baked clay. Verily herein are signs unto *men* of sagacity : and those *cities were punished,* to *point out* a right way *for men to walk in.* Verily

[1] See Chap. XI.
[2] What occasioned Abraham's apprehension was, either their sudden entering without leave or their coming at an unseasonable time ; or else their not eating with him.
[3] Which was into Syria ; or into Egypt. (Al Beidâwi, Jallalo'ddin.)
[4] Comp. Midr. Rabbah on Gen. Par. 50.
[5] Some will have these words spoken by the angels to Lot ; others, by GOD to Mohammed.

herein is a sign unto the true believers. The inhabitants of the wood *near Midian*[1] were also ungodly : wherefore we took vengeance on them.[2] And both of them were *destroyed*, to serve as a manifest rule *for men to direct their actions by*. And the inhabitants of Al Hejr[3] likewise heretofore accused the messengers *of God* of imposture : and we produced our signs unto them, but they retired afar off from the same. And they hewed houses out of the mountains, to secure themselves. But a terrible noise from heaven assailed them in the morning : neither was what they had wrought of any advantage unto them. We have not created the heavens and the earth, and whatever is *contained* between them, otherwise than in justice : and the hour *of judgment* shall surely come. Wherefore, *O Mohammed*, forgive *thy people* with a gracious forgiveness.[4] Verily thy LORD is the creator *of thee and of them*, and knoweth *what is most expedient*. We have already brought unto thee seven *verses* which are *frequently to be* repeated,[5] and the glorious Korân. Cast not thine eyes on the *good things* which we have bestowed on several of *the unbelievers, so as to covet the same* ;[6] neither be thou grieved on their account. Behave thyself with meekness towards the true believers ; and say, I am a public preacher. *If they believe not, we will inflict a like punishment on them,* as we have inflicted on the dividers,[7] who distinguished the Korân

---

[1] To whom Shoaib was also sent, as well as to the inhabitants of Midian. Abulfeda says these people dwelt near Tabûc, and that they were not of the same tribe with Shoaib. (See also Geog. Nub. 110.)

[2] Destroying them, for their incredulity and disobedience, by a hot suffocating wind. (Al Beidâwi.)

[3] Who were the tribe of Thamûd. (Chap. VII., and Sale, Prel. Disc. Sect. I.)

[4] This verse, it is said, was abrogated by that of the sword.

[5] That is, the first chapter of the Korân, which consists of so many verses : though some suppose the seven long chapters (see Chap. IX.) are here intended.

[6] That is, Do not envy or covet their worldly prosperity, since thou hast received, in the Korân, a blessing, in comparison whereof all that we have bestowed on them ought to be contemned as of no value. Al Beidâwi mentions a tradition, that Mohammed meeting at Adhriât (a town of Syria) seven caravans, very richly laden, belonging to some Jews of the tribes of Koreidha and Al Nadîr, his men had a great mind to plunder them, saying, That those riches would be of great service for the propagation of GOD's true religion. But the prophet represented to them, by this passage, that they had no reason to repine, GOD having given them the *seven verses*, which were infinitely more valuable than those seven caravans. (Al Beidâwi.)

[7] Some interpret the original word, the *obstructors*, who hindered men from entering Mecca, to visit the temple, lest they should be persuaded to embrace Islâm : and this, it is said, was done by ten men, who were all slain at Bedr. Others translate the word, *who bound themselves by oath* ; and suppose certain Thamûdites, who swore to kill Sâleh by night, are here meant. But the sentence more probably relates to the Jews and Christians,

into *different* parts ; for by thy LORD, we will demand an
account from them all, of that which they have wrought.
Wherefore publish that which thou hast been commanded,
and withdraw from the idolaters. We will surely take thy
part against the scoffers,[1] who associate with GOD another
god ; they shall surely know *their folly*. And now we well
know that thou art deeply concerned on account of that
which they say : but do thou celebrate the praise of thy
LORD ; and be *one* of those who worship ; and serve thy
LORD, until death[2] shall overtake thee.

XVI

THE CHAPTER OF THE BEE [3]

Revealed at Mecca.[4]

IN THE NAME OF THE MOST MERCIFUL GOD.

THE sentence of GOD will surely come *to be executed* ;
wherefore do not hasten it. Praise be unto him !
and far be that from him which they associate *with him* !
He shall cause the angels to descend with a revelation by his
command, unto such of his servants as he pleaseth, *saying*,
Preach that there is no GOD, except myself ; therefore fear
me. He hath created the heavens and the earth to *manifest
his* justice : far be that from him which they associate *with*

who (say the Mohammedans) receive some part of the Scriptures, and
reject others ; and also approved of some passages of the Korân, and disapproved of others, according to their prejudices ; or else to the unbelieving
Meccans, some of whom called the Korân a piece of witchcraft ; others,
flights of divination ; others, old stories ; and others, a poetical composition. (Al Beidâwi, Jallalo'ddin.)

[1] This passage, it is said, was revealed on account of five noble Koreish,
whose names were Al Walîd Ebn al Mogheira, Al As Ebn Wayel, Oda Ebn
Kais, Al Aswad Ebn Abd Yaghûth, and Al Aswad Ebn al Motalleb. These
were inveterate enemies of Mohammed, continually persecuting him, and
turning him into ridicule ; wherefore at length Gabriel came and told him
that he was commanded to take his part against them ; and on the angel's
making a sign towards them one after another, Al Walîd passing by
some arrows, one of them hitched in his garment, and he, out of pride,
not stooping to take it off, but walking forward, the head of it cut a vein in
his heel, and he bled to death ; Al As was killed with a thorn, which stuck
into the sole of his foot, and caused his leg to swell to a monstrous size ;
Oda died with violent and perpetual sneezing ; Al Aswad Ebn Abd Yaghûth
ran his head against a thorny tree and killed himself ; and Al Aswad Ebn al
Motalleb was struck blind. (Al Beidâwi.)

[2] Literally, *That which is certain*.

[3] This insect is mentioned about the middle of the chapter.

[4] Except the three last verses.

him ! He hath created man of seed ; and *yet* behold, he is a professed disputer *against the resurrection.*[1] He hath likewise created the cattle for you : from them ye have wherewith to keep yourselves warm,[2] and *other* advantages ; and of them do ye *also* eat. And they are likewise a credit unto you,[3] when ye drive *them* home *in the evening*, and when ye lead *them* forth to feed *in the morning* : and they carry your burthens to a *distant* country, at which ye could not *otherwise* arrive, unless with *great* difficulty to yourselves ; for your LORD *is* compassionate and merciful. And *he hath also created* horses, and mules, and asses, that ye may ride thereon, and for an ornament *unto you* ; and *he likewise* createth *other things* which ye know not. *It appertaineth* unto GOD, to instruct *men* in the *right* way ; and *there is* who turneth aside from the same : but, if he had pleased, he would certainly have directed you all. It is he who sendeth down from heaven *rain* water, whereof ye have to drink, and from which plants, whereon ye feed *your cattle, receive their nourishment. And* by means thereof he causeth corn, and olives, and palm-trees, and grapes, and all *kinds* of fruits to spring forth for you. Surely herein is a sign *of the divine power and wisdom* unto people who consider. And he hath subjected the night and the day to your service ; and the sun, and the moon, and the stars, which are compelled to serve by his command. Verily herein are signs unto people of understanding. And *he hath also given you dominion over* whatever he hath created for you in the earth, distinguished by its different colour.[4] Surely herein is a sign unto people who reflect. It is he who hath subjected the sea *unto you*, that ye might eat fish[5] thereout, and take from thence ornaments[6] for you to wear : and thou seest the ships ploughing *the waves* thereof, that ye may seek *to enrich yourselves* of his abundance, *by commerce* ; and that ye might give thanks.

[1] The person particularly intended in this place was Obba Ebn Khalf, who came to Mohammed with a rotten bone, and asked him whether it was possible for GOD to restore it to life. (Al Beidâwi.)

[2] viz., Their skins, wool, and hair, which serve you for clothing.

[3] Being a grace to your court-yards, and a credit to you in the eyes of your neighbours. (Al Beidâwi.)

[4] That is, of every kind ; the various colours of things being one of their chief distinctions. (Al Beidâwi.)

[5] Literally, *fresh flesh* ; by which fish is meant, as being naturally more fresh, and sooner liable to corruption, than the flesh of birds and beasts. The expression is thought to have been made use of here the rather, because the production of such fresh food from salt water is an instance of GOD's power. (Al Beidâwi.)

[6] As pearls and coral.

And he hath thrown upon the earth *mountains* firmly rooted, lest it should move with you,[1] and *also* rivers, and paths, that ye might be directed : and *he hath likewise ordained* marks *whereby men may know their way* ; and they are directed by the stars.[2] *Shall God* therefore who createth, *be* as he who createth not ? Do ye not therefore consider ? If ye *attempt to* reckon up the favours of GOD, ye shall not *be able to* compute their number : GOD *is* surely gracious, *and* merciful ; and GOD knoweth that which ye conceal and that which ye publish. But the *idols* which ye invoke, besides GOD, create nothing, but are themselves created. *They are* dead, *and* not living ; neither do they understand when they shall be raised.[3] Your GOD *is* one GOD. As to those who believe not in the life to come, their hearts deny *the plainest evidence*, and they proudly reject *the truth*. There is no doubt but GOD knoweth that which they conceal and that which they discover : verily he loveth not the proud. And when it is said unto them, What hath your LORD sent down *unto Mohammed* ? they answer, Fables of ancient *times*. *Thus are they given up to error*, that they may bear their own burthens without diminution on the day of resurrection, and *also a part* of the burthens of those whom they caused to err, without knowledge. *Will it* not *be an* evil *burthen* which they shall bear ? Their predecessors devised plots heretofore ; but GOD came unto their building, *to overthrow it* from the foundations : and the roof fell on them from above, and a punishment came upon them, from whence they did not expect.[4] Also on the day of resurrection he will cover them with shame ; and will say, Where are my companions, concerning whom ye disputed ? Those unto whom

[1] The Mohammedans suppose that the earth, when first created, was smooth and equal, and thereby liable to a circular motion as well as the celestial orbs ; and that the angels asking, who could be able to stand on so tottering a frame, GOD fixed it the next morning by throwing the mountains on it.

[2] Which are their guides, not only at sea, but also on land, when they travel by night through the deserts. The stars which they observe for this purpose, are either the *Pleiades*, or some of those near the Pole.

[3] *i.e.*, At what time they or their worshippers shall be raised to receive judgment.

[4] Some understand this passage figuratively, of God's disappointing their wicked designs ; but others suppose the words literally relate to the tower which Nimrod (whom the Mohammedans will have to be the son of Canaan, the son of Ham, and so the nephew of Cush, and not his son) built in Babel, and carried to an immense height (five thousand cubits, say some), foolishly purposing thereby to ascend to heaven and wage war with the inhabitants of that place ; but GOD frustrated his attempt, utterly overthrowing the tower by a violent wind and earthquake. (Al Beidâwi, Jallalo'ddin. D'Herbel. Bibl. Orient. Art. Nimrod.)

knowledge shall have been given,[1] shall answer, This day *shall* shame and misery *fall* upon the unbelievers. They whom the angels shall cause to die, having dealt unjustly with their own souls, shall offer to make their peace[2] *in the article of death, saying*, We have done no evil. *But the angels shall reply*, Yea ; verily GOD well knoweth that which ye have wrought : wherefore enter the gates of hell, therein to remain *for ever* ; and miserable shall be the abode of the proud. And it shall be said unto those who shall fear *God*, What hath your LORD sent down ? They shall answer, Good : unto those who do right *shall be given* an excellent reward in this world ; but the dwelling of the next life *shall be* better ; and happy *shall be* the dwelling of the pious ! *namely*, gardens of eternal abode,[3] into which they shall enter ; rivers shall flow beneath the same ; therein *shall* they enjoy whatever they wish. Thus will GOD recompense the pious. Unto the righteous whom the angels shall cause to die, they shall say, Peace be upon you ; enter ye into paradise, *as a reward* for that which ye have wrought. Do *the unbelievers* expect *any other* than that the angels come unto them, *to part their souls from their bodies* ; or that the sentence of thy LORD come *to be executed on them* ? So did they act who were before them ; and GOD was not unjust towards them *in that he destroyed them* ; but they dealt unjustly with their own souls : the evils of that which they committed, reached them ; and the *divine judgment* which they scoffed at, fell upon them. The idolaters say, If GOD had pleased, we had not worshipped anything besides him, neither *had* our fathers : neither had we forbidden anything, without him.[4] So did they who were before them. But is the duty of the apostles *any other*, than public preaching ? We have heretofore raised up in every nation an apostle *to admonish them, saying*, Worship GOD, and avoid TAGHUT.[5] And of them *there were* some whom GOD directed, and *there were* others of them who were decreed to go astray. Wherefore go through the earth, *O tribe of Koreish*, and see what hath been the end of those who accused *their apostles* of imposture. If thou, *O prophet*,

[1] viz., The prophets, and the teachers and professors of GOD's unity ; or, the angels.

[2] Making their submission, and humbly excusing their evil actions, as proceeding from ignorance, and not from obstinacy or malice.

[3] Literally, *gardens of* Eden.

[4] This they spoke in a scoffing manner, justifying their idolatry and superstitious abstaining from certain cattle (Chap. VI.), by pretending, that had these things been disagreeable to GOD, he would not have suffered them to be practised. [5] See Chap. II.

dost earnestly wish for their direction ; verily GOD will not direct him whom he *hath resolved* to lead into error; neither shall they have any helpers. And they swear most solemnly by GOD, *saying*, GOD will not raise the dead. Yea ; the promise thereof is true : but the greater part of men know *it* not. *He will raise them* that he may clearly show them the *truth* concerning which they *now* disagree, and that the unbelievers may know that they are liars. Verily our speech unto anything, when we will the same, *is*, that we only say unto it, Be ; and it is. *As for* those who have fled their country for the sake of GOD, after they had been unjustly persecuted ;[1] we will surely provide them an excellent habitation in this world, but the reward of the next life shall be greater ; if they knew *it*.[2] They who persevere patiently, and p : their trust in their LORD, *shall not fail of happiness in this life and in that which is to come.* We have not sent *any* before thee, *as our apostles*, other than men, unto whom we spake by revelation. Inquire therefore of those who have the custody of the scriptures, if ye know not *this to be truth.* We sent *them* with evident *miracles*, and written revelations ; and we have sent down unto thee this Korân,[3] that thou mayest declare unto mankind that which hath been sent down unto them, and that they may consider. Are they who have plotted evil against *their prophet* secure, that GOD will not cause the earth to cleave under them, or that a punishment will not come upon them, from whence they do not expect ; or that he will not chastise them while they are busied *in travelling from one place to another, and in traffic* ? (for they shall not be able to elude *the power of God*,) or that he will not chastise them by a gradual destruction ? But your LORD is truly gracious and merciful *in granting you respite*. Do they not consider the things which GOD hath created ; whose shadows are cast on the right hand and on the left, worshipping GOD,[4] and become contracted ? Whatever moveth

---

[1] Some suppose the prophet and the companions of his flight in general are here intended ! others suppose that those are particularly meant in this place, who, after Mohammed's departure, were imprisoned at Mecca on account of their having embraced his religion, and suffered great persecution from the Koreish ; as, Belâl, Soheib, Khabbab, Ammâr, Abes, Abu'l Jandal, and Sohail. (Al Beidâwi.)

[2] It is uncertain whether the pronoun *they* relates to the infidels, or to the true believers. If to the former, the consequence would be, that they would be desirous of attaining to the happiness of the Mohajerîn, by professing the same faith ; if to the latter, the knowledge of this is urged as a motive to patience and perseverance. (Al Beidâwi.)

[3] Literally, *this admonition.* (Sale, Prel. Disc. Sect. III. p. 61.)

[4] See Chap. XIII.

both in heaven and on earth, worshippeth GOD, and the angels *also* ; and they are not exalted with pride, *so as to disdain his service* : they fear their LORD, *who is exalted* above them, and perform that which they are commanded. GOD said, Take not *unto yourselves* two gods ; for there is but one GOD : and revere me. Unto him *belongeth* whatsoever is in heaven and on earth ; and unto him is obedience eternally *due*. Will ye therefore fear *any* besides GOD ? Whatever favours ye have received, are certainly from GOD ; and when evil afflicteth you, unto him do ye make your supplication ; yet when he taketh the evil from off you, behold, a part of you give a companion unto their LORD, to show their ingratitude for *the favours* we have bestowed on them. Delight yourselves *in the enjoyments of this life :* but hereafter shall ye know *that ye cannot escape the divine vengeance.* And they set apart unto *idols* which have no knowledge,[1] a part of the food which we have provided for them. By GOD, ye shall surely be called to account for that which ye have falsely devised. They attribute daughters unto GOD ;[2] (far be it from him !) but unto themselves *children of the sex* which they desire.[3] And when any of them is told the news of *the birth of* a female, his face becometh black,[4] and he *is* deeply afflicted : he hideth himself from the people, because of the ill tidings which have been told him ; *considering within himself* whether he shall keep it with disgrace, or whether he shall bury it in the dust. Do they not make an ill judgment ? Unto those who believe not in the next life, the similitude of evil *ought to be applied*, and unto GOD the most sublime similitude :[5] for he *is* mighty *and* wise. If GOD should punish men for their iniquity he would not leave on the *earth* any moving thing : but he giveth them respite unto an appointed time ;

---

[1] Or, *which they know not* ; foolishly imagining that they have power to help them, or interest with GOD to intercede for them.

As to the ancient Arabs setting apart a certain portion of the produce of their lands for their idols, and their superstitious abstaining from the use of certain cattle, in honour to the same, see Chaps. V. and VI.

[2] See Sale, Prel. Disc. Sect. I. Al Beidâwi says, that the tribes of Khozâah and Kenâna, in particular, used to call the angels the daughters of GOD.

[3] viz., Sons : for the birth of a daughter was looked on as a kind of misfortune among the Arabs ; and they often used to put them to death by burying them alive. (Chap. LXXXI.)

[4] *i.e.*, Clouded with confusion and sorrow.

[5] This passage condemns the Meccans' injudicious and blasphemous application of such circumstances to GOD as were unworthy of him, and not only derogatory to the perfections of the Deity, but even disgraceful to man, while they arrogantly applied the more honourable circumstances to themselves.

and when their time shall come, they shall not be respited an hour, neither shall *their punishment* be anticipated. They attribute unto GOD that which they dislike themselves,[1] and their tongues utter a lie ; *namely*, that the reward of *paradise* is for them. There is no doubt but that the fire *of hell is prepared* for them, and that they shall be sent thither before *the rest of the wicked*. By GOD, we have heretofore sent *messengers* unto the nations before thee : but Satan prepared their works for them : he *was* their patron in this world,[2] and *in that which is to come* they shall suffer a grievous torment. We have not sent down the book *of the Korân* unto thee, *for any other purpose*, than that thou shouldest declare unto them that *truth* concerning which they disagree ; and for a direction and mercy unto people who believe. GOD sendeth down water from heaven, and causeth the earth to revive after it hath been dead. Verily herein is a sign *of the resurrection* unto people who hearken. Ye have also in cattle an example of instruction : we give you to drink of that which is in their bellies, *a liquor* between digested dregs, and blood ;[3] *namely* pure milk,[4] which is swallowed with pleasure by those who drink *it*. And of the fruits of palm-trees, and of grapes, ye obtain an inebriating liquor, and also good nourishment.[5] Verily herein is a sign unto people who understand. Thy LORD spake by inspiration unto the bee, *saying*, provide *thee* houses[6] in the mountains, and in the trees, and of *those materials* wherewith *men* build *hives for thee* : then eat of every *kind of* fruit, and walk in the beaten paths of thy LORD.[7] There proceedeth from their bellies

---

[1] By giving him daughters, and associates in power and honour ; by disregarding his messengers ; and by setting apart the better share of the presents and offerings for their idols, and the worse for him. (Al Beidâwi.)

[2] Or, *He is the patron of them* (viz. the Koreish) *this day*, &c.

[3] The milk consisting of certain particles of the blood, supplied from the finer parts of the aliment. Ebn Abbas says, that the grosser parts of the food subside into excrement, and that the finer parts are converted into milk, and the finest of all into blood.

[4] Having neither the colour of the blood, nor the smell of the excrements.

[5] Not only wine, which is forbidden, but also lawful food, as dates, raisins, a kind of honey flowing from the dates, and vinegar. Some have supposed that these words allow the moderate use of wine ; but the contrary is the received opinion.

[6] So the apartments which the bee builds are here called, because of their beautiful workmanship, and admirable contrivance, which no geometrician can excel. (Al Beidâwi.)

[7] *i.e.*, The ways through which, by GOD's power, the nectar from the flowers becomes honey ; or, the methods of making bee-bread from pollen, which he has taught the bee by instinct ; or else the ready way home from the distant places to which that insect flies.

a liquor of various colours :[1] wherein *is* a medicine for men.[2]
Verily herein *is* a sign unto people who consider.   GOD hath
created you, and he will hereafter cause you to die : and some
of you shall have his life prolonged to a decrepit age, so that
he shall forget whatever he knew ; for GOD *is* wise *and* powerful.   GOD causeth some of you to excel others in worldly
possessions : yet they who are caused to excel, do not give
their wealth unto *the slaves* whom their right hands possess,
that they *may become* equal *sharers* therein.[3]   Do they therefore deny the beneficence of GOD ?   GOD hath ordained you
wives from among yourselves,[4] and of your wives hath
granted you children and grandchildren ; and hath bestowed
on you good things for food.   Will they therefore believe in
that which is vain, and ungratefully deny the goodness of
GOD ?   They worship, besides GOD, *idols* which possess
nothing wherewith to sustain them, either in heaven, or on
earth ; and have no power.   Wherefore liken not *anything*
unto GOD :[5] for GOD knoweth, but ye know not.   GOD propoundeth as a parable a possessed slave, who hath power over
nothing, and him on whom we have bestowed a good provision from us, and who giveth alms thereout *both* secretly and
openly :[6] shall these *two* be esteemed equal ?   GOD forbid !
But the greater part of them know *it* not.   GOD also propoundeth as a parable two men ; one of them born dumb,

[1] viz., Honey ; the colour of which is very different, occasioned by the
different plants on which the bees feed ; some being white, some yellow,
some red, and some black.   (Al Beidâwi.)

[2] The same being not only good food, but a useful remedy in several dis-
tempers, particularly those occasioned by phlegm.   There is a story, that a
man came once to Mohammed, and told him that his brother was afflicted
with a violent pain in his belly ; upon which the prophet bade him give him
some honey.   The fellow took his advice ; but soon after coming again,
told him that the medicine had done his brother no manner of service :
Mohammed answered, *Go and give him more honey, for* GOD *speaks truth, and
thy brother's belly lies.*   And the dose being repeated, the man, by GOD's
mercy, was immediately cured.   (Al Beidâwi.)

[3] These words reprove the idolatrous Meccans, who could admit created
beings to a share of the divine honour, though they suffered not their slaves
to share with themselves in what GOD had bestowed on them. (Al Beidâwi.)

[4] That is, of your own nations and tribes.   Some think the formation of
Eve from Adam is here intended.

[5] Or propound no similitudes or comparisons between him and his creatures.
One argument the Meccans employed in defence of their idolatry, it seems,
was, that the worship of inferior deities did honour to GOD in the same
manner as the respect showed to the servants of a prince does honour to the
prince himself.   (Al Beidâwi.)

[6] The idols are here likened to a slave, who is so far from having anything
of his own, that he is himself in the possession of another ; whereas GOD
is as a rich free man, who provideth for his family abundantly, and also
assisteth others who have need, both in public and in private.   (Al Beidâwi,
Jallalo'ddin.)

who is unable to *do or understand* anything, but is a burthen unto his master ; whithersoever he shall send him, he shall not return with any good *success* : shall this *man*, and he *who hath his speech and understanding, and* who commandeth that which is just, and followeth the right way, be esteemed equal ?[1] Unto GOD *alone is* the secret of heaven and earth *known*. And the business of the *last* hour[2] shall be only as the twinkling of an eye, or even more quick : for GOD is almighty. GOD hath brought you forth from the wombs of your mothers ; ye knew nothing, and he gave you *the senses of* hearing and seeing, and understanding, that ye might give thanks. Do they not behold the fowls which are enabled to fly in the open firmament of heaven ? none supporteth them except GOD. Verily herein *are* signs unto people who believe. GOD hath also provided your houses for habitations for you ; and hath *also* provided you tents of the skins of cattle, which ye find light *to be removed* on the day of your departure *to new quarters*, and *easy to be pitched* on the day of your sitting down *therein* : and of their wool, and their fur, and their hair *hath he supplied you with* furniture and household-stuff for a season. And GOD hath provided for you, of that which he hath created, conveniences to shade you *from the sun*,[3] and he hath *also* provided you places of retreat in the mountains,[4] and he hath given you garments to defend you from the heat,[5] and coats *of mail* to defend you in your wars. Thus doth he accomplish his favour towards you, that ye may resign yourselves *unto him*. But if they turn back ; verily thy duty is public preaching *only*. They acknowledge the goodness of GOD, and afterwards they deny the same ;[6] but the greater part of them are unbelievers.[7] On a *certain* day we will raise a witness out of every nation :[8] then they who shall

---

[1] The idol is here again represented under the image of one who, by a defect in his senses, is a useless burthen to the man who maintains him ; and GOD, under that of a person completely qualified either to direct or to execute any useful undertaking. Some suppose the comparison is intended of a true believer and an infidel.

[2] That is, The resurrection of the dead.

[3] As trees, houses, tents, mountains, &c.

[4] viz., Caves and grottos, both natural and artificial.

[5] Al Beidâwi says, that one extreme, and that the most insupportable in Arabia, is here put for both ; but Jallalo'ddin supposes that by *heat* we are in this place to understand *cold*.

[6] Confessing GOD to be the author of all the blessings they enjoy ; and yet directing their worship and thanks to their idols, by whose intercession they imagine blessings are obtained.

[7] Absolutely denying GOD's providence, either through ignorance or perverseness.

[8] See Chap. IV.

have been unbelievers shall not be suffered *to excuse them-selves*, neither shall they be received into favour. And when they who shall have acted unjustly shall see the torment *prepared for them* ; (it shall not be mitigated unto them, neither shall they be respited ;) and when those who shall have been guilty of idolatry shall see their false gods,[1] they shall say, O LORD, these are our idols which we invoked, besides thee. But they shall return an answer unto them, *saying*, Verily ye are liars.[2] And on that day shall *the wicked* offer submission unto GOD ; and the *false deities* which they imagined shall abandon them. *As for* those who shall have been infidels, and shall have turned aside *others* from the way of GOD, we will add unto them punishment upon punish-ment, because they have corrupted *others*. On a *certain* day we will raise up in every nation a witness against them, from among themselves ; and we will bring thee, *O Mohammed*, as a witness against these *Arabians*. We have sent down unto thee the book *of the Korân*, for an explication of everything *necessary both as to faith and practice*, and a direction, and mercy, and good tidings unto the Moslems. Verily GOD commandeth justice, and the doing of good, and the giving unto kindred *what shall be necessary* ; and he for-biddeth wickedness, and iniquity, and oppression : he admonisheth you that ye may remember.[3] Perform *your* covenant with GOD,[4] when ye enter into covenant *with him* ; and violate not *your* oaths, after the ratification thereof ; since ye have made GOD a witness over you. Verily GOD knoweth that which ye do. And be not like unto her who undoeth that which she hath spun, untwisting it after she hath twisted it strongly ;[5] taking your oaths between you

---

[1] Literally, *Their companions*.

[2] For that we are not the companions of GOD, as ye imagined ; neither did ye really serve us, but your own corrupt affections and lusts ; nor yet were ye led into idolatry by us, but ye fell into it of your own accord. (Al Beidâwi.)

[3] This verse, which was the occasion of the conversion of Othmân Ebn Matûn, the commentators say, containeth the whole which it is a man's duty either to perform or to avoid ; and is alone a sufficient demonstration of what is said in the foregoing verse. Under the three things here commanded, they understand the belief of GOD's unity, without inclining to atheism, on the one hand, or polytheism, on the other ; obedience to the commands of GOD ; and charity towards those in distress. And under the three things forbidden, they comprehend all corrupt and carnal affections ; all false doctrines and heretical opinions : and all injustice towards man. (Al Beidâwi.)

[4] By persevering in his true religion. Some think that the oath of fidelity taken to Mohammed by his followers is chiefly intended here.

[5] Some suppose that a particular woman is meant in this passage, who used (like Penelope) to undo at night the work that she had done in the day.

deceitfully, because one party is more numerous than *another* party.[1]   Verily GOD only tempteth you therein ; and he will make that manifest unto you, on the day of resurrection, concerning which ye now disagree.   If GOD had pleased, he would surely have made you one people :[2] but he will lead into error whom he pleaseth, and he will direct whom he pleaseth ; and ye shall surely give an account of that which ye have done.   Therefore take not your oaths between you deceitfully, lest *your* foot slip, after it hath been stead-fastly fixed, and ye taste evil *in this life,* for that ye have turned aside from the way of GOD ; and ye *suffer* a grievous punishment *in the life to come.*   And sell not the covenant of GOD for a small price ;[3] for with GOD is a better *recompence prepared* for you, if ye be *men* of understanding.   That which *is* with you will fail ; but that which *is* with GOD *is* per-manent : and we will surely reward those who shall persevere, according to the utmost *merit* of their actions.   Whoso worketh righteousness, whether he be male or female, and is a true believer, we will surely raise him to a happy life ; and we will give them their reward, according to the utmost *merit* of their actions.   When thou readest the Korân, have recourse unto GOD, *that he may preserve thee* from Satan driven away with stones :[4] he hath no power over those who believe, and who put their confidence in their LORD ; but his power is over those only, who take him for their patron, and who give companions unto *God.*   When we substitute *in the Korân* an *abrogating* verse in lieu of a verse *abrogated,* (and GOD best knoweth *the fitness of* that which he revealeth,) the *infidels* say, Thou art only a forger *of these verses* : but the greater

Her name, they say, was Reita Bint Saad Ebn Teym, of the tribe of Koreish. (Al Beidâwi.)

[1] Of this insincerity in their alliances the Koreish are accused ; it being usual with them, when they saw the enemies of their confederates to be superior in force, to renounce their league with their old friends, and strike up one with the others.   (Al Beidâwi.)

[2] Or, of one religion.

[3] That is, Be not prevailed on to renounce your religion, or your engage-ments with your prophet, by any promises or gifts of the infidels.   For, it seems, the Koreish, to tempt the poorer Moslems to apostatize, made them offers, not very considerable indeed, but such as they imagined might be worth their acceptance.   (Al Beidâwi.)

[4] Mohammed one day when reading the Korân, uttered a horrid blasphemy, to the great scandal of those who were present, as will be observed in another place (Chap. XXII.) ; to excuse which he assured them that those words were put into his mouth by the devil ; and to prevent any such accident for the future, he is here taught to beg GOD's protection before he entered on that duty.   (Jallalo'ddin, Al Beidâwi, Yahya, &c.)   Hence the Mohammedans, before they begin to read any part of this book, repeat these words, *I have recourse unto God for assistance against Satan driven away with stones.*

part of them know not *truth from falsehood*. Say, The holy spirit[1] hath brought the same down from thy LORD with truth; that he may confirm those who believe, and for a direction and good tidings unto the Moslems. We *also* know that they say, Verily, a *certain* man teacheth him *to compose the Korân*. The tongue of *the person* unto whom they incline, is a foreign *tongue*; but this, *wherein the Korân is written*, is the perspicuous Arabic tongue.[2] Moreover as for those who

---

[1] viz., Gabriel. See Chap. II.

[2] This was a great objection made by the Meccans to the authority of the Korân; for when Mohammed insisted, as a proof of its divine original, that it was impossible a man so utterly unacquainted with learning as himself could compose such a book, they replied, that he had one or more assistants in the forgery; but as to the particular person or persons suspected of this confederacy, the traditions differ. One says it was Jabar, a Greek, servant to Amer Ebn al Hadrami, who could read and write well (Al Zamakhshari, Al Beidâwi, Yahya); another, that they were Jabar and Yesâr, two slaves who followed the trade of sword-cutlers at Mecca, and used to read the pentateuch and gospel, and had often Mohammed for their auditor, when he passed that way (Al Zamakh., Al Beidâwi. Prid. Life of Mah. p. 32). Another tells us, it was one Aïsh, or Yâïsh, a domestic of Al Haweiteb, Ebn Abd al Uzza, who was a man of some learning, and had embraced Mohammedism (Al Zamakh., Al Beidâwi). Another supposes it was one Kais, a Christian, whose house Mohammed frequented (Jallalo'ddin); another, that it was Addas, a servant of Otba Ebn Rabia (Al Zamakh., Yahya); and another, that it was Salmân the Persian (Al Zamakh., Al Beidâwi). According to some Christian writers (Ricardi Confut. Legis Saracenicæ, c. 13. Joh. Andreas, de Confus. Sectæ Mohametanæ, c. 2. Prid. Life of Mah. pp. 33, 34), Abdallah Ebn Salâm, the Jew who was so intimate with Mohammed (named by one, according to the Hebrew dialect, Abdias Ben Salon and by another, Abdala Celen), was assistant to him in the compiling his pretended revelations. This Jew Dr. Prideaux confounds with Salmân the Persian, who was a very different man, as a late author (Gagnier not. in Abulf. Vit. Moh. p. 74) has observed before me; wherefore, and for that we may have occasion to speak of Salmân hereafter, it may be proper to add a brief extract of his story as told by himself. He was of a good family of Ispahan, and, in his younger years, left the religion of his country to embrace Christianity; and travelling into Syria, was advised by a certain monk of Amuria to go into Arabia, where a prophet was expected to arise about that time, who should establish the religion of Abraham; and whom he should know, among other things, by the *seal of prophecy* between his shoulders. Salmân performed the journey, and meeting with Mohammed at Koba, where he rested in his flight to Medina, soon found him to be the person he sought, and professed Islâm (Ex Ebn Ishak. Vide Gagnier, p. 74). The general opinion of the Christians however is, that the chief help Mohammed had in the contriving his Korân, was from a Nestorian monk named Sergius, supposed to be the same person with the monk Boheira, with whom Mohammed in his younger years had some conference at Bosra, a city of Syria Damascena, where that monk resided (Prid. ubi sup. p. 35, &c. Gagnier, ubi sup. pp. 10, 11. Marrac. de Alcor. p. 37). To confirm which supposition, a passage has been produced from an Arab writer (Al Masudi), who says that Boheira's name in the books of the Christians, is Sergius; but this is only a conjecture; and another (Abu'l Hasan al Becri in Korân) tells us, his true name was Saïd, or Felix, and his surname Boheira. But be that as it will, if Boheira and Sergius were the same man, I find not the least intimation in the Mohammedan writers that he ever quitted his monastery to go into Arabia (as is supposed by the Christians); and his acquaintance with Mohammed at Bosra was too early to favour the surmise of his assisting him in the

believe not in the signs of GOD, GOD will not direct them, and they shall suffer a painful torment : verily they imagine a falsehood who believe not in the signs of GOD, and they are *really* the liars. Whoever denieth GOD, after he hath believed, except him who shall be compelled against his will, and whose heart continueth steadfast in the faith, *shall be severely chastised :*[1] but whoever shall voluntarily profess

Korân, which was composed long after ; though Mohammed might, from his discourse, gain some knowledge of Christianity and of the Scriptures, which might be of use to him therein. From the answer given in this passage of the Korân to the objection of the infidels, viz., that the person suspected by them to have a hand in the Korân spoke a foreign language, and therefore could not, with any face of probability, be supposed to assist in a composition written in the Arabic tongue, and with so great elegance, it is plain this person was no Arabian. The word Ajami, which is here used, signifies any *foreign* or *barbarous* language in general ; but the Arabs applying it more particularly to the Persian, it has been thence concluded by some that Salmân was the person ; however, if it be true that he came not to Mohammed till after the Hejra, either he could not be the man here intended, or else this verse must have been revealed at Medina, contrary to the common opinion.

[1] These words were added for the sake of Ammâr Ebn Yaser, and some others, who being taken and tortured by the Koreish, renounced their faith out of fear, though their hearts agreed not with their mouths. (Al Beidâwi, Al Zamakh, Yahya.) It seems Ammâr wanted the constancy of his father and mother, Yâser and Sommeya, who underwent the like trial at the same time with their son, and resolutely refusing to recant, were both put to death, the infidels tying Sommeya between two camels, and striking a lance through her privy parts. (Al Beidâwi.) When news was brought to Mohammed, that Ammâr had denied the faith, he said, it could not be, for that Ammâr was full of faith from the crown of his head to the sole of his foot, faith being mixed and incorporated with his very flesh and blood ; and when Ammâr himself came weeping to the prophet, he wiped his eyes, saying, *What fault was it of thine, if they forced thee ?* But though it be here said, that those who apostatize in appearance only, to avoid death or torments, may hope for pardon from GOD, yet it is unanimously agreed by the Mohammedan doctors, to be much more meritorious and pleasing in the sight of GOD to persist courageously and nobly in the true faith, and rather to suffer death itself than renounce it, even in words. Nor did the Mohammedan religion want its martyrs, in the strict sense of the word ; of which I will here give two instances, besides the above-mentioned. One is that of Khobaib Ebn Ada, who being perfidiously sold to the Koreish, was by them put to death in a cruel manner, by mutilation, and cutting off his flesh piecemeal ; and being asked, in the midst of his tortures, whether he did not wish Mohammed was in his place, answered, *I would not wish to be with my family, my substance, and my children, on condition that Mohammed was only to be pricked with a thorn.* (Ebn Shohnah.) The other is that of a man who was put to death by Moseilama, on the following occasion. That false prophet having taken two of Mohammed's followers, asked one of them, what he said of Mohammed ? the man answered, That he was the apostle of GOD : *And what sayest thou of me ?* added Moseilama ; to which he replied, *Thou also art the apostle of God* ; whereupon he was immediately dismissed in safety. But the other, having returned the same answer to the former question, refused to give any to the last, though required to do it three several times, but pretended to be deaf, and was therefore slain. It is related that Mohammed, when the story of these two men was told him, said, *The first of them threw himself on* GOD's *mercy* ; *but the latter professed the truth* ; *and he shall find his account in it* (Al Beidâwi.)

infidelity, on those shall the indignation of GOD *fall*, and they shall suffer a grievous punishment. This *shall be their sentence*, because they have loved the present life above that which is to come, and for that GOD directeth not the unbelieving people. These *are* they whose hearts, and hearing, and sight GOD hath sealed up ; and these are the negligent : there is no doubt but that in the next life they shall perish. Moreover thy LORD *will be favourable* unto those who have fled their country, after having suffered persecution,[1] *and been compelled to deny the faith by violence*, and *who* have since fought *in defence of the true religion*, and have persevered with patience ; verily *unto these will* thy LORD *be* gracious and merciful, after *they shall have shown their sincerity*. On a certain day shall every soul come to plead for itself,[2] and every soul shall be repaid that which it shall have wrought ; and they shall not be treated unjustly. GOD propoundeth as a parable a city[3] which was secure *and* quiet, unto which her provisions came in abundance from every side ; but she ungratefully denied the favours of GOD : wherefore GOD caused her to taste the extreme famine, and fear, because of that which they had done. And now is an apostle come unto the *inhabitants of Mecca* from among themselves ; and they accuse him of imposture : wherefore a punishment shall be inflicted on them, while they are acting unjustly. Eat of what GOD hath given you for food, *that which is* lawful *and* good ; and be thankful for the favours of GOD, if ye serve him. He hath only forbidden you that which dieth of itself, and blood, and swine's flesh, and that which hath been slain in the name of any, besides GOD.[4] But unto him who shall be compelled by necessity *to eat of these things*, not lusting nor *wilfully* transgressing, GOD *will* surely *be* gracious *and* merciful. And say not that wherein your tongues utter a lie ; This is lawful, and this is unlawful ;[5] that ye may devise a lie

[1] As did Ammâr, who made one in both the flights. Some, reading the verb with different vowels, render the last words, *after having persecuted* the true believers ; and instance Al Hadrami, who obliged a servant of his to renounce Mohammedism, by force, but afterwards, together with that servant, professed the same faith, and fled for it. (Al Beidâwi.)

[2] That is, Every person shall be solicitous for his own salvation, not concerning himself with the condition of another, but crying out, *My own soul, my own soul.* (Al Beidâwi.)

[3] This example is applied to every city which having received great blessings from GOD, becometh insolent and unthankful, and is therefore chastised by some signal judgment ; or rather to Mecca in particular, on which the calamities threatened in this passage, viz. both famine and sword, were inflicted. (Al Beidâwi.)　　　　[4] See Chap. V.

[5] Allowing what GOD hath forbidden, and superstitiously abstaining from what he hath allowed. See Chap. VI.

270 THE KORÂN [CHAP. XVI.

concerning GOD : for they who devise a lie concerning GOD, shall not prosper. *They shall have* small enjoyment *in this world*, and *in that which is to come* they shall suffer a grievous torment. Unto the Jews did we forbid that which we have told thee formally :[1] and we did them no injury *in that respect* ; but they injured their own souls.[2] Moreover thy LORD *will be favourable* unto those who do evil through ignorance ; and afterwards repent and amend : verily *unto these will* thy LORD *be* gracious and merciful, after *their repentance*. Abraham was a model of true religion, obedient unto GOD, orthodox, and was not an idolater :[3] *he was also* grateful for his benefits : *wherefore God* chose him, and directed him into the right way. And we bestowed on him good in this world ; and in the next he shall surely be *one* of the righteous. We have also spoken unto thee, *O Mohammed*, by revelation, *saying*, Follow the religion of Abraham, *who was* orthodox, and was no idolater. The sabbath was only appointed unto those who differed from *their prophet* concerning it ;[4] and thy LORD will surely judge between them, on the day of resurrection, as to that concerning which they differed. Invite *men* unto the way of thy LORD, by wisdom, and mild exhortation ; and dispute with them in the most condescending *manner* : for thy LORD well knoweth him who strayeth from his path, and he well knoweth those who are *rightly* directed. If ye take vengeance *on any*, take a vengeance proportionable to the wrong which hath been done you ;[5] but if ye suffer *wrong*

[1] viz., In Chap. VI.

[2] *i.e.*, They were forbidden things which were in themselves indifferent, as a punishment for their wickedness and rebellion.

[3] This was to reprehend the idolatrous Koreish, who pretended that they professed the religion of Abraham.

[4] These were the Jews ; who being ordered by Moses to set apart Friday (the day now observed by the Mohammedans) for the exercise of divine worship, refused it, and chose the sabbath-day, because on that day GOD rested from his works of creation : for which reason they were commanded to keep the day they had chosen in the strictest manner. (Al Beidâwi, Jallalo'ddin.)

[5] This passage is supposed to have been revealed at Medína, on occasion of Hamza, Mohammed's uncle, being slain at the battle of Ohod. For the infidels having abused his dead body, by taking out his bowels, and cutting off his ears and his nose, when Mohammed saw it, he swore that if GOD granted him success, he would retaliate those cruelties on seventy of the Koreish ; but he was by these words forbidden to execute what he had sworn, and he accordingly made void his oath. (Al Beidâwi, Jallalo'ddin.) Abulfeda makes the number on which Mohammed swore to wreak his vengeance to be but thirty (Abulf. Vit. Moh. p. 68) : but it may be observed, by the way, that the translator renders the passage in that author, GOD *hath revealed unto me that I shall retaliate*, &c., instead of, *If* GOD *grant me victory over the* Koreish, *I will retaliate*, &c., reading *Lam adhharni*, for *adhfarni* ; GOD, far from putting this design into the prophet's head by a revelation, expressly forbidding him to put it in execution.

patiently, verily this will be better for the patient.[1]   Wherefore do thou bear *opposition* with patience ; but thy patience shall not be *practicable*, unless with GOD's *assistance*.   And be not thou grieved on account of the *unbelievers* ; neither be thou troubled for that which they subtly devise · for GOD is with those who fear *him*, and are upright.

XVII

THE CHAPTER OF THE NIGHT-JOURNEY [2]
Revealed at Mecca.[3]

IN THE NAME OF THE MOST MERCIFUL GOD.

(XV.) [4] PRAISE be unto him, who transported his servant by night, from the sacred temple *of Mecca* to the farther temple *of Jerusalem*,[5] the circuit of which we have blessed, that we might show him *some* of our signs ; for *God is* he who heareth, *and* seeth.   And we gave unto Moses the book *of the law*, and appointed the same *to be* a direction unto the children of Israel, *commanding them, saying, Beware* that ye take not any other patron besides me.   O posterity of those whom we carried *in the ark* with Noah :[6] verily he was

---

[1] Here, says Al Beidâwi, the Korân principally points at Mohammed, who was of all men the most conspicuous for meekness and clemency.

[2] The reason of this inscription appears in the first words. Some entitle the chapter, *The children of Israel*.

[3] Some except eight verses, beginning at these words, *It wanted little but*, &c. (p. 279).   [4] Section XV begins.

[5] From whence he was carried through the seven heavens to the presence of GOD, and brought back again to Mecca the same night.   This journey of Mohammed to heaven is so well known that I may be pardoned if I omit the description of it.   The English reader may find it in Dr. Prideaux's Life of Mahomet (see Morgan's Mahometism Explained, vol. 2), and the learned in Abulfeda (Vit. Moham. cap. 19), whose annotator has corrected several mistakes in the relation of Dr. Prideaux, and in other writers.   It is a dispute among the Mohammedan divines, whether their prophet's nightjourney was really performed by him corporeally, or whether it was only a dream or vision.   Some think the whole was no more than a vision ; and allege an express tradition of Moâwiyah (Vit. Moham, c. 18), one of Mohammed's successors, to that purport.   Others suppose he was carried bodily to Jerusalem, but no farther ; and that he ascended thence to heaven in spirit only.   But the received opinion is, that it was no vision, but that he was actually transported in the body to his journey's end ; and if any impossibility be objected, they think it a sufficient answer to say, that it might easily be effected by an omnipotent agent. (Al Beidâwi.)

[6] The commentators are put to it to find out the connection of these words with the foregoing.   Some think the accusative case is here put for the vocative, as I have translated it ; and others explain the words thus, *Take not for your patrons besides me, the posterity of those*, &c., meaning, mortal men.

a grateful servant. And we expressly declared unto the children of Israel in the book *of the law, saying*, Ye will surely commit evil in the earth twice,[1] and ye will be elated with great insolence. And when the *punishment* threatened for the first of those *transgressions* came *to be executed*, we sent against you our servants,[2] endued with exceeding strength *in war*, and they searched the inner apartments of *your* houses; and the prediction became accomplished. Afterwards we gave you the victory over them,[3] *in your turn*, and we granted you increase of wealth and children, and we made you a more numerous people, *saying*, If ye do well, ye will do well to your own souls; and if ye do evil, *ye will do it* unto the same. And when the *punishment* threatened or *your* latter *transgression* come *to be executed, we sent enemies against you* to afflict you,[4] and to enter the temple, as they entered it the first time, and utterly to destroy that which they had conquered. Peradventure your LORD will have mercy on you *hereafter*; but if ye return *to transgress a third time* we

---

[1] Their first transgression was their rejecting the decisions of the law, their putting Isaiah to death (Al Beidâwi), and their imprisoning of Jeremiah (Jallalo'ddin); and the second, was their slaying of Zachariah and John the Baptist, and their imagining the death of JESUS. (Jallalo'ddin.)

[2] These were Jalût, or Goliath, and his forces (Jallalo'ddin, Yahya); or Sennacherib the Assyrian; or else Nebuchadnezzar, whom the Eastern writers called Bakhtnasr (which was, however, only his surname, his true name being Gudarz, or Raham), the governor of Babylon under Lohorasp, king of Persia (Al Zamakhshari, Al Beidâwi), who took Jerusalem, and destroyed the temple.

[3] By permitting David to kill Goliath; or by the miraculous defeat of Sennacherib's army; or for that GOD put it into the heart of Bahman the son of Isfandiyar, when he succeeded his grandfather Lohorasp, to order Kiresh, or Cyrus, then governor of Babylon, to send home the Jews from their captivity, under the conduct of Daniel; which he accordingly did, and they prevailed against those whom Bakhtnasr had left in the land. (Al Zamakh., Al Beidâwi.)

[4] Some imagine the army meant in this place was that of Bakhtnasr (Yahya, Jallalo'ddin); but others say the Persians conquered the Jews this second time, by the arms of Gudarz (by whom they seem to intend Antiochus Epiphanes), one of the successors of Alexander at Babylon. It is related that the general in this expedition, entering the temple, saw blood bubbling up on the great altar, and asking the reason of it, the Jews told him it was the blood of a sacrifice which had not been accepted of GOD; to which he replied, that they had not told him the truth, and ordered a thousand of them to be slain on the altar; but the blood not ceasing, he told them, that if they would not confess the truth, he would not spare one of them; whereupon they acknowledged it was the blood of John: and the general said, *Thus hath your* LORD *taken vengeance on you*; and then cried out, O John, my LORD *and thy* LORD *knoweth what hath befallen thy people for thy sake*; *wherefore let thy blood stop, by* GOD's *permission, lest I leave not one of them alive*; upon which the blood immediately stopped. (Al Beidâwi.) These are the explanations of the commentators, wherein their ignorance in ancient history is sufficiently manifest; though perhaps Mohammed himself, in this latter passage, intended the destruction of Jerusalem by the Romans

also will return *to chastise you* ;[1] and we have appointed hell *to be* the prison of the unbelievers. Verily this Korân directeth unto *the way* which is most right, and declareth unto the faithful, who do good works, that they shall receive a great reward ; and that for those who believe not in the life to come, we have prepared a grievous punishment. Man prayeth for evil, as he prayeth for good ;[2] for man is hasty.[3] We have ordained the night and the day for two signs *of our power* : afterwards we blot out the sign of the night, and we cause the sign of the day to shine forth, that ye may endeavour to obtain plenty from your LORD *by doing your business therein*, and that ye may know the number of years, and the computation *of time* ; and everything *necessary* have we explained by a *perspicuous* explication. The fate[4] of every man have we bound about his neck ;[5] and we will produce unto him, on the day of resurrection, a book *wherein his actions shall be recorded* : it shall be offered him open, *and the angels shall say unto him*, Read thy book ; thine own soul will be a sufficient accountant against thee, this day.[6] He who shall be *rightly* directed, shall be directed to *the advantage* only *of* his own soul ; and he who shall err, shall err only against the same : neither shall any laden *soul* be charged with the burthen of another. We did not punish *any people*, until we had *first* sent an apostle *to warn them*. And when we resolved to destroy a city, we commanded the inhabitants

---

[1] And this came accordingly to pass : for the Jews being again so wicked as to reject Mohammed, and conspire against his life, God delivered them into his hands ; and he exterminated the tribe of Koreidha, and slew the chiefs of Al Nadîr, and obliged the rest of the Jewish tribes to pay tribute. (Al Beidâwi.)

[2] Out of ignorance, mistaking evil for good ; or making wicked imprecations on himself and others, out of passion and impatience.

[3] Or inconsiderate, not weighing the consequence of what he asks. It is said that the person here meant is Adam, who, when the breath of life was breathed into his nostrils, and had reached so far as his navel, though the lower part of his body was, as yet, but a piece of clay, must needs try to rise up, and got an ugly fall in consequence. But others pretend the passage was revealed on the following occasion. Mohammed committed a certain captive to the charge of his wife, Sawda bint Zamáa, who, moved with compassion at the man's groans, unbound him, and let him escape : upon which the prophet, in the first moments of his anger, wished her hand might fall off ; but immediately composing himself, said aloud, *O God, I am but a man ; therefore turn my curse into a blessing.* (Jallalo'ddin.)

[4] Literally, *the bird*, which is here used to signify a man's *fortune* or *success* ; the Arabs, as well as the Greeks and Romans, taking omens from the flight of birds, which they supposed to portend good luck, if they flew from the left to the right, but if from the right to the left, the contrary ; the like judgment they also made when certain beasts passed before them.

[5] Like a collar, which he cannot by any means get off. See Sale, Prel. Disc. Sect. IV.

[6] Sale, Prel. Disc. Sect. IV.

thereof, who lived in affluence, *to obey our apostle* ; but they acted corruptly therein : wherefore the sentence was justly pronounced against *that city* ; and we destroyed it with an utter destruction. And how many generations have we consumed since Noah ? for thy LORD sufficiently knoweth and seeth the sins of his servants. Whosoever chooseth *this* transitory *life*, we will bestow on him therein beforehand that which we please ; on him, *namely*, whom we please : afterwards will we appoint him hell *for his abode* ; he shall be thrown into the same to be scorched, covered with ignominy, *and* utterly rejected *from mercy*. But whosoever chooseth the life to come, and directeth his endeavour towards the same, being also a true believer ; the endeavour of these shall be acceptable *unto God*. On all will we bestow *the blessings of this life*, both on these and on those, of the gift of thy LORD ; for the gift of thy LORD shall not be denied *unto any*. Behold, how we have caused some of them to surpass others *in wealth and dignity* : but the next life shall be more considerable in degrees *of honour*, and greater in excellence. Set not up another god with *the true* GOD, lest thou sit down in disgrace *and* destitute. Thy LORD hath commanded that ye worship none, besides him ; and *that ye show* kindness unto *your* parents, whether the one of them, or both of them attain to old age with thee.[1] Wherefore say not unto them, Fie *on you* ! neither reproach them, but speak respectfully unto them ; and submit to behave humbly[2] towards them, out of tender affection, and say, O LORD, have mercy on them both, as they nursed me *when I was* little. Your LORD well knoweth that which is in your souls ; whether ye be men of integrity : and he will be gracious unto those who sincerely return *unto him*. And give unto him who is of kin *to you* his due,[3] and *also* unto the poor, and the traveller. And waste not *thy substance* profusely : for the profuse are brethren of the devils :[4] and the devil was ungrateful unto his LORD. But if thou turn from them, in expectation of the mercy which thou hopest from thy LORD ;[5] *at least*, speak kindly unto

[1] That is, receiving their support and maintenance from thee.

[2] Literally, *Lower the wing of humility*, &c.

[3] That is, friendship and affection, and assistance in time of need.

[4] Prodigality, and squandering away one's substance in folly or luxury, being a very great sin. The Arabs were particularly guilty of extravagance in killing camels, and distributing them by lot, merely out of vanity and ostentation ; which they are forbidden by this passage, and commanded to bestow what they could spare on their poor relations, and other indigent people. (Al Beidâwi.)

[5] That is, If thy present circumstances will not permit thee to assist others, defer thy charity till GOD shall grant thee better ability.

them. And let not thy hand be tied up to thy neck ; neither open it with an unbounded expansion,[1] lest thou become worthy of reprehension, and be reduced to poverty. Verily thy LORD will enlarge the store of whom he pleaseth, and will be sparing *unto whom he pleaseth* ; for he knoweth and regardeth his servants. Kill not your children for fear of being brought to want ; we will provide for them and for you : verily the killing them is a great sin.[2] Draw not near unto fornication ; for it is wickedness, and an evil way. Neither slay the soul which GOD hath forbidden *you to slay,* unless for a just cause ;[3] and whosoever shall be slain unjustly we have given his heir power *to demand satisfaction* ;[4] but let him not exceed the bounds *of moderation* in putting to death *the murderer in too cruel a manner,* or *by* revenging *his friend's blood on any other than the person who killed him* ; since he is assisted *by this law.*[5] And meddle not with the substance of the orphan, unless it be to improve it, until he attain his age of strength :[6] and perform *your* covenant ; for the *performance of your* covenant shall be inquired into *hereafter.* And give full measure, when you measure *aught* ; and weigh with a just balance. This will be better, and more easy for determining *every man's due.*[7] And follow not that whereof thou hast no knowledge ;[8] for the hearing, and the sight, and the heart, each of these shall be examined *at the last day.* Walk not proudly in the land, for thou canst not cleave the earth, neither shalt thou equal the mountains in stature. All this is evil, *and* abominable in the sight of thy LORD. These *precepts are a part* of the wisdom which thy LORD hath revealed unto thee. Set not up any other god *as equal* unto GOD, lest thou be cast into hell, reproved *and* rejected. Hath

---

[1] *i.e.,* Be neither niggardly nor profuse, but observe the mean between the two extremes, wherein consists true liberality. (Al Beidâwi.)

[2] See Chaps. VI. and LXXXI.

[3] The crimes for which a man may justly be put to death are these : apostasy, adultery and murder. (Al Beidâwi.)

[4] It being at the option of the heir, or next of kin, either to take the life of the murderer or to accept of a fine in lieu of it. (See Chap. II.)

[5] Some refer the pronoun *he* to the person slain, for the avenging whose death this law was made ; some to the heir, who has a right granted him to demand satisfaction for his friend's blood (Yahya) ; and others to him who shall be slain by the heir, if he carry his vengeance too far. (Al Beidâwi.)

[6] See Chap. IV.

[7] Or, *more advantageous in the end.* (Al Beidâwi, Al Zamakh.)

[8] *i.e.,* Vain and uncertain opinions, which thou hast not good reason to believe true or at least probable. Some interpret the words, *Accuse not* another of a crime *whereof thou hast no knowledge* : supposing they forbid the bearing false witness, or the spreading or giving credit to idle reports of others. (Al Beidâwi, Al Zamakh.)

your LORD preferably granted unto you sons, and taken *for himself* daughters from among the angels ?[1] Verily *in asserting this* ye utter a grievous saying.   And now have we used various *arguments and repetitions* in this Korân, that they may be warned ; yet it only rendereth them more disposed to fly *from the truth.*   Say *unto the idolaters,* If there were *other* gods with him, as ye say, they would surely seek an occasion *of making some attempt* against the possessor of the throne : [2] GOD forbid ! and far, very far, be that from him which they utter !   The seven heavens praise him, and the earth, and all who are therein : neither is there anything which doth not celebrate his praise ; but ye understand not their celebration *thereof* : he is gracious and merciful.   When thou readest the Korân, we place between thee and those who believe not in the life to come, a dark veil ; and we put coverings over their hearts, lest they should understand it, and in their ears thickness of hearing.   And when thou makest mention, in *repeating* the Korân, of thy LORD only,[3] they turn their backs, flying *the doctrine of his unity.*   We well know with what *design* they hearken when, they hearken unto thee, and when they privately discourse together : when the ungodly say, Ye follow no other than a madman.   Behold ! what epithets they bestow on thee.   But they are deceived ; neither can they *find* any *just* occasion *to reproach thee.*   They also say, After we shall have become bones and dust, shall we surely be raised a new creature ?   Answer, Be ye stones, or iron, or some creature more improbable in your opinions *to be raised to life.*   But they will say, Who shall restore us *to life* ?   Answer, He who created you the first time : and they will wag their heads at thee, saying, When *shall* this *be* ?   Answer, Peradventure it is nigh.   On *that* day shall GOD call you *forth from your sepulchres,* and ye shall obey, with celebration of his praise ;[4] and ye shall think that ye tarried[5] but a little while.   Speak unto my servants, that they speak mildly *unto the unbelievers, lest ye exasperate them* ; for Satan soweth discord among them, and Satan is a declared enemy unto man.   Your LORD well knoweth you ; if he pleaseth, he will

[1] See Chap. XVI.

[2] *i.e.,* They would in all probability contend with GOD for superiority, and endeavour to dethrone him, in the same manner as princes act with one another on earth.

[3] Not allowing their gods to be his associates, nor praying their intercession with him.

[4] The dead, says Al Beidâwi, at his call shall immediately rise, and shaking the dust off their heads, shall say, *Praise be unto thee, O God.*

[5] viz., In your graves ; or, in the world.

have mercy on you, or, if he pleaseth, he will punish you :[1] and we have not sent thee *to be* a steward over them. Thy LORD well knoweth all persons in heaven and on earth.[2] We have bestowed peculiar favours on some of the prophets, preferably to others ; and we gave unto David the psalms.[3] Say, Call upon those whom ye imagine *to be gods* besides him ; yet they will not be able to free you from harm, or to turn *it on others*. Those whom ye invoke,[4] do *themselves* desire *to be admitted to* a near conjunction with their LORD ; *striving* which of them shall approach nearest *unto him* : they also hope for his mercy, and dread his punishment ; for the punishment of thy LORD is terrible. There is no city but we will destroy the same before the day of resurrection, or we will punish it with a grievous punishment. This is written in the book *of our eternal decrees*. Nothing hindered us from sending *thee* with miracles, except that the former *nations* have charged them with imposture. We gave unto *the tribe of* Thamûd, *at their demand*, the she-camel visible *to their sight* ; yet they dealt unjustly with her :[5] and we send not *a prophet* with miracles, but to strike terror. *Remember* when we said unto thee, Verily thy LORD encompasseth men *by his knowledge and power*. We have appointed the vision which we showed thee,[6] and also the tree [7] cursed in the Korân

[1] These words are designed as a pattern for the Moslems to follow, in discoursing with the idolaters ; by which they are taught to use soft and dubious expressions, and not to tell them directly that they are doomed to hell fire ; which, besides the presumption in offering to determine the sentence of others, would only make them more irreconcilable enemies.

[2] And may choose whom he pleases for his ambassador. This is an answer to the objections of the Koreish, that Mohammed was the orphan pupil of Abu Taleb, and followed by a parcel of naked and hungry fellows. (Al Beidâwi.)

[3] Which were a greater honour to him than his kingdom ; and wherein Mohammed and his people are foretold by these words, among others (Marracc. in Alc. p. 28, &c. Prid. Life of Mah. p. 122) : *The righteous shall inherit the earth* (Psal. xxxvii. 28. Al Beidâwi).

[4] viz., The angels and prophets, who are the servants of GOD as well as yourselves.   [5] See Chap. VII.

[6] Mohammed's journey to heaven is generally agreed to be intended in this place ; which occasioned great heats and debates among his followers, till they were quieted by Abu Becr's bearing testimony to the truth of it. (Abulf. Vit. Moh. p. 39, and not. ibid. Prideaux, Life of Mah. p. 50, and Sale, Prel. Disc. Sect. II.). The word *vision*, here used, is urged by those who take this journey to have been no more than a dream, as a plain confirmation of their opinion. Some, however, suppose the vision meant in this passage was not the night-journey, but the dream Mohammed saw at Al Hodeibiya, wherein he seemed to make his entrance into Mecca (see Chap. XLVIII.); or that at Bedr (see Chap. VIII.) ; or else a vision he had relating to the family of Ommeya, whom he saw mount his pulpit, and jump about in it like monkeys ; upon which he said, This is their portion in this world, which they have gained by their profession of Islâm (Al Beidâwi). But if any of these latter expositions be true, the verse must have been revealed at Medina.

[1] Called Al Zakkûm, which springs from the bottom of hell.

only for an occasion of dispute unto men, and to strike *them* with terror ; but it shall cause them to transgress only the more enormously. And *remember* when we said unto the angels, Worship Adam ; and they *all* worshipped him except Eblîs, *who* said, Shall I worship him whom thou hast created *of* clay ? *And* he said, What thinkest thou, *as to* this *man* whom thou hast honoured above me ? verily, if thou grant me respite until the day of resurrection, I will extirpate his offspring, except a few. *God* answered, Begone, *I grant thee respite* : but whosoever of them shall follow thee, hell shall surely be your reward ; an ample reward *for your demerits* ![1] And entice to vanity such of them as thou canst, by thy voice ; and assault them on all sides with thy horsemen and thy footmen ;[2] and partake with them in *their* riches, and *their* children ;[3] and make them promises ; (but the devil shall make them no other than deceitful promises :) *as to* my servants, thou shalt have no power over them ; for thy LORD is a sufficient protector *of those who trust in him.* It is your LORD who driveth forward the ships for you in the sea, that ye may seek *to enrich yourselves* of his abundance *by commerce* ; for he is merciful towards you. When a misfortune befalleth you at sea, the *false deities* whom ye invoke are forgotten *by you*, except him *alone* : yet when he bringeth you safe to dry land, ye retire afar off *from him, and return to your idols* ; for man is ungrateful.[4] Are ye therefore secure that he will not cause the dry land to swallow you up, or *that he will not* send against you a *whirlwind* driving the sands *to overwhelm you* ? then ye find none to protect you. Or are ye secure that he will not cause you again to commit yourselves to *the sea* another time, and send against you a tempestuous wind, and drown you ; for that ye have been ungrateful ? then shall ye find none to defend *you* against us, in that *distress.* And now have we honoured the children of Adam *by sundry peculiar privileges and endowments* ; and we have given them conveniences of carriage by land and by sea, and have provided food for them of good things ; and we have preferred them before many of *our creatures* which we have created, by granting *them great* prerogatives. On a

[1] See Chap II. and Chap. VII.
[2] *i.e.*, With all thy forces.
[3] Instigating them to get wealth by unlawful means, and to spend it in supporting vice and superstition ; and tempting them to incestuous mixtures, and to give their children names in honour of their idols, as Abd Yaghûth, Abd' al Uzza, &c. (Al Beidâwi.)
[4] See Chap. X.

certain day we will call all men *to judgment* with their *respective* leaders :[1] and whosoever shall have his book given him into his right hand, they shall read their book *with joy and satisfaction* ;[2] and they shall not be wronged a hair.[3] And whoever hath been blind in this *life*, shall be also blind in the next, and shall wander more widely from the path *of salvation*. It wanted little but *the unbelievers* had tempted thee to swerve from *the instructions* which we had revealed unto thee, that thou shouldest devise concerning us a different thing ;[4] and then would they have taken thee for *their* friend : and unless we had confirmed thee, thou hadst certainly been very near inclining unto them a little. Then would we surely have caused thee to taste the punishment of life, and the punishment of death ;[5] and thou shouldest not have found any to protect thee against us. The *unbelievers* had likewise almost caused thee to depart the land, that they might have expelled thee thence :[6] but then should they not have tarried

[1] Some interpret this of the prophet sent to every people ; others, of the heads of sects ; others, of the various religions professed in the world ; others, of the books which shall be given to every man at the resurrection, containing a register of his good and bad actions.

[2] See Sale, Prel. Disc. Sect. IV.

[3] See Chap. IV., p. 80, note 5.

[4] These are generally supposed to have been the tribe of Thakîf, the inhabitants of Al Tâyef, who insisted on Mohammed's granting them several very extraordinary privileges, as the terms of their submission to him ; for they demanded that they might be free from the legal contribution of alms, and from observing the appointed times of prayer ; that they might be allowed to keep their idol Allât for a certain time (Sale, Prel. Disc. Sect. I.), and that their territory might be declared a place of security and not be violated, like that of Mecca, &c. And they added, that if the other Arabs asked him the reason of these concessions, he should say, that GOD had commanded him so to do (Al Beidâwi, Jallalo'ddin. Abulf. Vit. Moham. p. 126, &c.). According to which explanation it is plain this verse must have been revealed long after the Hejra. Some, however, will have the passage to have been revealed at Mecca, on occasion of the Koreish ; who told Mohammed they would not suffer him to kiss the black stone in the wall of Caaba, unless he also visited their idols, and touched them with his hand, to show his respect.

[5] *i.e.,* Both of this life and the next. Some interpret the first of the punishment in the next world, and the latter of the torture of the sepulchre. (Al Beidâwi.)

[6] The commentators differ as to the place where this passage was delivered, and the occasion of it. Some think it was revealed at Mecca, and that it refers to the violent enmity which the Koreish bore Mohammed, and their restless endeavours to make him leave Mecca (Al Beidâwi), as he was at length obliged to do. But as the persons here spoken of seem not to have prevailed in their project, others suppose that the verse was revealed at Medina, on the following occasion. The Jews, envious of Mohammed's good reception and stay there, told him, by way of counsel, that Syria was the land of the prophets, and that if he was really a prophet he ought to go thither. Mohammed seriously reflecting on what they had said, began to think they had advised him well ; and actually set out, and proceeded a day's journey on his way to Syria : whereupon GOD acquainted

therein after thee, except a little while.[1] *This is* the method of dealing *which we have prescribed ourselves* in respect to our apostles, whom we have already sent before thee : and thou shalt not find any change in our *prescribed* method. Regularly perform *thy* prayer at the declension of the sun,[2] at the first darkness of the night,[3] and the prayer of daybreak ;[4] for the prayer of daybreak is borne witness unto *by the angels.*[5] And watch *some part* of the night in the same *exercise,* as a work of supererogation for thee ; peradventure thy LORD will raise thee to an honourable station.[6] And say, O LORD, cause me to enter with a favourable entry, and cause me to come forth with a favourable coming forth ;[7] and grant me from thee an assisting power. And say, Truth is come, and falsehood is vanished : for falsehood is of short continuance.[8] We send down of the Korân that which is a medicine and a mercy unto the true believers, but it shall only increase the perdition of the unjust. When we bestow favours on man, he retireth and withdraweth himself *ungratefully from us* : but when evil toucheth him, he despaireth *of our mercy.* Say, Every one acteth after his own manner :[9] but your LORD

him with their design by the revelation of this verse ; and he returned to Medina (Al Beidâwi, Jallalo'ddin).

[1] This was fulfilled, according to the former of the above-mentioned explanations, by the loss of the Koreish at Bedr ; and according to the latter, by the great slaughter of the Jews of Koreidha and Al Nadîr. (Al Beidâwi, Jallalo'ddin.)

[2] *i.e.,* At the time of noon prayer, when the sun declines from the meridian ; or, as some choose to translate the words, *at the setting of the sun,* which is the time of the first evening prayer.

[3] The time of the last evening prayer.

[4] Literally, *the reading of the daybreak* ; whence some suppose the reading of the Korân at that time is here meant.

[5] viz., The guardian angels, who, according to some, are relieved at that time ; or else the angels appointed to make the change of night into day, &c. (Al Beidâwi.)

[6] According to a tradition of Abu Horeira, the honourable station here intended is that of intercessor for others. (Al Beidâwi.)

[7] That is, Grant that I may enter my grave with peace, and come forth from it, at the resurrection, with honour and satisfaction. In which sense this petition is the same with that of Balaam, *Let me die the death of the righteous, and let my last end be like his* (Numb. xxiii. 10). But as the person here spoken to is generally supposed to be Mohammed, the commentators say he was commanded to pray in these words for a safe departure from Mecca, and a good reception at Medina ; or for a sure refuge in the cave, where he hid himself when he fled from Mecca (Sale, Prel. Disc. Sect. II.); or (which is the more common opinion) for a victorious entrance into Mecca, and a safe return thence (Al Beidâwi, Jallalo'ddin.)

[8] These words Mohammed repeated, when he entered the temple of Mecca, after the taking of that city, and cleansed it of the idols ; a great number of which are said to have fallen down on his touching them with the end of the stick he held in his hand. (Al Beidâwi, Jallalo'ddin. Vide Gagnier, Vie de Mahomet, tom. 2, p. 127.)

[9] *i.e.,* According to his judgment or opinion, be it true or false ; or according

best knoweth who is most truly directed in *his* way. They will ask thee concerning the spirit :[1] answer, The spirit *was created* at the command of my LORD :[2] but ye have no knowledge given unto you, except a little.[3] If we pleased, we should certainly take away that which we have revealed unto thee ;[4] in such case thou couldest not find any to assist thee therein against us, unless through mercy from thy LORD ; for his favour towards thee hath been great. Say, Verily, if men and genii were purposely assembled, that they might produce *a book* like this Korân, they could not produce *one* like unto it, although the one of them assisted the other. And we have variously propounded unto men in this Korân, every *kind of* figurative argument ; but the greater part of men refuse *to receive it*, merely out of infidelity. And they say, We will by no means believe on thee, until thou cause a spring of water to gush forth for us out of the earth ;[5] or thou hast a garden of palm-trees and vines, and thou cause rivers to spring forth from the midst thereof in abundance ; or thou cause the heaven to fall down upon us, as thou hast given out, in pieces ; or thou bring down GOD and the angels to vouch *for thee* ; or thou hast a house of gold ; or thou ascend by a ladder to heaven : neither will we believe thy ascending *thither alone*,[6] until thou cause a book to descend unto us, *bearing witness of thee*, which we may read. Answer, My LORD be praised ! Am I *other* than a man, *sent as an apostle* ?

---

to the bent of his mind, and the natural constitution of his body. (Al Beidâwi.)

[1] Or the soul of man. Some interpret it of the angel Gabriel, or of the divine revelation. (Al Beidâwi.)

[2] viz., By the word *Kun, i.e., Be* ; consisting of an immaterial substance, and not generated, like the body. But, according to a different opinion, this passage should be translated, *The spirit is of those things, the knowledge of which thy Lord hath reserved to himself*. For it is said that the Jews bid the Koreish ask Mohammed to relate the history of those who slept in the cave, and of Dhu'lkarnein (see the next chapter), and to give them an account of the soul of man ; adding, that if he pretended to answer all the three questions, or could answer none of them, they might be sure he was no prophet, but if he gave an answer to one or two of the questions and was silent as to the other, he was really a prophet. Accordingly, when they propounded the questions to him, he told them the two histories, but acknowledged his ignorance as to the origin of the human soul. (Al Beidâwi.)

[3] All your knowledge being acquired from the information of your senses, which must necessarily fail you in spiritual speculations, without the assistance of divine revelation. (Al Beidâwi.)

[4] viz., The Korân ; by erasing it both from the written copies, and the memories of men.

[5] This and the following miracles were demanded of Mohammed by the Koreish, as proofs of his mission.

[6] As thou pretendest to have done in thy night-journey ; but of which no man was witness.

And nothing hindereth men from believing, when a direction is come unto them, except that they say, Hath GOD sent a man *for his* apostle ? Answer, If the angels had walked on earth *as* familiar inhabitants *thereof*, we had surely sent down unto them from heaven an angel *for our* apostle. Say, GOD is a sufficient witness between me and you : for he knoweth and regardeth his servants. Whom GOD shall direct, he shall be the *rightly* directed ; and whom he shall cause to err, thou shalf find none to assist, besides him. And we will gather them together on the day of resurrection, *creeping* on their faces, blind, and dumb, and deaf :[1] their abode *shall be* hell ; so often as *the fire thereof* shall be extinguished, we will rekindle a burning flame to *torment* them.[2] This shall be their reward, because they disbelieve in our signs, and say, When we shall have been *reduced to* bones and dust, shall we surely be raised new creatures ? Do they not perceive that GOD, who created the heavens and the earth, *is* able to create *other bodies*, like *their present* ? And he hath appointed them a limited term ;[3] there is no doubt thereof : but the ungodly reject *the truth*, merely out of unbelief. Say, If ye possessed the treasures of the mercy of my LORD, ye would surely refrain *from using them*, for fear of spending *them* ;[4] for man is covetous. We heretofore gave unto Moses *the power of working* nine evident signs.[5] And do thou ask the children of Israel *as to the story of Moses* ;[6] when he came unto them, and Pharaoh said unto him, Verily I esteem thee, O Moses,

---

[1] See Sale, Prel. Disc. Sect. IV.

[2] *i.e.*, When the fire shall go out or abate for want of fuel, after the consumption of the skins and flesh of the damned, we will add fresh vigour to the flames by giving them new bodies. (Al Beidâwi. See Chap. IV.)

[3] Of life, or resurrection.

[4] That is, lest they should be exhausted.

[5] These were, the changing his rod into a serpent, the making his hand white and shining, the producing locusts, lice, frogs, and blood, the dividing of the Red Sea, the bringing water out of the rock, and the shaking of Mount Sinai over the children of Israel. In lieu of the three last some reckon the inundation of the Nile, the blasting of the corn, and scarcity of the fruits of the earth. (Al Beidâwi, Jallalo'ddin.) These words, however, are interpreted by others, not of *nine miracles*, but of *nine commandments*, which Moses gave his people, and were thus numbered up by Mohammed himself to a Jew, who asked him the question, *viz.*, That they should not be guilty of idolatry, nor steal, nor commit adultery or murder, nor practise sorcery or usury, nor accuse an innocent man to take away his life, or a modest woman of whoredom, nor desert the army ; to which he added the observing of the sabbath, as a tenth commandment, but which peculiarly regarded the Jews : upon which answer, it is said, the Jew kissed the prophet's hands and feet. (Al Beidâwi.)

[6] Some think these words are directed to Moses, who is hereby commanded to *demand the children of* Israel *of* Pharaoh, that he might let them go with him.

to be deluded by sorcery.　*Moses* answered, Thou well knowest that none hath sent down these evident signs except the LORD of heaven and earth ; and I surely esteem thee, O Pharaoh, a lost *man*.　Wherefore *Pharaoh* sought to drive them out of the land ; but we drowned him, and all those who were with him.　And we said unto the children of Israel, after *his destruction*, Dwell ye in the land : and when the promise of the next life shall come *to be fulfilled*, we will bring you *both* promiscuously *to judgment*.　We have sent down *the Korân* with truth, and it hath descended with truth : and we have not sent thee *otherwise* than *to be* a bearer of good tidings, and a denouncer *of threats*.　And we have divided the Korân, *revealing it by parcels*, that thou mightest read it unto men with deliberation ; and we have sent it down, causing *it* to descend *as occasion required*.[1]　Say, Whether ye believe therein, or do not believe, verily those who have been favoured with the knowledge *of the scriptures which were revealed* before it, when the same is rehearsed unto them, fall down on *their* faces,[2] worshipping, and say, Our LORD be praised, for that the promise of our LORD is surely fulfilled !　And they fall down on *their* faces, weeping ; and *the hearing thereof* increaseth their humility.　Say, Call upon GOD, or call on the Merciful : by whichsoever *of the two names* ye invoke *him, it is equal* ; for he hath most excellent names.[3]　Pronounce not thy prayer aloud, neither pronounce it with too low a voice,[4] but follow a *middle* way between these : and say, Praise *be* unto GOD, who hath not begotten any child ; who hath no partner in the kingdom, nor hath any to protect him from contempt ; and magnify him by proclaiming his greatness.

[1] See Sale, Prel. Disc. Sect. III.
[2] Literally, *on their chins*.
[3] The infidels hearing Mohammed say, O GOD, and *O Merciful*, imagined *the Merciful* was the name of a deity different from GOD, and that he preached the worship of two ; which occasioned this passage.　See Chap. VII.
[4] Neither so loud, that the infidels may overhear thee, and thence take occasion to blaspheme and scoff ; nor so softly as not to be heard by the assistants.　Some suppose that by the word *prayer*, in this place, is meant the reading of the Korân.

XVIII

THE CHAPTER OF THE CAVE [1]

Revealed at Mecca. [2]

IN THE NAME OF THE MOST MERCIFUL GOD.

PRAISE be unto GOD, who hath sent down unto his servant the book *of the Korân,* and hath not inserted therein any crookedness, *but hath made it* a straight *rule* : that he should threaten a grievous punishment *unto the unbelievers* from his presence ; and should bear good tidings unto the faithful, who work righteousness, that they shall receive an excellent reward, *namely, paradise,* wherein they shall remain for ever : and that he should warn those who say, GOD hath begotten issue ; of which matter they have no knowledge, neither *had* their fathers. A grievous saying *it is,* which proceedeth from their mouths : they speak no other than a lie. Peradventure thou wilt kill thyself with grief after them, *out of thy earnest zeal for their conversion,* if they believe not in this new revelation *of the Korân.* Verily we have ordained whatsoever is on the earth for the ornament thereof, that we might make trial of *men, and see* which of them excelleth in works ; and we will surely reduce whatever is thereon, to dry dust. Dost thou consider that the companions of the cave,[3] and Al Rakim,[4] were *one* of our signs,

---

[1] The chapter is thus inscribed because it makes mention of the cave wherein the Seven Sleepers concealed themselves.

[2] Some except one verse, which begins thus, *Behave thyself with constancy,* &c.

[3] These were certain Christian youths, of a good family in Ephesus, who, to avoid the persecution of the emperor Decius, by the Arab writers called Decianus, hid themselves in a cave, where they slept for a great number of years. (Al Beidâwi, Jallalo'ddin, &c.) This apocryphal story, for Baronius—Martyrol. ad 27 Julii—treats it as no better, and Father Marracci (Alcor. p. 425 ; Prodr. part 4, p. 103) acknowledges it to be partly false, or at least doubtful, though he calls Hottinger *a monster of impiety,* and the *off-scum of heretics,* for terming it a fable (Hotting. Hist. Orient. p. 40) was borrowed by Mohammed from the Christian traditions (Greg. Turon. et Simeon, Metaphrast), but has been embellished by him and his followers with several additional circumstances. (D'Herbelot, Bibl. Orient. p. 189.)

[4] What is meant by this word the commentators cannot agree. Some will have it to be the name of the mountain, or the valley, wherein the cave was ; some say it was the name of their dog ; and others (who seem to come nearest the true signification) that it was a brass plate, or stone table, placed near the mouth of the cave, on which the names of the young men were written. There are some, however, who take the companions of Al Rakim to be different from the Seven Sleepers : for they say the former were three men who were driven by ill weather into a cave for shelter, and were shut in there by the falling down of a vast stone, which stopped the cave's mouth ; but on their begging GOD's mercy, and their relating each of them a meritorious action which they hoped might entitle them to it, were miraculously

and a great miracle? When the young men took refuge in the cave, they said, O LORD, grant us mercy from before thee, and dispose our business for us to a right *issue.* Wherefore we struck their ears *with deafness, so that they slept without disturbance* in the cave for a *great* number of years : then we waked them, that we might know which of the two parties[1] was more exact in computing the space which they had remained *there.* We will relate unto thee their history with truth. Verily they were young men who had believed in their LORD ; and we had abundantly directed them : and we fortified their hearts with constancy when they stood *before the tyrant* ; and they said, Our LORD is the LORD of heaven and earth : we will by no means call on any god besides him ; *for* then should we surely utter an extravagance. These our *fellow* people have taken *other* gods, besides him ; although they bring no demonstrative argument for them : and who is more unjust than he who deviseth a lie concerning GOD ? And *they said the one to the other,* When ye shall separate yourselves from them, and *from the deities* which they worship, except GOD,[2] fly into the cave : your LORD will pour his mercy on you abundantly, and will dispose your business for you to advantage. And thou mightest have seen the sun, when it had risen, to decline from their cave towards the right hand ; and when it went down, to leave them on the left hand :[3] and they were in the spacious part *of the cave.*[4] This *was one* of the signs of GOD. Whomsoever GOD shall direct, he *shall be rightly* directed ; and whomsoever he shall cause to err, thou shalt not find any to defend *or* to direct. And thou wouldest have judged them to have been awake, while they were sleeping ;[5] and we caused them to turn themselves to the right hand, and to the left.[6] And their dog[7] stretched forth his fore-legs in the

delivered by the rock's rending in sunder to give them passage. (Al Beidâwi, ex trad. Noomân Ebn Bashir.)

[1] *viz.,* Of the sleepers themselves, or others, who were divided in opinion as to the length of their stay in the cave.

[2] For they, like other idolaters, worshipped the true GOD and idols also. (Al Beidâwi.)

[3] Lest it should be offensive to them, the cave opening towards the south. (Al Beidâwi.)

[4] *i.e.,* In the midst of it, where they were incommoded neither by the heat of the sun nor the closeness of the cave. (Al Beidâwi.)

[5] Because of their having their eyes open, or their frequent turning themselves from one side to the other. (Al Beidâwi.)

[6] Lest their lying so long on the ground should consume their flesh. (Al Beidâwi, Jallalo'ddin.)

[7] This dog had followed them as they passed by him when they fled to the

mouth of the cave : if thou hadst come suddenly upon them,
verily thou wouldest have turned thy back and fled from
them, and thou wouldest have been filled with fear *at the
sight* of them.[1]   And so we waked them from *their* sleep,
that they might ask questions of one another.   One of them
spake and said, How long have ye tarried *here* ?   They answered, We have tarried a day, or part of a day.   *The others*
said, Your LORD best knoweth the *time* ye have tarried :[2]
and now send one of you with this your money into the city,[3]
and let him see which of its *inhabitants* hath the best and
cheapest food, and let him bring you provision from him ;
and let him behave circumspectly, and not discover you to
any one.   Verily, if they come up against you. they will stone
you, or force you to return to their religion ; and then shall
ye not prosper for ever.   And so we made *their people*
acquainted with *what had happened to* them ; that they might
know that the promise of GOD is true, and that there is no
doubt of the *last* hour ;[4] when they disputed among themselves concerning their matter.[5]   And they said, Erect a

cave, and they drove him away ; whereupon GOD caused him to speak, and
he said, *I love those who are dear unto God* ; *go to sleep therefore, and I will
guard you.*   But some say, it was a dog belonging to a shepherd who followed
them, and that the dog followed the shepherd ; which opinion is supported
by reading, as some do, *câlebohom*, their dog's master, instead of *calbohom*, their
dog. (Al Beidâwi.)   Jallalo'ddin adds, that the dog behaved as his masters
did, in turning himself, in sleeping, and in waking.   The Mohammedans
have a great respect for this dog, and allow him a place in paradise with some
other favourite brutes : and they have a sort of proverb which they use in
speaking of a covetous person, *that he would not throw a bone to the dog of
the seven sleepers* ; nay, it is said that they have the superstition to write his
name, which they suppose to be Katmír (though some, as is observed above,
think he was called Al Rakim), on their letters which go far, or which pass
the sea, as a protection, or kind of talisman, to preserve them from mis-
carriage. (La Roque, Voy. de l'Arabie Heur. p. 74. D'Herbel. ubi sup.)
 [1] For that GOD had given them terrible countenances ; or else because of
the largeness of their bodies, or the horror of the place.   It is related that
the Khalif Moâwiyah, in an expedition he made against Natolia, passed by
the cave of the Seven Sleepers, and would needs send somebody into it,
notwithstanding Ebn Abbâs remonstrated to him the danger of it, saying,
That a better man than him (meaning the prophet) had been forbidden to
enter it, and repeated this verse ; but the men the Khalif sent in had no
sooner entered the cave, than they were struck dead by a burning wind.
(Al Beidâwi.)
 [2] As they entered the cave in the morning, and waked about noon, they at
first imagined they had slept half a day, or a day and a half at most ; but
when they found their nails and hair grown very long, they used these
words. (Al Beidâwi.)
 [3] Which some commentators suppose was Tarsus.
 [4] The long sleep of these young men, and their waking after so many years,
being a representation of the state of those who die, and are afterwards raised
to life.
 [5] *i.e.,* Concerning the resurrection ; some saying that the souls only should
be raised, others, that they should be raised with the body : or, concerning,

building over them : their LORD best knoweth *their condition.* Those who prevailed in their affair answered, We will surely build a chapel over them.[1] *Some say, The sleepers were* three ; *and* their dog *was* the fourth :[2] and *others* say, *They were* five ; and their dog *was* the sixth ;[3] guessing at a secret matter : and *others* say, *They were* seven ; and their dog *was* the eighth.[4] Say, My LORD best knoweth their number : none shall know them, except a few. Wherefore dispute not concerning them, unless with a clear disputation, *according to what hath been revealed unto thee* : and ask not any of *the Christians* concerning them. Say not of any matter, I will surely do this to-morrow ; unless *thou add,* If GOD please.[5] And remember thy LORD, when thou forgettest,[6] and say, My LORD is able to direct me with ease, that I may draw near unto *the truth of* this *matter* rightly. And they remained in their cave three hundred years, and nine *years* over.[7] Say, GOD best knoweth how long they continued *there* : unto him *are* the secrets of heaven and

the sleepers, after they were really dead ; one saying, that they were dead, and another, they were only asleep : or else concerning the erecting a building over them, as it follows in the next words ; some advising a dwelling-house to be built there, and others a temple. (Al Beidâwi.)

[1] When the young man who was sent into the city, went to pay for the provision he had bought, his money was so old, being the coin of Decius, that they imagined he had found a treasure, and carried him before the prince, who was a Christian, and having heard his story, sent some with him to the cave, who saw and spoke to the others ; after which they fell asleep again and died ; and the prince ordered them to be buried in the same place, and built a chapel over them.

[2] This was the opinion of Al Seyid, a Jacobite Christian of Najrân.

[3] Which was the opinion of certain Christians, and particularly of a Nestorian prelate.

[4] And this is the true opinion. (Al Beidâwi, Jallalo'ddin.)

[5] It is said, that when the Koreish, by the direction of the Jews, put the three questions above mentioned to Mohammed, he bid them come to him the next day, and he would give them an answer, but added not, *if it please God* ; for which reason he had the mortification to wait above ten days before any revelation was vouchsafed him concerning those matters, so that the Koreish triumphed, and bitterly reproached him as a liar ; but at length Gabriel brought him directions what he should say ; with this admonition, however, that he should not be so confident for the future. (Al Beidâwi.)

[6] *i.e.,* Give the glory to him, and ask pardon for thy omission, in case thou forget to say, *If it please God.*

[7] Jallalo'ddin supposes the whole space was three hundred solar years, and that the odd nine are added to reduce them to lunar years. Some think these words are introduced as spoken by the Christians, who differed among themselves about the time ; one saying it was three hundred years, and another, three hundred and nine years. (Al Beidâwi.) The interval between the reigns of Decius, and that of Theodosius the younger, in whose time the sleepers are said to have awaked, will not allow them to have slept quite two hundred years ; though Mohammed is somewhat excusable, since the number assigned by Simeon Metaphrastes (ubi sup.) is three hundred and seventy-two years.

earth *known* ; do thou make him to see and to hear.[1]   The *inhabitants thereof* have no protector besides him ; neither doth he suffer any one to have a share in *the establishment or knowledge of* his decree.   Read that which hath been revealed unto thee, of the book of thy LORD, *without presuming to make any change therein* :[2] there is none who hath power to change his words ; and thou shalt not find any to fly to, besides him, *if thou attempt it*.   Behave thyself with constancy towards those who call upon their LORD morning and evening, and who seek his favour ; and let not thine eyes be turned away from them, seeking the pomp of this life ;[3] neither obey him whose heart we have caused to neglect the remembrance of us,[4] and who followeth his lusts, and leaveth *the truth* behind him, and say, The truth *is* from your LORD ; wherefore let him who will, believe, and let him who will, be incredulous.   We have surely prepared for the unjust *hell* fire, the flame and smoke whereof shall surround them like a pavilion : and if they beg relief, they shall be relieved with water like molten brass, which shall scald *their* faces ; O how miserable a portion, and how unhappy a couch ! As to those who believe and do good works, we will not suffer the reward of him who shall work righteousness to perish : for them *are prepared* gardens of eternal abode,[5] which shall be watered by rivers ; they shall be adorned therein with bracelets of gold, and shall be clothed in green garments of fine silk and brocades ; reposing themselves therein on thrones.   O how happy a reward, and how easy a couch ! And propound unto them as a parable two men :[6] on the one of whom we had bestowed two vineyards,

[1] This is an ironical expression, intimating the folly and madness of man's presuming to instruct GOD. (Al Beidâwi, Jallalo'ddin.) Palmer renders it, "He can see ! and hear ! "
[2] As the unbelievers would persuade thee to do. (Al Beidâwi, Jallalo'ddin.)
[3] That is, Despise not the poor believers because of their meanness, nor honour the rich because of their wealth and grandeur.
[4] The person more particularly intended here, it is said, was Ommeya Ebn Khalf, who desired Mohammed to discard his indigent companions, out of respect to the Koreish. See Chap. VI.
[5] Literally of Eden. See Chap. IX.
[6] Though these seem to be general characters only, designed to represent the different end of the wicked, and of the good ; yet it is supposed, by some, that two particular persons are here meant.   One says they were two Israelites and brothers, who had a considerable sum left them by their father, which they divided between them ; and that one of them, being an unbeliever, bought large fields and possessions with his portion, while the other, who was a true believer, disposed of his to pious uses ; but that in the end, the former was ruined, and the latter prospered.   Another thinks they were two men of the tribe of Makhzûm : the one named Al Aswad Ebn Abd'al Ashadd, an infidel ; and the other Abu Salma Ebn Abd'allah,

and had surrounded them with palm-trees, and had caused corn *to grow* between them. Each of the gardens brought forth its fruit *every season*, and failed not at all ; and we caused a river to flow in the midst thereof : and he had great abundance. And he said unto his companion by way of debate, I am superior to thee in wealth, and have a more powerful family. And he went into his garden,[1] being guilty of injustice against his own soul, *and* said, I do not think that this *garden* will decay for ever ; neither do I think that the *last* hour will come : and although I should return unto my LORD, verily I shall find a better *garden* than this in exchange.[2] *And* his companion said unto him, by way of debate, Dost thou not believe in him who created thee of the dust, and afterwards of seed ; and then fashioned thee into a perfect man ? But *as for me*, GOD is my LORD ; and I will not associate any *other deity* with my LORD. And when thou enterest thy garden, wilt thou not say, What GOD pleaseth *shall come to pass* ; there is no power but in GOD *alone* ? Although thou seest me to be inferior to thee in wealth and *number of* children, my LORD is well able to bestow on me a better *gift* than thy garden, and to shoot *his* arrows against the same from heaven, so that it shall become barren dust ; or its water may sink deep *into the earth*, that thou canst not draw thereof. And his possessions were encompassed *with destruction, as his companion had fore-warned him* : wherefore he began to turn down the palms of his hands *out of sorrow and regret* for that which he had expended thereon ; for *the vines thereof* were fallen down on their trails : and he said, Would to GOD that I had not associated any *other deity* with my LORD ! And he had no party to assist him, besides GOD, neither was he able to defend himself *against his vengeance*. In such case protection *belongeth* of right unto GOD *alone* ; he is the best rewarder, and the best giver of success. And propound to them a similitude of the present life. *It is* like water which we send down from heaven ; and the herb of the earth is mixed therewith, and *after it hath been green and flourishing*, in the morning it becometh dry stubble, which the winds scatter abroad : and GOD is able to do all things. Wealth and

the husband of Omm Salma (whom the prophet married after his death), and a true believer. (Al Beidâwi.)

[1] Carrying his companion with him, out of ostentation, and to mortify him with the view of his large possessions. (Al Beidâwi.)

[2] Vainly imagining that his prosperity was not so much the free gift of GOD, as due to his merit. (Al Beidâwi.)

children *are* the ornament of this present life : but good *works*, which are permanent, *are* better in the sight of thy LORD, with respect to the reward, and better with respect to hope. On a *certain* day we will cause the mountains to pass away,[1] and thou shalt see the earth appearing plain *and even* ; and we will gather *mankind* together, and we will not leave any one of them behind. And they shall be set before thy LORD in *distinct* order, *and he shall say unto them*, Now are ye come unto us *naked*, as we created you the first time : but ye thought that we should not perform *our* promise unto you. And the book *wherein every one's actions are recorded* shall be put *into his hand* ; and thou shalt see the wicked in great terror, because of that which *is written* therein, and they shall say, Alas for us ! what *meaneth* this book ? it omitteth neither a small *action* nor a great *one*, but it compriseth the same ; and they shall find that which they have wrought, present *before their eyes* : and thy LORD will not deal unjustly with any one. *Remember* when we said unto the angels, Worship ye Adam : and they *all* worshipped *him* except Eblîs,[2] *who* was *one* of the genii,[3] and departed from the command of his LORD. Will ye therefore take him and his offspring for *your* patrons besides me, notwithstanding they are your enemies ? Miserable *shall such* a change *be* to the ungodly ! I called not them to be present at the creation of the heavens and of the earth, nor at the creation of themselves, neither did I take *those* seducers for *my* assistants. On a *certain* day, GOD shall say *unto the idolaters*, Call those whom ye imagined *to be* my companions, *to protect you* ; and they shall call them, but they shall not answer them ; and we will place a valley of destruction between them :[4] and the wicked shall see *hell* fire ; and they shall know that they shall be thrown into the same, and they shall find no way to avoid it. And now have we variously propounded unto men, in this Korân, a parable of every kind ; but man cavilleth at most things *therein*. Yet nothing

---

[1] For being torn up by the roots, they shall fly in the air, and be reduced to atoms. (Al Beidâwi. Sale, Prel. Disc. Sect. IV.)

[2] See Chaps. II. and VII.

[3] Hence some imagine the *genii* are a species of angels : others suppose the devil to have been originally a *djin*, which was the occasion of his rebellion, and call him *the father of the genii*, whom he begat after his fall (Jallalo'ddin, &c.) ; it being a constant opinion among the Mohammedans, that the angels are impeccable, and do not propagate their species (Prelim. Disc. Sect. IV. &c.).

[4] *i.e.*, Between the idolaters and their false gods. Some suppose the meaning is no more than that GOD will set them at variance and division.

hindereth men from believing, now a direction is come unto them, and from asking pardon of their LORD, excepting that *they wait until* the punishment of *their* predecessors come *to be inflicted* on them, or that the chastisement *of the next life* come upon them publicly. We send not *our* messengers, but to bear good tidings, and to denounce threats. Those who believe not, dispute with vain *arguments*, that they may thereby render the truth of no effect : and they hold my signs, and the admonitions which have been made them, in derision. And who is more unjust than he who hath been acquainted with the signs of his LORD, and retireth afar off from the same, and forgetteth that which his hands have formerly committed ? Verily we have cast veils over their hearts, lest they should understand *the Korân*, and into their ears thickness of hearing : if thou invite them to the *true* direction, yet will they not therefore be directed for ever. Thy LORD *is* gracious, endued with mercy ; if he would have punished them for that which they have committed, he would doubtless have hastened their punishment : but a threat *hath been denounced* against them,[1] and they shall find no refuge, besides him. And those *former* cities[2] did we destroy, when they acted unjustly ; and we gave them previous warning of their destruction. And *remember* when Moses said unto his servant *Joshua, the son of Nun*, I will not cease *to go forward*, until I come to the place where the two seas meet ; or I will travel for a long space of time.[3] But when they were arrived at the meeting of the two *seas*,[4] they forgot their fish *which they had taken with them* ;[5] and

[1] viz. Of their calamity at Bedr (for the Koreish are the infidels here intended), or their punishment at the resurrection. (Al Beidâwi.)

[2] That is, the towns of the Adites, Thamûdites, Sodomites, &c.

[3] The original word properly signifies the space of eighty years and upwards. To explain this long passage the commentators tell the following story. They say that Moses once preaching to the people, they admired his knowledge and eloquence so much, that they asked him whether he knew any man in the world who was wiser than himself ; to which he answered in the negative : whereupon GOD, in a revelation, having reprehended him for his vanity (though some pretend that Moses asked GOD the question of his own accord), acquainted him that his servant Al Khedr was more knowing than he ; and, at Moses's request, told him he might find that person at a certain rock, where the two seas met ; directing him to take a fish with him in a basket, and that where he missed the fish, that was the place. Accordingly Moses set out, with his servant Joshua, in search of Al Khedr ; which expedition is here described. (Al Beidâwi, Al Zamakhshari, Al Bokhari, in Sonna, &c.)

[4] viz., Those of Persia and Greece. Some fancy that the meeting of Moses and Al Khedr is here intended, as of the two *seas* of knowledge. (Al Beidâwi.)

[5] Moses forgot to inquire concerning it, and Joshua forgot to tell him when he missed it. It is said that when they came to the rock, Moses falling

the fish took its way freely[1] in the sea.   And when they had
passed beyond *that place, Moses* said unto his servant, Bring
us our dinner : for now are we fatigued with this our journey.
His servant answered, Dost thou know *what has befallen me* ?
When we took up our lodging at the rock, ve⁻¹v I forgot the
fish : and none made me to forget it except Satan, that I
should not remind *thee* of it.   And *the fish* took its way in
the sea, in a wonderful manner.   *Moses* said, This is what
we sought after.   And they both went back, returning by
the way they came.   And *coming to the rock* they found one
of our servants,[2] unto whom we had granted mercy from us,
and whom we had taught wisdom from before us.   *And*
Moses said unto him, Shall I follow thee, that thou mayest
teach me *part* of that which thou hast been taught, for a
direction *unto me* ?   He answered, Verily thou canst not
bear with me : for how canst thou patiently suffer those
things, the knowledge whereof thou dost not comprehend ?
Moses replied, Thou shalt find me patient, if GOD please ;
neither will I be disobedient unto thee in anything.   He said,
If thou follow me therefore, ask me not concerning anything,
until I shall declare the meaning thereof unto thee.   So they
both went on *by the sea-shore,* until they went up into a ship ;
and he made a hole therein.[3]   *And Moses* said *unto him,*
Hast thou made a hole therein, that thou mightest drown
those who are on board ? now hast thou done a strange
thing.   He answered, Did I not tell thee that thou couldest
not bear with me ?   *Moses* said, Rebuke me not, because I

asleep, the fish, which was roasted, leaped out of the basket into the sea ;
some add, that Joshua making the ablution at the fountain of life (of which
immediately), some of the water happened to be sprinkled on the fish,
which immediately restored it to life. (Al Beidâwi.)

[1] The word here translated *freely,* signifying also a pipe or arched channel
for conveyance of water, some have imagined that the water of the sea was
miraculously kept from touching the body of the fish, which passed through
it as under an arch. (Al Beidâwi).

[2] This person, according to the general opinion, was the prophet Al
Khedr ; whom the Mohammedans usually confound with Phineas, Elias,
and St. George, saying that his soul passed by a metempsychosis successively
through all three. Some, however, say his true name was Balya Ebn
Malcân, and that he lived in the time of Afridûn, one of the ancient kings of
Persia, and that he preceded Dhu'lkarnein, and lived to the time of Moses.
They suppose Al Khedr, having found out the fountain of life and drunk
thereof, became immortal ; and that he had therefore this name from his
flourishing and continual youth (Al Beidâwi.   D'Herbelot, Bibl. Orient. Art.
Khedher, Septemcastrens, de Turcar. Moribus. Busbeq. Epist. 1, p. 93, &c.
Hotting. Hist. Orient. p. 58, &c., 99, &c., 292, &c.). Part of these fictions
they took from the Jews, some of whom also fancy Phineas was Elias (R.
Levi. Ben Gerson in Append. l. 1, Reg. 1, 27).

[3] For Al Khedr took an axe, and knocked out two of her planks.
(Al Beidâwi.)

did forget ; and impose not on me a difficulty in what I am commanded. Wherefore they *left the ship and* proceeded, until they met with a youth ; and he slew him.[1] *Moses* said, Hast thou slain an innocent person, without *his having killed* another ? Now hast thou committed an unjust action. (XVI.) [2] He answered, Did I not tell thee that thou couldest not bear with me ? *Moses* said, If I ask thee concerning anything hereafter, suffer me not to accompany thee : now hast thou received an excuse from me. They went forwards, therefore, until they came to the inhabitants of a *certain* city:[3] *and* they asked food of the inhabitants thereof ; but they refused to receive them. And they found therein a wall, which was ready to fall down ; and he set it upright.[4] *Whereupon Moses* said *unto him,* If thou wouldest thou mightest doubtless have received a reward for it. He answered, This shall be a separation between me and thee : *but* I will *first* declare unto thee the signification of that which thou couldest not bear with patience. The vessel belonged to certain poor men,[5] who did their business in the sea : and I was minded to render it unserviceable, because there was a king[6] behind them, who took every *sound* ship by force. As to the youth, his parents were true believers, and we feared lest he, *being an unbeliever,* should oblige them to suffer *his* perverseness and ingratitude : wherefore we desired that their LORD might give them a more righteous *child* in exchange for him, and one more affectionate *towards them.*[7] And the wall belonged to two orphan youths[8] in the city, and under it was a treasure *hidden which belonged* to them ; and their father was a righteous man : and thy LORD was pleased that they should attain their full age, and take forth their treasure, through the mercy of thy LORD. And I did not *what thou hast seen* of mine own will, *but by God's direction.* This is the interpretation of that which thou couldest not bear with

[1] By twisting his neck round, or dashing his head against a wall, or else by throwing him down and cutting his throat. (Al Beidâwi.)

[2] Here the sixteenth section begins. See Sale, Prel. Disc. p. 63.

[3] This city was Antioch ; or, as some rather think, Obollah, near Basra, or else Bâjirwân in Armenia. (Al Beidâwi.)

[4] By only stroking it with his hand ; though others say he threw it down and rebuilt it. (Al Beidâwi.)

[5] They were ten brothers, five of whom were past their labour by reason of their age. (Al Beidâwi).

[6] Named Jaland Ebn Karkar, or Minwâr Ebn Jaland al Azdi.

[7] It is said that they had afterwards a daughter, who was the wife and the mother of a prophet ; and that her son converted a whole nation. (Al Beidâwi.)

[8] Their names were Asram and Sarim. (Al Beidâwi.)

patience. The Jews will ask thee concerning Dhu'lkarnein.[1]
Answer, I will rehearse unto you an account of him. We
made him powerful in the earth, and we gave him means to
accomplish everything *he pleased*. And he followed *his* way,
until he came to the place where the sun setteth ; *and* he
found it to set in a spring of black mud ;[2] and he found near
the same a certain people.[3] And we said, O Dhu'lkarnein,
either punish *this people*, or use gentleness towards them.[4]
He answered, Whosoever *of them* shall commit injustice, we
will surely punish him *in this world* ; afterwards shall he
return unto his LORD, and he shall punish him with a
severe punishment. But whosoever believeth, and doth
that which is right, shall receive the most excellent reward,
and we will give him in command that which is easy. Then
he continued *his* way, until he came to the place where the
sun riseth ;[5] *and* he found it to rise on certain people, unto
whom we had not given anything wherewith to shelter themselves therefrom.[6] Thus *it was* ; and we comprehended

---

[1] Or, The two-horned. The generality of the commentators (Al Beidâwi,
Al Zamakhshari, Jallalo'ddin, Yahya) suppose the person here meant
to be Alexander the Great, or, as they call him, Iscander al Rûmi, king of
Persia and Greece ; but there are very different opinions as to the reason of
this surname. Some think it was given him because he was king of the
East and of the West, or because he had made expeditions to both those
extreme parts of the earth ; or else because he had two horns on his diadem,
or two curls of hair, like horns, on his forehead ; or, which is most probable,
by reason of his great valour. Several modern writers (Scaliger, de Emend.
temp. L'Empereur, not. in Jachiad. Dan. viii. 5. Gol. in Alfrag. p. 58,
&c.) rather suppose the surname was occasioned by his being represented
in his coins and statues with horns, as the son of Jupiter Ammon ; or else by
his being compared by the prophet Daniel to a he-goat (Schickard. Tarikh
Reg. Pers. p. 73) ; though he is there represented with but one horn (Dan.
viii.). There are some good writers, however, who believe the prince intended
in this passage of the Korân was not Alexander the Grecian, but another
great conqueror, who bore the same name and surname, and was much
more ancient than he, being contemporary with Abraham, and one of the
kings of Persia of the first race (Abulfeda, Khondemir, Tarikh Montakhab,
&c. D'Herbel. Bibl. Orient. Art. Escander) ; or, as others suppose, a king
of Yaman, named Asaab Ebn al Râyesh (Ex trad. Ebn. Abbas. Poc. Spec. p.
58). They all agree he was a true believer, but whether he was a prophet
or no, is a disputed point.

[2] That is, it seemed so to him, when he came to the ocean, and saw nothing
but water. (Al Beidâwi, Jallalo'ddin.)

[3] An unbelieving nation, who were clothed in the skins of wild beasts,
and lived upon what the sea cast on shore. (Al Beidâwi, Jallalo'ddin.)

[4] For GOD gave Dhu'lkarnein his choice, either to destroy them for their
infidelity, or to instruct them in the true faith ; or, according to others,
either to put them to the sword, or to take them captive : but the words
which follow confirm the former interpretation, by which it appears he
chose to invite them to the true religion, and to punish only the disobedient
and incredulous.

[5] *i.e.*, That part of the habitable world on which the sun first rises.

[6] Who had neither clothes nor houses, their country not bearing any buildings, but dwelt in holes underground, into which they retreated from the heat

with our knowledge the *forces* which were with him. And he prosecuted *his* journey *from south to north*, until he came between the two mountains ;[1] beneath which he found certain people, who could scarce understand what was said.[2] *And* they said, O Dhu'lkarnein, verily Gog and Magog waste the land ;[3] shall we therefore pay the tribute, on condition that thou build a rampart between us and them ? He answered, The *power* wherewith my LORD hath strengthened me, is better *than your tribute* : but assist me strenuously, and I will set a strong wall between you and them. Bring me iron in large pieces, until it fill up *the space* between the two sides *of these mountains. And* he said *to the workmen,* Blow *with your bellows,* until it makes *the iron red hot as* fire. *And* he said *further,* Bring me molten brass, that I may pour upon it. Wherefore, *when this wall was finished, Gog and Magog* could not scale it, neither could they dig through it.[4] *And Dhu'lkarnein* said, This *is* a mercy from my LORD : but when the prediction of my LORD shall come *to be fulfilled,*[5] he shall reduce *the wall* to dust ; and the prediction of my LORD is true. On that day we will suffer some of them to

of the sun. (Al Beidâwi, Jallalo'ddin.) Jallalo'ddin says they were the Zenj, a black nation lying south-west of Ethiopia. They seem to be the Troglodytes of the ancients.

[1] Between which Dhu'lkarnein built the famous rampart, mentioned immediately, against the irruptions of Gog and Magog. These mountains are situate in Armenia and Adherbiján, or, according to others, much more northwards, on the confines of Turkestan. (Al Beidâwi.) The relation of a journey taken to this rampart, by one who was sent on purpose to view it by the Khalíf Al Wathek, may be seen in D'Herbelot (Bibl. Orient. Art. Jagiouge).

[2] By reason of the strangeness of their speech and their slowness of apprehension ; wherefore they were obliged to make use of an interpreter. (Al Beidâwi.)

[3] The Arabs call them Yajûi and Majûj, and say they are two nations or tribes descended from Japhet the son of Noah, or, as others write, Gog are a tribe of the Turks, and Magog of those of Gilân (Al Beidâwi. D'Herbel. ubi supra), the Geli and Gelæ of Ptolemy and Strabo. (Gol. in Alfrag. p. 207.) It is said these barbarous people made their irruptions into the neighbouring countries in the spring, and destroyed and carried off all the fruits of the earth ; and some pretend they were man-eaters. (Al Beidâwi.)

[4] The commentators say the wall was built in this manner. They dug till they found water, and having laid the foundation of stone and melted brass, they built the superstructure of large pieces of iron, between which they laid wood and coals, till they equalled the height of the mountains ; and then setting fire to the combustibles, by the help of large bellows, they made the iron red hot, and over it poured melted brass, which filling up the vacancies between the pieces of iron, rendered the whole work as firm as a rock. Some tell us that the whole was built of stones joined by cramps of iron, on which they poured melted brass to fasten them. (Al Beidâwi.)

[5] That is, when the time shall come for Gog and Magog to break forth from their confinement ; which shall happen some time before the resurrection. (Sale, Prel. Disc. Sect. IV.)

press tumultuously like waves on others ;[1] and the trumpet shall be sounded, and we will gather them in a body together. And we will set hell, on that day, before the unbelievers ; whose eyes have been veiled from my remembrance, and who could not hear *my words*. Do the unbelievers think *that I will not punish them*, for that they take my servants for *their* protectors besides me ? Verily we have prepared hell for the abode of the infidels. Say, Shall we declare unto you those whose works are vain, whose endeavour in the present life hath been wrongly directed, and who think they do the work which is right ? These are they who believe not in the signs of their LORD, or that they shall be assembled before him ; wherefore their works are vain, and we will not allow them any weight on the day of resurrection. This *shall be* their reward, *namely*, hell ; for that they have disbelieved, and have held my signs and my apostles in derision. But *as for* those who believe and do good works, they shall have the gardens of paradise for their abode ; they shall remain therein for ever ; they shall wish for no change therein. Say, If the sea were ink to *write* the words of my LORD, verily the sea would fail, before the words of my LORD would fail ; although we added *another sea* like unto it as a further supply. Say, Verily I am only a man as ye are. It is revealed unto me that your GOD is one only GOD : let him therefore who hopeth to meet his LORD, work a righteous work ; and let him not make any other to partake in the worship of his LORD.

XIX

THE CHAPTER OF MARY [2]

Revealed at Mecca.[3]

IN THE NAME OF THE MOST MERCIFUL GOD.

C H. Y. A. S.[4] A commemoration of the mercy of thy LORD *towards* his servant Zacharias.[5] When he called upon his LORD, invoking *him* in secret, *and* said, O LORD,

---

[1] These words represent either the violent irruption of Gog and Magog, or the tumultuous assembly of all creatures, men, genii, and brutes, at the resurrection. (Sale, Prel. Disc. Sect IV.)

[2] Several circumstances relating to the Virgin Mary being mentioned in this chapter, her name was chosen for the title.

[3] Except the verse of *Adoration*.

[4] See Sale, Prel. Disc. Sect. III.   [5] See Chap. III.

verily my bones are weakened, and my head is become white with hoariness, and I have never been unsuccessful in my prayers to thee, O LORD. But now I fear my nephews, who are to succeed after me,[1] for my wife is barren : wherefore give me a successor *of my own body* from before thee ; who may be my heir, and may be an heir of the family of Jacob ;[2] and grant, O LORD, that he may be acceptable *unto thee. And the angel answered him,* O Zacharias, verily we bring thee tidings of a son, whose name *shall be* John ; we have not caused any to bear the same name before him.[3] *Zacharias* said, LORD, how shall I have a son, seeing my wife is barren, and I am now arrived at a great age,[4] *and am* decrepit ? *The angel* said, So *shall it be* : thy LORD saith, This is easy with me ; since I created thee heretofore, when thou wast nothing. *Zacharias* answered, O LORD, give me a sign. *The angel* replied, Thy sign *shall be* that thou shalt not speak to men for three nights, *although thou be* in perfect health. And he went forth unto his people, from the chamber, and he made signs unto them,[5] *as if he should say,* Praise ye *God* in the morning and in the evening. *And we said unto his son,* O John, receive the book *of the law,* with a resolution to *study and observe it.* And we bestowed on him wisdom, *when he was yet* a child, and mercy from us, and purity *of life* ;[6] and he was a devout person, and dutiful towards his parents, and was not proud *or* rebellious. Peace be on him the day whereon he was born, and the day whereon he shall die, and the day whereon he shall be raised to life. And

---

[1] These were his brother's sons, who were very wicked men, and Zacharias was apprehensive lest, after his death, instead of confirming the people in the true religion, they should seduce them to idolatry. (Al Beidâwi, Jallalo'ddin.) And some commentators imagine that he made his prayer in private, lest his nephews should overhear him.

[2] viz., In holiness and knowledge ; or in the government and superintendence of the Israelites. There are some who suppose it is not the patriarch who is here meant, but another Jacob, the brother of Zacharias, or of Imrân Ebn Mâthân, of the race of Solomon. (Al Beidâwi, Jallalo'ddin.)

[3] For he was the first who bore the name of John, or Yahya (as the Arabs pronounce it) ; which fancy seems to be occasioned by the words of St. Luke misunderstood, *that none of* Zacharias's *kindred was called by that name* (Luke i. 61) ; for otherwise John, or, as it is written in Hebrew, Johanan, was a common name among the Jews. Some expositors avoid this objection, by observing that the original word *samiyyan* signifies, not only one who is *actually called by the same name,* but also one who by reason of his possessing the like qualities and privileges, *deserves,* or *may pretend to the same name.*

[4] The Mohammedan traditions greatly differ as to the age of Zacharias at this time ; we have mentioned one already : Jallalo'ddin says, he was an hundred and twenty, and his wife ninety-eight ; and the Sonna takes notice of several other opinions.

[5] Some say he wrote the following words on the ground.

[6] Or, as the word also signifies, *The love of alms-deeds.*

remember in the book *of the Korân the story of* Mary ; when she retired from her family to a place towards the east,[1] and took a veil *to conceal herself* from them ; and we sent our spirit *Gabriel* unto her, and he appeared unto her *in the shape of* a perfect man.[2]   She said, I fly for refuge unto the merciful *God, that he may defend me* from thee : if thou fearest *him, thou wilt not approach me.*   He answered, Verily I am the messenger of thy LORD, *and am sent* to give thee a holy son. She said, how shall I have a son, seeing a man hath not touched me, and I am no harlot ?   *Gabriel* replied, So *shall it be* : thy LORD saith, This is easy with me ; and *we will perform it,* that we may obtain him for a sign unto men, and a mercy from us : for it is a thing which is decreed.   Wherefore she conceived him :[3] and she retired aside with him *in her womb* to a distant place ;[4] and the pains of childbirth came upon her near the trunk of a palm-tree.[5]   She said, Would to GOD I had died before this, and had become a *thing* forgotten, and lost in oblivion !   And he who was beneath her

[1] viz., To the eastern part of the temple ; or to a private chamber in the house, which opened to the east : whence, says Al Beidâwi, the Christians pray towards that quarter.   There is a tradition, that when the virgin was grown to years of puberty, she used to leave her apartment in the temple, and retire to Zacharias's house to her aunt, when her courses came upon her ; and so soon as she was clean, she returned again to the temple : and that at the time of the angel's visiting her, she was at her aunt's on the like occasion, and was sitting to wash herself, in an open place, behind a veil to prevent her being seen (Yahya, Al Beidâwi).   But others more prudently suppose the design of her retirement was to pray (Al Zamakh.).

[2] Like a full-grown but beardless youth.   Al Beidâwi, not contented with having given one good reason why he appeared in that form, viz., to moderate her surprise, that she might hear his message with less shyness, adds, that perhaps it might be to raise an emotion in her, and assist her conception.

[3] For Gabriel blew into the bosom of her shift, which he opened with his fingers (Yahya), and his breath reaching her womb, caused the conception (Jallalo'ddin, Al Beidâwi).   The age of the Virgin Mary at the time of her conception was thirteen, or, as others say, ten ; and she went six, seven, eight, or nine months with him, according to different traditions ; though some say the child was conceived at its full growth of nine months, and that she was delivered of him within an hour after (Al Beidâwi, Yahya).

[4] To conceal her delivery, she went out of the city by night, to a certain mountain.

[5] The palm to which she fled, that she might lean on it in her travail, was a withered trunk, without any head or verdure, and this happened in the winter season ; notwithstanding which it miraculously supplied her with fruits for her refreshment (Al Beidâwi, Yahya, Al Zamakh.) as is mentioned immediately.   It has been observed, that the Mohammedan account of the delivery of the Virgin Mary very much resembles that of Latona, as described by the poets (Sikii not. in Evang. Infant. p. 9, 21 &c.), not only in this circumstance of their laying hold on a palm-tree—Homer, Hymn. in Apoll. Callimach. Hymn. in Delum—(though some say Latona embraced an olive-tree, or an olive and a palm, or else two laurels), but also in that of their infants speaking ; which Apollo is fabled to have done in the womb. (Callimach. ibid.   See Kor. Chap. III.)

called to her,[1] *saying*, Be not grieved : now hath GOD provided a rivulet under thee ; and do thou shake the body of the palm-tree, and it shall let fall ripe dates upon thee, ready gathered.[2]   And eat, and drink, and calm thy mind.[3] Moreover if thou see any man, *and he question thee*, say, Verily I have vowed a fast unto the Merciful ; wherefore I will by no means speak to a man this day.[4]   So she brought *the child* to her people, carrying him *in her arms*.   *And* they said *unto her*, O Mary, now hast thou done a strange thing : O sister of Aaron,[5] thy father was not a bad man, neither was thy mother a harlot.   But she made signs unto *the child to answer them* ; *and* they said, How shall we speak to him, who is an infant in the cradle ?   *Whereupon the child* said, Verily I am the servant of God ;[6] he hath given me the book *of the gospel*, and hath appointed me a prophet.   And he hath made me blessed, wheresoever I shall be ; and hath commanded me *to observe* prayer, and *to give* alms, so long as I shall live ; and *he hath made me* dutiful towards my mother, and hath not made me proud, *or* unhappy.   And peace *be* on me the day whereon I was born, and the day whereon I shall die, and the day whereon I shall be raised to life.   This *was* JESUS, the son of Mary ; the Word of truth,[7] concerning whom they doubt.   It is not *meet* for GOD, that he should have any son : GOD forbid !   When he decreeth a thing, he

[1] This some imagine to have been the child himself ; but others suppose it was Gabriel, who stood somewhat lower than she did. (Al Beidâwi, Jallalo'ddin.) According to a different reading this passage may be rendered, *And he called to her from beneath her, &c.*   And some refer the pronoun, translated *her*, to the palm-tree ; and then it should be *beneath it*, &c.

[2] And accordingly she had no sooner spoken it than the dry trunk revived, and shot forth green leaves, and a head loaded with ripe fruit.

[3] Literally, *thine eye.*

[4] During which she was not to speak to anybody, unless to acquaint them with the reason of her silence : and some suppose she did that by signs.

[5] Several Christian writers think the Korân stands convicted of a manifest falsehood in this particular, but I am afraid the Mohammedans may avoid the charge (Chap. III.) ; as they do by several answers. Some say the Virgin Mary had really a brother named Aaron, who had the same father, but a different mother ; others suppose Aaron the brother of Moses is here meant, but say Mary is called *his sister*, either because she was of the Levitical race (as by her being related to Elizabeth, it should seem she was), or by way of comparison ; others say that it was a different person of that name who was contemporary with her, and conspicuous for his good or bad qualities, and that they likened her to him either by way of commendation or reproach, &c. (Al Zamakh., Al Beidâwi, Jallalo'ddin, Yahya, &c.)

[6] These were the first words which were put into the mouth of JESUS, to obviate the imagination of his partaking of the divine nature, or having a right to the worship of mankind, on account of his miraculous speaking so soon after his birth. (Al Beidâwi, &c.)

[7] This expression may either be referred to JESUS, as *the Word of GOD* ; or to the account just given of him.

only saith unto it, Be ; and it is. And verily GOD is my
LORD, and your LORD ; wherefore serve him : this is the
right way. Yet the sectaries differ among themselves *concerning Jesus* ; but woe be unto those who are unbelievers,
because of *their* appearance at the great day. Do thou
cause them to hear, and do thou cause *them* to see,[1] *on* the
day *whereon* they shall come unto us *to be judged* : but the
ungodly are this day in a manifest error. And do thou fore-
warn them of the day of sighing, when the matter shall be
determined, while they are *now sunk* in negligence and do
not believe. Verily we will inherit the earth, and whatever
creatures are therein :[2] and unto us shall they *all* return.
And remember Abraham in the book *of the Korân* ; for he
was one of great veracity, *and* a prophet. When he said
unto his father,[3] O my father, why dost thou worship that
which heareth not, neither seeth, nor profiteth thee at all ?
O my father, verily *a degree* of knowledge hath been bestowed
on me, which hath not been bestowed on thee : wherefore
follow me ; I will lead thee into an even way. O my father,
serve not Satan ; for Satan was rebellious unto the Merciful.
O my father, verily I fear lest a punishment be inflicted on
thee from the Merciful, and thou become a companion of
Satan. *His father* answered, Dost thou reject my gods, O
Abraham ? If thou forbear not, I will surely stone thee :
wherefore leave me for a long time. *Abraham* replied, Peace
be on thee : I will ask pardon for thee of my LORD ; for he
is gracious unto me. And I will separate myself from you,
and from the *idols* which ye invoke besides GOD ; and I will
call upon my LORD : it may be that I shall not be unsuccessful in calling on my LORD, *as ye are in calling upon them.*
And when he had separated himself from them, and from
the *idols* which they worshipped besides GOD,[4] we gave him
Isaac and Jacob ; and we made each of them a prophet ;
and we bestowed on them, through our mercy, *the gift of
prophecy, and children and wealth* ; and we caused them

---

[1] These words are variously expounded : some taking them to express
admiration (Chap. XVIII.) at the quickness of those senses in the wicked,
on the day of judgment, when they shall plainly perceive the torments prepared for them, though they have been deaf and blind in this life ; and others
supposing the words contain a threat to the unbelievers, of what they shall
then hear and see ; or else a command to Mohammed to lay before them the
terrors of that day. (Al Beidâwi.)

[2] *i.e.*, Alone surviving, when all creatures shall be dead and annihilated.
See Chap. XV.

[3] See Chap. VI.

[4] By flying to Harrân, and thence to Palestine.

to deserve the highest commendations.[1] And remember Moses in the book *of the Korân* : for he was sincerely upright, and was an apostle *and* a prophet. And we called unto him from the right side of mount *Sinai*, and caused him to draw near, *and* to discourse privately *with us*.[2] And we gave him, through our mercy, his brother Aaron, a prophet, *for his assistant.* Remember also Ismael in the *same* book : for he was true to *his* promise ;[3] and was an apostle, *and* a prophet. And he commanded his family *to observe* prayer, and *to give* alms ; and he was acceptable unto his LORD. And remember Edrîs[4] in the *same* book ; for he was a just person, *and* a prophet : and we exalted him to a high place.[5] These are they unto whom GOD hath been bounteous, of the prophets of the posterity of Adam, and of those whom we carried *in the ark* with Noah ; and of the posterity of Abraham, and of Israel, and of those whom we have directed and chosen. When the signs of the Merciful were read unto them, they fell down, worshipping, and wept : but a succeeding generation have come after them, who neglect prayer, and follow *their* lusts ; and they shall surely fall into evil : except him who repenteth, and believeth, and doth that which is right ; these shall enter paradise, and they shall not in the least be wronged ; gardens of perpetual abode *shall be their reward,* which the Merciful hath promised unto his servants, as an object of faith ; for his promise will surely come *to be fulfilled.* Therein shall they hear no vain discourse, but peace ;[6] and

---

[1] Literally, *We granted them a lofty tongue of truth.*

[2] Or, as some expound it, *And we raised him on high* ; for, say they, he was raised to so great an elevation, that he heard the creaking of the pen writing on the table of GOD's decrees. (Al Beidâwi.)

[3] Being celebrated on that account ; and particularly for his behaving with that resignation and constancy which he had promised his father, on his receiving GOD's command to sacrifice him (Al Beidâwi) ; for the Mohammedans say it was Ismael, and not Isaac, whom he was commanded to offer.

[4] Or Enoch, the great-grandfather of Noah, who had that surname from his great *knowledge* ; for he was favoured with no less than thirty books of divine revelations, and was the first who wrote with a pen, and studied the sciences of astronomy and arithmetic, &c. (Al Beidâwi, Jallalo'ddin, &c.) The learned Bartolocci endeavours to show, from the testimonies of the ancient Jews, that Enoch, surnamed Edrîs, was a very different person from the Enoch of Moses, and many ages younger. (Bartol. Bibl. Rabb. part 2, p. 845.)

[5] Some understand by this the honour of the prophetic office, and his familiarity with GOD ; but others suppose his translation is here meant : for they say that he was taken up by God into heaven at the age of three hundred and fifty, having first suffered death, and been restored to life ; and that he is now alive in one of the seven heavens, or in paradise. (Al Beidawi, Jallalo'ddin, Abulfeda.)

[6] *i.e.,* Words of peace and comfort ; or the salutations of the angels, &c. (Chap. X.)

their provision shall be prepared for them therein morning
and evening. This is paradise, which we will give for an
inheritance unto such of our servants as shall be pious. We
descend not *from heaven*, unless by the command of thy
LORD : unto him *belongeth* whatsoever is before us, and
whatsoever is behind us, and whatsoever is in the intermediate space ; neither is thy LORD forgetful *of tnee*.[1]   *He is*
the LORD of heaven and earth, and of whatsoever is between
them : wherefore worship him, and be constant in his worship. Dost thou know any named like him ?[2]   Man saith,[3]
After I shall have been dead, shall I really be brought forth
alive *from the grave* ?   Doth not man remember that we
created him heretofore, when he was nothing ?   But by thy
LORD we will surely assemble them and the devils *to judgment* ;[4] then will we set them round about hell on their
knees : afterwards we will draw forth from every sect such
of them as *shall have been* a more obstinate rebel against the
Merciful ;[5] and we best know which of them are more worthy
to be burned therein.[6]   There shall be none of you but shall
approach near the same :[7] *this* is an established decree with
thy LORD.   Afterwards we will deliver those who shall have
been pious, but we will leave the ungodly therein on their
knees.   When our manifest signs are read unto them, the
infidels say unto the true believers, Which of the two parties

[1] These are generally supposed to have been the words of the angel Gabriel,
in answer to Mohammed's complaint for his long delay of fifteen, or, according to another tradition, of forty days, before he brought him instructions
what solution he should give to the questions which had been asked him
concerning the sleepers, Dhu'lkarnein, and the spirit. (See before.)   Others,
however, are of opinion that they are the words which the godly will use
at their entrance into paradise ; and that their meaning is, *We take up our
abode here at the command and through the mercy of God alone, who ruleth all
things, past, future, and present* ; *and who is not forgetful of the works of his
servants*. (Al Beidâwi.)

[2] That is, Deserving, or having a right to the name and attributes of GOD.

[3] Some suppose a particular person is here meant, namely, Obba Ebn
Khalf.   (Chap. XVI, p. 195.)

[4] It is said that every infidel will appear, at the day of judgment, chained
to the devil who seduced him.   (Al Beidâwi.)

[5] Hence, says Al Beidâwi, it appears that GOD will pardon some of the
rebellious people.   But perhaps the distinguishing the unbelievers into
different classes, in order to consign them to different places and degrees
of torment, is here meant.

[6] viz., The more obstinate and perverse, and especially the heads of sects,
who will suffer double punishment for their own errors and their seducing
of others.

[7] For the true believers must also pass by or through hell, but the fire
will be damped, and the flames abated, so as not to hurt them, though it
will lay hold on the others.   Some, however, suppose that the words intend
no more than the passage over the narrow bridge, which is laid over hell.
(Al Beidâwi.   Prelim. Disc. Sect. IV.)

is in the more eligible condition, and *formeth* the more excellent assembly ?[1] But how many generations have we destroyed before them, which excelled them in wealth, and in outward appearance ? Say, Whosoever is in error, the Merciful will grant him a long and prosperous life ; until they see that with which they are threatened, whether it be the punishment *of this life*, or *that of* the *last* hour ; and hereafter they shall know who is in the worse condition, and the weaker in forces. GOD shall more fully direct those who receive direction ; and the good works which remain *for ever*, are better in the sight of thy LORD *than worldly possessions*, in respect to the reward, and more eligible in respect to the future recompence. Hast thou seen him who believeth not in our signs, and faith, I shall surely have riches and children bestowed on me ?[2] Is he acquainted with the secrets *of futurity* ; or hath he received a covenant from the Merciful *that it shall be so* ? By no means. We will surely write down that which he saith ; and increasing we will increase his punishment : and we will be his heir as to that which he speaketh of,[3] and *on the last day* he shall appear before us alone *and naked*. They have taken *other* gods, besides GOD, that they may be a glory unto them. By no means. Hereafter shall they deny their worship ;[4] and they shall become adversaries[5] unto them. Dost thou not see that we send the devils against the infidels, to incite them *to sin* by *their* instigations ? Wherefore be not in haste *to call down destruction* upon them ; for we number unto them a *determined* number *of days of respite*. On a certain day we will assemble the pious before the Merciful *in an honourable manner*, as ambassadors come *into the presence of a prince* ; but we will drive the wicked into hell, *as cattle are driven*

[1] viz., Of us, or of you. When the Koreish were unable to produce a composition to equal the Korân, they began to glory in their wealth and nobility, valuing themselves highly on that account, and despising the followers of Mohammed.

[2] This passage was revealed on account of Al As Ebn Wayel, who being indebted to Khabbâb, when he demanded the money, refused to pay it, unless he would deny Mohammed ; to which proposal Khabbâb answered, that he would never deny that prophet, neither alive, nor dead, nor when he should be raised to life at the last day ; therefore replied Al As, when thou art raised again, come to me, for I shall then have abundance of riches, and children, and I will pay you. (Al Beidâwi, Jallalo'ddin.)

[3] *i.e.*, He shall be obliged to leave all his wealth and his children behind him at his death.

[4] viz., At the resurrection ; when the idolaters shall disclaim their idols and the idols their worshippers, and shall mutually accuse one another (Chaps. VI. and X.)

[5] Or, *the contrary* ; that is to say, a *disgrace* instead of an *honour*.

to water : they shall obtain no intercession, except he only
who hath received a covenant from the Merciful.[1]   They say,
The Merciful hath begotten issue.   Now have ye uttered an
impious thing : it wanteth little but that on occasion thereof
the heavens be rent, and the earth cleave in sunder, and the
mountains be overthrown and fall, for that they attribute
children unto the Merciful ; whereas it becometh not GOD
to beget children.   Verily there is none in heaven or on earth,
but shall approach the Merciful *as his* servant.   He encompasseth them *by his knowledge and power*, and numbereth
them with an *exact* computation : and they shall all come
unto him on the day of resurrection, destitute *both of helpers
and followers*.   But as for those who believe and do good
works, the Merciful will bestow on them love.[2]   Verily we
have rendered the *Korân* easy for thy tongue, that thou
mayest thereby declare *our* promises unto the pious, and
mayest thereby denounce threats unto contentious people.
And how many generations have we destroyed before them ?
Dost thou find one of them *remaining* ?   Or dost thou hear
so much as a whisper concerning them ?[3]

[1] That is, except he who shall be a subject properly disposed to receive
that favour, by having possessed Islâm.   Or, the words may also be translated, according to another exposition, *They shall not obtain the intercession*
of any, *except* the intercession *of him*, &c.   Or else, *None shall be able to
make intercession* for others, *except he who shall have received a covenant* (or
permission) from God ; *i.e.*, who shall be qualified for that office by faith, and
good works, according to GOD'S promise, or shall have special leave given
him by GOD for that purpose.   (Al Beidâwi.   Chap II.)

[2] viz., The love of GOD and all the inhabitants of heaven.   Some suppose
this verse was revealed to comfort the Moslems who were hated and despised
at Mecca, on account of their faith, by the promise of their gaining the love
and esteem of mankind in a short time.   Rodwell's rendering is, "But
love will the God of Mercy vouchsafe to those who believe and do the things
that be right."

[3] Of so many generations which we have annihilated, canst thou call
back even one man ?   Do they make the slightest murmur heard ?   (Savary.)

XX

THE CHAPTER OF T. H.[1]

Revealed at Mecca.

IN THE NAME OF THE MOST MERCIFUL GOD.

T. H. We have not sent down the Korân unto thee, that thou shouldest be unhappy;[2] but for an admonition unto him who feareth *God* : being sent down from him who created the earth, and the lofty heavens. The Merciful sitteth on *his* throne : unto him *belongeth* whatsoever is in heaven and on earth, and whatsoever is between them, and whatsoever is under the earth. If thou pronounce *thy prayers* with a loud voice, *know that it is not necessary in respect to God* ; for he knoweth that which is secret, and what is yet more hidden. GOD ! there is no god but he : he hath most excellent names.[3] Hast thou been informed of the history of Moses ?[4] When he saw fire, and said unto his family, Tarry ye *here* ; for I perceive fire : peradventure I may bring you a brand thereout, or may find a direction *in our way* by the fire.[5] And when he was come near unto it,

[1] The signification of these letters, which being prefixed to the chapter are therefore taken for the title, is uncertain. (Sale, Prel. Disc. Sect. III.) Some, however, imagine they stand for *Ya rajol,* i.e. *O man* ! which interpretation, seeming not easily to be accounted for from the Arabic, is by a certain tradition deduced from the Ethiopic (Moham. Ebn Abd al Baki, ex trad. Acremæ Ebn Abi Sofian); or for *Ta,* i.e. *tread* ; telling us that Mohammed, being employed in watching and prayer the night this passage was revealed, stood on one foot only, but was hereby commanded to ease himself by setting both feet to the ground. Others fancy the first letter stands for *Túba, beatitude* ; and the latter for *Háwiyat,* the name of the lower apartment of hell. *Tah* is also an interjection commanding silence, and may properly enough be used in this place.

[2] Either by reason of thy zealous solicitude for the conversion of the infidels, or thy fatiguing thyself by watching and other religious exercises ; for, it seems, the Koreish urged the extraordinary fatigues he underwent in those respects, as the consequence of his having left their religion. (Al Beidâwi.)

[3] See Chaps. VII. and XVII.

[4] The relation of the story of Moses, which takes up the greatest part of this chapter, was designed to encourage Mohammed, by his example, to discharge the prophetic office with firmness of mind, as being assured of receiving the like assistance from GOD : for it is said this chapter was one of the first that were revealed. (Al Beidâwi.)

[5] The commentators say, that Moses having obtained leave of Shoaib, or Jethro, his father-in-law, to visit his mother, departed with his family from Midian towards Egypt ; but coming to the valley of Towa, wherein Mount Sinai stands, his wife fell in labour, and was delivered of a son, in a very dark and snowy night ; he had also lost his way, and his cattle were scattered from him ; when on a sudden he saw a fire by the side of a mountain, which on his nearer approaching he found burning in a green bush. (Al Beidâwi.)

a voice called unto him, *saying*, O Moses! verily I am thy
LORD : wherefore put off thy shoes ;[1] for thou art in the sacred
valley Towa.   And I have chosen thee ; therefore hearken
with attention unto that which is revealed *unto thee*.   Verily
I am GOD ; there is no god beside me : wherefore worship
me, and perform *thy* prayer in remembrance of me.   Verily
the hour cometh : I will surely manifest the same, that every
soul may receive its reward for that which it hath deliberately
done.   Let not him who believeth not therein, and who
followeth his lust, prevent thee from *believing in* the same,
lest thou perish.   Now what *is* that in thy right hand, O
Moses ?   He answered, It is my rod whereon I lean, and
with which I beat down leaves for my flock ; and I have
other uses for it.[2]   *God* said *unto him*, Cast it down, O Moses.
And he cast it down, and behold, it *became* a serpent,[3] which
ran about.   *God* said, Take hold on it, and fear not :[4] we will
reduce it to its former condition.   And put thy *right* hand
under thy *left* arm : it shall come forth white,[5] without any
hurt.   *This shall be* another sign : that we may show thee
some of our greatest signs.   Go unto Pharaoh : for he is
exceedingly impious.   *Moses* answered, LORD, enlarge my
breast, and make what thou hast commanded me easy unto
me : and loose the knot of my tongue, that they may understand my speech.[6]   And give me a counsellor[7] of my family,
namely, Aaron my brother.   Gird up my loins by him, and

[1] This was a mark of humility and respect : though some fancy there was
some uncleanness in the shoes themselves, because they were made of the
skin of an ass not dressed.   (Al Beidâwi.)

[2] As to drive away wild beasts from my flock, to carry my bottle of water
on, to stick up and hang my upper garment on to shade me from the sun ;
and several other uses enumerated by the commentators.

[3] Which was at first no bigger than the rod, but afterwards swelled to a
prodigious size.   (Al Beidâwi.)

[4] When Moses saw the serpent move about with great nimbleness, and
swallow stones and trees, he was greatly terrified, and fled from it ; but
recovering his courage at these words of GOD, he had the boldness to take
the serpent by the jaws.   (Al Beidâwi.)

[5] See Chap. VII.

[6] For Moses had an impediment in his speech, which was occasioned by
the following accident.   Pharaoh one day carrying him in his arms, when a
child, he suddenly laid hold of his beard, and plucked it in a very rough
manner, which put Pharaoh into such a passion, that he ordered him to be
put to death : but Asia, his wife, representing to him that he was but a child,
who could not distinguish between a burning coal and a ruby, he ordered the
experiment to be made ; and a live coal and a ruby being set before Moses,
he took the coal and put it into his mouth, and burnt his tongue : and
thereupon he was pardoned.   This is a Jewish story a little altered.   (Shalsh.
Hakkab., p. 11.)

[7] The Arabic word is Wazîr, which signifies one who has the chief administration of affairs under a prince.

make him my colleague in the business : that we may praise thee greatly, and may remember thee often ; for thou regardest us. *God* replied, Now hast thou obtained thy request, O Moses : and we have heretofore been gracious unto thee, another time ; when we revealed unto thy mother that which was revealed *unto her*,[1] *saying*, Put him into the ark, and cast him into the river, and the river shall throw him on the shore ; *and* my enemy and his enemy shall take him *and bring him up* :[2] and I bestowed on thee love from me,[3] that thou mightest be bred up under my eye. When thy sister went and said, Shall I bring you unto one who will nurse *the child* ?[4] *So* we returned thee unto thy mother, that her mind might be set at ease, and that she might not be afflicted. And thou slewest a soul, and we delivered thee from trouble ;[5] and we proved thee by *several* trials :[6] and *afterwards* thou didst dwell some years[7] among the inhabitants of Madian. Then thou camest *hither* according to *our* decree, O Moses ; and I have chosen thee for myself : *wherefore* go thou and thy brother[8] with my signs ; and be not

---

[1] The commentators are not agreed by what means this revelation was made; whether by private inspiration, by a dream, by a prophet, or by an angel.

[2] The commentators say, that his mother accordingly made an ark of the *papyrus*, and pitched it, and put in some cotton ; and having laid the child therein, committed it to the river, a branch of which went into Pharaoh's garden : that the stream carried the ark thither into a fishpond, at the head of which Pharaoh was then sitting, with his wife Asia, the daughter of Mozahem ; and that the king, having commanded it to be taken up and opened, and finding in it a beautiful child, took a fancy to it, and ordered it to be brought up. (Al Beidâwi.) Some writers mention a miraculous preservation of Moses before he was put into the ark ; and tell us, that his mother having hid him from Pharaoh's officers in an oven, his sister, in her mother's absence, kindled a large fire in the oven to heat it, not knowing the child was there, but that he was afterwards taken out unhurt. (Abulfed., &c.)

[3] That is, I inspired the love of thee into the hearts of those who saw thee, and particularly into the heart of Pharaoh.

[4] The Mohammedans pretend that several nurses were brought, but the child refused to take the breast of any, till his sister Miriam, who went to learn news of him, told them she would find a nurse, and brought his mother. (Al Beidâwi.)

[5] Moses killed an Egyptian, in defence of an Israelite, and escaped the danger of being punished for it, by flying to Midian, which was eight days' journey distant from Mesr. (Al Beidâwi.) The Jews pretend he was actually imprisoned for the fact, and condemned to be beheaded, but that, when he should have suffered, his neck became as hard as ivory, and the sword rebounded on the executioner. (Shalsh Hakkab., p. 11.)

[6] For he was obliged to abandon his country and his friends, and to travel several days, in great terror and want of necessary provisions, to seek a refuge among strangers ; and was afterwards forced to serve for hire, to gain a livelihood. [7] *i.e.*, Ten. (Al Beidâwi.)

[8] Aaron being by this time come out to meet his brother, either by divine inspiration, or having notice of his design to return to Egypt. (Al Beidâwi.)

negligent in remembering me. Go ye unto Pharaoh, for he is excessively impious : and speak mildly unto him ; peradventure he will consider, or will fear *our threats.* They answered, O LORD, verily we fear lest he be precipitately violent against us, or lest he transgress *more exorbitantly.* *God* replied, Fear not ; for I am with you : I will hear and will see. Go ye therefore unto him, and say, Verily we are the messengers of thy LORD : wherefore send the children of Israel with us, and do not afflict them. Now are we come unto thee with a sign from thy LORD : and peace be upon him who shall follow the *true* direction. Verily it hath been revealed unto us, that a punishment *shall be inflicted* on him who shall charge *us* with imposture, and shall turn back. *And when they had delivered their message, Pharaoh* said, Who is your LORD, O Moses ? He answered, Our LORD is he who giveth all things : he hath created them, and directeth them *by his providence. Pharaoh* said, What therefore is the condition of the former generations ?[1] *Moses* answered, The knowledge thereof is with my LORD, in the book *of his decrees :* my LORD erreth not, neither doth he forget. *It is he* who hath spread the earth as a bed for you, and hath made you paths therein ; and who sendeth down rain from heaven, whereby we cause various kinds of vegetables to spring forth ; *saying,* Eat *of part,* and feed your cattle *with other part thereof.* Verily herein are signs unto those who are endued with understanding. Out of *the ground* have we created you ; and to the same will we cause you to return, and we will bring you forth from thence another time. And we showed *Pharaoh* all our signs *which we had empowered Moses to perform :* but he accused *him* of imposture, and refused *to believe ; and* he said, Art thou come unto us that thou mayest dispossess us of our land by thy enchantments, O Moses ? Verily we will meet thee with the like enchantments ; wherefore fix an appointment between us and thee ; we will not fail it, neither shalt thou, in an equal place. *Moses* answered, Let your appointment be on the day of *your* solemn feast ;[2] and let the people be assembled in open day. And Pharaoh turned away *from Moses,* and gathered together *the most expert magicians, to execute* his stratagem ; and they came *to the appointment.* Moses said

---

[1] viz., As to happiness or misery after death. " How do you explain the fact that the generations of men have always practised a different worship ? " (Rodwell.)

[2] Which was probably the first day of their new year.

unto them, Woe be unto you! do not devise a lie against
GOD,[1] lest he utterly destroy you by some judgment : for
he shall not prosper who deviseth lies. *And the magicians*
disputed concerning their affair among themselves, and
discoursed in private : and they said, These two are certainly magicians : they seek to dispossess you of your land
by their sorcery ; and to lead away *with them* your chiefest
and most considerable men. Wherefore collect *all* your
cunning, and then come in order : for he shall prosper this
day, who shall be superior. They said, O Moses, whether
wilt thou cast down *thy rod first,* or shall we be the first who
cast down *our rods* ? He answered, Do ye cast down *your
rods first.* And behold, their cords and their rods appeared
unto him, by their enchantment, to run about *like serpents* :[2]
wherefore Moses conceived fear in his heart. *But* we said
unto him, Fear not ; for thou shalt be superior : therefore
cast down *the rod* which is in thy right hand ; and it shall
swallow up *the seeming serpents* which they have made : for
what they have made is only the deceit of an enchanter ;
and an enchanter shall not prosper, whithersoever he cometh.
And the magicians, *when they saw the miracle which Moses
performed,* fell down and worshipped, saying, We believe
in the LORD of Aaron and of Moses. *Pharaoh* said *unto them,*
do ye believe in him before I give you permission ? Verily
this is your master, who hath taught you magic. But I
will surely cut off your hands and your feet on the opposite
sides ; and I will crucify you on trunks of palm-trees :[3] and
ye shall know which of us is more severe in punishing, and can
longer protract *your pains.* They answered, We will by no
means have greater regard unto thee, than unto those evident
miracles which have been shown us, or than unto him who
hath created us. Pronounce therefore that sentence *against
us* which thou art about to pronounce ; for thou canst only
give sentence *as to* this present life. Verily we believe in our
LORD, that he may forgive us our sins, and the sorcery which
thou hast forced us to *exercise* : for GOD is better *to reward,*
and more able to prolong *punishment than thou.* Verily
whosoever shall appear before his LORD *on the day of judgment,* polluted with crimes, shall have hell *for his reward* ;
he shall not die therein, neither shall he live. But whoever

---

[1] By saying the miracles performed in his name are the effects of magic.
[2] They rubbed them over with quicksilver, which being wrought upon
by the heat of the sun, caused them to move. (Al Beidâwi.)
[3] See Chap. VII.

shall appear before him, *having been a true* believer, *and* shall have worked righteousness, for these *are prepared* the highest degrees *of happiness* ; *namely* gardens of perpetual abode,[1] which shall be watered by rivers ; they shall remain therein for ever : and this shall be the reward of him who shall be pure. And we spake by revelation unto Moses, *saying*, Go forth with my servants *out of Egypt* by night ; and smite *the waters with the rod, and make* them a dry path through the sea :[2] be not apprehensive of *Pharaoh's* overtaking *thee* ; neither be thou afraid. And *when Moses had done so*, Pharaoh followed them with his forces ; and *the waters* of the sea which overwhelmed them, overwhelmed them. And Pharaoh caused his people to err, neither did he direct *them aright*. Thus, O children of Israel, we delivered you from your enemy ; and we appointed you the right side of mount *Sinai to discourse with Moses and to give him the law* ; and we caused manna and quails to descend upon you ;[3] *saying*, Eat of the good things which we have given you for food ; and transgress not therein,[4] lest my indignation fall on you : and on whomsoever my indignation shall fall, he shall go down headlong *into perdition*. But I *will be* gracious unto him who shall repent and believe, and shall do that which is right ; and *who* shall be rightly directed. What hath caused thee to hasten from thy people, O Moses, *to receive the law* ?[5] He answered, These *follow close* on my footsteps ; but I have hastened unto thee, O LORD, that thou mightest be well pleased *with me*. *God* said, We have already made a trial of thy people, since *thy departure* ;[6] and Al Sâmeri[7]

---

[1] Literally, *gardens of* Eden ; see Chap. IX.

[2] The expositors add, that the sea was divided into twelve separate paths, one for each tribe (Al Beidâwi. Abulfed. in Hist.) : a fable borrowed from the Jews. (R. Eliezer, Pirke, chapter 42.)

[3] Chap. II.

[4] By ingratitude, excess, or insolent behaviour.

[5] For Moses, it seems, outwent the seventy elders, who had been chosen, in obedience to the divine command, to accompany him to the mount (Chap. II., Chap. VII.), and appeared before GOD while they were at some, though no great, distance behind him.

[6] They continued in the worship of the true GOD for the first twenty days of Moses's absence, which, by taking the nights also into their reckoning, they computed to be forty, and at their expiration concluded they had stayed the full time which Moses had commanded them, and so fell into the worship of the golden calf. (Al Beidâwi.)

[7] This was not his proper name, but he had this appellation because he was of a certain tribe among the Jews called Samaritans (wherein the Mohammedans strangely betray their ignorance of history) ; though some say he was a proselyte, but a hypocritical one, and originally of Kirmân, or some other country. His true name was Moses, or Mûsa, Ebn Dhafar (Al Beidâwi.)

Selden is of opinion that this person was no other than Aaron himself

hath seduced them *to idolatry*. Wherefore Moses returned
unto his people[1] in great wrath, and exceedingly afflicted.
And he said, O my people, had not your LORD promised you
a most excellent promise ?[2] Did the time *of my absence*
seem long unto you ? Or did ye desire that indignation from
your LORD should fall on you, and therefore fail to keep the
promise which ye made me ? They answered, We have not
failed in what we promised thee of our own authority ; but
we were made to carry in *several* loads of *gold and silver, of*
the ornaments of the people,[3] and we cast them *into the fire* ;
and in like manner Al Sâmeri also cast in *what he had collected*,
and he produced unto them a corporeal calf,[4] which lowed.
And *Al Sâmeri and his companions* said, This is your god,
and the god of Moses ; but he hath forgotten *him, and is gone
to seek some other*. Did they not therefore see that *their idol*
returned them no answer, and was not able to cause them
either hurt or profit ? And Aaron had said unto them before, O my people, verily ye are only proved by this *calf* ; for
your LORD is the Merciful : wherefore follow me, and obey
my command. They answered, We will by no means cease
to be devoted to its *worship*, until Moses return unto us.
And when Moses was returned, he said, O Aaron, what hindered thee, when thou sawest that they went astray, that

(who was really the maker of the calf), and that he is here called Al Sâmeri,
from the Hebrew verb *shamar*, to *keep* (Selden, de Diis Syris, Synt. 1,
chapter 4); because he was the *Keeper or Guardian* of the children of Israel
during his brother's absence in the mount ; which is a very ingenious conjecture, not absolutely inconsistent with the text of the Korân (though
Mohammed seems to have mistaken Al Sâmeri for the name of a different
person), and offers a much more probable origin of that appellation, than to
derive it, as the Mohammedans do, from the Samaritans, who were not
formed into a people, nor bore that name till many ages after.

  [1] viz., After he had completed his forty days' stay in the mount, and had
received the law. (Al Beidâwi.)

  [2] *i.e.*, The law, containing a light and certain direction to guide you in
the right way.

  [3] These ornaments were rings, bracelets, and the like, which the Israelites
had borrowed of the Egyptians, under pretence of decking themselves out
for some feast, and had not returned to them ; or, as some think, what they
had stripped from the dead bodies of the Egyptians, cast on shore by the
sea : and Al Sâmeri, conceiving them unlawful to be kept, and the occasion
of much wicke.'ness, persuaded Aaron to let him collect them from the
people ; which being done, he threw them all into the fire, to melt them
down into one mass. (Al Beidâwi, D'Herbel. Bibl. Orient. p. 650, and
Kor. Chap. II.)

  It is observable, that the Mohammedans generally suppose the cast
metal's coming forth in the shape of a calf, was beside the expectation of Al
Sâmeri, who had not made a mould of that figure : and that when Aaron
excuses himself to his brother, in the Pentateuch, he seems as if he wou'.d
persuade him it was an accident. (Exod. xxxii. 24.)

  [4] See Chap. VII.

thou didst not follow me ?[1] Hast thou therefore been disobedient to my command ?   *Aaron* answered, O son of my
mother, drag *me* not by my beard, nor by *the hair of* my
head.   Verily I feared lest thou shouldest say, Thou hast
made a division among the children of Israel, and thou hast
not observed my saying.[2]   *Moses* said *unto Al Sameri*,
What *was* thy design, O Sâmeri ?   He answered, I saw that
which they saw not ; [3] wherefore I took a handful *of dust*
from the footsteps of the messenger *of God*, and I cast it *into
the molten calf* ; [4] for so did my mind direct me.   *Moses* said,
Get thee gone ; for thy *punishment* in *this* life shall be, that
thou shalt say *unto those who shall meet thee*, Touch *me* not ; [5]
and a threat *is denounced* against thee *of more terrible pains
in the life to come*, which thou shalt by no means escape.
And behold now thy god, to whose *worship* thou hast continued assiduously devoted :   verily we will burn it ,[6] and
we will reduce it to powder, and scatter it in the sea.   Your
GOD is *the true* GOD, besides whom there is no other god :
he comprehendeth all things by *his* knowledge.   Thus do
we recite unto thee, *O Mohammed*, relations of what hath
passed heretofore ; and we have given thee an admonition
from us.   He who shall turn aside from it, shall surely carry

---

[1] By these words Moses reprehends Aaron for not seconding his zeal in
taking arms against the idolaters ; or for not coming after him to the mountain, to acquaint him with their rebellion.

[2] *i.e.*, Lest if I had taken arms against the worshippers of the calf, thou
shouldest say that I had raised a sedition ; or if I had gone after thee, thou
shouldest blame me for abandoning my charge, and not waiting thy return
to rectify what was amiss.

[3] Or, I knew that which they knew not ; *viz.*, That the messenger sent
to thee from GOD was a pure spirit, and that his footsteps gave life to whatever they touched ; being no other than the angel Gabriel, mounted on the
horse of life : and therefore I made use of the dust of his feet to animate
the molten calf.   It is said Al Sâmeri knew the angel, because he had saved
and taken care of him when a child and exposed by his mother for fear of
Pharaoh.   (Al Beidâwi, Jallalo'ddin.)

[4] See Chap. II.

[5] Lest they infect thee with a burning fever : for that was the consequence
of any man's touching him, and the same happened to the persons he touched ;
for which reason he was obliged to avoid all communication with others,
and was also shunned by them, wandering in the desert like a wild beast.
(Al Beidâwi, Jallalo'ddin.)   Hence it is concluded that a tribe of Samaritan
Jews, said to inhabit a certain isle in the Red Sea, are the descendants of
our Al Sâmeri ; because it is their peculiar mark of distinction, at this day,
to use the same words, *viz. La mesâs*, i.e., *Touch me not*, to those they meet.
(Geogr. Nub. p. 45.)   It is not improbable that this story may owe its rise
to the known hatred borne by the Samaritans to the Jews, and their superstitiously avoiding to have any commerce with them, or any other strangers.
(Selden, ubi sup.)

[6] Or, as the word may also be translated, *We will file it down* ; but the
other is the more received interpretation.

a load *of guilt* on the day of resurrection : they shall continue thereunder *for ever* ; and a grievous burthen shall it
be unto them on the day of resurrection.[1] On *that* day the
trumpet shall be sounded ; and we will gather the wicked
together on that day, having grey eyes.[2] They shall speak
with a low voice to one another, *saying*, Ye have not tarried[3]
above ten days.   We well know what they will say ; when
the most conspicuous among them for behaviour shall say,
Ye have not tarried above one day.   They will ask thee concerning the mountains : Answer, My LORD will reduce them
to dust, and scatter them abroad ;[4] and he will leave them a
plain equally extended : thou shalt see no part of them
higher or lower than another.   On that day *mankind* shall
follow *the angel* who will call *them to judgment*,[5] none shall
have power to turn aside from him ; and *their* voices shall
be low before the Merciful, neither shalt thou hear any more
than the hollow sound *of their feet*.   On that day the intercession *of none* shall be of advantage *unto another*, except
the intercession of him to whom the Merciful shall grant
permission,[6] and who shall be acceptable unto him in what
he saith.   *God* knoweth that which is before them, and that
which is behind them ; but they comprehend not the same
by *their* knowledge : and their faces shall be humbled[7] before
the living, the self-subsisting *God* ; and he shall be wretched
who shall bear *his* iniquity.   But whosoever shall do good
works, being a true believer, shall not fear any injustice, or
any diminution *of his reward from God*.   And thus have we
sent down *this book, being* a Korân in the Arabic tongue ;
and we have inserted various threats and promises therein,
that *men* may fear *God*, or that it may awaken some consideration in them : wherefore let GOD be highly exalted, the King,
the Truth !   Be not overhasty in *receiving or repeating* the
Korân, before the revelation thereof be completed unto
thee ;[8] and say, LORD, increase my knowledge.   We hereto-

[1] See Chap. VI.
[2] For this, with the Arabs, is one mark of an enemy, or a person they
abominate ; to say a man has a black liver (though I think we express our
aversion by the term white-livered), reddish whiskers, and grey eyes, being
a periphrasis for a foe, and particularly a Greek, which nation were the most
inveterate enemies of the Arabs, and have usually hair and eyes of those
colours. (Al Beidâwi, Jawhari, in Lex.) The original word, however,
signifies also those who are squint-eyed, or even blind of a suffusion.
[3] viz., In the world ; or, in the grave.
[4] See Sale, Prelim. Disc. Sect. IV.	[5] Sale, Prelim. Disc. p. 88.
[6] Or, Except unto him, &c. See Chap. XIX.
[7] The original word properly expresses the humility and dejected looks of
captives in the presence of their conqueror.
[8] Mohammed is here commanded not to be impatient at any delay in

fore gave a command unto Adam ; but he forgot *the same*,[1] *and ate of the forbidden fruit* ; and we found not in him a firm resolution. And *remember* when we said unto the angels, Worship ye Adam ; and they worshipped *him* : but Eblîs refused.[2] And we said, O Adam, verily this is an enemy unto thee, and thy wife : wherefore *beware* lest he turn you out of paradise ; for *then* shalt thou be miserable. Verily *we have made a provision* for thee, that thou shalt not hunger therein, neither shalt thou be naked : and *there is* also *a provision made* for thee, that thou shalt not thirst therein, neither shalt thou be incommoded by heat. But Satan, whispered *evil suggestions* unto him, saying, O Adam, shall I guide thee to the tree of eternity, and a kingdom which faileth not ? And they both ate thereof : and their nakedness appeared unto them ; and they began to sew together the leaves of paradise, to cover themselves.[3] And *thus* Adam became disobedient unto his LORD, and was seduced. Afterwards his LORD accepted him, *on his repentance*, and was turned unto him, and directed *him*. *And God* said, Get ye down hence, all *of you* : the one of you *shall be* an enemy unto the other. But hereafter shall a direction come unto you from me :[4] and whosoever shall follow my direction, shall not err, neither shall he be unhappy ; but whosoever shall turn aside from my admonition, verily he shall *lead* a miserable life, and we will cause him to appear *before us* on the day of resurrection, blind.[5] *And* he shall say, O LORD, why hast thou brought me *before thee* blind, whereas before I saw clearly ? *God* shall answer, Thus *have we done, because* our signs came unto thee, and thou didst forget them ; and in the same manner shalt thou be forgotten this day. And thus will we reward him who shall be negligent, and shall not believe in the signs of his LORD : and the punishment of the life to come shall be more severe, and more lasting *than the punishment of this life*. Are not *the Meccans* therefore

Gabriel's bringing the divine revelations, or not to repeat it too fast after the angel, so as to overtake him before he had finished the passage. But some suppose the prohibition relates to the publishing any verse before the same was perfectly explained to him. (Al Beidâwi, Jallalo'ddin.)

[1] Adam's so soon forgetting the divine command, has occasioned some Arab etymologists to derive the word Insân, *i.e., man*, from *nasiya*, to *forget* ; and has also given rise to the following proverbial saying, *Awwalo nâsin awwalo 'nnâsi*, that is, *The first forgetful person was the first of men* ; alluding to the like sound of the words.

[2] Chap. II.; Chap. VII.

[3] Chap. VII.

[4] Chap. II.

[5] Prelim. Disc. Sect. IV. p. 91.

acquainted with how many generations we have destroyed before them; in whose dwellings they walk?[1] Verily herein are signs unto those who are endued with understanding. And unless a decree had previously gone forth from thy LORD *for their respite*, verily *their destruction* had necessarily followed : but there is a certain time determined *by God for their punishment*. Wherefore do thou, *O Mohammed*, patiently bear that which they say ; and celebrate the praise of thy LORD before the rising of the sun, and before the setting thereof, and praise *him* in the hours of the night, and in the extremities of the day,[2] that thou mayest be well-pleased *with the prospect of receiving favour from God*. And cast not thine eyes on that which we have granted divers of the *unbelievers* to enjoy, *namely*, the splendour of this present life,[3] that we may prove them thereby : for the provision of thy LORD[4] *is* better, and more permanent. Command thy family *to observe* prayer ; and do thou persevere therein. We require not of thee *that thou labour to gain necessary* provisions *for thyself and family* : we will provide for thee ; for the *prosperous* issue *shall attend* on piety.[5] *The unbelievers* say, Unless he come unto us with a sign from his LORD, *we will not believe on him*. Hath not a plain declaration come unto them, of that which *is contained* in the former volumes *of scripture, by the revelation of the Korân* ? If we had destroyed them by a judgment before *the same had been revealed*, they would have said, *at the resurrection*, O LORD, *how could we believe* since thou didst not send unto us an apostle, that we might follow thy signs, before we were humbled and covered with shame ? Say, Each *of us* awaits *the issue* : wait therefore ; for ye shall surely know hereafter who *have been* the followers of the even way, and who have been *rightly* directed.

[1] Seeing the footsteps of their destruction ; as of the tribes of Ad and Thamûd.

[2] *i.e.*, Evening and morning ; which times are repeated as the principal hours of prayer. But some suppose these words intend the prayer of noon ; the first half of the day ending, and the second half beginning at that time. (Al Beidâwi, Jallalo'ddin.)

[3] That is, do not envy or covet their pomp and prosperity in this world. (Chap. XV.)

[4] viz., The reward laid up for thee in the next life : or the gift of prophecy, and the revelations with which GOD has favoured thee.

[5] It is said that when Mohammed's family were in any strait or affliction, he used to order them to go to prayers and to repeat this verse. (Al Beidâwi.)

XXI

THE CHAPTER OF THE PROPHETS [1]

Revealed at Mecca.

IN THE NAME OF THE MOST MERCIFUL GOD.

(XVII.) *T*HE *time of giving up* their account draweth nigh unto the people *of Mecca* ; while they are *sunk* in negligence, turning aside *from the consideration thereof.* No admonition cometh unto them from their LORD, being lately revealed *in the Korân,* but when they hear it, they turn it to sport : their hearts *are* taken up with delights. And they who act unjustly discourse privately together, *saying,* Is this *Mohammed* any more than a man like yourselves ? Will ye therefore come to *hear* a piece of sorcery, when ye plainly perceive it *to be so* ? Say, My LORD knoweth whatever is spoken in heaven and on earth : *it is* he *who* heareth *and* knoweth. But they say, *The Korân* is a confused heap of dreams : nay, he hath forged it ; nay, he is a poet : let him come unto us therefore with some miracle, in like manner as the former *prophets* were sent. None of the cities which we have destroyed, believed *the miracles which they saw performed,* before them : will these therefore believe, *if they see a miracle* ? We sent none *as our apostles* before thee, other than men, unto whom we revealed *our will.* Ask those who are acquainted with the scripture, if ye know not *this.* We gave them not a body *which could be supported* without their eating food ; neither were they immortal. But we made good *our* promise unto them : wherefore we delivered them, and those whom we pleased ; but we destroyed the exorbitant transgressors. Now have we sent down unto you, *O Koreish,* the book *of the Korân ;* wherein there is *honourable* mention of you : will ye not therefore understand ? And how many cities have we overthrown, which were ungodly ; and caused other nations to rise up after them ? And when they felt our severe vengeance, behold, they fled swiftly from those *cities. And the angels said, scoffingly, unto them,* Do not fly ; but return to that wherein ye delighted, and to your habitations : peradventure ye will be asked.[2] They answered, Alas for

---

[1] The chapter bears this title, because particulars relating to several of the prophets are here recited. It begins the seventeenth section.

[2] *i.e.,* Concerning the present posture of affairs, by way of consultation : or, that ye may be examined as to your deeds, that ye may receive the reward thereof. (Al Beidâwi, Jallalo'ddin, Al Zamakh.)

us ! verily we have been unjust.[1]　And this their lamentation ceased not, until we had rendered them *like* corn which is mowed down, *and* utterly extinct.　We created not the heavens and the earth, and that which is between them, by way of sport.[2]　If we had pleased to take diversion, verily we had taken it with *that which beseemeth* us ;[3] if we had *resolved to have* done this.　But we will oppose truth to vanity, and it shall confound the same ; and behold, it shall vanish away.　Woe be unto you, for that which ye *impiously* utter *concerning God* ! since whoever *is* in heaven and on earth *is subject* unto him ; and *the angels* who are in his presence do not insolently disdain his service, neither are they tired *therewith*.　They praise *him* night and day : they faint not.　Have they taken gods from the earth ?　Shall they raise *the dead* to life ?　If there were either in *heaven or on earth* gods besides GOD, verily both would be corrupted.[4]　But far be that which they utter, from GOD, the LORD of the throne !　No account shall be demanded of him for what he shall do ; but an account shall be demanded of them.　Have they taken *other* gods besides him ?　Say, Produce your proof *thereof*.　This is the admonition of those who *are contemporary* with me, and the admonition of those who *have been* before me :[5] but the greater part of them know not the truth, and turn aside *from the same*.　We have sent no apostle before thee, but we revealed unto him that there is no god besides myself : wherefore serve me.　They say, The Merciful hath begotten issue ; *and the angels are his*

---

[1] It is related that a prophet was sent to the inhabitants of certain towns in Yaman, but instead of hearkening to his remonstrances, they killed him : upon which GOD delivered them into the hands of Nebuchadnezzar, who put them to the sword ; a voice at the same time crying from heaven, Vengeance for the blood of the prophets !　Upon which they repented, and used the words of this passage.

[2] But for the manifestation of our power and wisdom to people of understanding, that they may seriously consider the wonders of the creation, and direct their actions to the attainment of future happiness, neglecting the vain pomp and fleeting pleasures of this world.

[3] viz., We had sought our pleasure in our own perfections ; or, in the spiritual beings which are in our immediate presence ; and not in raising of material buildings, with painted roofs, and fine floors, which is the diversion of man.　Some think the original word, translated diversion, signifies in this place a wife, or a child ; and that the passage is particularly levelled against the Christians. (Al Beidâwi, Jallalo'ddin, Al Zamakh.)

[4] That is the whole creation would necessarily fall into confusion and be overturned, by the competition of such mighty antagonists.

[5] *i.e.*, This is the constant doctrine of all the sacred books ; not only of the Korán, but of those which were revealed in former ages ; all of them bearing witness to the great and fundamental truth of the unity of God.

daughters.[1] GOD forbid! They are his honoured servants: they prevent him not in anything which they say;[2]
and they execute his command. He knoweth that which
is before them, and that which is behind them: they shall
not intercede *for any*, except for whom it shall please him;
and they tremble for fear of him. Whoever of them shall
say, I am a god besides him; that *angel* will we reward with
hell; *for* so will we reward the unjust. Do not the unbelievers therefore know, that the heavens and the earth were
solid, and we clave the same in sunder;[3] and made every
living thing of water? Will they not therefore believe?
And we placed stable *mountains* on the earth, lest it should
move with them;[4] and we made broad passages between
them for paths, that they might be directed *in their journeys*:
and we made the heaven a roof well supported. Yet they
turn aside from the signs thereof, *not considering that they
are the workmanship of God*. It is he who hath created the
night, and the day, and the sun, and the moon; all *the
celestial bodies* move swiftly, *each* in *its respective* orbit. We
have not granted unto any man before thee, *eternal* per-
manency *in this world*; if thou die therefore, will they be
immortal?[5] Every soul shall taste of death: and we will
prove you with evil, and with good, for a trial *of you*; and
unto us shall ye return. When the unbelievers see thee,
they receive thee only with scoffing, *saying, Is* this he who
mentioneth your gods *with contempt*? Yet themselves
believe not what is mentioned *to them* of the Merciful.[6] Man
is created of precipitation.[7] Hereafter will I show you my
signs, so that ye shall not wish them to be hastened. They

[1] This passage was revealed on account of the Khozâites, who held the
angels to be the daughters of GOD.
[2] *i.e.*, They presume not to say anything, until he hath spoken it; behaving as servants who know their duty.
[3] That is, They were one continuous mass of matter, till we separated them,
and divided the heaven into seven heavens, and the earth into as many
stories; and distinguished the various orbs of the one, and the different climates
of the other, &c. Or, as some choose to translate the words, *The heavens
and the earth were shut up, and we opened the same*: their meaning being,
that the heavens did not rain, nor the earth produce vegetables, till GOD
interposed his power. (Al Beidâwi, Jallalo'ddin.)
[4] Chap. XVI.
[5] This passage was revealed when the infidels said, We expect to see
Mohammed die, like the rest of mankind.
[6] Denying his unity; or rejecting his apostles and the scriptures which
were given for their instruction, and particularly the Korân.
[7] Being hasty and inconsiderate. (Chap. XVII.) It is said this passage
was revealed on account of Al Nodar Ebn al Hareth, when he desired Mohammed to hasten the divine vengeance with which he threatened the unbelievers. (Al Beidâwi.)

say, When *will* this threat *be accomplished*, if ye speak truth ? If they who believe not, knew *that the time will surely come* when they shall not *be able to* drive back the fire *of hell* from their faces, nor from their backs, neither shall they be helped, *they would not hasten it.* But *the day of vengeance* shall come upon them suddenly, and shall strike them with astonishment : they shall not be able to avert it ; neither shall they be respited. *Other* apostles have been mocked before thee : but the *punishment* which they scoffed at, fell upon such of them as mocked. Say *unto the scoffers*, Who shall save you by night and by day from the Merciful ? Yet they utterly neglect the remembrance of their LORD. Have they gods who will defend them, besides us ? They are not able to help themselves ; neither shall they be assisted against us by their companions. But we have permitted these *men* and their fathers to enjoy *worldly prosperity*, so long as life was continued unto them. Do they not perceive that we come unto the land *of the unbelievers, and* straiten the borders thereof ? Shall they therefore be the conquerors ? Say, I only preach unto you the revelation *of God* ; but the deaf will not hear *thy* call, whenever they are preached unto. Yet *if the least* breath of the punishment of thy LORD touch them, they will surely say, Alas for us ! verily we have been unjust. We will appoint just balances for the day of resurrection ; neither shall any soul be injured at all : although *the merit or guilt of an action* be of the weight of a grain of mustard-seed *only*, we will produce it *publicly* ; and there will be sufficient accountants with us. We formerly gave unto Moses and Aaron the *Law, being a* distinction[1] *between good and evil*, and a light and admonition unto the pious ; who fear their LORD in secret, and who dread the hour *of judgment*. And this *book also* is a blessed admonition ; which we have sent down *from heaven* : will ye therefore deny it ? And we gave unto Abraham his direction [2] heretofore, and we knew him *to be worthy of the revelations wherewith he was favoured. Remember* when he said unto his father, and his people, What are these images, to which ye are *so* entirely devoted ?[3] They answered, We found our fathers worshipping them. He said, Verily both ye and your fathers have been in a manifest error. They said, Dost thou

[1] Arab,. Al Forkân. Prelim. Disc. Sect. III.

[2] viz., The ten books of divine revelations which were given him. (Sale, Prel. Disc. Sect. IV.)

[3] See Chap. VI., Chap. XIX., and Chap. II.

seriously tell us the truth, or art thou one who jestest *with us* ?
He replied, Verily your LORD is the LORD of the heavens
and the earth ; *it is he* who hath created them : and I am
one of those who bear witness thereof.   By GOD, I will surely
devise a plot against your idols, after ye shall have retired
from them, and shall have turned your backs.   And *in the
people's absence he went into the temple where the idols stood,
and* he brake them *all* in pieces, except the biggest of them ;
that they might lay the blame upon that.[1]   *And when they
were returned, and saw the havoc which had been made*, they
said, Who hath done this to our gods ?   He is certainly an
impious person.   *And certain of them* answered, We heard
a young man speak *reproachfully* of them : he is named
Abraham.   They said, Bring him therefore before the eyes
of the people, that they may bear witness *against him.   And
when he was brought before the assembly*, they said *unto him*,
Hast thou done this unto our gods, O Abraham ?   He
answered, Nay, that biggest of them hath done it : but ask
them, if they *can* speak.   And they returned unto themselves,[2] and said *the one to the other*, Verily ye are the impious
persons.   Afterwards they relapsed into their former
obstinacy[3] *and said*, Verily thou knowest that these speak not.
Abraham answered, Do ye therefore worship, besides GOD,
that which cannot profit you at all, neither can it hurt you ?
Fie on you ; and upon that which ye worship besides GOD !
Do ye not understand ?   They said, Burn him, and avenge
your gods ; if ye do this *it will be well*.[4]   *And when Abraham*

---

[1] Abraham took his opportunity to do this while the Chaldeans were
abroad in the fields, celebrating a great festival ; and some say he hid himself in the temple : and when he had accomplished his design, that he might
the more evidently convince them of their folly in worshipping them, he
hung the axe, with which he had hewn and broken down the images, on the
neck of the chief idol, named by some writers, Baal ; as if he had been the
author of all the mischief. (Al Beidâwi, Jallalo'ddin, &c. Hyde, de Rel.
Vet. Pers. c. 2.) For this story, which, though it be false, is not ill invented,
Mohammed stands indebted to the Jews, who tell it with a little variation :
for they say Abraham performed this exploit in his father's shop, during his
absence ; that Terah, on his return, demanding the occasion of the disorder,
his son told him that the idols had quarrelled and fallen together by the ears
about an offering of fine flour, which had been brought them by an old
woman ; and that the father, finding he could not insist on the impossibility of what Abraham pretended, without confessing the impotence of his
gods, fell into a violent passion and carried him to Nimrod that he might be
exemplarily punished for his insolence. (R. Gedal. in Shalshel. hakkab. p.
8. Vide Maimon. Yad hazzaka. c. 1, de idol.)
[2] That is, They became sensible of their folly.
[3] Literally, *They were turned down upon their heads*.
[4] Perceiving they could not prevail against Abraham by dint of argument,
says Al Beidâwi, they had recourse to persecution and torments. The same
commentator tells us the person who gave this counsel was a Persian Curd

was cast into the burning pile, we said, O fire, be thou cold, and a preservation unto Abraham.[1]   And they sought to lay a plot against him : but we caused them to be the sufferers.[2]   And we delivered him, and Lot, *by bringing them*

(D' Herbel. Bibl. Orient. Art. Dhokak. et Schultens, Indic. Geogr. in Vit. Saladini, voce Curdi.), named Heyyûn, and that the earth opened and swallowed him up alive : some, however, say it was Andeshân, a Magian priest (D'Herbel., p. 115) ; and others, that it was Nimrod himself.

[1] The commentators relate that, by Nimrod's order, a large space was enclosed at Cûtha, and filled with a vast quantity of wood, which being set on fire burned so fiercely, that none dared to venture near it : then they bound Abraham, and putting him into an engine (which some suppose to have been of the devil's invention), shot him into the midst of the fire ; from which he was preserved by the angel Gabriel who was sent to his assistance ; the fire burning only the cords with which he was bound. (Al Beidâwi, Jallalo'ddin, &c. Vide Morgan's Mahometism Expl., v. 1, chapter 4.)   They add that the fire having miraculously lost its heat, in respect to Abraham, became an odoriferous air, and that the pile changed to a pleasant meadow ; though it raged so furiously otherwise, that, according to some writers, about two thousand of the idolaters were consumed by it. (The MS. Gospel of Barnabas, Chapter 28.)   This story seems to have had no other foundation than that passage of Moses, where GOD is said to have brought Abraham *out of* Ur *of the* Chaldees (Genes. xv. 7) misunderstood : which words the Jews, the most trifling interpreters of scripture, and some moderns who have followed them, have translated, *out of the fire of the* Chaldees ; taking the word *Ur*, not for the proper name of a city, as it really is, but for an appellative, signifying *fire*. (Targ. Jonath. et Hierosol. in Genes. c. 11 et 15 ; et Hyde, de Rel. Vet. Pers. p. 74, &c.)   However it is a fable of some antiquity, and credited, not only by the Jews, but by several of the Eastern Christians ; the twenty-fifth of the second Canun, or January, being set apart in the Syrian calendar, for the commemoration of Abraham's being cast into the fire. (Hyde, ibid. p. 73.)   The Jews also mention some other persecutions which Abraham underwent on account of his religion, particularly a ten years' imprisonment (R. Eliez. Pirke, c. 26, &c. Maim. More Nev. l. 3. c. 29) ; some saying he was imprisoned by Nimrod (Glossa Talmud. in Gemar. Bava bathra, 91, 1) ; and others, by his father Terah (In Aggada).

[2] Some tell us that Nimrod, on seeing this miraculous deliverance from his palace, cried out, that he would make an offering to the GOD of Abraham ; and that he accordingly sacrificed four thousand kine. (Al Beidâwi.)   But, if he ever relented, he soon relapsed into his former infidelity : for he built a tower that he might ascend to heaven to see Abraham's GOD ; which being overthrown (Chap. XVI.), still persisting in his design, he would be carried to heaven in a chest borne by four monstrous birds ; but after wandering for some time through the air, he fell down on a mountain with such a force, that he made it shake, whereto (as some fancy) a passage in the Korân (Chap. XIV.) alludes, which may be translated, *although their contrivances be such as to make the mountains tremble.*   Nimrod, disappointed in his design of making war with GOD, turned his arms against Abraham, who being a great prince, raised forces to defend himself ; but GOD, dividing Nimrod's subjects, and confounding their language, deprived him of the greater parts of his people, and plagued those who adhered to him by swarms of gnats, which destroyed almost all of them : and one of those gnats having entered into the nostril, or ear, of Nimrod, penetrated to one of the membranes of his brain, where, growing bigger every day, it gave him such intolerable pain, that he was obliged to cause his head to be beaten with a mallet, in order to procure some ease, which torture he suffered four hundred years ; GOD being willing to punish, by one of the smallest of his creatures, him who insolently boasted himself to be lord of all. (D'Herbel. Bibl. Orient. Art. Nimrod.   Hyde, ub¹

into the land wherein we have blessed all creatures.[1]   And
we bestowed on him Isaac, and Jacob, as an additional gift :
and we made all *of them* righteous persons.   We also made
them models of religion,[2] that they might direct *others* by
our command : and we inspired into them the doing of good
works, and the observance of prayer, and the giving of alms ;
and they served us.   And unto Lot we gave wisdom and
knowledge, and we delivered him out of the city which
committed filthy crimes ; for they were a wicked *and* insolent
people :[3] and we led him into our mercy ; for he was an
upright person.   And *remember* Noah, when he called *for
destruction on his people,*[4] before *the prophets above mentioned* ; and we heard him, and delivered him and his family
from a great strait : and we protected him from the people
who accused our signs of falsehood ; for they were a wicked
people, wherefore we drowned them all.   And *remember*
David, and Solomon, when they pronounced judgment
concerning a field, when the sheep of *certain* people had fed
therein by night, having no shepherd ; and we were witnesses
of their judgment : and we gave the understanding thereof
unto Solomon.[5]   And on all *of them* we bestowed wisdom,
and knowledge.   And we compelled the mountains to praise
us with David ; and the birds also :[6] and we did *this*.   And

---

supra.) A Syrian calendar places the death of Nimrod, as if the time were
well known, on the eighth of Thamûz, or July. (Hyde, ibid.)

[1] *i.e.*, Palestine ; in which country the greater part of the prophets
appeared.

[2] See Chap. II. p. 19.

[3] See Chap. VII. p. 150, and Chap. XI. p. 220.

[4] See Chap. VIII.

[5] Some sheep, in their shepherd's absence, having broken into another
man's field (or vineyard, say others), by night, and eaten up the corn, a
dispute arose thereupon : and the cause being brought before David and
Solomon, the former said, that the owner of the land should take the sheep,
in compensation of the damage which he had sustained ; but Solomon, who
was then but eleven years old, was of opinion that it would be more just
for the owner of the field to take only the profit of the sheep, *viz.,* their milk,
lambs, and wool, till the shepherd should, by his own labour and at his own
expense, put the field into as good condition as when the sheep entered it ;
after which the sheep might be returned to their master. And this judgment of Solomon was approved by David himself as better than his own.
(Al Beidâwi, Jallalo'ddin, &c.)

[6] Mohammed, it seems, taking the visions of the Talmudists for truth,
believed that when David was fatigued with singing psalms, the mountains,
birds, and other parts of the creation, both animate and inanimate, relieved
him in chanting the divine praises. This consequence the Jews draw from
the words of the psalmist, when he calls on the several parts of nature to
join with him in celebrating the praise of God (Psalm cxlviii.) ; it being
their perverse custom to expound passages in the most literal manner, which
cannot bear a literal sense without a manifest absurdity ; and, on the contrary, to turn the plainest passages into allegorical fancies.

we taught him the art of making coats of mail for you,[1] that they may defend you in your wars : will ye therefore be thankful ?　And unto Solomon *we subjected* a strong wind ;[2] it ran at his command to the land whereon we had bestowed *our* blessing :[3] and we knew all things.　And *we also subjected unto his command certain* of the devils, who might dive *to get pearls* for him, and perform *other* work besides this ;[4] and we watched over them.[5]　And *remember* Job ;[6] when he cried unto his LORD, *saying*, Verily evil hath afflicted me : but thou art the most merciful of those who show mercy. Wherefore we heard him, and relieved *him from* the evil

[1] Men, before his inventing them, used to arm themselves with broad plates of metal.　Lest this fable should want something of the marvellous, one writer tells us, that the iron which David used became soft in his hands like wax.　(Tarikh Montakkab, D'Herbel. p. 284.)　In nearly all Mohammedan countries the blacksmith is respected as treading in the path of David, the father of the craft.　(See Burton, Footsteps in East. Af., p. 33.)

[2] Which transported his throne with prodigious swiftness.　Some say, this wind was violent or gentle, just as Solomon pleased.　See Chap. XXVII.

[3] viz., Palestine : whither the wind brought back Solomon's throne in the evening, after having carried it to a distant country in the morning.

[4] Such as the building of cities and palaces, the fetching of rare pieces of art from foreign countries, and the like.

[5] Lest they should swerve from his orders, or do mischief according to their natural inclinations.　Jallalo'ddin says, that when they had finished any piece of building, they pulled it down before night, if they were not employed in something new.

[6] The Mohammedan writers tell us, that Job was of the race of Esau, and was blessed with a numerous family, and abundant riches ; but that GOD proved him, by taking away all that he had, even his children, who were killed by the fall of a house ; notwithstanding which he continued to serve GOD, and to return him thanks, as usual : that he was then struck with a filthy disease, his body being full of worms, and so offensive, that as he lay on the dunghill none could bear to come near him : that his wife, however (whom some call Rahmat the daughter of Ephraim the son of Joseph, and others Makhir the daughter of Manasses), attended him with great patience, supporting him with what she earned by her labour ; but that the devil appeared to her one day, after having reminded her of her past prosperity, promised her that if she would worship him, he would restore all they had lost : whereupon she asked her husband's consent, who was so angry at the proposal, that he swore, if he recovered, to give his wife a hundred stripes : that Job having pronounced the prayer recorded in this passage, GOD sent Gabriel, who taking him by the hand raised him up ; and at the same time a fountain sprang up at his feet, of which having drank, the worms fell off his body, and washing therein he recovered his former health and beauty : that GOD then restored all to him double : his wife also becoming young and handsome again, and bearing him twenty-six sons : and that Job, to satisfy his oath, was directed by GOD to strike her one blow with a palmbranch having a hundred leaves.　(Al Beidâwi, Jallalo'ddin, Abulfeda, &c. D'Herbel. Bibl. Orient. Art. Aioub.)　Some, to express the great riches which were bestowed on Job after his sufferings, say he had two threshingfloors, one for wheat, and the other for barley, and that GOD sent two clouds which rained gold on the one, and silver on the other, till they ran over. (Jallalo'ddin.)　The traditions differ as to the continuance of Job's calamities ; one will have it to be eighteen years, another thirteen, another three, and another exactly seven years seven months and seven hours.

which was upon him : and we restored unto him his family,
and as many more with them, through our mercy, and for
an admonition unto those who serve GOD. And *remember*
Ismael, and Edrîs,[1] and Dhu'lkefl.[2] All *these* were patient
persons : wherefore we led them into our mercy ; for they
were righteous doers. And *remember* Dhu'lnun,[3] when he
departed in wrath,[4] and thought that we could not exercise
our power over him. And he cried out in the darkness,[5]
saying, There is no GOD, besides thee : praise be unto thee !
Verily I have been one of the unjust. Wherefore we heard
him, and delivered him from affliction :[6] for so do we deliver
the true believers. And *remember* Zacharias, when he called
upon his LORD, *saying*, O LORD, leave me not childless :
yet thou art the best heir. Wherefore we heard him, and
we gave him John ; and we rendered his wife fit *for bearing
a child* unto him. These strove to excel in good works, and
called upon us with love, and with fear ; and humbled themselves before us. And *remember* her who preserved her
virginity,[7] and into whom we breathed of our spirit ; ordain-
ing her and her son for a sign unto all creatures. Verily this
your religion is one religion ;[8] and I am your LORD ; wherefore serve me. But *the Jews and Christians* have made
schisms in the affair of their *religion* among themselves :
but all of them shall appear before us. Whosoever shall do
good wcrks, being a true believer, there shall be no denial
of the reward due to his endeavours ; and we will surely

[1] See Chap. XIX. p. 301.

[2] Who this prophet was is very uncertain. One commentator will have
him to be Elias, or Joshua, or Zacharias (Al Beidâwi) ; another supposes
him to have been the son of Job, and to have dwelt in Syria ; to which some
add, that he was first a very wicked man, but afterwards repenting, died ;
upon which these words appeared miraculously written over his door, *Now
hath God been merciful unto Dhu'lkefl* (Abulf.) ; and the third tells us he
was a person of great strictness of life, and one who used to decide causes
to the satisfaction of all parties, because he was never in a passion ; and
that he was called Dhu'lkefl from his continual fasting, and other religious
exercises (Jallalo'ddin).

[3] This is the surname of Jonas ; which was given him because he was
swallowed by the fish. See Chap. X.

[4] Some suppose Jonas's anger was against the Ninevites, being tired with
preaching to them for so long a time, and greatly disgusted at their obstinacy
and ill-usage of him ; but others, more agreeably to Scripture, say the reason
of his ill-humour was GOD's pardoning of that people on their repentance,
and averting the judgment which Jonas had threatened them with. so that
he thought he had been made a liar. (Al Beidâwi.)

[5] Out of the belly of the fish.

[6] Chap. XXXVII.

[7] Namely, the Virgin Mary.

[8] Being the same which was professed by all the prophets, and holy men
and women, without any fundamental difference or variation.

write *it* down unto him. An inviolable prohibition *is laid* on *every* city which we shall have destroyed ; for that they shall not return *any more into the world* ; until Gog and Magog shall have a passage opened for them,[1] and they shall hasten from every high hill ;[2] and the certain promise shall draw near *to be fulfilled* : and behold, the eyes of the infidels shall be fixed *with astonishment, and they shall say,* Alas for us ! we were formerly regardless of this *day* ; yea, we were wicked doers. Verily *both* ye, *O men of Mecca,* and *the idols* which ye worship besides GOD, *shall be* cast *as fuel* into hell *fire* : ye shall go down into the same. If these were *really* gods, they would not go down into the same : and all *of them* shall remain therein for ever. In that *place* shall they groan *for anguish* ; and they shall not hear *aught* therein.[3] *As for* those unto whom the most excellent *reward of paradise* hath been predestinated by us, they shall be transported far off from the same ;[4] they shall not hear the least sound thereof : and they shall continue for ever in the *felicity* which their souls desire. The greatest terror shall not trouble them ; and the angels shall meet them *to congratulate them, saying,* This is your day which ye were promised. On *that* day we will roll up the heavens, as *the angel* Al Sijil[5] rolleth up the book *wherein every man's actions are recorded.* As we made the first creature *out of nothing, so* we will also reproduce it *at the resurrection. This is* a promise *which it lieth* on us *to fulfil* : we will surely perform *it.* And now have we written in the psalms, after *the promulgation of* the law, that my servants the righteous shall inherit the

---

[1] *i.e.,* Until the resurrection ; one sign of the approach whereof will be the irruption of those barbarians. (Sale, Prel. Disc. Sect. IV.)

[2] In this passage some copies, instead of *hadabin,* i.e., *an elevated part of the earth,* have *jadathin,* which signifies *a grave* ; and if we follow the latter reading, the pronoun *they* must not refer to Gog and Magog, but to mankind in general.

[3] Because of their astonishment and the insupportable torments they shall endure ; or, as others expound the words, *They shall not hear therein* anything which may give them the least comfort.

[4] One Ebn ?l Zabári objected to the preceding words, *Both ye and that which ye worship besides* GOD, *shall be cast into hell,* because, being general, they asserted an absolute falsehood ; some of the objects of idolatrous worship being so far from any danger of damnation, that they were in the highest favour with GOD, as JESUS, Ezra, and the angels : wherefore this passage was revealed, excepting those who were predestined to salvation. (Al Beidâwi, Jallalo'ddin.)

[5] Whose office it is to write down the actions of every man's life, which, at his death, he rolls up, as completed. Some pretend one of Mohammed's scribes is here meant : and others take the word Sijil, or, as it is also written, Sijjill, for an appellative, signifying a *book* or *written scroll* ; and accordingly render the passage, *as a written scroll is rolled up.* (Al Beidâwi, Jallalo'ddin.)

earth.[1] Verily in this *book are contained* sufficient means
of salvation, unto people who serve *God*. We have not
sent thee, *O Mohammed*, but *as* a mercy unto all creatures.
Say, No other hath been revealed unto me, than that your
GOD is one GOD : *will* ye therefore *be* resigned *unto him* ?
But if they turn their backs *to the confession of God's unity*,
say, I proclaim *war* against you *all* equally :[2] but I know not
whether that which ye are threatened with[3] *be* nigh, or
whether *it be* far distant.   Verily, *God* knoweth the discourse
which is spoken in public ; and he *also* knoweth that which
ye hold in private.   I know not *but* peradventure *the respite
granted you is for* a trial of you ; and that he may enjoy
the prosperity of this world for a time.   Say, LORD, judge
between me and my adversaries with truth.   Our LORD is the
Merciful ; whose assistance *is* to be implored against the
blasphemies and calumnies which ye utter.

XXII

THE CHAPTER OF THE PILGRIMAGE [4]

Revealed at Mecca.[5]

IN THE NAME OF THE MOST MERCIFUL GOD.

O MEN *of Mecca*, fear your LORD. Verily the shock of
the *last* hour[6] *will be* a terrible thing.   On the day
whereon ye shall see it, every woman who giveth suck shall
forget *the infant* which she suckleth,[7] and every *female* that
is with young shall cast her burthen ; and thou shalt see
men *seemingly* drunk, yet they shall not be *really* drunk :
but the punishment of GOD *will be* severe.   There is a man
who disputeth concerning GOD without knowledge,[8] and

---

[1] These words are taken from Psalm xxxvii. v. 29.

[2] Or, *I have publicly declared unto you* what I was commanded.

[3] viz., The losses and disgraces which ye shall suffer by the future successes of the Moslems ; or, the day of judgment.

[4] Some ceremonies used at the pilgrimage of Mecca being mentioned in this chapter, gave occasion to the inscription.

[5] Some (Jallalo'ddin) except two verses, beginning at these words, *There are some men who serve* GOD *in a wavering manner*, &c. And others (Al Beidâwi) six verses, beginning at, *These are two opposite parties*, &c.

[6] Or, the earthquake which, some say, is to happen a little before the sun rises from the west ; one sign of the near approach of the day of judgment. (Sale, Prelim. Disc. Sect. IV. p. 88.)

[7] See Sale, Prelim. Disc. Sect. IV. p. 88.

[8] This passage was revealed on account of Al Nodar Ebn al Hareth, who maintained that the angels were the daughters of GOD, that the Korân was a fardel of old fables, and denied the resurrection. (Al Beidâwi.)

followeth every rebellious devil : against whom it is written,
that whoever shall take him for his patron, he shall surely
seduce him, and shall lead him into the torment of hell. O
men, if ye be in doubt concerning the resurrection, *consider
that we first* created you of the dust of the ground ; afterwards
of seed ; afterwards, of a little coagulated blood ; afterwards, of a piece of flesh, perfectly formed *in part*, and *in
part* imperfectly formed ; that we might make *our power*
manifest unto you : and we cause that of which we please
to rest in the wombs, until the appointed time *of delivery*.
Then we bring you forth infants ; and afterwards *we permit*
you to attain your age of full strength : and one of you
dieth *in his youth*, and another of you is postponed to a
decrepit age, so that he forgetteth whatever he knew. Thou
seest the earth *sometimes* dried up and barren : but when we
send down rain thereon, it is put in motion, and swelleth,
and produceth every kind of luxuriant *vegetables*. This
showeth that GOD is the truth, and that he raiseth the dead
to life, and that he is almighty ; and that the hour *of judgment* will surely come (there is no doubt thereof), and that
GOD will raise again those who are in the graves. There is
a man who disputeth concerning GOD without either knowledge, or a direction, or an enlightening book ; proudly
turning his side,[1] that he may seduce *men* from the way of
GOD. Ignominy *shall attend* him in this world ;[2] and on the
day of resurrection we will make him take the torment of
burning, *when it shall be said unto him*, This *thou sufferest*
because of that which thy hands have formerly committed ;
for GOD is not unjust towards mankind. There are some
men who serve GOD *in a wavering manner, standing, as it
were*, on the verge[3] *of the true religion*. If good befall *one of*

---

[1] That is "turning aside in scorn."

[2] The person here meant, it is said, was Abu Jahl (Jallalo'ddin), a principal man among the Koreish, and a most inveterate enemy of Mohammed
and his religion. His true name was Amru Ebn Heshâm, of the family
of Makhzûm ; and he was surnamed Abu'lhocm, i.e., *the father of wisdom*,
which was afterwards changed into Abu Jahl, or *the father of folly*. He was
slain in the battle of Bedr. (Chap. VIII. p. 173.)

[3] This expression alludes to one who being posted in the skirts of an army,
if he sees the victory inclining to his own side, stands his ground, but if the
enemy is likely to prevail, takes to his heels. The passage, they say, was
revealed on account of certain Arabs of the desert, who came to Medina, and
having professed Mohammedism, were well enough pleased with it so long
as their affairs prospered, but if they met with any adversity, were sure to
lay the blame on their new religion. A tradition of Abu Sa'd mentions
another accident as the occasion of this passage, viz., that a certain Jew
embraced Islâm, but afterwards taking a dislike to it, on account of some
misfortunes which had befallen him, went to Mohammed, and desired he

them, he resteth satisfied therein ; but if any tribulation befall him, he turneth himself round, with the loss *both* of this world, and of the life to come. This is manifest perdition. He will call upon that besides GOD, which can neither hurt him, nor profit him. This is an error remote *from truth*. He will invoke him who will sooner be of hurt *to his worshipper* than of advantage. *Such is* surely a miserable patron, and a miserable companion. But GOD will introduce those who shall believe, and do righteous works, into gardens through which rivers flow ; for GOD doth that which he pleaseth. Whoso thinketh that GOD will not assist *his apostle* in this world, and in the world to come, let him strain a rope towards heaven, then let him put an end to his life, and see whether his devices can render that ineffectual, for which he was angry.[1] Thus do we send down *the Korân, being* evident signs ; for GOD directeth whom he pleaseth. *As to* the true believers, and those who Judaize, and the Sabians, and the Christians, and the Magians, and the idolaters ; verily GOD shall judge between them on the day of resurrection ; for GOD is witness of all things. Dost thou not perceive that all *creatures* both in heaven and on earth adore GOD ;[2] and the sun, and the moon, and the stars, and the mountains, and the trees, and the beasts, and many men ? But many are worthy of chastisement : and whomsoever GOD shall render despicable, there shall be none to honour ; for GOD doth that which he pleaseth. These are two opposite parties, who dispute concerning their LORD.[3] And they who believe not, shall have garments of fire fitted unto them : boiling water shall be poured on their heads ; their bowels shall be dissolved thereby, and *also* their skins ; and they shall *be beaten* with maces of iron. So often as they shall endeavour to get out of *hell*, because of the anguish

---

might renounce it, and be freed from the obligations of it : but the prophet told him that no such thing was allowed in his religion. (Al Beidâwi.)

[1] Or, *Let him tie a rope to the roof of his house, and hang himself* ; that is, let him carry his anger and resentment to ever so great a height, even to be driven to the most desperate extremities, and see whether with all his endeavours he will be able to intercept the divine assistance. (Al Beidâwi.)

[2] Confessing his power, and obeying his supreme command.

[3] viz., The true believers and the infidels. The passage is said to have been revealed on occasion of a dispute between the Jews and the Mohammedans ; the former insisting that they were in greater favour with GOD, their prophet and revelations being prior to those of the latter ; and these replying, that they were more in GOD's favour, for that they believed not only in Moses but also in Mohammed, and in all the scriptures without exception ; whereas the Jews rejected Mohammed, though they knew him to be a prophet, out of envy. (Al Beidâwi.)

of their torments, they shall be dragged back into the same ; and *their tormentors shall say unto them,* Taste ye the pain of burning. GOD will introduce those who shall believe, and act righteously, into gardens through which rivers flow : they shall be adorned therein with bracelets of gold, and pearls ; and their vestures therein shall be silk. They are directed unto a good saying ;[1] and are directed into the honourable way. But they who shall disbelieve, and obstruct the way of GOD, and *hinder men from visiting* the holy temple *of Mecca,* which we have appointed *for a place of worship* unto *all* men : the inhabitant thereof, and the stranger *have an* equal *right to visit it* : and whosoever shall seek impiously to profane it we will cause him to taste a grievous torment. *Call to mind* when we gave the site of the house *of the Caaba* for an abode unto Abraham,[2] *saying,* Do not associate anything with me ; and cleanse my house for those who compass *it,* and who stand up, and who bow down to worship. And proclaim unto the people a solemn pilgrimage ;[3] let them come unto thee on foot, and on every lean *camel,* arriving from every distant road ; that they may be witnesses of the advantages *which accrue* to them *from the visiting this holy place,*[4] and may commemorate the name of GOD on the appointed days,[5] *in gratitude* for the brute cattle which he hath bestowed on them. Wherefore eat thereof, and feed the needy, *and* the poor. Afterwards let them put an end to the neglect of their persons';[6]

[1] viz., The profession of GOD's unity ; or these words, which they shall use at their entrance into paradise, *Praise be unto GOD, who hath fulfilled his promise unto us.* (Al Beidâwi.)

[2] *i.e.* For a place of religious worship ; showing him the spot where it had stood, and also the model of the old building, which had been taken up to heaven at the flood. (Sale, Prelim. Disc. Sect. IV. p. 125.)

[3] It is related that Abraham, in obedience to this command, went up to Mount Abu Kobeis, near Mecca, and cried from thence, *O men, perform the pilgrimage to the house of your* LORD ; and that GOD caused those who were then in the loins of their fathers, and the wombs of their mothers, from east to west, and who, he knew beforehand, would perform the pilgrimage, to hear his voice. Some say, however, that these words were directed to Mohammed, commanding him to proclaim the pilgrimage of valediction (Al Beidâwi) : according to which exposition the passage must have been revealed at Medina.

[4] viz., The temporal advantage made by the great trade driven at Mecca during the pilgrimage, and the spiritual advantage of having performed so meritorious a work.

[5] Namely, The ten first days of Dhu'lhajja ; or the tenth day of the same month, on which they slay the sacrifices, and the three following days. (Al Beidâwi, Jallalo'ddin.)

[6] By shaving their heads, and other parts of their bodies, and cutting their beards and nails in the valley of Mina ; which the pilgrims are not allowed to do from the time they become Mohrims, and have solemnly

and let them pay their vows,[1] and compass the ancient house.[2] This *let them do*. And whoever shall regard the sacred ordinances of GOD ;[3] this will be better for him in the sight of his LORD. *All sorts of cattle* are allowed you *to eat*, except what hath been read unto you, *in former passages of the Korân, to be forbidden*. But depart from the abomination of idols, and avoid speaking that which is false :[4] being orthodox in respect to GOD, associating *no other god* with him ; for whoever associateth *any other* with GOD, is like that which falleth from heaven, and which the birds snatch away, or the wind bloweth to a far distant place.[5] This *is so*. And whoso maketh valuable offerings unto God ;[6] verily they *proceed* from the piety of *men's* hearts. Ye receive various advantages from the *cattle designed for sacrifices*, until a determined time *for slaying them* : then the place of sacrificing them *is* at the ancient house. Unto the possessors of every religion[7] have we appointed certain rites, that they may commemorate the name of GOD on *slaying* the brute cattle which he hath provided for them. Your GOD is one GOD : wherefore resign yourselves *wholly* unto him. And do thou bear good tidings unto those who

dedicated themselves to the performance of the pilgrimage, till they have finished the ceremonies, and slain their victims. (Al Beidâwi. Jallalo'ddin. Chap. II., Chap. V., and Bobov. de Peregr. Meccana, p. 15, &c.)

[1] By doing the good works which they have vowed to do in their pilgrimage. Some understand the words only of the performance of the requisite ceremonies.

[2] *i.e.*, The Caaba ; which the Mohammedans pretend was the first edifice built and appointed for the worship of God. (See Chap. III., and Sale, Prelim. Disc. Sect. IV.) The going round this chapel is a principal ceremony of the pilgrimage, and is often repeated ; but the last time of their doing it, when they take their farewell of the temple, seems to be more particularly meant in this place.

[3] By observing what he has commanded, and avoiding what he has forbidden, or, as the words also signify, *Whoever shall honour what* GOD *hath sanctified*, or commanded not to be profaned ; as the temple and territory of Mecca, and the sacred months, &c.

[4] Either by asserting wrong and impious things of the Deity ; or by bearing false witness against your neighbours.

[5] Because he who falls into idolatry, sinketh from the height of faith into the depth of infidelity, has his thoughts distracted by wicked lusts, and is hurried by the devil into the most absurd errors. (Al Beidâwi.)

[6] By choosing a well-favoured and costly victim in honour of him to whom it is destined. They say Mohammed once offered a hundred fat camels, and among them one which had belonged to AbuJahl, having in his nose a ring of gold : and that Omar offered a noble camel, for which he had been bid three hundred *dinârs*. (Al Beidâwi.) The original may also be translated generally, *Whoso regardeth the rites of the pilgrimage*, &c. But the *victims* seem to be more particularly intended in this place.

[7] Jallalo'ddin understands this passage in a restricted sense, of the former nations who were true believers ; to whom GOD appointed a sacrifice, and a fixed place and proper ceremonies for the offering of it.

humble themselves ; whose hearts, when mention is made of GOD, are struck with fear ; and *unto* those who patiently endure that which befalleth them ; and who duly perform their prayers, and give alms out of what we have bestowed on them.   The camels *slain for sacrifice* have we appointed for you as symbols of your obedience unto GOD : ye *also* receive *other* advantages from them.   Wherefore commemorate the name of GOD over them, *when ye slay them*, standing on their feet, disposed in right order :[1] and when they are fallen down *dead*, eat of them ; and give to eat *thereof both* unto him who is content *with what is given him, without asking*, and unto him who asketh.[2]   Thus have we. given you dominion over them, that ye might return *us* thanks. Their flesh is not accepted of GOD, neither their blood ; but your piety is accepted of him.   Thus have we given you dominion over them, that ye might magnify GOD, for *the revelations* whereby he hath directed you.   And bear good tidings unto the righteous, that GOD will repel *the ill designs of the infidels* from the true believers ; for GOD loveth not every perfidious unbeliever.   Permission is granted unto those who take arms *against the unbelievers*, for that they have been unjustly persecuted *by them* ; (and GOD is certainly able to assist them :) who have been turned out of their habitations injuriously, *and for no other reason* than because they say, Our LORD is GOD.[3]   And if GOD did not repel *the violence of* some men by others, verily monasteries, and churches, and synagogues, and the temples *of the Moslems*, wherein the name of GOD is frequently commemorated, would be utterly demolished.[4]   And GOD will certainly assist him who shall be on his side : for GOD *is* strong *and* mighty.   *And he will assist those* who, if we establish them in the earth, will observe prayer, and give alms and command

[1] That is, as some expound the word, standing on three feet, having one of their fore feet tied up, which is the manner of tying camels to prevent their moving from the place.   Some copies instead of *sawáffa* read *sawáffena* from the verb *safana*, which properly signifies the posture of a horse, when he stands on three feet, the edge of the fourth only touching the ground.

[2] Or, as the words may also be rendered, *Unto him who asketh in a modest and humble manner, and unto him who wanteth but dare not ask.*

[3] This was the first passage of the Korân which allowed Mohammed and his followers to defend themselves against their enemies by force, and was revealed a little before the flight to Medina ; till which time the prophet had exhorted his Moslems to suffer the injuries offered them with patience, which is also commanded in above seventy different places of the Korân. (Al Beidâwi, &c. S le Prelim. Disc. Sect. II.)

[4] That is, The public exercise of any religion, whether true or false, is supported only by force ; and therefore, as Mohammed would argue, the true religion must be established by the same means.

that which is just, and forbid that which is unjust. And
unto GOD *shall be* the end of *all* things. If they accuse thee,
O Mohammed, of imposture ; *consider that*, before them, the
people of Noah, and *the tribes of* Ad and Thamûd, and the
people of Abraham, and the people of Lot, and the inhabitants of Madian, accused *their prophets* of imposture : and
Moses was also charged with falsehood. And I granted a
long respite unto the unbelievers : *but* afterwards I chastised
them ; and how *different* was the change I made *in their
condition* ! How many cities have we destroyed, which
were ungodly, and which *are now* fallen to ruin on their
roofs ? And *how many* wells have been abandoned,[1] and
lofty castles ? Do they not therefore journey through the
land ? And have they not hearts to understand with, or
ears to hear with ? Surely as to these things *their* eyes
are not blind, but the hearts are blind which *are* in *their*
breasts. They will urge thee to hasten the *threatened*
punishment ; but GOD will not fail *to perform* what he hath
threatened : and verily *one* day with thy LORD *is* as a
thousand years, of those which ye compute.[2] Unto how
many cities have I granted respite, though they were wicked ?
Yet afterwards I chastised them : and unto me shall they
come *to be judged, at the last day*. Say, O men, verily I am
only a public preacher unto you. And they who believe
and do good works ; shall obtain forgiveness and an honourable provision. But those who endeavour to make our
signs of none effect, *shall be* the inhabitants of hell. We
have sent no apostle, or prophet, before thee, but, when he
read, Satan suggested *some error* in his reading.[3] But GOD

---

[1] That is, How many spots in the deserts, which were formerly inhabited,
are now abandoned ? a neglected well being the proper sign of such a deserted
dwelling in those parts, as ruins are of a demolished town. Some imagine
that this passage intends more particularly a well at the foot of a certain hill
in the province of Hadramaut, and a castle built on the top of the same hill,
both belonging to the people of Handha Ebn Safwân, a remnant of the
Thamûdites, who having killed their prophet, were utterly destroyed by GOD,
and their dwelling abandoned. (Al Beidâwi, &c.)

[2] See 2 Pet. iii. 8.

[3] The occasion of the passage is thus related. Mohammed one day
reading the 53rd chapter of the Korân, when he came to this verse, *What
think ye of* Allât, *and* Al Uzza, *and of* Manâh, *the other third goddess* ? the devil
put the following words into his mouth, which he pronounced through
inadvertence, or, as some tell us, because he was then half asleep (Yahya),
viz., *These are the most high and beauteous damsels, whose intercession is to
be hoped for*. The Koreish, who were sitting near Mohammed, greatly
rejoiced at what they had heard, and when he had finished the chapter, joined
with him and his followers in making their adoration : but the prophet,
being acquainted by the angel Gabriel with the reason of their compliance,
and with what he had uttered, was deeply concerned at his mistake, till this

shall make void that which Satan hath suggested : then shall GOD confirm his signs ; for GOD *is* knowing *and* wise. *But this he permitteth*, that he may make that which Satan hath suggested, a temptation unto those in whose hearts there is an infirmity, and whose hearts are hardened : (for the ungodly are certainly in a wide disagreement *from the truth* :) and that they on whom knowledge hath been bestowed may know that *this book* is the truth from thy LORD, and may believe therein ; and that their hearts may acquiesce in the same : for GOD *is* surely the director of those who believe, into the right way.   But the infidels will not cease to doubt concerning it, until the hour *of judgment* cometh suddenly upon them ; or until the punishment of a grievous day[1] overtake them.   On that day the kingdom shall be GOD'S : he shall judge between them.   And they who shall have believed, and shall have wrought righteousness, *shall be* in gardens of pleasure : but they who shall have disbelieved, and shall have charged our signs with falsehood, those shall suffer a shameful punishment.   And *as to those* who shall have fled their country for the sake of GOD's true religion, and afterwards shall have been slain, or shall have died ; on them will GOD bestow an excellent provision ; and GOD is the best provider.   He will surely introduce them with an introduction with which they shall be well pleased : for GOD *is* knowing *and* gracious.   This *is so*.   Whoever shall take a vengeance equal to the injury which hath been done him,[2] and shall afterwards be unjustly treated ;[3] verily GOD will assist him : for GOD *is* merciful, *and* ready to forgive.   This *shall be done*, for that GOD causeth the night to succeed the day, and he causeth the day to succeed the night ; and for that GOD *both* heareth *and* seeth.   This, because GOD is truth, and because what they invoke besides him is vanity ; and for that GOD is the high, the mighty.

verse was revealed for his consolation. (Al Beidâwi, Jallalo'ddin, Yahya, &c. Chap. XVI.)   We are told however by Al Beidâwi, that the more intelligent and accurate persons reject the aforesaid story ;   and the verb, here translated *read*, signifying also *to wish for* anything, interpret the passage of the suggestions of the devil to debauch the affections of those holy persons, or to employ their minds in vain wishes and desires.

[1] Or, *a day which maketh childless* ; by which some great misfortune in war is expressed : as the overthrow the infidels received at Bedr.   Some suppose the resurrection is here intended.

[2] And shall not take a more severe revenge than the fact deserves.

[3] By the aggressor's seeking to revenge himself again on the person injured, by offering him some further violence.   The passage seems to relate to the vengeance which the Moslems should take of the infidels, for their unjust persecution of them.

Dost thou not see that GOD sendeth down water from heaven, and the earth becometh green ? for GOD *is* gracious *and* wise. Unto him *belongeth* whatsoever is in heaven and on earth : and GOD is self-sufficient, worthy to be praised. Dost thou not see that GOD hath subjected whatever is in the earth to your service, and *also* the ships which sail in the sea, by his command ? And he withholdeth the heaven that it fall not on the earth, unless by his permission :[1] for GOD *is* gracious unto mankind, *and* merciful. It is he who hath given you life, and will hereafter cause you to die ; afterwards he will *again* raise you to life, *at the resurrection* : but man *is* surely ungrateful. Unto the professors of every religion have we appointed certain rites, which they observe. Let them not therefore dispute with thee concerning *this* matter ; but invite *them* unto thy LORD : for thou followest the right direction. But if they enter into debate with thee, answer, GOD well knoweth that which ye do : GOD will judge between you, on the day of resurrection, concerning that wherein ye *now* disagree. Dost thou not know that GOD knoweth whatever is in heaven and on earth ? Verily this *is written* in the book *of his decrees* : this is easy with GOD. They worship, besides GOD, that concerning which he hath sent down no convincing proof, and concerning which they have no knowledge : but the unjust doers shall have none to assist them. And when our evident signs are rehearsed unto them, thou mayest perceive, in the countenances of the unbelievers, a disdain *thereof* : it wanteth little but that they rush with violence on those who rehearse our signs unto them. Say, Shall I declare unto you a worse thing than this ? The fire *of hell*, which GOD hath threatened unto those who believe not, *is worse* ; and an unhappy journey *shall it be thither*. O men, a parable is propounded *unto you* ; wherefore hearken unto it. Verily, *the idols* which ye invoke, besides GOD, can never create a single fly, although they were *all* assembled for that *purpose* : and if the fly snatch anything from them, they cannot recover the same from it.[2] Weak is

---

[1] Which it will do at the last day.

[2] The commentators say, that the Arabs used to anoint the images of their gods with some odoriferous composition, and with honey, which the flies eat, though the doors of the temple were carefully shut, getting in at the windows or crevices. Perhaps Mohammed took this argument from the Jews, who pretend that the temple of Jerusalem, and the sacrifices there offered to the true GOD, were never annoyed by flies (Pirke Aboth, c. 5, Sect. 6, 7) ; whereas swarms of those insects infested the heathen temples,

the petitioner, and the petitioned.   They judge not of GOD
according to his due estimation : for GOD *is* powerful *and*
mighty.   GOD chooseth messengers from among the angels,[1]
and from among men : for GOD *is* he who heareth *and*
seeth.   He knoweth that which is before them, and that
which is behind them, and unto GOD shall *all* things return.
O true believers, bow down, and prostrate yourselves, and
worship your LORD ;   and work righteousness, that ye may
be happy : and fight in defence of GOD'S true religion, as
it behoveth *you* to fight for the same.   He hath chosen
you, and hath not imposed on you any difficulty in the
religion *which he hath given you,* the religion of your father
Abraham : he hath named you Moslems heretofore, and
in this *book* ; that *our* apostle may be a witness against
you *at the day of judgment,* and that ye may be witnesses
against *the rest of* mankind.   Wherefore be ye constant at
prayer ; and give alms : and adhere firmly unto GOD.   He
is your master ; and he is the best master ; and the best
protector.

XXIII

THE CHAPTER OF THE TRUE BELIEVERS [2]

Revealed at Mecca.

IN THE NAME OF THE MOST MERCIFUL GOD.

(XVIII.)[3] **N**OW are the   true believers   happy :   who
humble themselves in their   prayer, and
who eschew *all* vain discourse, and who *are* doers of alms-
deeds ;   and who keep themselves from carnal knowledge
of any women except their wives, or the *captives* which
their right hands possess ; (for *as to them* they shall be
blameless : but whoever coveteth any *woman* beyond these,
they *are* transgressors : and who acquit themselves faithfully of their trust, and *justly perform* their covenant ; and
who observe their *appointed times of* prayer :) these shall
be the heirs, who shall inherit paradise ; they shall continue therein for ever.   We formerly created man of a

---

being drawn thither by the steam of the sacrifices (Selden, de Diis Syris,
Synt. 2, c. 6).
    [1] Who are the bearers of the divine revelations to the prophets ; but ought
not to be the objects of worship.
    [2] Otherwise rendered *Believers*.   [3] Section XVIII begins.

finer sort of clay; afterwards we placed him *in the form of seed* in a sure receptacle : afterwards we made the seed coagulated blood ; and we formed the coagulated blood into a piece of flesh ; then we formed the piece of flesh into bones ; and we clothed those bones with flesh : then we produced the same by another creation.[1] Wherefore blessed be GOD, the most excellent Creator ![2] After this shall ye die : and afterwards shall ye be restored to life, on the day of resurrection. And we have created over you seven heavens :[3] and we are not negligent of what we have created. And we send down rain from heaven, by measure ; and we cause it to remain on the earth : we are also certainly able to deprive you of the same. And we cause gardens of palm-trees, and vineyards, to spring forth for you by means thereof ; wherein ye have many fruits, and whereof ye eat. And *we also raise for you* a tree springing from Mount Sinai ;[4] which produceth oil, and a sauce for those who eat. Ye have likewise an instruction in the cattle : we give you to drink of the *milk* which *is* in their bellies, and ye receive many advantages from them ; and of them do ye eat : and on them, and on ships, are ye carried.[5] We sent Noah heretofore unto his people, and he said, O my people, serve GOD : ye have no GOD besides him ; will ye not therefore fear *the consequence of your worshipping other gods* ? And the chiefs of his people, who believed not, said, This is no other than a man, as ye are : he seeketh to raise himself to a superiority over you. If GOD had pleased *to have sent a messenger unto you*, he would surely have sent angels : we have not heard this of our forefathers. Verily he is no other than a man *disturbed* with frenzy : wherefore wait concerning him for a time. *Noah* said, O LORD, do thou protect me ; for that they accuse me of falsehood. And we revealed *our orders* unto him, *saying,* Make the ark in our sight ; and *according to*

---

[1] *i.e.*, Producing a perfect man, composed of soul and body.

[2] See Chap. VI. p. 129.

[3] Literally, *seven paths* ; by which the heavens are meant, because, according to some expositors, they are the *paths* of the angels and of the celestial bodies : though the original word also signifies things which are *folded* or *placed like stories* one above another, as the Mohammedans suppose the heavens to be.

[4] viz., The olive. The gardens near this mountain are yet famous for the excellent fruit trees of almost all sorts which grow there. (Voyages de Thevenot, liv. 2, ch. 9.)

[5] The beast more particularly meant in this place is the camel, which is chiefly used for carriage in the East ; being called by the Arabs, the *land ship*, on which they pass those *seas of sand*, the deserts.

our revelation. And when our decree cometh *to be executed*, and the oven shall boil *and pour forth water*, carry into it of every *species of animals* one pair ; and also thy family, except such of them on whom a previous sentence *of destruction* hath passed :[1] and speak not unto me in behalf of those who have been unjust ; for they *shall be* drowned. And when thou and they who *shall be* with thee, shall go up into the ark, say, Praise be unto GOD, who hath delivered us from the ungodly people ! And say, O LORD, cause me to come down *from this ark* with a blessed descent ; for thou art best able to bring me down *from the same with safety*. Verily herein *were signs of our omnipotence*; and we proved *mankind thereby*. Afterwards we raised up another generation[2] after them ; and we sent unto them an apostle from among them,[3] *who said*, Worship GOD : ye have no GOD besides him ; will ye not therefore fear *his vengeance* ? And the chiefs of his people, who believed not, and who denied the meeting of the life to come, and on whom we had bestowed affluence in this present life, said, This is no other than a man, as ye are ; he eateth of that whereof ye eat, and he drinketh of that whereof ye drink : and if ye obey a man like unto yourselves, ye will surely be sufferers. Doth he threaten you that after ye shall be dead, and shall become dust and bones, ye shall be brought forth *alive from your graves* ? Away, away with that ye are threatened with ! There is *no other life* besides our present life : we die, and we live ; and we shall not be raised again. This is no other than a man, who deviseth a lie concerning GOD : but we will not believe him. *Their apostle* said, O LORD, defend me ; for that they have accused me of imposture. *God* answered, After a little while they shall surely repent *their obstinacy*. Wherefore a severe punishment was justly inflicted on them, and we rendered them *like* the refuse *which is carried down by a stream*. Away therefore with the ungodly people ! Afterwards we raised up other generations[4] after them. No nation shall be punished before their determined time ; neither shall they be respited *after*. Afterwards we sent our apostles, one after another. So often as their apostle came unto any nation, they charged him with imposture : and we caused

---

[1] See Chap. XI.
[2] Namely, the tribe of Ad, or of Thamûd.
[3] viz., The prophet Hûd, or Sâleh.
[4] As the Sodomites, Midianites, &c.

them successively to follow one another *to destruction* ; and we made them *only subjects of* traditional stories. Away therefore with the unbelieving nations! Afterwards we sent Moses, and Aaron his brother, with our signs and manifest power, unto Pharaoh and his princes : but they proudly refused *to believe on him* ; for they were a haughty people. And they said, Shall we believe on two men like unto ourselves ; whose people are our servants ? And they accused them of imposture : wherefore they became of *the number of* those who were destroyed. And we heretofore gave the book *of the law* unto Moses, that *the children of Israel* might be directed *thereby*. And we appointed the son of Mary, and his mother, for a sign : and we prepared an abode for them in an elevated part of the earth,[1] being *a place* of quiet *and security, and* watered with running springs. O apostles, eat of those things which are good ;[2] and work righteousness : for I well know that which ye do. This your religion is one religion[3] ; and I am your LORD : wherefore fear me. But *men* have rent the affair of their *religion* into various sects : every party rejoiceth in that which they follow. Wherefore leave them in their confusion, until a certain time.[4] Do they think that we hasten unto them the wealth and children which we have abundantly bestowed on them, for their good ? But they do not understand. Verily they who stand in awe, for fear of their LORD, and who believe in the signs of their LORD, and who attribute not companions unto their LORD ; and who give that which they give *in alms*, their hearts being struck with dread, for that they must return unto their LORD : these hasten unto good, and are foremost to *obtain* the same. We will not impose any difficulty on a soul, except according to its ability ; with us *is* a book, which speaketh the truth ; and they shall not be injured.

---

[1] The commentators tell us the place here intended is Jerusalem, or Damascus, or Ramlah, or Palestine, or Egypt. (Al Beidâwi, Jallalo'ddin.) But perhaps the passage means the hill to which the Virgin Mary retired to be delivered, according to the Mohammedan tradition. (Chap. XIX.)

[2] These words are addressed to the apostles in general, to whom it was permitted to eat of all clean and wholesome food ; and were spoken to them severally at the time of their respective missions. Some, however, think them directed particularly to the Virgin Mary and JESUS, or singly to the latter (in which case the plural number must be used out of respect only), proposing the practice of the prophets for their imitation. Mohammed probably designed in this passage to condemn the abstinence observed by the Christian monks. (Al Beidâwi.)

[3] See Chap. XXI.

[4] *i.e.*, Till they shall be slain, or shall die a natural death.

But their hearts are *drowned* in negligence, as to this *matter*; and they have works different from those *we have mentioned*; which they will continue to do, until, when we chastise such of them as enjoy an affluence of fortune, by a *severe* punishment,[1] behold, they cry aloud for help: *but it shall be answered them,* Cry not for help to-day: for ye shall not be assisted by us. My signs were read unto you, but ye turned back on your heels: proudly elating yourselves because of *your possessing the holy temple*; discoursing together by night, *and* talking foolishly. Do they not therefore attentively consider that which is spoken *unto them*; whether *a revelation* is come unto them which came not unto their forefathers? Or do they not know their apostle; and therefore reject him? Or do they say, He is a madman? Nay, he hath come unto them with the truth; but the greater part of them detest the truth. If the truth had followed their desires, verily the heavens and the earth, and whoever therein *is*, had been corrupted.[2] But we have brought them their admonition; and they turn aside from their admonition. Dost thou ask of them any maintenance *for thy preaching*? since the maintenance of thy LORD is better; for he is the most bounteous provider. Thou certainly invitest them to the right way: and they who believe not in the life to come, do surely deviate from *that* way. If we had had compassion on them, and had taken off from them the calamity which had befallen them,[3] they would surely have more obstinately persisted in their error, wandering *in confusion*. We formerly chastised them with a punishment:[4] yet they did not humble themselves before their LORD, neither did they make supplications *unto him*; until, when we have opened upon

[1] By which is intended either the overthrow at Bedr, where several of the chief Koreishites lost their lives; or the famine with which the Meccans were afflicted, at the prayer of the prophet, conceived in these words, O GOD, *set thy foot strongly on Modar* (an ancestor of the Koreish), *and give them years like the years of Joseph*: whereupon so great a dearth ensued, that they were obliged to feed on dogs, carrion, and burnt bones. (Al Beidâwi.)

[2] That is, If there had been a plurality of gods, as the idolaters contend (Chap. XXI.): or, if the doctrine taught by Mohammed had been agreeable to their inclinations, &c.

[3] viz., The famine. It is said that the Meccans being reduced to eat ilhiz, which is a sort of miserable food made of blood and camels' hair, used by the Arabs in time of scarcity, Abu Sofiân came to Mohammed, and said, *Tell me. I adjure thee by God and the relation that is between us, dost thou think thou art sent as a mercy unto all creatures; since thou hast slain the fathers with the sword and the children with hunger?* (Al Beidâwi.)

[4] Namely, the slaughter at Bedr.

them a door, from which a severe punishment[1] *hath issued,* behold, they are driven to despair thereat.   It is *God* who hath created in you *the senses of* hearing and *of* sight, *that ye may perceive our judgments,* and hearts, *that ye may seriously consider them* : *yet* how few of ȳou give thanks ! It is he who hath produced you in the earth ; and before him shall ye be assembled.   It is he who giveth life, and putteth to death ; and to him *is to be attributed* the vicissitude of night and day : do ye not therefore understand ? But the *unbelieving Meccans* say as *their* predecessors said : they say, When we shall be dead, and shall have become dust and bones, shall we really be raised to life ?   We have already been threatened with this, and our fathers also heretofore : this is nothing but fables of the ancients.   Say, Whose is the earth and whoever therein *is* ; if ye know ? They will answer, GOD'S.   Say, Will ye not therefore consider ?   Say, Who is the LORD of the seven heavens, and the LORD of the magnificent throne ?   They will answer, *They are* GOD'S.   Say, Will ye not therefore fear *him* ? Say, In whose hand is the kingdom of all things ; who protecteth *whom he pleaseth,* but is himself protected of none ; if ye know ?   They will answer, *In* GOD'S.   Say, How therefore are ye bewitched ?   Yea, we have brought them the truth ; and they are certainly liars *in denying the same.*   GOD hath not begotten issue ; neither is there any *other* god with him : otherwise every god had surely taken away that which he had created ;[2] and some of them had exalted themselves above the others.[3]   Far be that from GOD, which they affirm of *him* !   He knoweth that which is concealed, and that which is made public : wherefore far be it from him *to have those sharers in his honour,* which they attribute to him !   Say, O LORD, If thou wilt surely cause me to see *the vengeance* with which they have been threatened ; O LORD, set me not among the ungodly people : for we are surely able to make thee to see that with which we have threatened them.   Turn aside evil with that which is better :[4] we well know *the calumnies*

---

[1] viz., Famine : which is more terrible than the calamities of war. (Al Beidâwi.)   According to these explanations, the passage must have been revealed at Medina ; unless it be taken in a prophetical sense.

[2] And set up a distinct creation and kingdom of his own.

[3] See Chap. XVII.

[4] That is, By forgiving injuries, and returning of good for them : which rule is to be qualified, however, with this proviso ; that the true religion receive no prejudice by such mildness and clemency. (Al Beidâwi.)

which they utter *against thee*. And say, O LORD, I fly
unto thee for refuge, against the suggestions of the devils:
and I have recourse unto thee, O LORD, *to drive them away*,
that they be not present with me.[1] *The gainsaying of the
unbelievers ceaseth not* until, when death overtaketh any
of them, he saith, O LORD, suffer me to return *to life*, that
I may do that which is right ; in *professing the true faith*
which I have neglected.[2] By no means. Verily these
are the words which he shall speak : but behind them there
shall be a bar,[3] until the day of resurrection. When therefore the trumpet shall be sounded, there shall be no relation
between them *which shall be regarded* on that day ; neither
shall they ask *assistance* of each other. They whose balances
shall be heavy *with good works*, shall be happy : but
they whose balances shall be light, are those who shall lose
their souls, *and* shall remain in hell for ever.[4] The fire
shall scorch their faces, and they shall writhe their mouths
therein *for anguish* : *and it shall be said unto them*, Were
not my signs rehearsed unto you ; and did you not charge
them with falsehood ? They shall answer, O LORD, our
unhappiness prevailed over us, and we were people who
went astray. O LORD, take us forth from this *fire* : if we
return *to our former wickedness*, we shall surely be unjust.
God will say *unto them*, Be ye driven away with ignominy
thereinto : and speak not unto me *to deliver you*. Verily
they were a party of my servants, who said, O LORD, we

---

[1] To besiege me : or, as it may also be translated, *That they hurt me not.*

[2] Or, as the word may also import, *In the world which I have left* ; that is,
during the further term of life which shall be granted me, and from which
I have been cut off. (Al Beidâwi.)

[3] The original word *barzakh*, here translated " bar," primarily signifies
any partition, or interstice, which divides one thing from another ; but is
used by the Arabs not always in the same, and sometimes in an obscure sense.
They seem generally to express by it what the Greeks did by the word Hades ;
one while using it for the place of the dead, another while for the time of
their continuance in that state, and another while for the state itself. It is
defined by their critics to be the interval or space between this world and
the next, or between death and the resurrection ; every person who dies
being said to enter into *al barzakh* ; or, as the Greek expresses it, καταβῆναι
εἰς ᾅδου. (Vide Pocock. not. in Port. Mosis, p. 248, &c., and Sale, Prel.
Disc. Sect. IV.) One lexicographer (Ebn Maruf, apud Gol. Lex. Arab.
col. 254) tells us that in the Korân it denotes the grave : but the commentators on this passage expound it a bar, or invincible obstacle, cutting off
all possibility of return into the world, after death. See Chap. XXV.,
where the word again occurs. Some interpreters understand the words
we have rendered " behind them," to mean " before them " (it being one of
those words, of which there are several in the Arabic tongue, that have directly
contrary significations), considering *al barzakh* as a future space, and lying
before, and not behind them.

[4] Sale, Prelim. Disc. Sect. IV.

believe : wherefore forgive us, and be merciful unto us ; for thou art the best of those who show mercy. But ye received them with scoffs, so that they suffered you to forget my admonition,[1] and ye laughed them to scorn. I have this day rewarded them, for that they suffered *the injuries ye offered them* with patience : verily they enjoy great felicity. *God* will say, What number of years have ye continued on earth ? They will answer, We have continued *there* a day, or part of a day :[2] but ask those who keep account.[3] *God* will say, Ye have tarried but a little, if ye knew *it*. Did ye think that we had created you in sport, and that ye should not be brought again before us ? Wherefore let GOD be exalted, the King, the Truth ! There is no GOD besides him, the LORD of the honourable throne. Whoever together with *the true* GOD shall invoke another god, concerning whom he hath no demonstrative proof, shall surely be brought to an account for the same before his LORD. Verily the infidels shall not prosper. Say, O LORD, pardon, and show mercy ; for thou art the best of those who show mercy.

XXIV

THE CHAPTER OF LIGHT [4]
Revealed at Medina.

IN THE NAME OF THE MOST MERCIFUL GOD.

*T*HIS Sura have we sent down *from heaven* ; and have ratified the same : and we have revealed therein evident signs, that ye may be warned. The whore, and the whoremonger, shall ye scourge with an hundred stripes.[5]

---

[1] Being unable to prevail on you by their remonstrances, because of the contempt wherein ye held them.

[2] The time will seem thus short to them in comparison to the eternal duration of their torments, or because the time of their living in the world was the time of their joy and pleasure ; it being usual for the Arabs to describe what they like as of short, and what they dislike, as of long continuance.

[3] That is the angels, who keep account of the length of men's lives and of their works, or any other who may have leisure to compute ; and not us, whose torments distract our thoughts and attention.

[4] This title is taken from an allegorical comparison made between light and GOD, or faith in him, about the middle of the chapter.

[5] This law is not to be understood to relate to married people, who are of free condition ; because adultery in such, according to the Sonna, is to be punished by stoning. (Chap. IV.)

And let not compassion towards them prevent you from *executing* the judgment of GOD ;[1] if ye believe in GOD and the last day : and let some of the true believers be witnesses of their punishment.[2] The whoremonger shall not marry *any other* than a harlot, or an idolatress. And a harlot shall no *man* take in marriage, except a whoremonger, or an idolater. And this *kind of marriage* is forbidden the true believers.[3] But *as to* those who accuse women of reputation *of whoredom*,[4] and produce not four witnesses *of the fact*,[5] scourge them with fourscore stripes, and receive not their testimony for ever ; for such are infamous prevaricators : excepting those who shall afterwards repent, and amend ; for *unto such will* GOD *be* gracious *and* merciful. They who shall accuse *their wives* of adultery, and shall have no witnesses *thereof* besides themselves ; the testimony *which shall be required* of one of them *shall be*, that he swear four times by GOD that he speaketh the truth : and the fifth *time that he imprecate* the course of GOD on him, if he be a liar. And it shall avert the punishment from *the wife*, if she swear four times by GOD that he is a liar ; and if the fifth *time she imprecate* the wrath of GOD on her, if he speaketh the truth.[6] If *it were* not *for* the

[1] *i.e.*, Be not moved by pity, either to forgive the offenders, or to mitigate their punishment. Mohammed was for so strict and impartial an execution of the laws, that he is reported to have said, *If Fâtema the daughter of Mohammed steal, let her hand be struck off.* (Al Beidâwi.)

[2] That is, Let the punishment be inflicted in public, and not in private because the ignominy of it is more intolerable than the smart, and more likely to work a reformation on the offender. Some say there ought to be three persons present at the least ; but others think two, or even one, to be sufficient. (Al Beidâwi.)

[3] The preceding passage was revealed on account of the meaner and more indigent Mohâjerins, or refugees, who sought to marry the whores of the infidels, taken captives in war, for the sake of the gain which they made by prostituting themselves. Some think the prohibition was special, and regarded only the Mohâjerins before mentioned ; and others are of opinion it was general ; but it is agreed to have been abrogated by the words which follow in this chapter, *Marry the single women among you* ; harlots being comprised under the appellation of *single women*. (Al Beidâwi, Jallalo'ddin.) It is supposed by some that not *marriage*, but *unlawful commerce* with such women is here forbidden.

[4] The Arabic word, *mohsinât*, properly signifies *women of unblamable conduct*; but to bring the chastisement after mentioned on the calumniator, it is also requisite that they be free women, of ripe age, having their understandings perfect, and of the Mohammedan religion. Though the word be of the feminine gender, yet *men* are also supposed to be comprised in this law. Abu Hanîfa was of opinion that the slanderer ought to be scourged in pu' lic, as well as the fornicator; but the generality are against him. (Al Beidâwi.)

[5] Chap. IV. p. 74.

[6] In case both swear, the man's oath discharges him from the imputation and penalty of slander, and the woman's oath frees her from the imputation

indulgence of GOD towards you, and his mercy, and that GOD is easy to be reconciled, *and* wise ; *he would immediately discover your crimes. As to* the party among you who have published the falsehood *concerning Ayesha*,[1] think it not to be an evil unto you : on the contrary, it is better for you.[2] Every man of them *shall be punished* according to the injustice of which he hath been guilty ;[3] and he among them who hath undertaken to aggravate the same,[4]

and penalty of adultery : but though the woman do swear to her innocence yet the marriage is actually void, or ought to be declared void by the judge because it is not fit they should continue together after they have come to these extremities. (Al Beidâwi.)

[1] For the understanding of this passage, it is necessary to relate the following story. Mohammed having undertaken an expedition against the tribe of Mostalek, in the sixth year of the Hejra, took his wife Ayesha with him, to accompany him. On their return, when they were not far from Medina, the army removing by night, Ayesha, on the road, alighted from her camel, and stepped aside on a private occasion : but, on her return, perceiving she had dropped her necklace, which was of onyxes of Dhafâr, she went back to look for it ; and in the meantime her attendants, taking it for granted that she had got into her pavilion (or little tent surrounded with curtains, wherein women are carried in the East), set it again on the camel, and led it away. When she came back to the road, and saw her camel was gone, she sat down there, expecting that when she was missed some would be sent back to fetch her ; and in a little time she fell asleep. Early in the morning, Safwân Ebn al Moattel, who had stayed behind to rest himself, coming by, and perceiving somebody asleep, went to see who it was, and knew her to be Ayesha ; upon which he waked her, by twice pronouncing with a low voice these words, *We are God's, and unto him must we return.* Then Ayesha immediately covered herself with her veil ; and Safwân set her on his own camel, and led her after the army, which they overtook by noon, as they were resting. This accident had like to have ruined Ayesha, whose reputation was publicly called in question, as if she had been guilty of adultery with Safwân : and Mohammed himself knew not what to think, when he reflected on the circumstances of the affair, which were improved by some malicious people very much to Ayesha's dishonour ; and notwithstanding his wife's protestations of her innocence, he could not get rid of his perplexity, nor stop the mouths of the censorious, till about a month after, when this passage was revealed, declaring the accusation to be unjust. (Al Bokhari in Sonna, Al Beidâwi, Jallalo'ddin, &c. Vide Abulf. Vit. Moh. p. 82, &c., and Gagnier, Vie de Mahomet, lib. 4. c. 7.)

[2] The words are directed to the prophet, and to Abu Becr, Ayesha, and Safwân, the persons concerned in this false report ; since, besides the amends they might expect in the next world, GOD had done them the honour to clear their reputations by revealing eighteen verses expressly for that purpose. (Al Beidâwi.)

[3] The persons concerned in spreading the scandal were Abd'allah Ebn Obba (who first raised it, and inflamed the matter to the utmost, out of hatred to Mohammed)), Zeid Ebn Refâa, Hassân Ebn Thabet, Mestah Ebn Othâtha, a great-grandson of Abd'almotalleb's, and Hamna Bint Jahash : and every one of them received fourscore stripes, pursuant to the law ordained in this chapter, except only Abd'allah, who was exempted, being a man of great consideration. (Abulfeda, Vit. Moh. p. 83) It is said that, as a further punishment, Hassân and Mestah became blind, and that the former of them also lost the use of both his hands. (Al Beidâwi.)

[4] viz., Abd'allah Ebn Obba, who had not the grace to become a true believer, but died an infidel. (Chap. IX. p. 191.)

shall suffer a grievous punishment. Did not the faithful men, and the faithful women, when ye heard this, judge in their own minds for the best ; and say, This is a manifest falsehood ? Have they produced four witnesses thereof ? wherefore since they have not produced the witnesses, they are surely liars in the sight of GOD. *Had it* not *been for* the indulgence of GOD towards you, and his mercy, in this world and in that which is to come, verily a grievous punishment had been inflicted on you, for the *calumny* which ye have spread : when ye published that with your tongues, and spoke that with your mouths, of which ye had no knowledge ; and esteemed it to be light, whereas it was a matter of importance in the sight of GOD. When ye heard it, did ye say, It belongeth not unto us, that we should talk of this *matter* : GOD forbid ! this is a grievous calumny ? GOD warneth you, that ye return not to the like *crime* for ever ; if ye be true believers. And GOD declareth unto you *his* signs ; for GOD *is* knowing *and* wise. Verily they who love that scandal be published of those who believe, shall receive a severe punishment *both* in this world, and in the next. GOD knoweth, but ye know not. *Had it* not *been for* the indulgence of GOD towards you, and his mercy, and that GOD *is* gracious *and* merciful, *ye had felt his vengeance.* O true believers, follow not the steps of the devil : for whosoever shall follow the steps of the devil, he will command him filthy crimes, and that which is unlawful. If *it were* not *for* the indulgence of GOD, and his mercy towards you, there had not been so much as one of you cleansed *from his guilt* for ever : but GOD cleanseth whom he pleaseth ; for GOD *both* heareth *and* knoweth. Let not those among you who possess abundance *of wealth*, and *have* ability, swear that they will not give unto *their* kindred, and the poor, and those who have fled their country for the sake of GOD's true religion : but let them forgive, and act with benevolence *towards them.* Do ye not desire that GOD should pardon you ?[1] And GOD *is* gracious *and* merciful. Moreover they who falsely accuse modest women, who behave in a negligent manner,[2] *and*

---

[1] This passage was revealed on account of Abu Becr ; who swore that he would not for the future bestow anything on Mestah, though he was his mother's sister's son, and a poor Mohâjer or refugee, because he had joined in scandalizing his daughter Ayesha. But on Mohammed's reading this verse to him, he continued Mestah's pension. (Al Beidâwi, Jallalo'ddin.)

[2] *i.e.*, Who may be less careful in their conduct, and more free in their behaviour, as being conscious of no ill.

are true believers, shall be cursed in this world, and *in* the world to come ; and they shall suffer a severe punishment.[1] One day their own tongues shall bear witness against them, and their hands, and their feet, concerning that which they have done. On that day shall GOD render unto them their just due ; and they shall know that GOD is the evident truth. The wicked women *should be joined* to the wicked men, and the wicked men to the wicked women ; but the good women *should be married* to the good men, and the good men to the good women. These shall be cleared from *the calumnies* which *slanderers* speak *of them* :[2] they shall obtain pardon, and an honourable provision. O true believers, enter not any houses, besides your own houses, until ye have asked leave, and have saluted the family thereof :[3] this *is* better for you ; peradventure ye will be admonished. And if ye shall find no person in the *houses*, yet do not enter them, until leave be granted you : and if it be said unto you, Return back ; do ye return back. This *will be* more decent for you ;[4] and GOD knoweth that which ye do. It shall be no crime in you, that ye enter uninhabited houses,[5] wherein ye may meet with a convenience. GOD knoweth that which ye discover, and that which ye conceal. Speak unto the true believers, that they restrain their eyes, and keep themselves from immodest actions : this will be more pure for them ; for GOD is well acquainted with that which they do. And speak unto the believing

[1] Though the words be general, yet they principally regard those who should calumniate the prophet's wives. According to a saying of Ebn Abbas, if the threats contained in the whole Korân be examined, there are none so severe as those occasioned by the false accusation of Ayesha ; wherefore he thought even repentance would stand her slanderers in no stead. (Al Beidâwi.)

[2] Al Beidâwi observes, on this passage, that GOD cleared four persons, by four extraordinary testimonies : for he cleared Joseph by the testimony of a child in his mistress's family (Chap. XII. p. 172) ; Moses, by means of the stone which fled away with his garments (Chap. II. and Chap. XXXIII.); Mary, by the testimony of her infant (Chap. XIX.) ; and Ayesha, by these verses of the Korân.

[3] To enter suddenly or abruptly into any man's house or apartment, is reckoned a great incivility in the East ; because a person may possibly be surprised in an indecent action or posture, or may have something discovered which he would conceal. It is said, that a man came to Mohammed, and wanted to know whether he must ask leave to go in to his sister ; which being answered in the affirmative, he told the prophet that his sister had nobody else to attend upon her, and it would be troublesome to ask leave every time he went in to her. *What*, replied Mohammed, *wouldest thou see her naked* ? (Al Beidâwi.)

[4] Than to be importunate for admission, or to wait at the door.

[5] *i.e.*, Which are not the private habitation of a family ; such as public inns, shops, sheds, &c.

women, that they restrain their eyes, and preserve their modesty, and discover not their ornaments,[1] except what *necessarily* appeareth thereof :[2] and let them throw their veils over their bosoms,[3] and not show their ornaments, unless to their husbands,[4] or their fathers, or their husbands' fathers, or their sons, or their husbands' sons, or their brothers, or their brothers' sons, or their sisters' sons,[5] or their women,[6] or the *captives* which their right hands shall possess,[7] or unto such men as attend *them*, and have no need *of women*,[8] or unto children, who distinguish not the nakedness of women.   And let them not make a noise with their feet, that their ornaments which they hide may *thereby* be discovered.[9]   And be ye all turned unto GOD, O

[1] As their clothes, jewels, and the furniture of their toilet ; much less such parts of their bodies as ought not be seen.

[2] Some think their outward garments are here meant ; and others their hands and faces : it is generally held, however, that a free woman ought not to discover even those parts, unless to the persons after excepted, or on some unavoidable occasion, as their giving evidence in public, taking advice or medicine in case of sickness, &c.

[3] Taking care to cover their heads, necks, and breasts.

[4] For whose sake it is that they adorn themselves, and who alone have the privilege to see their whole body.

[5] These near relations are also excepted, because they cannot avoid seeing them frequently, and there is no great danger to be apprehended from them. They are allowed, therefore, to see what cannot be well concealed in so familiar an intercourse (Al Beidâwi), but no other part of their body, particularly whatever is between the navel and the knees.   (Jallalo'ddin.)   Uncles not being here particularly mentioned, it is a doubt whether they may be admitted to see their nieces. Some think they are included under the appellation of *brothers* : but others are of opinion that they are not comprised in this exception ; and give this reason for it, *viz.*, lest they should describe the persons of their nieces to their sons.   (Al Beidâwi.)

[6] That is, such as are of the Mohammedan religion ; it being reckoned by some unlawful, or, at least, indecent, for a woman, who is a true believer, to uncover herself before one who is an infidel, because she will hardly refrain describing her to the men : but others suppose all women in general are here excepted ; for, in this particular, doctors differ. (Al Beidâwi, Jallalo'ddin.)

[7] Slaves of either sex are included in this exception, and, as some think, domestic servants who are not slaves ; as those of a different nation.   It is related, that Mohammed once made a present of a man-slave to his daughter Fâtema ; and when he brought him to her, she had on a garment which was so scanty that she was obliged to leave either her head or her feet uncovered : and that the prophet, seeing her in great confusion on that account, told her, she need be under no concern, for that there was none present besides her father and her slave. (Al Beidâwi.)

[8] Or have no desire to enjoy them ; such as decrepit old men, and deformed or silly persons, who follow people as hangers-on, for their spare victuals, being too despicable to raise either a woman's passion, or a man's jealousy.   Whether eunuchs are comprehended under this general designation, is a question among the learned.   (Al Beidâwi, Yahya, &c.)

[9] By shaking the rings, which the women in the East wear about their ankles, and are usually of gold or silver.   (Al Beidâwi.)   The pride which the Jewish ladies of old took in making *a tinkling* with these *ornaments of their feet*, is—among other things of that nature—severely reproved by the prophet Isaiah. (Isaiah iii. 16 and 18.)

true believers, that ye may be happy. Marry those who are single[1] among you, and such as are honest of your men-servants, and your maid-servants : if they be poor, GOD will enrich them of his abundance ; for GOD *is* bounteous *and* wise. And let those who find not a match, keep themselves *from fornication,* until GOD shall enrich them of his abundance. And unto such of your slaves [2] as desire a written instrument *allowing them to redeem themselves on paying a certain sum*'[3] write *one,* if ye know good in them ;[4] and give them of the riches of GOD, which he hath given you.[5]   And compel not your maid-servants to prostitute themselves, if they be willing to live chastely ; that ye may seek the casual *advantage* of this present life :[6] but whoever shall compel them *thereto,* verily GOD *will be* gracious *and* merciful *unto such women* after their compulsion. And now have we revealed unto you evident signs, and a *history* like unto some *of the histories* of those who have gone before you,[7] and an admonition unto the pious. GOD *is* the light of heaven and earth : the similitude of his light is as a niche in a wall, wherein a lamp *is placed, and* the lamp *enclosed* in a *case of* glass ; the glass *appears* as it were a shining star. It is lighted with *the oil of* a blessed tree, an olive neither of the east, nor of the west :[8] it wanteth little but that the oil thereof would give light, although no fire touched it. *This is* light *added* unto light :[9] GOD will direct unto his

---

[1] *i.e.,* Those who are unmarried of either sex ; whether they have been married before or not.

[2] Of either sex.

[3] Whereby the master obliges himself to set his slave at liberty, on receiving a certain sum of money, which the slave undertakes to pay.

[4] That is, if ye have found them faithful, and have reason to believe they will perform their engagement.

[5] Either by bestowing something on them of your own substance, or by abating them a part of their ransom.   Some suppose these words are directed, not to the masters only, but to all Moslems in general ; recommending it to them to assist those who have obtained their freedom, and paid their ransom, either out of their own stock, or by admitting them to have a share in the public alms.   (Al Beidâwi.)

[6] It seems Abda'llah Ebn Obba had six women-slaves, on whom he laid a certain tax, which he obliged them to earn by the prostitution of their bodies : and one of them made her complaint to Mohammed, which occasioned the revelation of this passage.   (Al Beidâwi, Jallalo'ddin.)

[7] *i.e.,* The story of the false accusation of Ayesha, which resembles those of Joseph and the Virgin Mary.   (Al Beidâwi.)

[8] But of a more excellent kind.   Some think the meaning to be that the tree grows neither in the eastern nor the western parts, but in the midst of the world, namely, in Syria, where the best olives grow.   (Al Beidâwi.)

[9] Or a light whose brightness is doubly increased by the circumstances above mentioned.   The commentators explain this allegory, and every particular of it, with great subtlety ; interpreting the *light* here described

light whom he pleaseth. GOD propoundeth parables unto men ; for GOD knoweth all things. In the houses which GOD hath permitted to be raised,[1] and that his name be commemorated therein : men celebrate his praise in the same morning and evening, whom neither merchandizing, nor selling diverteth from the remembering of GOD, and the observance of prayer, and the giving of alms ; fearing the day whereon *men's* hearts and eyes shall be troubled ; that GOD may recompense them according to the utmost merit of what they shall have wrought, and may add unto them of his abundance *a more excellent reward* ; for GOD bestoweth on whom he pleaseth without measure. But *as to* the unbelievers, their works are like the vapour in a plain,[2] which the thirsty *traveller* thinketh to be water, until, when he cometh thereto, he findeth it *to be* nothing ; but he findeth GOD with him,[3] and he will fully pay him his account ; and GOD is swift in taking an account : or, as the darkness in a deep sea, covered by waves *riding* on waves, above which are clouds, being *additions of* darkness one over the other ; when *one* stretcheth forth his hand, he is far from seeing it. And unto whomsoever GOD shall not grant *his* light, he shall enjoy no light at all. Dost thou not perceive that all *creatures* both in heaven and earth praise GOD ; and the birds *also*, extending their wings ? Every one knoweth his prayer, and his praise : and GOD knoweth that which they do. Unto GOD *belongeth* the kingdom of heaven and earth ; and unto GOD *shall be* the return *at the last day*. Dost thou not see that GOD gently driveth forward the clouds, and

to be the *light* revealed in the Korân, or God's *enlightening grace* in the heart of man ; and in divers other manners.

[1] The connection of these words is not very obvious. Some suppose they ought to be joined with the preceding words, " Like a niche," or " It is lighted in the houses," &c., and that the comparison is more strong and just, by being made to the lamps in Mosques, which are larger than those in private houses. Some think they are rather to be connected with the following words, " Men praise," &c. And others are of opinion they are an imperfect beginning of a sentence, and that the words, Praise ye God, or the like, are to be understood. However, the houses here intended are those set apart for divine worship ; or particularly the three principal temples of Mecca, Medina, and Jerusalem. (Al Beidâwi.)

[2] The Arabic word *Seráb* signifies that false appearance or mirage which, in the East, is often seen in sandy plains about noon, resembling a large lake of water in motion, and is occasioned by the reverberation of the sunbeams. It sometimes tempts thirsty travellers out of their way, but deceives them when they come near, either going forward (for it always appears at the same distance), or quite vanishing. (Vide Q. Curt. de rebus Alex. lib. 7, et Gol. in Alfrag. p. iii, et in Adag. Arab. ad calcem Gram. Erp. p. 93.)

[3] That is, He will not escape the notice or vengeance of GOD.

gathereth them together, and then layeth them in heaps? Thou also seest the rain, which falleth from the midst thereof; and GOD sendeth down from heaven *as it were* mountains, wherein there is hail; he striketh therewith whom he pleaseth, and turneth the same away from whom he pleaseth: the brightness of his lightning wanteth but little of taking away the sight. GOD shifteth the night, and the day: verily herein is an instruction unto those who have sight. And GOD hath created every animal of water;[1] one of them goeth on his belly, and another of them walketh upon two feet, and another of them walketh upon four *feet*: GOD createth that which he pleaseth; for GOD is almighty. Now have we sent down evident signs: and GOD directeth whom he pleaseth into the right way. The *hypocrites* say, We believe in GOD, and on *his* apostle; and we obey *them*: yet a part of them turneth back, after this; but these are not *really* believers. And when they are summoned before GOD and his apostle, that he may judge between them; behold, a part of them retire: but if the right had been on their side, they would have come and submitted themselves unto him. Is there an infirmity in their hearts? Do they doubt? Or do they fear lest GOD and his apostle act unjustly towards them? But themselves are the unjust doers.[2] The saying of the true believers, when they are summoned before GOD and his apostle, that he may judge between them, is no other than that they say, We have heard, and do obey: and these are they who shall prosper. Whoever shall obey GOD and his apostle, and shall fear GOD, and shall be devout towards him; these shall enjoy great felicity. They swear by GOD, with a most solemn oath, that if thou commandest them, they will go forth *from their houses and possessions.* Say, Swear not *to a falsehood*: obedience *is more* requisite: and GOD is well acquainted with that which ye do. Say, Obey GOD, and obey the apostle: but if ye turn back, verily *it is expected* of him *that he perform* his duty, and of you *that ye perform* your duty;

---

[1] This assertion, which has already occurred in another place (Chap. XXI. p. 243) being not true in strictness, the commentators suppose that by water is meant seed; or else that water is mentioned only as the chief cause of the growth of animals, and a considerable and necessary constituent part of their bodies.

[2] This passage was occasioned by Bashir the hypocrite, who, having a controversy with a Jew, appealed to Caab Ebn al Ashraf, whereas the Jew appealed to Mohammed (Chap. IV. p. 81); or, as others tell us, by Mogheira Ebn Wayel, who refused to submit a dispute he had with Ali to the prophet's decision. (Al Beidâwi.)

and if ye obey him, ye shall be directed : but the duty of *our* apostle is only public preaching. GOD promiseth unto such of you as believe, and do good works, that he will cause them to succeed *the unbelievers* in the earth, as he caused those who were before you to succeed *the infidels of their time ;*[1] and that he will establish for them their religion which pleaseth them, and will change their fear into security. They shall worship me ; and shall not associate any *other* with me. But whoever shall disbelieve after this ; they will be the wicked doers. Observe prayer, and give alms, and obey the apostle : that ye may obtain mercy. Think not that the unbelievers shall frustrate *the designs of* GOD on earth : and their abode *hereafter* shall be *hell* fire ; a miserable journey *shall it be thither* ! O true believers, let your slaves, and those among you who shall not have attained the age of puberty, ask leave of you, *before they come into your presence,* three times *in the day ;*[2] *namely,* before the morning prayer,[3] and when ye lay aside your garments at noon,[4] and after the evening prayer.[5] *These are the* three times for you *to be private* : it shall be no crime in you, or in them, *if they go in to you without asking permission* after these *times,* while ye are in frequent attendance, the one of you on the other. Thus GOD declareth *his* signs unto you ; for GOD *is* knowing *and* wise. And when your children attain *the age of* puberty, let them ask leave *to come into your presence at all times,* in the same manner as those who *have attained that age* before them, ask leave. Thus GOD declareth his signs unto you ; and GOD *is* knowing *and* wise. *As to* such women as are past child-bearing, who hope not to marry *again, because of their advanced age* ; it shall be

---

[1] *i.e.,* As he caused the Israelites to dispossess the Canaanites and other nations.

[2] Because there are certain times when it is not convenient, even for a domestic, or a child, to come in to one without notice. It is said this passage was revealed on account of Asma Bint Morthed, whose servant entered suddenly upon her, at an improper time ; but others say, it was occasioned by Modraj Ebn Amru, then a boy, who, being sent by Mohammed to call Omar to him, went directly into the room where he was, without giving notice, and found him taking his noon's nap, and in no very decent posture ; at which Omar was so ruffled, that he wished GOD would forbid even their fathers, and children, to come in to them abruptly, at such times. (Al Beidâwi.)

[3] Which is the time of people's rising from their beds, and dressing themselves for the day.

[4] That is, when ye take off your upper garments to sleep at noon ; which is a common custom in the East, and all warm countries.

[5] When ye undress yourselves to prepare for bed. Al Beidâwi adds a fourth season, when permission to enter must be asked, *viz.,* at night : but this follows of course.

no crime in them, if they lay aside their *outer* garments, not
showing *their* ornaments ; but if they abstain *from this, it
will be better* for them. GOD *both* heareth *and* knoweth. It
shall be no crime in the blind, nor shall it be any crime in
the lame, neither shall it be any crime in the sick, or in yourselves, that ye eat in your houses,[1] or in the house of your
fathers, or the houses of your mothers, or in the houses of
your brothers, or the houses of your sisters, or the houses of
your uncles on the father's side, or the houses of your aunts
on the father's side, or the houses of your uncles on the
mother's side, or the houses of your aunts on the mother's
side, or *in those houses* the keys whereof ye have in your
possession, or *in the house* of your friend. It shall not be
any crime in you whether ye eat together, or separately.[2]
And when ye enter any houses, salute one another[3] on the
part of GOD, with a blessed and a welcome salutation. Thus
GOD declareth his signs unto you, that ye may understand.
Verily they only *are* true believers, who believe in GOD and
his apostle, and when they are assembled with him on any
affair,[4] depart not, until they have obtained leave of him.
Verily they who ask leave of thee, are those who believe in
GOD and his apostle. When therefore they ask leave of
thee *to depart*, on account of any business of their own,
grant leave unto such of them as thou shalt think fit, and
ask pardon for them of GOD ;[5] for GOD *is* gracious *and* merci-

---

[1] *i.e.*, Where your wives or families are ; or in the houses of your sons,
which may be looked on as your own. This passage was designed to remove
some scruples or superstitions of the Arabs in Mohammed's time ; some of
whom thought their eating with maimed or sick people defiled them ; others
imagined they ought not to eat in the house of another, though ever so nearly
related to them, or though they were entrusted with the key and care of
the house in the master's absence, and might therefore conclude it would
be no offence ; and others declined eating with their friends though invited,
lest they should be burthensome. (Al Beidâwi, Jallolo'ddin.) The whole
passage seems to be no more than a declaration that the things scrupled
were perfectly innocent ; however, the commentators say it is now abrogated, and that it related only to the old Arabs, in the infancy of Mohammedism.
[2] As the tribe of Leith thought it unlawful for a man to eat alone ; and
some of the Ansârs, if they had a guest with them, never ate but in his company ; so there were others who refused to eat with any, out of a superstitious caution lest they should be defiled, or out of a hoggish greediness.
(Al Beidâwi, Jallalo'ddin.)
[3] Literally yourselves ; that is, according to Al Beidâwi, the people of
the house, to whom ye are united by the ties of blood, and by the common
bond of religion. And if there be nobody in the house, says Jallalo'ddin,
salute yourselves, and say, *Peace be on us, and on the righteous servants of
God* : for the angels will return your salutation.
[4] As at public prayers, or a solemn feast, or at council, or on a military
expedition.
[5] Because such departure, though with leave, and on a reasonable excuse,

ful. Let not the calling of the apostle be esteemed among you, as your calling the one to the other.[1] GOD knoweth such of you as privately withdraw themselves *from the assembly*, taking shelter behind one another. But let those who withstand his command, take heed ; lest some calamity befall them *in this world*, or a grievous punishment be inflicted on them *in the life to come*. *Doth* not whatever is in heaven and on earth *belong* unto GOD ? He well knoweth what ye are about : and on a certain day they shall be assembled before him ; and he shall declare unto them that which they have done ; for GOD knoweth all things.

XXV

THE CHAPTER OF AL FORKÂN [2]

Revealed at Mecca.

IN THE NAME OF THE MOST MERCIFUL GOD.

BLESSED be he who hath revealed the Forkân unto his servant, that he may be a preacher unto all creatures : unto whom *belongeth* the kingdom of heaven and of earth : who hath begotten no issue ; and hath no partner in *his* kingdom : *who* hath created all things ; and disposed the same according to his determinate will. Yet have they taken *other* gods besides him ; which have created nothing, but are themselves created,[3] and are able neither to avert evil from, nor to procure good unto themselves ; and have not the power of death, or of life, or of raising *the dead*. And the unbelievers say, This *Korân* is no other than a forgery which he hath contrived ; and other people have

is a kind of failure in the exact performance of their duty ; seeing they prefer their temporal affairs to the advancement of the true religion.　(Al Beidâwi.)

[1] These words are variously interpreted : for their meaning may be, either, Make not light of the apostle's summons, as ye would of another person's of equal condition with yourselves, by not obeying it, or by departing out of, or coming into, his presence without leave first obtained ; or, Think not that when the apostle calls upon God in prayer, it is with him, as with you, when ye prefer a petition to a superior, who sometimes grants but as often denies, your suit ; or, Call not to the apostle, as ye do to one another, that is, by name, or familiarly and with a loud voice ; but make use of some honourable compellation, as, O apostle of GOD, or, O prophet of GOD, and speak in an humble, modest manner.　(Al Beidâwi, Jallalo'ddin, &c.)

[2] Which is one of the names of the Korân, and means, *The Discrimination*, which Palmer adopts as the title of the chapter.　See Sale, Prelim. Disc. Sect. III.

[3] Being either the heavenly bodies ; or idols, the work of men's hands.

assisted him therein :[1] but they utter an unjust thing, and a falsehood. They also say, *These are* fables of the ancients, which he hath caused to be written down ; and they are dictated unto him morning and evening. Say, He hath revealed it, who knoweth the secrets in heaven and earth : verily he is gracious *and* merciful. And they say, What *kind* of apostle is this ? He eateth food, and walketh in the streets,[2] *as we do* : unless an angel be sent down unto him, and become a *fellow* preacher with him ; or *unless* a treasure be cast down unto him ; or he have a garden, *of the fruit* whereof he may eat ; *we will not believe.* The ungodly also say, Ye follow no other than a man who is distracted. Behold, what they liken thee unto. But they are deceived ; neither can they *find a just* occasion *to reproach thee.* Blessed be he, who, if he pleaseth, will make for thee a better *provision* than this *which they speak of, namely,* gardens through which rivers flow : and he will provide thee palaces. But they reject the belief of the hour *of judgment,* as a falsehood : and we have prepared for him, who shall reject the belief of *that* hour, burning fire ; when it shall see them from a distant place, they shall hear it furiously raging, and roaring. And when they shall be cast bound together into a strait place thereof, they shall there call for death : *but it shall be answered them,* Call not this day for one death, but call for many deaths. Say, Is this better, or a garden of eternal duration, which is promised unto the pious ? It shall be *given* unto them for a reward, and a retreat : therein shall they have whatever they please ; continuing *in the same* for ever. *This* is a promise to be demanded at the hands of thy LORD. On a certain day he shall assemble them, whatever they worship besides GOD ; and shall say *unto the worshipped,* Did ye seduce these my servants ; or did they wander *of themselves* from the *right* way ? They shall answer, GOD forbid ! It was not fitting for us, that we should take any protectors besides thee : but thou didst permit them and their fathers to enjoy abundance ; so that

---

[1] See Chap. XVI. p. 267. It is supposed the Jews are particularly intended in this place ; because they used to repeat passages of ancient history to Mohammed, on which he used to discourse and make observations. (Al Beidâwi.)

[2] Being subject to the same wants and infirmities of nature, and obliged to submit to the same low means of supporting himself and his family, with ourselves. The Meccans were acquainted with Mohammed, and with his circumstances and way of life, too well to change their old familiarity into the reverence due to the messenger of GOD : for a prophet hath no honour in his own country.

they forgot *thy* admonition, and became lost people. *And God shall say unto their worshippers,* Now have these convinced you of falsehood, in that which ye say : they can neither avert *your punishment,* nor *give you* any assistance. And whoever of you shall be guilty of injustice, him will we cause to taste a grievous torment. We have sent no messengers before thee, but they ate food, and walked through the streets : and we make some of you an occasion of trial unto others.[1]   Will ye persevere with patience ? since your LORD regardeth *your perseverance.* (XIX.)[2] They who hope not to meet us *at the resurrection* say, Unless the angels be sent down unto us, or we see our LORD *himself, we will not believe.* Verily they behave themselves arrogantly ; and have transgressed with an enormous transgression. The day *whereon* they shall see the angels, there shall be no glad tidings on that day for the wicked ; and they shall say, *Be this* removed far from us ! and we will come unto the work which they shall have wrought, and we will make it *as* dust scattered abroad. On that day shall they who are destined to paradise be more happy in an abode, and have a preferable place of repose at noon.[3] On that day the heaven shall be cloven in sunder by the clouds, and the angels shall be sent down, descending *visibly therein.*[4]   On that day the kingdom shall of right belong wholly unto the Merciful ; and that day shall be grievous for the unbelievers. On that day, the unjust person[5] shall

---

[1] Giving occasion of envy, repining, and malice ; to the poor, mean, and sick, for example, when they compare their own condition with that of the rich, the noble, and those who are in health : and trying the people to whom prophets are sent, by those prophets. (Al Beidâwi, Jallal.)

[2] The nineteenth section begins here.

[3] For the business of the day of judgment will be over by that time ; and the blessed will pass their noon in paradise, and the damned in hell. (Al Beidâwi.)

[4] *i.e.*, They shall part and make way for the clouds which shall descend with the angels, bearing the books wherein every man's actions are recorded.

[5] It is supposed by some that these words particularly relate to Okba Ebn Abi Moait, who used to be much in Mohammed's company, and having once invited him to an entertainment, the prophet refused to taste of his meat unless he would profess Islâm ; which accordingly he did. Soon after, Okba, meeting Obba Ebn Khalf, his intimate friend, and being reproached by him for changing his religion, assured him that he had not, but had only pronounced the profession of faith to engage Mohammed to eat with him, because he could not for shame let him go out of his house without eating. However, Obba protested that he would not be satisfied, unless he went to Mohammed, and set his foot on his neck, and spit in his face : which Okba, rather than break with his friend, performed in the public hall, where he found Mohammed sitting ; whereupon the prophet told him that if ever he met him out of Mecca, he would cut off his head. And he was as good as his word : for Okba, being afterwards taken prisoner at the battle of Bedr,

bite his hands *for anguish and despair, and* shall say, O that I had taken the way *of truth* with the apostle! Alas for me! O that I had not taken such a one[1] for *my* friend! He seduced me from the admonition *of God*, after it had come unto me: for the devil is the betrayer of man. And the apostle shall say, O LORD, verily my people esteemed this Korân *to be* a vain *composition*. In like manner did we ordain unto every prophet an enemy from among the wicked: but thy LORD is a sufficient director, and defender. The unbelievers say, Unless the Korân be sent down unto him entire at once,[2] *we will not believe. But* in this manner *have we revealed it*, that we might confirm thy heart thereby,[3] and we have dictated it gradually, by distinct parcels. They shall not come unto thee with any strange question; but we will bring thee the truth *in answer*, and a most excellent interpretation. They who shall be dragged on their faces into hell, shall be in the worst condition, and shall stray most widely from the way *of salvation*. We heretofore delivered unto Moses the book *of the law*; and we appointed him Aaron his brother for a counsellor. And we said *unto them*, Go ye to the people who charge our signs with falsehood. And we destroyed them with a *signal* destruction. *And remember* the people of Noah, when they accused *our* apostles of imposture: we drowned them, and made them a sign unto mankind. And we have prepared for the unjust a painful torment. *Remember* also Ad, and Thamûd, and those who dwelt at Al Rass;[4] and many

had his head struck off by Ali at Mohammed's command. As for Obba, he received a wound from the prophet's own hand, at the battle of Ohod, of which he died on his return to Mecca. (Al Beidâwi. Vide Gagnier, Vie de Mahom. vol. 1, p. 362.)

[1] According to the preceding note, this was Obba Ebn Khalf.

[2] As were the Pentateuch, Psalms, and Gospel, according to the Mohammedan notion; whereas it was twenty-three years before the Korân was completely revealed. (Sale, Prelim. Disc. Sect. III.)

[3] Both to infuse courage and constancy into thy mind, and to strengthen thy memory and understanding. For, say the commentators, the prophet's receiving the divine direction, from time to time, how to behave, and to speak, on any emergency, and the frequent visits of the angel Gabriel, greatly encouraged and supported him under all his difficulties: and the revealing of the Korân by degrees was a great, and to him, a necessary help for his retaining and understanding it; which it would have been impossible for him to have done with any exactness, had it been revealed at once; Mohammed's case being entirely different from that of Moses, David, and Jesus, who could all read and write, whereas he was perfectly illiterate. (Al Beidâwi, &c.)

[4] The commentators are at a loss where to place Al Rass. According to one opinion it was the name of a well (as the word signifies) near Midian, about which some idolaters having fixed their habitations, the prophet Shoaib was sent to preach to them; but they not believing on him, the

other generations, within this *period*. Unto each *of them* did we propound examples *for their admonition* ; and each *of them* did we destroy with an *utter* destruction. *The Koreish* have passed *frequently* near the city which was rained on by a fatal rain ;[1] have they not seen *where* it *once stood* ? Yet have they not dreaded the resurrection. When they see thee, they will receive thee only with scoffing, *saying*, Is this he, whom GOD hath sent *as his* apostle ? Verily he had almost drawn us aside from *the worship of* our gods ; if we had not firmly persevered *in our devotion* towards them. But they shall know hereafter, when they shall see the punishment *prepared for them*, who hath strayed more widely from the *right* path. What thinkest thou ? He who taketh his lust for his god ; canst thou be his guardian ?[2] Dost thou imagine that the greater part of them hear, or understand ? They are no other than like the *brute* cattle ; yea, they stray more widely from the *true* path. Dost thou not consider *the works of* thy LORD, how he stretcheth forth the shadow *before sunrise* ? If he had pleased, he would have made it immovable *for ever*. Then we cause the sun to *rise, and to* show the same ; *and* afterwards we contract it by an easy *and gradual* contraction. It is he who hath ordained the night to *cover* you *as* a garment ; and sleep *to give you* rest ; and hath ordained the day for waking. It is he who sendeth the winds, driving abroad the pregnant clouds, as the forerunners of his mercy :[3] and we send down pure water[4] from heaven, that we may thereby revive

well fell in, and they and their houses were all swallowed up. Another supposes it to have been a town in Yamâma, where a remnant of the Thamûdites settled, to whom a prophet was also sent ; but they, slaying him, were utterly destroyed. Another thinks it was a well near Antioch, where Habîb al Najjâr (whose tomb is still to be seen there, being frequently visited by the Mohammedans) was martyred (Abulf. Geog. Vide Vit. Saladini, p. 86). And a fourth takes Al Rass to be a well in Hadramaut, by which dwelt some idolatrous Thamûdites, whose prophet was Handha, or Khantala (for I find the name written both ways) Ebn Safwân (Chap. XXII.). These people were first annoyed by certain monstrous birds, called Ankâ, which lodged in the mountain above them, and used to snatch away their children, when they wanted other prey : but this calamity was so far from humbling them, that on their prophet's calling down a judgment upon them, they killed him, and were all destroyed. (Al Beidâwi, Jallalo'ddin.)

[1] viz., Sodom ; for the Koreish often passed by the place where it once stood, in the journeys they took to Syria for the sake of trade.

[2] *i.e.*, Dost thou expect to reclaim such a one from idolatry and infidelity ?

[3] See Chap. VII. p. 145. There is the same various reading here as is mentioned in the notes to that passage.

[4] Properly, *purifying* water ; which epithet may perhaps refer to the cleansing quality of that element, of so great use both on religious and on common occasions.

a dead country, and give to drink thereof unto what we have created, both of cattle and men, in great numbers ;[1] and we distribute the same among them at various times, that they may consider : but the greater part of men refuse *to consider*, only out of ingratitude.[2] If we had pleased, we had sent a preacher unto every city :[3] wherefore do not thou obey the unbelievers ; but oppose them herewith, with a strong opposition. It is he who hath let loose the two seas ; this fresh *and* sweet, and that salt *and* bitter : and hath placed between them a bar,[4] and a bound which cannot be passed. It is he who hath created man of water ;[5] and hath made him *to bear the double relation of* consanguinity and affinity ; for the LORD is powerful. They worship, besides GOD, that which can neither profit them nor hurt them : and the unbeliever is an assistant *of the devil* against his LORD.[6] We have sent thee *to be* no other than a bearer of good tidings, and a denouncer of threats. Say, I ask not of you any reward for this *my preaching* ; besides *the conversion* of him who shall desire to take the way unto his LORD.[7] And do thou trust in him who liveth, and dieth not ; and celebrate his praise : (he is sufficiently acquainted with the faults of his servants :) who hath created the heavens and the earth, and whatever is between them, in six days ; and then ascended *his* throne ; the Merciful. Ask now the knowing concerning him. When it is said unto *the unbelievers*, Adore the Merciful ; they reply, And who *is* the Merciful ?[8] Shall we adore that which thou commandest

[1] That is, To such as live in the dry deserts, and are obliged to drink rain-water ; which the inhabitants of towns, and places well-watered, have no occasion to do.

[2] Or, out of *infidelity* : for the old Arabs used to think themselves indebted for their rains, not to GOD, but to the influence of some particular stars.

[3] And had not given thee, O Mohammed, the honour and trouble of being a preacher to the whole world in general. (Sale, Prelim. Disc. Sect. IV. p. 76.)

[4] To keep them asunder, and prevent their mixing with each other. The original word is *barzakh* ; which has been already explained. (In not. to Chap. XXIII. p. 341.)

[5] With which Adam's primitive clay was mixed ; or, of *seed*. See Chap. XXIV.

[6] Joining with him in his rebellion and infidelity. Some think Abu Jahl is particularly struck at in this passage. The words may also be translated, *The unbeliever is contemptible in the sight of his Lord*.

[7] Seeking to draw near unto him, by embracing the religion taught by *ine* his apostle ; which is the best return I expect from you for my labours. (Al Beidâwi.) The passage, however, is capable of another meaning, viz., that Mohammed desires none to give, but him who shall contribute freely and voluntarily towards the advancement of GOD's true religion.

[8] See Chap. XVII. p. 283.

us ? And this *precept* causeth them to fly the faster *from the faith*. Blessed be he who hath placed *the twelve* signs in the heavens ; and hath placed therein a lamp[1] *by day*, and the moon which shineth *by night* ! It is he who hath ordained the night and the day to succeed each other, for *the observation of* him who will consider, or desireth *to show his* gratitude. The servants of the Merciful are those who walk meekly on the earth, and, when the ignorant speak unto them, answer, Peace :[2] and who pass the night adoring their LORD, and standing up *to pray unto him ;* and who say, O LORD, avert from us the torment of hell, for the torment thereof *is* perpetual ; verily the same is a miserable abode, and *a wretched* station : and who, when they bestow, are neither profuse nor niggardly ; but *observe* a just medium between these ;[3] and who invoke not another god together with *the true* GOD ; neither slay the soul, which GOD hath forbidden *to be slain*, unless for a just cause : and who are not guilty of fornication. But he who shall do this, shall meet the reward of *his* wickedness : *his* punishment shall be doubled unto him on the day of resurrection ; and he shall remain therein, covered with ignominy, *for ever* : except him who shall repent, and believe, and shall work a righteous work ; unto them will GOD change their *former* evils into good ;[4] for GOD is ready to forgive, *and* merciful. And whoever repenteth, and doth that which is right ; verily he turneth unto GOD with an *acceptable* conversion. And they who do not bear false witness ; and when they pass by vain discourse, pass by the same with decency : and who, when they are admonished by the signs of their LORD, fall not down *as if they were* deaf and blind, *but stand up and are attentive* thereto : and who say, O LORD, grant us of our wives and our offspring such as may be the satisfaction of *our* eyes ; and make us patterns unto those who fear *thee*. These shall be rewarded with the highest apartments *in paradise*, because they have persevered with constancy ; and they shall meet therein with greeting and salutation ; they shall remain in the same for ever : it shall be an excellent abode and a *delightful* station. Say, My LORD is not solicitous on your account, if ye do not invoke him : ye

---

[1] *i.e.*, The sun.
[2] This is intended here not as a salutation, but as a waiving all further discourse and communication with the idolaters.
[3] See Chap. XVII.
[4] Blotting out their former rebellion, on their repentance, and confirming and increasing their faith and obedience. (Al Beidâwi.)

have already charged *his apostle* with imposture ; but hereafter shall there be a lasting punishment *inflicted on you.*

XXVI

IN THE NAME OF THE MOST MERCIFUL GOD.

T S. M.[3] These *are* the signs of the perspicuous book.
. Peradventure thou afflictest thyself unto death,
lest *the Meccans* become not true believers. If we pleased,
we could send down unto them a *convincing* sign from heaven,
unto which their necks would humbly submit. But there
cometh unto them no admonition from the Merciful, being
newly revealed *as occasions require,* but they turn aside from
the same ; and they have charged *it* with falsehood : but a
message shall come unto them, which they shall not laugh
to scorn. Do they not behold the earth, how many *vegetables* we cause to spring up therein, of every noble species ?
Verily herein is a sign : but the greater part of them do not
believe. Verily thy LORD is the mighty, the merciful *God.*
Remember when thy LORD called Moses, *saying,* Go to the
unjust people, the people of Pharaoh ; will they not dread
me ? *Moses* answered, O LORD, verily I fear lest they accuse
me of falsehood, and lest my breast become straitened, and
my tongue be not ready *in speaking* :[4] send therefore unto
Aaron, *to be my assistant.* Also they have a crime *to object*
against me ;[5] and I fear they will put me to death. *God*
said, *They shall* by no means *put thee to death* : wherefore
go ye with our signs ; for we *will be* with you, *and will* hear
what passes between you and them. Go ye therefore unto
Pharaoh, and say, Verily we are the apostle[6] of the LORD
of all creatures : send away with us the children of Israel.
And when they had delivered their message, Pharaoh answered,

[1] The chapter bears this inscription because at the conclusion of it the
Arabian poets are severely censured.
[2] The five last verses, beginning at these words, *And those who err follow
the poets,* &c., some take to have been revealed at Medina.
[3] See Sale, Prelim. Disc. Sect. III. p. 64.
[4] See Chap XX. p. 306.
[5] viz., The having killed an Egyptian. (See Chap. XXVIII.)
[6] The word is in the singular number in the original ; for which the
commentators give several reasons.

Have we not brought thee up among us, *when* a child ; and hast thou not dwelt among us for *several* years of thy life ?[1] Yet hast thou done thy deed which thou hast done : and thou art an ungrateful person. *Moses* replied, I did it indeed, and I was *one* of those who erred ;[2] wherefore I fled from you, because I feared you : but my LORD hath bestowed on me wisdom, and hath appointed me *one* of *his* apostles. And this is the favour which thou hast bestowed on me, that thou hast enslaved the children of Israel. Pharaoh said, And who is the LORD of all creatures ? *Moses* answered, The LORD of heaven and earth, and of whatever is between them : if ye are men of sagacity. *Pharaoh* said unto those who were about him, Do ye not hear ? *Moses* said, Your LORD, and the LORD of your forefathers. *Pharaoh* said *unto those who were present*, Your apostle, who is sent unto you, is certainly distracted.[3] *Moses* said, The LORD of the east, and of the west, and of whatever is between them ; if ye are men of understanding. *Pharaoh* said unto him, Verily if thou take any god besides me,[4] I will make thee *one* of those who are imprisoned.[5] *Moses* answered, What, although I come unto you with a convincing *miracle* ? *Pharaoh* replied, Produce it, therefore, if thou speakest truth. And he cast down his rod, and behold, it *became* a visible serpent : and he drew forth his hand *out of his bosom* ; and behold, it *appeared* white unto the spectators. *Pharaoh* said unto the princes *who were* about him, Verily this *man* is a skilful magician : he seeketh to dispossess you of your land by his sorcery ; what therefore do ye direct ? They answered, Delay him and his brother *by good words for a time* ; and send through the cities *men* to assemble and

---

[1] It is said that Moses dwelt among the Egyptians 30 years, and then went to Midian, where he stayed 10 years ; after which he returned to Egypt, and spent 30 years in endeavouring to convert them ; and that he lived after the drowning of Pharaoh 50 years. (Al Beidâwi.)

[2] Having killed the Egyptian undesignedly.

[3] Pharaoh, it seems, thought Moses had given but wild answers to his question : for he wanted to know the person and true nature of the GOD whose messenger Moses pretended to be ; whereas he spoke of his works only. And because this answer gave so little satisfaction to the king, he is therefore supposed by some to have been a Dahrite, or one who believed in the eternity of the world. (Al Beidâwi.)

[4] From this and a parallel expression in the twenty-eighth chapter, it is inferred that Pharaoh claimed the worship of his subjects, as due to his supreme power.

[5] These words, says Al Beidâwi, were a more terrible menace than if he had said *I will imprison thee* ; and gave Moses to understand that he must expect to keep company with those wretches whom the tyrant had thrown, as was his custom, into a deep dungeon, where they remained till they died.

bring unto thee every skilful magician. So the magicians were assembled at an appointed time, on a solemn day. And it was said unto the people, Are ye assembled together ? Perhaps we may follow the magicians, if they do get the victory. And when the magicians were come, they said unto Pharaoh, Shall we certainly receive a reward, if we do get the victory ? He answered, Yea ; and ye shal! surely be of those who approach *my person*. Moses said unto them, Cast down what ye are about to cast down. Wherefore they cast down their ropes and their rods, and said, By the might of Pharaoh, verily we *shall be* the conquerors. And Moses cast down his rod, and behold, it swallowed up that which they had *caused* falsely *to appear* changed *into serpents*. Whereupon the magicians prostrated themselves, worshipping, *and* said, We believe in the LORD of all creatures, the LORD of Moses and of Aaron. *Pharaoh* said *unto them*, Have ye believed on him, before I have given you permission ? Verily he is your chief, who hath taught you magic :[1] but hereafter ye shall surely know *my power*. I will cut off your hands and your feet, on the opposite sides, and I will crucify you all. They answered, *It will be* no harm *unto us* ; for we shall return unto our LORD. We hope that our LORD will forgive us our sins, since we are the first who have believed.[2] And we spake by revelation unto Moses, *saying*, March forth with my servants by night ; for ye will be pursued. And Pharaoh sent *officers* through the cities to assemble *forces, saying*, Verily these are a small company ; and they are enraged against us : but we are a multitude well provided. So we caused them to quit *their* gardens, and fountains, and treasures, and fair dwellings : thus *did we do* ; and we made the children of Israel to inherit the same.[3] And they pursued them at sunrise. And when the two armies were come in sight of each other, the companions of Moses said, We shall surely be overtaken. *Moses* answered, By no means ; for my LORD *is* with me, who will surely direct me. And we commanded Moses by revelation, *saying*, Smite the sea with thy rod. And *when he had smitten it*, it became divided *into twelve parts, between which*

---

[1] But has reserved the most efficacious secrets to himself. (Al Beidâwi.)
[2] See Chap. VII. p. 154.
[3] Hence some suppose the Israelites, after the destruction of Pharaoh and his host, returned to Egypt, and possessed themselves of the riches of that country (Jallalo'ddin, Yahya). But others are of opinion that the meaning is no more than that GOD gave them the like possessions and dwellings in another country (Al Zamakh. See Chap. VII.).

were as many paths, and every part was like a vast mountain. And we drew thither the others ; and we delivered Moses and all those who were with him : then we drowned the others. Verily herein was a sign ; but the greater part of them did not believe. Verily thy LORD is the mighty, *and* the merciful. And rehearse unto them the story of Abraham : when he said unto his father and his people, What do ye worship ? They answered, We worship idols ; and we constantly serve them all the day long. *Abraham* said, Do they hear you, when ye invoke *them* ? Or do they either profit you, or hurt you ? They answered, But we found our fathers do the same. He said, What think ye ? *The gods* which ye worship, and your forefathers *worshipped,* are my enemy : except only the LORD of all creatures, who hath created me and directeth me ; and who giveth me to eat and to drink, and when I am sick, healeth me ; and who will cause me to die, and will afterwards restore me to life ; and who, I hope, will forgive my sins on the day of judgment. O LORD, grant me wisdom ; and join me with the righteous ; and grant that I may be spoken of with honour[1] among the latest *posterity* ; and make me an heir of the garden of delight : and forgive my father, for that he hath been *one* of those who go astray.[2] And cover me not with shame on the day of resurrection ; on the day *in which* neither riches nor children shall avail, unless unto him who shall come unto GOD with a sincere heart : *when* paradise shall be brought near to *the view of* the pious, and hell shall appear plainly to those who shall have erred ; and it shall be said unto them, Where *are your deities* which ye served besides GOD ? will they deliver you *from punishment,* or will they deliver themselves ? And they shall be cast into the same, *both* they,[3] and those who have been seduced *to their worship* ; and all the host of Eblîs. The *seduced* shall dispute therein *with their false gods,* saying, By GOD, we were in a manifest error, when we equalled you with the LORD of all creatures : and none seduced us but the wicked. We have *now* no intercessors, nor any friend who careth *for*

---

[1] Literally, *Grant me a tongue of truth,* that is, a high encomium. The same expression is used in Chap. XIX.

[2] By disposing him to repentance, and the receiving of the true faith. Some suppose Abraham pronounced this prayer after his father's death, thinking that possibly he might have been inwardly a true believer, but have concealed his conversion for fear of Nimrod, and before he was forbidden to pray for him. (See Chaps. IX. and XIV.)

[3] See Chap. XXI.

us. If we were allowed to return once more *into the world*, we would certainly become true believers. Verily herein was a sign : but the greater part of them believed not. Thy LORD is the mighty, the merciful. The people of Noah accused *God's* messengers of imposture : when their brother Noah said unto them, Will ye not fear *God* ? Verily I am a faithful messenger unto you ; wherefore fear GOD and obey me. I ask no reward of you for *my preaching unto you* ; *I expect* my reward from no other than the LORD of all creatures : wherefore fear GOD, and obey me. They answered, Shall we believe on thee, when *only* the most abject *persons* have followed thee ? *Noah* said, I have no knowledge of that which they did ;[1] *it appertaineth* unto my LORD alone to bring them to account, if ye understand ; wherefore I will not drive away the believers :[2] I am no more than a public preacher. They replied, Assuredly, unless thou desist, O Noah, thou shalt be stoned. He said, O LORD, verily my people take me for a liar : wherefore judge publicly between me and them ; and deliver me and the true believers who are with me. Wherefore we delivered him, and those who were with him, in the ark filled *with men and animals* ; and afterwards we drowned the rest. Verily herein was a sign : but the greater part of them believed not. Thy LORD is the mighty, the merciful. *The tribe of* Ad charged *God's* messengers with falsehood : when their brother Hûd said unto them, Will ye not fear *God* ? Verily I am a faithful messenger unto you ; wherefore fear GOD, and obey me. I demand not of you any reward for *my preaching unto you* : *I expect* my reward from no other than the LORD of all creatures. Do ye build a landmark on every high place, to divert yourselves ?[3] And do ye erect *magnificent* works, *hoping* that ye may continue *in their possession* for ever ? And when ye exercise your power, do ye exercise it with cruelty and rigour ?[4] Fear GOD, *by leaving these things* ; and obey me. And fear him who hath bestowed on you that which ye know ; he hath bestowed on you cattle, and children, and gardens, and springs of

---

[1] *i.e.*, Whether they have embraced the faith which I have preached, out of the sincerity of their hearts, or in prospect of some worldly advantage.

[2] See Chap. XI. p. 213.

[3] Or to mock the wayfarers who direct themselves in their journeys by the stars. and have no need of such buildings ? (Al Beidâwi.)

[4] Putting to death, and inflicting other corporal punishments without mercy, and rather for the satisfaction of your passion than the amendment of the sufferer. (Al Beidâwi.)

water. Verily I fear for you the punishment of a grievous day. They answered, It is equal unto us whether thou admonish us, or dost not admonish *us* : this *which thou preachest* is only a device of the ancients ; neither shall we be punished *for what we have done*. And they accused him of imposture : wherefore we destroyed them. Verily herein was a sign : but the greater part of them believed not. Thy LORD is the mighty, the merciful. *The tribe of* Thamûd *also* charged the messengers *of God* with falsehood. When their brother Sâleh said unto them, Will ye not fear *God* ? Verily I am a faithful messenger unto you : where-fore fear GOD, and obey me. I demand no reward of you for *my preaching unto you ; I expect* my reward from no other than the LORD of all creatures. Shall ye be left *for ever* secure in *the possession of* the things which *are* here ; among gardens, and fountains, and corn, and palm-trees, whose branches sheathe their flowers ? And will ye *continue to* cut habitations *for yourselves* out of the mountains, behaving with insolence ?[1] Fear GOD, and obey me ; and obey not the command of the transgressors, who act corruptly in the earth, and reform not *the same*. They answered, Verily thou art distracted : thou art no *other* than a man like unto us : produce now some sign, if thou speakest truth. *Sâleh* said, This she-camel *shall be a sign unto you* : she shall have *her* portion of water, and ye shall have *your* portion of water *alternately*, on a *several* day appointed *for you* ;[2] and do her no hurt, lest the punishment of a terrible day be inflicted on you. But they slew her ; and were made to repent *of their impiety* : for the punishment *which had been threatened* overtook them. Verily herein was a sign ; but the greater part of them did not believe. Thy LORD is the mighty, the merciful. The people of Lot *likewise* accused *God's* messengers of imposture. When their brother Lot said unto them, Will ye not fear *God* ? Verily I am a faithful messenger unto you : wherefore fear GOD, and obey me. I demand no reward of you for *my preaching : I expect* my reward from no other than the LORD of all creatures. Do ye approach unto the males among mankind, and leave your wives which your LORD hath created for you ? Surely, ye are people who transgress. They answered, Unless

---

[1] Or, as the original word may also be rendered, *showing art and ingenuity* in your work.

[2] That is, they were to have the use of the water by turns, the camel drinking one day, and the Thamûdites drawing the other day ; for when this camel drank, she emptied the wells or brooks for that day. See Chap. VII. p. 149.

thou desist, O Lot, thou shalt certainly be expelled *our city*. He said, Verily I am *one* of those who abhor your doings : O LORD deliver me and my family, from that which they do. Wherefore we delivered him, and all his family ; except an old woman, *his wife, who perished* among those who remained behind : then we destroyed the rest ; and we rained on them a shower *of stones* ; and terrible was the shower *which fell on* those who had been warned *in vain*. Verily herein was a sign ; but the greater part of them did not believe. Thy LORD is the mighty, the merciful. The inhabitants of the wood[1] *also* accused GOD's messengers of imposture. When Shoaib said unto them, Will ye not fear *God* ? Verily I am a faithful messenger unto you : wherefore fear GOD, and obey me. I ask no reward of you for *my preaching* : *I expect* my reward from no other than the LORD of all creatures. Give just measure, and be not defrauders ; and weigh with an equal balance ; and diminish not unto men *aught* of their matters ; neither commit violence in the earth, acting corruptly. And fear him who hath created you, and *also* the former generations. They answered, Certainly thou art distracted : thou art no more than a man, like unto us ; and we do surely esteem thee to be a liar. Cause now a part of the heaven to fall upon us, if thou speakest truth. *Shoaib* said, My LORD best knoweth that which ye do. And they charged him with falsehood : wherefore the punishment of the day of the shadowing cloud[2] overtook them ; *and* this was the punishment of a grievous day. Verily herein was a sign ; but the greater part of them did not believe. Thy LORD is the mighty, the merciful. This *book* is certainly a revelation from the LORD of all creatures, which the faithful spirit[3] hath caused to descend upon thy heart, that thou mightest be a preacher *to thy people,* in the perspicuous Arabic tongue : and it is *borne witness to* in the scriptures of former ages. Was it not a sign unto them, that the wise men among the children of Israel knew it ? Had we revealed

[1] See Chap. XV. p. 255. Shoaib being not called the *brother* of these people, which would have preserved the conformity between this passage and the preceding, it has been thought they were not Midianites, but of another race ; however, we find the p ophet taxes them with the same crimes as he did those of Midian. (Chap. VII.)

[2] GOD first plagued them with such intolerable heat for seven days that all their waters were dried up, and then brought a cloud over them, under whose shade they ran, and were all destroyed by a hot wind and fire which proceeded from it. (Al Beidâwi.)

[3] *i.e.,* Gabriel, who is entrusted with the divine secrets and revelations.

it unto any of the foreigners, and he had read the same unto them, yet they would not have believed therein. Thus have we caused *obstinate infidelity* to enter the hearts of the wicked : they shall not believe therein, until they see a painful punishment. It shall come suddenly upon them, and they shall not foresee it : and they shall say, Shall we be respited ? Do they therefore desire our punishment to be hastened ?[1] What thinkest thou ? If we suffer them to enjoy *the advantage of this life* for several years, and afterwards that with which they are threatened come upon them ; what will that which they have enjoyed profit them ? We have destroyed no city, but preachers *were first sent* unto it, to admonish *the inhabitants thereof* ; neither did we treat *them* unjustly. The devils did not descend with the *Korân, as the infidels give out* : it is not for their purpose, neither are they able *to produce such a book* ; for they are far removed from hearing *the discourse of the angels in heaven.*[2] Invoke no other god with *the true* GOD, lest thou become *one* of those who are doomed to punishment. And admonish thy more near relations.[3] And behave thyself with meekness[4] towards the true believers who follow thee : and if they be disobedient unto thee, say, Verily I am clear of that which ye do. And trust in the most mighty, the merciful *God* ; who seeth thee when thou risest up, and thy behaviour among those who worship ;[5] for he *both* heareth *and* knoweth. Shall I declare unto you upon whom the devils descend ?

[1] The infidels were continually defying Mohammed to bring some signal and miraculous destruction on them, as a shower of stones, &c.

[2] See Chap. XV.

[3] The commentators suppose the same command to have been virtually contained in the 74th chapter, which is prior to this in point of time. (See the notes thereon, and Sale, Prelim. Disc. Sect II. p. 46.) It is said that Mohammed, on receiving the passage before us, went up immediately to Mount Safâ, and having called the several families to him, one by one, when they were all assembled, asked them whether, if he should tell them tha. mountain would bring forth a smaller mountain, they would believe him ; to which they answering in the affirmative, *Verily*, says he, *I am a warner sent unto you, before a severe chastisement.* (Al Beidâwi.)

[4] Literally, "lower thy wing."

[5] *i.e.*, Who seeth thee when thou risest up to watch and spend the night in religious exercises, and observeth thy anxious care for the Moslems' exact performance of their duty. It is said that the night on which the precept of watching was abrogated, Mohammed went privately from one house to another, to see how his companions spent the time ; and that he found them so intent in reading the Korân, and repeating their prayers, that their houses, by reason of the humming noise they made, seemed to be so many nests of hornets. (Al Beidâwi.) Some commentators, however, suppose that by the prophet's *behaviour*, in this place, are meant the various postures he used in praying at the head of his companions ; as standing, bowing, prostration, and sitting. (Al Beidâwi, Jallalo'ddin.)

They descend upon every lying *and* wicked person :[1] they learn what is heard ;[2] but the greater part of them *are* liars. And those who err follow the *steps of the poets* : dost thou not see that they rove *as bereft of their senses* through every valley, and that they say that which they do not ?[3] except those who believe, and do good works, and remember GOD frequently ; and who defend themselves, after they have been unjustly treated.[4] And they who act unjustly shall know hereafter, with what treatment they shall be treated.

XXVII

THE CHAPTER OF THE ANT [5]

Revealed at Mecca.

IN THE NAME OF THE MOST MERCIFUL GOD.

T S. These *are* the signs of the Korân, and of the . perspicuous book : a direction, and good tidings unto the true believers ; who regularly perform *their* prayer, and

---

[1] The prophet, having vindicated himself from the charge of having communication with the devils, by the opposition between his doctrine and their designs, and their inability to compose so consistent a book as the Korân, proceeds to show that the persons most likely to a correspondence with those evil spirits were liars and slanderers, that is, his enemies and opposers.

[2] *i.e.*, They are taught by the secret inspiration of the devils, and receive their idle and inconsistent suggestions for truth. It being uncertain whether the *slanderers* or the *devils* be the nominative case to the verb, the words may also be rendered, *They impart what they hear* ; that is, The devils acquaint their correspondents on earth with such incoherent scraps of the angels' discourse as they can hear by stealth. (Al Beidâwi.)

[3] Their compositions being as wild as the actions of a distracted man : for most of the ancient poetry was full of vain imaginations ; as fabulous stories and descriptions, love verses, flattery, excessive commendations of their patrons, and as excessive reproaches of their enemies, incitements to vicious actions, vainglorious vauntings, and the like. (Al Beidâwi.)

[4] That is, such poets as had embraced Mohammedism ; whose works, free from the profaneness of the former, run chiefly on the praises of GOD, and the establishing his unity, and contain exhortations to obedience and other religious and moral virtues, without any satirical invectives, unless against such as have given just provocations, by having first attacked them, or some others of the true believers, with the same weapons. In this last case, Mohammed saw it was necessary for him to borrow assistance from the poets of his party, to defend himself and religion from the insults and ridicule of the others, for which purpose he employed the pens of Labîd Ebn Rabîa (see Sale, Prel. Disc. Sect. III.), Abda'llah Ebn Rawâha, Hassân Ebn Thabet, and the two Caabs. It is related that Mohammed once said to Caab Ebn Malec, *Ply them with satires ; for, by him in whose hand my soul is, they wound more deeply than arrows.* (Al Beidâwi.)

[5] In this chapter is related, among other strange things, an odd story of the ant, which has therefore been chosen for the title.

give alms, and firmly believe in the life to come. *As to those who believe not in the life to come, we have prepared their works for them* ;[1] and they shall be struck with astonishment *at their disappointment, when they shall be raised again* ; these *are* they whom an evil punishment *awaiteth in this life* ; and in that which is to come they shall be the greatest losers. Thou hast certainly received the Korân from the presence of a wise, a knowing *God. Remember* when Moses said unto his family, Verily I perceive fire : *I* will bring you tidings thereof, or I will bring you a lighted brand, that ye may be warmed.[2]   And when he was come near unto it, *a voice* cried unto him, *saying,* Blessed be he who is in the fire, and whoever is about it ;[3] and praise be unto GOD, the LORD of all creatures ! O Moses, verily I am GOD, the mighty, the wise : cast down now thy rod. And when he saw it, that it moved, as though it *had been* a serpent, he retreated and fled, and returned not. *And* GOD *said*, O Moses, fear not ; for *my* messengers are not disturbed with fear in my sight : except he who shall have done amiss, and shall have afterwards substituted good in lieu of evil ; for I am gracious *and* merciful.[4]   Moreover put thy hand into thy bosom ; it shall come forth white, without hurt : *this shall be one* among the nine signs [5] unto Pharaoh and his people ; for they are a wicked people.   And when our visible signs had come unto them, they said, This is manifest sorcery.   And they denied them, although their souls certainly knew them *to be from God*, out of iniquity and pride : but behold what was the end of the corrupt doers.   We heretofore bestowed knowledge on David and Solomon ; and they said, Praise be unto GOD, who hath made us more excellent than many of his faithful servants ! And Solomon was David's heir ;[6] and he said, O men, we have been

[1] By rendering them pleasing and agreeable to their corrupt natures and inclinations.

[2] See Chap. XX. p. 305.

[3] Some suppose GOD to be intended by the former words, and by the latter, the angels who were present (Yahya) ; others think Moses and the angels are here meant, or all persons in general in this holy plain, and the country round it. (Jallalo'ddin, Al Beidâwi.)

[4] This exception was designed to qualify the preceding assertion, which seemed too general ; for several of the prophets have been subject to sins, though not great ones, before their mission, for which they had reason to apprehend GOD's anger, though they are here assured that their subsequent merits entitle them to his pardon.   It is supposed that Moses's killing the Egyptian undesignedly is hinted at.   (Al Beidâwi.)

[5] See Chap. XVII. p. 282.

[6] Inheriting not only his kingdom, but also the prophetical office, preferably to his other sons, who were nineteen in number.   (Al Beidâwi.)

taught the speech of birds,[1] and have had all things bestowed on us ; this is manifest excellence.   And his armies
were gathered together unto Solomon, *consisting of* genii,[2]
and men, and birds ; and they were led in distinct bands,
until they came unto the valley of ants.[3]   *And* an ant,
seeing the hosts approaching, said, O ants, enter ye into your
habitations, lest Solomon and his army tread you underfoot,
and perceive *it* not.   And *Solomon* smiled, laughing at her
words, and said, O LORD, excite me that I may be thankful
for thy favour, wherewith thou hast favoured me, and my
parents ; and that I may do that which is right, *and* well-
pleasing unto thee : and introduce me, through thy mercy,
into paradise, among thy servants, the righteous.   And he
viewed the birds, and said, What is the reason that I see not
the lapwing ?[4]   Is she absent ?   Verily I will chastise her
with a severe chastisement,[5] or I will put her to death, unless

---

[1] That is, the meaning of their several voices, though not articulate ; of
Solomon's interpretation whereof the commentators give several instances.
(Maracc. not. in loc. p. 511.)

[2] For this fancy, as well as the former, Mohammed was obliged to the
Talmudists (Midrash. Yalkut Shemuni, p. 11, f. 29, et Millium, de Mohammedismo ante Mohammed. p. 232), who, according to their manner, have
interpreted the Hebrew words of Solomon (Eccles. ii. 8), which the English
version renders, *I gat men-singers and women-singers*, as if that prince had
forced *demons* or *spirits* to serve him at his table, and in other capacities ;
and particularly in his vast and magnificent buildings, which they could not
conceive he could otherwise have performed.

[3] The valley seems to be so called from the great numbers of ants which
are found there.   Some place it in Syria, and others in Tâyef.   (Al Beidâwi,
Jallalo'ddin.)

[4] The Arab historians tell us that Solomon, having finished the temple of
Jerusalem, went on pilgrimage to Mecca, where, having stayed as long as he
pleased, he proceeded towards Yaman ; and leaving Mecca in the morning,
he arrived by noon at Sama, and being extremely delighted with the country,
rested there ; but wanting water to make the ablution, he looked among
the birds for the lapwing, called by the Arabs Al Hudbud, whose business
it was to find it ; for it is pretended she was sagacious or sharp-sighted enough
to discover water underground, which the devils used to draw, after she
had marked the place by digging with her bill : they add, that this bird was
then taking a tour in the air, whence, seeing one of her companions alighting,
she descended also, and having had a description given her by the other of
the city of Saba, whence she was just arrived, they both went together to
take a view of the place, and returned soon after Solomon had made the
inquiry which occasioned what follows.   (Al Beidâwi.)   It may be proper
to mention here what the eastern writers fable of the manner of Solomon's
travelling.   They say that he had a carpet of green silk, on which his throne
was placed, being of a prodigious length and breadth, and sufficient for all
his forces to stand on, the men placing themselves on his right hand, and
the spirits on his left ; and that when all were in order, the wind, at his command, took up the carpet, and transported it, with all that were upon it,
wherever he pleased (Chap. XXI.) ; the army of birds at the same time flying
over their heads, and forming a kind of canopy, to shade them from the sun.

By plucking off her feathers, and setting her in the sun, to be tormented
by the insects ; or by shutting her up in a cage.   (Al Beidâwi, Jallalo'ddin.)

she bring me a just excuse. And she tarried not long *before she presented herself unto Solomon*, and said, I have viewed *a country* which thou hast not viewed; and I come unto thee from Saba, with a certain piece of news. I found a woman[1] to reign over them, who is provided with every-thing *requisite for a prince*, and hath a magnificent throne.[2] I found her and her people to worship the sun, besides GOD: and Satan hath prepared their works for them, and hath turned them aside from the way *of truth* (wherefore they are not *rightly* directed), lest they should worship GOD, who bringeth to light that which is hidden in heaven and earth, and knoweth whatever they conceal and whatever they discover. GOD! there is no GOD but he; the LORD of the magnificent throne. *Solomon* said, We shall see whether thou hast spoken the truth, or whether thou art a liar. Go with this my letter, and cast it down unto them; then turn aside from them, and wait *to know* what *answer* they will return. *And when the queen of Saba had received the letter*,[3] she said, O nobles, verily an honourable letter hath been delivered unto me; it is from Solomon, and *this* is *the tenour thereof*: In the name of the most merciful GOD, Rise not up against me: but come, and surrender your-selves unto me.[4] *She* said, O nobles, advise me in my business: I will not resolve on anything, until ye be wit-nesses *and approve* thereof. *The nobles* answered, We are endued with strength, and *are* endued with great prowess in war; but the command *appertaineth* unto thee: see therefore what thou wilt command.[5] She said, Verily

[1] This queen the Arabs name Balkîs: some make her the daughter of Al Hodhâd Ebn Sharhabil (Pocock, Spec. p. 59), and others of Sharahîl Ebn Malec. (Al Beidâwi, &c. D'Herbel. Bibl. Orient. p. 182); but they all agree she was a descendant of Yárab Ebn Kahtân. She is placed the twenty-second in Dr. Pocock's list of the kings of Yaman.

[2] Which the commentators say was made of gold and silver, and crowned with precious stones. But they differ as to the size of it; one making it fourscore cubits long, forty broad, and thirty high; while some say it was fourscore, and others thirty cubits every way.

[3] Jallalo'ddin says that the queen was surrounded by her army when the lapwing threw the letter into her bosom; but Al Beidâwi supposes she was in an apartment of her palace, the doors of which were shut, and that the bird flew in at the window. The former commentator gives a copy of the epistle somewhat more fully than in the text; viz., *From the servant of GOD, Solomon, the son of David, unto Balkîs queen of Saba. In the name of the most merciful GOD. Peace be on him who followeth the true direction. Rise not up against me, but come and surrender yourselves unto me.* He adds that Solomon perfumed this letter with musk, and sealed it with his signet.

[4] Or, *Come unto me and resign yourselves* unto the divine direction, and profess the true religion which I preach.

[5] *i.e.*, Whether thou wilt obey the summons of Solomon, or give us orders to make head against him.

kings, when they enter a city *by force*, waste the same, and abase the most powerful of the inhabitants hereof : and so will *these* do *with us*.   But I will send gifts unto them ; and will wait for what *farther information* those who shall be sent shall bring back.   And when *the queen's ambassador* came unto Solomon,[1] *that prince* said, Will ye present me with riches ?   Verily that which GOD hath given me, is better than what he hath given you, but ye do glory in your gifts.   Return unto *the people of Saba*.   We will surely come unto them with forces, which they shall not be able to with-stand ; and we will drive them out from *their city*, humbled ; and they *shall become* contemptible.   And *Solomon* said, O nobles, which of you will bring unto me her throne, before they come and surrender themselves unto me ?   A terrible genius[2] answered, I will bring it unto thee, before thou arise from thy place :[3] for I am able to *perform* it, and may be trusted.   *And one* with whom was the knowledge of the scriptures[4] said, I will bring it unto thee, in the twinkling of an eye.[5]   And when *Solomon* saw *the throne* placed before him, he said, This is a favour of my LORD, that he may make trial of me, whether I will be grateful, or whether I will be ungrateful : and he who is grateful, is grateful to his own *advantage*, but if any shall be ungrateful, verily my LORD *is* self-sufficient *and* munificent.   *And Solomon* said *unto his servants*, Alter her throne, that she may not know it,

---

[1] Bearing the presents, which they say were five hundred young slaves of each sex, all habited in the same manner, five hundred bricks of gold, a crown enriched with precious stones, besides a large quantity of musk, amber, and other things of value. (Jallalo'ddin.)   Some add that Balkîs, to try whether Solomon was a prophet or no, dressed the boys like girls, and the girls like boys, and sent him, in a casket, a pearl not drilled, and an onyx drilled with a crooked hole ; and that Solomon distinguished the boys from the girls by the different manner of their taking water, and ordered one worm to bore the pearl, and another to pass a thread through the onyx. (Al Beidâwi.)   They also tell us that Solomon, having notice of this embassy, by means of the lapwing, even before they set out, ordered a large square to be enclosed with a wall built of gold and silver bricks, wherein he ranged his forces and attendants to receive them.   (Jallalo'ddin.)

[2] This was an Ifrît, or one of the wicked and rebellious genii ; and his name, says Al Beidâwi, was Dhacwân or Sakhr.

[3] *i.e.*, From thy seat of justice.   For Solomon used to sit in judgment every day till noon.

[4] This person, as is generally supposed, was Asaf the son of Baracnia, Solomon's Wazîr (or Visir), who knew the great or ineffable name of GOD, by pronouncing of which he performed this wonderful exploit (Jallalo'ddin). Others, however, suppose it was Al Khedr, or else Gabriel, or some other angel ; and some imagine it to have been Solomon himself (Al Beidâwi).

[5] The original is, *Before thou canst look at any object, and take thy eye off it.* It is said that Solomon, at Asaf's desire, looked up to heaven, and before he cast his eye downwards, the throne made its way underground, and appeared before him.

to the end we may see whether she be *rightly* directed, or whether she be *one* of those who are not *rightly* directed. And when she was come *unto Solomon*,[1] it was said *unto her*, Is thy throne like this ? She answered, As though it were the same. And we have had knowledge bestowed on us before this, and have been resigned *unto God*.[2] But that which she worshipped, besides GOD, had turned her aside *from the truth* ; for she was of an unbelieving people. It was said unto her, Enter the palace.[3] And when she saw it, she imagined it to be a great water ; and she discovered her legs, *by lifting up her robe to pass through it*.[4] *Whereupon Solomon* said *unto her*, Verily this is a palace evenly floored with glass. *Then* said *the queen*, O LORD, verily I have dealt unjustly with my own soul ; and I resign myself, together with Solomon, unto GOD, the LORD of all creatures.[5] Also we heretofore sent unto *the tribe of* Thamûd their brother Sâleh ; *who said unto them*, Serve ye GOD. And behold they *were divided into* two parties, who disputed among themselves.[6] *Sâleh* said, O my people, why do you hasten evil rather than good ?[7] Unless ye ask pardon of GOD, that ye may obtain mercy, *ye are lost*. They answered, We presage evil from thee, and from those who *are* with thee. *Sâleh* replied, The evil which ye presage is with GOD:[8] but ye *are* a people who are proved *by a vicissitude of prosperity*

[1] For, on the return of her ambassador, she determined to go and submit herself to that prince ; but before her departure, she secured her throne, as she thought, by locking it up in a strong castle, and setting a guard to defend it ; after which she set out, attended by a vast army. (Jallalo'ddin.)

[2] It is uncertain whether these be the words of Balkis, acknowledging her conviction by the wonders she had already seen ; or of Solomon and his people, acknowledging the favour of GOD, in calling them to the true faith before her.

[3] Or, as some understand the word, *the court* before the palace, which Solomon had commanded to be built against the arrival of Balkis ; the floor or pavement being of transparent glass, laid over running water, in which fish were swimming. Fronting this pavement was placed the royal throne, on which Solomon sat to receive the queen. (Jallalo'ddin, Al Beidâwi).

[4] Some Arab writers tell us Solomon had been informed that Balkîs's legs and feet were covered with hair, like those of an ass, of the truth of which he had hereby an opportunity of being satisfied by ocular demonstration.

[5] The queen of Saba having by these words professed Islâm, and renounced idolatry, Solomon had thoughts of making her his wife ; but could not resolve to do it, till the devils had by a depilatory taken off the hair from her legs (Jallalo'ddin). Some (Al Beidâwi), however, will have it that she did not marry Solomon, but a prince of the tribe of Hamdân.

[6] Concerning the doctrine preached by Sâleh ; one party believing on him, and the other treating him as an impostor.

[7] *i. e.*, Why do ye urge and defy the divine vengeance with which ye are threatened, instead of averting it by repentance ?

[8] See Chap. VII., where the Egyptians in the same manner accuse Moses as being the cause of their calamities.

and adversity. And there were nine men in the city, who acted corruptly in the earth, and behaved not with integrity. And they said *unto one another,* Swear ye reciprocally by GOD, that we will fall upon *Sâleh* and his family by night : and afterwards we will say unto him who hath right to avenge his blood, We were not *so much as* present at the destruction of his family ; and we certainly speak the truth. And they devised a plot *against him* : but we devised a plot *against them* ; and they perceived it not. And see what was the issue of their plot :[1] we utterly destroyed them and their whole people ; and these their habitations *remain* empty, because of the injustice which they committed. Verily herein *is* a sign, unto people who understand. And we delivered those who believed and feared GOD. And *remember* Lot, when he said unto his people, Do ye commit a wickedness, though ye see *the heinousness thereof* ? Do ye approach lustfully unto men, leaving the women ? Ye are surely an ignorant people. (XX.)[2] But the answer of his people was no other than that they said, Cast the family of Lot out of your city : for they are men who preserve themselves pure *from the crimes of which ye are guilty.* Wherefore we delivered him and his family, except his wife, whom we decreed *to be one* of those who remained behind *to be destroyed.* And we rained on them a shower *of stones* : and dreadful was the shower which fell on those who had been warned *in vain.* Say, Praise *be* unto GOD ; and peace *be* upon his servants whom he hath chosen ! Is GOD more worthy, or the *false gods* which they associate *with him* ? *Is not* he *to be preferred,* who hath created the heavens and the earth, and sendeth down rain for you from heaven, whereby we cause delicious groves to spring up ? It is not in your power to cause the trees thereof to shoot forth. Is there *any other* god *partner* with *the true* GOD ? Verily these are a people who deviate *from the truth. Is not he more worthy to be adored* who hath established the earth, and hath caused rivers *to flow* through the midst thereof, and placed thereon immovable *mountains,* and set a bar between

---

[1] It is related that Sâleh, and those who believed on him, usually meeting to pray in a certain narrow place between the mountains, the infidels said, *He thinks to make an end of us after three days* (Chap. VII.), *but we will be beforehand with him* ; and that a party of them went directly to the straits above mentioned, thinking to execute their design, but were terribly disappointed ; for instead of catching the prophet, they were caught themselves, their retreat being cut off by a large piece of rock, which fell down at the mouth of the straits, so that they perished there in a miserable manner.

[2] Here begins the twentieth section.

the two seas ?[1]　Is there *any other* god *equal* with *the true*
GOD ?　Yet the greater part of them know *it* not.　*Is not he
more worthy* who heareth the afflicted,[2] when he calleth upon
him, and taketh off the evil *which distressed him* ;　and *who*
hath made you the successors *of your forefathers* in the earth ?
Is there *any other* god *who can be equalled* with *the true* GOD ?
How few consider *these things* !　*Is not he more worthy* who
directeth you in the dark *paths* of the land and of the sea ;
and who sendeth the winds driving abroad the clouds as
the forerunners of his mercy ?[3]　Is there *any other god who
can be equalled* with *the true* GOD ?　Far be GOD from *having*
those *partners in his power*, which ye associate *with him* !
Is not he more worthy, who produceth a creature, and after
it hath been dead restoreth it *to life*, and who giveth you food
from heaven and earth ?　Is there *any other* god with *the
true* GOD, *who doth this* ?　Say, produce your proof *thereof*,
if ye speak truth.　Say, None either in heaven or earth
knoweth that which is hidden, besides GOD :　neither do
they understand when they shall be raised.　However
their knowledge attaineth *some notion* of the life to come :[4]
yet they are in an uncertainty concerning the same ;　yea,
they are blind as to *the real circumstances* thereof.　And the
unbelievers say, When we and our fathers shall have been
reduced to dust, shall we be taken forth *from the grave* ?
Verily we have been threatened with this, *both we* and our
fathers, heretofore.　This *is* no other than fables of the
ancients.　Say *unto them*, Pass through the earth, and see
what hath been the end of the wicked.　And be not thou
grieved for them ;　neither be thou in any concern on account
of *the plots* which they are contriving *against thee*.　And
they say, When *will* this threat *be accomplished*, if ye speak
true ?　Answer, Peradventure some part of that *punishment*, which ye desire to be hastened, may follow close
behind you :　verily thy LORD is endued with indulgence
towards mankind ;　but the greater part of them are not
thankful.　Verily thy LORD knoweth what their breasts
conceal, and what they discover :　and there is nothing
hidden in heaven or on earth, but it *is written* in a clear book.
Verily this Korân declareth unto the children of Israel

[1] See Chap. XXV. p. 358.　The word *barzakh* is not used here, but
another of equivalent import.
[2] Literally, *Him who is driven* by distress to implore GOD's assistance.
[3] See Chap. XXV. p. 357.
[4] Or the words may be translated thus : *Yea, their knowledge faileth as
to the life to come* ; *yea*, &c.

most of those *points* concerning which they disagree :[1]
and it *is* certainly a direction, and a mercy unto the true
believers. Thy LORD will decide the controversy between
them, by his definitive sentence ; and he *is* the mighty,
the wise. Therefore put thy trust in GOD ; for thou art
in the manifest truth. Verily thou shalt not make the
dead to hear, neither shalt thou make the deaf to hear *thy*
call to *the true faith,* when they retire and turn their backs :
neither shalt thou direct the blind *to extricate themselves*
out of their error. Thou shalt make none to hear *thee,*
except him who shall believe in our signs : and they are
wholly resigned *unto us.* When the sentence shall *be ready
to* fall upon them, we will cause a beast[2] to come forth unto
them from out of the earth, which shall speak unto them :[3]
verily men do not firmly believe in our signs. On the
day *of resurrection* we will assemble, out of every nation, a
company of those who shall have charged our signs with
falsehood ; and they shall be prevented from mixing together, until they shall arive *at the place of judgment. And*
GOD shall say *unto them,* Have ye charged my signs with
falsehood, although ye comprehended them not with *your*
knowledge ? Or what is it that ye were doing ? And the
sentence *of damnation* shall fall on them, for that they have
acted unjustly : and they shall not speak *in their own excuse.*
Do they not see that we have ordained the night, that they
may rest therein, and the day giving open light ? Verily
herein *are* signs unto people who believe. On *that* day the
trumpet shall be sounded ; and whoever are in heaven and
on earth shall be struck with terror, except those whom GOD
shall please *to exempt therefrom :*[4] and all shall come before
him, in humble guise. And thou shalt see the mountains,
and shalt think them firmly fixed ; but they shall pass away,

[1] Such as the comparing of GOD to sensible things, or to created beings :
the removing all imperfections from the description of the Deity ; the state
of paradise and hell ; the stories of Ezra and Jesus Christ, &c. (Al Beidâwi.)
[2] The Mohammedans call this beast, whose appearance will be one sign
of the approach of the day of judgment, Al Jassâsa, or the Spy. I have
given the description of her elsewhere (Sale, Prel. Disc. Sect. IV. p. 85), to
which should be added that she is to have two wings.
[3] Or, according to a different reading, viz., *taclimohom* instead of *tocallimo-
hom, who shall wound them.*
[4] See Sale, Prelim. Disc. Sect. IV. p. 88. Some say the only persons
exempted from this general consternation will be the angels Gabriel, Michael,
Israfil, and Azrael (Jallalo'ddin, Al Beidâwi) ; others suppose them to be the
virgins of paradise, and the angels who guard that place and carry
GOD's throne (Al Beidâwi) ; and others will have them to be the martyrs
(Ebn Abbas).

even as the clouds pass away. *This will be* the wòrk of GOD, who hath rightly disposed all things : and he is well acquainted with that which ye do. Whoever shall have wrought righteousness, shall receive *a reward* beyond the desert thereof ; and they shall be secure from the terror of that day ;[1] but whoever shall have wrought evil, shall be thrown on their faces into *hell* fire. Shall ye receive the reward *of any other* than of that which ye shall have wrought ? Verily I am commanded to worship the LORD of this territory *of Mecca*, who hath sanctified the same : unto him *belong* all things. And I am commanded to be a Moslem, and to rehearse the Korân : he who shall be directed *thereby*, will be directed to his own *advantage* ; and *to* him who shall go astray, say, Verily I am a warner *only*. And say, Praise *be* unto GOD ! he will show you his signs,[2] and ye shall know them ; and thy LORD is not regardless of that which they do.

XXVIII

THE CHAPTER OF THE STORY [3]

Revealed at Mecca.[4]

IN THE NAME OF THE MOST MERCIFUL GOD.

T. S. M.[5] These *are* the signs of the perspicuous book. We will dictate unto thee, *O Mohammed, some parts* of the history of Moses and Pharaoh, with truth ; for *the sake of* people who believe. Now Pharaoh lifted himself up in the land *of Egypt* ; and he caused his subjects to be divided into parties :[6] he weakened one party of them,[7] by slaying their male children, and preserving their females alive ; for he was an oppressor. And we were minded to

---

[1] That is, from the fear of damnation, and the other terrors which will disturb the wicked ; not from the general terror or consternation before mentioned.

[2] viz., The successes of the true believers against the infidels, and particularly the victory of Bedr.

[3] The title is taken from the 26th verse, where Moses is said to have related *the story* of his adventures to Shoaib.

[4] Some except a verse towards the latter end, beginning with these words : *He who hath given thee the Korân for a rule of faith and practice*, &c.

[5] See Sale, Prelim. Disc. Sect. III. p. 64.

[6] *i.e.*, Either into companies, that they might the better attend his order and perform the services he exacted of them ; or into opposite factions, to prevent their attempting anything against them, to deliver themselves from his tyranny. (Al Beidâwi.)

[7] viz., The Israelites.

be gracious unto those who were weakened in the land, and
to make them models of religion ; and to make them the
heirs *of the wealth of Pharaoh and his people*,[1] and to establish
a place for them in the earth ; and to show Pharaoh, and
Haman,[2] and their forces, that *destruction of their kingdom
and nation* by them, which they sought to avoid.[3]   And we
directed the mother of Moses by revelation, *saying*, Give
him suck : and if thou fearest for him, cast him into the
river ; and fear not, neither be afflicted ; for we will restore
him unto thee, and we will appoint him *one* of *our* apostles.[4]
And *when she had put the child in the ark, and had cast it into
the river*, the family of Pharaoh took him up ; *providence
designing* that he should become an enemy and a sorrow unto
them.   Verily Pharaoh, and Haman, and their forces were
sinners.   And the wife of Pharaoh said, *This child is* a delight
of the eye to me and to thee :[5] kill him not ; peradventure
it may happen that he may be serviceable unto us ; or we
may adopt him for *our* son.   And they perceived not *the
consequence of what they were doing*.   And the heart of the
mother of Moses became oppressed *with fear* ; and she had
almost discovered him, had we not armed her heart with
constancy, that she might be *one* of those who believe *the
promises of* God.   And she said unto his sister, Follow him.
And she watched him at a distance ; and they perceived
it *not*.   And we suffered him not *to take* the breasts *of the
nurses who were provided* before *his sister came up* :[6] and

[1] See Chap. XXVI.

[2] This name is given to Pharaoh's chief minister ; whence it is generally
inferred that Mohammed has here made Haman, the favourite of Ahasuerus
king of Persia, and who indisputably lived many ages after Moses, to be that
prophet's contemporary.   But how probable soever this mistake may seem
to us, it will be very hard, if not impossible, to convince a Mohammedan of
it ; for, as has been observed in a parallel case (see p. 46, note 2), two very
different persons may bear the same name.   (Reland. de Rel. Moham. p. 217.)

[3] For Pharaoh had either dreamed, or been told by some diviners, that
one of the Herew nation should be the ruin of his kingdom ; which prophecy
is supposed to have been the occasion of his cruelty to them (Chap. VII,
p. 117).   This circumstance is owing to the invention of the Jews (Shalshel. hakkab, p. 11, et R. Eliez. pirke, c. 48).

[4] It is related that the midwife appointed to attend the Hebrew women,
terrified by a light which appeared between the eyes of Moses at his birth,
and touched with an extraordinary affection for the child, did not discover
him to the officers, so that his mother kept him in her house, and nursed
him three months ; after which it was impossible for her to conceal him any
longer, the king then giving orders to make the searches more strictly.   (Al
Beidâwi.   See the notes to Chap. XX.)

[5] This sudden affection or admiration was raised in them either by his
uncommon beauty, or by the light which shone on his forehead, or because,
when they opened the ark, they found him sucking his thumb, which supplied
him with milk.   (Al Beidâwi, Jallalo'ddin.)

[6] See Chap. XX. p. 307.

she said, Shall I direct you unto some of his nation, who may nurse him for you, and will be careful of him ? *And, at their desire, she brought his mother to them.* So we restored him to his mother, that her mind might be set at ease, and that she might not be afflicted ; and that she might know that the promise of GOD *was* true : but the greater part of *mankind* know not *the truth.* And when *Moses* had attained his age of full strength, and was become a perfect man, we bestowed on him wisdom and knowledge : and thus do we reward the upright. And he went into the city, at a time when the inhabitants thereof observed not *what passed in the streets* :[1] and he found therein two men fighting ; the one *being* of his own party, and the other of his enemies.[2] And he who *was* of his party, begged his assistance against him who *was* of the contrary party ; and Moses struck him with his fist, and slew him : *but being sorry for what had happened,* he said, This is of the work of the devil ;[3] for he is a seducing *and* an open enemy. *And* he said, O LORD, verily I have injured my own soul : wherefore forgive me. So GOD forgave him ; for he *is* ready to forgive, *and* merciful. He said, O LORD, by the *favours* with which thou hast favoured me, I will not be an assistant to the wicked *for the future.* And the next morning he was afraid in the city, and looked about him, *as one apprehensive of danger* : and behold, he whom he had assisted the day before, cried out unto him *for help a second time.* *But* Moses said unto him, Thou art plainly a quarrelsome fellow. And when he sought to lay hold on him who was an enemy unto them both, he said, O Moses, dost thou intend to kill me, as thou killedst a man yesterday ?[4] Thou seekest only to be an oppressor in the earth, and seekest not to be a reconciler *of quarrels.* And a *certain* man[5] came from the farther part of the city, running hastily, *and* said, O Moses, verily the

---

[1] viz., At noon ; at which time it is usual in those countries for people to retire to sleep ; or, as others rather suppose, a little within night.

[2] *i.e.,* The one being an Israelite of his own religion and nation, and the other an idolatrous Egyptian.

[3] Mohammed allows that Moses killed the Egyptian wrongfully ; but, to excuse it, supposes that he struck him without designing to kill him.

[4] Some suppose these words to have been spoken by the Israelite, who, because Moses had reprimanded him, imagined he was going to strike him ; and others, by the Egyptian, who either knew or suspected that Moses had killed his countryman the day before.

[5] This person, says the tradition, was an Egyptian, and Pharaoh's uncle's son, but a true believer ; who, finding that the king had been informed of what Moses had done, and designed to put him to death, gave him immediate notice to provide for his safety by flight.

magistrates are deliberating concerning thee, to put thee to death : depart therefore ; I certainly advise thee well. Wherefore he departed out of the *city* in great fear, looking this way and that, *lest he should be pursued. And* he said, O LORD, deliver me from the unjust people. And when he was journeying towards Madian, he said, Peradventure my LORD will direct me in the right way.[1] And when he arrived at the water of Madian, he found about the *well* a company of men, who were watering *their flocks.* And he found, besides them, two women, who kept off *their sheep at a distance. And* he said *unto them,* What is the matter with you ? They answered, We shall not water *our flock,* until the shepherds shall have driven away *theirs* : for our father is an old man, stricken in years. So *Moses* watered *their sheep* for them ;[2] and afterwards retired to the shade, saying, O LORD, verily I stand in need of the good which thou shalt send down unto me. And one of the *damsels*[3] came unto him, walking bashfully, and said, My father calleth thee, that he may recompense thee for the *trouble which thou hast taken in* watering *our sheep* for us. And when he was come unto *Shoaib,* and had told him the story *of his adventures,* he said *unto him,* Fear not ; thou hast escaped from unjust people. And one of the *damsels* said, My father, hire him for *certain* wages : the best *servant* thou canst hire, *is* an able *and* trusty person.[4] *And Shoaib said unto Moses,* Verily I will give thee one of these my two daughters in marriage, on condition that thou serve me for hire eight years : and if thou fulfil ten *years,* it *is* in thine own breast ; for I seek not to impose a hardship on thee : *and* thou shalt find me, if GOD please, a man of probity. *Moses* answered, *Let* this *be the covenant* between me and

---

[1] For Moses knew not the way, and coming to a place where three roads met, committed himself to the guidance of GOD, and took the middle road, which was the right ; providence likewise so ordering it, that his pursuers took the other two roads, and missed him. (Al Beidâwi.) Some say he was led by an angel in the appearance of a traveller. (Jallalo'ddin.)

[2] By rolling away a stone of a prodigious weight, which had been laid over the mouth of the well by the shepherds, and required no less than seven men (though some name a much larger number) to remove it. (Jallalo'ddin, interp. Yahya.)

[3] This was Sefûra (or Zipporah) the elder, or, as others suppose, the younger daughter of Shoaib, whom Moses afterwards married.

[4] The girl, being asked by her father how she knew Moses deserved this character, told him that he had removed the vast stone above mentioned without any assistance, and that he looked not in her face, but held down his head till he heard her message, and desired her to walk behind him because the wind ruffled her garments a little, and discovered some part of her legs. (Jallalo'ddin.)

thee : whichsoever of the two terms I shall fulfil, let it be no crime in me *if I then quit thy service* ; and GOD is witness of that which we say. And when Moses had fulfilled the term,[1] and was journeying with his family *towards Egypt,* he saw fire on the side of Mount *Sinai.* *And* he said unto his family, Tarry ye *here* ; for I see fire : peradventure I may bring you thence some tidings *of the way,*[2] or *at least* a brand out of the fire, that ye may be warmed. And when he was come thereto, *a voice* cried unto him from the right side of the valley, in the sacred bottom, from the tree, *saying,* O Moses, verily I am GOD, the LORD of all creatures : cast down now thy rod. And when he saw it that it moved, as though it *had been* a serpent, he retreated and fled, and returned not. *And God said unto him,* O Moses, draw near, and fear not ; for thou art safe. Put thy hand into thy bosom, *and* it shall come forth white, without any hurt ; and draw back thy hand[3] unto thee *which thou stretchest forth* for fear. These shall be two evident signs from thy LORD, unto Pharaoh and his princes ; for they are a wicked people. *Moses* said, O LORD, verily I have slain one of them ; and I fear they will put me to death : but my brother Aaron is of a more eloquent tongue than I *am* ; wherefore send him with me for an assistant, that he may gain me credit ; for I fear lest they accuse me of imposture. *God* said, We will strengthen thine arm by thy brother, and we will give each of you *extraordinary* power, so that they shall not come up to you, in our signs. Ye two, and whoever shall follow you. *shall be* the conquerors. And when Moses came unto them with our evident signs, they said, This *is* no other than a deceitful piece of sorcery : neither have we heard of *anything like* this among our forefathers. And Moses said, My LORD best knoweth who cometh with a direction from him ; and who shall have success in this life, *as well as the next* : but the unjust shall not prosper. And Pharaoh said, O princes, I did not know that ye had any *other* god besides

---

[1] viz., The longest term of ten years. The Mohammedans say, after the Jews (vide Shals. hakkab. p. 12.   R. Eliez, pirke, c. 40, &c.), that Moses received from Shoaib the rod of the prophets (which was a branch of a myrtle of paradise, and had descended to him from Adam) to keep off the wild beasts from his sheep ; and that this was the rod with which he performed all those wonders in Egypt.

[2] See Chap. XX. p. 305.

[3] Literally, *thy wing* : the expression alludes to the action of birds, which stretch forth their wings to fly away when they are frightened, and fold them together again when they think themselves secure. (Al Beidâwi.)

me.[1] Wherefore do thou, O Haman, burn me clay *into bricks* ; and build me a high tower,[2] that I may ascend unto the GOD of Moses : for I verily believe him to be a liar. And both he and his forces behaved themselves insolently and unjustly in the earth ; and imagined that they should not be brought before us *to be judged*. Wherefore we took him and his forces, and cast them into the sea. Behold, therefore, what was the end of the unjust. And we made them *deceitful* guides, inviting *their followers* to *hell* fire ; and on the day of resurrection they shall not be screened *from punishment*. We pursued them with a curse in this *life*, and on the day of resurrection they *shall be* shamefully rejected. And we gave the book *of the law* unto Moses, after we had destroyed the former generations, to enlighten *the minds* of men, and for a direction and a mercy ; that peradventure they might consider. Thou, *O prophet*, wast not on the west side *of Mount Sinai*, when we delivered Moses *his* commission : neither wast thou *one* of those who were present *at his receiving it* : but we raised up *several* generations *after Moses* : and life was prolonged unto them. Neither didst thou dwell among the inhabitants of Madian, rehearsing unto them our signs ; but we have sent *thee fully instructed in every particular*. Nor wast thou *present* on the side of the mount, when we called unto Moses : but *thou art sent as* a mercy from thy LORD ; that thou mightest preach unto a people to whom no preacher hath come before thee,[3] that peradventure they may be warned ; and lest, if a calamity had befallen them, for that which their hands had previously committed, they should have said, O LORD, since thou hast not sent an apostle unto us, that we might follow thy signs, and become true believers, *are we not excusable* ? Yet when the truth is come unto them from before us, they say, Unless he receive the same *power to work miracles* as Moses received, *we will not believe*. Have they not likewise rejected the *revelation* which was

---

[1] See Chap. XXVI.

[2] It is said that Haman, having prepared bricks and other materials, employed no less than fifty thousand men, besides labourers, in the building ; which they carried to so immense a height that the workmen could no longer stand on it ; that Pharaoh, ascending this tower, threw a javelin towards heaven, which fell back again stained with blood, whereupon he impiously boasted that he had killed the GOD of Moses ; but at sunset GOD sent the angel Gabriel, who, with one stroke of his wing, demolished the tower, a part whereof, falling on the king's army, destroyed a million of men. (Al Zamakhshari.)

[3] That is, to the Arabians ; to whom no prophet had been sent, at least since Ismael.

heretofore given unto Moses ? They say, Two cunning impostures[1] have mutually assisted one another : and they say, Verily we reject them both. Say, Produce therefore a book from GOD, which is more right than these two, that I may follow it ; if ye speak truth. But if they return thee no answer, know that they only follow their own desires : and who erreth more widely *from the truth* than he who followeth his own desire, without a direction from GOD ? verily GOD directeth not the unjust people. And now have we caused *our* word to come unto them, that they may be admonished. They unto whom we have given the scriptures *which were revealed* before it, believe in the same ; and when it is read unto them, say, We believe therein ; it is certainly the truth from our LORD : verily we were Moslems before this.[2] These shall receive their reward twice,[3] because they have persevered, and repel evil by good, and distribute *alms* out of that which we have bestowed on them ; and when they hear vain discourse, avoid the same, saying, We have our works, and ye have your works : peace be on you ;[4] we covet not the acquaintance of the ignorant. Verily thou canst not direct whom thou wilt : but GOD directeth whom he pleaseth ; and he best knoweth those who will submit to be directed. *The Meccans* say, If we follow the *same* direction with thee, we shall be forcibly expelled our land.[5] Have we not established for them a secure asylum ;[6] to which fruits of every sort are brought, as a provision of our bounty ? but the greater part of them do not understand. How many cities have we destroyed, *whose inhabitants* lived in ease and plenty ? and these their dwellings are not inhabited after them, unless

---

[1] viz., The Pentateuch and the Korân. Some copies read, *Two impostors*, meaning Moses and Mohammed.

[2] Holding the same faith in fundamentals, before the revelation of the Korân, which we receive because it is consonant to the scriptures, and attested to by them. The passage means those Jews and Christians who had embraced Mohammedism.

[3] Because they have believed both in their own scriptures and in the Korân.

[4] See Chap. XXV. p. 359.

[5] This objection was made by Al Hareth Ebn Othmân Ebn Nawfal Ebn Abd Menâf, who came to Mohammed and told him that the Koreish believed he preached the truth, but were apprehensive that if they made the Arabs their enemies by quitting their religion, they would be obliged likewise to quit Mecca, being but a handful of men, in comparison to the whole nation. (Al Beidâwi.)

[6] By giving them for their habitation the sacred territory of Mecca, a place protected by GOD, and reverenced by man.

for a little while ;[1] and we were the inheritors *of their wealth*.[2]
But thy LORD did not destroy *those* cities, until he had sent
unto their capital an apostle, to rehearse our signs unto
them : neither did we destroy *those* cities, unless their
inhabitants *were* injurious *to their apostle*. The things which
are given you, are the provisions of this present life, and the
pomp thereof ; but that which is with GOD, is better and
more durable : will ye not therefore understand ? Shall
he then, unto whom we have promised an excellent promise
of future happiness, and *who* shall attain the same, *be* as he
on whom we have bestowed the provision of this present
life, and who, on the day of resurrection, *shall be one* of those
who are delivered up *to eternal punishment* ? On *that* day
GOD shall call unto them, and shall say, Where are my
partners, which ye imagined *to be so* ? And they upon whom
the sentence *of damnation* shall be justly pronounced, shall
answer, These, O LORD, *are* those whom we seduced ; we
seduced them as we *also* had been seduced : *but now* we
clearly quit them, *and turn* unto thee. They did not worship us, *but their own lusts*.[3] And it shall be said *unto the
idolaters*, Call *now* upon those whom ye associated *with* GOD :
and they shall call upon them, but they shall not answer
them ; and they shall see the punishment *prepared for them,
and shall wish* that they had submitted to be directed. On
that day GOD shall call unto them, and shall say, What
answer did ye return to *our* messengers ? But they shall
not be able to give an account *thereof* on that day ;[4] neither
shall they ask one another *for information*. Howbeit whoso
shall repent and believe, and shall do that which is right,
may expect to be happy. Thy LORD createth what he
pleaseth ; and chooseth freely : *but* they have no free choice.
Praise be unto GOD ; and far be he removed from *the idols*
which they associate *with him* ! Thy LORD knoweth *both
the secret malice* which their breasts conceal, and *the open
hatred* which they discover. He is GOD ; there is no GOD
but he. Unto him *is* the praise *due*, both in this life and *in
†*that which is to come : unto him *doth* judgment *belong*, and

---

[1] That is, for a day, or a few hours only, while travellers stay there to
rest and refresh themselves ; or, as the original may also signify, *unless by a
few inhabitants* : some of those ancient cities and dwellings being utterly
desolate, and others thinly inhabited.

[2] There being none left to enjoy it after them.

[3] See Chap. X. p. 202.

[4] Literally, *The account thereof shall be dark unto them* ; for the consternation they shall then be under, will render them stupid, and unable to return
an answer.

before him shall ye be assembled *at the last day.* Say, What
think ye ? If GOD should cover you with perpetual night,
until the day of resurrection ; what god, besides GOD,
would bring you light ? Will ye not therefore hearken ?
Say, What think ye ? If GOD should give you continual day, until the day of resurrection ; what god, besides
GOD, would bring you night, that ye might rest therein ?
Will ye not therefore consider ? Of his mercy he hath
made for you the night and the day, that ye may rest in
the one, and may seek *to obtain provision for yourselves* of
his abundance, *by your industry, in the other* ; and that
ye may give thanks. On a *certain* day GOD shall call
unto them, and shall say, Where are my partners, which
ye imagined *to share the divine power with me* ? And we will
produce a witness out of every nation,[1] and will say, Bring
hither your proof *of what ye have asserted.* And they shall
know that the right *is* GOD's *alone* ; and the *deities* which
they have devised shall abandon them. Karûn was of the
people of Moses ;[2] but he behaved insolently towards them :
for we had given him so much treasure, that his keys would
have loaded several strong men.[3] When his people said

---

[1] viz.. The prophet who shall have been sent to each nation.

[2] The commentators say, Karûn was the son of Yeshar (or Izhar), the
uncle of Moses, and consequently, make him the same with the Korah of
the Scriptures. This person is represented by them as the most beautiful
of the Israelites, and so far surpassing them all in opulency that the riches
of Karûn have become a proverb. The Mohammedans are indebted to the
Jews for this last circumstance, to which they have added several other
fables : for they tell us that he built a large palace overlaid with gold, the
doors whereof were of massy gold ; that he became so insolent, because of
his immense riches, as to raise a sedition against Moses, though some pretend
the occasion of his rebellion to have been his unwillingness to give alms, as
Moses had commanded ; that one day, when that prophet was preaching
to the people, and, among other laws which he published, declared that
adulterers should be stoned, Karûn asked him what if he should be found
guilty of the same crime ? To which Moses answered, that in such case
he would suffer the same punishment ; and thereupon Karûn produced a
harlot, whom he had hired to swear that Moses had lain with her, and charged
him publicly with it ; but on Moses adjuring the woman to speak the truth,
her resolution failed her, and she confessed that she was suborned by Karûn
to accuse him wrongfully ; that then GOD directed Moses, who had complained
to him of this usage, to command the earth what he pleased, and it should
obey him ; whereupon he said, *O earth, swallow them up* ! and that immediately the earth opened under Karûn and his confederates, and swallowed them
up, with his palace and all his riches. (Abulfeda, Jallalo'ddin, Al Beidâwi, &c.)
There goes a tradition, that as Karûn sank gradually into the ground, first
to his knees, then to his waist, then to his neck, he cried out four several
times, *O Moses, have mercy on me* ! but that Moses continued to say, *O earth,
swallow them up,* till at last he wholly disappeared : upon which GOD said
to Moses, *Thou hast no mercy on Karûn, though he asked pardon of thee four
times ; but I would have had compassion on him if he had asked pardon of me
but once.* (Al Beidâwi. D'Herbel. Bibl. Orient. Art. Carun.)

[3] The original word properly signifies any number of persons from ten to

unto him, Rejoice not *immoderately* ; for GOD loveth not
those who rejoice *in their riches immoderately* : but seek to
attain, by means of *the wealth* which GOD hath given thee,
the future mansion *of paradise.*[1]   And forget not thy portion
in this world ; but be thou bounteous *unto others,* as GOD
hath been bounteous unto thee : and seek not to act corruptly in the earth ; for GOD loveth not the corrupt doers.
He answered, I have received *these riches,* only because of
the knowledge which is with me.[2]   Did he not know that
GOD had already destroyed, before him, several generations,
who were mightier than he in strength, and had amassed
more abundance *of riches ?*   And the wicked shall not be
asked *to discover* their crimes.   And *Karûn* went forth unto
his people, in his pomp.[3]   *And* they who loved this present
life said, Oh that we had the like *wealth* as hath been given
unto Karûn ! verily he is master of a great fortune.   But
those on whom knowledge had been bestowed, answered,
Alas for you ! the reward of GOD *in the next life* will be
better unto him who shall believe and do good works : but
none shall attain the same, except those who persevere with
constancy.   And we caused the ground to cleave in sunder,
and to swallow up him and his palace : and he had no
forces to defend him, besides GOD ; neither was he rescued
from punishment.   And the next morning, those who had
coveted his condition the day before, said, Aha ! verily
GOD bestoweth abundant provision on such of his servants
as he pleaseth ; and he is sparing *unto whom he pleaseth.*
Unless GOD had been gracious unto us, certainly *the earth*
had swallowed us up *also.*   Aha ! the unbelievers shall not
prosper.   *As to* this future mansion *of paradise,* we will give
it unto them who seek not to exalt themselves in the earth,
or to do wrong ; for the *happy* issue shall attend the pious.
Whoso doth good, shall receive a reward which shall exceed
the merit thereof : but *as to him* who doth evil, they who

forty.   Some pretend these keys were a sufficient load for seventy men ; and
Abulfeda says forty mules used to be employed to carry them.

　[1] This passage is parallel to that in the New Testament, *Make to yourselves
friends of the mammon of unrighteousness ; that when ye fail, they may receive
you into everlasting habitations.* (Luke xvi. 9.)

　[2] For some say he was the most learned of all the Israelites, and the best
versed in the law, after Moses and Aaron ; others pretend he was skilled in
chemistry, or in merchandizing, or other arts of gain, and others suppose,
as the Jews also fable—Vide R. Ghedal. Shalsh. hakkab. p. 13—that he
found out the treasures of Joseph in Egypt (Jallalo'ddin, Al Beidâwi).

　[3] It is said he rode on a white mule adorned with trappings of gold, and
that he was clothed in purple, and attended by four thousand men, all well
mounted and richly dressed.

work evil shall be rewarded *according to the merit* only of that which they shall have wrought. Verily he who hath given thee the Korân for a rule *of faith and practice*, will certainly bring thee back home *unto Mecca*.[1] Say, My LORD best knoweth who cometh with a *true* direction, and who is in a manifest error. Thou didst not expect that the book *of the Korân* should be delivered unto thee : but *thou hast received it* through the mercy of thy LORD. Be not therefore assisting to the unbelievers ; neither let them turn thee aside from the signs of GOD, after they have been sent down unto thee : and invite *men* unto thy LORD. And be not thou an idolater ; neither invoke any other god, together with the *true* GOD : there is no god but he. Everything shall perish, except himself ; unto him *belongeth* judgment ; and before him shall ye be assembled *at the last day*.

XXIX

THE CHAPTER OF THE SPIDER [2]

Revealed at Mecca.[3]

IN THE NAME OF THE MOST MERCIFUL GOD.

A. L. M.[4] Do men imagine that it shall be sufficient for them[5] to say, We believe ; while they be not proved ?[6] We heretofore proved those who *were* before them ; for GOD will surely know those who are sincere, and he will surely know the liars. Do they who work evil think that they shall prevent us *from taking vengeance on them* ? An ill judgment do they make. Whoso hopeth to meet

---

[1] This verse, some say, was revealed to Mohammed when he arrived at Johsa, in his flight from Mecca to Medina, to comfort him and still his complaints.

[2] Transient mention is made of the spider towards the end of the chapter.

[3] Some think the first ten verses, ending with these words, *And he well knoweth the hypocrites*, were revealed at Medina, and the rest at Mecca ; and others believe the reverse.

[4] See Sale, Prel. Disc. Sect. III. p. 64.

[5] Literally, *That they shall be let alone*, &c.

[6] This passage reprehends the impatience of some of the prophet's companions, under the hardships which they sustained in defence of their religion, and the losses which they suffered from the infidels ; representing to them that such trials and afflictions were necessary to distinguish the sincere person from the hypocrite, and the steady from the wavering. Some suppose it to have been occasioned by the death of Mahja, Omar's slave, killed by an arrow at the battle of Bedr, which was deeply lamented and laid to heart by his wife and parents. (Al Beidâwi.)

GOD, verily GOD's appointed time will certainly come ; and he *both* heareth *and* knoweth. Whoever striveth *to promote the true religion*, striveth for *the advantage of* his own soul ; for GOD needeth not any of *his* creatures : and *as to those* who believe and work righteousness, we will expiate their evil deeds from them ; and we will give them a reward according to the utmost merit of their actions. We have commanded man *to show* kindness towards his parents : but if they endeavour to prevail with thee to associate with me that concerning which thou hast no knowledge, obey them not.[1] Unto me shall ye return ; and I will declare unto you what ye have done. Those who shall believe, and shall work righteousness, we will surely introduce *into paradise*, among the upright. There are some men who say, We believe in GOD : but when *such a one* is afflicted for GOD's sake, he esteemeth the persecution of men *to be as grievous* as the punishment of GOD. Yet if success cometh from thy LORD, they say, Verily we are with you. Doth not GOD well know that which is in the breasts of *his* creatures ? Verily GOD well knoweth the true believers, and he well knoweth the hypocrites. The unbelievers say unto those who believe, Follow our way ; and we will bear your sins. Howbeit they shall not bear any part of their sins ; for they are liars : but they shall surely bear their own burdens, and *other* burdens besides their own burdens ;[2] and they shall be examined, on the day of resurrection, concerning that which they have falsely devised. We heretofore sent Noah unto his people ; and he tarried among them one thousand years, save fifty years,[3] and the deluge took them away, while they

---

[1] That is, If they endeavour to pervert thee to idolatry. The passage is said to have been revealed on account of Saad Ebn Abi Wakkâs, and his mother Hamna, who, when she heard that her son had embraced Mohammedism, swore that she would neither eat nor drink till he returned to his old religion, and kept her oath for three days. (Al Beidâwi.)

[2] viz., The guilt of seducing others, which shall be added to the guilt of their own obstinacy without diminishing the guilt of such as shall be seduced by them.

[3] This is true, if the whole life of Noah be reckoned ; and accordingly Abulfeda says he was sent to preach in his two hundred and fiftieth year, and that he lived in all nine hundred and fifty : but the text seeming to speak of those years only which he spent in preaching to the wicked ante-diluvians, the commentators suppose him to have lived much longer. Some say the whole length of his life was a thousand and fifty years ; that his mission happened in the fortieth year of his age, and that he lived after the Flood sixty years (Al Beidâwi, Ai Zamakhari) : and others give different numbers ; one, in particular, pretending that Noah lived near sixteen hundred years (Caab. apud Yahyam). This circumstance, says Al Beidâwi, was mentioned to encourage Mohammed, and to assure him that GOD, who supported Noah so many years against the opposi-

were acting unjustly ; but we delivered him and those who were in the ark, and we made the same[1] a sign unto *all* creatures. *We* also *sent* Abraham ; when he said unto his people, Serve GOD, and fear him : this *will be* better for you, if ye understand. Ye only worship idols besides GOD, and forge a lie. Verily those which ye worship, besides GOD, are not able to make any provision for you : seek therefore *your* provision from GOD ; and serve him and give thanks unto him ; unto him shall ye return. If ye charge *me* with imposture,[2] verily *sundry* nations before you *likewise* charged *their prophets* with imposture : but public preaching only *is incumbent* on an apostle. Do they not see how GOD produceth creatures, and afterwards restoreth them ?[3] Verily this is easy with GOD. Say, Go through the earth, and see how he originally produceth creatures : afterwards will GOD reproduce another production ; for GOD *is* almighty. He will punish whom he pleaseth, and he will have mercy on whom he pleaseth. Before him shall ye be brought *at the day of judgment* : and ye shall not escape *his reach*, either in earth, or in heaven ;[4] neither shall ye have any patron or defender besides GOD. *As for* those who believe not in the signs of GOD, or that they shall meet him *at the resurrection*, they shall despair of my mercy, and for them *is* a painful punishment *prepared*. And the answer of his people was no other than that they said, Slay him, or burn him. But GOD saved him from the fire.[5] Verily herein were signs unto people who believed. And *Abraham* said, Ye have taken idols, besides GOD, *to cement* affection between you in this life : but on the day of resurrection, the one of you shall deny the other, and the one of you shall curse the other ; and your abode shall be *hell* fire, and there shall be none to deliver you. And Lot believed on him. And *Abraham* said, Verily I fly *from my people*, unto *the place which* my LORD

tion and plots of the antediluvian infidels, would not fail to defend him against all attempts of the idolatrous Meccans and their partisans.

[1] *i.e.*, The ark.

[2] This seems to be part of Abraham's speech to his people : but some suppose that GOD here speaks, by way of apostrophe, first to the Koreish, and afterwards to Mohammed ; and that the parenthesis is continued to these words, *And the answer of his people was no other*, &c. In which case we should have said, *If ye charge* Mohammed your apostle *with imposture*, &c.

[3] The infidels are bidden to consider how GOD causeth the fruits of the earth to spring forth, and reneweth them every year, as in the preceding ; which is an argument of his power to raise man, whom he created at first, to life again after death, at his own appointed time.

[4] See Psalm cxxxix. 7, &c.

[5] See Chap. XXI. p. 321.

hath commanded me ; for he *is* the mighty, the wise. And
we gave him Isaac and Jacob ; and we placed among his
descendants the gift of prophecy and the scriptures : and
we gave him his reward in this world ; and in the next he
shall be *one* of the righteous. *We* also *sent* Lot ; when he
said unto his people, Do ye commit filthiness which no creature hath committed before you ?   Do ye approach *lustfully*
unto men, and lay wait in the highways,[1] and commit wickedness in your assembly ?[2]   And the answer of his people was
no other than that they said, Bring down the vengeance of
GOD upon us, if thou speakest truth.   *Lot* said, O LORD,
defend me against the corrupt people.   And when our
messengers came unto Abraham with good tidings,[3] they
said, We will surely destroy the inhabitants of this city ;
for the inhabitants thereof are unjust doers. *Abraham*
answered, Verily Lot *dwelleth* there.   They replied, We well
know who *dwelleth* therein : we will surely deliver him and
his family except his wife ; she shall be *one* of those who
remain behind.   And when our messengers came unto Lot,
he was troubled for them, and his arm was straitened concerning them.[4]   But they said, Fear not, neither be grieved ;
for we will deliver thee and thy family, except thy wife ;
for she shall be *one* of those who remain behind.   We will
surely bring down upon the inhabitants of this city vengeance from heaven, for that they have been wicked doers :
and we have left thereof a manifest sign[5] unto people who
understand.   And unto *the inhabitants of* Madian *we sent*
their brother Shoaib ; and he said *unto them,* O my people,
serve GOD, and expect the last day ; and transgress not,
acting corruptly in the earth.   But they accused him of
imposture ; wherefore a storm from heaven[6] assailed them,
and in the morning they were found in their dwellings *dead
and* prostrate.   And *we also destroyed the tribes of* Ad and
Thamûd ; and *this* is well known unto you from *what yet
remains of* their dwellings.   And Satan prepared their works

---

[1] Some suppose the Sodomites robbed and murdered the wayfarers ;
others, that they unnaturally abused their bodies.
[2] Their meetings being scenes of obscenity and riot.
[3] See Chap. XI. p. 219.
[4] See ibid.
[5] viz., The story of its destruction, handed down by common tradition ;
or else its ruins, or some other traces of this signal judgment ; it being pretended that several of the stones which fell from heaven on those cities, are
still to be seen, and that the ground where they stood appears burnt and
blackish.
[6] See Chap. VII. p. 152.

for them, and turned them aside from the way *of truth* ; although they were sagacious *people*. And *we likewise destroyed* Karûn, and Pharaoh, and Haman. Moses came unto them with evident *miracles* ; and they behaved themselves insolently in the earth : but they could not escape *our vengeance*. Every of them did we destroy in his sin. Against some of them we sent a violent wind :¹ some of them did a terrible noise from heaven destroy : ² some of them did we cause the earth to swallow up :³ and some of them we drowned.⁴ Neither was GOD *disposed* to treat them unjustly ; but they dealt unjustly with their own souls. The likeness of those who take *other* patrons besides GOD, is as the likeness of the spider, which maketh herself a house : but the weakest of *all* houses surely is the house of the spider ; if they knew *this*. Moreover GOD knoweth what things they invoke, besides him ; and he *is* the mighty, the wise. These similitudes do we propound unto men : but none understand them, except the wise. GOD hath created the heavens and the earth in truth : verily herein *is* a sign unto the true believers. (XXI.) ⁵ Rehearse that which hath been revealed unto thee of the book *of the Korân* : and be constant at prayer ; for prayer preserveth *a man* from filthy crimes, and *from* that which is blameable ; and the remembering of GOD is surely a most important *duty*. GOD knoweth that which ye do. Dispute not against those who have received the scriptures, unless in the mildest manner ;⁶ except against such of them as behave injuriously *towards you* : and say, We believe in the *revelation* which hath been sent down unto us, and *also in that which* hath been sent down unto you ; our GOD and your GOD is one, and unto him are we resigned. Thus have we sent down the book *of the Korân* unto thee : and they unto whom we have given the *former* scriptures, believe therein ; and of these *Arabians also there is* who believeth therein : and none reject our signs except the *obstinate* infidels. Thou couldst not read any book before this ; neither couldst thou write it with thy right hand : then had the gainsayers *justly* doubted *of the divine*

¹ The original word properly signifies a wind that *drives the gravel and small stones* before it ; by which the storm, or shower of stones, which destroyed Sodom and Gomorrah, seems to be intended.

² Which was the end of Ad and Thamûd.

³ As it did Karûn.

⁴ As the unbelievers in Noah's time.   ⁵ Section XXI. begins here.

⁶ *i.e.*, Without ill language or passion. This verse is generally supposed to have been abrogated by that of *the sword* ; though some think it relates only to those who are in alliance with the Moslems.

origin thereof. But the same *is* evident signs in the breasts of those who have received understanding : for none reject our signs, except the unjust. They say, Unless a sign be sent down unto him from his LORD, *we will not believe.* Answer, Signs are in the power of GOD alone ; and I am *no more than* a public preacher. Is it not sufficient for them that we have sent down unto thee the book *of the Korân,* to be read unto them ? Verily herein *is* a mercy, and an admonition unto people who believe. Say, GOD is a sufficient witness between me and you : he knoweth whatever is in heaven and earth ; and those who believe in vain *idols,* and deny GOD, they shall perish. They will urge thee to hasten the punishment *which they defy thee to bring down upon them :*[1] if *there had* not *been* a determined time *for their respite,* the punishment had come upon them *before this* ; but it shall surely overtake them suddenly, and they shall not foresee it. They urge thee to bring down vengeance swiftly *upon them* : but hell shall surely encompass the unbelievers. On *a certain* day *their* punishment shall suddenly assail them, *both* from above them, and from under their feet ; and *God* shall say, Taste ye *the reward of* that which ye have wrought. O my servants who have believed, verily my earth is spacious ; wherefore serve me.[2] Every soul shall taste death : afterwards shall ye return unto us ; and *as for* those who shall have believed, and wrought righteousness, we will surely lodge them in a higher apartment of paradise ; rivers shall flow beneath them, *and* they shall continue therein for ever. How excellent *will be* the reward of the workers *of righteousness ;* who persevere with patience, and put their trust in their LORD ! How many beasts *are there,* which provide not their food ? *It is* GOD *who* provideth food for them and for you ; and he *both* heareth *and* knoweth. Verily, if thou ask *the Meccans,* who hath created the heavens and the earth, and hath obliged the sun and the moon to serve *in their courses* ; they will answer, GOD. How therefore do they lie, *in acknowledging of other gods* ? GOD maketh abundant provision for such of his servants as he pleaseth ;

---

[1] See Chap. VI.

[2] That is, if ye cannot serve me in one city or country, fly unto another, where ye may profess the true religion in safety ; for the earth is wide enough, and ye may easily find places of refuge. Mohammed is said to have declared, that whoever flies for the sake of his religion, though he stir but the distance of a span, merits paradise, and shall be the companion of Abraham and of himself. (Al Beidâwi.)

and is sparing unto him, *if he pleaseth* : for GOD knoweth all things.[1]   Verily if thou ask them, who sendeth rain from heaven, and thereby quickeneth the earth, after it hath been dead ; they will answer, GOD.   Say, GOD be praised !   But the greater part of them do not understand.   This present life is no other than a toy and a plaything ; but the future mansion *of paradise* is life indeed : if they knew *this, they would not prefer the former to the latter.*   When they sail in a ship, they call upon GOD, sincerely exhibiting unto him the *true* religion : but when he bringeth them safe to land, behold, they return to their idolatry ; to show themselves ungrateful for that which we have bestowed on them, and that they may enjoy *the delights of this life* ; but they shall hereafter know *the issue.*   Do they not see that we have made *the territory of Mecca* an inviolable and secure *asylum,* when men are spoiled *in the countries* round about them ? Do they therefore believe in that which is vain, and acknowledge not the goodness of GOD ?   But who is more unjust than he who deviseth a lie against GOD, or denieth the truth, when it hath come unto him ?   Is there not in hell an abode for the unbelievers ?   Whoever do their utmost endeavour to promote our true religion, we will direct them into our ways ; for GOD is with the righteous.

XXX

THE CHAPTER OF THE GREEKS [2]

Revealed at Mecca.[3]

IN THE NAME OF THE MOST MERCIFUL GOD.

A. L.M.[4] The Greeks have been overcome *by the Persians,*[5]

[1] And particularly who will make a good, and who will make a bad use of their riches.

[2] The original word is Al Rûm ; by which the later Greeks, or subjects of the Constantinopolitan empire, are here meant ; though the Arabs give the same name also to the Romans, and other Europeans.

[3] Some except the verse beginning at these words, *Praise be unto* GOD

[4] See note to Chap. II, and Sale, Prel. Disc. Sect. III. p. 64.

[5] The accomplishment of the prophecy contained in this passage, which is very famous among the Mohammedans, being insisted on by their doctors as a convincing proof that the Korân really came down from heaven, it may be excusable to be a little particular.   The passage is said to have been revealed on occasion of a great victory obtained by the Persians over the Greeks, the news whereof coming to Mecca, the infidels became strangely elated, and began to abuse Mohammed and his followers, imagining that

in the nearest part of the land;[1] but after their
defeat, they shall overcome *the others in their turn,*

this success of the Persians, who, like themselves, were idolaters, and supposed to have no scriptures, against the Christians, who pretended as well
as Mohammed to worship one GOD, and to have divine scriptures, was an
earnest of their own future successes against the prophet and those of his
religion : to check which vain hopes, it was foretold, in the words of the
text, that how improbable soever it might seem, yet the scale should be
turned in a few years, and the vanquished Greeks prevail as remarkably
against the Persians. That this prophecy was exactly fulfilled the commentators fail not to observe, though they do not exactly agree in the
accounts they give of its accomplishment ; the number of years between the
two actions being not precisely determined. Some place the victory gained
by the Persians in the fifth year before the Hejra, and their defeat by the
Greeks in the second year after it, when the battle of Bedr was fought
(Jallalo'ddin, &c.) : others place the former in the third or fourth year before
the Hejra, and the latter in the end of the sixth or beginning of the seventh
year after it, when the expedition of Al Hodeibiyah was undertaken (Al
Zamakh., Al Beidâwi). The date of the victory gained by the Greeks, in
the first of these accounts, interferes with a story which the commentators
tell, of a wager laid by Abu Becr with Obba Ebn Khalf, who turned this
prophecy into ridicule. Abu Becr at first laid ten young camels that the
Persians should receive an overthrow within three years ; but on his acquainting Mohammed with what he had done, that prophet told him that the word
bed', made use of in this passage, signified no determinate number of years,
but any number from three to nine (though some suppose the tenth year is
included), and therefore advised him to prolong the time, and to raise the
wager ; which he accordingly proposed to Obba, and they agreed that the
time assigned should be nine years, and the wager a hundred camels. Before
the time was elapsed, Obba died of a wound he had received at Ohod, in the
third year of the Hejra (see Chap. XXV.); but the event afterwards showing
that Abu Becr had won, he received the camels of Obba's heirs, and brought
them in triumph to Mohammed (Al Beidâwi, Jallalo'ddin, &c.). History
informs us that the successes of Khosru Parviz, king of Persia, who carried
on a terrible war against the Greek empire, to revenge the death of Maurice,
his father-in-law, slain by Phocas, were very great, and continued in an
uninterrupted course for two and twenty years. Particularly in the year
of Christ 615, about the beginning of the sixth year before the Hejra, the
Persians, having the preceding year conquered Syria, made themselves
masters of Palestine, and took Jerusalem ; which seems to be that signal
advantage gained over the Greeks mentioned in this passage, as agreeing
best with the terms here used, and most likely to alarm the Arabs by reason
of their vicinity to the scene of action : and there was so little probability, at that time, of the Greeks being able to retrieve their losses, much
less to distress the Persians, that in the following years the arms of the
latter made still farther and more considerable progresses, and at length
they laid siege to Constantinople itself. But in the year 625, in which
the fourth year of the Hejra began, about ten years after the taking of
Jerusalem, the Greeks, when it was least expected, gained a remarkable
victory over the Persians, and not only obliged them to quit the territories
of the empire, by carrying the war into their own country, but drove them
to the last extremity, and spoiled the capital city of Madâyen ; Heraclius
enjoying thenceforward a continued series of good fortune, to the deposition
and death of Khosru. For more exact information in these matters, and
more nicely fixing the dates, either so as to correspond with or to overturn
this pretended prophecy (neither of which is my business here), the reader
may have recourse to the historians and chronologers. (Vide etiam Asseman,
Bibl. Orient. t. 3. part i. p. 411, &c., et Boulainy. Vie de Mahom p. 333,
&c.)

[1] Some interpreters, supposing that the land here mean. is the land of
Arabia, or else that of the Greeks. place the scene of action on the confines

within a few years. Unto GOD *belongeth* the disposal *of this matter*, both for what is past, and for what is to come : and on that day shall the believers rejoice in the success granted by GOD ; for he granteth success unto whom he pleaseth, and he *is* the mighty, the merciful. *This is* the promise of GOD : GOD will not act contrary to his promise; but the greater part of men know not *the veracity of God*. They know the outward appearance of this present life ; but they are careless as to the life to come. Do they not consider within themselves that GOD hath not created the heavens and the earth, and whatever *is* between them, otherwise than in truth, and *hath set them* a determined period ? Verily a great number of men reject the belief of *their future* meeting their LORD *at the resurrection*. Do they not pass through the earth, and see what hath been the end of those who *were* before them ? They excelled *the Meccans* in strength, and broke up the earth,[1] and inhabited it in greater affluence and prosperity than they inhabit the same : and their apostles came unto them with evident *miracles* ; and GOD was not *disposed* to treat them unjustly, but they injured their own souls *by their obstinate infidelity* ; and the end of those who had done evil, was evil, because they charged the signs of GOD with falsehood, and laughed the same to scorn. GOD produceth creatures, and will hereafter restore them *to life* : then shall ye return unto him. And on the day whereon the hour shall come, the wicked shall be struck dumb for despair ; and they shall have no inter- cessors from among the *idols* which they associated *with God*. And they shall deny *the false gods* which they associated *with him*. On the day whereon the hour shall come, on that day shall *the true believers and the infidels* be separated : and they who shall have believed, and wrought righteousness, shall take their pleasure in a delightful meadow : but *as for* those who shall have disbelieved, and rejected our signs, and the meeting of the next life, they shall be delivered up to punishment. Wherefore glorify GOD, when the evening overtaketh you, and when ye rise in the morning : and unto him be praise in heaven and earth ; and at sunset, and when

of Arabia and Syria, near Bostra and Adhraât (Yahya, Al Beidâwi) ; others imagine the land of Persia is intended, and lay the scene in Mesopotamia, on the frontiers of that kingdom (Mojahed, apud Zamakh. Jallalo'ddin) ; but Ebn Abbas, with more probability, thinks it was in Palestine.

[1] To dig for water and minerals, and to till the ground for seed, &c. (Al Beidâwi.)

ye rest at noon.[1] He bringeth forth the living out of the dead, and he bringeth forth the dead out of the living ;[2] and he quickeneth the earth after it hath been dead : and in like manner shall ye be brought forth *from your graves*. Of his signs *one is*, that he hath created you of dust ; and behold, ye *are become* men, spread *over the face of the earth*. And of his signs *another is*, that he hath created for you, out of yourselves, wives, that ye may cohabit with them ; and hath put love and compassion between you : verily herein are signs unto people who consider. And of his signs *are also* the creation of the heavens and the earth, and the variety of your languages, and of your complexions :[3] verily herein are signs unto men of understanding. And of his signs *are* your sleeping by night and by day, and your seeking *to provide for yourselves* of his abundance : verily herein *are* signs unto people who hearken. Of his signs *others are*, that he showeth you the lightning, to *strike* terror, and to *give* hope *of rain*, and that he sendeth down water from heaven, and quickeneth thereby the earth, after it hath been dead : verily herein *are* signs unto people who understand. And of his signs *this also is one, namely*, that the heaven and the earth stand firm at his command : hereafter, when he shall call you out of the earth at one summons, behold, ye shall come forth. Unto him *are subject* whosoever are in the heavens and on earth, all are obedient unto him. It is he who originally produceth a creature, and afterwards restoreth the same *to life* : and this is most easy with him. He justly challengeth the most exalted comparison, in heaven and earth ;[4] and he *is* the mighty, the wise. He propoundeth unto you a comparison *taken* from yourselves. Have ye among the *slaves* whom your right hands possess, any partner in the *substance* which we have bestowed on you, so that ye become equal *sharers* therein *with them, or that* ye fear them as ye fear one another ?[5]

---

[1] Some are of opinion that the five times of prayer are intended in this passage ; the evening including the time both of the prayer of sunset, and of the evening prayer properly so called, and the word I have rendered *at sunset*, marking the hour of afternoon prayer, since it may be applied also to the time a little before sunset.

[2] See Chap. III. p. 46.

[3] Which are certainly most wonderful, and, as I conceive, very hard to be accounted for, if we allow the several nations in the world to be all the offspring of one man, as we are assured by Scripture they are without having recourse to the immediate omnipotency of GOD.

[4] That is, in speaking of him we ought to make use of the most noble and magnificent expressions we can possibly devise.

[5] See Chap. XVI. p. 263.

Thus do we distinctly explain *our* signs, unto people who
understand. But those who act unjustly *by attributing
companions unto God*, follow their own lusts, without knowledge : and who shall direct him whom GOD shall cause to
err ? They shall have none to help them. Wherefore be
thou orthodox, and set thy face towards the *true* religion,
the institution of GOD, to which he hath created mankind
disposed : there is no change in what GOD hath created.[1]
This *is* the right religion ; but the greater part of men know
it not. *And be ye* turned unto him, and fear him, and be
constant at prayer, and be not idolaters. Of those who
have made a schism in their religion, and are *divided* into
various sects ; every sect rejoice in their own *opinion*.
When adversity befalleth men, they call upon their LORD,
turning unto him : afterwards, when he hath caused them
to taste of his mercy, behold, a part of them associate *other
deities* with their LORD ; to show themselves ungrateful for
the *favours* which we have bestowed on them. Enjoy
therefore *the vain pleasures of this life* ; but hereafter
shall ye know *the consequence.* Have we sent down unto
them any authority, which speaketh of the *false gods* which
they associate with him ?[2] When we cause men to taste
mercy, they rejoice therein ; but if evil befalleth them, for
that which their hands have before committed, behold,
they despair.[3] Do they not see that GOD bestoweth provision abundantly on whom he pleaseth, and is sparing *unto
whom he pleaseth* ? Verily herein *are* signs unto people who
believe. Give unto him who is of kin *to thee* his reasonable
due ; and also to the poor and the stranger : this is better
for those who seek the face of GOD ; and they shall prosper.
Whatever ye shall give in usury,[4] to be an increase of men's
substance, shall not be increased by *the blessing of* GOD :
but whatever ye shall give in alms, for GOD's sake, they shall
receive a twofold *reward. It is* GOD who hath created you,
and hath provided food for you : hereafter will he cause you

[1] *i.e.*, The immutable law, or rule, to which man is naturally disposed to
conform, and which every one would embrace, as most fit for a rational
creature, if it were not for the prejudices of education. The Mohammedans
have a tradition that their prophet used to say, *That every person is born
naturally disposed to become a Moslem ; but that a man's parents make him
a Jew, a Christian, or a Magian.*
[2] That is, Have we either by the mouth of any prophet, or by any written
revelation, commanded or encouraged the worship of more gods than one ?
[3] And seek not to regain the favour of GOD by timely repentance.
[4] Or by way of bribe. The word may include any sort of extortion or
illicit gain.

to die ; and after that will he raise you again to life. *Is there* any of your false gods, who is able to do the least of these things ? Praise be unto him ; and far be he removed from what they associate *with him* ! Corruption[1] hath appeared by land and by sea, for *the crimes* which men's hands have committed ; that it might make them to taste[2] a part of the *fruits of that* which they had wrought, that peradventure they might turn *from their evil ways*. Say, Go through the earth, and see what hath been the end of those who have been before *you* : the greater part of them were idolaters. Set thy face therefore towards the right religion, before the day cometh, which none can put back from GOD. On that day shall they be separated into two companies : whoever shall have been an unbeliever, on him *shall* his unbelief *be charged* ; and whoever shall have done that which is right, shall spread themselves *couches of repose in paradise* ; that he may reward those who shall believe and work righteousness, of his abundant liberality ; for he loveth not the unbelievers. Of his signs *one is*, that he sendeth the winds, bearing welcome tidings *of rain*, that he may cause you to taste of his mercy ; and that ships may sail at his command, that ye may seek *to enrich yourselves* of his abundance *by commerce* ; and that ye may give thanks. We sent apostles, before thee, unto their *respective* people, and they came unto them with evident proofs : and we took vengeance on those who did wickedly ; and it was incumbent on us to assist the true believers. *It is* GOD who sendeth the winds, and raiseth the clouds, and spreadeth the same in the heaven, as he pleaseth ; and *afterwards* disperseth the same : and thou mayest see the rain issuing from the midst thereof ; and when he poureth the same down on such of his servants as he pleaseth, behold, they are filled with joy ; although before it was sent down unto them, before *such relief*, they were despairing. Consider therefore the traces of GOD's mercy ; how he quickeneth the earth, after its *state of* death : verily the same will raise the dead ; for he is almighty. Yet if we should send a *blasting* wind, and they should see *their corn* yellow *and burnt up*, they would surely become ungrateful, after *our former favours*. Thou canst not make the dead to hear, neither canst thou make

---

[1] viz., Mischief and public calamities, such as famine, pestilence, droughts, shipwrecks, &c., or erroneous doctrines, or a general depravity of manners.
[2] Some copies read in the first person plural, *That we might cause them to taste*, &c.

the deaf to hear *thy* call, when they retire and turn their
backs ; neither canst thou direct the blind out of their error :
thou shalt make none to hear, except him who shall believe
in our signs ; for they are resigned *unto us*. *It is* GOD who
created you in weakness, and after weakness hath given *you*
strength ; and after strength, he will *again* reduce *you*
to weakness, and grey hairs : he createth that which he
pleaseth ; and he *is* the wise, the powerful. On the day
whereon the *last* hour shall come, the wicked will swear that
they have not tarried[1] above an hour : in like manner did
they utter lies *in their lifetime*. But those on whom knowledge hath been bestowed, and faith, will say, Ye have tarried, according to the book of GOD,[2] until the day of resurrection : for this *is* the day of resurrection ; but ye knew
it not. On that day their excuse shall not avail those who
have acted unjustly ; neither shall they be invited *any
more* to make themselves acceptable *unto God*. And now
have we propounded unto men, in this Korân, parables of
every kind : yet if thou bring them a verse *thereof*, the
unbelievers will surely say, Ye *are* no other than publishers
of vain falsehoods. Thus hath GOD sealed up the hearts
of those who believe not. But do thou, *O Mohammed*,
persevere with constancy, for the promise of GOD is true ;
and let not those induce thee to waver, who have no certain
knowledge.

XXXI

THE CHAPTER OF LOKMÂN[3]

Revealed at Mecca.[4]

IN THE NAME OF THE MOST MERCIFUL GOD.

A. L. M.[5] These are the signs of the wise book, a direction, and a mercy unto the righteous ; who observe

[1] viz., In the world or in their graves. See Chap. XXIII. p. 342.

[2] That is, according to his foreknowledge and decree in the preserved
table ; or according to what is said in the Korân, where the state of the
dead is expressed by these words (Chap. XXIII.) : *Behind them there shall
be a bar until the day of resurrection* (Al Beidâwi).

[3] The chapter is so entitled from a person of this name mentioned therein,
of whom more immediately.

[4] Some except the fourth verse, beginning at these words, *Who observe
the appointed times of prayer, and give alms*, &c. And others three verses,
beginning at these words, *If all the trees in the earth were pens*, &c.

[5] See note to Chap. II;, and Sale, Prel. Disc. Sect. III. p. 64.

the appointed times of prayer, and give alms, and have firm assurance in the life to come : these are directed by their LORD, and they shall prosper. There is a man who purchaseth a ludicrous story,[1] that he may seduce *men* from the way of GOD, without knowledge, and may laugh the same to scorn : these shall suffer a shameful punishment. And when our signs are rehearsed unto him, he disdainfully turneth his back, as though he heard them not, as though there were a deafness in his ears : wherefore denounce unto him a grievous punishment. But they who shall believe and work righteousness, shall enjoy gardens of pleasure ; they shall continue therein for ever : *this is* the certain promise of GOD ; and he *is* the mighty, the wise. He hath created the heavens without visible pillars *to sustain them,* and hath thrown on the earth *mountains* firmly rooted, lest it should move with you ;[2] and he hath replenished the same with all kinds of beasts : and we send down rain from heaven and cause every kind of noble *vegetable* to spring forth therein. This is the creation of GOD : show me now what they have created, who *are worshipped* besides him ? verily the ungodly are in a manifest error. We heretofore bestowed wisdom on Lokmân,[3] *and commanded him, saying,* Be thou

---

[1] *i.e.,* Vain and silly fables. The passage was revealed, it is said, on occasion of Al Nodar Ebn al Hareth, who, having brought from Persia the romance of Rostam and Isfandiyar, the two heroes of that country, recited it in the assemblies the Koreish, highly extolling the power and splendour of the ancient Persian kings, and preferring their stories to those of Ad and Thamûd, David and Solomon, and the rest which are told in the Korân. Some say that Al Nodar bought singing girls, and carried them to those who were inclined to become Moslems to divert them from their purpose by songs and tales.   (Al Beidâwi.)

[2] See Chap. XVI.   A learned writer (Gol. in Append. ad. Erpemi Gram. p. 187), in his notes on this passage, says the original word *rawâsiya,* which the commentators in general will have to signify *stable mountains,* seems properly to express the Hebrew word *mechonim, i.e., bases* or *foundations ;* and therefore he thinks the Korân has here translated that passage of the Psalms, *He laid the foundations of the earth, that it should not be moved for ever* (Ps. civ. 5).   This is not the only instance which might be given that the Mohammedan doctors are not always the best interpreters of their own scriptures.

[3] The Arab writers say, that Lokmân was the son of Baûra, who was tne son or grandson of a sister or aunt of Job ; and that he lived several centuries, and to the time of David with whom he was conversant in Palestine. According to the description they give of his person, he must have been deformed enough ; for they say he was of a black complexion (whence some call him an Ethiopian), with thick lips and splay feet : but in return he received from GOD wisdom and eloquence in a great degree, which some pretend were given him in a vision, on his making choice of wisdom preferably to the gift of prophecy, either of which were offered him.   The generality of the Mohammedans, therefore, hold him to have been no prophet, but only a wise man.   As to his condition, they say he was a slave, but obtained his liberty on the following occasion : His master having one day given him

thankful unto GOD : for whoever is thankful, shall be thankful to *the advantage of* his own soul ; and if any shall be unthankful, verily GOD is self-sufficient, and worthy to be praised. And *remember* when Lokmân said unto his son,[1] as he admonished him, O my son, Give not a partner unto GOD ; for polytheism *is* a great impiety. We have commanded man concerning his parents,[2] (his mother carrieth him *in her womb* with weakness and faintness, and he is weaned in two years), *saying*, Be grateful unto me and to thy parents. Unto me shall all come *to be judged*. But if *thy parents* endeavour to prevail on thee to associate with me that concerning which thou hast no knowledge, obey them not : bear them company in this world in what shall be reasonable ;[3] but follow the way of him who sincerely turneth unto me.[4] Hereafter unto me shall ye return, and then will I declare unto you that which ye have done. O my son, verily *every matter, whether good or bad*, though it be of the weight of a grain of mustard-seed, and be *hidden* in a rock, or in the heavens, or in the earth, GOD will bring the same *to light* ; for GOD *is* clear-sighted *and* knowing.

a bitter melon to eat, he paid him such exact obedience as to eat it all ; at which his master being surprised, asked him how he could eat so nauseous a fruit ? To which he replied, it was no wonder that he should for once accept a bitter fruit from the same hand from which he had received so many favours. (Al Zamakh., Al Beidâwi, &c. Vide D'Herbel. Bibl. Orient. p. 516, et Marracc. in Alc. p. 547). The commentators mention several quick repartees of Lokmân, which, together with the circumstances above mentioned, agree so well with what Maximus Planudes has written of Esop, that from thence, and from the fables attributed to Lokmân by the Orientals, the latter has been generally thought to have been no other than the Esop of the Greeks. However that be (for I think the matter will bear a dispute), I am of opinion that Planudes borrowed great part of his life of Esop from the traditions he met with in the East concerning Lokmân, concluding them to have been the same person, because they were both slaves, and supposed to be the writers of those fables which go under their respective names, and bear a great resemblance to one another ; for it has long since been observed by learned men that the greater part of that monk's performance is an absurd romance, and supported by no evidence of the ancient writers. (Vide la Vie d'Esope, par M. de Meziriac, et Bayle, Dict. Hist. Art. Esope. Rem. B.)

[1] Whom some name Anám (which comes pretty near the Ennus of Planudes), some Ashcam, and others Mathan.

[2] The two verses which begin at these words, and end with the following, viz., *And then will I declare unto you that which ye have done*, are no part of Lokmân's advice to his son, but are inserted by way of parenthesis, as very pertinent and proper to be repeated here, to show the heinousness of idolatry : they are to be read (excepting some additions) in the twenty-ninth chapter, and were originally revealed on account of Saad Ebn Abi Wakkâs, as has been already observed. (See Chap. XXIX., and the notes thereon.)

[3] That is, show them all deference and obedience, so far as may be consistent with thy duty towards GOD.

[4] The person particularly meant here was Abu Becr, at whose persuasion Saad had become a Moslem.

O my son, be constant at prayer, and command that which is just, and forbid that which is evil : and be patient under the *afflictions* which shall befall thee ; for this *is* a duty absolutely incumbent *on all men*. Distort not thy face *out of contempt* to men, neither walk in the earth with insolence ; for GOD loveth no arrogant, vain-glorious person. And be moderate in thy pace : and lower thy voice ; for the most ungrateful of *all* voices surely *is* the voice of asses.[1] Do ye not see that GOD hath subjected whatever is in heaven and on earth to your service, and hath abundantly poured on you his favours, *both* outwardly and inwardly ?[2] *There are* some who dispute concerning GOD without knowledge, and without a direction, and without an enlightening book. And when it is said unto them, Follow that which GOD hath revealed ; they answer, Nay, we will follow that which we found our fathers to practise. What, though the devil invite them to the torment of hell ? Whoever resigneth himself unto GOD, being a worker of righteousness, taketh hold on a strong handle ; and unto GOD *belongeth* the issue of *all* things. But whoever shall be an unbeliever, let not his unbelief grieve thee : unto us shall they return ; then will we declare unto them that which they have done, for GOD knoweth the innermost parts of the breasts *of men*. We will suffer them to enjoy *this world* for a little while : afterwards we will drive them to a severe punishment. If thou ask them who hath created the heavens and the earth, they will surely answer, GOD. Say, GOD be praised ! But the greater part of them do not understand. Unto GOD *belongeth* whatever *is* in heaven and earth : for GOD *is* the self-sufficient, the praiseworthy. If whatever trees *are* in the earth *were* pens, and he should after that swell the sea into seven seas *of ink*, the words of GOD would not be exhausted ;[3] for GOD *is* mighty *and* wise. Your creation and your resuscitation are but as *the creation and resuscitation of* one soul :[4] verily GOD *both* heareth *and* seeth. Dost thou not see that GOD causeth the night to succeed the day, and causeth the day to succeed the night, and compelleth the sun and the moon to serve *you* ? Each *of those lumin-*

---

[1] To the braying of which animal the Arabs liken a loud and disagreeable voice.

[2] *i.e.*, All kinds of blessings, regarding the mind as well as the body.

[3] This passage is said to have been revealed in answer to the Jews, who insisted that all knowledge was contained in the law. (Al Beidâwi.)

[4] GOD being able to produce a million of worlds by the single word Kun, *i.e.*, Be, and to raise the dead in general by the single word Kum, *i.e.* Arise.

aries hasteneth *in its course* to a determined period : and GOD *is* well acquainted with that which ye do. This *is declared concerning the divine knowledge and power*, for that GOD is the true Being, and for that whatever ye invoke, besides him, *is* vanity ; and for that GOD is the high, the great *God*. Dost thou not see that the ships run in the sea, through the favour of GOD, that he may show you of his signs ? Verily herein *are* signs, unto every patient, grateful person. When waves cover them, like overshadowing *clouds*, they call upon GOD, exhibiting the pure religion unto him ; but when he bringeth them safe to land, *there* is of them who halteth *between the true faith and idolatry*. Howbeit, none rejecteth our signs, except every perfidious, ungrateful person. O men, fear your LORD, and dread the day whereon a father shall not make satisfaction for his son, neither shall a son make satisfaction for his father at all : the promise of GOD is assuredly true. Let not this present life, therefore, deceive you ; neither let the deceiver[1] deceive you concerning GOD. Verily the knowledge of the hour *of judgment* is with GOD : and he causeth the rain to descend, *at his own appointed time* ; and he knoweth what *is* in the wombs *of females*. No soul knoweth what it shall gain on the morrow ; neither doth any soul know in what land it shall die :[2] but GOD *is* knowing *and* fully acquainted *with all things*.

[1] viz., The devil.

[2] In this passage five things are enumerated which are known to GOD alone, viz., The time of the day of judgment ; the time of rain ; what is forming in the womb, as whether it be male or female, &c. ; what shall happen on the morrow ; and where any person shall die. These the Arabs, according to a tradition of their prophet, call *the five keys of secret knowledge*. The passage, it is said, was occasioned by Al Hareth Ebn Amru, who propounded questions of this nature to Mohammed. As to the last particular, Al Beidâwi relates the following story : The angel of death passing once by Solomon in a visible shape, and looking at one who was sitting with him, the man asked who he was, and upon Solomon's acquainting him that it was the angel of death, said, He seems to want me ; wherefore order the wind to carry me from hence into India ; which being accordingly done the angel said to Solomon, I looked so earnestly at the man out of wonder ; because I was commanded to take his soul in India, and found him with thee in Palestine.

XXXII

THE CHAPTER OF ADORATION [1]

Revealed at Mecca.

IN THE NAME OF THE MOST MERCIFUL GOD.

A. L. M.[2] The revelation of *this* book, *there is* no doubt thereof, *is* from the LORD of all creatures. Will they say, *Mohammed* hath forged it? Nay, it is the truth from thy LORD, that thou mayest preach to a people, unto whom no preacher hath come before thee;[3] peradventure they will be directed. *It is* GOD who hath created the heavens and the earth, and whatever *is* between them, in six days; and then ascended *his* throne. Ye have no patron or intercessor besides him. Will ye not therefore consider? He governeth *all* things from heaven even to the earth: hereafter shall they return unto him, on the day whose length shall be a thousand years,[4] of those which ye compute. This *is* he who knoweth the future and the present; the mighty, the merciful. *It is he* who hath made everything which he hath created exceeding good; and first created man of clay and afterwards made his posterity of an extract of despicable water;[5] and then formed him *into proper shape*, and breathed of his spirit into him; and hath given you *the senses of* hearing and seeing, and hearts *to understand*. How small thanks do ye return! And they say, When we shall lie hidden in the earth, shall we be *raised thence* a new creature? Yea, they deny the meeting of their LORD *at the resurrection*. Say, The angel of death,[6] who is set over you, shall cause you to die: then shall ye

---

[1] The title is taken from the middle of the chapter, where the believers are said *to fall down adoring*.

[2] See note to Chap. II., and Sale, Prel. Disc. Sect. III. p. 64.

[3] See Chap. XXVIII. p. 382.

[4] As to the reconciliation of this passage with another (Chap. XX.), which seems contradictory, see Sale, Prel. Disc. Sect. IV. Some, however, do not interpret the passage before us of the resurrection, but suppose that the words here describe the making and executing of the decrees of GOD, which are sent down from heaven to earth, and are returned (or *ascend*, as the verb properly signifies) back to him after they have been put in execution; and present themselves, as it were, so executed, to his knowledge, in the space of a day with GOD, but with man, of a thousand years. Others imagine this space to be the time which the angels, who carry the divine decrees, and bring them back executed, take in descending and reascending, because the distance from heaven to earth is a journey of five hundred years: and others fancy that the angels bring down at once decrees for a thousand years to come, which being expired, they return back for fresh orders, &c. (Al Beidâwi.)

[5] *i.e.*, Seed.

[6] See Sale, Prel. Disc. Sect. IV. p. 77

be brought back unto your LORD. If thou couldst see, when the wicked shall bow down their heads before their LORD, *saying*, O LORD, we have seen and have heard : suffer us therefore to return *into the world*, and we will work that which is right ; since we are now certain *of the truth of what hath been preached to us : thou wouldst see an amazing sight.* If we had pleased, we had certainly given unto every soul its direction : but the word *which hath proceeded* from me must necessarily be fulfilled, *when I said*, Verily I will fill hell with genii and men, altogether.[1] Taste therefore *the torment prepared for you*, because ye have forgotten the coming of this your day : we also have forgotten you ; taste therefore a punishment of eternal duration, for that which ye have wrought. Verily they only believe in our signs, who, when they are warned thereby, fall down adoring, and celebrate the praise of their LORD, and are not elated with pride : their sides are raised from *their* beds, calling on their LORD with fear and with hope ; and they distribute alms out of what we have bestowed on them. No soul [2] knoweth the complete satisfaction [3] which is secretly prepared for them, as a reward for that which they have wrought. Shall he, therefore, who is a true believer, *be* as he who is an impious transgressor ? They shall not be held equal. As to those who believe and do that which is right, they shall have gardens of *perpetual* abode, an ample recompence for that which they shall have wrought : but as for those who impiously transgress, their abode *shall be hell* fire ; so often as they shall endeavour to get thereout, they shall be dragged back into the same, and it shall be said unto them, Taste ye the torment of *hell* fire, which ye rejected as a falsehood. And we will cause them to taste the nearer punishment *of this world*, besides the more grievous punishment *of the next* ; peradventure they will repent. Who is more unjust than he who is warned by the signs of his LORD, and then turneth aside from the same ? We will surely take vengeance on the wicked. We heretofore delivered the book *of the law* unto Moses ; wherefore be not thou in doubt as to the

[1] See Chaps. VII. p. 143, and XI. p. 224.
[2] Not even an angel of those who approach nearest GOD's throne, nor any prophet who hath been sent by him. (Al Beidâwi.)
[3] Literally, *The Joy of the eyes.* The commentators fail not, on occasion of this passage, to produce that saying of their prophet, which was originally none of his own : GOD *saith, I have prepared for my righteous servants, what eye hath not seen, nor hath ear heard, not hath entered into the heart of man to conceive.*

revelation thereof :[1] and we ordained the same *to be* a direction unto the children of Israel ; and we appointed teachers from among them, who should direct *the people* at our command, when they had persevered with patience, and had firmly believed in our signs. Verily thy LORD will judge between them, on the day of resurrection, concerning that wherein they have disagreed. Is it not known unto them how many generations we have destroyed before them, through whose dwellings they walk ?[2] Verily herein are signs : will they not therefore hearken ? Do they not see that we drive rain unto a land bare of grass and parched up, and thereby produce corn, of which their cattle eat, and themselves *also* ? Will they not therefore regard ? The *infidels* say *to the true believers*, When *will* this decision *be made between us*, if ye speak truth ? Answer, On the day of *that* decision,[3] the faith of those who shall have disbelieved shall not avail them ; neither shall they be respited *any longer*. Wherefore avoid them, and expect *the issue* : verily they expect *to obtain some advantage over thee*.

XXXIII

THE CHAPTER OF THE CONFEDERATES [4]
Revealed at Medina.

IN THE NAME OF THE MOST MERCIFUL GOD.

O PROPHET, fear GOD, and obey not the unbelievers and the hypocrites :[5] verily GOD is knowing *and* wise.

---

[1] Or, as some interpret it, *of the revelation of the Korân to thyself* ; since the delivery of the law to Moses proves that the revelation of the Korân to thee is not the first instance of the kind. Others think the words should be translated thus : *Be thou not in doubt as to thy meeting of that prophet*; supposing that the interview between Moses and Mohammed in the sixth heaven, when the latter took his night-journey thither, is here intended. (Al Beidâwi.)

[2] The Meccans frequently passing by the places where the Adites, Thamûdites, Midianites, Sodomites, &c., once dwelt.

[3] That is, on the day of judgment ; though some suppose the day here intended to be that of the victory at Bedr, or else that of the taking of Mecca, when several of those who had been proscribed were put to death without remission. (Sale, Prel. Disc. Sect. II. p. 59.)

[4] Part of this chapter was revealed on occasion of the war of the ditch, which happened in the fifth year of the Hejra, when Medina was besieged, for above twenty days, by the joint and *confederate* forces of several Jewish tribes, and of the inhabitants of Mecca, Najd, and Tehâma, at the instigation of the Jews of the tribe of Nadhir, who had been driven out of their settlement near Medina, by Mohammed, the year before. (Vide Abulfeda, Vit. Moh. p. 73, et Gagnier, Vit. de Mahomet, l. 4, c. 1.)

[5] It is related that Abu Sofiân, Acrema Ebn Abi Jahl, and Abu'l A'war

But follow that which is revealed unto thee from thy
LORD; for GOD is well acquainted with that which ye
do: and put thy trust in GOD; for GOD is a sufficient
protector. GOD hath not given a man two hearts
within him, neither hath he made your wives (some of
whom ye divorce, regarding them hereafter as your
mothers) your *true* mothers; nor hath he made your
adopted sons your *true* sons.[1] This *is* your saying in your
mouths; but GOD speaketh the truth; and he directeth
the *right* way. Call *such as are adopted*, the sons of their
natural fathers: this *will be* more just in the sight of
GOD. And if ye know not their fathers, *let them be as* your
brethren in religion, and your companions: and it shall be
no crime in you, that ye err[2] *in this matter*; but that *shall be
criminal* which your hearts purposely design; for GOD is
gracious *and* merciful. The prophet *is* nigher unto the true
believers than their own souls;[3] and his wives *are* their

al Salami, having an amicable interview with Mohammed, at which were
present also Abda'llah Ebn Obba, Moatteb Ebn Kosheir, and Jadd Ebn
Kais, they proposed to the prophet that if he would leave off preaching
against the worship of their gods, and acknowledge them to be mediators,
they would give him and his LORD no further disturbance; upon which
these words were revealed. (Al Beidâwi.)
 [1] This passage was revealed to abolish two customs among the old Arabs.
The first was their manner of divorcing their wives, when they had no
mind to let them go out of their house, or to marry again: and this the
husband did by saying to the woman, *Thou art henceforward to me as the back of
my mother*; after which words pronounced he abstained from her bed, and
regarded her in all respects as his mother, and she became related to all his
kindred in the same degree as if she had been really so. The other custom
was the holding their adopted sons to be as nearly related to them as their
natural sons, so that the same impediments of marriage arose from that
supposed relation, in the prohibited degrees, as it would have done in the
case of a genuine son. The latter Mohammed had a peculiar reason to
abolish—viz., his marrying the divorced wife of his freedman Zeid, who
was also his adopted son, of which more will be said by-and-bye. By the
declaration which introduces this passage, that GOD *has not given a man
two hearts*, is meant, that a man cannot have the same affection for supposed
parents and adopted children, as for those who are really so. They tell us
the Arabs used to say, of a prudent and acute person, that he had two hearts;
whence one Abu Mámer, or, as others write, Jemil Ebn Asad al Fihri, was
surnamed Dhu'lkalbein, or *the man with two hearts*. (Al Beidâwi, Jallalo'ddin,
&c.)
 [2] Through ignorance or mistake; or, that ye have erred for the time past.
 [3] Commanding them nothing but what is for their interest and advantage,
and being more solicitous for their present and future happiness even than
themselves; for which reason he ought to be dear to them, and deserves their
utmost love and respect. In some copies these words are added, *And he
is a father unto them*; every prophet being the spiritual father of his people,
who are therefore brethren. It is said that this passage was revealed on
some of Mohammed's followers telling him, when he summoned them to
attend him in the expedition of Tabûc (see Chap. IX.), that they would ask
leave of their fathers and mothers. (Al Beidâwi.)

mothers.[1] Those who are related by consanguinity *are* nigher of kin the one of them unto the others, according to the book of GOD, than the *other* true believers, and the Mohâjerin :[2] unless that ye do what is fitting and reasonable to your relations *in general*. This is written in the book *of God*.[3] *Remember* when we accepted their covenant from the prophets,[4] and from thee, *O Mohammed*, and from Noah, and Abraham, and Moses, and Jesus the son of Mary, and received from them a firm covenant ;[5] that *God* may examine the speakers of truth concerning their veracity ;[6] and he hath prepared a painful torment for the unbelievers. O true believers, remember the favour of GOD towards you, when armies *of infidels* came against you,[7] and we sent against them a wind, and hosts *of angels* which ye saw not :[8] and

---

[1] Though the spiritual relation between Mohammed and his people, declared in the preceding words, created no impediment to prevent his taking to wife such women among them as he thought fit ; yet the commentators are of opinion that they are here forbidden to marry any of his wives. (Sale, Prel. Disc. Sect. VI.)

[2] These words, which also occur, excepting the latter part of the sentence, in the eighth chapter, abrogate that law concerning inheritances, published in the same chapter, whereby the Mohâjerin and Ansârs were to be the heirs of one another, exclusive of their nearer relations, who were infidels. (Chap. VIII. p. 180.)

[3] *i.e.*, In the preserved table, or the Korân ; or, as others suppose, in the Pentateuch.

[4] Jallalo'ddin supposes this covenant was made when Adam's posterity were drawn forth from his loins, and appeared before GOD like small ants (Chap. VII.) : but Marracci conjectures that the covenant here meant was the same which the Talmudists pretend all the prophets entered into with GOD on Mount Sinai, where they were all assembled in person with Moses. (Chap. III. p. 55.)

[5] Whereby they undertook to execute their several commissions, and promised to preach the religion commanded them by GOD.

[6] *i.e.*, That he may at the day of judgment demand of the prophets in what manner they executed their several commissions, and how they were received by their people ; or, as the words may also import, that he may examine those who believed on them, concerning their belief, and reward them accordingly.

[7] These were the forces of the Koreish and the tribe of Ghatfân, confederated with the Jews of Al Nadhir and Koreidha, who besieged Medina to the number of twelve thousand men, in the expedition called the *war of the ditch*.

[8] On the enemies' approach, Mohammed, by the advice of Salmân, the Persian, ordered a deep ditch or entrenchment to be dug round Medina, for the security of the city, and went out to defend it with three thousand men. Both sides remained in their camps near a month, without any other acts of hostility than shooting of arrows and slinging of stones ; till, in a winter's night, GOD sent a piercing cold east wind, which benumbed the limbs of the confederates, blew the dust in their faces, extinguished their fires, overturned their tents, and put their horses in disorder, the angels at the same time crying, *Allah acbar*! round about their camp ; whereupon Toleiha Ebn Khowailed, the Asadite, said aloud, *Mohammed is going to attack you with enchantments, wherefore provide for your safety by flight*: and accordingly the Koreish first, and afterwards the Ghatfânites, broke up the siege, and returned home, which retreat was also not a little owing to

GOD beheld that which ye did. When they came against you from above you, and from below you,[1] and when *your* sight became troubled, and *your* hearts came even to *your* throats *for fear*, and ye imagined of GOD *various* imaginations.[2]   Then were the faithful tried, and made to tremble with a violent trembling. And when the hypocrites, and those in whose heart was an infirmity, said, GOD and his apostle have made you no other than a fallacious promise.[3] And when a party of them[4] said, O inhabitants of Yathreb,[5] *there is* no place *of security* for you *here*; wherefore return *home*. And a part of them asked leave of the prophet *to depart*, saying, Verily our houses are defenceless *and exposed to the enemy* : but they were not defenceless, *and* their intention was no other than to fly. If *the city* had been entered upon then *by the enemy* from the parts adjacent, and they had been asked to desert *the true believers, and to fight against them* ; they had surely consented thereto : but they had not, *in such case*, remained in the same[6] but a little while. They had before made a covenant with GOD, that they would not turn *their* backs :[7] and the *performance of their* covenant with GOD shall be examined into *hereafter*. Say, Flight shall not profit you, if ye fly from death or from slaughter : and *if it would*, yet shall ye not enjoy *this world* but a little. Say, Who *is* he who shall defend you against GOD, if he is pleased *to bring* evil on you, or is pleased *to show* mercy

the dissensions among the confederate forces, the raising and fomenting whereof the Mohammedans also ascribe to GOD. It is related that when Mohammed heard that his enemies were retired, he said, *I have obtained success by means of the east wind* ; *and Ad perished by the west wind*. (Al Beidâwi, Abulf. Vit. Moh. p. 77, &c.)

[1] The Ghatfânites pitched on the east side of the town, on the higher part of the valley ; and the Koreish on the west side, on the lower part of the valley. (Al Beidâwi.)

[2] The sincere and those who were more firm of heart fearing they should not be able to stand the trial ; and the weaker-hearted and hypocrites thinking themselves delivered up to slaughter and destruction.

[3] The person who uttered these words, it is said, was Moatteb Ebn Kosheir, who told his fellows that Mohammed had promised them the spoils of the Persians and the Greeks, whereas now not one of them dared to stir out of their entrenchment. (Al Beidâwi. Vide Abulf. ubi sup. p. 76.)

[4] viz., Aws Ebn Keidhi and his adherents.

[5] This was the ancient and proper name of Medina, or of the territory wherein it stands. Some suppose the town was so named from its founder, Yathreb, the son of Kâbiya, the son of Mahlayel, the son of Aram, the son of Sem, the son of Noah ; though others tell us it was built by the Amalekites. (Ahmed Ebn Yusof. Sale, Prel. Disc. Sect. I.)

[6] *i.e.*, In the city ; or, in their apostasy and rebellion, because the Moslems would surely succeed at last.

[7] The persons meant here were Banu Haretha, who having behaved very ill and run away on a certain occasion, promised they would do so no more. (Al Beidâwi.)

towards you ? They shall find none to patronize or protect them, besides GOD. GOD already knoweth those among you who hinder *others from following his apostle,* and who say unto their brethren, Come hither unto us ; and who come not to battle, except a little ; [1] being covetous towards you : [2] but when fear cometh *on them,* thou seest them look unto thee *for assistance,* their eyes rolling about, like *the eyes* of him who fainteth by reason of *the agonies of* death : yet when *their* fear is past, they inveigh against you with sharp tongues, being covetous of the best *and most valuable part of the spoils.* These believe not *sincerely* ; wherefore GOD hath rendered their works of no avail ; and this is easy with GOD. They imagined that the confederates would not depart *and raise the siege* : and if the confederates should come *another time,* they would wish to live in the deserts among the Arabs who dwell in tents ;[3] and there to inquire of news concerning you ; and although they were with you *this time,* yet they fought not, except a little. Ye have in the apostle of GOD an excellent example,[4] unto him who hopeth in GOD and the last day, and remembereth GOD frequently. When the true believers saw the confederates, they said, This *is* what GOD and his apostle have foretold us ;[5] and GOD and his apostle have spoken the truth : and it only increased their faith and resignation. Of the true believers, *some* men justly performed what they had promised unto GOD ;[6] and some of them have finished their course,[7] and some of them wait *the same advantage* ;[8] and

[1] Either coming to the army in small numbers, or staying with them but a little while, and then returning on some feigned excuse ; or behaving ill in time of action. Some expositors take these words to be part of the speech of the hypocrites, reflecting on Mohammed's companions for lying idle in the trenches, and not attacking the enemy.

[2] *i.e.,* Sparing of their assistance either in person or with their purse ; or being greedy after the booty.

[3] That they might be absent, and not obliged to go to war.

[4] viz., Of firmness in time of danger, of confidence in the divine assistance, and of piety by fervent prayer for the same.

[5] Namely, That we must not expect to enter paradise without undergoing some trials and tribulations. There is a tradition that Mohammed actually foretold this expedition of confederates some time before, and the success of it. (Al Beidâwi.)

[6] By standing firm with the prophet, and strenuously opposing the enemies of the true religion, according to their engagement.

[7] Or, as the words may be translated, *have fulfilled their vow,* or *paid their debt* to nature, by falling martyrs in battle ; as did Hamza, Mohammed's uncle, Masab Ebn Omair, and Ans Ebn al Nadr (Al Beidâwi), who were slain at the battle of Ohod. The martyrs in the war of the ditch were six, including Saad Ebn Moadh, who died of his wound about a month after. (Abulf. Vit. Moh. p. 79.)

[8] As Othmân and Telha. (Al Beidâwi.)

they changed not *their promise*, by deviating *therefrom in the least* : that GOD may reward the just performers *of their covenant* for their fidelity ; and may punish the hypocritical, if he pleaseth, or may be turned unto them ; for GOD *is* ready to forgive, *and* merciful. GOD hath driven back the infidels in their wrath : they obtained no advantage ; and GOD was *a* sufficient *protector* unto the faithful in battle ; for GOD is strong *and* mighty. And he hath caused such of those who have received the scriptures, as assisted *the confederates*, to come down out of their fortresses,[1] and he cast into their hearts terror *and dismay* :[2] a part *of them* ye slew, and a part ye made captives ; and GOD hath caused you to inherit their land, and their houses, and their wealth,[3]

[1] These were the Jews of the tribe of Koreidha, who, though they were in league with Mohammed, had, at the incessant persuasion of Caab Ebn Asad, a principal man among them, perfidiously gone over to his enemies in this war of the ditch, and were severely punished for it. For the next morning, after the confederate forces had decamped, Mohammed and his men returned to Medina, and, laying down their arms, began to refresh themselves after their fatigue ; upon which Gabriel came to the prophet and asked him whether he had suffered his people to lay down their arms, when the angels had not laid down theirs ; and ordering him to go immediately against the Koreidhites, assuring him that himself would lead the way. Mohammed, in obedience to the divine command, having caused public proclamation to be made that every one should pray that afternoon for success against the sons of Koreidha, set forward upon the expedition without loss of time ; and being arrived at the fortress of the Koreidhites, besieged them for twenty-five days, at the end of which those people, being in great terror and distress, capitulated, and at length, not daring to trust to Mohammed's mercy, surrendered at the discretion of Saad Ebn Moadh (see Chap. VIII.), hoping that he, being the prince of the tribe of Aws, their old friends and confederates, would have some regard for them. But they were deceived ; for Saad, being greatly incensed at their breach of faith, had begged of GOD that he might not die of the wound he had received at the ditch till he saw vengeance taken on the Koreidhites, and therefore adjudged that the men should be put to the sword, the women and children made slaves, and their goods be divided among the Moslems ; which sentence Mohammed had no sooner heard than he cried out, *That Saad had pronounced the sentence of* GOD : and the same was accordingly executed, the number of men who were slain amounting to six hundred, or, as others say, to seven hundred, or very near, among whom were Hoyai Ebn Akhtab, a great enemy of Mohammed's, and Caab Ebn Asad, who had been the chief occasion of the revolt of their tribe : and soon after Saad, who had given judgment against them, died, his wound, which had been skinned over, opening again. (Al Beidâwi, Abulf. Vit. Moh. p. 77, &c. Vide Gagnier, Vie de Mah. l. 4, c. 2.)

[2] This was the work of Gabriel, who, according to his promise, went before the army of Moslems. It is said that Mohammed, a little before he came to the settlement of the Koreidhites, asking some of his men whether anybody had passed them, they answered, that Dohya Ebn Kholeifa, the Calbite, had just passed by them, mounted on a white mule, with housings of satin : to which he replied, *That person was the angel Gabriel, who is sent to the sons of Koreidha to shake their castles, and to strike their hearts with fear and consternation.* (Ebn Ishak.)

[3] Their immovable possessions Mohammed gave to the Mohâjerin, saying, that the Ansârs were in their own houses, but that the others were destitute of habitations. The movables were divided among his followers, but he

and a land on which ye have not trodden ;[1] for GOD is almighty. O prophet, say unto thy wives, If ye seek this present life, and the pomp thereof, come, I will make a handsome provision for you, and I will dismiss you with an honourable dismission :[2] but if ye seek GOD and his apostle, and the life to come, verily GOD hath prepared for such of you as work righteousness a great reward. O wives of the prophet, whosoever of you shall commit a manifest wickedness, the punishment *thereof* thall be doubled unto her twofold ;[3] and this is easy with GOD : (XXII.)[4] but whosoever of you shall be obedient unto GOD and his apostle, and shall do that which is right, we will give her her reward twice,[5] and we have prepared for her an honourable provision *in paradise.* O wives of the prophet, ye are not as other women ; if ye fear GOD, be not too complaisant in speech, lest he should covet, in whose heart is a disease *of incontinence* : but speak the speech which is convenient. And sit still in your houses ; and set not out yourselves with the ostentation of the former *time of* ignorance :[6] and observe the appointed times of prayer, and give alms ; and obey GOD and his apostle ; for GOD desireth only to remove from you the abomination *of vanity, since ye are* the household *of the prophet,* and to purify you by a *perfect* purification.[7]

remitted the fifth part, which was usual to be taken in other cases. (Al Beidâwi.)

[1] By which some suppose Persia and Greece are meant ; others, Khaibar ; and others, whatever lands the Moslems may conquer till the day of judgment. (Al Beidâwi.)

[2] This passage was revealed on Mohammed's wives asking for more sumptuous clothes, and an additional allowance for their expenses ; and he had no sooner received it than he gave them their option, either to continue with him or to be divorced, beginning with Ayesha, who chose GOD *and his apostle,* and the rest followed her example ; upon which the prophet thanked them, and the following words were revealed, viz., *It shall not be lawful for thee to take other women to wife hereafter,* &c. (see after, in this chapter). From hence some have concluded that a wife who has her option given her, and chooses to stay with her husband, shall not be divorced, though others are of a contrary opinion. (Al Beidâwi.)

[3] For the crime would be more enormous and unpardonable in them, because of their superior condition, and the grace which they have received from GOD ; whence it is that the punishment of a free person is ordained to be double to that of a slave, and prophets are more severely reprimanded for their faults than other men (Al Beidâwi). [4] Section XXII. begins.

[5] viz., Once for her obedience, and a second time for her conjugal affection to the prophet, and handsome behaviour to him.

[6] That is, in the old time of idolatry. Some suppose the times before the Flood, or the time of Abraham, to be here intended, when women adorned themselves with all their finery, and went abroad into the streets to show themselves to the men. (Al Beidâwi.)

[7] The pronouns of the second person in this part of the passage being of the masculine gender. the Shiites pretend the sentence has no connection

And remember that which is read in your houses, of the signs of GOD, and of the wisdom *revealed in the Korân* ; for GOD is clear-sighted, *and* well acquainted *with your actions*. Verily the Moslems of either sex, and the true believers of either sex, and the devout men, and the devout women, and the men of veracity, and the women of veracity, and the patient *men*, and the patient *women*, and the humble *men*, and the humble *women*, and the alms-givers of either sex, and the *men* who fast, and the *women* who fast, and the chaste *men*, and the chaste *women*, and those of either sex who remember GOD frequently ; for them hath GOD prepared forgiveness and a great reward. It is not *fit* for a true believer of either sex, when GOD and his apostle have decreed a thing, that they should have the liberty of choosing a *different* matter of their own :[1] and whoever is disobedient unto GOD and his apostle, surely erreth with a manifest error. And *remember* when thou saidst to him unto whom GOD had been gracious,[2] and on whom thou *also* hadst conferred favours,[3] Keep thy wife to thyself and fear GOD : and thou didst conceal that in thy mind which GOD had *determined* to discover,[4] and didst fear men ; whereas it *was*

with the foregoing or the following words ; and will have it that by *the household of the prophet* are particularly meant Fâtema and Ali, and their two sons, Hasan and Hosein, to whom these words are directed. (Al Beidâwi.)

[1] This verse was revealed on account of Zeinab (or Zenobia), the daughter of Jahash, and wife of Zeid, Mohammed's freedman, whom the prophet sought in marriage, but received a repulse from the lady and her brother Abdallah, they being at first averse to the match : for which they are here reprehended. The mother of Zeinab, it is said, was Amima, the daughter of Abd'almotalleb, and aunt to Mohammed. (Al Beidâwi, Jallalo'ddin.)

[2] viz., Zeid Ebn Haretha, on whom GOD had bestowed the grace early to become a Moslem.

[3] By giving him his liberty, and adopting him for thy son, &c. Zeid was of the tribe of Calb, a branch of the Khodaites, descended from Hamyar, the son of Saba ; and being taken in his childhood by a party of freebooters, was bought by Mohammed, or, as others say, by his wife Khadijah before she married him. Some years after, Haretha, hearing where his son was, took a journey to Mecca, and offered a considerable sum for his ransom ; whereupon, Mohammed said, *Let Zeid come hither ; and if he chooses to go with you, take him without ransom : but if it be his choice to stay with me, why should I not keep him ?* And Zeid being come, declared that he would stay with his master, who treated him as if he were his only son. Mohammed no sooner heard this, but he took Zeid by the hand, and led him to the black stone of the Caaba, where he publicly adopted him for his son, and constituted him his heir, with which the father acquiesced, and returned home well satisfied. From this time Zeid was called the son of Mohammed, till the publication of Islâm, after which the prophet gave him to wife Zeinab. (Al Jannabi. Vide Gagnier, Vie de Moh. i. 4, p. 3.)

[4] Namely, thy affection to Zeinab. The whole intrigue is artfully enough unfolded in this passage. The story is as follows :—Some years after his marriage, Mohammed, going to Zeid's house on some affair, and not finding him at home, accidentally cast his eyes on Zeinab, who was then in a dress

more just that thou shouldst fear GOD. But when Zeid[1] had determined the matter concerning her, *and had resolved to divorce her*, we joined her in marriage unto thee ;[2] lest a crime should be *charged* on the true believers, in *marrying* the wives of their adopted *sons*, when they have determined the matter concerning them :[3] and the command of GOD is to be performed. No crime is *to be charged* on the prophet, as to what GOD hath allowed him, *conformable to* the ordinance of GOD with regard to those who preceded *him* (for the command of GOD is a determinate decree), who brought the messages of GOD, and feared him, and feared none besides GOD : and GOD is a sufficient accountant. Mohammed is not the father of any man among you ; but the apostle of GOD, and the seal of the prophets : and GOD knoweth all things. O true believers, remember GOD with a frequent remembrance, and celebrate his praise morning and evening. It is he who is gracious unto you, and his angels *intercede for you*, that he may lead you forth from darkness into light ; and he is merciful towards the true believers. Their salutation, on the day *whereon* they shall meet him, *shall be*, Peace ! and he hath prepared for them an honourable recompence. O prophet, verily we have sent thee *to be* a witness, and a bearer of good tidings, and a denouncer of threats, and an inviter unto GOD, through his good pleasure, and a shining light. Bear good tidings therefore unto the true believers, that they shall receive great abundance from GOD. And obey not the unbelievers and hypocrites, and mind not

which discovered her beauty to advantage, and was so smitten at the sight, that he could not forbear crying out, GOD *be praised, who turneth the hearts of men as he pleaseth*! This Zeinab failed not to acquaint her husband with on his return home ; whereupon, Zeid, after mature reflection, thought he could do no less than part with his wife in favour of his benefactor, and therefore resolved to divorce her, and acquainted Mohammed with his resolution ; but he, apprehending the scandal it might raise, offered to dissuade him from it, and endeavoured to stifle the flames which inwardly consumed him ; but at length, his love for her being authorized by this revelation, he acquiesced, and after the term of her divorce was expired, married her in the latter end of the fifth year of the Hejra. (Al Beidâwi, Al Jannabi, &c.)

[1] It is observed that this is the only person, of all Mohammed's companions, whose name is mentioned in the Korân.

[2] Whence Zeinab used to vaunt herself above the prophet's other wives, saying that GOD had made the match between Mohammed and herself, whereas their matches were made by their relations. (Al Beidâwi.)

[3] For this feigned relation, as has been observed, created an impediment of marriage among the old Arabs within the prohibited degrees, in the same manner as if it had been real ; and therefore Mohammed's marrying Zeinab, who had been his adopted son's wife, occasioned great scandal among his followers, which was much heightened by the Jews and hypocrites : but the custom is here declared unreasonable, and abolished for the future.

CHAP. XXXIII.] THE CONFEDERATES 415

their evil treatment : but trust in GOD ; and GOD is a sufficient protector. O true believers, when ye marry *women
who are* believers, and afterwards put them away before ye
have touched them, *there is* no term prescribed you to fulfil
towards them[1] *after their divorce* ; but make them a present,[2]
and dismiss them freely, with an honourable dismission.
O prophet, we have allowed thee thy wives unto whom thou
hast given their dower, and also the *slaves* which thy right
hand possesseth, of the *booty* which GOD hath granted thee ;[3]
and the daughters of thy uncle, and the daughters of thy
aunts, both on thy father's side and on thy mother's side,
who have fled with thee *from Mecca,*[4] and any *other* believing woman, if she give herself unto the prophet ;[5] in case
the prophet desireth to take her to wife. *This is* a peculiar
privilege *granted* unto thee, above the rest of the true believers.[6] We know what we have ordained them concerning their wives, and the *slaves* whom their right hands
possess : lest it should be *deemed* a crime in thee *to make use
of the privilege granted thee* ; for GOD is gracious *and* merciful.
Thou mayest postpone the turn of such of *thy wives* as thou
shalt please, *in being called to thy bed* ; and thou mayest take
unto thee her whom thou shalt please, and her whom thou
shalt desire of those whom thou shalt have *before* rejected :

[1] That is, Ye are not obliged to keep them any certain time before ye
dismiss them, as ye are those with whom the marriage has been consummated.
(See Chap. II. p. 32.)
[2] *i.e.*, If no dower has been assigned them : for if a dower has been assigned,
the husband is obliged, according to the Sonna, to give the woman half the
dower agreed on, besides a present. (Al Beidâwi.) This is still to be understood of such women with whom the marriage has not been consummated.
[3] It is said, therefore, that the women slaves which he should buy are
not included in this grant.
[4] But not the others. It is related of Omm Hâni, the daughter of Abu
Taleb, that she would say, *The apostle of GOD courted me for his wife, but
I excused myself to him, and he accepted of my excuse : afterwards this verse
was revealed ; but he was not thereby allowed to marry me, because I fled not
with him.* (Al Beidâwi.) It may be observed that Dr. Prideaux is much
mistaken when he asserts that Mohammed, in this chapter, brings in GOD
exempting him from the law in the fourth chapter, whereby the Moslems
are forbidden to marry within certain degrees, and giving him an especial
privilege to take to wife the daughter of his brother, or the daughter of his
sister. (See Prid. Life of Mahomet, p. 116.)
[5] Without demanding any dower. According to a tradition of Ebn
Abbas, the prophet, however, married no woman without assigning her a
dower. The commentators are not agreed who was the woman particularly
meant in this passage : but they name four who are supposed to have thus
given themselves to the prophet, viz., Maimûna Bint al Hareth, Zeinab Bint
Khozaima, Ghozia Bint Jâber, surnamed Omm Shoraic (which three he
actually married), and Khawla Bint Hakim, whom as it seems, he rejected.
[6] For no Moslem can legally marry above four wives, whether free women
or slaves ; whereas Mohammed is, by the preceding passage, left at liberty
to take as many as he pleased, though with some restrictions.

and *it shall be* no crime in thee.[1] This *will be* more easy, that they may be entirely content, and may not be grieved, but may be well pleased with what thou shalt give every of them : GOD knoweth whatever *is* in your hearts ; and GOD is knowing *and* gracious. It shall not be lawful for thee *to take other* women *to wife* hereafter,[2] nor to exchange *any* of *thy* wives for them,[3] although their beauty please thee ; except the *slaves* whom thy right hand shall possess : and GOD observeth all things. O true believers, enter not the houses of the prophet, unless it be permitted you to *eat* meat *with him*, without waiting his convenient time : but when ye are invited, then enter. And when ye shall have eaten, disperse yourselves ; and *stay* not to enter into familiar discourse : for this incommodeth the prophet. He is ashamed *to bid* you *depart* ; but GOD is not ashamed of the truth. And when ye ask of *the prophet's wives* what ye may have occasion for, ask *it* of them from behind a curtain.[4] This will be more pure for your hearts and their hearts. Neither is it *fit* for you to give any uneasiness to the apostle of GOD, or to marry his wives after him for ever :[5] for this

---

[1] By this passage some further privileges were granted unto Mohammed ; for, whereas other men are obliged to carry themselves equally towards their wives (Chap. IV.), in case they had more than one, particularly as to the duties of the marriage bed, to which each has a right to be called in her turn— which right was acknowledged in the most early ages—(See Gen. xxx. 14, &c.), and cannot take again a wife whom they have divorced the third time, till she has been married to another and divorced by him (Chap. II.), the prophet was left absolutely at liberty to deal with them in these and other respects as he thought fit.

[2] The commentators differ as to the express meaning of these words. Some think Mohammed was thereby forbidden to take any more wives than nine, which number be then had, and is supposed to have been his stint, as four was that of other men ; some imagine that after this prohibition, though any of the wives he then had should die or be divorced, yet he could not marry another in her room : some think he was only forbidden from this time forward to marry any other woman than one of the four sorts mentioned in the preceding passage ; and others (as Abul Kasem Hebatallah) are of opinion that this verse is abrogated by the two preceding verses, or one of them, and was revealed before them, though it be read after them. (Al Zamakh., Al Beidâwi, Jallalo'ddin, &c.)

[3] By divorcing her and marrying another. Al Zamakhshari tells us that some are of opinion this prohibition is to be understood of a particular kind of exchange used among the idolatrous Arabs, whereby two men made a mutual exchange of their wives without any other formality.

[4] That is, let there be a curtain drawn between you, or let them be veiled while ye talk with them. As the design of the former precept was to prevent the impertinence of troublesome visitors, the design of this was to guard against too near an intercourse or familiarity between his wives and his followers ; and was occasioned, it is said, by the hand of one of his companions accidentally touching that of Ayesha, which gave the prophet some uneasiness. (Al Beidâwi.)

[5] *i.e.*, Eitner such as he shall divorce in his lifetime, or his widows after

would be a grievous thing in the sight of GOD. Whether ye divulge a thing, or conceal it, verily GOD knoweth all things. *It shall be* no crime in them as to their fathers, or their sons, or their brothers, or their brothers' sons, or their sisters' sons, or their women, or the *slaves* which their right hands possess, *if they speak to them unveiled* :[1] and fear ye GOD ;[2] for GOD is witness of all things.   Verily GOD and his angels bless the prophet : O true believers, do ye *also* bless him, and salute *him* with *a respectful* salutation.[3]   *As to* those who offend GOD and his apostle, GOD shall curse them in this world and in the next ; and he hath prepared for them a shameful punishment.   And they who shall injure the true believers of either sex, without their deserving it, shall surely bear *the guilt of* calumny and a manifest injustice.[4]   O prophet, speak unto thy wives, and thy daughters, and the wives of the true believers, that they cast their outer garments[5] over them *when they walk abroad* ;   this *will be* more proper, that they may be known *to be matrons of reputation*, and may not be affronted *by unseemly words or actions*. GOD is gracious *and* merciful.   Verily if the hypocrites, and those in whose hearts is an infirmity, and they who raise disturbances in Medina, do not desist ; we will surely stir thee up against them, *to chastise them* :   henceforth they shall not *be suffered to* dwell near thee therein, except for a little *time, and* being accursed ;   wherever they are found they shall be taken, and killed with a *general* slaughter, *according to* the sentence of GOD concerning those who have been before ; and thou shalt not find any change in the sentence of GOD.   Men will ask thee concerning the *approach of the last* hour :   answer, Verily the knowledge thereof *is* with GOD alone ;   and he will not inform thee :   peradventure the hour is nigh *at hand*.   Verily GOD hath cursed the

his death. This was another privilege peculiar to the prophet. It is related that, in the Khalîfat of Omar, Ashath Ebn Kais married the woman whom Mohammed had dismissed without consummating his marriage with her, upon which the Khalîf at first was thinking to stone her, but afterwards changed his mind, on its being represented to him that this prohibition related only to such women to whom the prophet had gone in.   (Al Beidâwi.)

[1] Chap. XXIV. p. 352.

[2] The words are directed to the prophet's wives.

[3] Hence the Mohammedans seldom mention his name without adding, *On whom be the blessing of* GOD *and peace* ! or the like words.

[4] This verse was revealed, according to some, on occasion of certain hypocrites who had slandered Ali ; or, according to others, on occasion of those who falsely accused Ayesha, &c. (Chap. XXIV.)

[5] The original word properly signifies the large wrappers, usually of white linen, with which the women in the East cover themselves from head to foot when they go abroad.

infidels, and hath prepared for them a fierce fire, wherein they shall remain for ever : they shall find no patron or defender. On the day *whereon* their faces shall be rolled in *hell* fire, they shall say, Oh that we had obeyed GOD, and had obeyed *his* apostle ! And they shall say, O LORD, verily we have obeyed our lords and our great men ; and they have seduced us from the *right* way. O LORD, give them the double of *our* punishment ; and curse them with a heavy curse ! O true believers, be not as those who injured Moses ; but GOD cleared him from *the scandal* which they had spoken *concerning him* ;[1] and he was of great consideration in the sight of GOD.[2] O true believers, fear GOD, and speak words well directed ; that *God* may correct your works for you, and may forgive you your sins : and whoever shall obey GOD and his apostle, shall enjoy great felicity. We proposed the faith unto the heavens, and the earth, and the mountains : and they refused to undertake the same, and were afraid thereof ; but man undertook it :[3] verily

[1] The commentators are not agreed what this injury was. Some say that Moses using to wash himself apart, certain malicious people gave out that he had a rupture (or, say others, that he was a leper, or an hermaphrodite), and for that reason was ashamed to wash with them ; but GOD cleared him from this aspersion by causing the stone on which he had laid his clothes while he washed to run away with them into the camp, whither Moses followed it naked ; and by that means the Israelites, in the midst of whom he was gotten ere he was aware, plainly perceived the falsehood of the report. Others suppose Karûn's accusation of Moses is here intended (Chap. XXVIII.), or else the suspicion of Aaron's murder, which was cast on Moses because he was with him when he died on Mount Hor ; of which latter he was justified by the angels bringing his body and exposing it to public view, or, say some, by the testimony of Aaron himself, who was raised to life for that purpose. (Jallalo'ddin, Al Beidâwi.) The passage is said to have been occasioned by reflections which were cast on Mohammed, in his dividing certain spoils ; and that when they came to his ear, he said, GOD *be merciful unto my brother Moses : he was wronged more than this, and bore it with patience.* (Al Bokhari.)

[2] Some copies for *inda* read *abda*, according to which the words should be translated, *And he was an illustrious servant of* GOD.

[3] By faith is here understood entire obedience to the law of GOD, which is represented to be of so high concern (no less than eternal happiness or misery depending on the observance or neglect thereof), and so difficult in the performance, that if GOD should propose the same on the conditions annexed, to the vaster parts of the creation, and they had understanding to comprehend the offer, they would decline it, and not dare to take on them a duty, the failing wherein must be attended with so terrible a consequence ; and yet man is said to have undertaken it, notwithstanding his weakness and the infirmities of his nature. Some imagine this proposal is not hypothetical, but was actually made to the heavens, earth, and mountains, which at their first creation were endued with reason, and that GOD told them he had made a law, and had created paradise for the recompence of such as were obedient to it, and hell for the punishment of the disobedient ; to which they answered they were content to be obliged to perform the services for which they were created, but would not undertake to fulfil the divine law on those conditions, and therefore desired neither reward nor punishment ; they add that when Adam was created, the same offer was made to him,

he was unjust *to himself*, and foolish :[1] that GOD may punish the hypocritical men and the hypocritical women, and the idolaters, and the idolatresses ; and that GOD may be turned unto the true believers, both men and women ; for GOD is gracious *and* merciful.

XXXIV

THE CHAPTER OF SABA [2]

Revealed at Mecca.

IN THE NAME OF THE MOST MERCIFUL GOD.

PRAISE be to GOD, unto whom *belongeth* whatever *is* in the heavens and on earth : and unto him *be* praise in the world to come ; for he *is* wise *and* intelligent. He knoweth whatsoever entereth into the earth,[3] and whatsoever cometh out of the same,[4] and whatsoever descendeth from heaven,[5] and whatsoever ascendeth thereto :[6] and he *is* merciful *and* ready to forgive. The unbelievers say, The hour *of judgment* will not come unto us. Answer, Yea, by my LORD, it will surely come unto you ; *it is he* who knoweth the hidden secret : the weight of an ant, either in heaven or in earth, is not absent from him, nor anything lesser than this, or greater, but *the same is written* in the perspicuous book *of his decrees* ; that he may recompense those who shall have believed and wrought righteousness : they shall receive pardon and an honourable provision. But they who endeavour to render our signs of none effect, shall receive a punishment of painful torment. Those unto whom knowledge hath been given, see that the book which hath been revealed unto thee from thy LORD is the truth, and directeth into the glorious and laudable way. The unbelievers say *to one another*, Shall we show you a man who shall prophesy unto you, that when ye shall

and he accepted it. (Jallalo'ddin, Al Beidâwi.) The commentators have other explications of this passage, which it would be too prolix to transcribe.

[1] Unjust to himself in not fulfilling his engagements and obeying the law he had accepted, and foolish in not considering the consequence of his disobedience and neglect.

[2] Mention is made of the people of Saba in the fifteenth verse.

[3] As the rain, hidden treasures, the dead, &c.

[4] As animals, plants, metals, spring water, &c.

[5] As the angels, scriptures, decrees of GOD, rain, thunder and lightning, &c.

[6] As the angels, men's works, vapours, smoke, &c. (Al Beidâwi.)

have been dispersed with a total dispersion, ye shall *be raised* a new creature? He hath forged a lie concerning GOD, or rather he is distracted. But they who believe not in the life to come, shall *fall* into punishment and a wide error. Have they not therefore considered what is before them, and what is behind them, of the heaven and the earth? If we please, we will cause the earth to open and swallow them up, or will cause a piece of the heaven to fall upon them: verily herein is a sign unto every servant, who turneth *unto God*. We heretofore bestowed on David excellence from us: *and we said*, O mountains, sing alternate praises with him; and *we obliged* the birds *also to join therein*.[1] And we softened the iron for him, *saying*, Make *thereof* complete coats of mail,[2] and rightly dispose the small plates *which compose the same*: and work ye righteousness, *O family of David*; for I see that which ye do. And *we made* the wind *subject* unto Solomon:[3] *it blew* in the morning for a month, and in the evening for a month. And we made a fountain of molten brass to flow for him.[4] And some of the genii *were obliged* to work in his presence, by the will of his LORD; and whoever of them turned aside from our command, we will cause him to taste the pain of hell fire.[5] They made for him whatever he pleased, of palaces, and statues,[6] and large dishes like fishponds,[7] and cauldrons standing firm *on their trevets*;[8] *and we said*, Work *righteousness, O* family of David, with thanksgiving; for few of my servants are thankful. And when we had decreed that *Solomon* should die, nothing discovered his death unto them, except the creeping thing of the earth, which gnawed his

[1] Chap. XXI.

[2] See ibid.

[3] See ibid. and Chap. XXVII.

[4] This fountain they say was in Yaman, and flowed three days in a month. (Al Beidâwi, Jallalo'ddin.)

[5] Or, as some expound the words, *We caused him to taste the pain of burning*; by which they understand the correction the disobedient genii received at the hands of the angel set over them, who whipped them with a whip of fire.

[6] Some suppose these were images of the angels and prophets, and that the making of them was not then forbidden; or else that they were not such images as were forbidden by the law. Some say these spirits made him two lions, which were placed at the foot of his throne, and two eagles, which were set above it; and that when he mounted it the lions stretched out their paws, and when he sat down the eagles shaded him with their wings. (Al Beidâwi.)

[7] Being so monstrously large that a thousand men might eat out of each of them at once.

[8] These cauldrons, they say, were cut out of the mountains of Yaman, and were so vastly big that they could not be moved; and people went up to them by steps. (Jallalo'ddin.)

staff.[1] And when *his body* fell down, the genii plainly perceived that if they had known that which is secret, they had not continued in a vile punishment.[2] *The descendants of* Saba[3] had heretofore a sign in their dwelling ; *namely,* two gardens, on the right hand and on the left ;[4] *and it was said unto them,* Eat ye of the provision of your LORD, and give thanks unto him ; *ye have* a good country, and a gracious LORD. But they turned aside *from what we had commanded them* : wherefore we sent against them the inundation of Al Arem,[5] and we changed their two gardens for them into two gardens producing bitter fruit, and tamarisks,[6] and some little *fruit* of the lote-tree. This we gave them in reward, because they were ungrateful : is any *thus* rewarded

---

[1] The commentators, to explain this passage, tell us that David, having laid the foundations of the temple of Jerusalem, which was to be in lieu of the tabernacle of Moses, when he died, left it to be finished by his son Solomon, who employed the genii in the work : that Solomon, before the edifice was quite completed, perceiving his end drew nigh, begged of GOD that his death might be concealed from the genii till they had entirely finished it : that GOD therefore so ordered it, that Solomon died as he stood at his prayers, leaning on his staff, which supported the body in that posture a full year ; and the genii, supposing him to be alive, continued their work during that term, at the expiration whereof the temple being perfectly completed, a worm, which had gotten into the staff, ate it through, and the corpse fell to the ground and discovered the king's death. (Al Beidâwi, Jallalo'ddin.) Possibly this fable of the temple's being built by genii, and not by men, might take its rise from what is mentioned in Scripture, that *the house was built of stone made ready before it was brought thither ; so that there was neither hammer, nor axe, nor any tool of iron heard in the house while it was building* (1 Kings vi. 7) : the Rabbins indeed tell us of a worm, which might assist the workmen, its virtue being such as to cause the rocks and stones to fly in sunder. (Vide Kimhi, in loc. Buxt. Lex. Talm. p. 2456, et Schickardi Tarich reg. Pers. p. 62.) Whether the worm which gnawed Solomon's staff were of the same breed with this other, I know not ; but the story has perfectly the air of a Jewish invention.

[2] *i.e.,* They had not continued in servile subjection to the command of Solomon, nor had gone on with the work of the temple.

[3] Saba was the son of Yashhab, the son of Yárab, the son of Kahtân, whose posterity dwelt in Yaman, in the city of Mâreb, called also Saba, about three days' journey from Sanaa.

[4] That is, two tracts of land, one on this side of their city, and the other on that, planted with trees, and made into gardens, which lay so thick and close together, that each tract seemed to be one continued garden : or, it may be, every house had a garden on each hand of it. (Al Beidâwi.)

[5] The commentators set down several significations of the word Al Arem which are scarce worth mentioning : it most properly signifies *mounds* or *dams* for the stopping or containing of water, and is here used for that stupendous *mound* or building which formed the vast reservoir above the city of Saba, described in another place (Sale, Prel. Disc. Sect. I.), and which, for the great impiety, pride, and insolence of the inhabitants, was broken down in the night by a mighty flood, and occasioned a terrible destruction. Al Beidâwi supposes this mound was the work of Queen Balkîs, and that the above-mentioned catastrophe happened after the time of Jesus Christ ; wherein he seems to be mistaken.

[6] A low shrub bearing no fruit, and delighting in saltish and barren ground.

except the ungrateful ?   And we placed between them and
the cities which we have blessed,[1] cities situate near each
other ; and we made the journey easy between them,[2] *saying*,
Travel through the same by night and by day in security.
But they said, O LORD, put a *greater* distance between our
journeys :[3] and they were unjust unto themselves ; and we
made them the subject of discourse, and dispersed them
with a total dispersion.[4]   Verily herein *are* signs, unto every
patient, grateful person.   And Eblîs found his opinion of
them to be true :[5] and they followed him, except a party of
the true believers :[6] and he had no power over them, unless
to tempt them, that we might know him who believed in the
life to come, from him who doubted thereof.   Thy LORD
observeth all things.   Say *unto the idolaters*, Call upon those
whom ye imagine *to be gods*, besides GOD, they are not masters
of the weight of an ant in heaven or on earth, neither
have they any share in *the creation or government of* the
same ; nor is any of them assistant to him *therein*.   No
intercession will be of service in his presence, except *the intercession* of him to whom he shall grant permission *to intercede
for others* :[7] *and they shall wait in suspense* until, when the
terror shall be taken off from their hearts,[8] they shall say *to*

[1] viz., The cities of Syria.

[2] By reason of their near distance, so that during the whole journey a
traveller might rest in one town during the heat of the day, and in another
at night ; nor was he obliged to carry provisions with him.   (Jallal., Al
Beidâwi.)

[3] This petition they made out of covetousness, that the poor being obliged
to be longer on the road, they might make greater advantages in letting
out their cattle, and furnishing the travellers with provisions ; and GOD
was pleased to punish them by granting them their wish, and permitting
most of the cities, which were between Saba and Syria, to be ruined and
abandoned.   (Al Beidâwi.)

[4] For the neighbouring nations justly wondered at so sudden and un-
foreseen a revolution in the affairs of this once flourishing people : whence
it became a proverbial saying, to express a total dispersion, that *they were
gone and scattered like Saba.* (Al Beidâwi. Vide Gol. not in Alfrag. p. 87.)
Of the descendants of Saba, who quitted their country and sought new settlements on this inundation, the tribe of Ghassân went into Syria, the tribe of
Anmâr to Yathreb, the tribe of Jodhâm to Tehâmah, the tribe of Al Azd
to Omân (Al Beidâwi), the tribe of Tay to Najd, the tribe of Khozaah to
Batan Marr near Mecca, Banu Amela to a mountain, thence called the Mountain of Amela, near Damascus, and others went to Hira in Irâk, &c. (Vide
Poc. Spec. p. 42, 45, and 66.)

[5] Either his opinion of the Sabæans, when he saw them addicted to pride
and ingratitude, and the satisfying their lusts ; or else the opinion he entertained of all mankind at the fall of Adam, or at his creation, when he heard
the angels say, *Wilt thou place in the earth one who will do evil therein, and
shed blood* ?   (See Chaps. II., VII. and XV.)

[6] Who were saved from the common destruction.

[7] See Chap. XIX. p. 304.

[8] *i.e.*, From the hearts of the intercessors, and of those for whom GOD

one another, What doth your LORD say ?   They shall answer,
That which is just : and he *is* the high, the great *God*.   Say,
Who provideth food for you from heaven and earth ?
Answer, GOD ; and either we, or ye, follow *the true* direction,
or *are* in a manifest error.   Say, Ye shall not be examined
concerning what we shall have committed : neither shall
we be examined concerning what ye shall have done.   Say,
Our LORD will assemble us together *at the last day* : then
will he judge between us with truth ; and he is the judge,
the knowing.   Say, Show me those whom ye have joined *as*
partners with him ?   Nay ; rather he is the mighty, the wise
GOD.   We have not sent thee otherwise than unto mankind
in general, a bearer of good tidings, and a denouncer of
threats : but the greater part of men do not understand.
And they say, When *will* this threat *be fulfilled*, if ye speak
truth ?   Answer, A threat *is denounced* unto you of a day
which ye shall not retard one hour, neither shall ye hasten.
The unbelievers say, We will by no means believe in this
Korân, nor in that which *hath been revealed* before it.[1]   But
if thou couldst see when the unjust doers shall be set before
their LORD !   They will iterate discourse with one another :
those who were esteemed weak shall say unto those who
behaved themselves arrogantly,[2] *Had it not been for* you,
verily we had been true believers.   They who behaved
themselves arrogantly shall say unto those who were
esteemed weak, Did we turn you aside from the *true* direction, after it had come unto you ?   On the contrary, ye
acted wickedly *of your own free choice*.   And they who
were esteemed weak shall say unto those who behaved with
arrogance, Nay, but the crafty plot *which ye devised* by
night and by day, *occasioned our ruin*, when ye commanded
us that we should not believe in GOD, and that we should
set up *other gods as* equal unto him.   And they shall conceal
their repentance,[3] after they shall have seen the punishment
prepared for them.   And we will put yokes on the necks of
those who shall have disbelieved : shall they be rewarded any
otherwise than *according to* what they shall have wrought ?

shall allow them to intercede, by the permission which he shall then grant
them ; for no angel or prophet shall dare to speak at the last day without
the divine leave.

[1] It is said that the infidels of Mecca, having inquired of the Jews and
Christians concerning the mission of Mohammed, were assured by them that
they found him described as the prophet who should come, both in the Pentateuch and in the Gospel ; at which they were very angry, and broke out
into the words here recorded.   (Al Beidâwi.)

[2] See Chap. XIV. p. 247.   [3] See Chap. X. p. 204.

We have sent no warner unto *any* city but the inhabitants thereof who lived in affluence said, Verily we believe not that with which ye are sent. And *those of Mecca also* say, We abound in riches and children more *than ye*, and we shall not be punished *hereafter*. Answer, Verily my LORD will bestow provision in abundance unto whom he pleaseth, and will be sparing *unto whom he pleaseth* : but the greater part of men know not *this*. Neither your riches nor your children *are the things* which shall cause you to draw nigh unto us with a near approach : only whoever believeth, and worketh righteousness, they shall receive a double reward for that which they shall have wrought ; and they shall *dwell* in security, in the upper apartments *of paradise*. But they who shall endeavour to render our signs of none effect, shall be delivered up to punishment. Say, Verily my LORD will bestow provision in abundance unto whom he pleaseth of his servants, and will be sparing unto *whom he pleaseth* : and whatever thing ye shall give in alms, he will return it ; and he is the best provider of food. On a certain day he shall gather them all together : then shall he say unto the angels, Did these worship you ? *And the angels* shall answer, GOD forbid ! thou art our friend, and not these : but they worshipped devils ; the greater part of them believed in them. On this day the one of you shall not be able either to profit or to hurt the other. And we will say unto those who have acted unjustly, Taste ye the pain of *hell* fire, which ye rejected as a falsehood. When our evident signs are read unto them, they say *of thee, O Mohammed*, This is no other than a man, who seeketh to turn you aside from *the gods* which your fathers worshipped. And they say *of the Korân*, This is no other than a lie blasphemously forged. And the unbelievers say of the truth, when it is come unto them, This is no other than manifest sorcery : yet we have given them no books *of scripture* wherein to exercise themselves, nor have we sent unto them any warner before thee. They who were before them *in like manner* accused *their prophets* of imposture : but *these* have not arrived unto the tenth part of *the riches and strength* which we had bestowed on *the former* : and they accused my apostles of imposture ; and how *severe* was my vengeance ! Say, Verily I advise you unto one thing, *namely*, that ye stand before GOD by two and two, and singly ;[1] and then consider seriously, *and*

[1] *i.e.*, That ye set yourselves to deliberate and judge of me and my pretensions coolly and sincerely, as in the sight of GOD, without passion or

you will find that there is no madness in your companion *Mohammed* : he *is* no other than a warner unto you, *sent* before a severe punishment. Say, I ask not of you any reward *for my preaching* ;[1] it is your own, *either to give or not* :[2] my reward *is to be expected* from GOD alone ; and he is witness over all things. Say, Verily my LORD sendeth down the truth *to his prophets* : *he is* the knower of secrets. Say, Truth is come, and falsehood is vanished, and shall not return *any more*. Say, If I err, verily I shall err only against my own soul : but if I be *rightly* directed, *it will be* by that which my LORD revealeth unto me ; for he is ready to hear, and nigh *unto those who call upon him*. If thou couldst see, when the *unbelievers* shall tremble,[3] and *shall find* no refuge, and shall be taken from a near place,[4] and shall say, We believe in him ! But how shall they receive *the faith* from a distant place :[5] since they had before denied him, and reviled the mysteries of faith, from a distant place ? And a bar shall be placed between them and that which they shall desire ; as it hath been done with those who *behaved* like them heretofore : because they have been in a doubt which hath caused scandal.

prejudice. The reason why they are ordered to consider either alone, or by two and two at most together, is because in larger assemblies, where noise, passion, and prejudice generally prevail, men have not that freedom of judgment which they have in private. (Al Beidâwi.)

[1] Mohammed, having in the preceding words answered the imputation of madness or vain enthusiasm, by appealing to their cooler thoughts of him and his actions, endeavours by these to clear himself of the suspicion of any worldly view or interest, declaring that he desired no salary or support from them for executing his commission, but expected his wages from GOD alone.

[2] See Chap. XXV. p. 358.

[3] viz., At their death, or the day of judgment, or the battle of Bedr. (Al Beidâwi.)

[4] That is, from the outside of the earth to the inside thereof ; or, from before GOD's tribunal to hell fire ; or, from the plain of Bedr to the well into which the dead bodies of the slain were thrown. (Al Beidâwi.)

[5] *i.e.*, When they are in the other world ; whereas faith is to be received in this.

XXXV

THE CHAPTER OF THE CREATOR [1]

Revealed at Mecca.

IN THE NAME OF THE MOST MERCIFUL GOD.

PRAISE be unto GOD, the Creator of heaven and earth ;
who maketh the angels *his* messengers, furnished with
two, and three, and four *pairs* of wings :[2] GOD maketh what
he pleaseth unto *his* creatures ; for GOD *is* almighty. The
mercy which GOD shall freely bestow on mankind, *there is*
none who can withhold ; and what he shall withhold, *there
is* none who can bestow, besides him : and he *is* the mighty,
the wise. O men, remember the favour of GOD towards
you : is there any creator, besides GOD, who provideth food
for you from heaven and earth ? *There is* no GOD but he :
how therefore are ye turned aside *from acknowledging his
unity* ? If they accuse thee of imposture, apostles before
thee have also been accused of imposture ; and unto GOD
shall *all* things return. O men, verily the promise of GOD
is true : let not therefore the present life deceive you, neither
let the deceiver deceive you concerning GOD : for Satan *is*
an enemy unto you ; wherefore hold him for an enemy : he
only inviteth his confederates to be the inhabitants of hell.
For those who believe not *there is prepared* a severe torment : but for those who shall believe and do that which
is right, *is prepared* mercy and a great reward. Shall he
therefore for whom his evil work hath been prepared, and
who imagineth it to be good, *be as he who is rightly disposed
and discerneth the truth* ? Verily GOD will cause to err whom
he pleaseth, and will direct whom he pleaseth. Let not
thy soul therefore be spent in sighs for their sakes, *on account
of their obstinacy* ; for GOD well knoweth that which they
do. *It is* GOD who sendeth the winds, and raiseth a cloud ;
and we drive the same unto a dead country, and thereby
quicken the earth after it hath been dead : so *shall the*

---

[1] Some entitle this chapter *The Angels* : both words occur in the first verse.
[2] That is, some angels have a greater and some a lesser number of wings,
according to their different orders, the words not being designed to express
the particular number. Gabriel is said to have appeared to Mohammed
on the night he made his journey to heaven, with no less than six hundred
wings. (Al Beidâwi.)

resurrection be.[1] Whoever desireth excellence, unto GOD
doth all excellence *belong* : unto him ascendeth the good
speech ; and the righteous work will he exalt. But as for
them who devise wicked *plots*,[2] they shall suffer a severe
punishment ; and the device of those *men* shall be rendered
vain. GOD created you *first* of the dust, and afterwards of
seed :[3] and he hath made you man and wife. No female
conceiveth, or bringeth forth, but with his knowledge.
Nor is anything added unto the age of him whose life is prolonged, neither is anything diminished from his age, but
the same is written in the book *of God's decrees.* Verily
this is easy with GOD. The two seas are not to be held in
comparison : this *is* fresh *and* sweet, pleasant to drink ;
but that *is* salt *and* bitter :[4] yet out of each of them ye eat
fish,[5] and take ornaments[6] for you to wear. Thou seest
the ships also ploughing *the waves* thereof, that ye may
seek *to enrich yourselves by commerce*, of the abundance *of
God* : peradventure ye will be thankful. He causeth the
night to succeed the day, and he causeth the day to succeed
the night ; and he obligeth the sun and the moon to perform
their services : each *of them* runneth an appointed course.
This is GOD, your LORD : his *is* the kingdom. But the
idols which ye invoke besides him have not the power even
over the skin of a date-stone : if ye invoke them, they will
not hear your calling ; and although they should hear, yet
they would not answer you. On the day of resurrection
they shall disclaim your having associated *them with* God :
and none shall declare unto thee *the truth*, like one who is well
acquainted *therewith*. O men, ye have need of GOD ; but
GOD is self-sufficient, and to be praised. If he pleaseth, he
can take you away, and produce a new creature *in your
stead* : neither *will* this *be* difficult with GOD. A burdened
soul shall not bear the burden of another : and if a heavily
burdened *soul* call *on another* to bear part of its *burden*, no
part thereof shall be borne *by the person who shall be called
on*, although he be *ever so nearly* related. Thou shalt
admonish those who fear their LORD in secret, and are
constant at prayer : and whoever cleanseth himself *from the*

[1] See Chap. XXIX. p. 389.
[2] As the Koreish did against Mohammed. See Chap. VIII. p. 170.
[3] See Chap. XXII. p. 327.
[4] That is, the two collective bodies of salt water and fresh. See Chap.
XXV. p. 358.
[5] See Chap. XVI. p. 257.
[6] As pearls and coral.

guilt of disobedience, cleanseth himself to *the advantage of* his own soul ; for all shall be assembled before GOD *at the last day.* The blind and the seeing shall not be held equal ; neither darkness and light ; nor the cool shade and the scorching wind : neither shall the living and the dead be held equal.[1] GOD shall cause him to hear whom he pleaseth : but thou shalt not make those to hear who are in *their* graves.[2] Thou *art* no other than a preacher : verily we have sent thee with truth, a bearer of good tidings, and a denouncer of threats. *There hath been* no nation, but a preacher hath in past times been *conversant* among them : if they charge thee with imposture, they who were before them likewise charged *their apostles* with imposture. Their apostles came unto them with evident *miracles,* and with *divine* writings,[3] and with the enlightening book :[4] afterwards I chastised those who were unbelievers, and how *severe* was my vengeance ! Dost thou not see that GOD sendeth down rain from heaven, and that we thereby produce fruits of various colours ?[5] In the mountain also *there are* some tracts white and red, of various colours ; [6] and *others are* of a deep black : and of men, and beasts, and cattle *there are* whose colours *are* in like manner various. Such only of his servants fear GOD as are endued with understanding : verily GOD *is* mighty *and* ready to forgive. Verily they who read the book of GOD, and are constant at prayer, and give alms out of what we have bestowed on them, *both* in secret and openly, hope for a merchandise which shall not perish : that GOD may fully pay them their wages, and make them a *superabundant* addition of his liberality ; for he *is* ready to forgive *the faults of his servants, and* to requite *their endeavours.* That which we have revealed unto thee of the book *of the Korân,* is the truth, confirming the *scriptures* which *were revealed* before it ; for GOD knoweth *and* regardeth his servants. And we have given the book *of the Korân* in heritage unto such of our servants as we have chosen : of them *there is one* who injureth his own soul ;[7] and *there is another* of them

---

[1] This passage expresses the great difference between a true believer and an infidel, truth and vanity, and their future reward and punishment.

[2] *i.e.,* Those who obstinately persist in their unbelief, who are compared to the dead.

[3] As the volumes delivered to Abraham, and to other prophets before Moses.

[4] viz., The law or the gospel.

[5] That is, of different kinds. See Chap. XVI.

[6] Being more or less intense. (Al Beidâwi.)

[7] By not practising what he is taught and commanded in the Korân

who keepeth the middle way ;[1] and *there is another* of them who outstrippeth *others* in good *works*, by the permission of GOD. This is the great excellence. They shall be introduced into gardens of perpetual abode ; they shall be adorned therein with bracelets of gold and pearls, and their clothing therein *shall be of* silk : and they shall say, Praise be unto GOD, who hath taken away sorrow from us ! verily our LORD *is* ready to forgive *the sinners, and* to reward *the obedient* : who hath caused us to take up our rest in a dwelling of *eternal* stability, through his bounty, wherein no labour shall touch us, neither shall any weariness affect us. But for the unbelievers *is prepared* the fire of hell : it shall not be decreed them to die *a second time* ; neither shall *any part* of the punishment thereof be made lighter unto them. Thus shall every infidel be rewarded. And they shall cry out aloud in *hell, saying,* LORD, take us hence, and we will work righteousness, and not what we have *formerly* wrought. *But it shall be answered them,* Did we not grant you lives of length sufficient, that whoever would be warned might be warned therein ; and did not the preacher[2] come unto you ? taste, therefore, *the pains of hell.* And the unjust shall have no protector. Verily GOD knoweth the secrets *both* of heaven and earth, for he knoweth the innermost parts of the breasts *of men.* It is he who hath made you to succeed in the earth. Whoever shall disbelieve, on him *be* his unbelief : and their unbelief shall only gain the unbelievers greater indignation in the sight of their LORD ; and their unbelief shall only increase the perdition of the unbelievers. Say, what think ye of your deities which ye invoke besides GOD ? Shew me what *part* of the earth they have created. Or had they any share in *the creation of* the heavens ? Have we given unto *the idolaters* any book *of revelations,* so that they *may rely* on any proof therefrom *to authorize their practice* ? Nay : but the ungodly make unto one another only deceitful promises. Verily GOD sustaineth the heavens and the earth, lest they fail : and if they should fail, none could support the same besides him ; he is gracious *and* merciful. *The Koreish* swore by GOD, with a most solemn oath, that if a preacher had come unto them, they would surely have been more *willingly* directed than any nation. But now a preacher is come unto

---

[1] That is, who meaneth well, and performeth his duty for the most part, but not perfectly.
[2] viz., Mohammed.

them, it hath only increased in them *their* aversion *from the truth, their* arrogance in the earth, and *their* contriving of evil ; but the contrivance of evil shall only encompass the authors thereof. Do they expect any other than the punishment awarded against the *unbelievers* of former times ? For thou shalt not find any change in the ordinance of GOD ; neither shalt thou find any variation in the ordinance of GOD. Have they not gone through the earth, and seen what hath been the end of those who were before them ; although they were more mighty in strength than they ? GOD is not to be frustrated by anything either in heaven or on earth ; for he is wise *and* powerful. If GOD should punish men according to what they deserve, he would not leave on the back of *the earth* so much as a beast : but he respiteth them to a determined time ; and when their time shall come, verily GOD will regard his servants.

XXXVI

THE CHAPTER OF Y. S.

Revealed at Mecca.

IN THE NAME OF THE MOST MERCIFUL GOD.

Y. S.[1] *I swear* by the instructive Korân, that thou art *one* of the messengers *of God, sent* to *show* the right way. *This is* a revelation of the most mighty, the merciful *God* : that thou mayest warn a people whose fathers were not warned, and who live in negligence. *Our* sentence[2] hath justly been pronounced against the greater part of them ; wherefore they shall not believe. We have put yokes[3] on their necks, which *come* up to *their* chins ; and they are forced to hold up their heads : and we have set a bar before them, and a bar behind them ;[4] and we have covered them with

[1] The meaning of these letters is unknown. (See Sale, Prel. Disc. Sect. III) : some however, from a tradition of Ebn Abbas, pretend they stand for *Ya insân, i.e.,* O man. This chapter, it is said, had several other titles given it by Mohammed himself, and particularly that of *The heart of the Korân.* The Mohammedans read it to dying persons in their last agony. (Vide Bobov. De Visit. Ægrot. p. 17.)

[2] viz., The sentence of damnation, which GOD pronounced against the great part of genii and men at the fall of Adam. (See Chaps. VII. and XI.)

[3] Or collars, such as are described in Chap. XIII. p. 240.

[4] That is, we have placed obstacles to prevent their looking either forwards or backwards. The whole passage represents the blindness and invincible obstinacy with which GOD justly curses perverse and reprobate men.

darkness ; wherefore they shall not see.[1] *It shall be* equal unto them whether thou preach unto them, or do not preach unto them ; they shall not believe. But thou shalt preach *with effect* unto him only who followeth the admonition *of the Korân,* and feareth the Merciful in secret. Wherefore bear good tidings unto him, of mercy, and an honourable reward. Verily we will restore the dead to life, and will write down *their works* which they shall have sent before them, and their footsteps *which they shall have left behind them* ;[2] and everything do we set down in a plain register. Propound unto them as an example the inhabitants of the city *of Antioch,* when the apostles *of Jesus* came thereto :[3] when we sent unto them *two of the said apostles* ;[4] but they charged them with imposture. Wherefore we strengthened *them* with a third.[5]

---

[1] It is said that when the Koreish, in pursuance of a resolution they had taken, had sent a select number to beset Mohammed's house, and to kill him (see Sale, Prel. Disc. Sect. II.), the prophet, having caused Ali to lie down on his bed to deceive the assassins, went out and threw a handful of dust at them, repeating the nine first verses of this chapter, which end here ; and they were thereupon stricken with blindness, so that they could not see him. (Vide Abulf. Vit. Moh. p. 50.)

[2] As their good or evil example, doctrine, &c.

[3] To explain this passage, the commentators tell the following story : The people of Antioch being idolaters, Jesus sent two of his disciples thither to preach to them ; and when they drew near the city they found Habîb, surnamed Al Najjâr, or the *carpenter,* feeding sheep, and acquainted him with their errand ; whereupon he asked them what proof they had of their veracity, and they told him they could cure the sick, and the blind, and the lepers ; and to demonstrate the truth of what they said, they laid their hands on a child of his who was sick, and immediately restored him to health. Habîb was convinced by this miracle, and believed ; after which they went into the city and preached the worship of one true GOD, curing a great number of people of several infirmities : but at length, the affair coming to the prince's ear, he ordered them to be imprisoned for endeavouring to seduce the people. When Jesus heard of this, he sent another of his disciples, generally supposed to have been Simon Peter, who, coming to Antioch, and appearing as a zealous idolater, soon insinuated himself into the favour of the inhabitants and of their prince, and at length took an opportunity to desire the prince would order the two persons who, as he was informed, had been put in prison for broaching new opinions, to be brought before him to be examined ; and accordingly they were brought : when Peter, having previously warned them to take no notice that they knew him, asked them who sent them, to which they answered, GOD, who had created all things, and had no companion. He then required some convincing proof of their mission, upon which they restored a blind person to his sight and performed some other miracles, with which Peter seemed not to be satisfied, for that, according to some, he did the very same miracles himself, but declared that, if their GOD could enable them to raise the dead, he would believe them ; which condition the two apostles accepting, a lad was brought who had been dead seven days, and at their prayers he was raised to life ; and thereupon Peter acknowledged himself convinced, and ran and demolished the idols, a great many of the people following him, and embracing the true faith ; but those who believed not were destroyed by the cry of the angel Gabriel. (Al Zamakh., Al Beidâwi, &c. Vide etiam Marracc. in Alc. p. 580.)

Some say these two were John and Paul ; but others name different persons.　　　　[5] viz. Simon Peter.

And they said, Verily we *are* sent unto you *by God. The inhabitants* answered, Ye are no other than men, as we *are* ; neither hath the Merciful revealed anything *unto you* : ye only publish a lie. The *apostles* replied, Our LORD knoweth that we *are* really sent unto you : and our duty is only public preaching. *Those of Antioch* said, Verily we presage evil from you : if ye desist not *from preaching*, we will surely stone you, and a painful punishment shall be inflicted on you by us. The *apostles* answered, Your evil presage is with yourselves :[1] although ye be warned, *will ye persist in your errors* ? Verily ye *are* a people who transgress *exceedingly*. And a certain man[2] came hastily from the farther parts of the city, *and* said, O my people, follow the messengers *of God* ; follow him who demandeth not any reward of you : for these are *rightly* directed. (XXIII.) [3] What *reason* have I that I should not worship him who hath created me ? for unto him shall ye return. Shall I take *other* gods besides him ? If the Merciful be pleased to afflict me, their inter-cession will not avail me at all, neither can they deliver *me* : then should I be in a manifest error. Verily I believe in your LORD ; wherefore hearken unto me. *But they stoned him* : *and as he died*, it was said *unto him*, Enter thou into paradise. *And* he said, O that my people knew how merciful GOD hath been unto me ! for he hath highly honoured me. And we sent not down against his people, after *they had slain* him, an army from heaven, nor *the other instruments of destruction* which we sent down *on unbelievers in former days* :[4] there was only one cry *of Gabriel from heaven*, and behold, they *became* utterly extinct. O the misery of men ! No apostle cometh unto them, but they laugh him to scorn. Do they not con-sider how many generations we have destroyed before them ? Verily they shall not return unto them : but all of them in general *shall be* assembled before us. *One* sign *of the resurrection* unto them *is* the dead earth : we quicken the same *by the rain*, and produce thereout *various sorts of* grain, of which they eat. And we make therein gardens of palm-trees, and vines ; and we cause springs

---

[1] *i.e.*, If any evil befall you, it will be the consequence of your own obstin-acy and unbelief. See Chap. XXVII. p. 373.

[2] This was Habîb al Najjâr, whose martyrdom is here described. His tomb is still shown near Antioch, and is much visited by the Mohammedans. (Vide Schultens, Indic. Geogr. ad Calcem Vitæ Saladini, voce Antiochia.)

[3] The twenty-third section begins here. See Sale, Prel. Disc. p. 63.

[4] As a deluge, or a shower of stones, or a suffocating wind, &c. The words may also be translated, *Nor did we determine to send down* such executioners of our justice.

to gush forth in the same : that they may eat of the fruits thereof, and of the labour of their hands. Will they not therefore give thanks ? Praise be unto him who hath created all the different kinds, *both* of *vegetables*, which the earth bringeth forth, and of their own species, *by forming the two sexes*, and also *the various sorts* of things which they know not. The night also *is* a sign unto them : we withdraw the day from the same, and behold, they *are* covered with darkness : and the sun hasteneth to his place of rest.[1] This *is* the disposition of the mighty, the wise *God.* And for the moon have we appointed *certain* mansions,[2] until she *change and* return *to be* like the old branch of a palm-tree.[3] It is not expedient that the sun should overtake the moon *in her course* ; neither doth the night outstrip the day : but each *of these luminaries* moveth in a *peculiar* orbit. *It is* a sign also unto them, that we carry their offspring in the ship filled *with merchandise* ;[4] and that we have made for them *other conveniences* like unto it,[5] whereon they ride. If we please, we drown them, and *there is* none to help them ; neither are they delivered, unless through our mercy, and that they may enjoy *life* for a season. When it is said unto them, Fear that which is before you, and that which is behind you,[6] that ye may obtain mercy ; *they withdraw from thee* : and thou dost not bring them one sign, of the signs of their LORD, but they turn aside from the same. And when it is said unto them, Give alms of that which GOD hath bestowed on you ; the unbelievers say unto those who believe, *by way of mockery*, Shall we feed him whom GOD can feed, if he pleaseth ?[7] Verily ye *are* in no

[1] That is, he hasteneth to run his daily course, the setting of the sun resembling a traveller's going to rest. Some copies vary in this place, and instead of *limostakarrin laha*, read *la mostakarra laha* ; according to which the sentence should be rendered, *The sun runneth* his course without ceasing, *and hath not a place of rest.*

[2] viz., These are twenty-eight constellations, through one of which the moon passes every night, thence called the *mansions* or *houses of the moon.* (See Sale, Prel. Disc. Sect. I.)

[3] For when a palm-branch grows old, it shrinks, and becomes crooked and yellow, not ill representing the appearance of the new moon.

[4] Some suppose that the deliverance of Noah and his companions in the ark is here intended ; and then the words should be translated, *That we carried their progeny in the ark filled with living creatures.*

[5] As camels, which are the *land-ships* ; or lesser vessels and boats.

[6] *i.e.,* The punishment of this world and of the next.

[7] When the poor Moslems asked alms of the richer Koreish, they told them that if GOD could provide for them, as they imagined, and did not, it was an argument that they deserved not his favour so well as themselves : whereas GOD permits some to be in want, to try the rich and exercise their charity.

other than a manifest error. And they say. When will this promise *of the resurrection be fulfilled*, if ye speak truth? They only wait for one sounding *of the trumpet*,[1] which shall overtake them while they are disputing together; and they shall not *have time to* make any disposition *of their effects*, neither shall they return to their family. And the trumpet shall be sounded *again*;[2] and behold they shall come forth from *their* graves, and hasten unto their LORD. They shall say, Alas for us! who hath awakened us from our bed?[3] This is what the Merciful promised *us*; and *his* apostles spoke the truth. It shall be but one sound *of the trumpet*, and behold, they *shall be* all assembled before us. On this day no soul shall be unjustly treated in the least; neither shall ye be rewarded, but according to what ye shall have wrought. On this day the inhabitants of paradise shall be wholly taken up with joy; they and their wives *shall rest* in shady groves, leaning on magnificent couches. There shall they have fruit, and they shall obtain whatever they shall desire. Peace *shall be* the word spoken *unto the righteous*, by a merciful LORD: but *he shall say unto the wicked*, Be ye separated this day, O ye wicked, *from the righteous*. Did I not command you, O sons of Adam, that ye should not worship Satan; because he *was* an open enemy unto you? And *did I not say*, Worship me; this *is* the right way? But now hath he seduced a great multitude of you: did ye not therefore understand? This is hell, with which ye were threatened: be ye cast into the same this day, to be burned; for that ye have been unbelievers. On this day we will seal up their mouths, *that they shall not open them in their own defence*; and their hands shall speak unto us, and their feet shall bear witness of that which they have committed.[4] If we pleased we could put out their eyes, and they might run with emulation in the way *they use to take*; and how should they see *their error*? And if we pleased we could transform them *into other shapes*, in their places *where they should be found*; and they should not be able to depart: neither should they repent.[5] Unto whomsoever we grant a long life, him do we cause to bow

---

[1] See Sale, Prel. Disc. Sect. IV., and the notes to Chap. XXXIX.
[2] See Sale, Prel. Disc. Sect. IV. pp. 88, 89.
[3] For they shall sleep during the interval between these two blasts of the trumpet, and shall feel no pain. (Jallalo'ddin.)
[4] See Sale, Prel. Disc. Sect. IV. p. 93.
[5] That is, They deserve to be thus treated for their infidelity and disobedience; but we bear with them out of mercy, and grant them respite.

down his body *through age*. Will they not therefore understand ? We have not taught *Mohammed* the art of poetry ;[1]
nor is it expedient for him *to be a poet*. This *book is* no other
than an admonition *from God*, and a perspicuous Korân ;
that he may warn him who is living :[2] and the sentence *of
condemnation* will be justly executed on the unbelievers.
Do they not consider that we have created for them, among
the things which our hands have wrought, cattle *of several
kinds*, of which they are possessors ; and that we have put
the same in subjection under them ? Some of them *are* for
their riding ; and on some of them do they feed : and they
receive *other* advantages therefrom ; and *of their milk do
they* drink. Will they not, therefore, be thankful ? They
have taken *other* gods, besides GOD, *in hopes* that they may
be assisted *by them* : but they are not able to give them
any assistance : yet *are* they a party of troops ready to
defend them. Let not their speech, therefore, grieve thee :
we know that which they privately conceal, and that which
they publicly discover. Doth not man know that we have
created him of seed ? yet behold, he is an open disputer
against the resurrection ; and he propoundeth unto us a
comparison, and forgetteth his creation. He saith, Who
shall restore bones to life, when they are rotten ?[3] Answer,
He shall restore them to life who produced them the first
time : for he is skilled in every *kind of* creation : who giveth
you fire out of the green tree,[4] and behold, ye kindle *your
fuel* from thence. Is not he who hath created the heavens
and the earth, able to create *new creatures* like unto them ?
Yea, certainly : for he *is* the wise Creator. His command,
when he willeth a thing, *is* only that he saith unto it, Be ;
and it is. Wherefore praise be unto him, in whose hand
is the kingdom of all things, and unto whom ye shall return
at the last day.

[1] This is in answer to the infidels, who pretended the Korân was only a
poetical composition.

[2] *i.e.*, Endued with understanding ; the stupid and careless being like
dead persons. (Al Beidâwi.)

[3] See Chap. XVI. p. 257.

[4] The usual way of striking fire in the East is by rubbing together two
pieces of wood, one of which is commonly of the tree called markh, and the
other of that called afâr : and it will succeed even though the wood be green
and wet. (Vide Hyde, de Rel. Vet. Pers. c. 25, p. 333, &c.)

XXXVII

THE CHAPTER OF THOSE WHO RANK THEMSELVES IN ORDER
Revealed at Mecca.

IN THE NAME OF THE MOST MERCIFUL GOD.

BY *the angels* who rank themselves in order ;[1] and by those who drive forward and dispel *the clouds* :[2] and by those who read *the Korân* for an admonition ; verily your GOD is one : the LORD of heaven and earth, and of whatever *is* between them, and the LORD of the east.[3] We have adorned the lower heaven with the ornament of the stars : and *we have placed therein* a guard against every rebellious devil ; that they may not listen to *the discourse of* the exalted princes (for they are darted at from every side, to repel *them*, and a lasting torment *is prepared* for them) ; except him who catcheth a word by stealth, and is pursued by a shining flame.[4] Ask *the Meccans*, therefore, whether they be stronger by nature, or *the angels* whom we have created ? We have surely created them of stiff clay. Thou wonderest at *God's power, and their obstinacy* ; but they mock *at the arguments urged to convince them* : when they are warned, they do not take warning ; and when they see any sign, they scoff *thereat*, and say, This *is* no other than manifest sorcery : after we shall be dead, and become dust and bones, shall we be really raised to life, and our forefathers also ? Answer, Yea : and ye *shall then be* despicable. There shall be but one blast *of the trumpet*, and they shall see *themselves raised* : and they shall say, Alas for us ! this *is* the day of judgment ; this is the day of distinction *between the righteous and the wicked*, which ye

---

[1] Some understand by these words the *souls of men* who *range themselves* in obedience to GOD's laws, and *put away* from them all infidelity and corrupt doings ; or the *souls* of those who *rank themselves* in battle array to fight for the true religion, and *push on* their horses to charge the infidels, &c. (Al Beidâwi.)

[2] Or, who *put in motion* all bodies, in the upper and lower world, according to the divine command ; or, who *keep off* men from disobedience to GOD, by inspiring them with good thoughts and inclinations ; or, who drive away the devils from them, &c. (Al Beidâwi.)

[3] The original word, being in the plural number, is supposed to signify the different points of the horizon from whence the sun rises in the course of the year, which are in number 360 (equal to the number of days in the old civil year), and have as many corresponding points where it successively sets, during that space. (Al Beidâwi, Yahya.) Marracci groundlessly imagines this interpretation to be built on the error of the plurality of worlds. (Marracc. in Alc. p. 589.)

[4] See Chap. XV.

rejected as a falsehood. Gather together those who have acted unjustly, and their comrades, and the *idols* which they worshipped besides GOD, and direct them in the way to hell : and set them *before God's tribunal* ; for they *shall be* called to account. What aileth you that ye defend not one another ? But on this day they shall submit themselves *to the judgment of God* : and they shall draw nigh unto one another, and shall dispute among themselves. *And the seduced* shall say *unto those who seduced them*, Verily ye came unto us with presages of prosperity ;[1] *and the seducers* shall answer, Nay, rather ye were not true believers : for we had no power over you *to compel you* ; but ye were people who *voluntarily* transgressed : wherefore the sentence of our LORD hath been justly pronounced against us, *and* we shall surely taste *his vengeance*. We seduced you ; *but* we also erred ourselves. They *shall both* therefore *be* made partakers of the *same* punishment on that day. Thus will we deal with the wicked : because, when it is said unto them, There is no god besides *the true* GOD, they swell with arrogance, and say, Shall we abandon our gods for a distracted poet ? Nay ; he cometh with the truth, and beareth witness to the *former* apostles. Ye shall surely taste the painful torment *of hell* ; and ye shall not be rewarded, but according to your works. But *as for* the sincere servants of GOD, they shall have a certain provision *in paradise, namely, delicious* fruits : and they *shall be* honoured : *they shall be placed* in gardens of pleasure, *leaning* on couches, opposite to one another :[2] a cup shall be carried round unto them, *filled* from a limpid fountain, for the delight of those who drink : it shall not oppress the understanding, neither shall they be inebriated therewith. And near them *shall lie the virgins of paradise*, refraining their looks *from beholding any besides their spouses*, having large black eyes, *and* resembling the eggs *of an ostrich* covered *with feathers from the dust*.[3] And they shall turn the one unto the other, and shall ask one another questions. And one of them shall say, Verily I had an intimate friend *while I lived in the world*, who said *unto me*, Art thou one of those who assertest the truth *of the resurrection* ? After we shall be dead, and

---

[1] Literally, *from the right hand*. The words may also be rendered, *with force*, to compel us ; or *with an oath*, swearing that ye were in the right.

[2] See Chap. XV.

[3] This may seem an odd comparison to an European ; but the orientals think nothing comes so near the colour of a fine woman's skin as that of an ostrich's egg when perfectly clean.

reduced to dust and bones, shall we surely be judged ? *Then*
he shall say *to his companions,* Will ye look down ?   And
he shall look down, and shall see him in the midst of hell ;
and he shall say *unto him,* By GOD, it wanted little but thou
hadst drawn me into ruin ; and *had it* not *been* for the grace
of my LORD, I had surely been *one* of those who had been
delivered up *to eternal torment.* Shall we die any other
than our first death ; or do we suffer any punishment ?
Verily this is great felicity : for *the obtaining* a *felicity* like
this let the labourers labour. Is this a better entertainment, or the tree of Al Zakkûm ?[1]   Verily we have designed
the same for an occasion of dispute unto the unjust.[2]   It
is a tree which issueth from the bottom of hell : the fruit
thereof resembleth the heads of devils ;[3] and *the damned*
shall eat of the same, and shall fill *their* bellies therewith ;
there shall be given them thereon a mixture of filthy and boiling water to drink : afterwards shall they return into hell.[4]
They found their fathers going astray, and they trod hastily
in their footsteps : for the greater part of the ancients erred
before them.   And we sent warners unto them heretofore ;
and see how *miserable* was the end of those who were warned ;
except the sincere servants of GOD.   Noah called on us in
former days, and we heard him graciously : and we delivered
him and his family out of the great distress : and we caused
his offspring *to be* those who survived *to people the earth* :
and we left *the following salutation to be bestowed* on him by
the latest posterity, *namely,* Peace *be* on Noah among all
creatures !   Thus do we reward the righteous ; for he *was*
one of our servants the true believers.   Afterwards we
drowned the others.   Abraham also *was* of his religion :[5]
when he came unto his LORD with a perfect heart.   When
he said unto his father and his people, What do ye worship ?
Do ye choose false gods preferably to *the true* GOD ?   What
therefore *is* your opinion of the LORD of all creatures ?   And

[1] There is a thorny tree so called, which grows in Tehâma, and bears fruit
like an almond, but extremely bitter ; and therefore the same name is given
to this infernal tree.

[2] The infidels not conceiving how a tree could grow in hell, where the stones
themselves serve for fuel.

[3] Or of serpents ugly to behold ; the original word signifies both.

[4] Some suppose that the entertainment above mentioned will be the
welcome given the damned before they enter that place ; and others, that
they will be suffered to come out of hell from time to time, to drink their
scalding liquor.

[5] For Noah and he agreed in the fundamental points both of faith and
practice ; though the space between them was no less than 2640 years.
(Al Beidâwi.)

he looked and observed the stars, and said, Verily I *shall be* sick,[1] *and shall not assist at your sacrifices*: and they turned their backs and departed from him.[2] And *Abraham* went privately to their gods, and said *scoffingly unto them*, Do ye not eat *of the meat which is set before you*? What aileth you that ye speak not? And he turned upon them, and struck *them* with his right hand, *and demolished them*. And *the people* came hastily unto him: *and* he said, Do ye worship the *images* which ye carve? whereas GOD hath created you, and also that which ye make. They said, Build a pile for him, and cast him into the glowing fire. And they devised a plot against him; but we made them the inferior, *and delivered him*.[3] And *Abraham* said, Verily I *am* going unto my LORD,[4] who will direct me. O LORD grant me a righteous *issue*. Wherefore we acquainted him *that he should have a son who should be* a meek youth. And when he had attained to *years of* discretion,[5] *and could join in acts of religion* with him; *Abraham* said *unto him*, O my son, verily I saw in a dream that I should offer thee in sacrifice:[6] consider therefore what thou art of opinion I *should do*. He answered, O my father, do what thou art commanded: thou shalt find me, if GOD please, a patient person. And when they had submitted themselves *to the divine will*,

---

[1] He made as if he gathered so much from the aspect of the heavens—the people being greatly addicted to the superstitions of astrology—and made it his excuse for being absent from their festival, to which they had invited him.

[2] Fearing he had some contagious distemper. (Al Beidâwi.)

[3] See Chap. XXI.

[4] Whither he hath commanded me.

[5] He was then thirteen years old. (Al Beidâwi.)

[6] The commentators say, that Abraham was ordered in a vision, which he saw on the eighth night of the month Dhu'lhajja, to sacrifice his son; and to assure him that this was not from the devil, as he was inclined to suspect, the same vision was repeated a second time the night next, when he *knew* it to be from GOD, and also a third time the night following, when he resolved to obey it, and to *sacrifice* his son; and hence some think the eighth, ninth, and tenth days of Dhu'lhajja are called *Yawm altarwiya, yawm ar afat*, and *yawm alnehr*, that is, *the day of the vision, the day of knowledge*, and *the day of the sacrifice*. It is the most received opinion among the Mohammedans that the son whom Abraham offered was Ismael, and not Isaac, Ismael being his only son at that time: for the promise of Isaac's birth is mentioned lower as subsequent in time to this transaction. They also allege the testimony of their prophet, who is reported to have said, *I am the son of the two who were offered in sacrifice*; meaning his great ancestor, Ismael, and his own father Abd'allah: for Abd'almotalleb had made a vow that if GOD would permit him to find out and open the well Zemzem, and should give him ten sons, he would sacrifice one of them. Accordingly, when he had obtained his desire in both respects, he cast lots on his sons, and the lot falling on Abd'allah, he redeemed him by offering a hundred camels, which was therefore ordered to be the price of a man's blood in the Sonna. (Al Beidâwi, Jallalo'ddin, Al Zamakh.)

and *Abraham* had laid *his son* prostrate on his face,[1] we cried unto him, O Abraham, now hast thou verified the vision. Thus do we reward the righteous. Verily this was a manifest trial. And we ransomed him with a noble victim.[2] And we left *the following salutation to be bestowed* on him by the latest posterity, *namely*, Peace *be* on Abraham ! Thus do we reward the righteous : for he *was one* of our faithful servants. And we rejoiced him with the promise of Isaac, a righteous prophet ; and we blessed him and Isaac : and of their offspring *were* some righteous doers, and *others* who manifestly injured their own souls. We were also gracious unto Moses and Aaron, heretofore : and we delivered them and their people from a great distress. And we assisted them *against the Egyptians* ; and they became the conquerors. And we gave them the perspicuous book *of the law,* and we directed them into the right way : and we left *the following salutation to be bestowed* on them by the latest posterity, *namely,* Peace *be* on Moses and Aaron ! Thus do we reward the righteous ; for they *were two* of our faithful servants. And Elias[3] *was also one* of those who were sent *by us.* When he said unto his people, Do ye not fear *God* ? Do ye invoke Baal, and forsake the most excellent Creator ? GOD *is* your LORD, and the LORD of your forefathers. But they accused him of imposture : wherefore they shall be delivered up *to eternal punishment* ; except the sincere servants of GOD. And we left *the following salutation to be bestowed* on him by the latest posterity,

[1] The commentators add, that Abraham went so far as to draw the knife with all his strength across the lad's throat, but was miraculously hindered from hurting him. (Al Beidâwi, Jallalo'ddin.)

[2] The epithet of *great* or *noble* is here added, either because it was large and fat, or because it was accepted as the ransom of a prophet. Some suppose this victim was a ram, and, if we may believe in common tradition, the very same which Abel sacrificed, having been brought to Abraham out of paradise ; others fancy it was a wild goat, which came down from Mount Thabîr, near Mecca, for the Mohammedans lay the scene of this transaction in the valley of Mina ; as a proof of which they tell us that the horns of the victim were hung up on the spout of the Caaba, where they remained till they were burnt, together with that building, in the days of Abda'llah Ebn Zobeir (Al Beidâwi) ; though others assure us that they had been before taken down by Mohammed himself, to remove all occasion of idolatry. (Vide D'Herbel. Bibl. Orient. Art. Ismail.)

[3] This prophet the Mohammedans generally suppose to be the same with Al Khedr, and confound him with Phineas (see Chap. XVIII.), and sometimes with Edris, or Enoch. Some say he was the son of Yasin, and nearly related to Aaron ; and others suppose him to have been a different person. He was sent to the inhabitants of Baalbec, in Syria, the Heliopolis of the Greeks, to reclaim them from the worship of their idol Baal, or the sun, whose name makes part of that of the city, which was anciently called Becc. (Jallalo'ddin, Al Beidâwi.)

namely, Peace *be* on Ilyâsin![1] Thus do we reward the righteous : for he *was one* of our faithful servants. And Lot *was also one* of those who were sent *by us.* When we delivered him and his whole family, except an old woman, *his wife, who perished* among those that remained behind : afterwards we destroyed the others.[2] And ye, *O people of Mecca,* pass by *the places where they once dwelt,* as ye journey in the morning and by night : will ye not therefore understand ? Jonas *was also one* of those who were sent *by us.*[3] When he fled[4] into the loaded ship ; and *those who were on board* cast lots among themselves,[5] and he was condemned :[6] and the fish swallowed him ;[7] for he was worthy of reprehension. And if he had not been *one* of those who praised GOD,[8] verily he had remained in the belly thereof until the day of resurrection. And we cast him on the naked *shore,* and he *was* sick :[9] and we caused a plant of a gourd[10] to grow up over him ; and we sent him to a hundred thousand *persons,* or they were a greater number, and they believed : wherefore we granted them to enjoy *this life* for a season. Inquire of the *Meccans* whether thy LORD

---

[1] The commentators do not well know what to make of this word. Some think it is the plural of Elias, or, as the Arabs write it, Ilyâs, and that both that prophet and his followers, or those who resembled him, are meant thereby ; others divide the word, and read *ál Yasin, i.e., the family of Yasin,* who was the father of Elias according to an opinion mentioned above ; and others imagine it signifies Mohammed, or the Korân, or some other book of scripture. But the most probable conjecture is that Ilyâs and Ilyâsin are the same name, or design one and the same person, as Sinai and Sinin denote one and the same mountain ; the last syllable being added here, to keep up the rhyme or cadence, at the close of the verse.

[2] See Chap. VII. and Chap. XI.

[3] See Chap. X. p. 208.

[4] See Chap. XXI. p. 324.

[5] Al Beidâwi says the ship stood stock-still, wherefore they concluded that they had a fugitive servant on board, and cast lots to find him out.

[6] *i.e.,* He was taken by the lot.

[7] When the lot fell on Jonas he cried out, *I am the fugitive* ; and immediately threw himself into the sea. (Al Beidâwi.)

[8] The words seem to relate particularly to Jonas's supplication while in the whale's belly. (See Chap. XXI.)

[9] By reason of what he had suffered ; his body becoming like that of a new-born child. (Al Beidâwi.) It is said that the fish, after it had swallowed Jonas, swam after the ship with its head above water, that the prophet might breathe, who continued to praise GOD till the fish came to land and vomited him out. The opinions of the Mohammedan writers as to the time Jonas continued in the fish's belly differ very much : some suppose it was part of a day, others three days, others seven, others twenty, and others forty. (Al Beidâwi.)

[10] The original word signifies a plant which spreads itself upon the ground, having no erect stalk or stem to support it, and particularly a gourd ; though some imagine Jonas's plant to have been a fig, and others the small tree or shrub called mauz (Al Beidâwi), which bears very large leaves, and excellent fruit. (Vide J. Leon Descr. Afric. lib. 9. Gab. Sionit. de Urb. Orient. **ad**

hath daughters, and they sons ? [1] Have we created the angels of the female sex ? and *were* they witnesses *thereof* ? Do they not say of their own false invention, GOD hath begotten *issue* ? and are they not really liars ? Hath he chosen daughters preferably to sons ? Ye have no *reason* to judge thus. Will ye not therefore be admonished ? Or have ye a manifest proof *of what ye say* ? Produce now your book *of revelations*, if ye speak truth. And they make him to be of kin unto the genii ;[2] whereas the genii know that they *who affirm such things*, shall be delivered up *to eternal punishment* (far be that from GOD which they affirm *of him* !) except the sincere servants of GOD. Moreover ye and that which ye worship shall not seduce *any* concerning *God*, except him who *is destined* to be burned in hell. There *is* none of us, but hath an appointed place : we range ourselves in order, *attending the commands of God* ; and we celebrate *the divine praise*.[3] *The infidels* said, If we had been favoured with a book of divine revelations, of *those which were delivered to* the ancients, we had surely been sincere servants of GOD : yet *now the Korân is revealed*, they believe not therein ; but hereafter shall they know *the consequence of their unbelief*. Our word hath formerly been given unto our servants the apostles ; that they should certainly be assisted *against the infidels*, and that our armies should surely be the conquerors. Turn aside therefore from them, for a season : and see *the calamities which shall afflict* them ; for they shall see *thy future success and prosperity*. Do they therefore seek to hasten our vengeance ? Verily when it shall descend into their courts, an evil morning *shall it be* unto those who were warned *in vain*. Turn aside from them therefore for a season ; and see : hereafter shall they see *thy success and their punishment*. Praise be unto thy LORD, the LORD who is far exalted above what they affirm *of him* ! And peace *be* on *his* apostles ! And praise *be* unto GOD, the LORD of all creatures !

calcem Gogr. Nub. p. 32, et Hottinger. Hist. Orient. p. 78, &c.) The commentators add, that this plant withered the next morning, and that Jonas being much concerned at it, GOD made a remonstrance to him in behalf of the Ninevites, agreeable to what is recorded in scripture.
[1] See Chap. XVI. p. 262.
[2] That is, the angels, who are also comprehended under the name of genii, being a species of them. Some say that the infidels went so far as to assert that GOD and the devil were brothers (Al Beidâwi), which blasphemous expression may have been occasioned by the magian notions.
[3] These words are supposed to be spoken by the angels, disclaiming the worship paid to them by the idolaters, and declaring that they have each

XXXVIII

THE CHAPTER OF S.

Revealed at Mecca.

IN THE NAME OF THE MOST MERCIFUL GOD.

S.[1] BY the Korân full of admonition.[2] Verily the unbelievers *are addicted to* pride and contention. How many generations have we destroyed before them ; and they cried *for mercy*, but it was not a time to escape. They wonder that a warner from among themselves hath come unto them. And the unbelievers said, This *man is* a sorcerer *and* a liar : doth he affirm the gods *to be but* one GOD ? Surely this *is* a wonderful thing. And the chief men among them departed,[3] *saying to one another*, Go and persevere in *the worship of* your gods : verily this is the thing which is designed.[4] We have not heard *anything like* this in the last religion :[5] this *is* no other than a *false* contrivance. Hath an admonition been sent unto him *preferably to any other* among us ? Verily they are in a doubt concerning my admonition : but they have not yet tasted my vengeance. Are the treasuries of the mercy of thy LORD, the mighty, the munificent *God*, in their hands ? Is the kingdom of the heavens and the earth, and of whatever is between them, in their possession ? *If it be so*, let them ascend by steps *unto heaven*. *But* any army of the confederates shall *even* here be put to flight. The people of Noah, and *the tribe of* Ad, and Pharaoh the contriver of the

their station and office appointed them by GOD, whose commands they are at all times ready to execute, and whose praises they continually sing. There are some expositors, however, who think they are the words of Mohammed and his followers ; the meaning being, that each of them has a place destined for him in paradise, and that they are the men who range themselves in order before GOD, to worship and pray to him, and who celebrate his praise by rejecting every false notion derogatory to the divine wisdom and power.

[1] The meaning of this letter is unknown (see Sale, Prel. Disc. Sect. III); some guess it stands for *Sidk, i.e., Truth*; or for *Sadaka, i.e., He* (viz., Mohammed) *speaketh the truth* ; and others propose different conjectures, all equally uncertain. It may stand for Solomon.

[2] Something must be understood to answer this oath, which the commentators variously supply.

[3] On the conversion of Omar, the Koreish being greatly irritated, the most considerable of them went in a body to Abu Taleb, to complain to him of his nephew Mohammed's proceedings ; but being confounded and put to silence by the prophet's arguments, they left the assembly and encouraged one another in their obstinacy. (Al Beidâwi.)

[4] Namely, to draw us from their worship.

[5] *i.e*, In the religion which we received from our fathers ; or, in the religion of Jesus, which was the last before the mission of Mohammed. (Al Beidâwi.)

stakes,¹ and *the tribe of* Thamûd, and the people of Lot, and the inhabitants of the wood *near Madian*,² accused *the prophets* of imposture before them : these were the confederates *against the messengers of* GOD. All *of them did no other* than accuse *their* apostles of falsehood : wherefore my vengeance hath been justly executed *upon them*. And these wait only for one sounding *of the trumpet* ; which there shall be no deferring. And they *scoffingly* say, O LORD, hasten our sentence unto us, before the day of account. Do thou patiently bear that which they utter : and remind *them* of our servant David, endued with strength ;³ for he *was* one who seriously turned himself *unto God*. We compelled the mountains to celebrate *our* praise with him, in the evening and at sunrise, and also the birds, which gathered themselves together *unto him* :⁴ all *of them* returned frequently unto him *for this purpose*. And we established his kingdom, and gave him wisdom and eloquence of speech. Hath the story of the *two* adversaries⁵ come to *thy knowledge* ; when they ascended over the wall into the upper apartment, when they went in unto David, and he was afraid of them ?⁶ They said, Fear not : *we are* two adversaries *who have a controversy to be decided*. The one of us hath wronged the other : wherefore judge between us with truth, and be not unjust ; and direct us into the even way. This my brother had ninety and nine sheep ; and I had only one ewe : and he said, Give her me to keep ; and he prevailed against me in the discourse *which we had together*. *David* answered, Verily he hath wronged thee, in demanding thine ewe *as an addition* to his own sheep : and many of

¹ For they say Pharaoh used to tie those he had a mind to punish by the hands and feet to four stakes fixed in the ground, and so tormented them. (Jallalo'ddin.) Some interpret the words, which may also be translated the *lord or master of the stakes*, figuratively, of the firm establishment of Pharaoh's kingdom ; because the Arabs fix their tents with stakes (Al Beidâwi) ; but they may possibly intend that prince's *obstinacy* and *hardness of heart*.
² See Chap. XV. p. 255.
³ The commentators suppose that ability to undergo the frequent practice of religious exercises is here meant. They say David used to fast every other day, and to spend one-half of the night in prayer. (Al Beidâwi.)
⁴ See Chap. XXI. p. 322.
⁵ These were two angels, who came unto David in the shape of men, to demand judgment in the feigned controversy after mentioned. It is no other than Nathan's parable to David (2 Sam. xii.), a little disguised.
⁶ Because they came suddenly upon him, on a day of privacy ; when the doors were guarded, and no person admitted to disturb his devotions. For David, they say, divided his time regularly, setting apart one day for the service of GOD, another day for rendering justice to his people, another day for preaching to them, and another day for his own affairs. (Al Beidâwi, Jallalo'ddin.)

them who are concerned together *in business*, wrong one
another, except those who believe and do that which is
right ; but how few are they ! And David perceived that
we had tried him *by this parable*, and he asked pardon
of his LORD : and he fell down and bowed himself, and
repented.[1] Wherefore we forgave him this *fault* ; and he
shall be admitted to approach near unto us, and *shall have*
an excellent place of abode *in paradise*. O David, verily
we have appointed thee a sovereign prince in the earth :
judge therefore between men with truth ; and follow not
thy own lust, lest it cause thee to err from the way of GOD :
for those who err from the way of GOD shall suffer a severe
punishment, because they have forgotten the day of account.
We have not created the heavens and the earth, and whatever *is* between them, in vain.[2] This *is* the opinion of the
unbelievers : but woe unto those who believe not, because
of the fire *of hell*. Shall we deal with those who believe and
do good works, as with those who act corruptly in the earth ?
Shall we deal with the pious as with the wicked ? A blessed
book have we sent down unto thee, *O Mohammed*, that they
may attentively meditate on the signs thereof, and that
men of understanding may be warned. And we gave unto
David Solomon ; how excellent a servant ! for he frequently
turned himself *unto God*. When the *horses* standing on
three feet, and touching the ground with the edge of the
fourth foot, *and* swift in the course, were set in parade before
him in the evening,[3] he said, Verily I have loved the love of
earthly good above the remembrance of my LORD ; *and
have spent the time in viewing these horses*, until *the sun* is

[1] The crime of which David had been guilty, was the taking the wife of
Uriah, and ordering her husband to be set in the front of the battle to be
slain. (Al Beidâwi.) Some suppose this story was told to serve as an
admonition to Mohammed, who, it seems, was apt to covet what was another's.

[2] So as to permit injustice to go unpunished, and righteousness unre-
warded.

[3] Some say that Solomon brought these horses, being a thousand in
number, from Damascus and Nisibis, which cities he had taken ; others
say that they were left him by his father, who took them from the Amalekites ; while others, who prefer the marvellous, pretend that they came
up out of the sea, and had wings. However, Solomon, having one day a
mind to view these horses, ordered them to be brought before him, and
was so taken up with them that he spent the remainder of the day, till after
sunset, in looking on them ; by which means he neglected the prayer, which
ought to have been said at that time, till it was too late : but when he perceived his omission he was so greatly concerned at it, that ordering the
horses to be brought back, he killed them all as an offering to GOD, except
only a hundred of the best of them. But GOD made him ample amends
for the loss of these horses, by giving him dominion over the winds. (Al
Beidâwi, Al Zamakh., Yahya.)

hidden by the veil of *night* : bring the *horses* back unto me.
And when they were brought back, he began to cut off *their*
legs and *their* necks.   We also tried Solomon, and placed
on his throne a *counterfeit* body :¹ afterwards he turned *unto
God, and* said, O LORD, forgive me. and give me a kingdom
which may not be obtained by any after me ;² for thou *art*
the giver *of kingdoms.*   And we made the wind subject
to him ; it ran gently at his command, whithersoever he
directed.   And *we also put* the devils *in subjection under
him* ; *and among them* such as were every way skilled in
building, and in diving *for pearls* :³ and others *we delivered
to him* bound in chains ; *saying,* This *is* our gift : therefore
be bounteous, or be sparing *unto whom thou shall think fit,*⁴
without rendering an account.   And he shall approach near
unto us, and shall have an excellent abode *in paradise.*   And
remember our servant Job ;⁵ when he cried unto his LORD,
saying, Verily Satan hath afflicted me with calamity and
pain.   *And it was said unto him,* Strike *the earth* with thy
foot ; *which when he had done, a fountain*⁶ *sprang up, and
it was said to him,* This *is for thee* to wash in, to refresh *thee,*

¹ The most received exposition of this passage is taken from the following
Talmudic fable. (Vide Talm. En Jacob, part ii. et Yalkut in lib. Reg. p. 182.)
Solomon, having taken Sidon, and slain the king of that city, brought away
his daughter Jerâda, who became his favourite ; and because she ceased not
to lament her father's loss, he ordered the devils to make an image of him
for her consolation : which being done, and placed in her chamber, she and
her maids worshipped it morning and evening, according to their custom.
At length Solomon being informed of this idolatry, which was practised
under his roof, by his vizir Asâf, he broke the image, and having chastised
the woman, went out into the desert, where he wept and made supplications
to GOD ; who did not think fit, however, to let his negligence pass without
some correction.   It was Solomon's custom, when he eased or washed himself,
to entrust his signet, on which his kingdom depended, with a concubine of
his named Amina : one day, therefore, when she had the ring in her custody,
a devil, named Sakhar, came to her in the shape of Solomon, and received
the ring from her ; by virtue of which he became possessed of the kingdom,
and sat on the throne in the shape which he had borrowed, making what
alterations in the law he pleased.   Solomon, in the meantime, being changed
in his outward appearance, and known to none of his subjects, was obliged
to wander about and beg alms for his subsistence ; till at length, after the
space of forty days, which was the time the image had been worshipped in
his house, the devil flew away, and threw the signet into the sea : the signet
was immediately swallowed by a fish, which being taken and given to Solomon, he found the ring in its belly, and having by this means recovered the
kingdom, took Sakhar, and tying a great stone to his neck, threw him into
the lake of Tiberias. (Al Beidâwi, Jallalo'ddin, Abulfeda.)
   ² *i.e.,* That I may surpass all future princes in magnificence and power.
   ³ See Chaps. XXI. p. 323 and XXVII.
   ⁴ Some suppose these words to relate to the genii, and that Solomon is
thereby empowered to *release* or to *keep in chains* such of them as he pleased.
   ⁵ See Chap. XXI. p. 323.
   ⁶ Some say there were two springs, one of hot water, wherein he bathed ;
and the other of cold, of which he drank.   (Al Beidâwi.)

and to drink. And we restored unto him his family, and as many more with them, through our mercy; and for an admonition unto those who are endued with understanding. And *we said unto him*, Take a handful *of rods*[1] in thy hand, and strike *thy wife* therewith;[2] and break not thine oath.[3] Verily we found him a patient person: how excellent a servant *was he*! for he *was* one who frequently turned himself *unto us.* Remember also our servants Abraham, and Isaac, and Jacob, *who were* men strenuous and prudent. Verily we purified them with a *perfect* purification, through the remembrance of the life to come;[4] and they were, in our sight, elect *and* good *men.* And remember Ismael, and Elisha,[5] and Dhu'lkefl:[6] for all *these were* good *men.* This *is* an admonition. Verily the pious shall have an excellent place to return unto, *namely,* gardens of perpetual abode, the gates *whereof shall stand* open unto them. As they lie down therein, they shall there ask for many *sorts of* fruits, and for drink; and near them *shall sit the virgins of paradise,* refraining their looks *from beholding any besides their spouses, and* of equal age *with them.*[7] This *is* what ye are promised at the day of account. This *is* our provision; which shall not fail. This *shall be the reward of the righteous.* But for the transgressors *is prepared* an evil receptacle, *namely,* hell: they shall be cast into the same to be burned, and a wretched couch *shall it be.* This let them taste, *to wit,* scalding water, and corruption *flowing from the bodies of the damned,* and divers other things of the same kind. *And it shall be said to the seducers,* This troop *which was guided by you,* shall be thrown, together

---

[1] The original not expressing what this handful was to consist of, one supposes it was to be only a handful of dry grass or of rushes, and another that it was a branch of a palm-tree. (See Chap. XXI.)

[2] The commentators are not agreed what fault Job's wife had committed to deserve this chastisement: we have mentioned one opinion already (Chap. XXI.) Some think it was only because she stayed too long on an errand.

[3] For he had sworn to give her a hundred stripes if he recovered.

[4] Or, as the words may be interpreted, according to Al Zamakhshari, *We have purified them,* or *peculiarly destined and fitted them for paradise.*

[5] See Chap. VI. p. 128.

[6] See Chap. XXI. Al Beidâwi here takes notice of another tradition concerning this prophet, viz., that he entertained and took care of a hundred Israelites, who fled to him from certain slaughter, from which action he probably had the name of Dhu'lkefl given him, the primary signification of the verb *cafala* being to *maintain or take care of* another. If a conjecture might be founded on this tradition, I should fancy the person intended was Obadiah, the governor of Ahab's house. (See 1 Kings xviii. 4.)

[7] *i.e.*, About thirty or thirty-three. (See Sale, Prel. Disc. Sect. IV.)

with you, headlong *into hell* : they shall not be bidden wel-come ; for they shall enter the fire to be burned. *And the seduced* shall say *to their seducers,* Verily ye shall not be bidden welcome : ye have brought it upon us ; and a wretched abode *is hell.* They shall say, O LORD, doubly increase the torment of him who hath brought this *punish-ment* upon us, in the fire *of hell.* And *the infidels* shall say, Why do we not see the men whom we numbered among the wicked, *and* whom we received with scorn ? Or do *our* eyes miss them ? Verily this is a truth ; *to wit,* the disputing of the inhabitants of *hell* fire. Say, *O Mohammed, unto the idolaters,* Verily I *am* no other than a warner : and there *is* no god, except the one only GOD, the Almighty, the LORD of heaven and earth, and of whatsoever *is* be-tween them ; the mighty, the forgiver *of sins.* Say, It is a weighty message, from which ye turn aside. I had no knowledge of the exalted princes,[1] when they disputed *con-cerning the creation of man* (it hath been revealed unto me only *as a proof* that I am a public preacher) : when thy LORD said unto the angels, Verily I am about to create man of clay : when I shall have formed him, therefore, and shall have breathed my spirit into him, do ye fall down and worship him.[2] And all the angels worshipped *him,* in general ; except Eblîs, *who* was puffed up with pride, and became an unbeliever. *God* said *unto him,* O Eblîs, what hindereth thee from worshipping that which I have created with my hands ? Art thou elated with vain pride ? Or art thou *really* one of exalted merit ? He answered, I am more excellent than he : thou hast created me of fire, and hast created him of clay. *God* said *unto him,* Get thee hence therefore, for thou shalt be driven away *from mercy* : and my curse *shall be* upon thee, until the day of judgment. He replied, O LORD, Respite me, therefore, until the day of resurrection. *God* said, Verily thou shalt be *one* of those who are respited until the day of the determined time. *Eblîs* said, By thy might *do I swear,* I will surely seduce them all, except thy servants *who shall be* peculiarly chosen from among them. *God* said, *It is* a just sentence : and I speak the truth : I will surely fill hell with thee, and with such of them as shall follow thee, altogether.[3] Say *unto the Meccans,* I ask not of you any reward for this *my preach-*

---

[1] That is, the angels.   [2] See Chap. II. p. 6.
[3] See Chaps. VII. p. 140 and also XV. p. 253, where the seven gates are mentioned.

ing : neither am I *one* of those who assume a part which belongs not to them. *The Korân* is no other than an admonition unto all creatures : and ye shall surely know what is delivered therein *to be true*, after a season.

XXXIX

THE CHAPTER OF THE TROOPS [1]

Revealed at Mecca.[2]

IN THE NAME OF THE MOST MERCIFUL GOD.

THE revelation of *this* book *is* from the mighty, the wise GOD. Verily we have revealed *this* book unto thee with truth : wherefore serve GOD, exhibiting the pure religion unto him. *Ought* not the pure religion *to be exhibited* unto GOD ? But *as to* those who take other patrons besides him, *saying*, We worship them only that they may bring us nearer unto GOD ; verily GOD will judge between them concerning that wherein they disagree. Surely GOD will not direct him who is a liar, *or* ungrateful. If GOD had been minded to have had a son, he had surely chosen what he pleased out of that which he hath created.[3] But far be *such a thing* from him ! He is the sole, the almighty GOD. He hath created the heavens and the earth with truth : he causeth the night to succeed the day, and he causeth the day to succeed the night, and he obligeth the sun and the moon to perform their services ; each *of them* hasteneth to an appointed period. Is not he the mighty, the forgiver *of sins* ? He created you of one man, and afterwards out of him formed his wife : and he hath bestowed[4]

---

[1] This title is taken from the latter end of the chapter, where it is said the wicked shall be sent to hell, and the righteous admitted into paradise by troops.

[2] Except the verse beginning, Say, O my servants, who have transgressed against your own souls, &c. (Jallalo'ddin, Al Beidâwi.)

[3] Because, says Al Beidâwi, there is no being besides himself but what hath been created by him, since there cannot be two necessarily-existent beings ; and hence appears the absurdity of the imagination here condemned, because no creature can resemble the Creator, or be worthy to bear the relation of a son to him.

[4] Literally, *He hath sent down* ; from which expression some have imagined that these four kinds of beasts were created in paradise, and thence sent down to earth. (Al Zamakh.)

on you four pairs of cattle.[1]   He formeth you in the wombs
of your mothers, by several gradual formations,[2] within
three veils of darkness.[3]   This *is* GOD, your LORD : his *is*
the kingdom :   there is no GOD but he.   Why therefore
are ye turned aside *from the worship of him to idolatry* ?   If
ye be ungrateful, verily GOD hath no need of you ; yet he
liketh not ingratitude in his servants : but if ye be thankful,
he will be well pleased with you.   A burdened *soul* shall
not bear the burden of another : hereafter shall ye return
unto your LORD, and he shall declare unto you that which
ye have wrought, *and will reward you accordingly* ;   for he
knoweth the innermost parts of *your* breasts.   When harm
befalleth a man, he calleth upon his LORD, and turneth unto
him :   yet afterwards, when *God* hath bestowed on him favour
from himself, he forgetteth that *Being* which he invoked
before,[4] and setteth up equals unto GOD, that he may seduce
men from his way.   Say *unto such a man*, Enjoy *this life*
in thy infidelity for a little while :   *but hereafter* shalt thou
surely be *one* of the inhabitants of *hell* fire.   Shall he who
giveth himself up to prayer in the hours of the night, prostrate and standing, *and* who taketh heed as to the life to
come, and hopeth for the mercy of his LORD, *be dealt with as
the wicked unbeliever* ?   Say, Shall they who know *their
duty*, and they who know *it* not, be held equal ?   Verily the
men of understanding only will be warned.   Say, O my
servants who believe, fear your LORD.   They who do good
in this world, shall obtain good *in the next* ;[5] and GOD'S earth
is spacious :[6] verily those who persevere with patience shall
receive their recompence without measure.   Say, I am commanded to worship GOD, and to exhibit the pure religion
unto him :   and I am commanded to be the first Moslem.[7]
Say, Verily I fear, if I be disobedient unto my LORD, the
punishment of the great day.   Say, I worship GOD, exhibiting my religion pure unto him :   but do ye worship that
which ye will, besides him.   Say, Verily they *will be* the losers,
who shall lose their own souls, and their families, on the day
of resurrection :   is not this manifest loss ?   Over them *shall*

[1] See Chap. VI. p. 136.
[2] See Chap. XXII.
[3] *i.e.*, The belly, the womb, and the membranes which enclose the embryo.
[4] Or, *He forgetteth the evil which he before prayed against.*
[5] Or, *They who do good, shall obtain good even in this world.*
[6] Wherefore let him who cannot safely exercise his religion where he
was born or resides, fly to a place of liberty and security.   (Al Beidâwi.)
[7] *i.e.*, The first of the Koreish who professeth the true religion, or the leader
in chief of the Moslems.

be roofs of fire, and under them *shall be* floors *of fire*. With this doth GOD terrify his servants : wherefore, O my servants, fear me. But those who eschew the worship of idols, and are turned unto GOD, shall receive good tidings. Bear good tidings therefore unto my servants, who hearken unto *my* word, and follow that which is most excellent therein : these *are they* whom GOD directeth, and these are *men* of understanding. Him therefore on whom the sentence of *eternal* punishment shall be justly pronounced, canst thou, O *Mohammed*, deliver him who *is destined to dwell* in the fire *of hell*. But for those who fear their LORD *will be prepared* high apartments *in paradise*, over which *shall be other* apartments built ; *and* rivers shall run beneath them : *this is* the promise of GOD ; *and* GOD will not be contrary to the promise. Dost thou not see that GOD sendeth down water from heaven, and causeth the same to enter *and form* sources in the earth ; and produceth thereby corn of various sorts ? Afterwards he causeth *the same* to wither ; and thou seest it become yellow : afterwards he maketh it crumble into dust. Verily herein is an instruction to men of understanding. Shall he, therefore, whose breast GOD hath enlarged to *receive the religion of* Islâm, and who followeth the light from his LORD, *be as he whose heart is hardened* ? But woe unto those whose hearts are hardened against the remembrance of GOD ! they are in a manifest error. GOD hath revealed a most excellent discourse ; a book conformable to itself, *and* containing repeated *admonitions*. The skins of those who fear their LORD shrink for fear thereat : afterwards their skins grow soft, and their hearts *also*, at the remembrance of their LORD. This *is* the direction of GOD ; he will direct thereby whom he pleaseth ; and whomsoever GOD shall cause to err, he shall have no director. Shall he therefore who shall *be obliged to* screen himself with his face[1] from the severity of the punishment on the day of resurrection, *be as he who is secure therefrom* ? And it shall be said unto the ungodly, Taste that which ye have deserved. Those who *were* before them, accused *their apostles* of imposture ; wherefore a punishment came upon them from whence they expected *it* not : and GOD caused them to taste shame in this present life ; but the punishment of the life to come *will* certainly *be* greater. If they were men of understanding, *they would know this*. Now have we proposed unto mankind,

----

[1] For his hands shall be chained to his neck, and he shall not be able to oppose anything but his face to the fire. (Al Beidâwi.)

in this Korân, every kind of parable; that they may be
warned : an Arabic Korân, wherein there is no crookedness ;[1]
that they may fear *God*. GOD propoundeth as a parable
a man who hath *several* companions who are at mutual
variance, and a man who committeth himself wholly to one
person :[2] shall these be held in equal comparison ? GOD
forbid ! But the greater part of them do not understand.
Verily thou, *O Mohammed*, shalt die, and they also shall die :
and ye shall debate *the matter*[3] with one another before your
LORD, at the day of resurrection.   (XXIV.) [4] Who *is* more
unjust than he who uttereth a lie concerning GOD, and
denieth the truth, when it cometh unto him ?   Is there not a
dwelling *provided* in hell for the unbelievers ?   But he who
bringeth the truth, and giveth credit thereto,[5] these are
they who fear *God* ; they *shall obtain* whatever they shall
desire, in the sight of their LORD :   this *shall be* the recompence of the righteous :   that GOD may expiate from them
the *very* worst of that which they have wrought, and may
render them their reward according to the utmost merit of
the good which they have wrought.   Is not GOD a sufficient
protector of his servant ?   yet they will attempt to make
thee afraid of the *false deities* which *they worship* besides
GOD.[6]   But he whom GOD shall cause to err, shall have none
to direct *him* :   and he whom GOD shall direct, shall have
none to mislead *him*.   Is not GOD most mighty, able to
avenge ?   If thou ask them who hath created the heavens

---

[1] *i.e.*, No contradiction, defect, or doubt.

[2] This passage represents the uncertainty of the idolater, who is distracted
in the service of different masters ; and the satisfaction of mind which attends
the worshipper of the only true GOD.   (Al Beidâwi.)

[3] For the prophet will represent his endeavours to reclaim them from
idolatry, and their obstinacy ; and they will make frivolous excuses, as
that they obeyed their chiefs, and kept to the religion of their fathers, &c.
(Al Beidâwi.)   [4] Section XXIV. begins here.

[5] *i.e.*, Mohammed and his followers.   Some suppose that by the latter
words Abu Becr is particularly intended, because he asserted the prophet's
veracity in respect to his journey to heaven.

[6] The Koreish used to tell Mohammed that they feared their gods would
do him some mischief, and deprive him of the use of his limbs, or of his
reason, because he spoke disgracefully of them.   It is thought by some that
this passage was verified in Khâled Ebn al Walîd ; who, being sent by
Mohammed to demolish the idol Al Uzza, was advised by the keeper of
her temple to take heed what he did, because the goddess was able to avenge
herself severely ; but he was so little moved at the man's warning, that
he immediately stepped up to the idol, and broke her nose.   To support
the latter explanation, they say that what happened to Khâled is attributed
to Mohammed, because the former was then executing the prophet's orders.
(Al Beidâwi.)   A circumstance not much different from the above mentioned
is told of the demolition of Allat.   (Vide Gagnier, not. in Abulf. Vit. Moh.
p. 127.)

and the earth, they will surely answer, GOD. Say, Do ye think therefore that the *deities* which ye invoke besides GOD, if GOD be pleased to afflict me, are able to relieve *me* from his affliction ? or if he be pleased to show mercy unto me, that they are able to withhold his mercy ? Say, GOD is my sufficient support : in him let those put their trust, who *seek in whom to* confide. Say, O my people, do ye act according to your state ; verily I will act *according to mine* : hereafter shall ye know on which of us will be inflicted a punishment that shall cover him with shame, and on whom a lasting punishment shall fall. Verily we have revealed unto thee the book *of the Korân,* for *the instruction of* mankind, with truth. Whoso shall be directed *thereby, shall be directed* to *the advantage of* his own soul ; and whoso shall err, shall only err against the same : and thou *art* not a guardian over them. GOD taketh unto himself the souls *of men* at the time of their death ; and those which die not *he also taketh* in their sleep:[1] and he withholdeth those on whom he hath passed the decree of death,[2] but sendeth back the others till a determined period.[3] Verily, herein *are* signs unto people who consider. Have *the Koreish* taken idols for their intercessors *with God* ? Say, What, although they have not dominion over anything, neither do they understand ? Say, Intercession is altogether in the disposal of GOD :[4] his *is* the kingdom of heaven and earth ; and hereafter shall ye return unto him. When the one sole GOD is mentioned, the hearts of those who believe not in the life to come, shrink with horror : but when the *false gods,* which *are worshipped* besides him, are mentioned, behold, they are filled with joy. Say, O GOD, the creator of heaven and earth, who knowest that which is secret and that which is manifest ; thou shalt judge between thy servants concerning that wherein they disagree. If those who act unjustly were masters of whatever is in the earth, and as much more therewith, verily they would give it to ransom themselves from the evil of the punishment, on the day of resurrection : and there shall appear unto them, from GOD, *terrors* which they never imagined ; and there shall appear unto them the evils of that which they shall have gained ;

---

[1] That is, seemingly and to outward appearance, sleep being the image of death.

[2] Not permitting them to return again into their bodies.

[3] viz., Into their bodies when they awake. (Al Beidâwi.)

[4] For none can or dare presume to intercede with him, unless by his permission.

and that which they mocked at shall encompass them. When harm befalleth man, he calleth upon us; yet afterwards, when we have bestowed on him favour from us, he saith, I have received it merely because of *God's* knowledge *of my deserts.*[1] On the contrary, it *is* a trial; but the greater part of them know *it* not. Those who *were* before them, said the same:[2] but that which they had gained, profited them not; and the evils which they had deserved, fell upon them. And whoever of these *Meccans* shall have acted unjustly, on them likewise shall fall the evils which they shall have deserved;[3] neither shall they frustrate *the divine vengeance.* Do they not know that GOD bestoweth provision abundantly on whom he pleaseth, and is sparing *unto whom he pleaseth?* Verily herein *are* signs unto people who believe. Say, O my servants who have transgressed against your own souls, despair not of the mercy of GOD: seeing that GOD forgiveth all sins;[4] for he is gracious *and* merciful. And be turned unto your LORD, and resign yourselves unto him, before the *threatened* punishment overtake you; *for* then ye shall not be helped. And follow the most excellent *instructions* which have been sent down unto you from your LORD, before the punishment come suddenly upon you, and ye perceive not *the approach thereof;* *and* a soul say, Alas! for that I have been negligent in my duty to GOD: verily I have been *one* of the scorners: or say, If GOD had directed me, verily I had been one of the pious: or say, when it seeth the *prepared* punishment, If I could return once more *into the world* I would become *one* of the righteous. But *God shall answer,* My signs came unto thee heretofore, and thou didst charge them with falsehood, and wast puffed up with pride; and thou becamest *one* of the unbelievers. On the day of resurrection thou shalt see the faces of those who have uttered lies concerning GOD, become black: is there not an abode *prepared* in hell for the arrogant? But GOD shall deliver those who shall fear *him, and shall set them* in their place of safety: evil shall not touch them, neither shall they be grieved. GOD *is* the creator of all things, and he *is* the governor of all things. His are the keys of heaven and earth:

---

[1] Or by means of my own wisdom.

[2] As did Karûn in particular. (See Chap. XXVIII.)

[3] As it happened accordingly: for they were punished with a sore famine for seven years and had the bravest of their warriors cut off at the battle of Bedr. (Al Beidâwi.)

[4] To those who sincerely repent and profess his unity: for the sins of idolaters will not be forgiven. (See Chap. II. p. 13.)

and they who believe not in the signs of God, they shall perish. Say, Do ye therefore bid me to worship other than GOD, O ye fools ? since it hath been spoken by revelation unto thee, and also unto *the prophets* who *have been* before thee, *saying*, Verily if thou join any partners *with* GOD, thy work will be altogether unprofitable, and thou shalt certainly be *one* of those who perish : wherefore rather fear GOD, and be *one* of those who give thanks. But they make not a due estimation of GOD :[1] since the whole earth *shall be but* his handful, on the day of resurrection ; and the heavens *shall be* rolled together in his right hand. Praise be unto him ! and far be he exalted above the *idols* which they associate *with him* ! The trumpet shall be sounded,[2] and whoever *are* in heaven and whoever *are* on earth shall expire ; except those whom GOD shall please *to exempt from the common fate*.[3] Afterwards it shall be sounded again ; and behold, they shall arise and look *up*. And the earth shall shine by the light of its LORD : and the book shall be laid *open*,[4] and the prophets and the martrys shall be brought *as witnesses* ; and judgment shall be given between them with truth, and they shall not be treated unjustly. And every soul shall be fully rewarded, according to that which it shall have wrought ; for he perfectly knoweth whatever they do. And the unbelievers shall be driven unto hell by troops, until, when they shall arrive at the same, the gates thereof shall be opened : and the keepers thereof[5] shall say unto them, Did not apostles from among you come unto you, who rehearsed unto you the signs of your LORD, and warned you of the meeting of this your day ? They shall answer, Yea : but the sentence of *eternal* punishment hath been justly

---

[1] See Chap. VI. p. 128.

[2] The first time, says Al Beidâwi ; who consequently supposes there will be no more than two blasts (and two only are distinctly mentioned in the Korân), though others suppose there will be three. (See Sale, Prel. Disc. Sect. IV. p. 89.)

[3] These, some say, will be the angels Gabriel, Michael, and Israfil, and the angel of death, who yet will afterwards all die, at the command of GOD (Al Beidâwi, Yahya); it being the constant opinion of the Mohammedan doctors, that every soul, both of men and of animals, which live either on land or in the sea, and of the angels also, must necessarily taste of death (Vide Pocock, not. in Port. Mosis. p. 266): others suppose those who will be exempted are the angels who bear the throne of GOD (Al Beidâwi), or the black-eyed damsels, and other inhabitants of paradise (Jallalo'ddin). The space between these two blasts of the trumpet will be forty days, according to Yahya and others ; there are some, however, who suppose it will be as many years (see Sale, Prel. Disc. Sect. IV.)

[4] See Sale, Prel. Disc. Sect. IV. p. 93.

[5] See Chap. LXXIV., and Sale, Prel. Disc. Sect. IV. p. 97.

pronounced on the unbelievers.[1] It shall be said *unto them*, Enter ye the gates of hell, to dwell therein for ever ; and miserable *shall be* the abode of the proud ! But those who shall have feared their LORD, shall be conducted by troops towards paradise, until they shall arrive at the same : and the gates thereof shall be ready set open ; and the guards thereof shall say unto them, Peace *be* on you ! ye have been good : wherefore enter ye into *paradise*, to remain therein for ever. And they shall answer, Praise be unto GOD, who hath performed his promise unto us, and hath made us to inherit the earth,[2] that we may dwell in paradise wherever we please ! How excellent *is* the reward of those who work *righteousness* ! And thou shalt see the angels going in procession round the throne, celebrating the praises of their LORD : and judgment shall be given between them with truth ; and they shall say, Praise be unto GOD, the LORD of all creatures !

XL

THE CHAPTER OF THE TRUE BELIEVER [3]
Revealed at Mecca.

IN THE NAME OF THE MOST MERCIFUL GOD.

H. M.[4] The revelation of *this* book *is* from the mighty, the wise GOD ; the forgiver of sin, and the accepter of repentance ; severe in punishing ; long-suffering. There is no GOD but he : before him *shall be* the *general* assembly *at the last day*. None disputeth against the signs of GOD, except the unbelievers : but let not their prosperous dealing in the land[5] deceive thee *with vain allurement*. The people of Noah, and the confederated *infidels which were* after them, accused *their respective prophets* of imposture before these ; and each nation hatched *ill designs* against their apostle,

---

[1] See Chaps. VII. and XI. It seems as if the damned, by these words, attributed their ruin to GOD's decree of predestination.

[2] This is a metaphorical expression, representing the perfect security and abundance which the blessed will enjoy in paradise.

[3] This title, also rendered *The Believer*, is taken from the passage wherein mention is made of one of Pharaoh's family who believed in Moses.

[4] Sale, Prel. Disc. Sect. III. p. 64.

[5] By trading into Syria and Yaman. See Chap. III. p. 70.

that they might get him *into their power*; and they disputed with vain *reasoning*, that they might thereby invalidate the truth: wherefore I chastised them; and how *severe* was my punishment! Thus hath the sentence of thy LORD justly passed on the unbelievers; that they *shall be* the inhabitants of *hell* fire. *The angels* who bear the throne *of God*, and those who *stand* about it,[1] celebrate the praise of their LORD, and believe in him; and they ask pardon for the true believers, *saying*, O LORD, thou encompassest all things by *thy* mercy and knowledge; wherefore forgive those who repent and follow thy path, and deliver them from the pains of hell: O LORD, lead them also into gardens of eternal abode, which thou hast promised unto them, and unto every one who shall do right, of their fathers, and their wives, and their children; for thou art the mighty, the wise *God*. And deliver them from evil; for whomsoever thou shalt deliver from evil on that day, on him wilt thou show mercy; and this will be great salvation. But the infidels, *at the day of judgment*, shall hear a voice crying unto them, Verily the hatred of GOD *towards you is* more grievous than your hatred towards yourselves: since ye were called unto the faith, and would not believe. They shall say, O LORD, thou hast given us death twice, and thou hast twice given us life;[2] and we confess our sins: *is there* therefore no way to get forth *from this fire*? *And it shall be answered them*, This *hath befallen you*, for that when one GOD was preached *unto you*, ye believed not; but if *a plurality of gods* had been associated with him, ye had believed; and judgment *belongeth* unto the high, the great GOD. *It is* he who showeth you his signs, and sendeth down food unto you from heaven: but none will be admonished, except he who turneth himself *unto God*. Call therefore upon GOD, exhibiting *your* religion pure unto him, although the infidels be averse *thereto*. *He is the Being* of exalted degree, the possessor of the throne; who sendeth down the spirit, at his command, on such of his servants as he pleaseth; that he may warn *mankind*

---

[1] These are the Cherubim, the highest order of angels, who approach nearest to GOD's presence. (Al Beidâwi.)

[2] Having first created us in a state of death, or void of life and sensation, and then given life to the inanimate body (see Chap. II.); and afterwards caused us to die a natural death, and raised us again at the resurrection. Some understand the first death to be a natural death, and the second that in the sepulchre, after the body shall have been there raised to life in order to be examined (Sale, Prel. Disc. Sect. IV.); and consequently suppose the two revivals to be those of the sepulchre and the resurrection (Al Beidâwi, Jallal.)

of the day of meeting,[1] the day *whereon* they shall come forth *out of their graves, and* nothing of *what concerneth* them shall be hidden from GOD. Unto whom *will* the kingdom *belong* on that day? Unto the only, the almighty GOD. On that day shall every soul be rewarded according to its merits; *there shall be* no injustice *done* on that day. Verily GOD *will be* swift in taking an account. Wherefore warn them, *O prophet*, of the day which shall suddenly approach; when *men's* hearts *shall come up* to their throats, and strangle *them*. The ungodly shall have no friend or intercessor who shall be heard. *God* will know the deceitful eye, and that which *their* breasts conceal; and GOD will judge with truth: but *the false gods* which they invoke besides him, shall not judge at all; for GOD *is* he who heareth *and* seeth. Have they not gone through the earth and seen what hath been the end of those who were before them? They were more mighty than these in strength, and *left more considerable* footsteps *of their power* in the earth: yet GOD chastised them for their sins, and there was none to protect them from GOD. This *they suffered*, because their apostles had come unto them with evident *signs*, and they disbelieved: wherefore GOD chastised them; for he *is* strong, *and* severe in punishing. We heretofore sent Moses with our signs and manifest power, unto Pharaoh, and Haman, and Karûn; and they said, *He is* a sorcerer *and* a liar. And when he came unto them with the truth from us, they said, Slay the sons of those who have believed with him, and save their daughters alive:[2] but the stratagem of the infidels *was* no other than vain. And Pharaoh said, Let me alone, that I may kill Moses;[3] and let him call upon his LORD: verily I fear lest he change your religion, or cause violence to appear in the earth.[4] And Moses said *unto his people*, Verily I have recourse unto my LORD, and your LORD, *to defend me* against every proud person, who believeth not in the day of account. And a man *who was* a true believer, of the family of Pharaoh,[5] *and*

---

[1] When the Creator and his creatures (see Chap. VI. p. 120), the inhabitants of heaven and of earth, the false deities and their worshippers, the oppressor and the oppressed, the labourer and his works, shall meet each other. (Al Beidâwi, Jallal.)

[2] *i.e.*, Pursue the resolution which has been formerly taken, and execute it more strictly for the future. See Chap. VII. p. 155.

[3] For they advised him not to put Moses to death, lest it should be thought he was not able to oppose him by dint of argument. (Al Beidâwi.)

[4] By raising of commotions and seditions, in order to introduce his new religion.

[5] This seems to be the same person who is mentioned on p. 379.

concealed his faith, said, Will ye put a man to death, because he saith, GOD *is* my LORD ; seeing, he is come unto you with evident signs from your LORD ?   If he be a liar, on him *will the punishment of* his falsehood *light* ; but if he speaketh the truth, some of *those judgments* with which he threateneth you, will fall upon you : verily GOD directeth not him who is a transgressor *or* a liar.   O my people, the kingdom is yours this day ; *and ye are* conspicuous in the earth : but who shall defend us from the scourge of GOD, if it come unto us ?[1] Pharaoh said, I only propose to you what I think *to be most expedient* : and I guide you only into the right path.   And he who had believed, said, O my people, verily I fear for you a day like that of the confederates *against the prophets in former times* ; a condition like that of the people of Noah, and *the tribes of* Ad and Thamûd, and of those who *have lived* after them : for GOD willeth not *that* any injustice *be done* unto *his* servants.   O my people, verily I fear for you the day whereon men shall call unto one another ;[2] the day whereon ye shall be turned back *from the tribunal, and driven to hell* : *then* shall ye have none to protect you against GOD. And he whom GOD shall cause to err, shall have no director. Joseph came unto you, before *Moses*, with evident *signs* ; but ye ceased not to doubt of the *religion* which he preached unto you, until, when he died, ye said, GOD will by no means send *another* apostle, after him.   Thus doth GOD cause him to err, who is a transgressor *and* a sceptic.   They who dispute against the signs of GOD, without any authority which hath come unto them, are in great abomination with GOD, and with those who believe.   Thus doth GOD seal up every proud *and* stubborn heart.   And Pharaoh said, O Haman, build me a tower, that I may reach the tracts, the tracts of heaven, and may view the GOD of Moses ;[3] for I verily think him *to be* a liar.   And thus the evil of his work was prepared for Pharaoh, and he turned aside from the *right* path : and the stratagems of Pharaoh *ended* only in loss.   And he who had believed, said, O my people, follow me : I will guide you into the right way.   O my people, verily this present life *is* but a temporary enjoyment ; but *the life* to come is

---

[1] See the speech of Gamaliel to the Jewish Sanhedrim, when the apostles were brought before them.   (Acts v. 38, 39.)

[2] *i.e.*, The day of judgment, when the inhabitants of paradise and of hell shall enter into mutual discourse : when the latter shall call for help, and the seducers and the seduced shall cast the blame upon each other.   (Al Beidâwi, Jallalo'ddin.)

[3] See Chap. XXVIII. p. 332.

the mansion of firm continuance. Whoever worketh evil, shall only be rewarded in equal proportion to the same : but whoever worketh good, whether male or female, and *is* a true believer, they shall enter paradise ; they shall be provided for therein superabundantly. And, O my people, as for me, I invite you to salvation ; but ye invite me to *hell* fire : ye invite me to deny GOD, and to associate with him that whereof I have no knowledge ; but I invite you to the most mighty, the forgiver *of sins*. *There is* no doubt but that the *false gods* to which ye invite me, deserve not to be invoked, either in this world or in the next ; and that we must return unto GOD ; and that the transgressors shall be the inhabitants of *hell* fire : and ye shall *then* remember what I *now* say unto you. And I commit my affair unto GOD : for GOD regardeth his servants. Wherefore GOD delivered him from the evils which they had devised ; and a grievous punishment encompassed the people of Pharaoh.[1] They shall be exposed to the fire *of hell* morning and evening :[2] and the day whereon the hour *of judgment* shall come, *it shall be said unto them*, Enter, O people of Pharaoh, into a most severe torment. And *think on the time* when *the infidels* shall dispute together in *hell* fire ; and the weak shall say unto those who behaved with arrogance,[3] Verily we were your followers : will ye, therefore, relieve us from *any* part of *this* fire ? Those who behaved with arrogance shall answer, Verily we *are* all *doomed to suffer* therein : for GOD hath now judged between *his* servants. And they who *shall be* in the fire, shall say unto the keepers of hell,[4] Call ye on your LORD, that he would ease us, for one day, from *this* punishment. They shall answer, Did not your apostles come unto you with evident *proofs* ? They shall say, Yea. *The keepers* shall reply, Do ye therefore call *on God* : but the calling of the unbelievers *on him* shall be only in vain. We will surely assist our apostles, and those who believe in

[1] Some are of opinion that those who were sent by Pharaoh to seize the true believer, his kinsman, are the persons more particularly meant in this place : for they tell us that the said believer fled to a mountain, where they found him at prayers, guarded by the wild beasts, which ranged themselves in order about him, and that his pursuers thereupon returned in a great fright to their master, who put them to death for not performing his command. (Al Beidâwi.)

[2] Some expound these words of the previous punishment they are doomed to suffer according to a tradition of Ebn Masûd, which informs us that their souls are in the crops of black birds, which are exposed to hell fire every morning and evening until the day of judgment. (Al Beidâwi.)

[3] See Chap. XIV. p. 247.

[4] See Chap. LXXIV.

this present life, and on the day whereon the witnesses shall stand forth : a day, whereon the excuse of the un-believers shall not avail them ; but a curse *shall attend* them, and a wretched abode. We heretofore gave unto Moses a direction : and we left as an inheritance unto the children of Israel the book *of the law* ; a direction, and an admonition to *men* of understanding. Wherefore do thou, *O prophet*, bear *the insults of the infidels* with patience ; for the promise of GOD *is* true : and ask pardon for thy fault ;[1] and celebrate the praise of thy LORD, in the evening and in the morning. *As to* those who impugn the signs of GOD, without any con-vincing proof which hath been revealed unto them, there is nothing but pride in their breasts ;[2] *but* they shall not attain *their desire* : wherefore, fly for refuge unto GOD, for *it is* he who heareth *and* seeth. Verily the creation of heaven and earth *is* more considerable than the creation of man : but the greater part of men do not understand. The blind and the seeing shall not be held equal ; nor they who believe and work righteousness, and the evil-doer : how few revolve *these things* in their mind ! The *last* hour will surely come ; *there is* no doubt thereof : but the greater part of men believe *it* not. Your LORD saith, Call upon me, *and* I will hear you : but they who proudly disdain my service shall enter with ignominy into hell. *It is* GOD who hath appointed the night for you to take your rest therein, and the day to give *you* light : verily GOD *is* endued with beneficence to-wards mankind ; but the greater part of men do not give thanks. This *is* GOD, your LORD ; the creator of all things : *there is* no GOD besides him : how therefore are ye turned aside *from his worship* ? Thus are they turned aside who oppose the signs of GOD. *It is* GOD who hath given you the earth for a stable floor, and the heaven for a ceiling : and who hath formed you, and made your forms beautiful ; and feedeth you with good things. This *is* GOD, your LORD. Wherefore, blessed be GOD, the LORD of all creatures ! He *is* the living *God* : *there is* no GOD but he. Wherefore call upon him, exhibiting unto him the pure religion. Praise be unto GOD, the LORD of all creatures ! Say, Verily I am forbidden to worship the *deities* which ye invoke, besides GOD,

---

[1] In being too backward and negligent in advancing the true religion, for fear of the infidels. (Al Beidâwi.)

[2] This sentence may be understood generally, though it was revealed on account of the idolatrous Meccans or of the Jews, who said of Mohammed, *This man is not our lord, but the Messias the Son of David, whose kingdom will be extended over sea and land.* (Al Beidâwi.)

after that evident proofs have come unto me from my LORD ; and I am commanded to resign myself unto the LORD of all creatures. *It is* he who *first* created you of dust, and afterwards of seed, and afterwards of coagulated blood ; and afterwards brought you forth infants *out of your mothers' wombs* : then *he permitteth* you to attain your age of full strength, and afterwards to grow old men (but some of you die before *that age*), and to arrive at the determined period *of your life* ;[1] that peradventure ye may understand. *It is* he who giveth life, and causeth to die : and when he decreeth a thing, he only saith unto it, Be, and it is. Dost thou not observe those who dispute against the signs of GOD, how they are turned aside *from the true faith* ? They who charge with falsehood the book *of the Korân*, and *the other scriptures and revealed doctrines* which we sent our *former* apostles *to preach*, shall hereafter know *their folly* ; when the collars *shall be* on their necks, and the chains *by which* they shall be dragged into hell : then shall they be burned in the fire. And it shall be said unto them, Where are the *gods* which ye associated beside GOD ? They shall answer, They have withdrawn themselves from us : yea, we called on nothing[2] heretofore. Thus doth GOD lead the unbelievers into error. This *hath befallen you*, for that ye rejoiced *insolently* on earth in that which was false ; and for that ye were elated with immoderate joy. Enter ye the gates of hell, to remain therein *for ever* : and wretched *shall be* the abode of the haughty ! Wherefore persevere with patience, *O Mohammed* ; for the promise of GOD *is* true. Whether we cause thee to see any part of the *punishment* with which we have threatened them, or whether we cause thee to die *before thou see it* ; before us shall they be assembled *at the last day*. We have sent *a great number of* apostles before thee ;[3] *the histories of some* of whom we have related unto thee, and *the histories of others* of them we have not related unto thee : but no apostle had the power to produce a sign, unless by the permission of GOD. When the command of GOD, therefore, shall come, judgment shall be given with truth ; and then shall they perish who endeavour to render *the signs of God* of no effect. *It is* GOD who hath given you the cattle, that ye may ride on *some of* them, and may eat *of others* of them (ye also receive *other* advantages therefrom);[4]

[1] See Chap. XXII. p. 327.
[2] Seeing an idol is nothing in the world. (Al Beidâwi.)
[3] See Sale, Prel. Disc. Sect. IV. p. 81.   [4] See Chap. XVI. p. 258.

and that on them ye may arrive at the business *proposed* in your mind : and on them are ye carried *by land*, and on ships *by sea*. And he showeth you his signs : which, therefore, of the signs of GOD will ye deny ? Do they not pass through the earth, and see what hath been the end of those who *were* before them ? They were more numerous than these, and more mighty in strength, and *left more considerable monuments of their power* in the earth : yet that which they had acquired profited them not. And when their apostles came unto them with evident *proofs of their mission*, they rejoiced in the knowledge which was with them :[1] but that which they mocked at encompassed them. And when they beheld our vengeance, they said, We believe in GOD alone, and we renounce *the idols* which we associated with him : but their faith availed them not, after they had beholden our vengeance. *This was* the ordinance of GOD, which was formerly observed in respect to his servants : and then did the unbelievers perish.

XLI

THE CHAPTER OF THE DISTINCTLY EXPLAINED [2]

Revealed at Mecca.

IN THE NAME OF THE MOST MERCIFUL GOD.

H M.[3] *This is* a revelation from the most Merciful, a book the verses whereof are distinctly explained, an Arabic Korân for *the instruction of* people who understand ; bearing good tidings, and denouncing threats : but the greater part of them turn aside, and hearken not *thereto*. And they say, Our hearts are veiled from *the doctrine* to which thou invitest us ; and *there is* a deafness in our ears, and a curtain between us and thee : wherefore act thou *as thou shalt think fit* ; for we shall act *according to our own sentiments*. Say, Verily I am only a man like you. It is revealed unto me that your GOD is one GOD : wherefore direct your

---

[1] Being prejudiced in favour of their own erroneous doctrines, and despising the instructions of the prophets.

[2] Some entitle this chapter *Worship*, or *Adoration*, because the infidels are herein commanded to forsake the worship of idols, and to worship GOD : but the thirty-second chapter bearing the same title, that which we have here prefixed is, for distinction, generally used.

[3] See Sale, Prel. Disc. Sect. III. p. 64, and Chap. II. p. 2.

[4] See Chap. XI. p. 210.

way straight unto him; and ask pardon of him *for what is past*. And woe *be* to the idolaters; who give not the appointed alms, and believe not in the life to come! But *as to* those who believe and work righteousness; they shall receive an everlasting reward. Say, Do ye indeed disbelieve in him who created the earth in two days;[1] and do ye set up equals unto him? He is the LORD of all creatures. And he placed in *the earth mountains* firmly rooted,[2] *rising* above the same: and he blessed it; and provided therein the food *of the creatures designed to be the inhabitants* thereof, in four days;[3] equally for those who ask.[4] Then he set his mind to *the creation of* heaven; and it was smoke:[5] and he said unto it, and to the earth, Come, either obediently, or against your will. They answered, We come obedient *to thy command*. And he formed them into seven heavens, in two days;[6] and revealed unto every heaven its office. And he adorned the lower hea·-en with lights, and *placed therein a* guard *of angels*.[7] This *is* the disposition of the mighty, the wise *God*. If *the Meccans* withdraw *from these instructions*, say, I denounce unto you a sudden destruction, like the destruction of Ad and Thamûd. When the apostles came unto them before them and behind them,[8] *saying*, Worship GOD alone; they answered, If our LORD had been pleased *to send messengers*, he had surely sent angels: and we believe not *the message* with which ye are sent. As to *the tribe of* Ad, they behaved insolently in the earth, without reason, and said, Wɧɔ *is* more mighty than we in strength? Did they not see that GꝺD, who had created them, was more mighty than they in strength? And they knowingly

---

[1] viz., The two first days of the week. (Jallalo'ddin.)

[2] See Chap. XVI. p. 258.

[3] That is, including the two former days wherein the earth was created.

[4] *i.e.*, For all, in proportion to the necessity of each, and as their several appetites require. Some refer the word *sawâan*, here translated *equally*, and which also signifies *completely*, to the four days; and suppose the meaning to be that GOD created these things in just so many *entire* and *complete* days. (Jallalo'ddin, Al Beidâwi.)

[5] Or darkness. Al Zamakhshari says this smoke proceeded from the waters under the throne of GOD (which throne was one of the things created before the heavens and the earth), and rose above the water; that the water being dried up, the earth was formed out of it, and the heavens out of the smoke which had mounted aloft.

[6] viz., On the fifth and sixth days of the week. It is said the heavens were created on Thursday, and the sun, moon, and stars on Friday; in the evening of which last day Adam was made. (Al Beidâwi.)

[7] See Chap. XV. p. 252.

[8] That is, on every side; persuading and urging them continually, and by arguments drawn from past examples, and the expectation of future rewards or punishments.

rejected our signs. Wherefore we sent against them a piercing wind, on days of ill luck,[1] that we might make them taste the punishment of shame in this world : but the punishment of the life to come will be more shameful ; and they shall not be protected *therefrom*. And as to Thamûd, we directed them ; but they loved blindness better than the *true* direction : wherefore the terrible noise of an ignominious punishment assailed them, for that which they had deserved ; but we delivered those who believed and feared *God*.[2] And *warn them of* the day, on which the enemies of GOD shall be gathered together unto *hell* fire, and shall march in distinct bands ; until, when they shall arrive thereat, their ears, and their eyes, and their skins shall bear witness against them of that which they shall have wrought. And they shall say unto their skins, Wherefore do ye bear witness against us ? They shall answer, GOD hath caused us to speak, who giveth speech unto all things : he created you the first time ; and unto him are ye returned. Ye did not hide yourselves, *while ye sinned*, so that your ears, and your eyes, and your skins could not bear witness against you :[3] but ye thought that GOD was ignorant of many things which ye did. This *was* your opinion, which ye imagined of your LORD : it hath ruined you ; and ye are become lost *people*. Whether they bear *their torment, hell* fire *shall be* their abode ; or whether they beg for favour, they shall not obtain favour. And we will give them *the devils to be their* companions ; for they dressed up for them *the false notions which they entertained of* this present world, and *of* that which is to come ; and the sentence justly fitteth them, which was formerly pronounced on the nations of genii and men who were before them ; for they perished. The unbelievers say, Hearken not unto this Korân : but use vain discourse[4] during *the reading* thereof ; that ye may overcome *the voice of the reader by your scoffs and laughter*. Wherefore we will surely cause the unbelievers to taste a grievous punishment, and we will certainly reward them for the evils which they shall have wrought. This *shall be* the reward of the enemies

---

[1] It is said that this wind continued from Wednesday to Wednesday inclusive, being the latter end of the month Shawâl ; and that a Wednesday is the day whereon GOD sends down his judgments on a wicked people. (Al Beidâwi.)

[2] See Chap. VII. p. 148.

[3] *i.e.*, Ye hid your crimes from men, little thinking that your very members, from which ye could not hide them, would rise up as witnesses against you.

[4] Or, talk aloud.

of GOD, *namely, hell* fire ; therein *is prepared* for them an
everlasting abode, *as* a reward for that they have wittingly
rejected our signs.   And the infidels shall say *in hell*, O LORD,
show us the two who seduced us, of the genii and men,[1] and
we will cast them under our feet, that they may become
most base *and despicable.   As for* those who say, Our LORD
is GOD, and who behave uprightly ;   the angels shall descend
unto them,[2] *and shall say*, Fear not, neither be ye grieved ;
but rejoice in the hopes of paradise, which ye have been
promised.   We *are* your friends in this life, and in that which
is to come :   therein shall ye have that which your souls shall
desire, and therein shall ye obtain whatever ye shall ask for ;
as a gift from a gracious *and* merciful *God.*   Who speaketh
better than he who inviteth unto GOD, and worketh righteousness, and saith, I *am* a Moslem ?   Good and evil shall not be
held equal.   Turn away *evil* with that which is better ;   and
behold the *man* between whom and thyself *there was* enmity,
shall become, as it were, *thy* warmest friend :   but none shall
attain to this *perfection,* except they who are patient ;   nor
shall any attain thereto, except he who is endued with a
great happiness *of temper.*   And if a malicious suggestion
be offered unto thee from Satan, have recourse unto GOD ;
for *it is* he who heareth *and* knoweth.   Among the signs *of
his power are* the night, and the day, and the sun, and the
moon.   Worship not the sun, neither the moon :   but worship GOD, who hath created them ;   if ye serve him.   But
if ye proudly disdain *his service* ;   verily the *angels,* who
are with thy LORD, praise him night and day, and are not
wearied.   And among his signs *another is,* that thou seest
the land waste :   but when we send down rain thereon, it is
stirred and fermenteth.   And he who quickeneth *the earth,*
will surely quicken the dead ;   for he is almighty.   Verily
those who impiously wrong our signs, are not concealed from
us.   *Is* he, therefore, better, who shall be cast into *hell* fire,
or he who shall appear secure on the day of resurrection ?
Work that which ye will :   he certainly beholdeth whatever
ye do.   Verily they who believe not in the admonition *of
the Korân,* after it hath come unto them, *shall one day be dis-*

---

[1] *i.e.*, Those of either species, who drew us into sin and ruin.   Some suppose
that the two more particularly intended here are Eblis and Cain, the two
authors of infidelity and murder.   (Al Beidâwi, Jallalo'ddin.)

[2] Either while they are living on earth to dispose their minds to good,
to preserve them from temptations, and to comfort them ;   or at the hour
of death to support them in their last agony ;   or at their coming forth from
their graves at the resurrection.   (Al Beidâwi.)

covered. It *is* certainly a book of infinite value : vanity shall not approach it, either from before it or from behind it :[1] *it is* a revelation from a wise *God*, whose praise is justly to be celebrated. No other is said unto thee *by the infidels of Mecca*, than what hath been formerly said unto the apostles before thee : verily thy LORD *is* inclined to forgiveness, and *is also* able to chastise severely. If we had revealed *the Korân* in a foreign language,[2] they had surely said, Unless the signs thereof be distinctly explained, *we will not receive the same* : *is the book written in* a foreign tongue, and *the person unto whom it is directed* an Arabian ? Answer, It is, unto those who believe, a sure guide, and a remedy *for doubt and uncertainty* : but unto those who believe not, *it is* a thickness of hearing in their ears, and it is a darkness which covereth them ; these are *as they who are* called unto from a distant place.[3] We heretofore gave the book *of the law* unto Moses ; and a dispute arose concerning the same : and if a previous decree had not proceeded from thy LORD, *to respite the opposers of that revelation*, verily *the matter* had been decided between them, *by the destruction of the infidels* ; for they were in a very great doubt as to the same. He who doth right, *doth it* to *the advantage of* his own soul ; and he who doth evil, *doth it* against the same : for thy LORD *is* not unjust towards *his* servants. (XXV.)[4] Unto him is reserved the knowledge of the hour *of judgment* : and no fruit cometh forth from the knops which involve it ; neither doth any female conceive *in her womb*, nor is she delivered *of her burden*, but with his knowledge. On the day whereon he shall call them to him, *saying*, Where *are* my companions *which ye ascribed unto me* ? they shall answer, We assure thee *there is* no witness *of this matter* among us :[5] and *the idols* which they called on before, shall withdraw themselves from them ; and they shall perceive that *there will be* no way to escape. Man is not wearied with asking good ; but if evil befall him, he despondeth and despaireth. And if we cause him to taste mercy from us, after affliction hath touched him, he surely saith, This *is due* to me, *on account of my deserts* : I do not think the hour *of judgment* will *ever* come ; and if I be brought before my LORD, I shall surely

[1] That is, it shall not be prevailed against, or frustrated by any means or in any respect whatever.
[2] See Chap. XVI. p. 267.
[3] Being so far off that they hear not, or understand not the voice of him who calls to them. [4] Section XXV. begins here.
[5] For they shall disclaim their idols at the resurrection.

attain, with him, the most excellent *condition*. But we will *then* declare unto those who shall not have believed, that which they have wrought ; and we will surely cause them to taste a most severe punishment. When we confer favours on man, he turneth aside, and departeth *without returning thanks* : but when evil toucheth him, he *is* frequent at prayer. Say, What think ye ? if *the Korân* be from GOD, and ye believe not therein ; who will lie under a greater error, than he who dissenteth widely *therefrom* ? Hereafter we will show them our signs in the regions *of the earth*, and in themselves ;[1] until it become manifest unto them that *this book* is the truth. Is it not sufficient *for thee* that thy LORD is witness of all things ? Are they not in a doubt as to the meeting of their LORD *at the resurrection* ? Doth not he encompass all things ?

XLII

THE CHAPTER OF CONSULTATION [2]

Revealed at Mecca.[3]

IN THE NAME OF THE MOST MERCIFUL GOD.

H. M. A. S. K.[4] Thus doth the mighty, the wise GOD, reveal *his will* unto thee ; and *in like manner did he reveal it* unto the *prophets* who *were* before thee. Unto him *belongeth* whatever *is* in heaven and in earth ; and he is the high, the great *God*. It wanteth little but that the heavens be rent in sunder from above, *at the awfulness of his majesty* : the angels celebrate the praise of their LORD, and ask pardon for those who *dwell* in the earth. Is not GOD the forgiver *of sins*, the merciful ? But *as to* those who take *other gods for their* patrons, besides him, GOD observeth their *actions* : for thou art not a steward over them. Thus have we revealed unto thee an Arabic Korân, that thou mayest warn the metropolis *of Mecca*, and the *Arabs* who *dwell* round about

---

[1] By the surprising victories and conquests of Mohammed and his successors. (Al Beidâwi.)

[2] Palmer renders this *Counsel*. The title is taken from the verse wherein the believers are commended, among other things, for using deliberation in their affairs, and *consulting* together in order to act for the best. Some, instead of this word, prefix the five single letters with which the chapter begins.

[3] Jallalo'ddin excepts three verses, beginning with these words, *Say, I ask not of you, for this my preaching, any reward*, &c.

[4] See Sale, Prel. Disc. Sect. III. p. 64, and Chap. II. p. 2.

it ; and mayest threaten *them* with the day of the *general* assembly, of which there is no doubt : *one* part *shall then be placed* i'l paradise, and *another* part in hell. If GOD had pleased, he had made them *all* of one religion : but he leadeth whom he pleaseth into his mercy ; and the unjust shall have no patron or helper. Do they take *other* patrons, besides him ? whereas GOD is the *only true* patron : he quickeneth the dead ; and he *is* almighty. Whatever matter ye disagree about, the decision thereof *appertaineth* unto GOD. This is GOD, my LORD : in him do I trust, and unto him do I turn me : the creator of heaven and earth : he hath given you wives of your own species, and cattle both male and female ; by which means he multiplieth you : there is nothing like him ; and *it is* he who heareth *and* seeth. His are the keys of heaven and earth : he bestoweth provision abundantly on whom he pleaseth, and he is sparing *unto whom he pleaseth* ; for he knoweth all things. He hath ordained you the religion which he commanded Noah, and which we have revealed unto thee, *O Mohammed*, and which we commanded Abraham, and Moses, and Jesus :[1] *saying*, Observe *this* religion, and be not divided therein. The *worship of one God*, to which thou invitest them, is grievous unto the unbelievers : GOD will elect thereto whom he pleaseth, and will direct unto the same him who shall repent. *Those who lived in times past* were not divided among themselves, until after that the knowledge *of God's unity* had come unto them ; through their own perverseness : and unless a previous decree had passed from thy LORD, *to bear with them* till a determined time, verily *the matter* had been decided between them, *by the destruction of the gainsayers*. They who have inherited the scriptures after them,[2] *are* certainly in a perplexing doubt concerning *the same*.[3] Wherefore invite *them to receive the sure faith*, and be urgent *with them*, as thou hast been commanded ; and follow not their *vain* desires : and say, I believe in *all* the scriptures which GOD hath sent down ; and I am commanded to establish justice among you : GOD is our LORD and your LORD : unto us *will* our works *be imputed*, and unto you *will* your works *be imputed* : *let there be* no wrangling between us and you ; for GOD will assemble us *all at the last day*, and unto him shall

---

[1] See ibid. Sect. IV.
[2] viz., The modern Jews and Christians.
[3] Not understanding the true meaning, nor believing the real doctrines

we return. *As to* those who dispute concerning GOD, after obedience hath been paid him *by receiving his religion*, their disputing *shall be* vain in the sight of their LORD ; and wrath *shall fall* on them, and they shall suffer a grievous punishment. *It is* GOD who hath sent down the scripture with truth ; and the balance *of true judgment* : and what shall inform thee whether the hour be nigh at hand ? They who believe not therein, wish it to be hastened *by way of mockery* : but they who believe dread the same, and know it to be the truth. Are not those who dispute concerning the *last* hour in a wide error ? GOD is bounteous unto his servants : he provideth for whom he pleaseth ; and he is the strong, the mighty. Whoso chooseth the tillage of the life to come,[1] unto him will we give increase in his tillage : and whoso chooseth the tillage of this world, we will give him *the fruit* thereof ; but he shall have no part in the life to come. Have *the idolaters* deities which ordain them a religion which GOD hath not allowed ? But *had it* not *been* for the decree of *respiting their punishment to the day of* separating *the infidels from the true believers*, judgment had been *already* given between them : for the unjust shall surely suffer a painful torment. *On that day* thou shalt see the unjust in great terror, because of their demerits ; and *the penalty thereof* shall fall upon them : but they who believe and do good works, *shall dwell* in the delightful meadows of paradise ; they shall obtain whatever they shall desire, with their LORD. This *is* the greatest acquisition. This *is* what GOD promiseth unto his servants who believe and do good works. Say, I ask not of you, for this *my preaching*, any reward, except the love of *my* relations : and whoever shall have deserved well by *one* good action, unto him will we add *the merit of another* action thereto ; for GOD *is* inclined to forgive, *and* ready to reward. Do they say, *Mohammed* hath blasphemously forged a lie concerning GOD ? If GOD pleaseth, he will seal up thy heart :[2] and GOD will absolutely abolish

---

[1] Labouring here to obtain a reward hereafter ; for what is sown in this world will be reaped in the next.

[2] The meaning of these words is somewhat obscure. Some imagine they express a detestation of the forgery charged on the prophet by the infidels ; because none could be capable of so wicked an action but one whose heart was close shut, and knew not his LORD ; as if he had said, *God forbid that thou shouldst be so void of grace, or have so little sense of thy duty.* Others think the signification to be that GOD might strike all the revelations which had been vouchsafed to Mohammed, out of his heart at once ; and others, that GOD would strengthen his heart with patience against the insults of the unbelievers. (Al Beidâwi.)

vanity, and will establish the truth in his words ;[1] for he
knoweth the innermost parts of *men's* breasts. *It is* he who
accepteth repentance from his servants, and forgiveth sins,
and knoweth that which ye do.   He will incline his ear unto
those who believe and work righteousness, and will add unto
them *above what they shall ask or deserve*, of his bounty : but
the unbelievers shall suffer a severe punishment.   If GOD
should bestow abundance upon his servants, they would
certainly behave insolently in the earth : but he sendeth
down by measure *unto every one* that which he pleaseth ; for
he well knoweth *and* seeth *the condition of* his servants.   *It
is* he who sendeth down the rain, after *men* have despaired
thereof, and spreadeth abroad his mercy ;   and he is the
patron justly to be praised.   Among his signs *is* the creation
of heaven and earth, and of the living creatures with which
he hath replenished them both ;   and he *is* able to gather
them together *before his tribunal* whenever he pleaseth.
Whatever misfortune befalleth you *is sent you by God*, for
that which your hands have deserved ;   and *yet* he forgiveth
many things :   ye shall not frustrate *the divine vengeance*
in the earth ;   neither shall ye have any protector or helper
against GOD.   Among his signs *also are* the *ships* running in
the sea, like high mountains :   if he pleaseth he causeth the
wind to cease, and they lie still on the back of *the water*
(verily herein *are* signs, unto every patient *and* grateful
person) :   or he destroyeth them *by shipwreck*, because of
that which *their crews* have merited ;   though he pardoneth
many things.   And they who dispute against our signs shall
know that *there will be* no way for them to escape *our vengeance.*   Whatever things are given you, *they are* the provision of this present life : but the *reward* which is with GOD
is better and more durable, for those who believe and put
their trust in their LORD ;   and who avoid heinous and filthy
crimes, and when they are angry, forgive ;   and who hearken
unto their LORD, and are constant at prayer, and whose
affairs *are directed by* consultation among   themselves and
who give *alms* out of what we have bestowed on them ;   and
who, when an injury is done them, avenge themselves[2] (and

---

[1] Wherefore if the doctrine taught in this book be of man, it will certainly
fail and come to nothing ;   but if it be of GOD, it can never be overthrown.
(Al Beidâwi.)

[2] Using the means which GOD has put into their hands for their own defence.
This is added to complete the character here given ;   for valour and courage
are not inconsistent with clemency (Al Beidâwi), the rule being. *Parcere
subjectis, et debellare superbos.*

the retaliation of evil *ought to be* an evil proportionate thereto) : but he who forgiveth, and is reconciled *unto his enemy*, shall receive his reward from GOD ;[1] for he loveth not the unjust doers. And whoso shall avenge himself, after he hath been injured ; as to these, it is not lawful to punish them *for it* : but it is only lawful to punish those who wrong men, and act insolently in the earth, against justice ; these shall suffer a grievous punishment. And whoso beareth *injuries* patiently, and forgiveth ; verily this *is* a necessary work. Whom GOD shall cause to err, he shall afterwards have no protector. And thou shalt see the ungodly, who shall say, when they behold the punishment *prepared for them, Is there* no way to return back *into the world* ? And thou shalt see them exposed unto *hell fire* ; dejected, because of the ignominy *they shall undergo* : they shall look *at the fire* sideways and by stealth ; and the true believers shall say, Verily the losers are they who have lost their own souls, and their families, on the day of resurrection : *shall* not the ungodly *continue* in eternal torment ? They shall have no protectors to defend them against GOD : and whom GOD shall cause to err, he shall find no way *to the truth.* Hearken unto your LORD, before the day come, which GOD will not keep back ; ye shall have no place of refuge on that day ; neither shall ye be able to deny *your sins.* But if *those to whom thou preachest* turn aside *from thy admonitions*, verily we have not sent thee *to be* a guardian over them : thy duty is preaching only. When we cause man to taste mercy from us, he rejoiceth thereat : but if evil befall them, for that which their hands have formerly committed, verily man *becometh* ungrateful. Unto GOD *appertaineth* the kingdom of heaven and earth : he createth that which he pleaseth ; he giveth females unto whom he pleaseth, and he giveth males unto whom he pleaseth ; or he giveth them males and females jointly : and he maketh whom he pleaseth to be childless ; for he *is* wise *and* powerful. It is not *fit* for man that GOD should speak unto him otherwise than by *private* revelation, or from behind a veil, or by his sending of a messenger to reveal, by his permission, that which he pleaseth ; for he *is* high *and* wise. Thus have we revealed unto thee a revelation,[2] by our command. Thou didst not understand, *before this*, what the book *of the Korân* was, nor *what* the faith *was* :

---

[1] See Chap. V. p. 105.
[2] Or, as the words may be also translated, *Thus have we sent the spirit Gabriel unto thee with a revelation.*

but we have ordained the same *for* a light ; we will thereby direct such of our servants as we please : and thou shalt surely direct *them* into the right way, the way of GOD, unto whom *belongeth* whatever *is* in heaven and in earth. Shall not *all* things return unto GOD ?

XLIII

THE CHAPTER OF THE ORNAMENTS OF GOLD [1]

Revealed at Mecca. [2]

IN THE NAME OF THE MOST MERCIFUL GOD.

H M.[3] By the perspicuous book ; verily we have ordained the same an Arabic Korân, that ye may understand : and it *is* certainly *written* in the original book,[4] *kept* with us, *being* sublime and full of wisdom.   Shall we therefore turn away from you the admonition, and deprive *you thereof,* because ye are a people who transgress ?   And how many prophets have we sent among those of old ? and no prophet came unto them, but they laughed him to scorn : wherefore we destroyed *nations who were* more mighty than these in strength ; and the example of those who were of old, hath been already *set before them.*   If thou ask them who created the heavens and the earth, they will certainly answer, The mighty, the wise *God* created them : who hath spread the earth *as* a bed for you, and hath made you paths therein, that ye may be directed : and who sendeth down rain from heaven by measure, whereby we quicken a dead country (so shall ye be brought forth *from your graves*) : and who hath created all the *various* species *of things*, and hath given you ships and cattle, whereon ye are carried ; that ye may sit firmly on the backs thereof, and may remember the favour of your LORD, when ye sit thereon, and may say, Praise be unto him, who hath subjected these unto our service ! for we could not have mastered them *by our own power* : and unto our LORD shall we surely return.   Yet have they attributed unto him some of his servants *as his*

---

[1] The words chosen for the title of this chapter occur about the middle of it.

[2] Some except the verse beginning with these words, *And ask our apostles whom we have sent before thee,* &c.

[3] See Sale, Prel. Disc. Sect. III. p. 64, and Chap. II. p 2

[4] *i.e.,* The preserved table ; which is the original of all the scriptures in general.

offspring : verily man is openly ungrateful. Hath *God*
taken daughters out of *those beings* which he hath created ;
and hath he chosen sons for you ? But when one of them
hath the news brought of *the birth of a child of that sex* which
they attribute unto the Merciful, as *his* similitude, his face
becometh black, and he is oppressed with sorrow.[1] Do they
therefore *attribute unto God female issue*, which are brought
up among ornaments and are contentious without cause ?
And do they make the angels, who are the servants of the
Merciful, females ? Were they present at their creation ?
Their testimony shall be written down, and they shall be
examined *concerning the same, on the day of judgment.* And
they say, If the Merciful had pleased, we had not worshipped
them. They have no knowledge herein : they only utter a
vain lie. Have we given them a book *of revelations* before
this ; and do they keep the same in their custody ? But
they say, Verily we found our fathers practising a religion ;
and we *are* guided in their footsteps. Thus we sent no
preacher, before thee, unto *any* city, but the inhabitants
thereof who lived in affluence, said, Verily we found our
fathers practising a religion : and we tread in their footsteps.
And the preacher answered, What, although I bring you a
more right *religion* than that which ye found your fathers to
practise ? *And* they replied, Verily we believe not that
which ye are sent *to preach*. Wherefore we took vengeance
on them : and behold what hath been the end of those who
accused *our apostles* of imposture. *Remember* when Abraham said unto his father, and his people, Verily I am clear
of *the gods* which ye worship, except him who hath created
me ; for he will direct me *aright*. And he ordained this *to
be* a constant doctrine among his posterity ; that they should
be turned *from idolatry to the worship of the only true God*.
Verily I have permitted these *Meccans* and their fathers to
live in prosperity, until the truth should come unto them,
and a manifest apostle : but now the truth is come unto
them, they say, This *is* a piece of sorcery ; and we believe
not therein. And they say, Had this Korân been sent down
unto some great man of *either of* the two cities,[2] *we would
have received it.* Do they distribute the mercy of thy LORD ?[3]
We distribute their necessary provision among them, in this

---

[1] See Chap. XVI. p. 261.
[2] *i.e.*, To one of the principal inhabitants of Mecca, or of Tâyef, such as Al
Wâlid Ebn al Mogheira, or Orwa Ebn Masûd, the Thakifite. (Al Beidâwi.)
[3] By this expression the prophetic office is here particularly intended.

present life, and we raise some of them *several* degrees above the others, that the one of them may take the other to serve him : and the mercy of thy LORD is more valuable than the *riches* which they gather together. If *it were* not that mankind would have become one sect *of infidels*, verily we had given, unto those who believe not in the Merciful, roofs of silver to their houses, and stairs *of silver*, by which they might ascend *thereto*, and doors *of silver* to their houses, and couches *of silver* for them to lean on ; and ornaments of gold : for all this *is* the provision of the present life ; but the next *life* with thy LORD *shall be* for those who fear *him*. Whoever shall withdraw from the admonition of the Merciful, we will chain a devil unto him ; and he shall be his inseparable companion (and *the devils* shall turn them aside from the way *of truth* ; yet they shall imagine themselves *to be* rightly directed): until, when he shall appear before us *at the last day*, he shall say *unto the devil*,[1] Would to GOD that between me and thee *there was* the distance of the east from the west ! Oh how wretched a companion *art thou* ! But *wishes* shall not avail you on this day, since ye have been unjust ; for ye shall be partakers of the *same* punishment. Canst thou, *O prophet*, make the deaf to hear, or canst thou direct the blind, and him who is in a manifest error ? Whether we take thee away, we will surely take vengeance on them ; or whether we cause thee to see *the punishment* with which we have threatened them, *executed*, we will certainly prevail over them. Wherefore hold fast *the doctrine* which hath been revealed unto thee ; for thou *art* in a right way : and it is a memorial unto thee and thy people, and hereafter shall ye be examined *concerning your observance thereof*. And ask our apostles whom we have sent before thee,[2] whether we have appointed gods for them to worship, besides the Merciful. We formerly sent Moses with our signs unto Pharaoh and his princes, and he said, Verily I am the apostle of the LORD of all creatures. And when he came unto them with our signs, behold, they laughed him to scorn ; although we showed them no sign, but it was greater than the other :[3] and we inflicted a punishment[4] on them, that peradventure

[1] See Chap. XIX. p. 302.

[2] That is, ask those who profess the religions which they taught, and their learned men. (Al Beidâwi, Jallal., &c.)

[3] Literally, *Than its sister*. The meaning is that the miracles were *all very great and considerable*, or, as the French may express it, by a phrase nearly the same, *les uns plus grands que les autres*.

[4] viz., The successive plagues which they suffered, previous to their final destruction in the Red Sea.

they might be converted. And they said *unto Moses*, O magician, pray unto thy LORD for us, according to the covenant which he hath made with thee ; for we *will* certainly *be* directed. But when we took the plague from off them, behold, they broke their promise. And Pharaoh made proclamation among his people, saying, O my people, is not the kingdom of Egypt mine, and these rivers[1] which flow beneath me ? Do ye not see ? Am not I better than this *Moses* ; who is a contemptible person, and can scarce express himself intelligibly ?[2] Have bracelets of gold, therefore, been put upon him ;[3] or do the angels attend him in orderly procession ? And *Pharaoh* persuaded his people to light behaviour ; and they obeyed him : for they were a wicked people. And when they had provoked us to wrath, we took vengeance on them, and we drowned them all : and we made them a precedent and an example unto others. And when the son of Mary was proposed for an example ; behold, thy people cried out *through excess of joy* thereat ;[4] and they said, *Are* our gods better, or he ? They have proposed this *instance* unto thee no otherwise than for an occasion of dispute : yea, they are contentious men. *Jesus* is no other than a servant, whom we favoured *with the gift of prophecy* ; and we appointed him for an example[5] unto the children of Israel (if we pleased, verily we could from yourselves produce angels, to succeed *you* in the earth) :[6] and he *shall be* a sign of the *approach of the last* hour ;[7] wherefore doubt not thereof.

---

[1] To wit, the Nile and its branches. (Al Beidâwi.)

[2] See Chap. XX. p. 306.

[3] Such bracelets were some of the insignia of royalty : for when the Egyptians raised a person to the dignity of a prince, they put a collar or chain of gold about his neck (see Gen. xli. 42), and bracelets of gold on his wrists (Al Beidâwi, Jallalo'ddin).

[4] This passage is generally supposed to have been revealed on occasion of an objection made by one Ebn al Zahári to those words in Chap. XXI. (see Chap. XXI.), by which all in general, who were worshipped as deities, besides GOD, are doomed to hell ; whereupon the infidels cried out, *We are contented that our gods should be with Jesus : for he also is worshipped as God*. (Jallalo'ddin, Al Beidâwi.) Some, however, are of opinion it might have been revealed in answer to certain idolaters, who said that the Christians, who received the scriptures, worshipped Jesus, supposing him to be the son of GOD ; whereas the angels were more worthy of that honour than he. (Al Beidâwi.)

[5] Or an instance of our power, by his miraculous birth.

[6] As easily as we produced Jesus without a father. (Al Beidâwi.) The intent of the words is to show how just and reasonable it is to think that the angels should bear the relation of children to men, rather than to GOD ; they being his creatures, as well as men, and equally in his power.

[7] For some time before the resurrection Jesus is to descend on earth, according to the Mohammedans, near Damascus (see Sale, Prel. Disc. Sect. IV.), or, as some say, near a rock in the Holy Land named Afik with a lance

And follow me : this *is* the right way.   And let not Satan cause you to turn aside : for he *is* your open enemy. And when *Jesus* came with evident *miracles*, he said, Now am I come unto you with wisdom ; [1] and to explain unto you part of *those things* concerning which ye disagree : wherefore fear GOD, and obey me.   Verily GOD is my LORD and your LORD ; wherefore worship him : this *is* the right way.   And the confederated sects among them fell to variance :[2] but woe unto those who have acted unjustly, because of the punishment of a grievous day.   *Do the unbelievers* wait for any other than the hour *of judgment* ; that it may come upon them suddenly, while they foresee *it* not ? The intimate friends, on that day, *shall be* enemies unto one another ; except the pious.   O my servants, *there shall* no fear *come* on you this day, neither shall ye be grieved ; who have believed in our signs, and have been Moslems : enter ye into paradise, ye and your wives, with great joy.   Dishes of gold shall be carried round unto them, and cups without handles : and therein *shall they enjoy* whatever *their* souls shall desire, and *whatever their* eyes shall delight in : and ye shall remain therein for ever.   This is paradise, which ye have inherited *as a reward* for that which ye have wrought. Therein shall ye have fruits in abundance, of which ye shall eat.   But the wicked shall remain for ever in the torment of hell : it shall not be made lighter unto them ; and they *shall* despair therein.   We deal not unjustly with them, but they deal unjustly *with their own souls*.   And they shall call aloud, *saying*, O Malec,[3] *intercede for us* that thy LORD would end us *by annihilation*.   He shall answer,[4] Verily ye shall remain *here for ever*.   We brought you the truth heretofore, but the greater part of you abhorred the truth.   Have *the*

in his hand, wherewith he is to kill Antichrist, whom he will encounter at Ludd, or Lydda, a small town not far from Joppa (Sale, Prel. Disc. Sect. IV.). They add that he will arrive at Jerusalem at the time of morning prayer, that he shall perform his devotions after the Mohammedan institution, and officiate instead of the Imâm, who shall give place to him ; that he will break down the cross, and destroy the churches of the Christians, of whom he will make a general slaughter, excepting only such as shall profess Islâm, &c. (Al Beidâwi).

[1] That is, with a book of revelations, and an excellent system of religion.

[2] This may be understood either of the Jews in the time of Jesus, who opposed his doctrine, or of the Christians since, who have fallen into various opinions concerning him ; some making him to be GOD, others the Son of GOD, and others, one of the persons of the Trinity, &c.   (Al Beidâwi, Jallal.)

[3] This the Mohammedans suppose to be the name of the principal angel who has the charge of hell.

[4] Some say that this answer will not be given till a thousand years after the day of judgement.

infidels fixed on a method *to circumvent our apostle* ? Verily we wil: fix *on a method to circumvent them.* Do they imagine that we hear not their secrets, and their private discourse ? Yea ; and our messengers who attend them[1] write down *the same.* Say, If the Merciful had a son, verily I *would be* the first of those who should worship *him.* Far be the LORD of heaven and earth, the LORD of the throne, from that which they affirm *of him* ! Wherefore let them wade *in their vanity,* and divert themselves, until they arrive at their day with which they have been threatened. He who is GOD in heaven is GOD on earth also : and he *is* the wise, the knowing. And blessed be he unto whom *appertaineth* the kingdom of heaven and earth, and of whatever is between them ; with whom *is* the knowledge of the *last* hour ; and before whom ye shall be assembled. They whom they invoke besides him, have not the privilege to intercede *for others* ; except those who bear witness to the truth, and know *the same.*[2] If thou ask them who hath created them, they will surely answer, GOD. How therefore are they turned away *to the worship of others* ? GOD *also heareth* the saying of *the prophet,* O LORD, verily these *are* people who believe not : *and he answered,* Therefore turn aside from them ; and say, Peace :[3] hereafter shall they know *their folly.*

XLIV

THE CHAPTER OF SMOKE [4]

Revealed at Mecca.[5]

IN THE NAME OF THE MOST MERCIFUL GOD.

H. M.[6] By the perspicuous book *of the Korân* ; verily we have sent down the same on a blessed night[7]

---

[1] *i.e.,* The guardian angels.

[2] That is, to the doctrine of GOD's unity. The exception comprehends Jesus, Ezra, and the angels ; who will be admitted as intercessors, though they have been worshipped as gods. (Al Beidâwi.)

[3] See Chap. XXV. p. 359.

[4] This word occurs within a few lines from the beginning of the chapter.

[5] Some except the verse beginning, *We will take the plague off you a little,* &c.

[6] See Sale, Prel. Disc. Sect. III. p. 64, and Chap. II.

[7] Generally supposed to be that between the twenty-third and twenty-fourth of Ramadân. See Sale, Prel. Disc. Sect. III., and Chap. XCVII., and the notes there.

(for we had engaged *so to do*), *on the night* wherein is distinctly sent down the decree of every determined thing, *as* a command from us.[1] Verily we have *ever* used to send *apostles with revelations, at proper intervals, as* a mercy from thy LORD; for it is he who heareth *and* knoweth : the LORD of heaven and earth, and of whatever *is* between them ; if ye are *men* of sure knowledge. There *is* no GOD but he : he giveth life, and he causeth to die ; *he is* your LORD, and the LORD of your forefathers. Yet do they amuse themselves with doubt. But observe *them* on the day *whereon* the heaven shall produce a visible smoke, which shall cover mankind :[2] this *will be* a tormenting plague. *They shall say,* O LORD, take *this* plague from off us : verily we *will become* true believers. How *should* an admonition *be of avail* to them *in this condition* ; when a manifest apostle came unto them, but they retired from him, saying, *This man is* instructed *by others,*[3] *or is* a distracted person ? We will take the plague from off *you,* a little : *but* ye will certainly return *to your infidelity.*[4] On the day whereon we shall fiercely assault *them* with great power,[5] verily we will take vengeance *on them.* We made trial of the people of Pharaoh before them, and an honourable messenger came unto them, *saying,* Send

---

[1] For annually on this night, as the Mohammedans are taught, all the events of the ensuing year, with respect to life and death and the other affairs of this world, are disposed and settled (Jallaloddin, Al Beidâwi.) Some, however, suppose that these words refer only to that particular night on which the Korân, wherein are completely contained the divine determinations in respect to religion and morality, was sent down, (Al Beidâwi) ; and according to this exposition, the passage may be rendered, *The night whereon every determined* or *adjudged matter was sent down.*

[2] The commentators differ in their expositions of this passage. Some think it spoke of a smoke which seemed to fill the air during the famine which was inflicted on the Meccans in Mohammed's time (see Chap. XXIII.), and was so thick that, though they could hear, yet they could not see one another (Al Zamakh., Al Beidâwi, Yahya, Jallalo'ddin). But according to a tradition of Ali, the smoke here meant is that which is to be one of the previous signs of the day of judgment (Sale, Prel. Disc. Sect. IV.), and will fill the whole space from east to west, and last for forty days. This smoke, they say, will intoxicate the infidels, and issue at their nose, ears, and posteriors, but will very little inconvenience the true believers (Al Zamakh., Al Beidâwi).

[3] See Chap. XVI. p. 267.

[4] If we follow the former exposition, the words are to be understood, of the ceasing of the famine upon the intercession of Mohammed, at the desire of the Koreish, and on their promise of believing on him ; notwithstanding which, they fell back to their old incredulity ; but if we follow the latter exposition, they are to be understood of GOD's taking away the plague of the smoke, after the expiration of the forty days, at the prayer of the infidels, and on their promise of receiving the true faith, which being done, they will immediately return to their wonted obstinacy.

[5] Some expound this of the slaughter at Bedr, and others of the day of judgment.

unto me the servants of GOD ;¹ verily I *am* a faithful
messenger unto you : and lift not yourselves up against
GOD : for I come unto you with manifest power.   And I fly
for protection unto my LORD and your LORD, that ye stone
me not.²   If ye do not believe me, *at least* depart from me.³
And *when they accused him of imposture*, he called upon his
LORD, *saying*, These are a wicked people.   *And God said unto
him*, March forth with my servants by night ; for ye *will
be* pursued : and leave the sea divided, *that the Egyptians
may enter the same* ; for they *are* a host *doomed* to be drowned.
How many gardens, and fountains, and fields of corn, and
fair dwellings, and advantages which they enjoyed, did they
leave behind them ?   Thus *we dispossessed them thereof* ; and
we gave the same for an inheritance unto another people.⁴
Neither heaven or earth wept for them ;⁵ neither were they
respited *any longer*.   And we delivered the children of Israel
from a shameful affliction ; from Pharaoh ; for he was
haughty, and a transgressor : and we chose them, knowingly,⁶
above *all* people ; and we showed them *several* signs,⁷ wherein
was an evident trial.   Verily these *Meccans* say, Assuredly
our final end will be no other than our first *natural* death ;
neither shall we be raised again : bring now our forefathers
back to life, if ye speak truth.   Are they better, or the people
of Tobba,⁸ and those who *were* before them ? we destroyed
them, because they wrought wickedness.   We have not
created the heavens and the earth, and whatever *is* between
them, by way of sport : we have created them no otherwise
than in truth ;⁹ but the greater part of them do not under-

---

¹ *i.e.*, Let the Israelites go with me to worship their GOD.

² Or that ye injure me not, either by word or deed. (Al Beidâwi.)

³ Without opposing me or offering me any injury, which I have not
deserved from you.

⁴ See Chap. XXVI. p. 362.

⁵ That is, none pitied their destruction.

⁶ *i.e.*, Knowing that they were worthy of our choice ; or, notwithstanding
we knew they would, in time to come, fall into idolatry, &c.

⁷ As the dividing of the Red Sea, the cloud which shaded them, the raining
on them manna and quails, &c. (Al Beidâwi.)

⁸ The Hamyarites, whose kings had the title of Tobba. (Sale, Prel. Disc.
Sect. I.) The commentators tell us that the Tobba here meant was very
potent, and built Samarcand, or, as others say, demolished it ; and that
he was a true believer, but his subjects were infidels. (Al Beidâwi, Jallalo'-
ddin.) This prince seems to have been Abu Carb Asaad, who flourished
about seven hundred years before Mohammed, and embraced Judaism,
which religion he first introduced into Yaman (being the true religion at
that time, inasmuch as Christianity was not then promulgated), and was,
for that cause probably, slain by his own people. (Al Jannâbi. Vide
Poc. Spec. p. 60.)

⁹ See Chaps. XXI. p. 316, and XXXVIII. p. 445.

stand. Verily the day of separation[1] *shall be* the appointed term of them all ; a day, whereon the master and the servant shall be of no advantage to one another, neither shall they be helped ; excepting those on whom GOD shall have mercy : for he *is* the mighty, the merciful. Verily *the fruit of* the tree of Al Zakkum *shall be* the food of the impious : [2] as the dregs of oil shall it boil in the bellies *of the damned*, like the boiling of the hottest water. *And it shall be said to the tormentors*, Take him, and drag him into the midst of hell : and pour on his head the torture of boiling water, *saying*, Taste *this* ; for thou art that mighty *and* honourable person. Verily this is the *punishment* of which ye doubted. But the pious *shall be lodged* in a place of security ; among gardens and fountains : they shall be clothed in fine silk and in satin ; *and they shall sit* facing one another. Thus *shall it be* : and we will espouse them to fair damsels, having large black eyes. In that place shall they call for all *kinds of* fruits, in full security : they shall not taste death therein, after the first death ; and *God* shall deliver from the pains of hell : through the gracious bounty of thy LORD. This will be great felicity. Moreover we have rendered *the Korân* easy *for thee, by revealing it* in thine own tongue : to the end that they may be admonished : wherefore do thou wait *the event* ; for they wait *to see some misfortune befall thee.*

XLV

THE CHAPTER OF THE KNEELING[3]

Revealed at Mecca.

IN THE NAME OF THE MOST MERCIFUL GOD.

H M.[4] The revelation of *this* book *is* from the mighty, the wise GOD. Verily *both* in heaven and earth *are* signs of *the divine power* unto the true believers : and in the creation of yourselves, and of the beasts which are scattered *over the face of the earth, are* signs unto people of sound judgment ; and *also in* the vicissitude of night and day, and

---

[1] *i.e.*, The day of judgment ; when the wicked shall be separated from the righteous, &c.

[2] Jallalo'ddin supposes this passage to have been particularly levelled against Abu Jahl.

[3] The word from which this chapter is denominated occurs towards the end of it.

[4] Sale, Prel. Disc. Sect. III. p. 64, and Chap. II. page 2, note.

the rain which GOD sendeth down from heaven, whereby he quickeneth the earth after it hath been dead : in the change of the winds also *are* signs, unto people of understanding. These *are* the signs of GOD ; we rehearse them unto thee with truth. In what revelation therefore will they believe, after *they have rejected* GOD and his signs ? Woe unto every lying *and* impious person ; who heareth the signs of GOD, which are read unto him, and afterwards proudly persisteth *in infidelity*, as though he heard them not (denounce unto him a painful punishment) : and who, when he cometh to the knowledge of any of our signs, receiveth the same with scorn. For these *is prepared* a shameful punishment : before them *lieth* hell : and whatever they shall have gained shall not avail them at all, neither *shall* the *idols* which they have taken for *their* patrons, besides GOD : and they shall suffer a grievous punishment. This *is* a *true* direction : and for those who disbelieve the signs of their LORD, *is prepared* the punishment of a painful torment. *It is* GOD who hath subjected the sea unto you, that the ships may sail therein, at his command ; and that ye may seek *advantage unto yourselves by commerce*, of his bounty ; and that ye may give thanks : and he obligeth whatever *is* in heaven and on earth to serve you ; the whole *being* from him. Verily herein *are* signs, unto people who consider. Speak unto the true believers, that they forgive those who hope not for the days of GOD,[1] that he may reward people according to what they shall have wrought. Whoso doth that which is right *doth it* to *the advantage of* his own soul ; and whoso doth evil, *doth it* against the same : hereafter shall ye return unto your LORD, We gave unto the children of Israel the book *of the law*, and wisdom, and prophecy ; and we fed them with good things, and preferred them above all nations ; and we gave them plain *ordinances* concerning the business *of religion* ; neither did they fall at variance, except after that knowledge had come unto them, through envy amongst themselves : but thy LORD will decide the controversy between them on the day of resurrection, concerning that wherein they disagree. Afterwards we appointed thee, *O Mohammed*, to *promulgate* a law concerning the business *of religion* : where-

---

[1] By the days of GOD, in this place, are meant the prosperous successes of his people in battle against the infidels. (See p. 245, note 4.) The passage is said to have been revealed on account of Omar, who being reviled by one of the tribe of Ghifâr, was thinking to revenge himself by force. Some are of opinion that this verse is abrogated. (Al Beidâwi.)

fore follow the same, and follow not the desires of those who are ignorant.[1] Verily they shall not avail thee against GOD at all : the unjust *are* the patrons of one another ; but GOD *is* the patron of the pious. This *Korân* delivereth evident *precepts* unto mankind ; and *is* a direction and a mercy, unto people who judge aright. Do the workers of iniquity imagine that we will deal with them as with those who believe and do good works ; *so that* their life and their death *shall be* equal ? An ill judgment do they make. GOD hath created the heavens and the earth in truth ; that he may recompense every soul according to that which it shall have wrought : and they shall not be treated unjustly. What thinkest thou ? He who taketh his own lust for his GOD, and whom GOD causeth knowingly to err, and whose ears and whose heart he hath sealed up, and over whose eyes he hath cast a veil ; who shall direct him, after GOD *shall have forsaken him* ? Will ye not therefore be admonished ? They say, *There* is no *other life*, except our present life : we die and we live ; and nothing but time destroyeth us. But they have no knowledge in this *matter* ; they only follow a *vain* opinion. And when our evident signs are rehearsed unto them, their argument *which they offer against the same* is no other than that they say, Bring *to life* our fathers *who have been dead* ; if ye speak truth. Say, GOD giveth you life ; and afterwards causeth you to die : hereafter will he assemble you together on the day of resurrection ; there is no doubt thereof ; but the greater part of men do not understand. Unto GOD *appertaineth* the kingdom of heaven and earth ; and the day whereon the hour shall be fixed, on that day shall those who charge *the Korân* with vanity perish. And thou shalt see every nation[2] kneeling : every nation shall be called unto its book *of account ; and it shall be said unto them*, This day shall ye be rewarded according to that which ye have wrought. This our book will speak concerning you with truth ; *therein* have we written down whatever ye have done.[3] As to those who shall have believed and done good works, their LORD shall lead them into his mercy : this shall be manifest felicity. But as to the infidels, *it shall be said unto them*, Were not my signs rehearsed unto you ?

---

[1] That is, of the principal Koreish, who were urgent with Mohammed to return to the religion of his forefathers. (Al Beidâwi.)

[2] The original word *ommat* properly signifies a people who profess one and the same law or religion.

[3] See Chap. II. p. 2 note, and Sale, Prel. Disc. Sect IV. p. 96.

but ye proudly rejected *them*, and became a wicked people ?
And when it was said *unto you*, Verily the promise of GOD
is true ; and as to the hour *of judgment, there is* no doubt
thereof : ye answered, We know not what the hour *of
judgment is* : we hold an *uncertain* opinion only ; and we
are not well assured *of this matter*.   But *on that day* the evil
of that which they have wrought shall appear unto them ;
and that which they mocked at shall encompass them : and
it shall be said *unto them*, This day will we forget you, as ye
did forget the meeting of this your day : and your abode
shall be hell fire ; and ye shall have none to deliver you.   This
shall ye suffer, because ye turned the signs of GOD to ridicule ;
and the life of the world deceived you.   On this day, therefore, they shall not be taken forth from thence, neither shall
they be asked *any more* to render themselves well pleasing
unto God.   Wherefore praise be unto GOD, the LORD of the
heavens and the LORD of the earth ; the LORD of all creatures : and unto him be glory in heaven and earth ; for he
is the mighty, the wise *God* !

XLVI

THE CHAPTER OF AL AHKÂF [1]

Revealed at Mecca.

IN THE NAME OF THE MOST MERCIFUL GOD.

(XXVI.) H. M.[2] The revelation of *this* book *is* from
the mighty, the wise GOD.   We have
not created the heavens and the earth, and whatever is
between them, otherwise than in truth,[3] and for a determined period :[4] but the unbelievers turn away from the
warning which is given them.   Say, What think ye ?   Show
me what *part* of the earth *the idols* which ye invoke, besides
GOD, have created ?   Or had they any share in *the creation
of* the heavens ?   Bring me a book *of scripture revealed*
before this, or some footstep of *ancient* knowledge, *to countenance your idolatrous practices* ; if ye are men of veracity.

[1] Al Ahkâf is the plural of Hekf, and signifies lands which lie in a crooked
or winding manner ; whence it became the name of a territory in the province of Hadramaut, where the Adites dwelt.   It is mentioned about the
middle of the chapter.
[2] Section XXVI. begins with this chapter.   See Sale, Prel. Disc. Sect. III.
pp. 63, 64.
[3] See Chaps. XXI. p. 317 and XXXVIII. p. 445.
[4] Being to last but a certain space of time, and not for ever.

Who is in a wider error than he who invoketh, besides GOD, that which cannot return him an answer till the day of resurrection ; and *idols* which regard not their calling *on them* : and which, when men shall be gathered together *to judgment*, will become their enemies, and will ungratefully deny their worship ? When our evident signs are rehearsed unto them, the unbelievers say of the truth,[1] when it cometh unto them, This *is* a manifest piece of sorcery. Will they say, *Mohammed* hath forged it ? Answer, If I have forged it, verily ye shall not obtain for me any *favour* from GOD : he well knoweth the *injurious language* which ye utter concerning it : he is a sufficient witness between me and you ; and he *is* gracious *and* merciful. Say, I am not singular among the apostles ;[2] neither do I know what will be done with me or with you *hereafter* : I follow no other than what is revealed unto me ; neither am I any more than a public warner. Say, What is your opinion ? If *this book* be from GOD, and ye believe not therein ; and a witness of the children of Israel bear witness to its consonancy *with the law*,[3] and believeth therein ; and ye proudly reject *the same* : *are ye not unjust doers* ? Verily GOD directeth not unjust people. But those who believe not, say of the true believers, If *the doctrine of the Korân* had been good, they had not embraced the same before us.[4] And when they are not guided thereby, they say, This *is* an antiquated lie. Whereas the book of Moses *was revealed* before *the Korân, to be* a guide and a mercy : and this *is* a book confirming *the same, delivered* in the Arabic tongue ; to denounce threats unto those who act unjustly, and to bear good tidings unto the righteous doers. *As to* those who say, Our LORD *is* GOD ; and who behave uprightly : on them *shall* no fear *come*, neither shall they be grieved. These *shall be* the inhabitants of paradise, they shall remain therein forever : in recompence

---

[1] *i.e.*, Any part of the revelations of the Korân.

[2] That is, I do not teach a doctrine different from what the former apostles and prophets have taught, nor am I able to do what they could not, particularly to show the signs which every one shall think fit to demand. (Al Beidâwi.)

[3] This witness is generally supposed to have been the Jew Abd'allah Ebn Salàm, who declared that Mohammed was the prophet foretold by Moses. Some, however, suppose the witness here meant to have been Moses himself. (Al Beidâwi, Jallalo'ddin.)

[4] These words were spoken, as some thin ., by the Jews, when Abd'allah professed Islàm ; or, according to others, by the Koreish, because the first followers of Mohammed were for the most part poor and mean people ; or else by the tribes of Amer, Ghatfân, and Asad, on the conversion of those of Joheinah, Mozeinah, Aslam, and Ghifâr. (Al Beidâwi.)

for that which they have wrought.   We have commanded
man *to show* kindness to his parents : his mother beareth
him *in her womb* with pain, and bringeth him forth with
pain : and *the space of* his being carried *in her womb*, and
of his weaning, *is* thirty months ;[1] until, when he attaineth
his age of strength, and attaineth *the age of* forty years, he
saith,[2] O LORD, excite me, by thy inspiration, that I may be
grateful for thy favours, wherewith thou hast favoured me
and my parents ; and that I may work righteousness, which
may please thee : and be gracious unto me in my issue ;
for I am turned unto thee and am a Moslem.   These *are*
they from whom we accept the good work which they have
wrought, and whose evil *works* we pass by ; *and they shall be*
among the inhabitants of paradise : this *is* a true promise,
which they are promised *in this world.*   He who saith unto
his parents, Fie on you ! do ye promise me that I shall be
taken forth *from the grave, and restored to life* ; when *many*
generations have passed away before me, *and none of them
have returned back* ?[3]   And *his parents* implore GOD's assistance, *and say to their son,* Alas for thee !   Believe : for the
promise of GOD *is* true.   But he answereth, This *is* no other
than silly fables of the ancients.   These *are they* whom the
sentence *passed* on the nations which have been before them,
of genii and of men, justly fitteth : they shall surely perish.[4]
For every one *is prepared* a certain degree *of happiness or
misery,* according to that which they shall have wrought ;
that *God* may recompense them for their works ; and they
shall not be treated unjustly.   On a certain day, the unbelievers shall be exposed before the fire *of hell* ; *and it shall be
said unto them,* Ye received your good things in your lifetime, *while ye were* in the world ; and ye enjoyed yourselves
therein : wherefore this day ye shall be rewarded with the

---

[1] At the least.   For if the full time of suckling an infant be two years
(see Chap. II.), or twenty-four months, there remain but six months for the
space of his being carried in the womb ; which is the least that can be
allowed.   (Al Beidâwi.)

[2] These words, it is said, were evealed on account of Abu Becr, who professed Islâm in the fortieth year of his age, two years after Mohammed's
mission, and was the only person, either of the Mohâjerîn or the Ansârs,
whose father and mother were also converted ; his son Abd'alrahmân, and
his grandson Abu Atik, likewise embracing the same faith.   (Al Beidâwi,
Jallalo'ddin, &c.)

[3] The words seem to be general ; but it is said they were revealed particularly on occasion of Abd'alrahmân, the son of Abu Becr, who used these
expressions to his father and mother before he professed Islâm.   (Al Beidâwi.)

[4] Unless they redeem their fault by repentance, and embracing the true
tàith, as did Abd'alrahmân.

punishment of ignominy ; for that ye behaved insolently in the earth, without justice, and for that ye transgressed. Remember the brother of Ad,[1] when he preached unto his people in Al Ahkâf (and there were preachers before him and after him), *saying*, Worship none but GOD : verily I fear for you the punishment of a great day. They answered, Art thou come unto us that thou mayest turn us aside from *the worship of* our gods ? Bring on us now *the punishment* with which thou threatenest us, if thou art a man of veracity. He said, Verily the knowledge *of the time when your punishment will be inflicted is* with GOD ; and I *only* declare unto you that which I am sent *to preach* ; but I see ye are an ignorant people. And when they saw *the preparation made for their punishment, namely*, a cloud traversing *the sky, and* tending towards their valleys, they said, This *is* a traversing cloud, which bringeth us rain. *Hûd answered*, Nay ; it is what ye demanded to be hastened : a wind, wherein *is* a severe vengeance : it will destroy everything,[2] at the command of its LORD. And in the morning nothing was to be seen, besides their *empty* dwellings. Thus do we reward wicked people. We had established them in the *like flourishing condition* wherein we have established you, *O men of Mecca* ; and we had given them ears, and eyes, and hearts : yet neither their ears, nor their eyes, nor their hearts profited them at all, when they rejected the signs of GOD ; but the *vengeance* which they mocked at fell upon them. We heretofore destroyed the cities which *were* round about you ;[3] and we variously proposed *our* signs unto them, that they might repent. Did those protect them, whom they took for gods, besides GOD, *and imagined to be* honoured with his familiarity ? Nay ; they withdrew from them : yet this *was* their false opinion *which seduced them*, and *the blasphemy* which they had devised. *Remember* when we caused certain of the genii[4] to turn aside unto thee, that they might hear the Korân : and when they were present at *the reading of* the

---

[1] *i.e.*, The prophet Hûd.

[2] Which came to pass accordingly ; for this pestilential and violent wind killed all who believed not in the doctrine of Hûd, without distinction of sex, age, or degree ; and entirely destroyed their possessions. See Sale, Prel. Disc. Sect. I., and the notes to Chapter VII.

[3] As the settlements of the Thamûdites, Midianites, and the cities of Sodom and Gomorrah, &c.

[4] These genii, according to different opinions, were of Nisibin, or of Yaman, or of Ninive ; and in number nine or seven. They heard Mohammed reading the Korân by night, or after the morning prayer, in the valley of Al Nakhlah, during the time of his retreat to Al Tayef, and believed on him. (Al Beidâwi, Jallalo'ddin.)

same, they said *to one another*, Give ear : and when it was ended, they returned back unto their people, preaching *what they had heard*. They said, Our people, verily we have heard a book *read unto us*, which hath been revealed since Moses,[1] confirming the *scripture* which *was delivered* before it ; *and* directing unto the truth and the right way. Our people, obey God's preacher : and believe in him ; that he may forgive you your sins, and may deliver you from a painful punishment. And whoever obeyeth not GOD'S preacher, shall by no means frustrate *God's vengeance* on earth : neither shall he have any protectors besides him. These *will be* in a manifest error. Do they not know that GOD, who hath created the heavens and the earth, and was not fatigued with the creation thereof, *is* able to raise the dead to life ? Yea, verily : for he *is* almighty. On a certain day the unbelievers shall be exposed unto *hell* fire ; *and it shall be said unto them*, Is not this really *come to pass* ? They shall answer, Yea, by our LORD. *God* shall reply, Taste, therefore, the punishment *of hell*, for that ye have been unbelievers. Do thou, *O prophet*, bear *the insults of thy people* with patience, as *our* apostles, who were endued with constancy, bare *the injuries of their people* : and require not *their punishment* to be hastened unto them. On the day whereon they shall see the *punishment* wherewith they have been threatened, it shall seem as though they had tarried *in the world* but an hour of a day. *This is* a *fair* warning. Shall any perish except the people who transgress ?

XLVII

THE CHAPTER OF MOHAMMED [2]

Revealed at Medina.[3]

IN THE NAME OF THE MOST MERCIFUL GOD.

GOD will render of none effect the works of those who believe not, and *who* turn away *men* from the way of GOD : but as to those who believe, and work righteousness, and believe in *the revelation* which hath been sent down unto

---

[1] Hence the commentators suppose those genii, before their conversion to Mohammedism, to have been of the Jewish religion.

[2] Some entitle this chapter *War*, which is therein commanded to be vigorously carried on against the enemies of the Mohammedan faith. Others know it as *Fight*.

[3] Some suppose the whole to have been revealed at Mecca.

Mohammed (for it is the truth from their LORD), he will expiate their evil deeds from them, and will dispose their heart aright. This *will he do*, because those who believe not follow vanity, and because those who believe follow the truth from their LORD. Thus GOD propoundeth unto men their examples. When ye encounter the unbelievers, strike off *their* heads, until ye have made a great slaughter among them ; and bind *them* in bonds : and either *give them* a free dismissal afterwards, or *exact* a ransom ; until the war shall have laid down its arms.[1] This *shall ye do* : Verily if GOD pleased, he could take vengeance on them, *without your assistance* ; but *he commandeth you to fight his battles*, that he may prove the one of you by the other. And *as to* those who fight[2] in defence of GOD's true religion, *God* will not suffer their works to perish : he will guide them, and will dispose their heart aright ; and he will lead them into paradise, of which he hath told them. O true believers, if ye assist GOD, *by fighting for his religion,* he will assist you *against your enemies* ; and will set your feet fast : but *as for* the infidels, let them perish : and their works shall *God* render vain. This *shall befall them,* because they have rejected with abhorrence that which GOD hath revealed : wherefore their works shall become of no avail. Do they not travel through the earth, and see what hath been the end of those who *were* before them ? GOD utterly destroyed them : and the like *catastrophe* awaiteth the unbelievers. This *shall come to pass,* for that GOD is the patron of the true believers, and for that the infidels have no protector. Verily GOD will introduce those who believe, and do good works, into gardens beneath which rivers flow : but the unbelievers indulge themselves in pleasures, and eat as beasts eat ; and their abode *shall be hell* fire. How many cities were more mighty in strength than thy city which hath expelled thee :

[1] This law the Hanifites judge to be abrogated, or to relate particularly to the war of Bedr, for the severity here commanded, which was necessary in the beginning of Mohammedism (see Chap. VIII. pp. 169 and 175), they think too rigorous to be put in practice in its flourishing state. But the Persians and some others hold the command to be still in full force ; for, according to them, all the men of full age who are taken in battle are to be slain, unless they embrace the Mohammedan faith ; and those who fall into the hands of the Moslems after the battle are not to be slain, but may either be set at liberty gratis or on payment of a certain ransom, or may be exchanged for Mohammedan prisoners, or condemned to slavery, at the pleasure of the Imâm or prince. (Al Beidâwi. Vide Reland. Dissert. de Jure Militari Mohammedanor. p. 32.)

[2] Some copies, instead of *kâtilu,* read *kútilu,* according to which latter reading it should be rendered, *who are slain,* or *suffer martyrdom,* &c.

yet have we destroyed them, and *there was* none to help them ? Shall he, therefore, who followeth the plain declaration of his LORD, *be* as he whose evil works have been dressed up for him *by the devil* ; and who follow their own lusts ? The description of paradise, which is promised unto the pious : therein *are* rivers of incorruptible water ; and rivers of milk, the taste whereof changeth not ; and rivers of wine, pleasant unto those who drink ; and rivers of clarified honey : and therein shall they have *plenty* of all *kinds of* fruits ; and pardon from their LORD. *Shall the man for whom these things are prepared, be* as they who must dwell for ever in *hell* fire, and will have the boiling water given them to drink, which shall burst their bowels ? Of the *unbelievers there are* some who give ear unto thee, until, when they go out from thee, they say, *by way of derision*, unto those to whom know-ledge hath been given,[1] What hath he said now ? These *are they* whose hearts GOD hath sealed up, and who follow their own lusts : but *as to* those who are directed, *God* will grant them a more ample direction, and he will instruct them what to avoid.[2] Do *the infidels* wait for any other than the *last* hour, that it may come upon them suddenly ? Some signs thereof are already come :[3] and when it shall actually overtake them, how can they *then* receive admonition ? Know, therefore, that there is no god but GOD : and ask pardon for thy sin,[4] and for the true believers, both men and women. GOD knoweth your busy employment *in the world*, and the place of your abode *hereafter*. The true believers say, Hath not a Sura been revealed *commanding war against the infidels* ? But when a Sura without any ambiguity is revealed, and war is mentioned therein, thou mayest see those in whose hearts is an infirmity,[5] look to-wards thee with the look of one whom death overshadoweth. But obedience *would be* more eligible for them, and to speak that which is convenient. And when the command is firmly

---

[1] *i e.*, The more learned of Mohammed's companions, such as Ebn Masûd and Ebn Abbâs. (Jallalo'ddin.)

[2] Or, as the words may also be translated, *and he will reward them for their piety*.

[3] As the mission of Mohammed, the splitting of the moon, and the smoke (Jallalo'ddin, Al Beidâwi), mentioned in the forty-fourth chapter.

[4] Though Mohammed here and elsewhere (see Chap. XLVIII., in the beginning) acknowledges himself to be a sinner, yet several Mohammedan doctors pretend he was wholly free from sin, and suppose he is here com-manded to ask forgiveness, not that he wanted it, but that he might set an example to his followers ; wherefore he used to say of himself, if the tradition be true, *I ask pardon of* GOD *a hundred times a day*. (Jallalo'ddin.)

[5] As hypocrisy, cowardice, or instability in their religion.

established, if they give credit unto GOD, it will be better for them. Were ye ready, therefore, if ye had been put in authority,[1] to commit outrages in the earth, and to violate your ties of blood ? These *are they* whom GOD hath cursed, and hath rendered deaf, and whose eyes he hath blinded. Do they not therefore attentively meditate on the Korân ? Are there locks upon their hearts ? Verily they who turn their backs, after the *true* direction is made manifest unto them, Satan shall prepare *their wickedness* for them, and *God* shall bear with them for a time. This *shall befall them*, because they say *privately* unto those who detest what GOD hath revealed, We will obey you in part of the matter.[2] But GOD knoweth their secrets. How therefore *will* it *be with them*, when the angels shall cause them to die, *and* shall strike their faces and their backs ?[3] This *shall they suffer*, because they follow that which provoketh GOD to wrath, and are adverse to what is well pleasing unto him : and he will render their works vain. Do they in whose hearts is an infirmity, imagine that GOD will not bring their malice to light ? If we pleased, we could surely show them unto thee, and thou shouldst know them by their marks ; but thou shalt certainly know them by *their* perverse pronunciation of *their* words. GOD knoweth your actions : and we will try you, until we know those among you who fight valiantly, and who persevere with constancy ; and we will try the reports of your behaviour. Verily those who believe not, and turn away *men* from the way of GOD, and make opposition against the apostle,[4] after the *divine* direction hath been manifested unto them, shall not hurt GOD at all ; but he shall make their works to perish. O true believers, obey GOD ; and obey the apostle : and render not your works of no effect. Verily those who believe not, and who turn away *men* from the way of GOD, and then die, being unbelievers, GOD will by no means forgive. Faint not, therefore, neither invite *your enemies* to peace, while ye *are* the superior : for GOD *is* with you, and will not defraud

---

[1] Or, as the words may also be translated, *If ye had turned back*, and apostatized from your faith.

[2] *i.e.*, In part of what ye desire of us ; by staying at home and not going forth with Mohammed to war, and by private combination against him. (Al Beidâwi.)

[3] These words are supposed to allude to the examination of the sepulchre.

[4] These were the tribes of Koreidha and Al Nadir ; or those who distributed provisions to the army of the Koreish at Bedr. (Al Beidâwi. See Chap. VIII. p. 171.)

you *of the merit of* your works. Verily this present life *is* only a play and a vain amusement : but if ye believe, and fear *God*, he will give you your rewards. He doth not require of you your *whole* substance : if he should require the whole of you, and earnestly press you, ye would become niggardly, and it would raise your hatred *against his apostle*. Behold, ye *are* those who are invited to expend *part of your substance* for the support of GOD's true religion ; and *there are* some of you who are niggardly. But whoever shall be niggardly, shall be niggardly towards his own soul : for GOD wanteth nothing, but ye *are* needy : and if ye turn back, he will substitute *another* people in your stead, who shall not be like unto you.[1]

XLVIII

THE CHAPTER OF THE VICTORY

Revealed at Medina.

IN THE NAME OF THE MOST MERCIFUL GOD.

VERILY we have granted thee a manifest victory :[2] that GOD may forgive thee[3] thy preceding and thy subsequent sin,[4] and may complete his favour on thee, and

---

[1] *i.e.*, In backwardness and aversion to the propagation of the faith. The people here designed to be put in the place of these lukewarm Moslems are generally supposed to be the Persians, there being a tradition that Mohammed, being asked what people they were, at a time when Salmân was sitting by him, clapped his hand on his thigh, and said, *This man and his nation.* Others, however, are of opinion the Ansârs or the angels are intended in this place.

[2] This victory, from which the chapter takes its title, according to the most received interpretation, was the taking of the city of Mecca. The passage is said to have been revealed on Mohammed's return from the expedition of Al Hodeibiya, and contains a promise or prediction of this signal success, which happened not till two years after ; the preterite tense being therein used for the future, according to the prophetic style (Al Zamakh., Al Beidâwi, &c.) There are some, notwithstanding, who suppose the advantage here intended was the pacification of Al Hodeibiya, which is here called a *victory*, because the Meccans sued for peace, and made a truce there with Mohammed, their breaking of which occasioned the taking of Mecca. Others think the conquest of Khaibar, or the victory over the Greeks at Mûta, &c., to be meant in this place.

[3] That is to say, that GOD may give thee an opportunity of deserving forgiveness by eradicating idolatry, and exalting his true religion, and the delivering of the weak from the hands of the ungodly, &c.

[4] *i.e.*, Whatever thou hast done worthy reprehension ; or, thy sins committed as well in the time of ignorance as since. Some expound the words more particularly, and say the *preceding* or *former* fault was his lying with his handmaid Mary (see Chap LXVI., and the notes thereon), contrary to his oath ; and the *latter*, his marrying of Zeinab (see Chap. XXXIII.), the wife of Zeid his adopted son. (Al Zamakh.)

direct thee in the right way ; and that GOD may assist thee
with a glorious assistance. It is he who sendeth down
secure tranquillity into the hearts of the true believers,
that they may increase in faith, beyond their *former* faith
(the hosts of heaven and earth are GOD's ; and GOD is knowing *and* wise) : that he may lead the true believers of both
sexes into gardens beneath which rivers flow, to dwell therein
for ever ; and may expiate their evil deeds from them (this
will be great felicity with GOD) : and that he may punish
the hypocritical men, and the hypocritical women, and the
idolaters, and the idolatresses, who conceive an ill opinion
of GOD. They shall experience a turn of evil fortune ; and
GOD shall be angry with them, and shall curse them, and hath
prepared hell for them ; an ill journey shall it be *thither* !
Unto GOD *belong* the hosts of heaven and earth ; and GOD is
mighty *and* wise. Verily we have sent thee *to be* a witness,
and a bearer of good tidings, and a denouncer of threats ; that
ye may believe in GOD and his apostle ; and may assist him,
and revere him, and praise him morning and evening. Verily
they who swear fealty[1] unto thee, swear fealty unto GOD :
the hand of GOD *is* over their hands.[2] Whoever shall violate
his oath, will violate *the same* to the hurt only of his own soul :
but whoever shall perform that which he hath covenanted
with GOD, he will surely give him a great reward. The
Arabs of the desert who were left behind[3] will say unto thee,
Our substance and our families employed us, *so that we went
not forth with thee to war* ; wherefore ask pardon for us.
They speak that with their tongues, which *is* not in their
hearts. Answer, Who shall be able *to obtain* for you anything from GOD *to the contrary,* if he is pleased to afflict you,
or is pleased to be gracious unto you ? Yea verily, GOD
is well acquainted with that which ye do. Truly ye imagined that the apostle and the true believers would never
return to their families ; and this was prepared in your

---

[1] The original word signifies publicly to acknowledge or inaugurate a
prince, by swearing fidelity and obedience to him.

[2] That is, he beholdeth from above, and is witness to the solemnity of your
giving your faith to his apostle, and will reward you for it.   (Jallalo'ddin.)
The expression alludes to the manner of their plighting their faith on these
occasions.

[3] These were the tribes of Aslam, Joheinah, Mozeinah, and Ghifâr, who,
being summoned to attend Mohammed in the expedition of Al Hodeibiya,
stayed behind, and excused themselves by saying their families must suffer
in their absence, and would be robbed of the little they had (for these tribes
were of the poorer Arabs) ; whereas in reality they wanted firmness in the
faith, and courage to face the Koreish. (Jallalo'ddin, Al Beidâwi.)

hearts : but ye imagined an evil imagination ; and ye are a corrupt people. Whoso believeth not in GOD and his apostle, verily we have prepared burning fire for the unbelievers. Unto GOD *belongeth* the kingdom of heaven and earth : he forgiveth whom he pleaseth, and he punisheth whom he pleaseth ; and GOD is inclined to forgive, *and* merciful. Those who were left behind will say, when ye go forth to take the spoil,[1] Suffer us to follow you. They seek to change the word of GOD.[2] Say, Ye shall by no means follow us ; thus hath GOD said heretofore. They will reply, Nay ; ye envy us *a share of the booty.* But they are men of small understanding. Say unto the Arabs of the desert who were lef: behind, Ye shall be called forth against a mighty *and* a warlike nation :[3] ye shall fight against them, or they shall profess Islâm. If ye obey, GOD will give you a glorious reward : but if ye turn back, as ye turned back heretofore, he will chastise you with a grievous chastisement. It shall be no crime in the blind, neither shall it be a crime in the lame, neither shall it be a crime in the sick, *if they go not forth to war* : and whoso shall obey GOD and his apostle, he shall lead him into gardens beneath which rivers flow ; but whoso shall turn back, he will chastise him with a grievous chastisement. Now GOD was well pleased with the true believers, when they sware fidelity unto thee under the tree ;[4]

[1] viz., In the expedition of Khaibar. The prophet returned from Al Hodeibiya in Dhu'lhajja, i i the sixth year of the Hejra, and stayed at Medina the remainder of that month and the beginning of Moharram, and then set forward against the Jews of Khaibar, with those only who had attended him to Hodeibiya ; and having made himself master of the place, and all the castles and strongholds in that territory (vide Abulf. Vit. Moh. p. 87, &c.), took spoils to a great value, which he divided among those who were present at that expedition, and none else (Al Beidâwi).

[2] Which was his promise to those who attended the prophet to Al Hodeibiya, that he would make them amends for their missing of the plunder of Mecca at that time by giving them that of Khaibar in lieu thereof. Some think the *word* here intended, to be that passage in the ninth chapter (page 192), *Ye shall not go forth with me for the future,* &c., which yet was plainly revealed long after the taking of Khaibar, on occasion of the expedition of Tabûc. (Al Beidâwi.)

[3] These were Banu Honeifa, who inhabited Al Yamâma, and were the followers of Moseilama, Mohammed's competitor ; or any other of those tribes which apostatized from Mohammedism (Al Beidâwi), or, as others rather suppose, the Persians or the Greeks. (Jallalo'ddin).

[4] Mohammed, when at Al Hodeibiya, sent Jawwâs Ebn Omeyya the Khozaïte, to acquaint the Meccans that he was come with a peaceable intention to visit the temple ; but they, on some jealousy conceived, refusing to admit him, the prophet sent Othman Ebn Affân, whom they imprisoned, and a report ran that he was slain : whereupon Mohammed called his men about him, and they took an oath to be faithful to him, even to death ; during which ceremony he sat under a tree, supposed by some to have been an Egyptian thorn, and by others a kind of lote-tree. (Jallal'oddin, Al Beidâwi. Vide Abulf. Vit. Moh. p. 85.)

and he knew that which *was* in their hearts : wherefore he sent down on them tranquillity of mind,[1] and rewarded them with a speedy victory,[2] and many spoils which they took, for GOD is mighty *and* wise. GOD promised you many spoils which ye should take ; but he gave you these by way of earnest ; and he restrained the hands of men from you :[3] and the same may be a sign unto the true believers ; and that he may guide you into the right way. And *he also promiseth you* other *spoils*, which ye have not *yet* been able *to take* : but now hath GOD encompassed them *for you* ; and GOD is almighty. If the unbelieving *Meccans* had fought against you, verily they had turned *their* backs, and they would not have found a patron or protector : *according to* the ordinance of GOD, which hath been put in execution heretofore *against opposers of the prophets* ; for thou shalt not find any change in the ordinance of GOD. *It was* he who restrained their hands from you, and your hands from them, in the valley of Mecca ; after that he had given you the victory over them :[4] and GOD saw that which ye did. These *are they* who believed not, and hindered you from *visiting* the holy temple, and *also hindered* the offering being detained that it should not arrive at the place where it ought to be sacrificed.[5] Had it not been that ye might have trampled on *divers* true believers, *both* men and women, whom ye knew not, *being promiscuously assembled with the infidels*, and that a crime might therefore have lighted on

[1] The original word is *Sakinat*, of which notice has been taken elsewhere. (Chap. II. p. 36.)

[2] Namely, the success at Khaibar ; or, as some rather imagine, the taking of Mecca, &c.

[3] *i.e.*, The hands of those of Khaibar, or of their successors of the tribes of Asad and Ghatfân, or of the inhabitants of Mecca, by the pacification of Al Hodeibiya.   (Al Beidâwi.)

[4] Jallalo'ddin says that fourscore of the infidels came privately to Mohammed's camp at Al Hodeibiya, with an intent to surprise some of his men, but were taken and brought before the prophet, who pardoned them and ordered them to be set at liberty ; and this generous action was the occasion of the truce struck up by the Koreish with Mohammed ; for thereupon they sent Sohail Ebn Amru and some others to treat for peace. Al Beidâwi explains the passage by another story, telling us that Acrema Ebn Abu Jahl marching from Mecca at the head of five hundred men to Al Hodeibiya, Mohammed sent against him Khâled Ebn al Walid with a detachment, who drove the infidels back to the innermost part of Mecca (as the word here translated *valley* properly signifies), and then left them, out of respect to the place.

[5] Mohammed's intent, in the expedition of Al Hodeibiya, being only to visit the temple of Mecca in a peaceable manner, and to offer a sacrifice in the valley of Mina, according to the established rites, he carried beasts with him for that purpose ; but was not permitted by the Koreish either to enter the temple or to go to Mina.

you on their account, without *your* knowledge, *he had not restrained your hands from them : but this was done*, that GOD might lead whom he pleaseth into his mercy. If they had been distinguished from one another, we had surely chastised such of them as believed not, with a severe chastisement. When the unbelievers had put in their hearts an affected preciseness, the preciseness of ignorance, and GOD sent down his tranquillity on his apostle and on the true believers ;[1] and firmly fixed in them the word of piety,[2] and they were the most worthy of the same, and the most deserving thereof : for GOD knoweth all things. Now hath GOD in truth verified unto his apostle the vision,[3] *wherein he said*, Ye shall surely enter the holy temple *of Mecca*, if GOD please, in full security ; having your heads shaved, and your hair cut :[4] ye shall not fear : for GOD knoweth that which ye know not ; and he hath appointed *you*, besides this, a speedy victory.[5] *It is* he who hath sent his apostle with the direction, and the religion of truth ; that he may

---

[1] This passage was occasioned by the stiffness of Sohail and his companions in wording the treaty concluded with Mohammed ; for when the prophet ordered Ali to begin with the form, *In the name of the most merciful* GOD, they objected to it, and insisted that he should begin with this : *In thy name, O* GOD ; which Mohammed submitted to, and proceeded to dictate, *These are the conditions on which Mohammed, the apostle of* GOD, *has made peace with those of Mecca* ; to this Sohail again objected, saying, *If we had acknowledged thee to be the apostle of* GOD, *we had not given thee any opposition* ; whereupon Mohammed ordered Ali to write as Sohail desired, *These are the conditions which Mohammed, the son of Abdallah*, &c. But the Moslems were so disgusted thereat, that they were on the point of breaking off the treaty, and had fallen on the Meccans, had not GOD appeased and calmed their minds, as it follows in the text. (Al Beidâwi. Vide Abulf. Vit. Moh. p. 87.) The terms of this pacification were that there should be a truce for ten years ; that any person might enter into league either with Mohammed or with the Koreish, as he should think fit ; and that Mohammed should have the liberty to visit the temple of Mecca the next year for three days. (Al Beidâwi.)

[2] *i.e.*, The Mohammedan profession of faith ; or the *Bismillah*, and the words, *Mohammed, the apostle of* GOD, which were rejected by the infidels.

[3] Or dream which Mohammed had at Medina before he set out for Al Hodeibiya ; wherein he dreamed that he and his companions entered Mecca in security, with their heads shaven and their hair cut. This dream being imparted by the prophet to his followers, occasioned a great deal of joy among them, and they supposed it would be fulfilled that same year ; but when they saw the truce concluded, which frustrated their expectation for that time, they were deeply concerned ; whereupon this passage was revealed for their consolation, confirming the vision, which was not to be fulfilled till the year after, when Mohammed performed the visitation distinguished by the addition of Al Kadâ, or completion, because he then completed the visitation of the former year, when the Koreish not permitting him to enter Mecca, he was obliged to kill his victims, and to shave himself at Al Hodeibiya. (Al Beidâwi, Jallalo'ddin. Vide Abulf. Vit. Moh. pp. 84, 87.)

[4] *i.e.*, Some being shaved, and others having only their hair cut.

[5] viz., The taking of Khaibar.

exalt the same above every religion : and GOD is a sufficient witness *hereof.* Mohammed *is* the apostle of GOD : and those who are with him *are* fierce against the unbelievers, *but* compassionate towards one another. Thou mayest see them bowing down, prostrate, seeking a recompence from GOD, and *his* good will. Their signs *are* in their faces, being marks of *frequent* prostration. This *is* their description in the pentateuch, and their description in the gospel : *they are* as seed which putteth forth its stalk, and strengtheneth it, and swelleth in the ear, and riseth upon its stem ; giving delight unto the sower. *Such are the Moslems described to be :* that the infidels may swell with indignation at them. GOD hath promised unto such of them as believe and do good works, pardon and a great reward.

XLIX

THE CHAPTER OF THE INNER APARTMENTS

Revealed at Medina.

IN THE NAME OF THE MOST MERCIFUL GOD.

O TRUE believers, anticipate not *any matter* in the sight of GOD and his apostle :[1] and fear GOD ; for GOD *both* heareth *and* knoweth. O true believers, raise not your voices above the voice of the prophet ;[2] neither speak loud unto him in discourse, as ye speak loud unto one another, lest your works become vain, and ye perceive *it* not. Verily they who lower their voices in the presence of the apostle of GOD, *are* those whose hearts GOD hath disposed unto piety : they shall obtain pardon and a great reward. *As to* those who call unto thee from without the inner apartments ;[3] the greater part of them do not understand *the respect due to thee.* If they wait with patience, until thou come forth unto them, it will certainly be better for them : but GOD *is* inclined to forgive, *and* merciful. O true be-

---

[1] That is, do not presume to give your own decision in any case, before ye have received the judgment of GOD and his apostle.

[2] This verse is said to have been occasioned by a dispute between Abu Becr and Omar, concerning the appointing of a governor of a certain place ; in which they raised their voices so high, in the presence of the apostle, that it was thought proper to forbid such indecencies for the future. (Jallalo'ddin.)

[3] These, they say, were Oyeyna Ebn Osein, and Al Akrá Ebn Hâbes ; who wanting to speak with Mohammed, when he was sleeping at noon in his women's apartment, had the rudeness to call out several times. *Mohammed, come forth to us.* (Al Beidâwi.)

lievers, if a wicked man come unto you with a tale, inquire
strictly *into the truth thereof*; lest ye hurt people through
ignorance, and afterwards repent of what ye have done :[1]
and know that the apostle of GOD *is* among you : if he should
obey you in many things, ye would certainly be guilty of a
crime, *in leading him into a mistake*.　But GOD hath made
the faith amiable unto you, and hath prepared the same in
your hearts ; and hath rendered infidelity, and iniquity, and
disobedience hateful unto you.　These are they who walk
in the right way ; through mercy from GOD, and grace :
and GOD *is* knowing *and* wise.　If two parties of the believers
contend with one another, do ye *endeavour to* compose the
matter between them : and if the one of them offer an insult
unto the other, fight against that *party* which offered the
insult, until they return unto the judgment of GOD ; and
if they do return, make peace between them with equity :
and act with justice ; for GOD loveth those who act justly.[2]
Verily the true believers *are* brethren : wherefore reconcile
your brethren ; and fear GOD, that ye may obtain mercy.
O true believers, let not men laugh *other* men to scorn ; who
peradventure may be better than themselves ; neither *let*
women *laugh other* women *to scorn* ; who may possibly be
better than themselves.　Neither defame one another ; nor
call one another by *opprobrious* appellations.　An ill name
it is to be charged with wickedness, after *having embraced*
the faith : and whoso repenteth not, they will be the unjust
doers.[3]　O true believers, carefully avoid *entertaining* a suspicion *of another* : for some suspicions *are* a crime.　Inquire
not too curiously *into other men's failings* : neither let the
one of you speak ill of another in his absence.　Would

[1] This passage was occasioned, it is said, by the following accident. Al
Walid Ebn Okba being sent by Mohammed to collect the alms from the
tribe of Al Mostalek, when he saw them come out to meet him in great numbers, grew apprehensive they designed him some mischief, because of past
enmity between him and them in the time of ignorance, and immediately
turned back, and told the prophet they refused to pay their alms, and
attempted to kill him ; upon which Mohammed was thinking to reduce them
by force : but on sending Khâled Ebn al Walid to them, he found his former
messenger had wronged them, and that they continued in their obedience.
(Al Beidâwi, Jallal.)

[2] This verse is supposed to have been occasioned by a fray which happened between the tribes of Al Aws and Al Kazraj.

[3] It is said that this verse was revealed on account of Safiya Bint Hoyai,
one of the prophet's wives ; who came to her husband and complained
that the women said to her, *O thou Jewess, the daughter of a Jew and of a
Jewess* : to which he answered, *Canst thou not say, Aaron is my father, and
Moses is my uncle, and Mohammed is my husband* ? (Al Beidâwi. See
Prid. Life of Mahom. p. iii, &c.)

any of you desire to eat the flesh of his dead brother ? Surely ye would abhor it. And fear GOD : for GOD *is* easy to be reconciled, *and* merciful. O men, verily we have created you of a male and a female ; and we have distributed you into nations and tribes, that ye might know one another. Verily the most honourable of you, in the sight of GOD, *is* the most pious of you : and GOD *is* wise *and* knowing. The Arabs of the desert[1] say, We believe. Answer, Ye do by no means believe ; but say, We have embraced Islâm :[2] for the faith hath not yet entered into your hearts. If ye obey GOD and his apostle, he will not defraud you of any part *of the merit* of your works : for GOD *is* inclined to forgive, *and* merciful. Verily the true believers *are* those only who believe in GOD and his apostle, and afterwards doubt not ; and who employ their substance and their persons in the defence of GOD's true religion : these are they who speak sincerely. Say, Will ye inform GOD concerning your religion ?[3] But GOD knoweth whatever *is* in heaven and in earth : for GOD *is* omniscient. They upbraid thee that they have embraced Islâm. Answer, Upbraid me not with your having embraced Islâm : rather GOD upbraideth you, that he hath directed you to the faith ;[4] if ye speak sincerely. Verily GOD knoweth the secrets of heaven and earth : and GOD beholdeth that which ye do.

L

THE CHAPTER OF K

Revealed at Mecca.

IN THE NAME OF THE MOST MERCIFUL GOD.

K.[5] By the glorious Korân : verily they wonder that a preacher from among themselves is come unto them ;

[1] These were certain of the tribe of Asad, who came to Medina in a year of scarcity, and having professed Mohammedism, told the prophet that they had brought all their goods and their families, and would not oppose him, as some other tribes had done : and this they said to obtain a part of the alms, and to upbraid him with their having embraced his religion and party. (Al Beidâwi.)

[2] That is, Ye are not sincere believers, but outward professors only of the true religion.

[3] *i.e.*, Will ye pretend to deceive him, by saying ye are true believers ?

[4] The obligation being not on GOD's side, but on yours, for that he has favoured you so far as to guide you into the true faith, if ye are sincere believers.

[5] Some imagine that this letter is designed to express the mountain Kâf, which several eastern writers fancy encompasses the whole world. (Vide

and the unbelievers say, This *is* a wonderful thing : after we shall be dead, and become dust, *shall we return to life* ? This *is* a return remote *from thought.* Now we know what the earth consumeth of them ; and with us *is* a book which keepeth an account *thereof.* But they charge falsehood on the truth, after it hath come unto them : wherefore they *are plunged* in a confused business.[1] Do they not look up to the heaven above them, *and consider* how we have raised it and adorned it ; and that *there are* no flaws therein ? We have also spread forth the earth, and thrown thereon *mountains* firmly rooted :[2] and we cause every beautiful kind *of vegetables* to spring up therein ; for a subject of meditation, and an admonition unto every man who turneth *unto us.* And we send down rain as a blessing from heaven, whereby we cause gardens to spring forth, and the grain of harvest, and tall palm-trees having branches laden with dates hanging one above another, as a provision for mankind ; and we thereby quicken a dead country : so *shall be* the coming forth *of the dead from their graves.* The people of Noah, and those who dwelt at Al Rass,[3] and Thamûd, and Ad, and Pharaoh accused *the prophets* of imposture before *the Meccans* ; and also the brethren of Lot, and the inhabitants of the wood *near Midian,* and the people of Tobba :[4] all *these* accused the apostles of imposture ; wherefore *the judgments* which I threatened were justly inflicted *on them.* Is our power exhausted by the first creation ? Yea : they are in a perplexity, because of a new creation *which is foretold them, namely, the raising of the dead.* We created man, and we know what his soul whispereth within him ; and we *are* nearer unto him than *his* jugular vein. When the two *angels* deputed to take account *of a man's behaviour,* take an account *thereof* ; one sitting on the right hand, and *the other* on the left : he uttereth not a word, but *there is* with him a watcher, ready *to note it.*[5] And the agony of death shall come in truth :

D'Herbel. Bibl. Orient. Art. Caf.) Others say it stands for *Kada al amr, i.e., The matter is decreed,* viz., the chastisement of the infidels. (Al Beidâwi, Jallalo'ddin.) See Chap. II. p. 2, and Sale, Prel. Disc. Sect. III. p. 64.

[1] Not knowing what certainly to affirm of the Korân ; calling it sometimes a piece of poetry, at other times a piece of sorcery, and at other times a piece of divination, &c.

[2] See Chaps. XVI. p. 258, and XXXI. p. 400.

[3] See Chap. XXV. p. 356.

[4] See Chap. XLIV. p. 480.

[5] The intent of the passage is to exalt the omniscience of GOD, who wants not the information of the guardian angels, though he has thought fit, in his wisdom, to give them that employment ; for if they are so exact as to write down every word which falls from a man's mouth, how can we hope

this, *O man, is* what thou soughtest to avoid. And the trumpet shall sound : this *will be* the day which hath been threatened. And every soul shall come ; *and* therewith *shall be* a driver and a witness.[1] *And the former shall say unto the unbeliever,* Thou wast negligent heretofore of this *day* : but we have removed thy veil from off thee ; and thy sight *is become* piercing this day. And his companion shall say, This *is* what *is* ready with me *to be attested. And God shall say,* Cast into hell every unbeliever, *and* perverse person, *and every one* who forbade good, *and every* transgressor, and doubter *of the faith,* who set up another god with *the true* GOD ; and cast him into a grievous torment. His companion[2] shall say, O LORD, I did not seduce him ; but he was in a wide error.[3] *God* shall say, Wrangle not in my presence : since I threatened you beforehand *with the torments which ye now see prepared for you.* The sentence is not changed with me : neither do I treat *my* servants unjustly. On that day we will say unto hell, Art thou full ? and it shall answer, *Is there* yet any addition ?[4] And paradise shall be brought near unto the pious ; *and it shall be said unto them,* This *is* what ye have been promised ; unto every one who turned himself *unto God,* and kept *his commandments* ; who feared the Merciful in secret, and came *unto him* with a converted heart : enter the same in peace : this *is* the day of eternity. Therein shall they have whatever they shall desire ; and *there will be* a superabundant addition *of bliss* with us. How many generations have we destroyed before the *Meccans,* which were more mighty than they in strength ? Pass,

to escape the observation of him who sees our inmost thoughts ? The Mohammedans have a tradition that the angel who notes a man's good actions has the command over him who notes his evil actions ; and that when a man does a good action, the angel of the right hand writes it down ten times, and when he commits an ill action, the same angel says to the angel of the left hand, *Forbear setting it down for seven hours* ; *peradventure he may pray, or may ask pardon.* (Al Beidâwi.)

[1] *i.e.,* Two angels, one acting as a serjeant, to bring every person before the tribunal ; and the other prepared as a witness, to testify either for or against him. Some say the former will be the guardian angel who took down his evil actions, and the other the angel who took down his good actions. (Al Beidâwi.)

[2] viz., The devil which shall be chained to him.

[3] This will be the answer of the devil, whom the wicked person will accuse as his seducer ; for the devil has no power over a man to cause him to do evil, any otherwise than by suggesting what is agreeable to his corrupt inclinations. (See Chap. XIV.)

[4] *i.e.,* Are there yet any more condemned to this place, or is my space to be enlarged and rendered more capacious to receive them ?

The commentators suppose hell will be quite filled at the day of judgment, according to that repeated expression in the Korân, *Verily I will fill hell with you,* &c.

therefore, through the regions *of the earth, and see* whether *there be* any refuge *from our vengeance* ? Verily herein *is* an admonition unto him who hath a heart *to understand,* or giveth ear, and is present *with an attentive mind.* We created the heavens and the earth, and whatever *is* between them, in six days ; and no weariness affected us.[1] Wherefore patiently suffer what they say ;[2] and celebrate the praise of thy LORD before sunrise, and before sunset, and praise him *in some part* of the night : and *perform* the additional parts of worship.[3] And hearken unto the day whereon the crier shall call *men to judgment* from a near place :[4] the day whereon they shall hear the voice *of the trumpet* in truth : this *will be* the day of *men's* coming forth *from their graves* : we give life, and we cause to die ; and unto us *shall be* the return *of all creatures* : the day whereon the earth shall suddenly cleave in sunder over them. This *will be* an assembly easy for us *to assemble.* We well know what *the unbelievers* say ; and thou *art* not sent to compel them forcibly *to the faith.* Wherefore warn, by the Korân. him who feareth my threatening.

LI

THE CHAPTER OF THE DISPERSING [5]

Revealed at Mecca.

IN THE NAME OF THE MOST MERCIFUL GOD.

B Y the *winds* dispersing and scattering *the dust* ;[6] and by the *clouds* bearing a load *of rain* ;[7] by the *ships* running swiftly *in the sea* ;[8] and by the *angels* who distribute

---

[1] This was revealed in answer to the Jews, who said that GOD rested from his work of creation on the seventh day, and reposed himself on his throne, as one fatigued. (Al Beidâwi, Jallalo'ddin.)

[2] viz., Either what the idolaters say, in denying the resurrection ; or the Jews, in speaking indecently of GOD.

[3] These are the two inclinations used after the evening prayer, which are not necessary, or of precept, but voluntary, and of supererogation ; and may therefore be added, or omitted, indifferently.

[4] That is, from a place whence every creature may equally hear the call. This place, it is supposed, will be the mountain of the temple of Jerusalem, which some fancy to be nigher heaven than any other part of the earth ; whence Israfil will sound the trumpet, and Gabriel will make the following proclamation : *O ye rotten bones, and torn flesh, and dispersed hairs,* GOD *commandeth you to be gathered together to judgment.* (Al Beidâwi.)

[5] This chapter is otherwise entitled *The Scatterers.*

[6] Or, *by the* women *who bring forth* or *scatter* children, &c.

[7] Or, *by the* women *bearing a burden* in their womb, or *the* winds *bearing* the clouds, &c.

[8] Or, *by the* winds *passing swiftly* in the air, or *the* stars *moving swiftly* in their courses, &c.

things *necessary for the support of all creatures* :[1] verily that wherewith ye are threatened is certainly true ; and the *last* judgment will surely come. By the heaven furnished with paths,[2] ye widely differ in what ye say.[3] He will be turned aside from *the faith,* who shall be turned aside *by the divine decree.* Cursed be the liars ; who *wade* in deep waters *of ignorance,* neglecting *their salvation.* They ask, When *will* the day of judgment *come* ? On that day shall they be burned in *hell* fire ; *and it shall be said unto them,* Taste your punishment ; this *is* what ye demanded to be hastened. But the pious *shall dwell* among gardens and fountains, receiving that which their LORD shall give them ; because they were righteous doers before this *day.* They slept but a small part of the night ;[4] and early in the morning they asked pardon *of God* : and a due portion of their wealth *was given* unto him who asked, and unto him who was forbidden *by shame to ask. There are* signs *of the divine power and goodness* in the earth, unto *men* of sound understanding ; and also in your own selves : will ye not therefore consider ? Your sustenance *is* in the heaven ; and also that which ye are promised.[5] Wherefore by the LORD of heaven and earth *I swear* that this *is* certainly the truth ; according to what yourselves speak.[6] Hath not the story of Abraham's honoured guests[7] come to thy knowledge ? When they went in unto him, and said, Peace : he answered, Peace ; *saying within himself, These are* unknown people. And he went privately unto his family, and brought a fatted calf. And he set it before them, *and when he saw they touched it not,* he said, Do ye not eat ? And he began to entertain a fear of them. They said, Fear not :[8] and they declared unto him the promise of a wise youth. And his wife drew near with exclamation, and she smote her face, and said, *I am* an old

---

[1] Or, *by the* winds *which distribute* the rain, &c.

[2] *i.e.,* The paths or orbs of the stars, or the streaks which appear in the sky like paths, being thin and extended clouds.

[3] Concerning Mohammed, or the Korân, or the resurrection and day of judgment ; speaking variously and inconsistently of them.

[4] Spending the greater part in prayer and religious meditation.

[5] *i.e.,* Your food cometh from above, whence proceedeth the change of seasons and rain ; and your future reward is also there, that is to say, in paradise, which is situate above the seven heavens.

[6] That is, without any doubt-or reserved meaning, as ye affirm a truth unto one another.

[7] See Chaps. XI. p. 218 and XV. p. 254.

[8] Some add, that to remove Abraham's fear, Gabriel, who was one of these strangers, touched the calf with his wing, and it immediately rose up and walked to its dam ; upon which Abraham knew them to be the messengers of GOD, (Al Beidâwi.)

woman, *and* barren. The *angels* answered, Thus saith thy
LORD : Verily he is the wise, the knowing. (XXVII.)[1]
And Abraham said *unto them*, What is your errand, therefore,
O messengers *of God* ? They answered, Verily we are sent
unto a wicked people : that we may send down upon them
stones of *baked* clay, marked from thy LORD, for *the destruction of* transgressors. And we brought forth the true believers who were in *the city* : but we found not therein more
than *one* family of Moslems. And we *overthrew the same,
and* left a sign therein unto those who dread the severe chastisement *of God*. In Moses also *was a sign* : when we sent
him unto Pharaoh with manifest power. But he turned
back, with his princes, saying, *This man is* a sorcerer or a
madman. Wherefore we took him and his forces, and cast
them into the sea : and he was one worthy of reprehension.
And in *the tribe of* Ad *also was a sign* : when we sent against
them a destroying wind ; it touched not aught, whereon
it came, but it rendered the same as a thing rotten *and
reduced to dust*. In Thamûd *likewise was a sign* : when it
was said unto them, Enjoy *yourselves* for a time.[2] But they
insolently transgressed the command of their LORD : wherefore a terrible noise from heaven assailed them, while they
looked on ;[3] and they were not able to stand *on their feet*,
neither did they save themselves *from destruction*. And the
people of Noah *did we destroy* before *these* : for they were
a people who enormously transgressed. We have built the
heaven with might ; and we have given *it* a large extent :
and we have stretched forth the earth beneath ; and how
evenly have we spread *the same* ! And of everything have
we created two kinds,[4] that peradventure ye may consider.
Fly, therefore, unto GOD ; verily I *am* a public warner unto
you, from him. And set not up another god with *the true*
GOD : verily I *am* a public warner unto you, from him. In
like manner there came no apostle unto their predecessors,
but they said, *This man is* a magician or a madman. Have
they bequeathed this *behaviour* successively the one to the
other ? Yea ; they are a people who enormously transgress.
Wherefore withdraw from them ; and thou *shalt* not *be*

---

[1] Here begins the twenty-seventh of the Ajzá, or sections. (See Sale, Prel.
Disc. p. 63.
[2] *i.e.*, For three days. See Chap. XI. p. 218.
[3] For this calamity happened in the daytime.
[4] As for example : male and female ; the heaven and the earth ; the
sun and the moon ; light and darkness ; plains and mountains ; winter
and summer ; sweet and bitter, &c. (Jallalo'ddin.)

blameworthy *in so doing*.   Yet continue to admonish : for admonition profiteth the true believers.   I have not created genii and men *for any other end* than that they should serve me.   I require not any sustenance from them ; neither will I that they feed me.   Verily GOD is he who provideth *for all creatures* ;   possessed of mighty power.   Unto those who shall injure *our apostle shall be given* a portion like unto the portion of those who behaved like them *in times past* ;   and they shall not wish *the same* to be hastened.   Woe, therefore, to the unbelievers, because of their day with which they are threatened !

LII

THE CHAPTER OF THE MOUNTAIN
Revealed at Mecca.

IN THE NAME OF THE MOST MERCIFUL GOD.

BY the mountain *of Sinai* ; and by the book written in an expanded scroll ;[1] and by the visited house ;[2] and by the elevated roof *of heaven* ; and by the swelling ocean : verily the punishment of thy LORD will surely descend ; *there shall be* none to withhold it.   On that day the heaven shall be shaken, and shall reel ; and the mountains shall walk and pass away.   And on that day woe be unto those who accused *God's apostles* of imposture ; who amused themselves in wading *in vain disputes* !   On that day shall they be driven and thrust into the fire of hell ; *and it shall be said unto them*, This *is* the fire which ye denied as a fiction.   *Is* this a magic illusion ?   Or do ye not see ?   Enter the same to be scorched : whether ye bear *your torments* patiently, or impatiently, *it will be* equal unto you : ye shall surely receive the reward of that which ye have wrought.   But the pious *shall dwell* amidst gardens and pleasures ; delighting themselves in what their LORD shall have given them : and their LORD shall deliver them from the pains of hell.   *And it shall be said unto them*, Eat and drink with easy digestion ;

[1] The book here intended, according to different opinions, is either the book or register wherein every man's actions are recorded ; or the *preserved table* containing GOD's decrees ; or the book of the law, which was written by GOD, Moses hearing the creaking of the pen ; or else the Korân.   (Al Zamakh., Al Beidâwi.)

[2] *i.e*, The Caaba, so much visited by pilgrims ; or, as some rather think, the original model of that house in heaven, called Al Dorâh, which is visited and compassed by the angels, as the other is by men.   (Sale, Prel. Disc. Sect. IV. p. 125.)

because of that which ye have wrought : leaning on couches disposed in order : and we will espouse them unto virgins having large black eyes. And unto those who believe, and whose offspring follow them in the faith, we will join their offspring *in paradise* : and we will not diminish unto them aught· of *the merit of* their works. (Every man *is* given in pledge for that which he shall have wrought.[1]) And we will give them fruits in abundance, and flesh of the *kinds* which they shall desire. They shall present unto one another therein a cup *of wine*, wherein there shall be no vain discourse, nor any incitement unto wickedness. And youths *appointed* to *attend* them, shall go round them : *beautiful* as pearls hidden *in their shell*. And they shall approach unto one another, and shall ask mutual questions. *And* they shall say, Verily we were heretofore amidst our family, in great dread *with regard to our state after death* ; but GOD hath been gracious unto us, and hath delivered us from the pain of burning fire : for we called on him heretofore ; and he is the beneficent, the merciful. Wherefore do thou, *O prophet*, admonish *thy people*. Thou *art* not, by the grace of thy LORD, a soothsayer or a madman. Do they say, *He is* a poet : we wait, concerning him, some adverse turn of fortune ? Say, Wait ye *my ruin* : verily I wait, with you, *the time of your destruction*. Do their mature understandings bid them *say* this ; or *are* they people who perversely transgress ? Do they say, He hath forged *the Korân* ? Verily they believe not. Let them produce a discourse like unto it, if they speak truth. Were they created by nothing ; or were they the creators *of themselves* ? Did they create the heavens and the earth ? Verily they are not firmly persuaded *that God hath created them.*[2] Are the stores of thy LORD in their hands ? Are they the supreme dispensers *of all things* ? Have they a ladder, whereby they may *ascend to heaven and* hear *the discourses of angels* ? Let one, therefore, who hath heard them, produce an evident proof *thereof*. Hath *God* daughters, and have ye sons ?[3] Dost thou ask them a reward *for thy preaching* ? but they are laden with debts. Are the secrets of futurity with them ; and do they transcribe *the same from the table of God's decrees* ? Do they seek *to lay* a plot *against thee* ? But the unbelievers are *they who*

---

[1] *i.e.*, Every man is pledged unto GOD for his behaviour ; and if he does well, he redeems his pledge, but if evil, he forfeits it.

[2] For though they confess this with their tongues, yet they deny it by their averseness to render him his due worship.

[3] See Chap. XVI p. 261.

shall be circumvented.[1] Have they *any* god, besides GOD ?
Far be GOD exalted above the *idols* which they associate
with him ! If they should see a fragment of the heaven
falling down *upon them*, they would say, *It is only* a thick
cloud.[2] Wherefore leave them, until they arrive at their
day wherein they shall swoon for fear :[3] a day in which
their subtle contrivances shall not avail them at all, neither
shall they be protected. And those who act unjustly shall
surely suffer *another* punishment besides this :[4] but the
greater part of them do not understand. And wait thou
patiently the judgment of thy LORD *concerning them* ; for
thou *art* in our eye : and celebrate the praise of thy LORD,
when thou risest up ; and praise him in the night season,
and when the stars begin to disappear.

LIII

THE CHAPTER OF THE STAR

Revealed at Mecca.

IN THE NAME OF THE MOST MERCIFUL GOD.

BY the star,[5] when it setteth ;[6] your companion *Mohammed*
erreth not, nor is he led astray : neither doth he
speak of *his own* will. It is no other than a revelation, which
hath been revealed *unto him*. One mighty in power, endued
with understanding, taught *it* him :[7] and he appeared[8] in
the highest part of the horizon. Afterwards he approached
the prophet,[9] and drew near *unto him* ; until he was at the

[1] See Chap. VIII. p. 170.
[2] This was one of the judgments which the idolatrous Meccans defied
Mohammed to bring down upon them ; and yet, says the text, if they should
see a part of the heaven falling on them, they would not believe it till they
were crushed to death by it. (Al Beidâwi.)
[3] *i.e.*, At the first sound of the trumpet. (Sale, Prel. Disc. Sect. IV.)
[4] That is, besides the punishment to which they shall be doomed at the
day of judgment, they shall be previously chastised by calamities in this
life, as the slaughter at Bedr, and the seven years' famine, and also after
their death, by the examination of the sepulchre. (Al Beidâwi.)
[5] Some suppose the stars in general, and others the Pleiades in particular,
to be meant in this place.
[6] Or, according to a contrary signification of the verb here used, *when it
riseth*.
[7] Namely, the angel Gabriel.
[8] In his natural form, in which GOD created him, and in the eastern part
of the sky. It is said that this angel appeared in his proper shape to none
of the prophets, except Mohammed, and to him only twice : once when he
received the first revelation of the Korân, and a second time when he took
his night journey to heaven ; as it follows in the text.
[9] In a human shape.

distance of two bows' length[1] *from him,* or yet nearer : and he revealed unto his servant that which he revealed. The heart *of Mohammed* did not falsely represent that which he saw.[2] Will ye therefore dispute with him concerning that which he saw ? He also saw him another time, by the lote-tree beyond which there is no passing :[3] near it is the garden of *eternal* abode. When the lote-tree covered that which it covered,[4] *his* eyesight turned not aside, neither did it wander : and he really beheld *some* of the greatest signs of his LORD.[5] What think ye of Allât, and Al Uzza, and Manah, that other third *goddess* ?[6] Have ye male children, and *God* female ?[7] This, therefore, *is* an unjust partition. They are no other than *empty* names, which ye and your fathers have named *goddesses.* GOD hath not revealed concerning them anything to authorize *their worship.* They follow no other than a vain opinion, and what *their* souls desire : yet hath the *true* direction come unto them from their LORD. Shall man have whatever he wisheth for ?[8] The life to come and the present life *are* GOD'S : and how many angels soever *there be* in the heavens, their intercession shall be of no avail, until after GOD shall have granted permission unto whom he shall please and shall accept. Verily they who believe not in the life to come give unto the angels a female appellation. But they have no knowledge herein : they follow no other than a bare opinion ; and a bare opinion attaineth not anything of truth. Wherefore withdraw from him who turneth away from our admonition, and seek-eth only the present life. This *is* their highest pitch of

[1] Or, as the word also signifies, *two cubits' length.*
[2] But he saw it in reality.
[3] This tree, say the commentators, stands in the seventh heaven, on the right hand of the throne of GOD ; and is the utmost bounds beyond which the angels themselves must not pass ; or, as some rather imagine, beyond which no creature's knowledge can extend.
[4] The words seem to signify that what was under this tree exceeded all description and number. Some suppose the whole host of angels worshipping beneath it (Al Beidâwi) are intended, and others, the birds which sit on its branches. (Jallalo'ddin.)
[5] Seeing the wonders both of the sensible and the intellectual world. (Al Beidâwi.)
[6] Those were three idols of the ancient Arabs, of which Sale has spoken in his Preliminary Discourse (Sect I.). As to the blasphemy which some pretend Mohammed once uttered, through inadvertence as he was reading this passage, see Chap. XXII. p. 332.
[7] See Chap. XVI. p. 261.
[8] *i.e.,* Shall he dictate to GOD, and name whom he pleases for his inter-cessors, or for his prophet ; or shall he choose a religion according to his own fancy, and prescribe the terms on which he may claim the reward of this life and the next (Al Beidâwi, Jallalo'ddin.)

knowledge. Verily thy LORD well knoweth him who erreth from his way; and he well knoweth him who is *rightly* directed. Unto GOD *belongeth* whatever *is* in heaven and earth : that he may reward those who do evil, according to that which they shall have wrought ; and may reward those who do well, with the most excellent *reward*. *As to those* who avoid great crimes and heinous sins, *and are guilty* only *of* lighter faults ; verily thy LORD *will be* extensive in mercy *towards them*. He well knew you when he produced you out of the earth, and when ye *were* embryos in your mothers' wombs : wherefore justify not yourselves : he best knoweth *the man* who feareth *him*. What thinkest thou of him who turneth aside *from following the truth*, and giveth little, and covetously stoppeth his hand ?[1] *Is* the knowledge of futurity with him, so that he seeth *the same* ?[2] Hath he not been informed of that which *is contained* in the books of Moses, and of Abraham who faithfully performed *his engagements* ? *To wit* : that a burdened *soul* shall not bear the burden of another ; and that nothing *shall be imputed* to a man *for righteousness*, except his own labour ; and that his reward shall surely be made manifest hereafter, and *that* he shall be rewarded for the same with a most abundant reward ; and that unto thy LORD *will be* the end *of all things* ; and that he causeth to laugh, and causeth to weep ; and that he putteth to death, and giveth life ; and that he createth the two sexes, the male and the female, of seed when it is emitted ; and that unto him *appertaineth* another production, *namely, the raising of the dead again to life hereafter* ; and that he enricheth, and causeth to acquire possessions ; and that he is the LORD of the dog-star ;[3] and that he destroyed the ancient *tribe of* Ad and Thamûd, and left not *any of them* alive ; and also the people of Noah, before *them* ; for they were most unjust and wicked :

---

[1] This passage, it is said, was revealed on account of Al Walîd Ebn al Mogheira, who, following the prophet one day, was reviled by an idolater for leaving the religion of the Koreish, and giving occasion of scandal ; to which he answered, that what he did was out of apprehension of the divine vengeance : whereupon the man offered, for a certain sum, to take the guilt of his apostasy on himself ; and the bargain being made, Al Walîd returned to his idolatry, and paid the man part of what had been agreed on ; but afterwards, on further consideration, he thought it too much, and kept back the remainder. (Al Beidâwi.)

[2] That is, is he assured that the person with whom he made the above-mentioned agreement will be allowed to suffer in his stead hereafter ? (Al Beidâwi.)

[3] Sirius, or the greater dog-star, was worshipped by some of the old *f*rabs. Sale, Prel. Disc. Sect. I., and Hyde, not. in Ulug. Beig. Tab. Stell. fix. p. 53.)

and he overthrew the *cities which were* turned upside down ;[1] and that which covered *them,* covered them. Which, therefore, of thy LORD's benefits, *O man,* wilt thou call in question ? This *our apostle* is a preacher like the preachers who preceded *him.* The approaching *day of judgment* draweth near : there is none who can reveal *the exact time of* the same, besides GOD. Do ye, therefore, wonder at this new revelation ; and do ye laugh, and not weep, spending your time in idle diversions ? But rather worship GOD, and serve *him.*

LIV

THE CHAPTER OF THE MOON
Revealed at Mecca.

IN THE NAME OF THE MOST MERCIFUL GOD.

THE hour *of judgment* approacheth ; and the moon hath been split in sunder :[2] but if *the unbelievers* see a sign, they turn aside, saying, *This is* a powerful charm.[3] And they accuse *thee, O Mohammed,* of imposture, and follow their own lusts : but everything *will be* immutably fixed.[4] And now hath a message[5] come unto them, wherein *is* a determent *from obstinate infidelity* ; *the same being* consummate wisdom : but warners profit *them* not ; wherefore

[1] viz., Sodom, and the other cities involved in her ruin. See Chap. XI.

[2] This passage is expounded two different ways. Some imagine the words refer to a famous miracle supposed to have been performed by Mohammed ; for it is said that, on the infidels demanding a sign of him, the moon appeared cloven in two (see a long and fabulous account of this pretended miracle in Gagnier, Vie de Mah. c. 19), one part vanishing, and the other remaining ; and Ebn Masûd affirmed that he saw Mount Harâ interpose between the two sections. Others think the preterite tense is here used in the prophetic style for the future, and that the passage should be rendered, *The moon shall be split in sunder* : for this, they say, is to happen at the resurrection. The former opinion is supported by reading, according to some copies, *wakad inshakka 'lkamaro, i.e., since the moon hath already been split in sunder* ; the splitting of the moon being reckoned by some to be one of the previous signs of the last day. (Al Zamakh., Al Beidâwi.)

[3] Or, as the participle here used may also signify, *a continued series of magic,* or *a transient magical illusion.*

[4] Or will reach a final period of ruin or success in this world, and of misery or happiness in the next, which will be conclusive and unchangeable thenceforward for ever. (Al Beidâwi.)

[5] *i.e.,* The Korân, containing stories of former nations which have been chastised for their incredulity, and threats of a more dreadful punishment hereafter.

do thou withdraw from them. The day whereon the summoner shall summon *mankind* to an ungrateful business,[1] they shall come forth from *their graves* with downcast looks : *numerous* as locusts scattered far abroad ; hastening with terror unto the summoner. The unbelievers shall say, This is a day of distress. The people of Noah accused *that prophet* of imposture, before *thy people rejected thee* : they accused our servant of imposture, saying, *He is* a madman ; and he was rejected with reproach. He called, therefore, upon his LORD, *saying*, Verily, I *am* overpowered ; wherefore avenge *me.*[2] So we opened the gates of heaven, with water pouring down, and we caused the earth to break forth into springs ; so that the water *of heaven and earth* met, according to the decree which had been established. And we bare him on *a vessel* composed of planks and nails ; which moved forward under our eyes :[3] as a recompence unto him who had been ungratefully rejected. And we left the *said vessel* for a sign : but *is* any one warned *thereby*? And how *severe* was my vengeance and my threatening ! Now have we made the Korân easy for admonition : but *is* any one admonished *thereby*? Ad charged *their prophet* with imposture : but how *severe* was my vengeance and my threatening ! Verily we sent against them a roaring[4] wind, on a day of continued ill luck :[5] it carried men away, as though they *had been* roots of palm-trees forcibly torn up.[6] And how *severe* was my vengeance and my threatening ! Now have we made the Korân easy for admonition : but *is* any one admonished *thereby*? Thamûd charged the admonitions *of their prophet* with falsehood, and said, Shall we follow a single man among us ? verily we should then be guilty of error and preposterous madness : is the *office of* admonition committed unto him *preferably to the rest* of us ? Nay : he is a liar *and* an insolent fellow. *But God said to Sâleh,* To-morrow shall they know who *is* the liar *and* the insolent person : for we will surely send the she-camel for a trial of

---

[1] That is, when the angel Israfil shall call men to judgment.

[2] This petition was not preferred by Noah till after he had suffered repeated violence from his people ; for it is related that one of them having fallen upon him and almost strangled him, when he came to himself he said, *O* LORD, *forgive them, for they know not what they do.* (Al Beidâwi.)

[3] *i.e.,* Under our special regard and keeping.

[4] Or, a *cold wind.*

[5] viz., On a Wednesday. See Chap. XLI. p. 465.

[6] It is related that they sought shelter in the clefts of rocks, and in pits, holding fast by one another ; but that the wind impetuously tore them away, and threw them down dead. (Al Beidâwi.)

them ;[1] and do thou observe them, and bear *their insults*
with patience : and prophesy unto them that the water
shall be divided between them,[2] and each portion *shall be*
sat down to *alternately*.   And they called their companion :[3]
and he took *a sword*,[4] and slew *her*.   But how *severe* was my
vengeance and my threatening !   For we sent against them
one cry *of the angel Gabriel*, and they became like the dry
sticks used by him who buildeth a fold *for cattle*.[5]   And
now have we made the Korân easy for admonition ; but *is*
any one admonished *thereby* ?   The people of Lot charged
his preaching with falsehood : but we sent against them *a
wind* driving a shower of stones, *which destroyed them all*
except the family of Lot ; whom we delivered early in the
morning, through favour from us.   Thus do we reward those
who are thankful.   And *Lot* had warned them of our severity
in chastising ; but they doubted of that warning.   And
they demanded his guests of him, *that they might abuse
them* : but we put out their eyes,[6] *saying*, Taste my vengeance, and my threatening.   And early in the morning a
lasting punishment[7] surprised them.   Taste, therefore, my
vengeance, and my threatening.   Now have we made the
Korân easy for admonition : but *is* any one admonished
thereby ?   The warning *of Moses* also came unto the people
of Pharaoh ; *but* they charged every one of our signs with
imposture : wherefore we chastised them with a mighty
and irresistible chastisement.   Are your unbelievers, *O
Meccans*, better than these ?   Is immunity from punishment *promised* unto you in the scriptures ?   Do they say,
We are a body *of men* able to prevail *against our enemies* ?
The multitude shall surely be put to flight, and shall turn
their back.[8]   But the hour *of judgment is* their threatened

---

[1] See Chap. VII. p. 149.

[2] That is, between the Thamûdites and the camel. See p. 365.

[3] Namely, Kodâr Ebn Salef ; who was not an Arab, but a stranger dwelling among the Thamûdites. See Chap VII. p. 149.

[4] Or, as the word also imports, *He became resolute and daring*.

[5] The words may signify either the dry boughs with which, in the East,
they make folds or enclosures, to fence their cattle from wind and cold ;
or the stubble and other stuff with which they litter them in those folds
during the winter season.

[6] So that their sockets became filled up even with the other parts of their
faces. This, it is said, was done by one stroke of the wing of the angel
Gabriel. See Chap. XI. p. 220.

[7] Under which they shall continue till they receive their full punishment
in hell.

[8] This prophecy was fulfilled by the overthrow of the Koreish at Bedr.
It is related, from a tradition of Omar, that when this passage was revealed,
Mohammed professed himself to be ignorant of its true meaning ; but **on**

time *of punishment* :[1] and that hour *shall be* more grievous
and more bitter *than their afflictions in this life.* Verily the
wicked *wander* in error, and *shall be tormented hereafter* in
burning flames. On that day they shall be dragged into
the fire on their faces ; *and it shall be said unto them,* Taste
ye the touch of hell. All things have we created *bound* by
a fixed decree : and our command *is* no more than a single
word,[2] like the twinkling of an eye. We have formerly
destroyed *nations* like unto you ; but *is* any *of you* warned
by their example ? Everything which they do *is recorded*
in the books *kept by the guardian angels* : and every *action,*
both small and great, *is* written down *in the preserved table.*
Moreover the pious *shall dwell* among gardens and rivers,
in the assembly of truth, in the presence of a most potent
king.

LV

THE CHAPTER OF THE MERCIFUL
Revealed at Mecca.[3]

IN THE NAME OF THE MOST MERCIFUL GOD.

THE Merciful hath taught *his* servant the Korân. He
created man : he hath taught him distinct speech.
The sun and the moon *run their courses* according to a certain rule : and the vegetables which creep on the ground
and the trees submit *to his disposition.* He also raised the
heavens ; and he appointed the balance,[4] that ye should not
transgress in respect to the balance : wherefore observe a
just weight, and diminish not the balance. And the earth
hath he prepared for living creatures : therein *are various*
fruits, and palm-trees bearing sheaths of flowers ; and grain
having chaff, and leaves. Which, therefore, of your LORD's
benefits will ye ungratefully deny ?[5] He created man of

the day of the battle of Bedr, he repeated these words as he was putting
on his coat of mail. (Al Beidâwi.)
   [1] *i.e.*, The time when they shall receive their full punishment ; what they
suffer in this world being only the forerunner or earnest of what they shall
feel in the next.
   [2] viz., *Kun, i.e., Be.* The passage may also be rendered, *The execution*
of our purpose is but a single act, exerted in a moment. Some suppose it
refers to the business of the day of judgment. (Al Beidâwi.)
   [3] Most of the commentators doubt whether this chapter was revealed at
Mecca or at Medina ; or partly at the one place, and partly at the other.
   [4] Or justice and equity in mutual dealings.
   [5] The words are directed to the two species of rational creatures, men and
genii, the verb and the pronoun being in the dual number. This verse is

dried clay like an earthen vessel : but he created the genii
of fire clear from smoke. Which, therefore, of your LORD's
benefits will ye ungratefully deny ? *He is* the LORD of the
east, and the LORD of the west.[1] Which, therefore, of your
LORD's benefits will ye ungratefully deny ? He hath let
loose the two seas,[2] that they meet each other : between
them *is placed* a bar which they cannot pass. Which,
therefore, of your LORD's benefits will ye ungratefully deny ?
From them are taken forth unions and lesser pearls.[3] Which,
therefore, of your LORD's benefits will ye ungratefully deny ?
His also *are* the ships, carrying their sails aloft in the sea,
like mountains. Which, therefore, of your LORD's benefits
will ye ungratefully deny ? Every *creature* which *liveth*
on the earth *is* subject to decay: but the glorious and honourable countenance of thy LORD shall remain *for ever*. Which,
therefore, of your LORD's benefits will ye ungratefully deny ?
Unto him do all *creatures* which *are* in heaven and earth
make petition : every day *is* he *employed* in *some new* work.[4]
Which, therefore, of your LORD's benefits will ye ungratefully deny ? We will surely attend to *judge* you, O men and
genii, *at the last day.* Which, therefore, of your LORD's
benefits will ye ungratefully deny ? O ye collective body
of genii and men, if ye be able to pass out of the confines
of heaven and earth,[5] pass forth : ye shall not pass forth
but by absolute power. Which, therefore, of your LORD's
benefits will ye ungratefully deny ? A flame of fire without smoke, and a smoke without flame[6] shall be sent down
upon you ; and ye shall not be able to defend yourselves
therefrom. Which, therefore, of your LORD's benefits will
ye ungratefully deny ? And when the heaven shall be rent
in sunder, and shall become *red as* a rose, *and shall melt* like
ointment.[7] Which, therefore, of your LORD's benefits

intercalated, or repeated by way of burden, throughout the whole chapter
no less than thirty-one times, which was done, as Marracci guesses, in
imitation of David. (See Psalm cxxxvi.)

[1] The original words are both in the dual number, and signify the different
points of the horizon at which the sun rises and sets at the summer and
winter solstice. See Chap. XXXVII. p. 436.

[2] Of salt water and fresh (see Chap. XXV.) ; or the Persian and Mediter-
ranean seas. (Al Beidâwi.)　　[3] *Coral and pearls* (Savary).

[4] In executing those things which he hath decreed from eternity ; by
giving life and death, raising one and abasing another, hearing prayers and
granting petitions, &c. (Al Beidâwi, Jallalo'ddin.)

[5] To fly from the power and to avoid the decree of GOD.

[6] Or, as the word also signifies, molten brass, which shall be poured on
the heads of the damned.

[7] Or, *shall appear like red leather* ; according to a different signification
of the original word.

will ye ungratefully deny ? On that day neither man nor genius shall be asked concerning his sin.[1] Which, therefore, of your LORD's benefits will ye ungratefully deny ? The wicked shall be known by their marks[2] and they shall be taken by the forelocks and the feet, *and shall be cast into hell.* Which, therefore, of your LORD's benefits will ye ungratefully deny ? This *is* hell, which the wicked deny as a falsehood : they shall pass to and fro between the same and hot boiling water.[3] Which, therefore, of your LORD's benefits will ye ungratefully deny ? But for him who dreadeth the tribunal of his LORD, *are prepared* two gardens:[4] Which, therefore, of your LORD's benefits will ye ungratefully deny ? planted with shady trees. Which, therefore, of your LORD's benefits will ye ungratefully deny ? In each of them *shall be* two fountains flowing. Which, therefore, of your LORD's benefits will ye ungratefully deny ? In each of them *shall there be* of every fruit two kinds.[5] Which, therefore, of your LORD's benefits will ye ungratefully deny ? They shall repose on couches, the linings whereof *shall be* of thick silk interwoven with gold : and the fruit of the two gardens *shall be* near at hand *to gather.*[6] Which, therefore, of your LORD's benefits will ye ungratefully deny ? Therein *shall receive them beauteous* damsels, refraining their eyes *from beholding any besides their spouses :* whom no man shall have deflowered before them, neither any genius. Which, therefore, of your LORD's benefits will ye ungratefully deny ? *Having complexions* like rubies and pearls. Which, therefore, of your LORD's benefits will ye ungratefully deny ? *Shall* the reward of good works *be* any other than good ? Which, therefore, of your LORD's benefits will ye ungratefully deny ? And besides these *there shall be* two *other* gardens.[7] Which, therefore, of your

[1] For their crimes will be known by their different marks ; as it follows in the text. This, says Al Beidâwi, is to be understood of the time when they shall be raised to life, and shall be led towards the tribunal : for when they come to trial, they will then undergo an examination, as is declared in several places of the Korân. By genius is meant one of the genii or djinn.

[2] Sale, Prel. Disc. Sect. IV.

[3] For the only respite they shall have from the flames of hell, will be when they are suffered to go to drink this scalding liquor. Chap. XXXVII.

[4] *i.e.,* One distinct paradise for men, and another for genii, or, as some imagine, two gardens for each person ; one as a reward due to his works, and the other as a free and superabundant gift, &c.

[5] Some being known, and like the fruits of the earth ; and others of new and unknown species, or fruits both green and ripe.

[6] So that a man may reach them as he sits or lies down.

[7] For the inferior classes of the inhabitants of paradise.

LORD's benefits will ye ungratefully deny? Of a dark green.[1] Which, therefore, of your LORD's benefits will ye ungratefully deny? In each of them *shall be* two fountains pouring forth plenty of water. Which, therefore, of your LORD's benefits will ye ungratefully deny? In each of them *shall be* fruits, and palm-trees, and pomegranates. Which, therefore, of your LORD's benefits will ye ungratefully deny? Therein *shall be* agreeable and beauteous *damsels*, Which, therefore, of your LORD's benefits will ye ungratefully deny? Having fine black eyes; *and* kept in pavilions *from public view*. Which, therefore, of your LORD's benefits will ye ungratefully deny? Whom no man shall have deflowered, before *their destined spouses*, nor any genius.[2] Which, therefore, of your LORD's benefits will ye ungratefully deny? *Therein shall they delight themselves*, lying on green cushions and beautiful carpets. Which, therefore, of your LORD's benefits will ye ungratefully deny? Blessed be the name of thy LORD, possessed of glory and honour!

LVI

THE CHAPTER OF THE INEVITABLE

Revealed at Mecca.

IN THE NAME OF THE MOST MERCIFUL GOD.

WHEN the inevitable[3] *day of judgment* shall suddenly come, no *soul* shall charge *the prediction of* its coming with falsehood: it will abase *some*, and exalt *others*. When the earth shall be shaken with a violent shock; and the mountains shall be dashed in pieces, and shall become *as* dust scattered abroad; and ye shall be *separated into* three *distinct* classes: the companions of the right hand (how *happy shall* the companions of the right hand *be*!), and the companions of the left hand[4] (how *miserable shall*

---

[1] Whence, says Al Beidâwi, it may be inferred that these gardens will chiefly produce herbs or the inferior sorts of vegetables, whereas the former will be planted chiefly with fruit-trees. The following part of this description also falls short of that of the other gardens, prepared for the superior classes. [2] See p. 515 note.[1]

[3] The original word, the force whereof cannot well be expressed by a single one in English, signifies a calamitous accident, which falls surely and with sudden violence, and is therefore made use of here to design the day of judgment.

[4] That is, the blessed and the damned; who may be thus distinguished here, because the books wherein their actions are registered will be delivered into the right hands of the former and into the left hands of the latter

the companions of the left hand *be* !), and those who have preceded *others in the faith* shall precede *them to paradise.*[1] These *are* they who shall approach near *unto God* : *they shall dwell* in gardens of delight. (*There shall be* many of the former *religions* ; and few of the last.[2]) Reposing on couches adorned with gold and precious stones ; sitting opposite to one another thereon. Youths which shall continue *in their bloom* for ever, shall go round about *to attend* them, with goblets, and beakers, and a cup of flowing *wine :* their heads shall not ache by *drinking* the same, neither shall their reason be disturbed : and with fruits of the *sorts* which they shall choose, and the flesh of birds of the *kind* which they shall desire. And *there shall accompany them* fair damsels having large black eyes ; resembling pearls hidden *in their shells* : as a reward for that which they shall have wrought. They shall not hear therein any vain discourse, or any charge of sin ; but only the salutation, Peace ! Peace ! And the companions of the right hand (how *happy shall* the companions of the right hand *be* !) *shall have their abode* among lote-trees free from thorns, and trees of mauz[3] loaded regularly *with their produce* from top to bottom ; *under* an extended shade, *near* a flowing water,[4] and *amidst* fruits in abundance, which shall not fail, nor shall be forbidden *to be gathered* : and *they shall repose themselves* on lofty beds.[5] Verily we have created *the damsels of paradise*

(Al Beidâwi, Jallalo'ddin), though the words translated *right hand* and *left hand* do also signify *happiness* and *misery.*

[1] Either the first converts to Mohammedism, or the prophets, who were the respective leaders of their people, or any persons who have been eminent examples of piety and virtue, may be here intended. The original words literally rendered are, *The leaders, the leaders* : which repetition, as some suppose, was designed to express the dignity of these persons and the certainty of their future glory and happiness. (Al Beidâwi.)

[2] *i.e.*, There shall be more *leaders*, who have preceded others in faith and good works, among the followers of the several prophets from Adam down to Mohammed, than of the followers of Mohammed himself. (Al Beidâwi.)

[3] The original word *talh* is the name, not only of the mauz (see note p. 441), but also of a very tall and thorny tree, which bears abundance of flowers of an agreeable smell (vide J. Leon. Descript. Africæ, l. 2), and seems to be the acacia.

[4] Which shall be conveyed in channels to such places and in such manner as every one shall desire. (Al Beidâwi.) Al Beidâwi observes that the condition of the few who have preceded others in faith and good works, is represented by whatever may render a city life agreeable ; and that the condition of the companions of the right hand, or the generality of the blessed, is represented by those things which make the principal pleasure of a country life ; and that this is done to show the difference of the two conditions.

[5] The word translated *beds*, signifies also, by way of metaphor, *wives* or *concubines ;* and if the latter sense be preferred, the passage may be rendered thus, *And they shall enjoy damsels raised on lofty couches, whom we have created,* &c.

by a *peculiar* creation [1] : and we have made them virgins, beloved by their husbands, of equal age *with them* ; for *the
delight of* the companions of the right hand. *There shall
be* many of the former *religions*, and many ot the latter.[2]
And the companions of the left hand (how *miserable shall*
the companions of the left hand *be* !) *shall dwell* amidst
burning winds,[3] and scalding water, under the shade of a
black smoke, neither cool nor agreeable. For they enjoyed
the pleasures of life before this, *while on earth* ; and obsti-
ately persisted in a heinous wickedness : and they said,
After we shall have died, and become dust and bones, *shall*
we surely *be* raised to life ? *Shall* our forefathers also *be
raised with us* ? Say, Verily both the first and the last
shall surely be gathered together *to judgment*, at the prefixed time of a known day. Then ye, *O men*, who have
erred, *and* denied *the resurrection* as a falsehood, shall surely
eat of *the fruit of* the tree of Al Zakkum, and shall fill *your*
bellies therewith : and ye shall drink thereon boiling water ;
and ye shall drink as a thirsty camel drinketh. This *shall
be* their entertainment on the day of judgment. We have
created you : will ye not therefore believe *that we can raise
you from the dead* ? What think ye ? The *seed* which ye
emit, do ye create the same, or *are* we the creators *thereof* ?
We have decreed death unto you *all* ; and we shall not be
prevented. *We are able* to substitute *others* like unto you
in your stead, and to produce you *again* in the *condition
or form* which ye know not. Ye know the original production *by creation* ; will ye not therefore consider *that we are
able to reproduce you by resuscitation* ? What think ye ?
The *grain* which ye sow, do ye cause the same to spring forth,
or do we cause *it* to spring forth ? If we pleased, verily we
could render the same dry and fruitless, *so that* ye would

[1] Having created them purposely of finer materials than the females of
this world, and subject to none of those inconveniences which are natural to
the sex (Sale, Prel. Disc. Sect. IV.). Some understand this passage of
the beatified women ; who, though they died old and ugly, shall yet be
restored to their youth and beauty in paradise (see Sale, Prel. Disc. Sect.
IV. p. 110).

[2] Father Marracci thinks this to be a manifest contradiction to what is
said above, *There shall be many of the former and few of the latter* : but Al
Beidâwi obviates such an objection by observing that the preceding passage
speaks of the *leaders* only, and those who have preceded others in faith and
good works ; and the passage before us speaks of the righteous of inferior
merit and degree ; so that though there be many of both sorts, yet there
may be few of one sort, comparatively speaking, in respect to the
other.

[3] Which shall penetrate into the passages of their bodies.

not cease to wonder,[1] *saying,* Verily we have contracted debts[2] *for seed and labour* ; but we are not permitted[3] *to reap the fruit thereof.* What think ye ? The water which ye drink, do ye send down the same from the clouds, or *are* we the senders *thereof* ? If we pleased, we could render the same brackish. Will ye not therefore give thanks ? What think ye ? The fire which ye strike, do ye produce the tree *whence ye obtain* the same,[4] or *are* we the producers *thereof* ? We have ordained the same for an admonition,[5] and an advantage unto those who travel through the deserts. Wherefore praise the name of thy LORD, the great *God.* Moreover I swear[6] by the setting of the stars (and it *is* surely a great oath, if ye knew *it*) ; that this *is* the excellent Korân, *the original whereof is written* in the preserved book : none shall touch the same, except those who are clean.[7] *It is* a revelation from the LORD of all creatures. Will ye, therefore, despise this new revelation ? And do ye make *this return* for your food *which ye receive from God,* that ye deny *yourselves to be obliged to him for the same* ?[8] When *the soul of a dying person* cometh up to *his* throat, and ye at the same time are looking on (and we are nigher unto him than ye, but ye see not *his true condition*) : would ye not, if ye are not to be rewarded *for your actions hereafter,* cause the same to return *into the body,* if ye speak truth ?[9] And whether he be of those who shall approach near *unto God,*[10]

---

[1] Qr *to repent* of your time and labour bestowed to little purpose, &c.

[2] Or, *We are undone.*

[3] Or, *We are unfortunate wretches,* who are denied the necessaries of life.

[4] See Chap. XXXVI. p. 435.

[5] To put men in mind of the resurrection (see Chap. XXXVI.) ; which the production of fire in some sort resembles ; or, of the fire of hell. (Al Beidâwi.)

[6] The particle *la* is generally supposed to be intensive in this place ; but if it be taken for a negative, the words must be translated, *I will not* or *do not swear,* because what is here asserted is too manifest to need the confirmation of an oath. (Al Beidâwi.)

[7] Or, *Let none touch the same,* &c. Purity both of body and mind being requisite in him who would use this book with the respect he ought, and hopes to edify by it : for which reason these words are usually written on the cover. (Sale, Prel. Disc. Sect. III. p. 74.)

[8] By ascribing the rains, which fertilize your lands, to the influence of the stars. (Sale, Prel. Disc. Sect. I.) Some copies instead of *rizkacom, i.e., your food,* read *shocracom, i.e., your gratitude* ; and then the passage may be rendered thus, *And do ye make this return of gratitude,* for GOD's revealing the Korân, *that ye reject* the same *as a fiction* ?

[9] The meaning of this obscure passage is, if ye shall not be obliged to give an account of your actions at the last day, as by your denying the resurrection ye seem to believe, cause the soul of the dying person to return into his body ; for ye may as easily do that as avoid the general judgment. (Jallal., Al Beidâwi.)

[10] That is, of the *leaders,* or first professors of the faith.

his reward shall be rest, and mercy, and a garden of delights: or whether he be of the companions of the right hand, *he shall be saluted with the salutation*, Peace be unto thee ! by the companions of the right hand *his brethren* : or whether he be of those who have rejected *the true faith, and* gone astray, *his* entertainment *shall consist* of boiling water, and the burning of hell *fire.* Verily this *is* a certain truth. Wherefore praise the name of thy LORD, the great *God.*

LVII

THE CHAPTER OF IRON [1]

Revealed at Mecca, or at Medina. [2]

IN THE NAME OF THE MOST MERCIFUL GOD.

WHATEVER *is* in heaven and earth singeth praise unto GOD ; and he *is* mighty *and* wise. His *is* the kingdom of heaven and earth ; he giveth life, and he putteth to death ; and he *is* almighty. He *is* the first and the last ; the manifest and the hidden : and he knoweth all things. *It is* he who created the heavens and the earth in six days ; and then ascended *his* throne. He knoweth that which entereth into the earth, and that which issueth out of the same ; and that which descendeth from heaven, and that which ascendeth thereto : and he *is* with you wheresoever ye be : for GOD seeth that which ye do. His *is* the kingdom of heaven and earth ; and unto GOD shall *all* things return. He causeth the night to succeed the day, and he causeth the day to succeed the night ; and he knoweth the innermost part of *men's* breasts. Believe in GOD and his apostle, and lay out *in alms* a part of the *wealth* whereof GOD hath made you inheritors : for unto such of you as believe, and bestow alms, *shall be given* a great reward. And what aileth you, that ye believe not in GOD, when the apostle inviteth you to believe in your LORD ; and he hath received your covenant[3] *concerning this matter*, if ye believe *any proposition* ? *It is* he who hath sent down unto his servant evident signs, that he may lead you out of darkness into

---

[1] The word occurs towards the end of the chapter.

[2] It is uncertain which of the two places was the scene of revelation of this chapter.

[3] That is, ye are obliged to believe in him by the strongest arguments and motives.

light ; for GOD *is* compassionate *and* merciful unto you. And what aileth you, that ye contribute not *of your substance* for the defence of GOD's true religion ? Since unto GOD *appertaineth* the inheritance of heaven and earth. Those among you who shall have contributed and fought *in defence of the faith,* before the taking *of Mecca,* shall not be held equal *with those who shall contribute and fight for the same afterwards.*[1] These shall be superior in degree unto those who shall contribute and fight *for the propagation of the faith* after *the above-mentioned success :* but unto all hath GOD promised a most excellent *reward ;* and GOD well knoweth that which ye do. Who *is* he that will lend unto GOD an acceptable loan ? for he will double the same unto him, and he shall receive *moreover* an honourable reward. On a *certain* day, thou shalt see the true believers of both sexes : their light shall run before them, and on their right hands ;[2] *and it shall be said unto them,* Good tidings unto you this day : gardens through which rivers flow ; *ye* shall remain therein for ever. This will be great felicity. On that day the hypocritical men and the hypocritical women shall say unto those who believe, Stay for us,[3] that we may borrow *some* of your light. It shall be answered, Return back *into the world,* and seek light. And a high wall shall be set betwixt them, wherein *shall be* a gate, within which *shall be* mercy ; and without, it, over against the same, the torment *of hell.* The *hypocrites* shall call out unto *the true believers, saying,* Were we not with you ? They shall answer, Yea ; but ye seduced your own souls *by your hypocrisy :* and ye waited *our ruin ;* and ye doubted *concerning the faith,* and *your* wishes deceived you, until the decree of GOD came, *and ye died ;* and the deceiver deceived you concerning GOD. This day, therefore, a ransom shall not be accepted of you, nor of those who have been unbelievers. Your abode *shall be hell* fire : this *is* what ye have deserved ; and an unhappy journey *shall it be thither* ! Is not the time yet come unto those who believe, that their hearts should humbly submit to the admonition of GOD, and to that truth which hath been revealed ; and that they be not as those

---

[1] Because afterwards there was not so great necessity for either, the Mohammedan religion being firmly established by that great success.

[2] One light leading them the right way to paradise, and the other proceeding from the book wherein their actions are recorded, which they will hold in their right hand.

[3] For the righteous will hasten to paradise swift as lightning

unto whom the scripture was given heretofore, and to whom the time *of forbearance* was prolonged, but their hearts were hardened, and many of them *were* wicked doers ? Know that GOD quickeneth the earth, after it hath been dead. Now have we distinctly declared *our* signs unto you, that ye may understand. Verily *as to* the almsgivers, both men and women, and *those who* lend unto GOD an acceptable loan, he will double the same unto them ; and they shall *moreover* receive an honourable reward. And they who believe in GOD and his apostles, these are the men of veracity and the witnesses in the presence of their LORD : they *shall have* their reward and their light. But *as to* those who believe not, and accuse our signs of falsehood, they *shall be* the companions of hell. Know that this present life *is* only a toy and a vain amusement : and *worldly* pomp, and the affectation of glory among you, and the multiplying of riches and children, *are* as the plants nourished by the rain, the springing up whereof delighteth the husbandmen ; afterwards they wither, so that thou seest the same turn yellow, and at length they become dry stubble. And in the life to come *will be* a severe punishment *for those who covet worldly grandeur* ; and pardon from GOD, and favour *for those who renounce it* : for this present life *is* no other than a deceitful provision. Hasten with emulation to *obtain* pardon from your LORD, and paradise, the extent whereof equalleth the extent of heaven and earth, prepared for those who believe in GOD and his apostles. This *is* the bounty of GOD ; he will give the same unto whom he pleaseth ; and GOD is endued with great bounty. No accident happeneth in the earth, nor in your persons, but *the same was entered* in the book *of our decrees*, before we created it : verily this *is* easy with GOD : *and this is written* lest ye *immoderately* grieve for the *good* which escapeth you, or rejoice for that which happeneth unto you ; for GOD loveth no proud *or* vain-glorious person, *or those* who are covetous, and command men covetousness. And whoso turneth aside *from giving alms* ; verily GOD *is* self-sufficient, worthy to be praised. We formerly sent our apostles with evident *miracles and arguments* ; and we sent down with them the scriptures and the balance,[1] that men might observe justice : and we

---

[1] *i.e.*, A rule of justice. Some think that a balance was actually brought down from heaven by the angel Gabriel to Noah, the use of which he was ordered to introduce among his people.

sent *them* down iron,[1] wherein is mighty strength for war,[2] and *various* advantages unto mankind : that GOD may know who assisteth him and his apostles in secret ;[3] for GOD *is* strong *and* mighty. We formerly sent Noah and Abraham, and we established in their posterity the gift of prophecy, and the scripture : and of them *some were* directed, but many of them *were* evil-doers. Afterwards we caused our apostles to succeed in their footsteps ; and we caused Jesus the son of Mary to succeed *them,* and we gave him the gospel : and we put in the hearts of those who followed him, compassion and mercy : but *as to* the monastic state, they instituted the same (we did not prescribe it to them) only out of a desire to please GOD ; yet they observed not the same as it ought truly to be observed. And we gave unto such of them as believed, their reward : but many of them *were* wicked doers. O ye who believe *in the former prophets,*[4] fear GOD, and believe in his apostle *Mohammed* : he will give you two portions of his mercy,[5] and he will ordain you a light wherein ye may walk, and he will forgive you ; for GOD *is* ready to forgive *and* merciful : that those who have received the scriptures may know that they have not power over any of the favours of GOD,[6] and that good *is* the hand of GOD ; he bestoweth the same on whom he pleaseth, for GOD *is* endued with great beneficence.

---

[1] That is, we taught them how to dig the same from mines. Al Zamakhshari adds that Adam is said to have brought down with him from paradise five things made of iron, viz., an anvil, a pair of tongs, two hammers, a greater and a lesser, and a needle.

[2] Warlike instruments and weapons being generally made of iron.

[3] That is, sincerely and heartily.

[4] These words are directed to the Jews and Christians, or rather to the latter only.

[5] One as a recompence for their believing in Mohammed, and the other as a recompence for their believing in the prophets who preceded him ; for they will not lose the reward of their former religion, though it be now abrogated by the promulgation of Islâm. (Al Beidâwi.)

[6] *i.e.,* That they cannot expect to receive any of the favours above mentioned, because they believe not in his apostle, and those favours are annexed to faith in him ; or, that they have not power to dispose of GOD's favours, particularly of the greatest of them, the gift of prophecy, so as to appropriate the same to whom they please. (Al Beidâwi.)

LVIII

THE CHAPTER OF THE WOMAN WHO DISPUTED

Revealed at Medina.[1]

IN THE NAME OF THE MOST MERCIFUL GOD.

(XXVIII.) NOW hath GOD heard the speech of her who disputed with thee concerning her husband, and made her complaint unto GOD ;[2] and GOD hath heard your mutual discourse ; for GOD *both* heareth *and* seeth. *As to* those among you who divorce their wives by declaring that they will thereafter regard them as their mothers ; *let them know that* they *are* not their mothers. They only *are* their mothers who brought them forth ;[3] and they certainly utter an unjustifiable saying, and a falsehood : but GOD *is* gracious *and* ready to forgive. Those who divorce their wives by declaring that they will for the future regard them as their mothers, and afterwards would repair[4] what they have said, *shall be obliged* to free a captive,[5] before they touch one another. This *is* what ye are warned *to perform* : and GOD *is* well apprised of that which ye do. And whoso findeth not *a captive to redeem, shall observe* a fast of two consecutive months, before they touch one another. And whoso shall not be able *to fast that time,*

---

[1] Some are of opinion that the first ten verses of this chapter, ending with these words, *and fear* GOD, *before whom ye shall be assembled*, were revealed at Mecca. (Al Beidâwi.) Section XXVIII. begins with it.

[2] Rodwell entitles this chapter, " She who pleaded," which is a better rendering of the phrase to modern ears. Palmer calls it " The Chapter of the Wrangler." The woman was Khawla bint Thálaba, wife of Aws Ebn al Sâmat, who, being divorced by her husband by a form in use among the Arabs in the time of ignorance, viz., by saying to her, *Thou art to me as the back of my mother* (see Chap. XXXIII. p. 407), came to ask Mohammed's opinion whether they were necessarily obliged to a separation ; and he told her that it was not lawful for her to cohabit with her husband any more : to which she replying, that her husband had not put her away, the prophet repeated his former decision, adding that such form of speaking was by general consent understood to imply a perpetual separation. Upon this the woman, being greatly concerned because of the smallness of her children, went home, and uttered her complaint to GOD in prayer : and thereupon this passage was revealed (Al Beidâwi, Jallalo'ddin, &c.), allowing a man to take his wife again, notwithstanding his having pronounced the above-mentioned form of divorce, on doing certain acts of charity or mortification, by way of penance.

[3] And therefore no woman ought to be placed in the same degree of prohibition, except those whom GOD has joined with them, as nursing mothers, and the wives of the prophet. (Al Beidâwi. See Chaps. IV. and XXXIII.)

[4] This seems to be here the true meaning of the original word, which properly signifies *to return*, and is variously expounded by the Mohammedan doctors.

[5] Which captive, according to the most received decisions, ought to be a true believer, as is ordered for the expiation of manslaughter. (See Chap. IV.).

shall feed threescore poor men. *This is ordained you*, that ye may believe in GOD and his apostle. These *are* the statutes of GOD : and for the unbelievers *is prepared* a grievous torment. Verily they who oppose GOD and his apostle, shall be brought low, as *the unbelievers* who preceded them were brought low. And now have we sent down manifest signs : and an ignominious punishment awaiteth the unbelievers. On a *certain* day GOD shall raise them all to life, and shall declare unto them that which they have wrought. GOD hath taken an exact account thereof ; but they have forgotten the same : and GOD *is* witness over all things. Dost thou not perceive that GOD knoweth whatever *is* in heaven and in earth ? There is no private discourse among three persons, but he *is* the fourth of them ; nor *among* five, but he *is* the sixth of them ; neither *among* a smaller *number* than this, nor a larger, but he *is* with them, wheresoever they be : and he will declare unto them that which they have done, on the day of resurrection ; for GOD knoweth all things. Hast thou not observed those who have been forbidden to use clandestine discourse, but afterwards return to what they have been forbidden, and discourse privily among themselves of wickedness, and enmity, and disobedience towards the apostle ? [1] And when they come unto thee, they salute thee with that *form of salutation* wherewith GOD doth not salute thee : [2] and they say among themselves, *by way of derision*, Would not GOD punish us for what we say, *if this man were a prophet* ? Hell *shall be* their sufficient *punishment* : they shall go down into the same to be burned ; and an unhappy journey *shall it be* ! O true believers, when ye discourse privily together, discourse not of wickedness, and enmity, and disobedience towards the apostle ; but discourse of justice and piety : and fear GOD, before whom ye shall be assembled. Verily the clandestine discourse *of the infidels proceedeth* from Satan, that he may grieve the true believers : but there shall be none to hurt them in the least, unless by the permission of GOD ; wherefore in GOD let the faithful trust. O true believers, when it is said unto you, Make

---

[1] That is, the Jews and hypocritical Moslems, who caballed privately together against Mohammed, and made signs to one another when they saw the true believers ; and this they continued to do, notwithstanding they were forbidden.

[2] It seems they used, instead of *Al salâm aleica, i.e., Peace be upon thee,* to say, *Al sâm aleica, i.e., Mischief on thee,* &c. (Al Beidâwi, Jallalo'ddin.)

room in the assembly; make room :[1] GOD will grant you ample room *in paradise*. And when it is said *unto you*, Rise up; rise up: GOD will raise those of you who believe, and those to whom knowledge is given, to *superior* degrees of *honour* : and GOD *is* fully apprised of that which ye do. O true believers, when ye go to speak with the apostle, give alms previously to your discoursing *with him* :[2] this *will be* better for you and more pure. But if ye find not *what to give*, verily GOD *will be* gracious *and* merciful *unto you.* Do ye fear to give alms previously to your discoursing *with the prophet, lest ye should impoverish yourselves* ? Therefore if ye do *it* not, and GOD is gracious unto you, *by dispensing with the said precept for the future*, be constant at prayer, and pay the legal alms; and obey GOD and his apostle *in all other matters* : for GOD well knoweth that which ye do. Hast thou not observed those who have taken for their friends a people against whom GOD is incensed ?[3] They *are* neither of you nor of them :[4] and they swear to a lie[5] knowingly. GOD hath prepared for them a grievous punishment; for it is evil which they do. They have taken their oaths for a cloak, and they have turned *men* aside from the way of GOD : wherefore a shameful punishment awaiteth them; neither their wealth nor their children shall avail them at all against GOD. These *shall be* the inhabitants of *hell* fire; they shall abide therein for ever. On a *certain* day GOD shall raise them all : then will they swear unto him, as they swear *now* unto you, imagining that it will be of service to them. Are they not liars ? Satan hath prevailed against them, and hath caused them to forget the remembrance of GOD. These *are* the party of the devil; and *shall* not the party of the devil *be* doomed to perdition ? Verily they who oppose GOD and his apostle, *shall be placed among* the most vile. GOD hath written, Verily I will prevail, and my apostles : for GOD *is* strong *and* mighty. Thou shalt not find people who believe in GOD and the last day, to love

---

[1] In this passage the Moslems are commanded to give place, in the public assemblies, to the prophet and the more honourable of his companions; and not to press and crowd upon him, as they used to do, out of a desire of being near him, and hearing his discourse.

[2] To show your sincerity, and to honour the apostle. It is doubted whether this be a counsel or a precept; but, however, it continued but a very little while in force, being agreed on all hands to be abrogated by the following passage, *Do ye fear to give alms*, &c. (Al Beidâwi.)

[3] *i.e.*, The Jews.

[4] Being hypocrites, and wavering between the two parties.

[5] *i.e.*, They have solemnly professed Islâm, which they believe not in their hearts.

him who opposeth GOD and his apostle ; although they be their fathers, or their sons, or their brethren, or their nearest relations. In the hearts of these hath GOD written faith ; and he hath strengthened them with his spirit : and he will lead them into gardens, beneath which rivers flow, to remain therein for ever. GOD is well pleased in them, and they are well pleased in him. These are the party of GOD ; and shall not the party of GOD prosper ?

LIX

THE CHAPTER OF THE EMIGRATION [1]

Revealed at Medina.

IN THE NAME OF THE MOST MERCIFUL GOD.

WHATEVER *is* in heaven and earth celebrateth the praise of GOD : and he *is* the mighty, the wise. *It was* he who caused those who believed not, of the people who receive the scripture, to depart from their habitations at the first emigration.[2] Ye did not think that they would

---

[1] The original word signifies the quitting or removing from one's native country or settlement, to dwell elsewhere, whether it be by choice or compulsion.

[2] The people here intended were the Jews of the tribe of Al Nadîr, who dwelt in Medina, and when Mohammed fled thither from Mecca, promised him to stand neutral between him and his opponents, and made a treaty with him to that purpose. When he had gained the battle of Bedr, they confessed that he was the prophet described in the law : but upon his receiving that disgrace at Ohod, they changed their note ; and Caab Ebn al Ashraf, with forty horse, went and made a league with Abu Sofiân, which they confirmed by oath. Upon this, Mohammed got Caab dispatched, and, in the fourth year of the Hejra, set forward against Al Nadîr, and besieged them in their fortress, which stood about three miles from Medina, for six days, at the end of which they capitulated, and were allowed to depart, on condition that they should entirely quit that place : and accordingly some of them went into Syria, and others to Khaibar and Hira. This was the *first emigration*, mentioned in the passage before us. The other happened several years, after, in the reign of Omar, when that Khalîf banished those who had settled at Khaibar, and obliged them to depart out of Arabia. (Al Beidâwi, Jallal., &c. Vide Abulf. Vit. Moh. c. 35.). Dr. Prideaux, speaking of Mohammed's obliging those of Al Nadîr to quit their settlements, says that a party of his men pursued those who fled into Syria, and having overtaken them, put them all to the sword, excepting only one man that escaped. *With such cruelty*, continues he, *did those barbarians first set up to fight for that imposture they had been deluded into.* (Prid. Life of Mah. p. 82.) But a learned gentleman has already observed that this is all grounded on a mistake, which the doctor was led into by an imperfection in the printed edition of Elmacinus ; where, after mentioning the expulsion of the Nadîrites, are inserted some incoherent words relating to another action which happened the month before, and wherein seventy Moslems, instead of putting others to the sword, were surprised and put to the sword themselves

go forth : and they thought that their fortresses would
protect them against GOD. But *the chastisement of* GOD
came upon them, from whence they did not expect ; and
he cast terror into their hearts. They pulled down their
houses with their own hands,[1] and the hands of the true
believers. Wherefore take example *from them*, O ye who
have eyes. And if GOD had not doomed them to banish-
ment, he had surely punished them in this world ;[2] and in
the world to come they shall suffer the torment of *hell* fire.
This because they opposed GOD and his apostle : and whoso
opposeth GOD, verily GOD *will be* severe in punishing *him*.
What palm-trees ye cut down, or left standing on their
roots, *were so cut down or left* by the will of GOD ; and that
he might disgrace the wicked doers. And *as to the spoils*
of these *people* which GOD hath granted *wholly* to his apostle,[3]
ye did not push forward any horses or camels against the
same ;[4] but GOD giveth unto his apostles dominion over
whom he pleaseth : for GOD *is* almighty. *The spoils* of the
inhabitants of the towns which GOD hath granted to his
apostle, *are due* unto GOD and to the apostle, and him who
is of kin *to the apostle*, and the orphans, and the poor, and
the traveller ; that they may not be *for ever divided* in a
circle among such of you as are rich. What the apostle
shall give you, that accept ; and what he shall forbid you,
that abstain from : and fear GOD ; for GOD *is* severe in
chastising. *A part also belongeth* to the poor Mohâjerîn,[5]
who have been dispossessed of their houses and their substance, seeking favour from GOD, and *his* goodwill, and
assisting GOD and his apostle. These are the men of
veracity. And they who quietly possessed the town *of Medina*,
and *professed* the faith *without molestation*, before them,[6] love

together with their leader Al Mondar Ebn Omar, Caab Ebn Zeid alone
escaping. (Vide Gagnier, not. in Abulf. Vit. Moh. p 72.)

[1] Doing what damage they could, that the Moslems might make the less
advantage of what they were obliged to leave behind them.

[2] By delivering them up to slaughter and captivity, as he did those of
the Koreidha.

[3] It is remarkable that in this expedition the spoils were not divided according to the law given for that purpose in the Korân (Chap. VIII. p. 172), but
were granted to the apostle, and declared to be entirely in his disposition. The
reason was, because the place was taken without the assistance of horse,
which became a rule for the future. (Vide Abulf. Vit. Moh. p. 91.)

[4] For the settlement of those of Al Nadîr being so near Medina, the Moslems went all on foot thither, except only the prophet himself. (Al Beidâwi.)

[5] Wherefore Mohammed distributed those spoils among the Mohâjerîn,
or those who had fled from Mecca, only, and gave no part thereof to
the Ansârs, or those of Medina, except only to three of them, who were in
necessitous circumstances. (Al Beidâwi. Vide Abulf. ubi sup. p. 72).

[6] That is, the Ansârs ; who enjoyed their houses and the free exercise of

him who hath fled unto them, and find in their breasts no want of that which is given *the Mohâjerîn*,[1] but prefer *them* before themselves, although there be indigence among them. And whoso is preserved from the covetousness of his own soul, those shall surely prosper. And they who have come after them[2] say, O LORD, forgive us and our brethren who have preceded us in the faith, and put not into our hearts ill-will against those who have believed : O LORD, verily thou *art* compassionate *and* merciful. Hast thou not observed those who play the hypocrites ? They say unto their brethren who believe not, of those who have received the scriptures,[3] Verily if ye be expelled *your habitations*, we will surely go forth with you ; and we will not pay obedience, in your respect unto any one for ever : and if ye be attacked, we will certainly assist you. But GOD is witness that they *are* liars. Verily if they be expelled, they will not go forth with them ; and if they be attacked, they will not assist them ;[4] and if they do not assist them, they will surely turn their backs : and they shall not be protected. Verily ye *are* stronger *than they*, by reason of the terror *cast* into their breasts from GOD. This, because they *are* not people of prudence. They will not fight against you in a body, except in fenced towns, or from behind walls. Their strength in war among themselves *is* great :[5] thou thinkest them *to be* united ; but their hearts are divided. This, because they *are* people who do not understand. Like those who lately preceded them,[6] they have tasted the evil consequence of their deed ; and a painful torment *is prepared* for them *hereafter. Thus have the hypocrites deceived the Jews :* like the devil, when he saith unto a man, Be thou an infidel ; and when he is become an infidel, he saith, Verily I *am* clear of thee ; for I fear GOD, the LORD of all creatures.   Where-

their religion before the Hejra, while the converts of Mecca were persecuted and harassed by the idolaters.

[1] *i.e.*, And bear them no grudge or envy on that account.

[2] The persons here meant seem to be those who fled from Mecca after Mohammed began to gain strength, and his religion had made a considerable progress.

[3] That is, the Jews of the tribe of Al Nadîr.

[4] And it happened accordingly ; for Ebn Obba and his confederates wrote to the Nadîrites to this purpose, but never performed their promise. (Al Beidâwi.)

[5] *i.e.*, It is not their weakness or cowardice which makes them decline a field battle with you, since they show strength and valour enough in their wars with one another ; but both fail them when they enter into the lists with GOD and his apostle.

[6] viz., The idolaters who were slain at Bedr ; or the Jews of Kainokâ, who were plundered and sent into exile before those of Al Nadîr.

fore the end of them both shall be that they *shall dwell* in *hell* fire, abiding therein for ever : and this *shall be* the recompence of the unjust. O true believers, fear GOD; and let a soul look what it sendeth before for the morrow :[1] and fear GOD, for GOD *is* well acquainted with that which ye do. And be not as those who have forgotten GOD, and whom he hath caused to forget their own souls : these are the wicked doers. The inhabitants of *hell* fire and the inhabitants of paradise shall not be held equal. The inhabitants of paradise are they who shall enjoy felicity. If we had sent down this Korân on a mountain, thou wouldst certainly have seen the same humble itself, and cleave in sunder for fear of GOD. These similitudes do we propose unto men, that they may consider. He *is* GOD, besides whom there is no GOD ; who knoweth that which is future and that which is present : he *is* the most Merciful ; he *is* GOD, besides whom there is no GOD : the King, the Holy, the Giver of peace, the Faithful, the Guardian, the Powerful, the Strong, the most High. Far be GOD exalted above *the idols*, which they associate *with him*! He is GOD, the Creator, the Maker, the Former. He hath most excellent names.[2] Whatever *is* in heaven and earth praiseth him : and he *is* the Mighty, the Wise.

LX

THE CHAPTER OF THE WOMAN WHO IS TRIED [3]

Revealed at Medina.

IN THE NAME OF THE MOST MERCIFUL GOD.

O TRUE believers, take not my enemy and your enemy for *your* friends,[4] showing kindness toward them ;

---

[1] That is, for the next life, which may be called *the morrow*, as this present life may be called *to-day*.

[2] See Chap. VII. p. 163.

[3] This chapter bears this title because it directs the women who desert and come over from the infidels to the Moslems to be examined, and tried whether they be sincere in their profession of the faith. Palmer renders the title as *The Chapter of the Tried*.

[4] This passage was revealed on account of Hateb Ebn Abi Baltaa, who understanding that Mohammed had a design to surprise Mecca, wrote a letter to the Koreish, giving them notice of the intended expedition, and advised them to be on their guard : which letter he sent by Sarah, a maid-servant belonging to the family of Hâshem. The messenger had not been gone long, before Gabriel discovered the affair to the prophet, who immediately sent after her ; and having intercepted the letter, asked Hateb how

since they believe not in the truth which hath come unto you, having expelled the apostle and yourselves *from your native city*, because ye believe in GOD, your LORD. If ye go forth to fight in defence of my religion, and out of a desire to please me, and privately show friendship unto them ;[1] verily I well know that which ye conceal, and that which ye discover : and whoever of you doth this, hath already erred from the straight path. If they get the better of you, they will be enemies unto you, and they will stretch forth their hands and their tongues against you with evil : and they earnestly desire that ye should become unbelievers. Neither your kindred nor your children will avail you at all on the day of resurrection, which will separate you from one another : and GOD seeth that which ye do. Ye have an excellent pattern in Abraham, and those who were with him, when they said unto their people, Verily we *are* clear of you, and of the *idols* which ye worship, besides GOD : we have renounced you ; and enmity and hatred is begun between us and you for ever, until ye believe in GOD alone : except Abraham's saying unto his father, Verily I will beg pardon for thee ;[2] but I cannot obtain aught of GOD in thy behalf. O LORD, in thee do we trust, and unto thee are we turned ; and before thee shall we be assembled *hereafter*. O LORD, suffer us not to be put to trial by the unbelievers :[3] and forgive us, O LORD ; for thou *art* mighty *and* wise. Verily ye have in them an excellent example, unto him who hopeth in GOD and the last day : and whoso turneth back ; verily GOD *is* self-sufficient, *and* praiseworthy. Peradventure GOD will establish friendship between yourselves and such of them as ye *now* hold for enemies :[4] for GOD *is* power-

---

ne came to be guilty of such an action ?   To which he replied that it was not out of infidelity, or a desire to return to idolatry, but merely to induce the Koreish to treat his family, which was still at Mecca, with some kindness ; adding that he was well assured his intelligence would be of no service at all to the Meccans, because he was satisfied GOD would take vengeance on them. Whereupon Mohammed received his excuse and pardoned him ; but it was thought proper to forbid any such practices for the future. (Al Beidâwi. Vide Abulf. Vit. Moh. p. 192.)

[1] The verb here used has also a contrary signification, according to which the words may be rendered, *and yet openly show friendship unto them.*

[2] For in this, Abraham's example is not to be followed. See Chap. IX.

[3] *i.e.*, Suffer them not to prevail against us, lest they thence conclude themselves to be in the right, and endeavour to make us deny our faith by the terror of persecution. (Al Beidâwi.)

[4] And this happened accordingly on the taking of Mecca ; when Abu Sofiân and others of the Koreish, who had till then been inveterate enemies to the Moslems, embraced the same faith, and became their friends and

ful; and GOD *is* inclined to forgive, *and* merciful. As to
those who have not borne arms against you on account of
religion, nor turned you out of your dwellings, GOD forbiddeth you not to deal kindly with them, and to behave
justly towards them ;[1] for GOD loveth those who act justly.
But as to those who have borne arms against you on account
of religion, and have dispossessed you of your habitations,
and have assisted in dispossessing you, GOD forbiddeth you
to enter into friendship with them : and whosoever *of you*
entereth into friendship with them, those are unjust doers.
O true believers, when believing women come unto you as
refugees, try them : GOD well knoweth their faith. And
if ye know them *to be* true believers, send them not back
to the infidels : they *are* not lawful for the *unbelievers to have
in marriage* ; neither are *the unbelievers* lawful for them.
But give *their unbelieving husbands* what they shall have
expended *for their dowers.*[2]   Nor *shall it be* any crime in you
if ye marry them, provided ye give them their dowries.[3]
And retain not the patronage of the unbelieving *women* :
but demand back that which ye have expended *for the dowry
of such of your wives as go over to the unbelievers* ; and let
them demand back that which they have expended *for
the dowry of those who come over to you.*   This *is* the judgment
of GOD, which he establisheth among you : and GOD *is*
knowing *and* wise.   If any of your wives[4] escape from you
to the unbelievers, and ye have your turn *by the coming*

brethren.   Some suppose the marriage of Mohammed with Omm Habîba,
the daughter of Abu Sofîan, which was celebrated the year before, to be
here intended.   (Vide Gagnier, not. in Abulf. Vit. Moh. p. 91.)
   [1] This passage, it is said, was revealed on account of Koteila bint Abd'al
Uzza, who having, while she was an idolatress, brought some presents to
her daughter, Asma bint Abu Becr, the latter not only refused to accept
them, but even denied her admittance.   (Al Beidâwi.)
   [2] For, according to the terms of the pacification of Al Hodeibiya (see
Chap. XLVIII.), each side was to return whatever came into their power
belonging to the other ; wherefore when the Moslems were, by this passage,
forbidden to restore the married women who should come over to them,
they were at the same time commanded to make some sort of satisfaction,
by returning their dowry.   It is related that, after the aforesaid pacification,
while Mohammed was yet at Al Hodeibiya, Sobeia bint al Hareth, of the
tribe of Aslam, having embraced Mohammedism, her husband, Mosâfer
the Makhzumite, came and demanded her back ; upon which this passage
was revealed : and Mohammed, pursuant thereto, administered to her the
oath thereafter directed, and returned her husband her dower ; and then
Omar married her.   (Al Beidâwi.)
   [3] For what is returned to their former husbands is not to be considered
as their dower.
   [4] Literally, *anything of your wives* ; which some interpret, *any part of their
dowry.*

over of any of the unbelievers' wives to you ;[1] give unto those
believers whose wives shall have gone away, *out of the dowries
of the latter*, so much as they shall have expended *for the
dowers of the former* : and fear GOD, in whom ye believe.
O prophet, when believing *women* come unto thee, and
plight their faith unto thee,[2] that they will not associate
anything with GOD, nor steal, nor commit fornication, nor
kill their children,[3] nor come with a calumny which they
have forged between their hands and their feet,[4] nor be
disobedient to thee in that which shall be reasonable : then
do thou plight thy faith unto them, and ask pardon for
them of GOD ; for GOD *is* inclined to forgive, *and* merciful.
O true believers, enter not into friendship with a people
against whom GOD is incensed :[5] they despair of the life to
come,[6] as the infidels despair of *the resurrection of* those who
dwell in the graves.

LXI

THE CHAPTER OF BATTLE ARRAY

Revealed at Mecca.[7]

IN THE NAME OF THE MOST MERCIFUL GOD.

WHATEVER *is* in heaven and in earth celebrateth
the praise of GOD ; for he *is* mighty *and* wise.   O
true believers, why do ye say that which ye do not ?[8]   *It*

---

[1] Or, as the original verb may also be translated, *and ye take spoils* ;
in which case the meaning will be, that those Moslems, whose wives shall
have gone over to the infidels, shall have a satisfaction for their dower out
of the next booty.   This law, they say, was given because the idolaters,
after the preceding verse had been revealed, refused to comply therewith,
or to make any return of the dower of those women who went over to them
from the Moslems (Al Beidâwi) ; so that the latter were obliged to indemnify
themselves as they could.

[2] See Sale, Prel. Disc. Sect. II. p. 50.   Some are of opinion that this passage
was not revealed till the day of the taking of Mecca ; when, after having
received the solemn submission of the men, he proceeded to receive that of
the women.   (Al Beidâwi.)

[3] See Chap. LXXXI.

[4] Jallalo'ddin understands these words of their laying their spurious children to their husbands.

[5] *i.e.*, The infidels in general ; or the Jews in particular.

[6] By reason of their infidelity ; or because they well know they cannot
expect to be made partakers of the happiness of the next life, by reason
of their rejecting of the prophet foretold in the law, and whose mission is
confirmed by miracles.   (Al Beidâwi.)

[7] Or, as some rather judge, at Medina ; which opinion is confirmed by the
explanation in the next note.

[8] The commentators generally suppose these words to be directed to the

is most odious in the sight of GOD, that ye say that which ye do not. Verily GOD loveth those who fight for his religion in battle array, as though they *were* a well compacted building. *Remember* when Moses said unto his people, O my people, why do ye injure me ;[1] since ye know that I am the apostle of GOD *sent* unto you ? And when they had deviated *from the truth*, GOD made their hearts to deviate *from the right way* ; for GOD directeth not wicked people. And when Jesus the son of Mary said, O children of Israel, verily I *am* the apostle of GOD *sent* unto you, confirming the law which *was delivered* before me, and bringing good tidings of an apostle who shall come after me, *and* whose name *shall be* Ahmed.[2] And when he produced unto them evident miracles, they said, This *is* manifest sorcery. But who *is* more unjust than he who forgeth a lie against GOD, when he is invited unto Islâm ? And GOD directeth not the unjust people. They seek to extinguish GOD's light with their mouths : but GOD will perfect his light, though the infidels be averse *thereto*. *It is* he who hath sent his apostle with the direction, and the religion of truth, that he may exalt the same above every religion, although the idolaters be averse *thereto*. O true believers, shall I show you a merchandise which will deliver you from a painful torment *hereafter* ? Believe in GOD and his apostle ; and defend GOD's true religion with your substance, and in your own persons. This *will be* better for you, if ye knew *it*. He will forgive you your sins ; and will introduce you into gardens through which rivers flow, and agreeable habitations in gardens of perpetual abode. This *will be* great felicity. And *ye shall obtain* other things which ye desire, *namely*, assistance from GOD, and a speedy victory. And do thou bear good tidings to the true believers. O true believers, be ye the assistants of GOD ; as Jesus the son of Mary said to the apostles, Who *will be* my assistants with respect to

Moslems who, notwithstanding they had solemnly engaged to spend their lives and fortunes in defence of their faith, yet shamefully turned their backs at the battle of Ohod. (See Chap. III.) They may, however, be applied to hypocrites of all sorts, whose actions contradict their words.

[1] viz., By your disobedience ; or by maliciously aspersing me. (See Chap. XXXIII. p. 418.)

[2] For Mohammed also bore the name of Ahmed ; both names being derived from the same root, and nearly of the same signification. The Persian paraphrast, to support what is here alleged, quotes the following words of Christ, *I go to my father, and the* Paraclete *shall come* (see John xvi. 7, &c.) : the Mohammedan doctors unanimously teaching that by the Paraclete (or, as they choose to read it, the *Periclyte*, or *Illustrious*) their prophet is intended, and no other. (Sale, Prel. Disc. Sect. IV. p. 80.)

GOD ?[1] The apostles answered, We *will be* the assistants
of GOD. So a part of the children of Israel believed, and a
part believed not :[2] but we strengthened those who believed,
above their enemy ; wherefore they became victorious *over
them.*

LXII

THE CHAPTER OF THE ASSEMBLY

Revealed at Medina.

IN THE NAME OF THE MOST MERCIFUL GOD.

WHATEVER *is* in heaven and earth praiseth GOD,
the King, the Holy, the Mighty, the Wise. *It is*
he who hath raised up amidst the illiterate *Arabians*[3] an
apostle from among themselves,[4] to rehearse his signs unto
them, and to purify them, and to teach them the scriptures
and wisdom ; whereas before they were certainly in a
manifest error : and others of them have not yet attained
unto them, *by embracing the faith* ; though *they also* shall
be converted *in God's good time* ; for he *is* mighty *and* wise.
This *is* the free grace of GOD : he bestoweth the same on
whom he pleaseth : and GOD is endued with great beneficence. The likeness of those who were charged with the
observance of the law, and then observed it not, *is* as the
likeness of an ass laden with books.[5] How wretched *is*
the likeness of the people who charge the signs of GOD with
falsehood ! and GOD directeth not the unjust people. Say,
O ye who follow the Jewish religion, if ye say that ye are
the friends of GOD above *other* men, wish for death,[6] if ye
speak truth. But they will never wish for it, because of
that which their hands have sent before them :[7] and GOD
well knoweth the unjust. Say, Verily death, from which
ye fly, will surely meet you : then shall ye be brought
before him who knoweth as well what is concealed as what

---

[1] See Chap. III. p. 50.
[2] Either by rejecting him, or by affirming him to be GOD, and the son of
GOD. (Jallalo'ddin.)
[3] This is rendered by Palmer as *The Gentiles.*
[4] See Sale, Prel. Disc. Sect. II. p. 45.
[5] Because they understand not the prophecies contained in the law, which
bear witness to Mohammed, no more than the ass does the books he carries.
[6] *i.e.*, Make it your request to GOD that he would translate you from this
troublesome world to a state of never-fading bliss.
[7] See Chap. II. p. 15.

is discovered; and he will declare unto you that which ye have done. O true believers, when ye are called to prayer on the day of the assembly,[1] hasten to the commemoration of GOD, and leave merchandising. This *will be* better for you, if ye knew *it*. And when prayer is ended, then disperse yourselves through the land *as ye list*, and seek *gain* of the liberality of GOD:[2] and remember GOD frequently, that ye may prosper. But when they see any merchandising or sport, they flock thereto, and leave thee standing up *in thy pulpit*.[3] Say, The *reward* which is with GOD *is* better than any sport or merchandise; and GOD is the best provider.

LXIII

THE CHAPTER OF THE HYPOCRITES

Revealed at Medina.

IN THE NAME OF THE MOST MERCIFUL GOD.

WHEN the hypocrites come unto thee, they say, We bear witness that thou *art* indeed the apostle of GOD. And GOD knoweth that thou *art* indeed his apostle: but GOD beareth witness that the hypocrites *are* certainly liars. They have taken their oaths for a protection, and they turn *others* aside from the way of GOD: it is surely evil which they do. This *is testified of them*, because they believed, and afterwards became unbelievers: wherefore a

---

[1] That is, Friday, which being more peculiarly set apart by Mohammed for the public worship of GOD, is therefore called Yawm al jomá, *i.e.*, the day of the assembly or congregation; whereas before it was called Al Arûba. The first time this day was particularly observed, as some say, was on the prophet's arrival at Medina, into which city he made his first entry on a Friday: but others tell us that Caab Ebn Lowa, one of Mohammed's ancestors, gave the day its present name, because on that day the people used to be assembled before him. (Al Beidâwi.) One reason given for the observation of Friday, preferably to any other day of the week, is because on that day GOD finished the creation. (Vide Gol. in Alfrag. p. 15.)

[2] By returning to your commerce and worldly occupations, if ye think fit: for the Mohammedans do not hold themselves obliged to observe the day of their public assembly with the same strictness as the Christians and Jews do their respective Sabbath; or particularly to abstain from work, after they have performed their devotions. Some, however, from a tradition of their prophet, are of opinion that works of charity, and religious exercises, which may draw down the blessing of GOD, are recommended in this passage.

[3] It is related that one Friday, while Mohammed was preaching, a caravan of merchants happened to arrive with their drums beating, according to custom; which the congregation hearing, they all ran out of the mosque to see them, except twelve only. (Al Beidâwi, Jallalo'ddin.)

seal is set on their hearts, and they shall not understand. When thou beholdest them, their persons please thee :[1] and if they speak, thou hearest their discourse *with delight*. They resemble pieces of timber set up *against a wall*.[2] They imagine every shout *to be* against them.[3] They are enemies ; wherefore beware of them. GOD curse them : how are they turned aside *from the truth* ! And when it is said unto them, Come, that the apostle of GOD may ask pardon for you ; they turn away their heads, and thou seest them retire big with disdain. *It shall be* equal unto them, whether thou ask pardon for them, or do not ask pardon for them ; GOD will by no means forgive them : for GOD directeth not the prevaricating people. These *are the men* who say *to the inhabitants of Medina*, Do not bestow *anything* on *the refugees* who *are* with the apostle of GOD, that they may *be obliged to* separate *from him*. Whereas unto GOD *belong* the stores of heaven and earth : but the hypocrites do not understand. They say, Verily, if we return to Medina, the worthier shall expel thence the meaner.[4] Whereas superior worth *belongeth* unto GOD, and his apostle, and the true believers : but the hypocrites know *it* not. O true believers, let not your riches or your children divert you from the remembrance of GOD : for whosoever doth this, they will surely be losers. And give alms out of that which we have bestowed on you ; before death come unto one of you, and he say, O LORD, wilt thou not grant me respite for a short term ; that I may give alms, and become *one* of the righteous ? For GOD will by no means grant further respite to a soul, when its determined time is come : and GOD *is* fully apprised of that which ye do.

[1] The commentators tell us, that Abdallah Ebn Obba, a leading hypocrite, was a tall man of a very graceful presence, and of a ready and eloquent tongue ; and used to frequent the prophet's assembly, attended by several like himself ; and that these men were greatly admired by Mohammed, who was taken with their handsome appearance, and listened to their discourse with pleasure. (Al Beidâwi.)

[2] Being tall and big, but void of knowledge and consideration. (Al Beidâwi.)

[3] Living under continual apprehensions ; because they are conscious of their hypocrisy towards GOD, and their insincerity towards the Moslems.

[4] These, as well as the preceding, were the words of Ebn Obba to one of Medina, who in a certain expedition quarreling with an Arab of the desert about water, received a blow on the head with a stick, and made his complaint thereof to him. (Al Beidâwi.)

LXIV

THE CHAPTER OF MUTUAL DECEIT

Revealed at Mecca.[1]

IN THE NAME OF THE MOST MERCIFUL GOD.

WHATEVER *is* in heaven and earth celebrateth the praises of GOD ; his *is* the kingdom, and unto him *is* the praise *due* ; for he *is* almighty. *It is* he who hath created you ; and *one* of you *is predestined to be* an unbeliever, and *another* of you *is predestined to be* a believer ; and GOD beholdeth that which ye do. He hath created the heavens and the earth with truth ; and he hath fashioned you, and given you beautiful forms : and unto him must ye all go. He knoweth whatever *is* in heaven and earth : and he knoweth that which ye conceal, and that which ye discover ; for GOD knoweth the innermost part of *men's* breasts. Have ye not been acquainted with the story of those who disbelieved heretofore, and tasted the evil consequence of their behaviour ? And for them *is prepared, in the life to come,* a tormenting punishment. This *shall they suffer,* because their apostles came unto them with evident *proofs of their mission,* and they said, Shall men direct us ? Wherefore they believed not, and turned their backs. But GOD standeth in need of no person : for GOD *is* self-sufficient, *and* worthy to be praised. The unbelievers imagine that they shall not be raised again. Say, Yea, by my LORD, ye shall surely be raised again : then shall ye be told that which ye have wrought ; and this *is* easy with GOD. Wherefore believe in GOD and his apostle, and the light which we have sent down : for GOD *is* well acquainted with that which ye do. On a *certain* day he shall assemble you, at the day of the *general* assembly : that *will be* the day of mutual deceit.[2] And whoso shall believe in GOD, and shall do that which is right, from him will he expiate his evil deeds, and he will lead him into gardens beneath which rivers flow, to remain therein for ever. This *will be* great felicity. But those who shall not believe, and shall accuse our signs of falsehood, they *shall be* the inhabitants of *hell* fire, wherein they shall remain *for ever* ;

---

[1] The commentators are not agreed whether this chapter was revealed at Mecca, or at Medina ; or partly at the one place, and partly at the other.

[2] When the blessed will deceive the damned, by taking the places which they would have had in paradise had they been true believers ; and contrariwise. (Al Beidâwi, Jallalo'ddin, Yahya.)

and a wretched journey *shall it be thither*! No misfortune happeneth but by the permission of GOD; and whoso believeth in GOD, he will direct his heart: and GOD knoweth all things. Wherefore obey GOD, and obey the apostle: but if ye turn back, verily *the duty incumbent* on our apostle *is* only public preaching. GOD! there is no GOD but he: wherefore in GOD let the faithful put their trust. O true believers, verily of your wives and your children ye have an enemy:[1] wherefore beware of them. But if ye pass over *their offences*, and pardon and forgive *them*;[2] GOD *is* likewise inclined to forgive, *and* merciful. Your wealth and your children *are* only a temptation; but with GOD *is* a great reward. Wherefore fear GOD, as much as ye are able; and hear, and obey: and give alms, for the good of your souls; for whoso is preserved from the covetousness of his own soul, they shall prosper. If ye lend unto GOD an acceptable loan, he will double the same unto you, and will forgive you: for GOD *is* grateful *and* long-suffering, knowing both what is hidden and what is divulged; the Mighty, the Wise.

LXV

THE CHAPTER OF DIVORCE

Revealed at Medina.

IN THE NAME OF THE MOST MERCIFUL GOD.

O PROPHET, when ye divorce women, put them away at their appointed term;[3] and compute the term *exactly*: and fear GOD, your LORD. Oblige them not to go out of their apartments, neither let them go out, *until the term be expired*, unless they be guilty of manifest uncleanness. These *are* the statutes of GOD: and whoever trans-

---

[1] For these are apt to distract a man from his duty, especially in time of distress; (Al Beidâwi); a married man caring for the things that are of this world, while the unmarried careth for the things that belong to the LORD. (See 1 Cor. vii. 25, &c.)

[2] Considering that the hindrance they may occasion you proceeds from their affection, and their ill bearing your absence in time of war, &c.

[3] That is, when they shall have had their courses thrice after the time of their divorce, if they prove not to be with child; or, if they prove with child, when they shall have been delivered. Al Beidâwi supposes husbands are hereby commanded to divorce their wives while they are clean; and says that the passage was revealed on account of Ebn Omar, who divorced his wife when she had her courses upon her, and was therefore obliged to take her again.

gresseth the statutes of GOD, assuredly injureth his own soul. Thou knowest not whether GOD will bring something new to pass, *which may reconcile them,* after this. And when they shall have fulfilled their term, either retain them with kindness, or part from them honourably : and take witnesses from among you, men of integrity ; and give *your* testimony as in the presence of GOD. This admonition is given unto him who believeth in GOD and the last day : and whoso feareth GOD, unto him will he grant a *happy* issue *out of all his afflictions,* and he will bestow on him an ample provision from whence he expecteth *it* not : and whoso trusteth in GOD, he *will be* his sufficient support ; for GOD will surely attain his purpose. Now hath GOD appointed unto everything a determined period. *As to* such of your wives as shall despair having their courses, *by reason of their age* ; if ye be in doubt *thereof,* let their term *be* three months : and *let the same be the term of* those who have not yet had their courses. But *as to* those who are pregnant, their term *shall be,* until they be delivered of their burden.[1] And whoso feareth GOD, unto him will he make his command easy. This *is* the command of GOD, which he hath sent down unto you. And whoso feareth GOD, he will expiate his evil deeds from him, and will increase his reward. Suffer the women *whom ye divorce* to dwell in *some part* of *the houses* wherein ye dwell ; *according to the room and conveniences* of the *habitations* which ye possess : and make them not uneasy, that ye may reduce them to straits. And if they be with child, expend on them *what shall be needful,* until they be delivered of their burden. And if they suckle *their children* for you, give them their hire ;[2] and consult among yourselves, according to what shall be just and reasonable. And if ye be put to a difficulty *herein,* and another woman shall suckle *the child* for him, let him who hath plenty expend *proportionably, in the maintenance of the mother and the nurse,* out of his plenty : and let him whose income is scanty, expend *in proportion* out of that which GOD hath given him. GOD obligeth no man to more than he hath given him *ability to perform* : GOD will cause ease to succeed hardship. How many cities have turned aside from the command of their LORD and his apostles ? Wherefore we brought them to a severe account ; and we chas-

[1] See Chap. II. p. 32.
[2] Which ought at least to be sufficient to maintain and clothe them during the time of suckling. See Chap. II.

tised them with a grievous chastisement : and they tasted the evil consequence of their business ; and the end of their business was perdition. GOD hath prepared for them a severe punishment ; wherefore fear GOD, O ye who are endued with understanding. True believers, now hath GOD sent down unto you an admonition, an apostle who may rehearse unto you the perspicuous signs of GOD ; that he may bring forth those who believe and do good works, from darkness into light. And whoso believeth in GOD, and doth that which is right, him will he lead into gardens beneath which rivers flow, to remain therein for ever : now hath GOD made an excellent provision for him. *It is* GOD who hath created seven heavens, and as many *different stories* of the earth : the *divine* command descendeth between them ;[1] that ye may know that GOD is omnipotent, and that GOD comprehendeth all things by *his* knowledge.

LXVI

THE CHAPTER OF PROHIBITION
Revealed at Medina.

IN THE NAME OF THE MOST MERCIFUL GOD.

O PROPHET, why holdest thou that to be prohibited which GOD hath allowed thee, seeking to please thy wives ;[2] since GOD *is* inclined to forgive *and* merciful ?

[1] Penetrating and pervading them all with absolute efficacy.

[2] There are some who suppose this passage to have been occasioned by Mohammed's protesting never to eat honey any more, because, having once eaten some in the apartment of Hafsa, or of Zeinab, three other of his wives, namely, Ayesha, Sawda, and Safia, all told him they smelt he had been eating of the juice which distils from certain shrubs in these parts, and resembles honey in taste and consistence, but is of a very strong flavour, and which the prophet had a great aversion to (Al Zamakh., Al Beidâwi). But the more received opinion is, that the chapter was revealed on the following occasion. Mohammed having lain with a slave of his named Mary, of Coptic extraction (who had been sent him as a present by Al Mokawkas, governor of Egypt), on the day which was due to Ayesha, or to Hafsa, and, as some say, on Hafsa's own bed while she was absent : and this coming to Hafsa's knowledge, she took it extremely ill, and reproached her husband so sharply, that, to pacify her, he promised, with an oath, never to touch the maid again (Al Beidâwi, Jallal., Yahya): and to free him from the obligation of this promise was the design of the chapter. I cannot here avoid observing, as a learned writer (Gagnier, not. ad Abulf. Vit. Moh. p. 150) has done before me, that Dr. Prideaux has strangely misrepresented this passage. For having given the story of the prophet's amour with his maid Mary, a little embellished, he proceeds to tell us that in this chapter Mohammed orings in GOD allowing him, and all his Moslems, to lie with their maids when they will, notwithstanding their wives (whereas the words relate

GOD hath allowed you the dissolution of your oaths :[1] and GOD *is* your master ; and he *is* knowing *and* wise. When the prophet entrusted as a secret unto one of his wives a certain accident ; and when she disclosed the same, and GOD made it known unto him ; he acquainted *her* with part *of what she had done,* and forbore *to upbraid her with the other* part thereof. And when he had acquainted her therewith, she said, Who hath discovered this unto thee ? He answered, The knowing, the sagacious *God* hath discovered *it* unto me.[2] If ye both be turned unto GOD (for

to the prophet only, who wanted not any new permission for that purpose, because it was a privilege already granted him—see Chap. XXXIII.—though to none else) ; and then, to show what ground he had for his assertion, adds that the first words of the chapter are, *O prophet, why dost thou forbid what* GOD *hath allowed thee, that thou mayest please thy wives* ? GOD *hath granted unto you to lie with your maid-servants* (Prid. Life of Mah. p. 113). Which last words are not to be found here, or elsewhere in the Korân, and contain an allowance of what is expressly forbidden therein (see Chaps. XVII., IV. and XXIV.) ; though the doctor has thence taken occasion to make some reflections which might as well have been spared. I shall say nothing to aggravate the matter, but leave the reader to imagine what this reverend divine would have said of a Mohammedan if he had caught him tripping in the like manner. Having digressed so far, I will venture to add a word or two in order to account for one circumstance which Dr. Prideaux relates concerning Mohammed's concubine Mary ; viz., that after her master's death, no account was had of her or the son which she had borne him, but both were sent away into Egypt, and no mention made of either ever after among them ; and then he supposes (for he seldom is at a loss for a supposition) that Ayesha, out of the hatred which she bore her, procured of her father, who succeeded the impostor in the government, to have her thus disposed of (Prid. Life of Mah. p. 114). But it being certain, by the general consent of all the Eastern writers, that Mary continued in Arabia till her death, which happened at Medina about five years after that of her master, and was buried in the usual burying-place there, called Al Baki, and that her son died before his father, it has been asked, whence the doctor had this ? (Gagnier, ubi supra). I answer, that I guess he had it partly from Abulfaragius, according to the printed edition of whose work, the Mary we are speaking of is said to have been sent with her sister Shirin (not with her son) to Alexandria by Al Mokawkas (Abulfarag. Hist. Dynast. p. 165) ; though I make no doubt but we ought in that passage to read *min, from,* instead of *ila, to* (notwithstanding the manuscript copies of this author used by Dr. Pocock, the editor, and also a very fair one in my own possession, agree in the latter reading) ; and that the sentence ought to run thus, *quam* (viz., Mariam) *unâ cum sorore* Shirina *ab* Alexandria *miserat* Al Mokawkas.

[1] By having appointed an expiation for that purpose (see Chap. V) ; or, as the words may be translated, *God hath allowed you to use an exception in your oaths if it please* GOD ; in which case a man is excused from guilt if he perform not his oath (Al Beidâwi). The passage, though directed to all the Moslems in general, seems to be particularly designed for quieting the prophet's conscience in regard to the oath above mentioned : but Al Beidâwi approves not this opinion, because such an oath was to be looked upon as an inconsiderate one, and required no expiation.

[2] When Mohammed found that Hafsa knew of his having injured her, or Ayesha, by lying with his concubine Mary on the day due to one of them, he desired her to keep the affair secret, promising, at the same time, that he would not meddle with Mary any more ; and foretold her, as a piece of news which might soothe her vanity, that Abu Becr and Omar should succeed

your hearts have swerved) *it is well* : but if ye join against him, verily GOD is his patron ; and Gabriel, and the good men among the faithful, and the angels also *are his* assistants.[1] If he divorce you, his LORD can easily give him in exchange other wives better than you, *women* resigned *unto God*, true believers, devout, penitent, obedient, given to fasting, *both such as have been* known by other men, and virgins. O true believers, save your souls, and *those of* your families, from the fire whose fuel *is* men and stones, over which are *set* angels fierce *and* terrible ;[2] who disobey not GOD in what he hath commanded them, but perform what they are commanded. O unbelievers, excuse not yourselves this day ; ye shall surely be rewarded for what ye have done.[3] O true believers, turn unto GOD with a sincere repentance : peradventure your LORD will do away from you your evil deeds, and will admit you into gardens, through which rivers flow; on the day *whereon* GOD will not put to shame the prophet, or those who believe with him : their light shall run before them and on their right hands,[4] *and* they shall say, LORD, make our light perfect, and forgive us ; for thou *art* almighty. O prophet, attack the infidels *with arms*, and the hypocrites *with arguments* ; and treat them with severity : their abode shall be hell, and an ill journey *shall it be thither*. GOD propoundeth as a similitude unto the unbelievers, the wife of Noah, and the wife of Lot : they were under two of our righteous servants, and they deceived them both ;[5] wherefore *their*

---

him in the government of his people. Hafsa, however, could not conceal this from Ayesha, with whom she lived in strict friendship, but acquainted her with the whole matter : whereupon the prophet, perceiving, probably by Ayesha's behaviour, that his secret had been discovered, upbraided Hafsa with her betraying him, telling her that GOD had revealed it to him ; and not only divorced her, but separated him from all his other wives for a whole month, which time he spent in the apartment of Mary. In a short time, notwithstanding, he took Hafsa again, by the direction, as he gave out, of the angel Gabriel, who commended her for her frequent fasting and other exercises of devotion, assuring him likewise that she should be one of his wives in paradise. (Al Beidâwi, Al Zamakh., &c.)

[1] This sentence is directed to Hafsa and Ayesha ; the pronouns and verbs of the second person being in the dual number.

[2] See Chap. LXXIV., and Sale, Prel. Disc. Sect. IV. p. 99.

[3] These words will be spoken to the infidels at the last day.

[4] See Chap. LVII.

[5] Who were both unbelieving women, but deceived their respective husbands by their hypocrisy. Noah's wife, named Wâîla, endeavoured to persuade the people her husband was distracted ; and Lot's wife, whose name was Wâhela (though some writers give this name to the other, and that of Wâîla to the latter), was in confederacy with the men of Sodom, and used to give them notice when any strangers came to lodge with him, by a signal of smoke by day, and of fire by night. (Jallal., Al Zamakh.)

husbands were of no advantage unto them at all, in the sight of GOD :[1] and it shall be said *unto them at the last day,* Enter ye into *hell* fire, with those who enter *therein.* GOD also propoundeth as a similitude unto those who believe, the wife of Pharaoh ;[2] when she said, LORD, build me a house with thee in paradise, and deliver me from Pharaoh and his doings, and deliver me from the unjust people : and Mary the daughter of Imrân ; who preserved her chastity, and into whose womb we breathed of our spirit,[3] and who believed in the words of her LORD and his scriptures, and was a devout and obedient person.[4]

LXVII

THE CHAPTER OF THE KINGDOM [5]

Revealed at Mecca.

IN THE NAME OF THE MOST MERCIFUL GOD.

(XXIX.)[6] BLESSED be he in whose hand *is* the kingdom ; for he *is* almighty ! Who hath created death and life, that he might prove you, which of you is most righteous in *his* actions : and he *is* mighty, *and* ready to forgive. Who hath created seven heavens, one above another : thou canst not see in a creature of the most Merciful any unfitness or disproportion. Lift up thine eyes again *to heaven, and look* whether thou seest any

---

[1] For they both met with a disastrous end in this world (see Chap. XI.), and will be doomed to eternal misery in the next. In like manner, as Mohammed would insinuate, the infidels of his time had no reason to expect any mitigation of their punishment, on account of their relation to himself and the rest of the true believers.

[2] viz., Asia, the daughter of Mozâhem. The commentators relate, that because she believed in Moses, her husband cruelly tormented her, fastening her hands and feet to four stakes, and laying a large mill-stone on her breast, her face, at the same time, being exposed to the scorching beams of the sun. These pains, however, were alleviated by the angels shading her with their wings, and the view of the mansion prepared for her in paradise, which was exhibited to her on her pronouncing the prayer in the text. At length GOD received her soul ; or, as some say, she was taken up alive into paradise, where she eats and drinks. (Jallal., Al Zamakh.) [3] Chap. XIX. p. 298.

[4] On occasion of the honourable mention here made of these two extraordinary women, the commentators introduce a saying of their prophet, *That among men there had been many perfect, but no more than four of the other sex had attained perfection ; to wit, Asia, the wife of Pharaoh ; Mary, the daughter of Imrân ; Khadîjah, the daughter of Khowailed (the prophet's first wife) ; and Fâtema, the daughter of Mohammed.*

[5] It is also entitled by some, *The Saving,* or *The Delivering,* because, say they, it will save him who reads it from the torture of the sepulchre.

[6] Section XXIX. begins with this chapter.

flaw : then take two other views ; and thy sight shall return unto thee dull and fatigued. Moreover we have adorned the lowest heaven with lamps, and have appointed them to be darted at the devils,[1] for whom we have prepared the torment of burning fire : and for those who believe not in their LORD, *is also prepared* the torment of hell ; an ill journey *shall it be thither* ! When they shall be thrown thereinto, they shall hear it bray like an ass ;[2] and it shall boil, and almost burst for fury. So often as a company *of them* shall be thrown therein, the keepers thereof shall ask them, *saying*, Did not a warner come unto you ? They shall answer, Yea, a warner came unto us : but we accused *him* of imposture, and said, GOD hath not revealed anything ; ye *are* in no other than a great error : and they shall say. If we had hearkened, or had rightly considered, we should not have been among the inhabitants of burning fire : and they shall confess their sins ; but far be the inhabitants of burning fire *from obtaining mercy* ! Verily they who fear their LORD in secret, shall receive pardon and a great reward. Either conceal your discourse, or make it public ; he knoweth the innermost parts of *your* breasts : shall not he know *all things* who hath created *them* ; since he *is* the sagacious, the knowing ?   *It is* he who hath levelled the earth for you : therefore walk through the regions thereof, and eat of his provision ; unto him *shall be* the resurrection. Are ye secure that he who *dwelleth* in heaven will not cause the earth to swallow you up ? and behold, it shall shake. Or are ye secure that he who *dwelleth* in heaven will not send against you an *impetuous whirlwind*, driving the sands *to overwhelm you* ? then shall ye know how *important* my warning *was*. Those also who *were* before you disbelieved ; and how *grievous* was my displeasure ! Do they not behold the birds above them, extending and drawing back their wings ? None sustaineth them, except the Merciful ; for he regardeth all things. Or who *is* he that *will be as* an army unto you, to defend you against the Merciful ? Verily the unbelievers *are* in no other than a mistake. Or who *is* he that will give you food, if he withholdeth his provision ? yet they persist in perverseness, and flying *from the truth*. Is he, therefore, who goeth grovelling upon his face, better directed than he who walketh upright in a straight way ?[3] Say, *It is* he who hath given

---

[1] See Chap. XV. p. 252.   [2] See Chap. XXXI. p. 402.
[3] This comparison is applied by the expositors to the infidel and the true believer.

you being, and endued you with hearing, and sight, and
understanding ; *yet* how little gratitude have ye ! Say,
It is he who hath sown you in the earth, and unto him shall
ye be gathered together.   They say, When s... *'l* this menace
be put in execution, if ye speak truth ?   Answer, The knowledge *of this matter is* with GOD alone : for I *am* only a public
warner.   But when they shall see the same nigh at hand,
the countenance of the infidels shall grow sad : and it shall
be said *unto them,* This is what ye have been demanding.
Say, What think ye ?   Whether GOD destroy me and those
who are with me, or have mercy on us ; who will protect
the unbelievers from a painful punishment ? Say, He is
the Merciful ; in him do we believe, and in him do we put
our trust.   Ye shall hereafter know who is in a manifest
error.   Say, What think ye ?   If your water be in the
morning swallowed up by the earth, who will give you clear
and running water ?

LXVIII

THE CHAPTER OF THE PEN

Revealed at Mecca.

IN THE NAME OF THE MOST MERCIFUL GOD.

N[1] . BY the pen, and what they write,[2] thou, *O Mohammed,* through the grace of thy LORD, *art* not
distracted.   Verily *there is prepared* for thee an everlasting
reward ; for thou *art* of a noble disposition.[3]   Thou shalt

---

[1] This letter is sometimes made the title of the chapter, but its meaning
is confessedly uncertain.   They who suppose it stands for the word Nûn
are not agreed as to its signification in this place ; for it is not only the name
of the letter N in Arabic, but signifies also *an inkhorn* and a *fish* ; some are
of opinion the former signification is the most proper here, as consonant
to what is immediately mentioned of *the pen* and *writing,* and, considering
that the blood of certain *fish* is good ink, not inconsistent with the latter
signification ; which is, however, preferred by others, saying, that either
the whole species of *fish* in general is thereby intended, or the fish which
swallowed Jonas (who is mentioned in this chapter), or else that vast one
called Behemoth, fancied to support the earth, in particular.   Those who
acquiesce in none of the foregoing explanations have invented others of their
own, and imagine this character stands for the *table of* GOD's *decrees,* or
one of the rivers in paradise, &c.   (Al Zamakh., Al Beidâwi, Yahya.)

[2] Some understand these words generally, and others of the pen with
which GOD's decrees are written on the preserved table, and of the angels
who register the same.

[3] In that thou hast borne with so much patience and resignation the
wrongs and insults of thy people, which have been greater than those offered
to any apostle before thee. (Al Beidâwi.)

see, and *the infidels* shall see, which of you *are* bereaved of
your senses. Verily thy LORD well knoweth him who
wandereth from his path ; and he well knoweth those who
are *rightly* directed : wherefore obey not those who charge
thee with imposture. They desire that thou shouldst be
easy *with them*, and they will be easy *with thee*.[1] But obey
not any *who is* a common swearer, a despicable *fellow*, a
defamer, going about with slander, who forbiddeth that
which is good, *who is also* a transgressor, a wicked person,
cruel, *and* besides this, of spurious birth :[2] although he be
possessed of wealth and *many* children : when our signs
are rehearsed unto him, he saith, *They are* fables of the
ancients. We will stigmatize him on the nose.[3] Verily
we have tried *the Meccans*,[4] as we *formerly* tried the owners
of the garden ;[5] when they swore that they would gather
the fruit thereof[6] in the morning, and added not the exception, *if it please God* : wherefore a surrounding *destruction*
from thy LORD encompassed it, while they slept ; and in
the morning it became like *a garden* whose fruits had been
gathered.[7]   And they called *the one to the other* as they rose

---

[1] *i.e.*, If thou wilt let them alone in their idolatry and other wicked practices, they will cease to revile and persecute thee.

[2] The person at whom this passage was particularly levelled is generally
supposed to have been Mohammed's inveterate enemy, Al Walîd Ebn al
Mogheira, whom, to complete his character, he calls *bastard*, because Al
Mogheira did not own him for his son till he was eighteen years of age. (Al
Beidawi, Jallalo'ddin.)   Some, however, think it was Al Akhnas Ebn Shoreik,
who was really of the tribe of Thakîf, though reputed to be of that of Zahra.
(Al Beidâwi.)

[3] Which being the most conspicuous part of the face, a mark set thereon
is attended with the utmost ignominy.   It is said that this prophetical
menace was actually made good, Al Walîd having his nose slit by a sword
at the battle of Bedr, the mark of which wound he carried with him to his
grave. (Al Beidâwi, Jallalo'ddin.)

[4] By afflicting them with a grievous famine. See Chap. XXIII. p. 339.

[5] This garden was a plantation of palm-trees, about two parasangs from
Sanaa, belonging to a certain charitable man, who, when he gathered his
dates, used to give public notice to the poor, and to leave them such of the
fruit as the knife missed, or was blown down by the wind, or fell beside the
cloth spread under the tree to receive it : after his death, his sons, who
were then become masters of the garden, apprehending they should come
to want if they followed their father's example, agreed to gather the fruit
early in the morning, when the poor could have no notice of the matter :
but when they came to execute their purpose, they found, to their great
grief and surprise, that their plantation had been destroyed in the night.
(Al Beidâwi.)

[6] Literally, *that they would cut it* ; the manner of gathering dates being
to cut the clusters off with a knife.   Marracci supposes they intended to
cut down the trees, and destroy the plantation ; which, as he observes,
renders the story ridiculous and absurd.

[7] Or, as the original may also be rendered, *like a dark night* ; it being burnt
up and black.

in the morning, *saying,* Go out early to your plantation, if
ye intend to gather the fruit thereof : so they went on,
whispering to one another, No poor man shall enter *the
garden* before you this day. And they went forth early,
with a determined purpose. And when they saw *the garden
blasted and destroyed,* they said, We have certainly mistaken
our way : *but when they found it to be their own garden, they
cried,* Verily we are not permitted[1] *to reap the fruit thereof.*
The worthier of them said, Did I not say unto you, Will
ye not give praise unto GOD ? They answered, Praise be
unto our LORD ! Verily we have been unjust doers. And
they began to blame one another,[2] *and* they said, Woe be
unto us ! verily we have been transgressors : peradventure our LORD will give us in exchange a better *garden*
than this : and we earnestly beseech our LORD *to pardon
us.* Thus *is the* chastisement *of this life :* but the chastisement of the next *shall be* more grievous ; if they had known
it, they would have taken heed. Verily for the pious *are
prepared,* with their LORD, gardens of delight. Shall we
deal with the Moslems as with the wicked ?[3] What aileth
you that ye judge thus ? Have ye a book *from heaven,*
wherein ye read that ye are therein promised that which
ye shall choose ? Or have ye *received* oaths which shall be
binding upon us to the day of resurrection, that ye shall
enjoy what ye imagine ? Ask them, which of them *will be*
the voucher of this. Or have they companions[4] *who will
vouch for them* ? Let them produce their companions,
therefore, if they speak truth. On a *certain* day the leg
shall be made bare ;[5] and they shall be called upon to worship, but they shall not be able.[6] Their looks *shall be* cast
down : ignominy shall attend them : for that they were

---

[1] The same expression is used in Chap. LVI. p. 519.

[2] For one advised this expedition, another approved of it, a third gave
consent by his silence, but the fourth was absolutely against it. (Al Beidâwi.)

[3] This passage was revealed in answer to the infidels, who said, *If we
shall be raised again, as Mohammed and his followers imagine, they will not
excel us ; but we shall certainly be in a better condition than they in the next
world, as we are in this.* (Al Beidâwi.)

[4] Or, as some interpret the word, *idols* ; which can make their condition;
in the next life, equal to that of the Moslems ?

[5] This expression is used to signify a grievous and terrible calamity : thus
they say, *War has made bare the leg,* when they would express the fury and
rage of battle. (Al Beidâwi, Jallalo'ddin.)

[6] Because the time of acceptance shall be past. Al Beidâwi is uncertain
whether the words refer to the day of judgment, or the moment of death :
but Jallalo'ddin supposes them to relate to the former, and adds that the
infidels shall not be able to perform the act of adoration, because their backs
shall become stiff and inflexible.

invited to the worship *of God*, while they *were* in safety, *but would not hear*. Let me alone, therefore, with him who accuseth this new revelation of imposture. We will lead them gradually *to destruction*, by *ways* which they know not :[1] and I will bear with them for a long time ; for my stratagem *is* effectual. Dost thou ask them any reward *for thy preaching* ? But they are laden with debts. *Are* the secrets of futurity with them ; and do they transcribe the same *from the table of God's decrees* ?[2] Wherefore patiently wait the judgment of thy LORD : and be not like him who was swallowed by the fish ;[3] when he cried *unto God*, being inwardly vexed. Had not grace from his LORD reached him, he had surely been cast forth on the naked *shore*, covered with shame : but his LORD chose him, and made him *one* of the righteous. It wanteth little but that the unbelievers strike thee down with their *malicious* looks, when they hear the admonition *of the Korân* ; and they say, He *is* certainly distracted : but it *is* no other than an admonition unto all creatures.

LXIX

THE CHAPTER OF THE INFALLIBLE
Revealed at Mecca.

IN THE NAME OF THE MOST MERCIFUL GOD.

THE infallible ![4] What *is* the infallible ? And what shall cause thee to understand what the infallible *is* ? *The tribes of* Thamûd and Ad denied as a falsehood the *day* which shall strike[5] *men's hearts with terror*. But Thamûd were destroyed by a terrible noise : and Ad were destroyed by a roaring *and* furious wind ; which GOD caused to assail them for seven nights and eight days successively : thou mightest have seen people, during the same, lying

---

[1] *i.e.*, By granting them long life and prosperity in this world ; which will deceive them to their ruin.

[2] See Chap. LII. p. 506.

[3] That is, be not impatient and pettish, as Jonas was. See Chap. XXI.

[4] The original word Al Hâkkat is one of the names or epithets of the day of judgment. As the root from which it is derived signifies not only *to be* or *come to pass of necessity*, but also to *verify* ; some rather think that day to be so called because it will verify and *show the truth* of what men doubt of in this life, viz., the resurrection of the dead, their being brought to account, and the consequent rewards and punishments. (Al Beidâwi.)

[5] Arab. *al Kâriât*, or *the striking* ; which is another name or epithet of the last day.

prostrate, as though they *had been* the roots of hollow palm-trees ;[1] and couldst thou have seen any of them remaining ? Pharaoh also, and those who *were* before him, and the *cities* which were overthrown,[2] were guilty of sin ; and they *severally* were disobedient to the apostle of their LORD ; wherefore he chastised them with an abundant chastisement.   When the water *of the deluge* arose, we carried you in the *ark* which swam *thereon* ; that we might make the same a memorial unto you, and the retaining ear might retain it.   And when one blast shall sound the trumpet, and the earth shall be moved *from its place,* and the mountains also, and shall be dashed in pieces at one stroke : on that day the inevitable *hour of judgment* shall suddenly come ; and the heavens shall cleave in sunder, and shall fall in pieces, on that day : and the angels *shall be* on the sides thereof ;[3] and eight shall bear the throne of thy LORD above them, on that day.[4]   On that day ye shall be presented *before the judgment seat of God* ; and none of your secret *actions shall be* hidden.   And he who shall have his book delivered into his right hand, shall say, Take ye, read this my book ; verily I thought that I should be brought to this my account : he *shall lead* a pleasing life, in a lofty garden, the fruits whereof shall be near *to gather.*   Eat and drink with easy digestion ; because of the *good works* which ye sent before you, in the days which are past.   But he who shall have his book delivered into his left hand, shall say, Oh that I had not received this my book ; and that I had not known what this my account *was* !   Oh that *death* had made an end *of me* !   My riches have not profited me ; *and* my power is passed from me.   *And God shall say to the keepers of hell,* Take him, and bind him, and cast him into hell to be burned ; then put him into a chain of the length of seventy cubits :[5] because he believed not in the great GOD ; and was not solicitous to feed the poor : wherefore this day he shall have no friend here ; nor *any* food, but the filthy corruption *flowing from the bodies of the damned,* which none shall eat but the sinners.   I swear[6] by that which

---

[1] See Chap. LIV. p. 511.
[2] viz., Sodom and Gomorrah. See Chap. IX. p. 189.
[3] These words seem to intimate the death of the angels at the demolition of their habitation ; beside the ruins whereof they shall lie like dead bodies.
[4] The number of those who bear it at present being generally supposed to be but four ; to whom four more will be added at the last day, for the grandeur of the occasion. (Al Beidâwi.)
[5] *i.e.,* Wrap him round with it, so that he may not be able to stir.
[6] Or, *I will not swear.* See Chap. LVI. p. 519.

ye see, and that which ye see not, that this *is* the discourse of an honourable apostle, and not the discourse of a poet : how little do ye believe ! Neither *is it* the discourse of a soothsayer : how little are ye admonished ! *It is* a revelation from the LORD of all creatures. If *Mohammed* had forged any part of *these* discourses concerning us, verily we had taken him by the right hand, and had cut in sunder the vein of his heart ; neither would we have withheld any of you from *chastising* him. And verily this *book is* an admonition unto the pious ; and we well know that there are *some* of you who charge *the same* with imposture : but it *shall* surely *be* an *occasion of* grievous sighing unto the infidels ; for it *is* the truth of a certainty. Wherefore praise the name of thy LORD, the great *God*.

LXX

THE CHAPTER OF THE STEPS

Revealed at Mecca.

IN THE NAME OF THE MOST MERCIFUL GOD.

ONE[1] demanded and called for vengeance to fall on the unbelievers : there shall be none to avert the same from *being inflicted by* GOD, the possessor of the steps :[2] by *which* the angels ascend unto him, and the spirit *Gabriel also*, in a day whose space is fifty thousand years :[3] where-

---

[1] The person here meant is generally supposed to have been Al Nodar Ebn al Hareth, who said, *O* GOD, *if what Mohammed preaches be the truth from thee, rain down upon us a shower of stones, or send some dreadful judgment to punish us* (Al Zamakh, Al Beidâwi). Others, however, think it was Abu Jahl, who challenged Mohammed to cause a fragment of heaven to fall on them (Al Beidâwi).

[2] By which prayers and righteous actions ascend to heaven ; or by which the angels ascend to receive the divine commands, or the believers will ascend to paradise. Some understand thereby the different orders of angels ; or the heavens, which rise gradually one above another.

[3] This is supposed to be the space which would be required for their ascent from the lowest part of creation to the throne of GOD, if it were to be measured ; or the time which it would take a man to perform that journey ; and this is not contradictory to what is said elsewhere—Chap. XXXII.— (if it be to be interpreted of the ascent of the angels), that the length of the day whereon they ascend is one thousand years ; because that is meant only of their ascent from earth to the lower heaven, including also the time of their descent. But the commentators generally taking the day spoken of in both these passages to be the day of judgment, have recourse to several expedients to reconcile them, some of which we have mentioned in another place (Sale, Prel. Disc. Sect. IV.) : and as both passages seem to contradict what the Mohammedan doctors teach, that GOD will judge all creatures in the space of half a day, they suppose that large number of years is designed to express the time of the previous attendance of those who are to be judged (see ibid. p. 90); or else to the space wherein GOD will judge the unbelieving

fore bear *the insults of the Meccans* with becoming patience ;
for they see *their punishment* afar off, but we see it nigh at
hand. On a certain day the heaven shall become like
molten *brass*, and the mountains like wool of various colours,
scattered abroad by the wind : and a friend shall not ask a
friend *concerning his condition, although* they see one another.
The wicked shall wish to redeem himself from the punishment of that day, by *giving up* his children, and his wife,
and his brother, and his kindred who showed kindness
unto him, and all who *are* in the earth ; and that *this* might
deliver him : by no means : for hell fire, dragging *them*
by *their* scalps, shall call him who shall have turned his
back, and fled *from the faith*, and shall have amassed *riches*,
and covetously hoarded *them*. Verily man is created
extremely impatient :[1] when evil toucheth him, *he is* full
of complaint ; but when good befalleth him, *he becometh*
niggardly : except those who are devoutly given, and who
persevere in their prayers ; and those of whose substance
a due and certain portion *is ready to be given* unto him who
asketh, and him who is forbidden *by shame to ask* : and those
who sincerely believe the day of judgment, and who dread
the punishment of their LORD (for *there is* none secure from
the punishment of their LORD) : and who abstain from
the carnal knowledge of *women* other than their wives, or
the *slaves* which their right hands possess (for *as to them*
they shall be blameless ; but whoever coveteth *any women*
besides these, they *are* transgressors) : and those who faithfully keep what they are entrusted with, and their covenant ; and who are upright in their testimonies, and who
carefully observe *the requisite rites in* their prayers : these
shall dwell amidst gardens, highly honoured. What aileth
the unbelievers, that they run before thee in companies,
on the right hand and on the left ? Doth every man of
them wish to enter into a garden of delight ? By no means :
verily we have created them of that which they know.[2] I
swear[3] by the LORD of the east and of the west,[4] that we

nations, of which, they say, there will be fifty, the trial of each nation taking
up one thousand years, though that of the true believers will be over in the
short space above mentioned. (Al Zamakh.)

[1] See Chap. XVII. p. 273.

[2] viz., Of filthy seed, which bears no relation or resemblance to holy
beings ; wherefore it is necessary for him who would hope to be an inhabitant
of paradise, to perfect himself in faith and spiritual virtues, to fit himself
for that place. (Al Beidâwi.)

[3] Or, *I will not swear*, &c. See Chap. LVI. p. 519.

[4] The original words are in the plural number, and signify the different

are able to *destroy them, and to* substitute better than them *in their room*; neither *are* we to be prevented, *if we shall please so to do*. Wherefore suffer them to wade in vain disputes, and to amuse themselves with sport : until they meet their day with which they have been threatened ; the day *whereon* they shall come forth hastily from *their* graves, as though they were *troops* hastening to *their* standard : their looks *shall be* downcast ; ignominy shall attend them. This *is* the day with which they have been threatened.

LXXI

THE CHAPTER OF NOAH
Revealed at Mecca.

IN THE NAME OF THE MOST MERCIFUL GOD.

VERILY we sent Noah unto his people, *saying*, Warn thy people, before a grievous punishment overtake them. *Noah* said, O my people, verily I *am* a public warner unto you ; wherefore, serve GOD and fear him, and obey me : he will forgive you *part* of your sins,[1] and will grant you respite until a determined time : for GOD's determined time, when it cometh, shall not be deferred ; if ye were men of understanding *ye would know this*. He said, LORD, verily I have called my people night and day ; but my calling only increaseth their aversion : and whensoever I call them *to the true faith*, that thou mayest forgive them, they put their fingers in their ears, and cover themselves with their garments, and persist *in their infidelity*, and proudly disdain *my counsel*. Moreover I invited them openly, and I spake to them again in public ; and I also secretly admonished them in private : and I said, Beg pardon of your LORD ; for he is inclined to forgive : and he will cause the heaven to pour down rain plentifully upon you, and will give you increase of wealth and of children ;[2] and he will provide you gardens, and furnish you with rivers. What aileth you, that ye hope not for benevolence in GOD ;[3]

points of the horizon at which the sun rises and sets in the course of the year. See Chap. XXXVII. p. 436.

[1] *i.e.,* Your past sins, which are done away by the profession of the true faith.

[2] It is said that after Noah had for a long time preached to them in vain, GOD shut up the heaven for forty years, and rendered their women barren. (Al Beidâwi.)

[3] *i.e.,* That GOD will accept and amply reward those who serve him ?

since he hath created you variously ?[1] Do ye not see how
GOD hath created the seven heavens, one above another,
and hath placed the moon therein for a light, and hath
appointed the sun for a taper ? GOD hath also produced
and caused you to spring forth from the earth : hereafter
he will cause you to return into the same ; and he will
again take you *thence,* by bringing *you* forth *from your
graves.* And GOD hath spread the earth as a carpet for
you, that ye may walk therein through spacious paths.
Noah said, LORD, verily they are disobedient unto me, and
they follow him whose riches and children do no other than
increase his perdition. And they devised a dangerous plot
against Noah : and *the chief men* said *to the others,* Ye shall
by no means leave your gods ; neither shall ye forsake
Wadd, nor Sowâ, nor Yaghûth, and Yäûk, and Nesr.[2]
And they seduced many (for thou shalt only increase error
in the wicked) ; because of their sins they were drowned,
and cast into the fire *of hell* ; and they found none to protect
them against GOD. And Noah said, LORD, leave not any
families of the unbelievers on the earth : for if thou leave
them, they will seduce thy servants, and will beget none
but a wicked and unbelieving *offspring.*[3] LORD, forgive
me and my parents,[4] and every one who shall enter my
house,[5] being a true believer, and the true believers of
both sexes ; and add unto the unjust doers nothing but
destruction.

For some suppose Noah's people made him this answer, *If what we now
follow be the truth, we ought not to forsake it ; but if it be false, how will* GOD
accept, or be favourable unto us, who have rebelled against him ? (Al Beidâwi.)
  [1] That is, as the commentators expound it, by various steps or changes,
from the original matter, till ye became perfect men. (See Chaps. XXII.
and XXIII.)
  [2] These were five idols worshipped by the antediluvians, and afterwards
by the ancient Arabs. See Sale, Prel. Disc. Sect. I.
  [3] They say Noah preferred not this prayer for the destruction of his
people till after he had tried them for nine hundred and fifty years, and
found them incorrigible reprobates.
  [4] His father Lamech, and his mother, whose name was Shamkha, the
daughter of Enosh, being true believers.
  [5] The commentators are uncertain whether Noah's dwelling-house be
here meant, or the temple he had built for the worship of GOD, or the ark.

LXXII

THE CHAPTER OF THE GENII

Revealed at Mecca.

IN THE NAME OF THE MOST MERCIFUL GOD.

SAY, It hath been revealed unto me that a company of genii attentively heard *me reading the Korân,*[1] and said, Verily we have heard an admirable discourse ; which directeth unto the right institution : wherefore we believe therein, and we will by no means associate any *other* with our LORD. He (may the majesty of our LORD be exalted !) hath taken no wife, nor *hath he begotten* any issue. Yet the foolish among us[2] hath spoken that which is extremely false of GOD ; but we verily thought that neither man nor genius[3] would by any means have uttered a lie concerning GOD. And there are certain men who fly for refuge unto certain of the genii :[4] but they increase their folly and transgression : and they also thought, as ye thought,[5] that GOD would not raise any one to life. And we *formerly* attempted *to pry into what was transacting in* heaven ; but we found the same filled with a strong guard *of angels*, and with flaming darts : and we sat on *some of the* seats thereof to hear *the discourse of its inhabitants* ; but whoever listeneth now findeth a flame laid in ambush for him, *to guard the celestial confines.*[6] And we know not whether evil be *hereby* intended against those who *are* in the earth, or whether their LORD intendeth to direct them aright. *There are* some among us who are upright ; and *there are* some among us who are otherwise : we are of different ways. And we verily thought that we could by no means frustrate GOD in the earth, neither could we escape him by flight : wherefore, when we had heard the direction *contained in the Korân*, we believed therein. And whoever believeth in his LORD, need not fear any diminution *of his reward*, nor any injustice. *There are some* Moslems among us ; and *there are others* of

---

[1] See Chap. XLVI. p. 487.

[2] viz., Eblis, or the rebellious genii.   [3] See p. 372.

[4] For the Arabs, when they found themselves in a desert in the evening (the genii being supposed to haunt such places about that time), used to say, *I fly for refuge unto the Lord of this valley, that he may defend me from the foolish among his people.* (Al Beidâwi.)

[5] It is uncertain which of these pronouns is to be referred to mankind, and which to the genii, some expositors taking that of the third person to relate to the former, and that of the second person to the latter ; and others being of the contrary opinion.

[6] See Chap. XV. p. 252.

us who swerve from righteousness.[1]   And whoso embraceth
Islâm, they earnestly seek true direction ; but those who
swerve from righteousness shall be fuel for hell.   If they
tread in the way *of truth,* we will surely water them with
abundant rain :[2] that we may prove them thereby ; but
whoso turneth aside from the admonition of his LORD, him
will he send into a severe torment.   Verily the places of
worship *are set apart* unto GOD : wherefore invoke not any
other therein together with GOD.   When the servant of God [3]
stood up to invoke him, it wanted little but that *the
genii* had pressed on him in crowds, *to hear him rehearse
the Korân.*   Say, Verily I call upon my LORD only, and I
associate no *other god* with him.   Say, Verily I am not able
of myself, to procure you either hurt or a right institution.
Say, Verily none can protect me against GOD ; neither
shall I find any refuge besides him.   *I can do no more* than
publish *what hath been revealed unto me* from GOD, and his
messages.   And whosoever shall be disobedient unto GOD
and his apostle, for him *is* the fire of hell *prepared* ; they
shall remain therein for ever.   Until they see *the vengeance*
with which they are threatened, *they will not cease their
opposition* : but then shall they know who *were* the weaker
in a protector, and the fewer in number.   Say, I know not
whether *the punishment* with which ye are threatened *be*
nigh, or whether my LORD will appoint for it a distant
term.   He knoweth the secrets of futurity ; and he doth
not communicate his secrets unto any, except an apostle
in whom he is well pleased : and he causeth a guard *of
angels* to march before him and behind him, that he may
know that they have executed the commissions of their
LORD[4] : he comprehendeth whatever is with them, and
counteth all things by number.

---

[1] See Sale, Prel. Disc. Sect. IV.
[2] *i.e.,* We will grant them plenty of all good things.   Some think by these
words rain is promised to the Meccans, after their seven years' drought, on
their embracing Islâm.
[3] viz., Mohammed.
[4] That is to say, either that the prophet may know Gabriel and the
other angels, who bring down the revelation, have communicated it to him
pure and free from any diabolical suggestions; or that GOD may know that
the prophet has published the same to mankind.   (Al Beidâwi.)

LXXIII

THE CHAPTER OF THE WRAPPED UP

Revealed at Mecca.[1]

IN THE NAME OF THE MOST MERCIFUL GOD.

O THOU wrapped up,[2] arise *to prayer, and continue therein* during the night, except a small part ;[3] *that is to say, during* one half thereof : or do thou lessen the same a little, or add thereto.[4]   And repeat the Korân with a distinct and sonorous voice : for we will lay on thee a weighty word.[5]   Verily the rising by night[6] is more efficacious for steadfast continuance *in devotion,* and more conducive to decent pronunciation :[7] for in the daytime

---

[1] Some will have the last verse, beginning at these words, *Verily thy* LORD *knoweth,* &c., to have been revealed at Medina.

[2] When this revelation was brought to Mohammed, he was wrapped up in his garments, being affrighted at the appearance of Gabriel ; or, as some say, he lay sleeping unconcernedly, or, according to others, praying, wrapped up in one part of a large mantle or rug, with the other part of which Ayesha had covered herself to sleep (Al Zamakh., Al Beidâwi).   This epithet of *wrapped up,* and another of the same import given to Mohammed in the next chapter, have been imagined, by several learned men (Hotting. Hist. Orient. l. 1, c. 2.   Mɔrracc. in Alc. p. 763.   Vide Gagnier, not. ad Abulf. Vit. Moh. p. 9), pretty plainly to intimate his being subject to the falling sickness :   a malady generally attributed to him by the Christians (see Prideaux, Life of Mahomet, p.16, and the authors there cited), but mentioned by no Mohammedan writer.   Though such an inference may be made, yet I think it scarce probable, much less necessary (see Ockley's Hist. of the Saracens, vol. i. p. 300, &c.).

[3] For a half is such, with respect to the whole.   Or, as the sentence may be rendered, *Pray half the night, within a small matter,* &c.   Some expound these words as an exception to nights in general ; according to whom the sense will be, *Spend one-half of every night in prayer, except some few nights in the year,* &c.   (Al Beidâwi.)

[4] *i.e.,* Set apart either less than half the night, as one-third, for example, or more, as two-thirds.   Or the meaning may be, either take a small matter from a lesser part of the night than one-half, *e.g.,* from one-third, and so reduce it to a fourth ; or add to such lesser part, and make it a full half. (Al Beidâwi.)

[5] viz., The precepts contained in the Korân ; which are heavy and difficult to those who are obliged to observe them, and especially to the prophet whose care it was to see that his people observed them also.   (Al Beidâwi, Jallalo'ddin.)

[6] Or, *the person who riseth by night ;* or, *the hours,* or particularly *the first hours of the night,* &c.

[7] For the night time is most proper for meditation and prayer, and also for reading GOD's word distinctly and with attention, by reason of the absence of every noise and object which may distract the mind.   Marracci, having mentioned this natural explanation of the Mohammedan commentators, because he finds one word in the verse which may be taken in a sense tending that way, says the whole may with greater exactness be expounded of the fitness of the night season for amorous diversions and discourse ; and he paraphrases it in Latin thus : *Certe in principio noctis majus robur et vim habet homo, ad fœminas premendas et subagitandas, et ad clarioribus verbis amores suos propalandos.* (Marracc. in Alc. p. 759.)   A most effectual way, this, to turn a book into ridicule !

thou hast long employment. And commemorate the name of thy LORD: and separate thyself unto him, renouncing worldly vanities. *He is* the LORD of the east and of the west; *there is* no GOD but he. Wherefore take him for thy patron: and patiently suffer the *contumelies* which the *infidels* utter *against thee*; and depart from them with a decent departure. And let me alone with those who charge *the Korân* with falsehood, who enjoy the blessings of this life; and bear with them for awhile: verily with us *are* heavy fetters, and a burning fire, and food ready to choke *him who swalloweth it*,[1] and painful torment. On a certain day the earth shall be shaken, and the mountains *also*, and the mountains shall become a heap of sand poured forth. Verily we have sent unto you an apostle, to bear witness against you; as we sent an apostle unto Pharaoh: but Pharaoh was disobedient unto the apostle; wherefore we chastised him with a heavy chastisement. How, therefore, will ye escape, if ye believe not, the day which shall make children become grey-headed *through terror*? The heaven *shall be* rent in sunder thereby: the promise thereof shall surely be performed. Verily this *is* an admonition; and whoever is willing *to be admonished*, will take the way unto his LORD. Thy LORD knoweth that thou continuest *in prayer and meditation sometimes* near two-third parts of the night, and *sometimes* one half thereof, and *at other times* one third part thereof: and a part of *thy companions*, who *are* with thee, *do the same*. But GOD measureth the night and the day; he knoweth that ye cannot *exactly* compute the same: wherefore he turneth favourably unto you.[2] Read, therefore, so much of the Korân as may be easy *unto you*. He knoweth that there will be some infirm among you; and others travel through the earth, that they may obtain *a competency* of the bounty of GOD; and others fight in the defence of GOD's faith. Read, therefore, so much of the same as may be easy. And observe the stated times of prayer, and pay the legal alms; and lend unto GOD an acceptable loan; for whatever good ye send on before for

[1] As thorns and thistles, the fruit of the infernal tree Al Zakkûm. and the corruption flowing from the bodies of the damned.

[2] By making the matter easy to you, and dispensing with your scrupulous counting of the hours of the night which ye are directed to spend in reading and praying: for some of the Moslems, not knowing how the time passed, used to watch the whole night, standing and walking about till their legs and feet swelled in a sad manner. The commentators add that this precept of dedicating a part of the night to devotion, is abrogated by the institution of the five hours of prayer. (Al Beidâwi.)

your souls, ye shall find the same with GOD. This *will be* better, and will merit a greater reward.[1] And ask GOD forgiveness ; for GOD *is* ready to forgive *and* merciful.

LXXIV

THE CHAPTER OF THE COVERED

Revealed at Mecca.

IN THE NAME OF THE MOST MERCIFUL GOD.

O THOU covered,[2] arise and preach,[3] and magnify thy LORD. And cleanse thy garments : and flee *every* abomination :[4] and be not liberal, in hopes to receive more in return : and patiently wait for thy LORD. When the trumpet shall sound, verily that day *shall be* a day of distress and uneasiness unto the unbelievers. Let me alone with him whom I have created,[5] on whom I have bestowed abundant riches, and children dwelling in his presence,[6] and for whom I have disposed *affairs* in a smooth and easy manner,[7] and who desireth that I will yet add *other blessings unto him.* By no means : because he is an adversary to

---

[1] *i.e.*, The good which ye shall do in your lifetime will be much more meritorious in the sight of GOD than what ye shall defer till death, and order by will. (Al Beidâwi.)

[2] That is," wrapped up in a mantle." It is related, from Mohammed's own mouth, that being on Mount Hirâ, and hearing himself called, he looked on each hand, and saw nobody ; but looking upwards, he saw the angel Gabriel on a throne, between heaven and earth ; at which sight being much terrified, he returned to his wife Khadîjah, and bade her cover him up ; and that then the angel descended, and addressed him in the words of the text. From hence some think this chapter to have been the first which was revealed : but the more received opinion is, that it was the 96th. Others say that the prophet, having been reviled by certain of the Koreish, was sitting in a melancholy and pensive posture, wrapped up in his mantle, when Gabriel accosted him : and some say he was sleeping. See the second note to the preceding chapter.

[3] It is generally supposed that Mohammed is here commanded more especially to warn his near relations, the Koreish ; as he is expressly ordered to do in a subsequent revelation. (See Chap. XXVI., and Sale, Prel. Disc. Sect. II. p. 45.)

[4] By the word *abomination* the commentators generally agree idolatry to be principally intended.

[5] The person here meant is generally supposed to have been Al Walîd Ebn al Mogheira (Al Zamakh., Al Beidâwi, Jallal.), a principal man among the Koreish.

[6] Being well provided for, and not obliged to go abroad to seek their living, as most others of the Meccans were. (Al Beidâwi.)

[7] By facilitating his advancement to power and dignity ; which were so considerable that he was surnamed Rihâna Koreish, or *The sweet odour of the Koreish, and* Al Wahîd, *i.e., The only one,* or *The incomparable.* (Al Beidâwi.)

our signs.[1] I will afflict him with grievous calamities :[2]
for he hath devised and prepared *contumelious expressions
to ridicule the Korân.* May he be cursed : how *maliciously*
hath he prepared *the same* ! And again, may he be cursed :
how *maliciously* hath he prepared *the same* ! Then he
looked, and frowned, and put on an austere countenance :
then he turned back, and was elated with pride ; and he
said, This *is* no other than a piece of magic, borrowed from
others : these *are* only the words of a man. I will cast him
to be burned in hell. And what shall make thee to understand what hell *is* ? It leaveth not *anything unconsumed*,
neither doth it suffer *anything* to escape : it scorcheth
men's flesh : over the same *are* nineteen *angels appointed.*
We have appointed none but angels to preside over *hell*
fire :[3] and we have expressed the number of them only for
an occasion of discord to the unbelievers ;[4] that they to
whom the scriptures have been given, may be certain *of
the veracity of this book,*[5] and the true believers may increase
in faith ; and that those to whom the scriptures have been
given, and the true believers, may not doubt *hereafter* ;
and that those in whose hearts *there is* an infirmity, and
the unbelievers, may say, What mystery doth GOD intend
by this *number* ? Thus doth GOD cause to err whom
he pleaseth ; and he directeth whom he pleaseth. None
knoweth the armies of thy LORD,[6] besides him : and this[7]
is no other than a memento unto mankind. Assuredly.
By the moon, and the night when it retreateth, and the
morning when it reddeneth, *I swear* that this *is* one of the
most terrible *calamities,* giving warning unto men, as well

[1] On the revelation of this passage it is said that Walîd's prosperity began
to decay, and continued daily so to do to the time of his death.   (Al Beidâwi.)
[2] Or, as the words may be strictly rendered, *I will drive him up the crag
of a mountain* ; which some understand of a mountain of fire, agreeably to a
tradition of their prophet, importing that Al Walîd will be condemned to
ascend this mountain, and then to be cast down from thence, alternately
for ever ; and that he will be seventy years in climbing up, and as many in
falling down.   (Al Beidâwi.)
[3] The reason of which is said to be, that they might be of a different nature
and species from those who are to be tormented, lest they should have a
fellow-feeling for and compassionate their sufferings ; or else, because of their
great strength and severity of temper.   (Al Beidâwi.)
[4] Or, *for a trial of them* : because they might say this was a detail
borrowed by Mohammed of the Jews.
[5] And especially the Jews ; this being conformable to what is contained
in their books.   (Jallal.)
[6] *i.e.,* All his creatures ; or particularly the number and strength of the
guards of hell.
[7] The antecedent seems to be *hell.*

unto him among you who desireth to go forward, as *unto him who chooseth* to remain behind.   Every soul *is* given in pledge for that which it shall have wrought :[1] except the companions of the right hand ;[2] *who shall dwell* in gardens, and shall ask one another questions concerning the wicked, *and shall also ask the wicked themselves, saying,* What hath brought you into hell ?   They shall answer, We were not of those who were constant at prayer, neither did we feed the poor ; and we waded in vain disputes with the fallacious reasoners ; and we denied the day of judgment, until death[3] overtook us : and the intercession of the interceders shall not avail them.   What aileth them, therefore, that they turn aside from the admonition *of the Korân,* as though they *were* timorous asses flying from a lion ?   But every man among them desireth that he may have expanded scrolls delivered to him *from God.*[4] By no means.   They fear not the life to come.   By no means : verily this *is* a *sufficient* warning.   Whoso is willing *to be warned,* him shall it warn : but they shall not be warned, unless GOD shall please.   He *is* worthy to be feared ; and he *is* inclined to forgiveness.

LXXV

THE CHAPTER OF THE RESURRECTION

Revealed at Mecca.

IN THE NAME OF THE MOST MERCIFUL GOD.

VERILY I swear[5] by the day of resurrection ; and I swear by the soul which accuseth *itself* :[6] doth man think that we will not gather his bones together ?   Yea : *we are* able to put together the *smallest* bones of his fingers.

---

[1] See Chap. LII. p. 506.

[2] *i.e.,* The blessed (see Chap. LVI) ; who shall redeem themselves by their good works.   Some say these are the angels, and others, such as die infants.   (Al Beidâwi.)

[3] Literally, *That which is certain.*

[4] For the infidels told Mohammed that they would never obey him as a prophet till he brought each man a writing from heaven, to this effect, viz., *From* GOD *to such a one: Follow Mohammed.*   (Al Beidâwi.)

[5] Or, *I will not swear.*   See Chap. LVI.

[6] Being conscious of having offended, and of failing of perfection, notwithstanding its endeavours to do its duty ; or, *the* pious *soul which shall blame others,* at the last day, for having been remiss in their devotions, &c.   Some understand the words of the soul of Adam, in particular ; who is continually blaming himself for having lost paradise by his disobedience.   (Al Beidâwi.)

But man chooseth to be wicked, *for the time which is* before him. He asketh, When *will* the day of resurrection *be*? But when the sight shall be dazzled, and the moon shall be eclipsed, and the sun and the moon shall be in conjunction;[1] on that day man shall say, Where *is* a place of refuge? By no means: *there shall be* no place to fly unto. With thy LORD *shall be* the sure mansion of rest on that day: on that day shall a man be told that which he hath done first and last.[2] Yea, a man *shall be* an evidence against himself: and though he offer his excuses, *they shall not be received.* Move not thy tongue, *O Mohammed,* in *repeating the revelations brought thee by Gabriel, before he shall have finished the same,* that thou mayest quickly commit them to memory: for the collecting the *Korân* in thy mind, and the *teaching thee the true* reading thereof, *are incumbent* on us. But when we shall have read the same *unto thee by the tongue of the angel,* do thou follow the reading thereof: and afterwards *it shall be* our part to explain it *unto thee.* By no means *shalt thou be thus hasty for the future.* But ye love that which hasteneth away,[3] and neglect the life to come. *Some* countenances, on that day, *shall be* bright, looking towards their LORD; and *some* countenances, on that day *shall be* dismal: they shall think that a crushing calamity shall be brought upon them. Assuredly. When *a man's soul* shall come up to his throat, *in his last agony*; and *the standers-by* shall say, Who bringeth a charm *to recover him*? and shall think it *to be his* departure *out of this world*; and *one* leg shall be joined with *the other* leg:[4] on that day unto thy LORD shall he be driven. For he believed not,[5] neither did he pray; but he accused *God's apostle* of imposture, and

[1] Rising both in the west (Sale, Prel. Disc. Sect. IV.): which conjunction is no contradiction to what is mentioned just before, of the moon's being eclipsed; because those words are not to be understood of a regular eclipse, but metaphorically, of the moon's losing her light at the last day in a preternatural manner. Some think the meaning rather to be, that the sun and the moon shall be *joined* in the loss of their light. (Al Beidâwi.)
[2] Or, the good which he hath done, and that which he hath left undone, &c.
[3] *i.e.,* The fleeting pleasures of this life. The words intimate the natural hastiness and impatience of man (Chap. XVII. p. 273), who takes up with a present enjoyment, though short and bitter in its consequences, rather than wait for real happiness in futurity.
[4] *i.e.,* And when he shall stretch forth his legs together, as is usual with dying persons. The words may also be translated, *And when one affliction shall be joined with another affliction.*
[5] Or, *He did not give alms*; or, *He was not a man of veracity.* Some suppose Abu Jahl, and others one Adi Ebn Rabîa, to be particularly inveighed against in this chapter.

turned back *from obeying him* : then he departed unto his family, walking with a haughty mien. Wherefore, woe be unto thee ; woe ! And again, Woe be unto thee ; woe ! Doth man think that he shall be left at full liberty, *without control* ? Was he not a drop of seed, which was emitted ? Afterwards he became a little coagulated blood ; and *God* formed him, and fashioned him with just proportion : and made of him two sexes, the male and the female. Is not he *who hath done this* able to quicken the dead ?

LXXVI

THE CHAPTER OF MAN

Revealed at Mecca.[1]

IN THE NAME OF THE MOST MERCIFUL GOD.

DID there not pass over man a *long* space of time ; during which he was a thing not worthy of remembrance ?[2] Verily we have created man of the mingled seed of both sexes, that we might prove him : and we have made him to hear and to see.[3] We have surely directed him in the way ; whether *he be* grateful or ungrateful. Verily we have prepared for the unbelievers chains, and collars, and burning fire. But the just shall drink of a cup *of wine*, mixed with *the water of* Cafur,[4] a fountain whereof the servants of GOD shall drink ; they shall convey the same by channels *whithersoever they please. These* fulfil *their* vow, and dread the day, the evil whereof will disperse itself far abroad ; and give food unto the poor, and the orphan, and the bondman, for his sake, *saying,* We feed you for GOD's sake only : we desire no recompence from you, nor any thanks : verily we dread, from our LORD, a dismal *and* calamitous day.[5]

[1] It is somewhat doubtful whether this chapter was revealed at Mecca or Medina.

[2] Some take these words to be spoken of Adam, whose body, according to the Mohammedan tradition, was at first a figure of clay, and was left forty years to dry before GOD breathed life into it (Chap. II. p. 5) ; others understand them of man in general, and of the time he lies in the womb.

[3] That he might be capable of receiving the rules and directions given by GOD for his guidance (Al Beidâwi) ; and of meriting reward or punishment for his observance or neglect of them.

[4] Is the name of a fountain in paradise, so called from its resembling *camphor* (which the word signifies) in odour and whiteness. Some take the word for an appellative, and think the wine of paradise will be mixed with *camphor*, because of its agreeable coolness and smell. (Al Beidâwi.)

[5] It is related that Hasan and Hosein, Mohammed's grandchildren, on a certain time being both sick, the prophet, among others, visited them, and they wished Ali to make some vow to GOD for the recovery of his sons :

Wherefore GOD shall deliver them from the evil of that day, and shall cast on them brightness of countenance, and joy ; and shall reward them, for their patient persevering, with a garden, and silk *garments* : therein shall they repose themselves on couches ; they shall see therein neither sun nor moon :[1] and the shades thereof *shall be* near *spreading* above them, and the fruits thereof shall hang low, so as to be easily gathered. And *their attendants* shall go round about unto them, with vessels of silver, and goblets : the bottles shall be bottles of silver *shining like glass* ; they shall determine the measure thereof *by their wish*. And therein shall they be given to drink of a cup *of wine*, mixed with *the water* of Zenjebil,[2] a fountain in *paradise* named Salsabil :[3] and youths, which shall continue *for ever in their bloom*, shall go round *to attend* them ; when thou seest them, thou shalt think them *to be* scattered pearls : and when thou lookest, there shalt thou behold delights, and a great kingdom. Upon them *shall be* garments of fine green silk, and of brocades, and they shall be adorned with brace ets of silver : and their LORD shall give them to drink of a most pure liquor ; *and shall say unto them*, Verily this is your reward : and your endeavour is gratefully accepted. Verily we have sent down unto thee the Korân, by a *gradual* revelation. Wherefore patiently wait the judgment of the LORD ; and obey not any wicked person or unbeliever among them. And commemorate the name of thy LORD, in the morning and in the evening : and *during some part* of the night worship him, and praise him a long *part of the*

---

whereupon Ali, and Fâtema, and Fidda, their maid-servant, vowed a fast of three days in case they did well ; as it happened they did. This vow was performed with so great strictness, that the first day, having no provisions in the house, Ali was obliged to borrow three measures of barley of one Simeon, a Jew, of Khaibar, one measure of which Fâtema ground the same day, and baked five cakes of the meal, and they were set before them to break their fast with after sunset : but a poor man coming to them, they gave all their bread to him, and passed the night without tasting anything except water. The next day Fâtema made another measure into bread, for the same purpose ; but an orphan begging some food, they chose to let him have it, and passed that night as the first ; and the third day they likewise gave their whole provision to a famished captive. Upon this occasion Gabriel descended with the chapter before us, and told Mohammed that GOD congratulated him on the virtues of his family. (Al Beidâwi.)

[1] Because they shall not need the light of either. (See Revel. xxi. 23.) The word Zamharír, here translated *moon*, properly signifies *extreme cold* : for which reason some understand the meaning of the passage to be, that in paradise there shall be felt no excess either of *heat* or of *cold*.

[2] The word signifies *ginger*, which the Arabs delight to mix with the water they drink ; and therefore the water of this fountain is supposed to have the taste of that spice. (Al Beidâwi, Jallal.)

[3] Signifies water which flows gently and pleasantly down the throat.

night. Verily these *men* love the transitory *life*, and leave behind them the heavy day *of judgment.* We have created them, and have strengthened their joints ; and when we please, we will substitute *others* like unto them, in their stead. Verily this *is* an admonition : and whoso willeth, taketh the way unto his LORD : but ye shall not will, unless GOD willeth ; for GOD is knowing *and* wise. He leadeth whom he pleaseth unto his mercy : but for the unjust hath he prepared a grievous punishment.

LXXVII

THE CHAPTER OF THOSE WHICH ARE SENT
Revealed at Mecca.

IN THE NAME OF THE MOST MERCIFUL GOD.

BY the *angels* which are sent *by God*, following one another in a continual series ; and those which move swiftly, with a rapid motion ; and by those which disperse *his commands*, by divulging them *through the earth* ; and by those which separate *truth from falsehood*, by distinguishing *the same ;* and by those which communicate *the divine* admonitions, to excuse, or to threaten :[1] verily that which ye are promised[2] *is* inevitable. When the stars, therefore, shall be out, and when the heaven shall be cloven in sunder, and when the mountains shall be winnowed, and when the apostles shall have a time assigned them *to appear and bear testimony against their respective people* ; to what a day shall *that appointment* be deferred ! to the day of separation : and what shall cause thee to understand what the day of separation *is* ? On that day, woe be unto them who accused *the prophets* of imposture ! Have we not destroyed the *obstinate unbelievers* of old ? We will also cause those of the latter times to follow them. Thus do we deal with the wicked. Woe be, on that day, unto them who accused *the prophets* of imposture ! Have we not created you of a contemptible

[1] Some understand the whole passage of the *verses* of the Korân ; which *continued to be sent down*, parcel after parcel, during the space of several years, and which *rescind* (for so the verb *ásafa* may also be translated) and abolish all former dispensations, *divulging and making known* the ways of salvation, *distinguishing* truth from falsehood, and *communicating admonition*, &c. Some interpret the first three verses of the *winds, sent in a continual succession, blowing with a violent gust, and dispersing* rain over the earth ; and others give different explanations.

[2] viz., The day of judgment.

drop *of seed*, which we placed in a sure repository, until the fixed term *of delivery* ? And we were able *to do this* : for we are most powerful. On that day, woe be unto those who accused *the prophets* of imposture ! Have we not made the earth to contain the living and the dead, and placed therein stable *and* lofty *mountains*, and given you fresh water to drink ? Woe be, on that day, unto those who accused *the prophets* of imposture ! *It shall be said unto them*, Go ye to the *punishment* which ye denied as a falsehood : go ye into the shadow *of the smoke of hell*, which *shall ascend* in three columns, and shall not shade *you from the heat*, neither shall it be of service against the flame ; but it shall cast forth sparks *as big* as towers, resembling yellow camels *in colour*.[1] Woe be, on that day, unto those who accused *the prophets* of imposture ! This *shall be* a day whereon they shall not speak *to any purpose* ; neither shall they be permitted to excuse themselves. Woe be, on that day, unto those who accused *the prophets* of imposture ! This *shall be* the day of separation : we will assemble *both* you and your predecessors. Wherefore, if ye have any cunning stratagem, employ stratagems against me. Woe be, on that day, unto those who accused *the prophets* of imposture ! But the pious *shall dwell* amidst shades and fountains, and fruits of the *kinds* which they shall desire : *and it shall be said unto them*, Eat and drink with easy digestion, *in recompence* for that which ye have wrought ; for thus do we reward the righteous doers. Woe be, on that day, unto those who accused *the prophets* of imposture ! Eat, *O unbelievers*, and enjoy *the pleasures of this life*, for a little while : verily ye *are* wicked men. Woe be, on that day, unto those who accused *the prophets* of imposture ! And when it is said unto them, Bow down ; they do not bow down. Woe be, on that day, unto those who accused *the prophets* of imposture ! In what new revelation will they believe, after this ?

[1] Being of a fiery colour. Others, however, suppose these sparks will be of a dusky hue, like that of *black* camels, which always inclines a little to the yellow ; the word translated *yellow*, signifying sometimes *black*. Some copies, by the variation of a vowel, have *cables* instead of *camels*.

LXXVIII

THE CHAPTER OF THE NEWS

Revealed at Mecca.

IN THE NAME OF THE MOST MERCIFUL GOD.

(XXX.)[1] CONCERNING what do *the unbelievers* ask questions of one another? Concerning the great news *of the resurrection*, about which they disagree. Assuredly they shall hereafter know *the truth thereof*. Again, Assuredly they shall hereafter know *the truth thereof*. Have we not made the earth for a bed, and the mountains for stakes *to fix the same*? And have we not created you of two sexes; and appointed your sleep for rest; and made the night a garment *to cover you*; and destined the day to the gaining *your* livelihood; and built over you seven solid *heavens*; and placed *therein* a burning lamp? And do we not send down from the *clouds* pressing forth rain, water pouring down in abundance, that we may thereby produce corn, and herbs, and gardens planted thick *with trees*? Verily the day of separation is a fixed period: the day whereon the trumpet shall sound, and ye shall come in troops *to judgment*; and the heaven shall be opened, and shall be *full of* gates *for the angels to pass through*; and the mountains shall pass away, and become *as* a vapour; verily hell shall be a place of ambush, a receptacle for the transgressors, who shall remain therein for ages: they shall not taste any refreshment therein, or any drink, except boiling water, and filthy corruption: a fit recompence *for their deeds*! For they hoped that they should not be brought to an account, and they disbelieved our signs, accusing them of falsehood. But everything have we computed, and written down. Taste, therefore: we will not add unto you *any other* than torment.[2] But for the pious *is prepared* a place of bliss: gardens planted with trees, and vineyards, and *damsels* with swelling breasts, of equal age *with themselves*, and a full cup. They shall hear no vain discourse there, nor any falsehood. *This shall be their* recompence from thy LORD; a gift *fully* sufficient: *from* the LORD of heaven and earth, and of whatever *is* between them; the Merciful. *The inhabitants of heaven or of earth*

---

[1] Section XXX. the last of the Ajza, begins here. See Sale, Prel. Disc. p. 63.

[2] This, say the commentators, is the most severe and terrible sentence in the whole Korân pronounced against the inhabitants of hell; they being hereby assured that every change in their torments will be for the worse.

shall not dare to demand audience of him : the day whereon the spirit *Gabriel* and the *other* angels shall stand in order, they shall not speak *in behalf of themselves or others*, except he *only* to whom the Merciful shall grant permission, and who shall say that which is right. This *is* the infallible day. Whoso, therefore, willeth, let him return unto his LORD. Verily we threaten you with a punishment nigh at hand : the day whereon a man shall behold *the good or evil deeds* which his hands have sent before him ; and the unbeliever shall say, Would to GOD I were dust !

LXXIX

THE CHAPTER OF THOSE WHO TEAR FORTH

Revealed at Mecca.

IN THE NAME OF THE MOST MERCIFUL GOD.

BY the *angels* who tear forth *the souls of some* with violence ; and by those who draw forth *the souls of others* with gentleness :[1] by those who glide swimmingly *through the air with the commands of God* ; and those who precede and usher *the righteous to paradise* ; and those who subordinately govern the affairs *of this world* : on a *certain* day, the disturbing *blast of the trumpet* shall disturb *the universe* ; and the subsequent *blast* shall follow it. On that day *men's* hearts shall tremble : their looks *shall be* cast down. *The infidels* say, Shall we surely be made to return whence we came ?[2] After we shall have become rotten bones, *shall we be again raised to life* ? They say, This then *will be* a return to loss. Verily it *will be* but one sounding *of the trumpet*,[3] and behold, they *shall appear alive* on the face of the earth.[4] Hath not the story of Moses reached thee ? When his LORD called unto him in the holy valley Towa,[5]

[1] These are the angel of death and his assistants, who will take the souls of the wicked in a rough and cruel manner from the inmost part of their bodies, as a man drags up a thing from the bottom of the sea ; but will take the souls of the good in a gentle and easy manner from their lips, as when a man draws a bucket of water at one pull. (Al Beidâwi.) There are several other interpretations of this whole passage ; some expounding all the five parts of the oath of the stars, others of the souls of men, others of the souls of warriors in particular, and others of war-horses : a detail of which, I apprehend, would rather tire than please.

[2] *i.e.*, Shall we be restored to our former condition ?

[3] viz., The second or third blast, according to different opinions.

[4] Or, *they shall appear at the place of judgment.* The original word Al Sâhira is also one of the names of hell.

[5] See Chap. XX. p. 305.

saying, Go unto Pharaoh ; for he is insolently wicked : and say, Hast thou *a desire* to become just and holy ? and I will direct thee unto thy LORD, that thou mayest fear *to transgress*. And he showed him the very great sign *of the rod turned into a serpent*, but he charged *Moses* with imposture, and rebelled *against God*. Then he turned back hastily ; and he assembled *the magicians*, and cried aloud, saying, I *am* your supreme LORD. Wherefore GOD chastised him with the punishment of the life to come, and *also* of this present life. Verily herein *is* an example unto him who feareth *to rebel*. *Are* ye more difficult to create, or the heaven which *God* hath built ? He hath raised the height thereof, and hath perfectly formed the same : and he hath made the night thereof dark, and hath produced the light thereof. After this he stretched out the earth,[1] whence he caused to spring forth the water thereof, and the pasture thereof ; and he established the mountains, for the use of yourselves and of your cattle. When the prevailing, the great *day* shall come, on that day shall a man call to remembrance what he hath purposely done : and hell shall be exposed to the view of the spectator. And whoso shall have transgressed, and shall have chosen this present life ; verily hell shall be his abode : but whoso shall have dreaded the appearing before his LORD, and shall have refrained *his* soul from lust ; verily paradise shall be *his* abode. They will ask thee concerning the *last* hour, when *will be* the fixed time thereof. By what means *canst* thou *give* any information of the same ? Unto thy LORD *belongeth the knowledge of* the period thereof : and thou *art* only a warner, who fearest the same. The day whereon they shall see the same, *it shall seem to them* as though they had not tarried *in the world longer* than an evening or a morning thereof.

LXXX

THE CHAPTER OF HE FROWNED
Revealed at Mecca.

IN THE NAME OF THE MOST MERCIFUL GOD.

THE *prophet* frowned, and turned aside, because the blind *man* came unto him :[2] and how dost thou know

---

[1] Which had been created before the heavens, but without expansion. (Jallalo'ddin.)

[2] This passage was revealed on the following occasion. A certain blind

whether he shall peradventure be cleansed *from his sins*;
or *whether* he shall be admonished, and the admonition
shall profit him ? *The man* who is wealthy thou receivest
respectfully : whereas *it is* not *to be charged* on thee, that
he is not cleansed ; but him who cometh unto thee earnestly
seeking *his salvation*, and who feareth God, dost thou neglect.
By no means *shouldst thou act thus*. Verily *the Korân* is
an admonition (and he who is willing retaineth the same) ;
written, in volumes, honourable, exalted, *and* pure ; by the
hands of scribes honoured *and* just.[1] May man be cursed ?
What hath seduced him to infidelity ? Of what thing
doth God create him ? Of a drop of seed doth he create
him ; and he formeth him with proportion ; and then
facilitateth *his* passage *out of the womb* ; afterwards he
causeth him to die, and layeth him in the grave ; hereafter,
when it shall please him, he shall raise him to life. Assuredly.
He hath not hitherto fully performed what *God* hath commanded him. Let man consider his food ; *in what manner
it is provided*. We pour down water by showers ; afterwards we cleave the earth in clefts, and we cause corn to
spring forth therein, and grapes, and clover, and the olive,
and the palm, and gardens planted thick with trees, and
fruits, and grass, for the use of yourselves and of your cattle.
When the stunning sound *of the trumpet* shall be heard ; on
that day shall a man fly from his brother, and his mother,
and his father, and his wife, and his children. Every man
of them, on that day, shall have business *of his own* sufficient
to employ *his thoughts*. On that day *the* faces *of some shall
be* bright, laughing, *and* joyful : and upon *the faces of others*,
on that day, *shall there be* dust ; darkness shall cover them.
These are the unbelievers, the wicked.

man, named Abdallah Ebn Omm Mactûm, came and interrupted Mohammed
while he was engaged in earnest discourse with some of the principal Koreish,
whose conversion he had hopes of ; but the prophet taking no notice of him,
the blind man, not knowing he was otherwise busied, raised his voice, and
said, *O apostle of* God, *teach me some part of what* God *hath taught thee* ;
but Mohammed, vexed at this interruption, frowned and turned away from
him ; for which he is here reprehended. After this, whenever the prophet
saw Ebn Omm Mactûm, he showed him great respect, saying, *The man is
welcome, on whose account my* Lord *hath reprimanded me* ; and he made
him twice governor of Medina. (Jallalo'ddin, Al Beidâwi.)

[1] Being transcribed from the *preserved table*, highly honoured in the sight
of God, kept pure and uncorrupted from the hands of evil spirits, and touched
only by the angels. Some understand hereby the books of the prophets,
with which the Korân agrees in substance. (Al Zamakh.)

LXXXI

THE CHAPTER OF THE FOLDING UP

Revealed at Mecca.

IN THE NAME OF THE MOST MERCIFUL GOD.

WHEN the sun shall be folded up;[1] and when the stars shall fall; and when the mountains shall be made to pass away; and when the camels ten months gone with young shall be neglected;[2] and when the wild beasts shall be gathered together;[3] and when the seas shall boil;[4] and when the souls shall be joined *again to their bodies*; and when the girl who hath been buried alive shall be asked for what crime she was put to death;[5] and when the books shall be laid open; and when the heavens shall be removed;[6] and when hell shall burn fiercely; and when paradise shall be brought near: *every* soul shall know what it hath wrought. Verily I swear[7] by the stars which are retrograde, which move swiftly, *and* which hide themselves;[8] and by the night, when it cometh on; and by the morning, when it appeareth; that these *are* the words of an honourable messenger,[9] endued with strength, of established dignity in the sight of the possessor of the throne, obeyed *by the angels under his authority*, and faithful: and your companion *Mohammed* is not distracted. He had already seen him in the clear horizon:[10] and he suspected not[11] the secrets *revealed unto him.* Neither *are* these the words of

---

[1] As a garment that is laid by.

[2] See Sale, Prel. Disc. Sect. IV. p. 88.

[3] See ibid. p. 92.

[4] See ibid. p. 88.

[5] For it was customary among the ancient Arabs to bury their daughters alive as soon as they were born; for fear they should be impoverished by providing for them, or should suffer disgrace on their account. See Chap. XVI.

[6] Or plucked away from its place, as *the skin is plucked off* from a camel when flaying it; for that is the proper signification of the verb here used. Marracci fancies the passage alludes to that in the Psalms (Psalm civ. 2), where, according to the versions of the Septuagint and the Vulgate, GOD is said to have *stretched out the heavens like a skin.*

[7] Or, *I will not swear*, &c. See Chap. LVI. p. 519.

[8] Some understand hereby the stars in general, but the more exact commentators, five of the planets, viz., the two which accompany the sun, and the three superior planets; which have both a retrograde and a direct motion, and hide themselves in the rays of the sun, or when they set.

[9] *i.e.*, Gabriel.

[10] See Chap. LIII. p. 507.

[11] Some copies, by a change of one letter only, instead of *dhaninin*, read *daninin*; and then the words should be rendered, *He is not tenacious of*, or grudges not to communicate to you. *the secret revelations* which he has received.

an accursed devil.[1] Whither, therefore, are you going? This *is* no other than an admonition unto all creatures; unto him among you who shall be willing to walk uprightly: but ye shall not will, unless GOD willeth, the LORD of all creatures.

LXXXII

THE CHAPTER OF THE CLEAVING IN SUNDER

Revealed at Mecca.

IN THE NAME OF THE MOST MERCIFUL GOD.

WHEN the heaven shall be cloven in sunder; and when the stars shall be scattered; and when the seas shall be suffered to join their waters; and when the graves shall be turned upside down: *every* soul shall know what it hath committed, and *what* it hath omitted. O man, what hath seduced thee against thy gracious LORD, who hath created thee, and put thee together, and rightly disposed thee? In what form he pleased hath he fashioned thee. Assuredly. But ye deny the *last* judgment as a falsehood. Verily *there are appointed* over you guardian *angels,*[2] honourable *in the sight of God,* writing down *your actions*; who know that which ye do. The just *shall* surely *be* in *a place of* delight: but the wicked *shall* surely *be* in hell; they shall be cast therein to be burned, on the day of judgment, and they *shall* not *be* absent therefrom *for ever.* What shall cause thee to understand what the day of judgment *is*? Again, What shall cause thee to understand what the day of judgment *is*? *It is* a day whereon one soul shall not be able to obtain anything in behalf of *another* soul: and the command, on that day, *shall be* GOD'S.

---

[1] Who has overheard, by stealth, the discourse of the angels. The verse is an answer to a calumny of the infidels, who said the Korân was only a piece of divination, or magic; for the Arabs suppose the soothsayer, or magician, receives his intelligence from those evil spirits who are continually listening to learn what they can from the inhabitants of heaven.

[2] See Chap. L., and Sale, Prel. Disc. Sect. IV. p. 77.

LXXXIII

THE CHAPTER OF THOSE WHO GIVE SHORT MEASURE OR WEIGHT

Revealed at Mecca.

IN THE NAME OF THE MOST MERCIFUL GOD.

WOE be unto those who give short measure or weight; who, when they receive by measure from *other* men take the full; but when they measure unto them, or weigh unto them, defraud! Do not these think they shall be raised again at the great day; the day whereon mankind shall stand before the LORD of all creatures? By no means. Verily the register of *the actions of* the wicked *is* surely in Sejjin.[1] And what shall make thee to understand what Sejjin *is*? *It is* a book distinctly written. Woe be, on that day, unto those who accused *the prophets* of imposture; who denied the day of judgment as a falsehood! And none denieth the same as a falsehood, except every unjust *and* flagitious person: who, when our signs are rehearsed unto him, saith, *They are* fables of the ancients. By no means: but rather their lusts have cast a veil over their hearts. By no means. Verily they *shall be* shut out from their LORD on that day; and they shall be sent into hell to be burned: then shall it be said *unto them, by the infernal guards*, This *is* what ye denied as a falsehood. Assuredly. But the register of *the actions of* the righteous *is* in Illiyyûn:[2] and what shall cause thee to understand what Illiyyûn *is*? *It is* a book distinctly written: those who approach near *unto God* are witnesses thereto.[3] Verily the righteous *shall dwell* among delights: *seated* on couches they shall behold *objects of*

---

[1] Is the name of the general register, wherein the actions of all the wicked both men and genii, are distinctly entered. Sejn signifies a *prison*; and this book, as some think, derives its name from thence, because it will occasion those whose deeds are there recorded to be *imprisoned* in hell. Sejjin, or Sajin, is also the name of the dungeon beneath the seventh earth, the residence of Eblis and his host, where, it is supposed by some, that this book is kept, and where the souls of the wicked will be detained till the resurrection. (Jallalo'ddin, Al Beidâwi. See Sale, Prel. Disc. Sect. IV.) If the latter explanation be admitted, the words, *And what shall make thee to understand what Sejjin is*? should be enclosed within a parenthesis.

[2] The word is a plural, and signifies high places. Some say it is the general register wherein the actions of the righteous, whether angels, men, or genii, are distinctly recorded. Others will have it to be a place in the seventh heaven, under the throne of GOD, where this book is kept, and where the souls of the just, as many think, will remain till the last day. (Jallalo'ddin. Sale, Prel. Disc. ubi sup.) If we prefer the latter opinion, the words, *And what shall make thee to understand what Illiyyûn is*? should likewise be enclosed in a parenthesis.

[3] Or, *are present with*, and keep *the same*.

pleasure ; thou shalt see in their faces the brightness of joy. They shall be given to drink of pure wine, sealed ; the seal whereof *shall be* musk :[1] and to this let those aspire, who aspire *to happiness*.　And the *water* mixed therewith *shall be* of Tasnîm,[2] a fountain whereof those shall drink who approach near *unto the divine presence*.[3]　They who act wickedly laugh the true believers to scorn ; and when they pass by them, they wink at one another : and when they turn aside to their people, they turn aside making scurrilous jests : and when they see them, they say, Verily these *are* mistaken men.　But they are not sent *to be* keepers over them.[4] Wherefore one day the true believers, *in their turn*, shall laugh the infidels to scorn :[5] lying on couches, they shall look down *upon them in hell*.　Shall not the infidels be rewarded for that which they have done ?

LXXXIV

THE CHAPTER OF THE RENDING IN SUNDER

Revealed at Mecca.[6]

IN THE NAME OF THE MOST MERCIFUL GOD.

WHEN the heaven shall be rent in sunder, and shall obey its LORD, and shall be capable *thereof* ; and when the earth shall be stretched out,[7] and shall cast forth that which *is* therein,[8] and shall remain empty, and shall obey its LORD, and shall be capable *thereof* : O man, verily labouring thou labourest to *meet* thy LORD, and thou shalt meet him.[9]　And he who shall have his book given into his

---

[1] *i.e.*, The vessels containing the same shall be sealed with musk, instead of clay.　Some understand by the seal of this wine its farewell, or the flavour it will leave in the mouth after it is drunk.

[2] Is the name of a fountain in paradise, so called from its being conveyed to the highest apartments.

[3] For *they* shall drink the water of Tasnîm pure and unmixed, being continually and wholly employed in the contemplation of GOD ; but the other inhabitants of paradise shall drink it mixed with their wine.　(Al Beidâwi.)

[4] *i.e.*, The infidels are not commissioned by GOD to call the believers to account or to judge of their actions.

[5] When they shall see them ignominiously driven into hell.　It is also said, that a door shall be shown the damned, opening into paradise, and they shall be bidden to go in ; but when they come near the door it shall be suddenly shut, and the believers within shall laugh at them.　(Al Beidâwi.)

[6] There are some who take this chapter to have been revealed at Medina.

[7] Like a skin ; every mountain and hill being levelled.

[8] As the treasures hidden in its bowels, and the dead bodies which lie in their graves.

[9] Or, *and thou shalt meet thy labour* ; whether thy works be good, or whether they be evil.

right hand, shall be called to an easy account, and shall turn unto his family[1] with joy : but he who shall have his book given him behind his back,[2] shall invoke destruction *to fall upon him*, and he shall be sent into hell to be burned ; because he rejoiced insolently amidst his family *on earth.* Verily he thought that he should never return *unto God* : yea verily ; but his LORD beheld him.   Wherefore I swear[3] by the redness of the sky after sunset, and by the night, and the *animals* which it driveth together, and by the moon when she is at the full ; ye shall surely be transferred *successively* from state to state.[4]   What *aileth* them, therefore, that they believe not *the resurrection* ; and that, when the Korân is read unto them, they worship not ? [5]   Yea : the unbelievers accuse *the same* of imposture : but GOD well knoweth the *malice* which they keep hidden *in their breasts.*   Wherefore denounce unto them a grievous punishment, except those who believe and do good works : for them *is prepared* a never-failing reward.

LXXXV

THE CHAPTER OF THE CELESTIAL SIGNS
Revealed at Mecca.

IN THE NAME OF THE MOST MERCIFUL GOD.

BY the heaven *adorned* with signs ;[6] by the promised day *of judgment* ; by the witness, and the witnessed ;[7] cursed

---

[1] *i.e.,* His relations or friends who are true believers ; or rather, to his wives and servants, of the damsels and youths of paradise, who wait to receive him. (Al Beidâwi.)

[2] That is, into his left hand ; for the wicked will have that hand bound behind their back, and their right hand to their neck.

[3] Or, *I will not swear.* See Chap. LVI.

[4] *i.e.,* From the state of the living to that of the dead ; and from the state of the dead to a new state of life in another world.

[5] Or, *humble not themselves.*

[6] The original word properly signifies *towers,* which some interpret of real towers (Yahya), wherein it is supposed the angels keep guard (Chap. XV. p. 252); and others, of the stars of the first magnitude : but the generality of expositors understand thereby the twelve signs of the zodiac, wherein the planets make their several stations (Jallal., Al Beidâwi, Yahya).

[7] The meaning of these words is very uncertain, and the explanations of the commentators consequently vary. One thinks *the witness* to be Mohammed, and *that which is borne witness of* to be *the resurrection,* or *the professors of the Mohammedan faith* ; or else that these latter are *the witness,* and the professors of every other religion those who will be *witnessed against* by them. Another supposes *the witness* to be the *guardian angel,* and his charge the person *witnessed against.* Another expounds the words of the day of Arafat, the 9th of Dhu'lhajja, and of the day of slaying the victims, which is the day following, or else of Friday, the day of the weekly assembling of the Mohammedans at their mosques, and of the people who are assembled on those days, &c. (Al Beidâwi.)

were the contrivers of the pit [1] of fire supplied with fuel ;
when they sat round the same, and were witnesses of what
they did against the true believers :[2] and they afflicted them
for no other reason, but because they believed in the mighty,
the glorious GOD, unto whom *belongeth* the kingdom of heaven
and earth : and GOD *is* witness of all things. Verily for those
who prosecute the true believers of either sex, and afterwards
repent not, *is prepared* the torment of hell ; and they *shall
suffer* the pain of burning.[3] But for those who believe, and
do that which is right, are *destined* gardens beneath which
rivers flow : this *shall be* great felicity. Verily the vengeance
of thy LORD *is* severe. He createth, and he restoreth *to
life* : he *is* inclined to forgive, *and* gracious : the possessor
of the glorious throne ; who effecteth that which he pleaseth.
Hath not the story of the hosts of Pharaoh,[4] and of Thamûd,[5]
reached thee ? Yet the unbelievers cease not to accuse
the divine revelations of falsehood : but GOD encompasseth
them behind, *that they cannot escape.* Verily *that which they
reject* is a glorious Korân ; *the original whereof is written* in a
table kept *in heaven.*[6]

LXXXVI

THE CHAPTER OF THE STAR WHICH APPEARETH BY NIGHT
Revealed at Mecca.

IN THE NAME OF THE MOST MERCIFUL GOD.

BY the heaven, and that which appeareth by night : but
what shall cause thee to understand what that which

[1] Literally, *the lords of the pit.* These were the ministers of the persecution
raised by Dhu Nowâs, king of Yaman, who was of the Jewish religion, against
the inhabitants of Najrân : for they having embraced Christianity (at that
time the true religion, by the confession of Mohammed himself), the bigoted
tyrant commanded all those who would not renounce their faith to be cast
into a pit, or trench, filled with fire, and there burnt to ashes (Al Beidâwi.
Vide Poc. Spec. p. 62 ; Ecchellens. Hist. Arab. part i. c. 10 ; and Prid
Life of Mah. p. 61). Others, however, tell the story with different circumstances (Vide D'Herbel. Bibl. Orient. Art. Abou Navas).

[2] Or, as some choose to understand the words, *And shall be witnesses
against themselves, at the day of judgment, of their unjust treatment of the true
believers.*

[3] Which pain, it is said, the persecutors of the Christian martyrs above
mentioned felt in this life ; the fire bursting forth upon them from the pit,
and consuming them. (Al Beidâwi, Yahya.)

[4] See Chap. VII. p. 153.

[5] See ibid. p. 148.

[6] And preserved from the least change or corruption. See Sale, Prelim.
Disc. Sect. III. p. 69 and Sect. IV.

appeareth by night *is* ? *it is* the star of piercing brightness : [1] every soul hath a guardian *set* over it.   Let a man consider, therefore, of what he is created.   He is created of seed poured forth, issuing from the loins, and the breastbones.[2]   Verily *God is* able to restore him *to life,* the day whereon *all* secret thoughts and actions shall be examined into ; and he shall have no power *to defend himself,* nor any protector.   By the heaven which returneth *the rain ;* [3] and by the earth which openeth *to let forth vegetables and springs :* verily this *is* a discourse distinguishing *good from evil ;* and it *is* not *composed* with lightness.   Verily *the infidels* are laying a plot *to frustrate my designs :* but I will lay a plot *for their ruin.* Wherefore, *O prophet,* bear with the unbelievers : let them alone a while.

LXXXVII

THE CHAPTER OF THE MOST HIGH [4]

Revealed at Mecca.

IN THE NAME OF THE MOST MERCIFUL GOD.

PRAISE the name of thy LORD, the most high ; who hath created, and completely formed *his creatures :* and who determineth *them to various ends,*[5] and directeth *them to attain the same ;*[6] and who produceth the pasture *for cattle,* and *afterwards* rendereth the same dry stubble of a dusky hue.   We will enable thee to rehearse *our revelations ;*[7] and thou shalt not forget *any part thereof,* except what GOD shall please ;[8] for he knoweth that which is manifest, and that which is hidden.   And we will facilitate unto thee the most easy *way.*[9]

---

[1] Some take the words to signify any bright star, without restriction ; but others think some particular star or stars to be thereby intended ; which one supposes to be the morning star (peculiarly called *Al Tárek,* or *the appearing by nights*), another Saturn (that planet being by the Arabs surnamed *Al Thakeb,* or *the piercing,* as it was by the Greeks, *Phænon,* or the *shining*), and a third, the *Pleiades.*

[2] *i.e.,* From the loins of the man, and the breast-bones of the woman. (Al Beidâwi, Yahya.)

[3] Or, as some expound it, *Which performeth its periodic motion, returning* to the point from whence it began the same.   The words seem designed to express the alternate returns of the different seasons of the year.

[4] Some take the first word of this chapter, viz., *Praise,* for its title.

[5] Determining their various species, properties, ways of life, &c.   (Al Beidâwi.)

[6] Guiding the rational by their reason and also by revelation, and the irrational by instinct, &c.   (Al Beidâwi.)

[7] See Chap. LXXV. p. 562.

[8] *i.e.,* Except such revelations as GOD shall think fit to abrogate and blot out of thy memory.

[9] To retain the relations communicated to thee by Gabriel ; or, as some

Wherefore admonish *thy people*, if *thy* admonition shall be profitable *unto them*. Whoso feareth *God*, he will be admonished : but the most wretched *unbeliever* will turn away therefrom ; who shall be cast to be broiled in the greater fire *of hell*, wherein he shall not die, neither shall he live. Now hath he attained felicity who is purified *by faith*, and who remembereth the name cf his LORD, and prayeth. But ye prefer this present life : yet the life to come *is* better, and more durable. Verily this *is written* in the ancient books, the books of Abraham and Moses.

LXXXVIII

THE CHAPTER OF THE OVERWHELMING [1]

Revealed at Mecca.

IN THE NAME OF THE MOST MERCIFUL GOD.

HATH the news of the overwhelming *day of judgment* reached thee ? The countenances *of some*, on that day, *shall be* cast down ; labouring *and* toiling :[2] they shall be cast into scorching fire to be broiled : they shall be given to drink of a boiling fountain : they shall have no food, but of dry thorns and thistles ;[3] which shall not fatten, neither shall they satisfy hunger. *But* the countenances *of others*, on that day, *shall be* joyful ; well pleased with their *past* endeavour : they *shall be placed* in a lofty garden, wherein thou shalt hear no vain discourse : therein *shall be* a running fountain : therein *shall be* raised beds, and goblets placed *before them*, and cushions laid in order, and carpets ready spread. Do they not consider the camels,[4] how they are created ; and the heaven, how it is raised, and the mountains, how they are fixed ; and the earth, how it is extended ? Wherefore warn *thy people* ; for thou *art* a warner only : thou

understand the words, *We will dispose thee to the profession and strict observance of the most easy religion*, that is, *of Islâm*.

[1] This is a name, or epithet, of the last day ; because it will suddenly *overwhelm* all creatures with fear and astonishment. It is also a name, or epithet, of hell fire.

[2] *i.e.*, Dragging their chains, and labouring through hell fire, as camels labour through mud, &c. Or, *Employing and fatiguing themselves* in what shall not avail them. (Al Beidâwi.)

[3] Such as the camels eat when green and tender. Some take the original word *Al Darí* for the name of a thorny tree.

[4] These animals are of such use, or rather necessity, in the East, that the creation of a species so wonderfully adapted to those countries is a very proper instance, to an Arabian, of the power and wisdom of GOD. Some, however, think the *clouds* (which the original word *ibl* also signifies) are here intended : *the heaven* being mentioned immediately after.

art not empowered to act with authority over them. But whoever shall turn back,[1] and disbelieve, GOD shall punish him with the greater punishment *of the life to come.* Verily unto us shall they return : then shall it be our part to bring them to account.

LXXXIX

THE CHAPTER OF THE DAYBREAK

Revealed at Mecca.[2]

IN THE NAME OF THE MOST MERCIFUL GOD.

BY the daybreak, and ten nights ;[3] by that which is double, and that which is single ;[4] and by the night when it cometh on : *is there* not in this an oath formed with understanding ? Hast thou not considered how thy LORD dealt with Ad, *the people of* Irem,[5] adorned with lofty buildings,[6]

---

[1] Or, *Except him who shall turn back, and be an infidel : and GOD shall also punish him,* &c. By which exception some suppose that power is here given to Mohammed to chastise obstinate infidels and apostates.

[2] Some are of opinion this chapter was revealed at Medina.

[3] That is, the ten nights of Dhu'lhajja, or the 10th of that month (whence some understand the daybreak mentioned just before, of the morning of that day, or of the preceding) ; or the nights of the 10th of Moharram ; or, as others rather think, the 10th, 11th, and 12th of Dhu'lhajja ; all which are days peculiarly sacred among the Mohammedans.

[4] These words are variously interpreted. Some understand thereby all things in general ; some, all created beings, which are said to have been created by pairs, or of two kinds (see Chap. LI.), and the Creator, who is single ; some, of the *primum mobile,* and the other orbs ; some, of the constellations and the planets ; some, of the nights before mentioned, taken either together or singly ; and some, of the day of slaying the victims (the 10th of Dhu'lhajja), and of the day of Arafat, which is the day before, &c. (Al Zamakh.)

[5] Was the name of the territory or city of the Adites, and of the garden mentioned in the next note ; which were so called from Irem, or Aram, the grandfather of Ad, their progenitor. Some think Aram himself to be here meant, and his name to be added to signify the ancient Adites, his immediate descendants, and to distinguish them from the latter tribe of that name (Al Beidâwi, Jallalo'ddin) : but the adjective and relative joined to the word are, in the original, of the feminine gender, which seems to contradict this opinion.

[6] Or *pillars.* Some imagine these words are used to express the great size and strength of the old Adites (Al Beidâwi. Sale, Prel. Disc. Sect. I.); and then they should be translated, *who were of enormous stature.* But the more exact commentators take the passage to relate to the sumptuous palace and delightful gardens built and made by Sheddâd the son of Ad. For they say Ad left two sons, Sheddâd and Sheddîd, who reigned jointly after his decease, and extended their power over the greater part of the world : but Sheddîd dying, his brother became sole monarch ; who, having heard of the *celestial paradise,* made a garden in imitation thereof, in the deserts of Aden, and called it Irem, after the name of his great-grandfather : when it was finished he set out, with a great attendance, to take a view of it ; but when they were come within a day's journey of the place, they were all destroyed by a terrible noise from heaven. Al Beidâwi adds that one Abdalla

the like whereof hath not been erected in the land ;[1] and with Thamûd, who hewed the rocks in the valley[2] *into houses* ; and with Pharaoh, the contriver of the stakes :[3] who had behaved insolently in the earth, and multiplied corruption therein ?   Wherefore thy LORD poured on them various kinds[4] of chastisement : for thy LORD *is* surely in a watchtower, *whence he observeth the actions of men.*   Moreover man, when his LORD trieth him *by prosperity*, and honoureth him, and is bounteous unto him, saith, My LORD honoureth me : but when he proveth him *by afflictions*, and withholdeth his provisions from him, he saith, My LORD despiseth me.   By no means :[5] but ye honour not the orphan, neither do ye excite *one another* to feed the poor ; and ye devour the inheritance *of the weak*,[6] with undistinguishing greediness ; and ye love riches, with much affection.   By no means *should ye do thus.*   When the earth shall be minutely ground to dust ; and thy LORD shall come, and the angels rank by rank ; and hell, on that day, shall be brought nigh :[7] on that day shall man call to remembrance *his evil deeds* ; but how *shall* remembrance *avail* him ?   He shall say, Would to GOD that I had heretofore done *good works* in my lifetime ![8]   On

Ebn Kelâbah (whom, after D'Herbelot, I have elsewhere named Colabah) accidentally hit on this wonderful place, as he was seeking a camel.,

[1] If we suppose the preceding words to relate to the vast stature of the Adites, these must be translated, *The like of whom hath not been created*, &c.

[2] The learned Greaves, in his translation of Abulfeda's description of Arabia (p. 43.   It was published by Dr. Hudson, in the third vol. of the Geographiæ Veteris Scriptor. Gr. minor), has falsely rendered these words, which are there quoted, *Quibus petræ vallis responsum dederunt*, i.e., *To whom the rocks of the valley returned answer* : which slip being made by so great a man, I do not at all wonder that La Roque, and Petis de la Croix, from whose Latin version, and with whose assistance, La Roque made his French translation of the aforesaid treatise, have been led into the same mistake, and rendered those words, *A qui les pierres de la vallée rendirent réponse.* (Descr. de l'Arabie, mise à la suite du Voyage de la Palestine, par La Roque, p. 35.)   The valley here meant, say the commentators (Jallalo'ddin, Al Beidâwi), is Wâdi'lkora, lying about one day's journey (Ebn Hawkal, apud Abulf. ubi sup.   Geogr. Nub. p. 110)—not five and upwards, as Abulfeda will have it—from Al Hejr.

[3] See Chap. XXXVIII. p. 444.

[4] The original word signifies a *mixture*, and also a *scourge* of plaited thongs : whence some suppose the *chastisement of this life* is here represented by *scourge*, and intimated to be as much lighter than that of the next life, as *scourging* is lighter than death.   (Al Beidâwi.)

[5] For worldly prosperity or adversity is not a certain mark either of the favour or disfavour of GOD.

[6] Not suffering women or young children to have any share in the inheritance of their husbands or parents.   See Chap. IV. p. 72.

[7] There is a tradition that at the last day hell will be dragged towards the tribunal by 70,000 halters, each halter being hauled by 70,000 angels, and that it will come with great roaring and fury.   (Al Beidâwi, Jallalo'ddin.)

[8] Or, *for* this *my* latter *life.*

that day none shall punish with his punishment ; nor shall any bind with his bonds.[1] O thou soul which art at rest,[2] return unto thy LORD, well pleased *with thy reward, and* well pleasing *unto God* : enter among my servants ; and enter my paradise.

XC

THE CHAPTER OF THE TERRITORY

Revealed at Mecca.

IN THE NAME OF THE MOST MERCIFUL GOD.

I SWEAR[3] by this territory[4] (and thou, *O prophet*, residest in this territory),[5] and by the begetter, and that which he hath begotten ;[6] verily we have created man in misery.[7] Doth he think that none shall prevail over him ?[8] He saith, I have wasted plenty of riches.[9] Doth he think that none seeth him ? Have we not made him two eyes, and a tongue, and two lips ; and shown him the two highways *of good and evil* ? Yet he attempteth not the cliff. What shall make thee to understand what the cliff *is* ? *It is* to free the captive ; or to feed, in the day of famine, the orphan who is of kin, or the poor man who lieth on the ground.

[1] *i.e.*, None shall be able to punish or to bind, as GOD shall then punish and bind the wicked. (Al Beidâwi.)

[2] Some expound this of the soul, which, having, by pursuing the concatenation of natural causes, raised itself to the knowledge of that Being which produced them, and exists of necessity, *rests* fully contented, or *acquiesces* in the knowledge of him, and the contemplation of his perfections. By this the reader will observe that the Mohammedans are no strangers to *Quietism*. Others, however, understand the words of the soul, which, having attained the knowledge of the truth, *relies* satisfied, and *relies securely* thereon, undisturbed by doubts ; or of the soul which is *secure* of its salvation, and free from fear or sorrow. (Al Beidâwi.)

[3] Or, *I will not swear*, &c. See Chap. LVI. p. 519.

[4] viz., The sacred territory of Mecca.

[5] Or, *Thou shalt be allowed to do what thou pleasest in this territory* ; the words, in this sense, importing a promise of that absolute power which Mohammed attained on the taking of Mecca. (Al Beidâwi.)

[6] Some understand these words generally ; others of Adam or Abraham, and of their offspring, and of Mohammed in particular. (Al Beidâwi.)

[7] Or, *to trouble*. This passage was revealed to comfort the prophet under the persecutions of the Koreish. (Al Beidâwi.)

[8] Some expositors take a particular person to be here intended, who was one of Mohammed's most inveterate adversaries ; as Al Walîd Ebn al Mogheira (Al Zamakh.) ; others suppose Abu'l Ashadd Ebn Calda to be, the man, who was so very strong, that a large skin being spread under his feet, and ten men pulling at it, they could not make him fall, though they tore the skin to pieces. (Al Beidâwi.)

[9] In a vain and ostentatious manner, or in opposing of Mohammed. (Al Beidâwi.)

Whoso doth this, and is *one* of those who believe, and recommend perseverance unto each other, and recommend mercy unto each other ; these *shall be* the companions of the right hand.[1] But they who shall disbelieve our signs, shall be the companions of the left hand :[2] above them *shall be* arched fire.

[1] See Chap. LVI. p. 516.   [2] See ibid.

XCI

THE CHAPTER OF THE SUN

Revealed at Mecca.

IN THE NAME OF THE MOST MERCIFUL GOD.

BY the sun, and its rising brightness ; by the moon, when she followeth him ; [1] by the day, when it showeth his splendour ; by the night, when it covereth him with darkness ; by the heaven, and him who built it ; by the earth, and him who spread it forth ; by the soul, and him who completely formed it, and inspired into the same its *faculty of distinguishing, and power of choosing,* wickedness and piety : now is he who hath purified the same, happy ; but he who hath corrupted the same, is miserable. Thamûd accused *their prophet Sâleh* of imposture, through the excess of their wickedness : when the wretch[2] among them was sent *to slay the camel* ; and the apostle of GOD said unto them, *Let alone* the camel of GOD ; and *hinder not* her drinking. But they charged him with imposture ; and they slew her. Wherefore their LORD destroyed them, for their crime, and made *their punishment* equal *unto them all* : and he feareth not the issue thereof.

[1] *i.e.*, When she rises just after him, as she does at the beginning of the month ; or when she sets after him, as happens when she is a little past the full. (Al Beidâwi.)

[2] viz., Kedâr Ebn Sâlef. See Chaps. VII. p. 149 and LIV. p. 512.

XCII

THE CHAPTER OF THE NIGHT

Revealed at Mecca.

IN THE NAME OF THE MOST MERCIFUL GOD.

BY the night, when it covereth *all things* with darkness ; by the day, when it shineth forth ; by him who hath created the male and the female : verily your endeavour *is* different. Now whoso is obedient, and feareth *God,* and professeth the truth of that *faith* which is most excellent ; unto him will

we facilitate *the way* to happiness : but whoso shall be covetous, and shall be wholly taken up *with this world*, and shall
deny the truth of that which is most excellent ; unto him
will we facilitate *the way* to misery ; and his riches shall not
profit him, when he shall fall headlong *into hell.* Verily unto
us *appertaineth* the direction *of mankind* : and ours *is* the
life to come and the present life. Wherefore I threaten you
with fire which burneth fiercely, which none shall enter to
be burned except the most wretched ; who shall have disbelieved, and turned back. But he who strictly bewareth
idolatry and rebellion, shall be removed far from the same ;
who giveth his substance in alms, and by whom no benefit
is bestowed on any, that it may be recompensed, but *who
bestoweth the same* for the sake of his LORD, the most High :[1]
and hereafter he shall be well satisfied *with his reward.*

XCIII

THE CHAPTER OF THE BRIGHTNESS
Revealed at Mecca.

IN THE NAME OF THE MOST MERCIFUL GOD.

BY the brightness *of the morning* ;[2] and by the night, when
it groweth dark : thy LORD hath not forsaken thee,
neither doth he hate *thee*.[3] Verily the life to come *shall be*
better for thee than this present life : and thy LORD shall
give thee *a reward* wherewith thou shalt be well pleased.
Did he not find thee an orphan, and hath he not taken care
of thee ? And did he not find thee wandering in error, and
hath he not guided *thee into the truth ?* And did he not find
thee needy, and hath he not enriched *thee ?* Wherefore
oppress not the orphan : neither repulse the beggar : but
declare the goodness of thy LORD.

[1] Jallalo'ddin thinks this whole description belongs peculiarly to Abu
Becr : for when he had purchased Belâl, the Ethiopian (afterwards the
prophet's muedhdhin, or crier to prayers), who had been put to the rack on
account of his faith, the infidels said he did it only out of a view of interest ;
upon which this passage was revealed.

[2] The original word properly signifies the bright part of the day, when the
sun shines full out three or four hours after it is risen. Palmer translates
it *the forenoon.*

[3] It is related that no revelation having been vouchsafed to Mohammed
for several days, in answer to some questions put to him by the Koreish,
because he had confidently promised to resolve them the next day, without
adding the exception, *if it please* GOD (see Chap. XVIII)., or because he had
repulsed an importunate beggar, or else because a dead puppy lay under
his seat, or for some other reason ; his enemies said that GOD had left him :
whereupon this chapter was sent down for his consolation. (Al Beidâwi,
Jallalo'ddin.)

XCIV

THE CHAPTER OF HAVE WE NOT OPENED

Revealed at Mecca.

IN THE NAME OF THE MOST MERCIFUL GOD.

HAVE we not opened thy breast ;[1] and eased thee of thy burden,[2] which galled thy back ; and raised thy reputation for thee ? Verily a difficulty *shall be attended* with ease. Verily a difficulty *shall be attended* with ease. When thou shalt have ended *thy preaching,* labour *to serve God in return for his favours* ;[3] and make thy supplication unto thy LORD.

[1] By disposing and enlarging it to receive the truth, and wisdom, and prophecy ; or, by freeing thee from uneasiness and ignorance ? This passage is thought to intimate the *opening* of Mohammed's heart, in his infancy, or when he took his journey to heaven, by the angel Gabriel ; who having wrung out the black drop, or seed of original sin, washed and cleansed the same, and filled it with wisdom and faith (Al Beidâwi, Yahya. Vide Abulf. Vit. Moh. p. 8 and 33 ; Prid. Life of Mohamet, p. 105, &c.) : but some think it relates to the occasion of the preceding chapter (Al Beidâwi).

[2] *i.e.,* Of thy sins committed before thy mission ; or of thy ignorance, or trouble of mind.

[3] Or *When thou shalt have finished* thy prayer, *labour* in preaching the faith. (Al Beidâwi.)

XCV

THE CHAPTER OF THE FIG

Where it was revealed is disputed.

IN THE NAME OF THE MOST MERCIFUL GOD.

BY the fig, and the olive ;[1] and by Mount Sinai, and this territory of security ;[2] verily we created man of a most excellent fabric ; afterwards we rendered him the vilest of the vile :[3] except those who believe and work righteousness ;

[1] GOD, say the commentators, swears by these two fruits, because of their great uses and virtues : for the fig is wholesome and of easy digestion, and physically good to carry off phlegm, and gravel in the kidneys or bladder, and to remove obstructions of the liver and spleen, and also cures the piles and the gout, &c. ; the olive produces oil, which is not only excellent to eat, but otherwise useful for the compounding of ointments (Al Beidâwi, Al Zamakh.) ; the wood of the olive-tree, moreover, is good for cleansing the teeth, preventing their growing rotten, and giving a good odour to the mouth, for which reason the prophets, and Mohammed in particular, made use of no other for toothpicks (Al Zamakh.). Some, however, suppose that these words do not mean the fruits or trees above mentioned, but two mountains in the Holy Land, where they grow in plenty ; or else the temple of Damascus and that at Jerusalem (Al Zamakh., Yahya, Al Beidâwi, Jallal.)

[2] viz., The territory of Mecca. (Sale, Prel. Disc. Sect. IV.) These words seem to argue the chapter to have been revealed there.

[3] *i.e.,* As the commentators generally expound this passage, *We created man of comely proportion of body, and great perfection of mind ; and yet*

for they shall receive an endless reward. What therefore shall cause thee to deny the *day of* judgment after *this* ?[1] Is not GOD the most wise judge?

XCVI

THE CHAPTER OF CONGEALED BLOOD

Revealed at Mecca.[2]

IN THE NAME OF THE MOST MERCIFUL GOD

READ, in the name of thy LORD, who hath created *all things* ; who hath created man of congealed blood.[3] Read, by thy most beneficent LORD ;[4] who taught the use of the pen ; who teacheth man that which he knoweth not. Assuredly. Verily man becometh insolent, because he seeth himself abound in riches.[5] Verily unto thy LORD *shall be* the return *of all.* What thinkest thou *as to* him who forbiddeth *our* servant, when he prayeth ?[6] What thinkest thou ; if he follow the *right* direction ; or command piety ? What thinkest thou ; if he accuse *the divine revelations* of falsehood, and turn his back ? Doth he not know that GOD seeth ? Assuredly. Verily, if he forbear not, we will drag him by the forelock,[7] the lying, sinful forelock. And let him

we have doomed him, in case of disobedience, to be an inhabitant of hell. Some, however, understand the words of the vigorous constitution of man in the prime and strength of his age, and of his miserable decay when he becomes old and decrepit : but they seem rather to intimate the perfect state of happiness wherein man was originally created, and his fall from thence, in consequence of Adam's disobedience, to a state of misery in this world, and becoming liable to one infinitely more miserable in the next. (Vide Marracc. in loc. p. 809).

[1] Some suppose these words directed to Mohammed, and others to man in general, by way of apostrophe.

[2] The first five verses of this chapter, ending with the words, *Who taught man that which he knew not,* are generally allowed to be the first passage of the Korân which was revealed, though some give this honour to the seventy-fourth chapter, and others to the first, the next, they say, being the sixty-eighth.

[3] All men being created of thick or concreted blood (see Chap. XXII.), except only Adam, Eve, and Jesus. (Yahya.)

[4] These words, containing a repetition of the command, are supposed to be a reply to Mohammed, who, in answer to the former words spoken by the angel, had declared that he could not read, being perfectly illiterate ; and intimate a promise that GOD, who had inspired man with the art of writing, would graciously remedy this defect in him. (Al Beidâwi.)

[5] The commentators agree the remaining part of the chapter to have been revealed against Abu Jahl, Mohammed's great adversary.

[6] For Abu Jahl threatened that if he caught Mohammed in the act of adoration, he would set his foot on his neck ; but when he came and saw him in that posture, he suddenly turned back as in a fright, and, being asked what was the matter, said there was a ditch of fire between himself and Mohammed, and a terrible appearance of troops to defend him. (Al Beidâwi.)

[7] See Chap. XI. p. 217.

call his council[1] *to his assistance* : we also will call the infernal guards *to cast him into hell.* Assuredly. Obey him not : but *continue to* adore *God* ; and draw nigh *unto him.*

[1] *i.e.*, The council or assembly of the principal Meccans, the far greater part of whom adhered to Abu Jahl.

XCVII

THE CHAPTER OF AL KADR

Where it was revealed is disputed.

IN THE NAME OF THE MOST MERCIFUL GOD.

VERILY we sent down *the Korân* in the night of Al Kadr.[1] And what shall make thee understand *how excellent* the night of Al Kadr *is* ? The night of Al Kadr *is* better than a thousand months. Therein do the angels descend, and the spirit *Gabriel* also, by the permission of their LORD, *with his decrees* concerning every matter.[2] It *is* peace, until the rising of the morn.

[1] The word Al Kadr signifies *power*, and *honour* or *dignity*, and also the *divine decree* ; and the night is so named either from its excellence above all other nights in the year, or because, as the Mohammedans believe, the *divine decrees* for the ensuing year are annually on this night fixed and settled, or taken from the *preserved table* by GOD's throne, and given to the angels to be executed. (Chap. XLIV.) On this night Mohammed received his first revelations ; when the Korân say the commentators, was sent down from the aforesaid table, entire and in one volume, to the lowest heaven, from whence Gabriel revealed it to Mohammed by parcels, as occasion required. The Moslem doctors are not agreed where to fix the night of Al Kadr ; the greater part are of opinion that it is one of the last ten nights of Ramadân, and, as is commonly believed, the seventh of those nights, reckoning backwards ; by which means it will fall between the 23rd and 24th days of that month. (Al Zamakh., Al Beidâwi, Jallalo'ddin.)

[2] See the preceding note, and Chap. XLIV. p. 479.

XCVIII

THE CHAPTER OF THE EVIDENCE [1]

Where it was revealed is disputed.

IN THE NAME OF THE MOST MERCIFUL GOD.

THE unbelievers among those to whom the scriptures were given, and *among* the idolaters, did not stagger,[2] until the *clear* evidence[3] had come unto them : an

[1] Some entitle this chapter, from the first words, *Did not.*

[2] *i.e.*, Did not waver in their religion, or in their promises to follow the truth, when an apostle should come unto them. For the commentators pretend that before the appearance of Mohammed, the Jews and Christians, as well as the worshippers of idols, unanimously believed and expected the coming of that prophet, until which time they declared they would persevere in their respective religions, and then would follow him ; but when he came, they rejected him through envy. (Al Beidâwi.)

[3] viz., Mohammed, or the Korân.

apostle from GOD, rehearsing *unto them* pure books *of revelations* ; wherein *are contained* right discourses. Neither were they unto whom the scriptures were given divided among themselves, until after the *clear* evidence had come unto them.[1] And they were commanded no other *in the scriptures* than to worship GOD, exhibiting unto him the pure religion, and being orthodox ; and to be constant at prayer, and to give alms :[2] and this is the right religion. Verily those who believe not, among those who have received the scriptures, and among the idolaters, *shall be cast* into the fire of hell, to remain therein *for ever.* These are the worst of creatures. But they who believe, and do good works ; these are the best of creatures : their reward with their LORD *shall be* gardens of perpetual abode, through which rivers flow ; they shall remain therein for ever. GOD will be well pleased in them ; and they shall be well pleased in him. This *is prepared* for him who shall fear his LORD.

XCIX

THE CHAPTER OF THE EARTHQUAKE

Where it was revealed is disputed.

IN THE NAME OF THE MOST MERCIFUL GOD.

WHEN the earth shall be shaken by an earthquake ;[3] and the earth shall cast forth her burdens;[4] and a man shall say, What aileth her ? On that day *the earth* shall declare her tidings, for that thy LORD will inspire her.[5] On that day men shall go forward in distinct classes, that they may behold their works. And whoever shall have wrought good of the weight of an ant,[6] shall behold the same. And whoever shall have wrought evil of the weight of an ant, shall behold the same.

[1] But when the promised apostle was sent, and the truth became manifest to them, they withstood the clearest conviction, differing from one another in their opinions ; some believing and acknowledging Mohammed to be the prophet foretold in the scriptures, and others denying it. (Al Beidâwi.)
[2] But these divine precepts in the law and the gospel have they corrupted, changed, and violated. (Al Beidâwi.)
[3] This earthquake will happen at the first, or, as others say, at the second blast of the trumpet. (Al Zamakh., Al Beidâwi. Sale, Prel. Disc. Sect. IV.
[4] viz. The treasures and dead bodies within it. (Chap. LXXXIV.)
[5] *i.e.*, Will inform all creatures of the occasion of her trembling, and casting forth her treasures and her dead, by the circumstances which shall immediately attend them. Some say the earth will at the last day be miraculously enabled to speak, and will give evidence of the actions of her inhabitants. (Al Beidâwi. Sale, Prel. Disc. Sect. IV.)
[6] See Chap. IV. p. 78.

C

THE CHAPTER OF THE ~ WAR-HORSES WHICH RUN SWIFTLY

Where it was revealed is disputed.

IN THE NAME OF THE MOST MERCIFUL GOD.

BY the *war-horses* which run swiftly *to the battle*, with a panting noise; and by those which strike fire by dashing *their hoofs against the stones*; and by those which make a sudden incursion *on the enemy* early in the morning, and therein raise the dust, and therein pass through the midst of the *adverse* troops :[1] verily man *is* ungrateful unto his LORD ; and he *is* witness thereof : and he *is* immoderate in the love of *worldly* good. Doth he not know, therefore, when that which *is* in the graves shall be taken forth and that which *is* in *men's* breasts shall be brought to light, that their LORD *will*, on that day, *be* fully informed concerning them ?

[1] Some will have it that not horses, but the camels which went to the battle of Bedr, are meant in this passage (Yahya, ex trad. Ali Ebn Abi Taleb). Others interpret all the parts of the oath of the human soul (Al Beidâwi); but their explanations seem a little forced, and are therefore here omitted.

CI

THE CHAPTER OF THE STRIKING

Revealed at Mecca.

IN THE NAME OF THE MOST MERCIFUL GOD.

THE striking ![1] What *is* the striking ? And what shall make thee to understand how *terrible* the striking *will be* ? On that day men shall be like moths scattered abroad, and the mountains shall become like carded wool of various colours *driven by the wind*. Moreover he whose balance shall be heavy *with good works*, shall lead a pleasing life : but *as to* him whose balance shall be light, his dwelling *shall be* the pit *of hell*.[2] What shall make thee to understand how *frightful* the pit *of hell is* ? *It is* a burning fire.

[1] This is one of the names or epithets given to the last day, because it will *strike the hearts of all creatures with terror*. (Al Beidâwi, Jallalo'ddin.)
[2] The original word Hâwiyat is the name of the lowest dungeon of hell, and properly signifies a deep pit or gulf.

CII

THE CHAPTER OF THE EMULOUS DESIRE OF MULTIPLYING
Where it was revealed is disputed.

IN THE NAME OF THE MOST MERCIFUL GOD.

THE emulous desire of multiplying *riches and children* employeth you, until ye visit the graves.[1] By no means *should ye thus employ your time* : hereafter shall ye know *your folly*. Again, By no means : hereafter shall ye know *your folly*. By no means : if ye knew *the consequence hereof* with certainty of knowledge, *ye would not act thus*. Verily ye shall see hell : again, ye shall surely see it with the eye of certainty. Then shall ye be examined, on that day, concerning the pleasures *with which ye have amused yourselves in this life*.

[1] *i.e.*, Until ye die   According to the exposition of some commentators, the words should be rendered thus : *The contending* or vying *in numbers wholly employeth you, so that ye visit even the graves*, to number the dead : to explain which, they relate that there was a great dispute and contention between the descendants of Abd Menâf and the descendants of Sahm, which of the two families was the more numerous ; and it being found, on calculation, that the children of Abd Menâf exceeded those of Sahm, the Sahmites said that their numbers had been much diminished by wars in the time of ignorance, and insisted that the dead, as well as the living, should be taken into the account ; and by this way of reckoning they were found to be more than the descendants of Abd Menâf.   (Al Zamakh., Al Beidâwi, Jallal.)

CIII

THE CHAPTER OF THE AFTERNOON
Revealed at Mecca.

IN THE NAME OF THE MOST MERCIFUL GOD.

BY the afternoon ;[1] verily man *employeth himself in that which will prove of* loss[2] : except those who believe, and do that which is right ; and *who* mutually recommend the truth, and mutually recommend perseverance unto each other.

[1] Or the time from the sun's declination to his setting, which is one of the five appointed times of prayer.   The original word also signifies, *The age*, or *time* in general.

[2] Or, "verily man's lot is cast upon the road to ruin."   This sura was recited in the mosque at Mecca by Mohammed shortly before he died.

CIV

THE CHAPTER OF THE SLANDERER

Revealed at Mecca.

IN THE NAME OF THE MOST MERCIFUL GOD.

WOE unto every slanderer *and* backbiter :[1] who heapeth up riches, and prepareth the same *for the time to come* ! He thinketh that his riches will render him immortal. By no means. He shall surely be cast into Al Hotama.[2] And who shall cause thee to understand what Al Hotama *is* ? *It is* the kindled fire of GOD ;[3] which shall mount above the hearts *of those who shall be cast therein*. Verily it *shall be as* an arched vault above them, on columns of vast extent.

[1] This passage is said to have been revealed against Al Akhnas Ebn Shoreik, or Al Walîd Ebn al Mogheira, or Omeyya Ebn Khalf, who were all guilty of slandering others, and especially the prophet. (Al Beidâwi.)

[2] Is one of the names of hell, or the name of one of its apartments (Sale, Prel. Disc. Sect. IV.); which is so called because it will *break in pieces* whatever shall be thrown into it.

[3] And therefore shall not be extinguished by any. (Al Beidâwi.)

CV

THE CHAPTER OF THE ELEPHANT

Revealed at Mecca.

IN THE NAME OF THE MOST MERCIFUL GOD.

HAST thou not seen how thy LORD dealt with the masters of the elephant ?[1] Did he not make their treacherous

[1] This chapter relates to the following piece of history, which is famous among the Arabs. Abraha Ebn al Sabâh, surnamed Al Ashram, *i.e., the Slit-nosed,* king or viceroy of Yaman, who was an Ethiopian (Sale, Prel. Disc. Sect. I.), and of the Christian religion, having built a magnificent church at Sanaa, with a design to draw the Arabs to go in pilgrimage thither, instead of visiting the temple of Mecca, the Koreish, observing the devotion and concourse of the pilgrims at the Caaba began considerably to diminish, sent one Nofail, as he is named by some, of the tribe of Kenânah, who getting into the aforesaid church by night, defiled the altar and walls thereof with his excrements. At this profanation Abraha being highly incensed, vowed the destruction of the Caaba, and accordingly set out against Mecca at the head of a considerable army, wherein were several elephants, which he had obtained of the king of Ethiopia, their numbers being, as some say, thirteen, though others mention but one. The Meccans, at the approach of so considerable a host, retired to the neighbouring mountains, being unable to defend their city or temple : but GOD himself undertook the protection of both. For when Abraha drew near to Mecca, and would have entered it, the elephant on which he rode, which was a very large one, and named Mahmûd, refused to advance any nigher to the town, but knelt down whenever they endeavoured to force him that way, though he would rise and march briskly enough if they turned him towards any other quarter : and while matters were in this posture, on a sudden a large flock of birds, like swallows, came flying from the sea coast, every one of which carried three

design an occasion of drawing them into error ; and send
against them flocks of birds, which cast down upon them
stones of baked clay ;[1] and render them like the leaves of
corn eaten *by cattle* ?

stones, one in each foot, and one in its bill ; and these stones they threw
down upon the heads of Abraha's men, certainly killing every one they struck.
Then GOD sent a flood, which swept the dead bodies, and some of those who
had not been struck by the stones, into the sea : the rest fled towards Yaman,
but perished by the way ; none of them reaching Sanaa, except only Abraha
himself, who died soon after his arrival there, being struck with a sort of
plague or putrefaction, so that his body opened, and his limbs rotted off by
piecemeal. It is said that one of Abraha's army, named Abu Yacsûm, escaped
over the Red Sea into Ethiopia, and going directly to the king, told him the
tragical story : and upon that prince's asking him what sort of birds they
were that had occasioned such a destruction, the man pointed to one of them,
which had followed him all the way, and was at that time hovering directly
over his head, when immediately the bird let fall the stone, and struck him
dead at the king's feet. (Al Zamakh., Al Beidâwi, Jallalo'ddin, Abulf.
Hist. Gen. &c. See Prid. Life of Mahomet, p. 61, &c., and D'Herbel. Bibl.
Orient. Art. Abrahah.)   This remarkable defeat of Abraha happened the
very year Mohammed was born, and as this chapter was revealed before the
Hejra, and within fifty-four years, at least, after it came to pass, when several
persons who could have detected the lie, had Mohammed forged this story out
of his own head, were alive, it seems as if there was really something extraordinary in the matter, which might, by adding some circumstances, have
been worked up into a miracle to his hands.   Marracci (Refut. in Alcor. p.
823) judges the whole to be either a fable, or else a feat of some evil spirits,
of which he gives a parallel instance, as he thinks, in the strange defeat of
Brennus, when he was marching to attack the temple of Apollo at Delphi
(See Prid. Connection, part ii. book i. p. 25, and the authors there quoted.)
Dr. Prideaux directly charges Mohammed with coining this miracle, notwithstanding he might have been so easily disproved, and supposes, without
any foundation, that this chapter might not have been published till Othman's
edition of the Korân (Sale, Prel. Disc. Sect. III.), which was many years after,
when all might be dead who could remember anything of the above-mentioned
war. (Prid. Life of Mahomet, pp. 63, 64.) But Mohammed had no occasion
to coin such a miracle himself, to gain the temple of Mecca any greater
veneration : the Meccans were but too superstitiously fond of it, and obliged
him, against his inclinations and original design, to make it the chief place
of his newly invented worship. I cannot, however, but observe Dr. Prideaux's
partiality on this occasion, compared with the favourable reception he gives
to the story of the miraculous overthrow of Brennus and his army, which he
concludes in the following words : " Thus was GOD pleased in a very extraordinary manner to execute his vengeance upon those sacrilegious wretches
for the sake of religion in general, how false and idolatrous soever that particular religion was, for which that temple at Delphos was erected."   (Prid.
Connection, in the place above cited.) If it be answered, that the Gauls
believed the religion, to the devotions of which that temple was consecrated,
to be true (though that be not certain), and therefore it was an impiety in
them to offer violence to it, whereas Abraha acknowledged not the holiness
of the Caaba, or the worship there practised, I reply, That the doctor, on
occasion of Cambyses being killed by a wound he accidentally received in
the same part of the body where he had before mortally wounded the Apis,
or bull worshipped by the Egyptians, whose religion and worship that prince
most certainly believed to be false and superstitious, makes the same reflection;
" The Egyptians," says he, " reckoned this as an especial judgment from
heaven upon him for that fact, and perchance they were not much out in it :
for it seldom happening in an affront given to any mode of worship, how
erroneous soever it may be, but that religion is in general wounded thereby."

[1] These stones were of the same kind with those by which the Sodomites

CVI

THE CHAPTER OF KOREISH

Revealed at Mecca.

IN THE NAME OF THE MOST MERCIFUL GOD.

FOR the uniting of *the tribe of* Koreish ;[1] their uniting in *sending forth* the caravan *of merchants and purveyors*[2] in winter and summer : let them serve the LORD of this house ; who supplieth them with food against hunger,[3] and hath rendered them secure from fear.[4]

were destroyed (see Chap. XI.), and were no bigger than vetches, though they fell with such force as to pierce the helmet and the man through, passing out at his fundament. It is said also that on each stone was written the name of him who was to be slain by it.

[1] Some connect these words with the following, and suppose the natural order to be, *Let them serve the Lord of this house, for the uniting,* &c. Others connect them with the last words of the preceding chapter, and take the meaning to be, that GOD had so destroyed the army of Abraha *for the uniting of the* Koreish, &c. And the last opinion is confirmed by one copy, mentioned by Al Beidâwi, wherein this and the preceding make but one chapter. It may not be amiss to observe, that the tribe of Koreish, the most noble among all the Arabians, and of which was Mohammed himself, are the posterity of Fehr, surnamed Koreish, the son of Malec, the son of Al Nadr, who was descended in a right line from Ismael. Some writers say that Al Nadr bore the surname of Koreish, but the more received opinion is that it was his grandson Fehr, who was so called because of his intrepid boldness, the word being a diminutive of Karsh, which is the name of a sea monster, very strong and daring ; though there be other reasons given for its imposition. (Vide Gagnier, Vie de Mah. t. I, pp. 44 and 46.)

[2] It was Hâshem, the great-grandfather of Mohammed, who first appointed the two yearly caravans here mentioned (Sale, Prel. Disc. Sect. I.); one of which set out in the winter for Yaman, and the other in summer for Syria. (Al Zamakh., Jallal., Al Beidâwi.)

[3] By means of the aforesaid caravans of purveyors ; or, *Who supplied them with food in time of a famine,* which those of Mecca had suffered. (Al Beidâwi.)

[4] By delivering them from Abraha and his troops ; or, by making the territory of Mecca a place of security.

CVII

THE CHAPTER OF NECESSARIES

Where it was revealed is disputed.

IN THE NAME OF THE MOST MERCIFUL GOD.

WHAT thinkest thou of him who denieth the *future* judgment as a falsehood ? *It is* he who pusheth away the orphan ;[1] and stirreth not up *others* to feed the poor.

[1] The person here intended, according to some, was Abu Jahl, who turned away an orphan, to whom he was guardian, and who came to him naked, and asked for some relief out of his own money. Some say it was Abu Sofiân, who, having killed a camel, when an orphan begged a piece of the

Woe be unto those who pray, *and* who are negligent at their prayer ; who play the hypocrites, and deny necessaries[1] *to the needy.*

---

flesh, beat him away with his staff ; and others think it was Al Walîd Ebn al Mogheira, &c.

[1] The original word Al Maûn properly signifies utensils, or whatever is of necessary use, *as a hatchet, a pot, a dish, and a needle,* to which some add a *bucket and a handmill* ; or, according to a tradition of Ayesha, *fire, water, and salt* ; and this signification it bore in the time of ignorance : but since the establishment of the Mohammedan religion, the word has been used to denote alms, either legal or voluntary ; which seems to be the true meaning in this place.

CVIII

THE CHAPTER OF AL CAWTHAR

Revealed at Mecca.[1]

IN THE NAME OF THE MOST MERCIFUL GOD.

VERILY we have given thee Al Cawthar.[2] Wherefore pray unto thy LORD ; and slay *the victims.*[3] Verily he who hateth thee shall be childless.[4]

---

[1] There are some, however, who think it to have been revealed at Medina.

[2] This word signifies *abundance,* especially of *good,* and thence *the gift of wisdom and prophecy,* the Korân, the *office of intercessor,* &c. Or it may imply *abundance of children, followers,* and the like. It is generally, however, expounded of a river in paradise of that name, whence the water is derived into Mohammed's pond, of which the blessed are to drink before their admission into that place. (Sale, Prel. Disc. Sect. IV.) According to a tradition of the prophet's, this river, wherein his Lord promised him abundant good, is sweeter than honey, whiter than milk, cooler than snow, and smoother than cream ; its banks are of chrysolites, and the vessels to drink thereout of silver ; and those who drink of it shall never thirst. (Al Beidâwi, Jallal., &c.)

Euthymius Zigabenus (In Panoplia Dogmat. inter Sylburgii Saracenic, p. 29), instead of Cauthar, reading Canthar, supposes the word to have the same signification in Arabic as in Greek, and translates the two first verses of the chapter thus : ʻΗμεῖς δεδώκαμέν σοι τὸν κάνθαρον, κεὶ εὐξαῖ πρὸς τὸν κύριόν σου, καὶ σφάξον—*i.e., We have given thee the beetle ; wherefore pray unto thy* LORD, *and slay it* ; and then he cries out, O *wonderful and magnificent sacrifice, worthy of the legislator !*

[3] Which are to be sacrificed at the pilgrimage in the valley of Mina. Al Beidâwi explains the words thus : Pray with fervency and intense devotion, not out of hypocrisy ; and slay the fatted camels and oxen, and distribute the flesh among the poor ; for he says this chapter is the counterpart of the preceding, exhorting to those virtues which are opposite to the vices there condemned.

[4] These words were revealed against Al As Ebn Wayel, who, on the death of Al Kâsem, Mohammed's son, called that prophet Abtar, which signifies *me who has no children or posterity.* (Jallalo'ddin.)

CIX

THE CHAPTER OF THE UNBELIEVERS
Revealed at Mecca.

IN THE NAME OF THE MOST MERCIFUL GOD.

SAY: O unbelievers,[1] I will not worship that which ye worship; nor will ye worship that which I worship. Neither do I worship that which ye worship; neither do ye worship that which I worship. Ye have your religion, and I my religion.

[1] It is said that certain of the Koreish once proposed to Mohammed that if he would worship their gods for a year, they would worship his GOD for the same space of time; upon which this chapter was revealed. (Jallalo'-ddin, Al Beidâwi.)

CX

THE CHAPTER OF ASSISTANCE
Revealed at Mecca.

IN THE NAME OF THE MOST MERCIFUL GOD.

WHEN the assistance of GOD shall come, and the victory;[1] and thou shalt see the people enter into the religion of GOD by troops:[2] celebrate the praise of thy LORD, and ask pardon of him;[3] for he is inclined to forgive.

[1] i.e., When GOD shall cause thee to prevail over thy enemies, and thou shalt take the city of Mecca.
[2] Which happened in the ninth year of the Hejra, when, Mohammed having made himself master of Mecca, and obliged the Koreish to submit to him, the rest of the Arabs came in to him in great numbers, and professed Islâm. (Sale, Prel. Disc. Sect. II.)
[3] Most of the commentators agree this chapter to have been revealed before the taking of Mecca, and suppose it gave Mohammed warning of his death; for they say that when he read it Al Abbâs wept, and being asked by the prophet what was the reason of his weeping, answered, Because it biddeth thee to prepare for death; to which Mohammed replied, It is as thou sayest. (Al Beidâwi.) And hence, adds Jallalo'ddin, after the revelation of this chapter the prophet was more frequent in praising and asking pardon of GOD, because he thereby knew that his end approached; for Mecca was taken in the eighth year of the Hejra, and he died in the beginning of the tenth.

CXI

THE CHAPTER OF ABU LAHEB
Revealed at Mecca.

IN THE NAME OF THE MOST MERCIFUL GOD.

THE hands of Abu Laheb shall perish,[1] and he shall perish.[2] His riches shall not profit him, neither that which he hath gained.[3] He shall go down to be burned into flaming fire ; [4] and his wife *also*,[5] bearing wood,[6] *having* on her neck a cord of twisted fibres of a palm-tree.

[1] Abu Laheb was the surname of Abd'al Uzza, one of the sons of Abd'almotalleb, and uncle to Mohammed. He was a most bitter enemy to his nephew, and opposed the establishment of his new religion to the utmost of his power. When that prophet, in obedience to the command he had received to *admonish his near relations* (Sale, Prel. Disc. Sect. II.), had called them together, and told them *he was a warner sent unto them before a grievous chastisement*, Abu Laheb cried out, *Mayest thou perish! Hast thou called us together for this* ? and took up a stone to cast at him. Whereupon this passage was revealed. (Al Beidâwi, Jallalo'ddin, &c.) By the *hands* of Abu Laheb some commentators, by a synecdoche, understand his *person* ; others, by a metonymy, his *affairs* in general, they being transacted with those members ; or his hopes in this world and the next.

[2] He died of grief and vexation at the defeat his friends had received at Bedr, surviving that misfortune but seven days. (Abulf. Vit. Moh. p. 57.) They add, that his corpse was left above ground three days, till it stank, and then some negroes were hired to bury him. (Al Beidâwi.)

[3] And accordingly his great possessions, and the rank and esteem in which he lived at Mecca, were of no service to him, nor could protect him against the vengeance of GOD. Al Beidâwi mentions also the loss of his son Otha, who was torn to pieces by a lion in the way to Syria, though surrounded by the whole caravan.

[4] Arab, *nâr dhât laheb* ; alluding to the surname of Abu Laheb, which signifies the *father of flames*.

[5] Her name was Omm Jemil; she was the daughter of Harb, and sister of Abu Sofiân.

[6] For fuel in hell ; because she fomented the hatred which her husband bore to Mohammed ; or, *bearing a bundle of thorns and brambles*, because she carried such, and strewed them by night in the prophet's way. (Al Beidâwi, Jallalo'ddin.)

CXII

THE CHAPTER OF THE DECLARATION OF GOD'S UNITY [1]
Where it was revealed is disputed.

IN THE NAME OF THE MOST MERCIFUL GOD.

SAY, *God* is one GOD ; the eternal God : he begetteth not, neither is he begotten and there is not any one like unto him.

[1] This chapter is held in particular veneration by the Mohammedans, and declared, by a tradition of their prophet, to be equal in value to a third part of the whole Korân. It is said to have been revealed in answer to the Koreish, who asked Mohammed concerning the distinguishing attributes of the GOD he invited them to worship. (Al Beidâwi.)

CXIII

THE CHAPTER OF THE DAYBREAK

Where it was revealed is disputed.

IN THE NAME OF THE MOST MERCIFUL GOD.

SAY, I fly for refuge unto the LORD of the daybreak,[1] *that he may deliver me* from the mischief of *those things* which he hath created ;[2] and from the mischief of the night, when it cometh on ;[3] and from the mischief of *women* blowing on knots ;[4] and from the mischief of the envious, when he envieth.

[1] The original word properly signifies a *cleaving,* and denotes, says Al Beidâwi, the production of all things in general, from the darkness of privation to the light of existence, and especially of those things which proceed from others, as springs, rain, plants, children, &c., and hence it is used more particularly to signify the breaking forth of the light from darkness.

[2] *i.e.,* From the mischiefs proceeding either from the perverseness and evil choice of those beings which have a power to choose, or the natural effects of necessary agents, as fire, poison, &c., the world being good in the whole, though evils may follow from those two causes. (Al Beidâwi.)

[3] Or, *from the mischief of the moon, when she is eclipsed.*

[4] The commentators relate that Lobeid, a Jew, with the assistance of his daughters, bewitched Mohammed, by tying eleven knots on a cord, which they hid in a well ; whereupon Mohammed falling ill, GOD revealed this chapter and the following, and Gabriel acquainted him with the use he was to make of them, and of the place where the cord was hidden. The prophet sent Ali to fetch the cord, and the same being brought, he repeated the two chapters over it, and at every verse (for they consist of eleven) a knot was loosed, till on finishing the last words, he was entirely freed from the charm.

CXIV

THE CHAPTER OF MEN

Where it was revealed is disputed.[1]

IN THE NAME OF THE MOST MERCIFUL GOD.

SAY, I fly for refuge unto the LORD of men, the king of men, the GOD of men, *that he may deliver me* from the mischief of the whisperer who slyly withdraweth,[2] who whispereth evil suggestions into the breasts of men ; from genii and men.

[1] This chapter was revealed on the same occasion as Chap. CXIII.

[2] *i.e.,* The devil ; who withdraweth when a man mentioneth GOD, or hath recourse to his protection.

FINIS.

INDEX

TO THE KORÂN AND THE NOTES THEREON